This book offers a radical new survey of more than a thousand years of religious life at Rome: from the foundation of the city to its rise to world empire and its conversion to Christianity. Religion was central to Roman culture; it was part of the fabric of politics and warfare, imperial power and its opponents, domestic life and philosophical theorizing. This authoritative account sets religion in its full cultural context, whether in the primitive hamlet of the eighth century B.C. or the cosmopolitan, multicultural society of the first centuries of the Christian era.

The narrative account is structured around a series of broad themes: how to interpret the Romans' own theories of their religious system and its origins; the relationship of religion and the changing politics of Rome; the religious importance of the layout and monuments of the city itself; changing ideas of religious identity and community; religious invasion – and, ultimately, revolution.

The companion volume, *Religions of Rome 2: A Sourcebook*, sets out a wide range of documents (including painting, coins, sculpture and inscriptions) richly illustrating the religious life of the Roman world.

Religions of Rome
Volume 1

A History

Religions of Rome

VOLUME 1

A History

MARY BEARD
Lecturer in Classics in the University of Cambridge, and Fellow of Newnham College

JOHN NORTH
Professor of History, University College London

SIMON PRICE
Fellow and Tutor, Lady Margaret Hall, Oxford

CAMBRIDGE
UNIVERSITY PRESS

PUBLISHED BY THE PRESS SYNDICATE OF THE UNIVERSITY OF CAMBRIDGE
The Pitt Building, Trumpington Street, Cambridge CB2 1RP, United Kingdom

CAMBRIDGE UNIVERSITY PRESS
The Edinburgh Building, Cambridge CB2 2RU, United Kingdom
40 West 20th Street, New York, NY 10011–4211, USA
10 Stamford Road, Oakleigh, Melbourne 3166, Australia

First published 1998

Printed in United Kingdom at the University Press, Cambridge

Typeset in 11/13pt Adobe Garamond   [PND]

A catalogue record for this book is available from the British Library

ISBN 0 521 30401 6 hardback
ISBN 0 521 31682 0 paperback

Contents

Acknowledgements

Many people have helped in different ways and at different points over the decade that we have been working on this volume and its companion. We would like to thank Andreas Bendlin, Robin Cormack, Michael Crawford, John Curran, Denis Feeney, Martin Goodman, Keith Hopkins, Christopher Kelly, David MacMullen, Lucia Nixon, Nicholas Purcell, Joyce Reynolds, Helen Weston, Greg Woolf; and staff in the Ashmolean Library, Oxford, the Classics Faculty and Library, Cambridge, the Institute of Classical Studies, London, as well as the Institute of Advanced Studies, Princeton, the Libraries of the British and American Schools in Athens and the Ward Chipman Library of the University of New Brunswick at Saint John.

In particular, we have used (and enjoyed) the comments of John Henderson, who read the whole manuscript; and are grateful for the care and patience of Pauline Hire, who finally extracted it from us.

Earlier versions of three chapters have already appeared in volumes of *The Cambridge Ancient History* 2nd edn (Chapter 1 by J. A. N. in VII. 2; Chapter 3 by M. B. in IX; Chapter 4 by S. R. F. P. in X). Anyone who chooses to compare what is printed here with those earlier versions will see how profound the effects of collaboration have been.

M. B.
J. A. N.
S. R. F. P.

October 1996

Preface

In A.D. 495 (or thereabouts) the Bishop of Rome sent a stern letter to some of his fellow Christians in the city, denouncing those who continued to celebrate the ancient ritual of the *Lupercalia*.[1] Almost two hundred years after the emperor Constantine had started the process of making Christianity the 'official' religion of the Roman state, in a city that must in some ways have seemed a securely *Christian* environment (with its great churches – old St Peter's, St John Lateran – rivalling in size and splendour the most famous buildings of the pagan[2] past), Bishop Gelasius was faced with the problem of an old pagan ritual that would not die. Many members of his flock watched eagerly, it seems, as every 15 February a group of youths, very scantily clad, rushed around the city (as similar groups had done for more than a thousand years), lashing with a thong anyone who came across their path. But these Christians were not just eager, interested or curious spectators. It was even worse than this from Gelasius' point of view; for they claimed that it was vital to the safety and prosperity of Rome that this ancient ritual should continue to be performed – a claim that had always been one of the most powerful, and most commonly repeated, justifications of the traditional (pagan) gods and their cult. Proper worship of the Roman gods ensured the success of Rome: that was an axiom not easily overthrown, even by Christians in the late fifth century A.D.

In mounting his attack, Gelasius looked back over more than a millennium of Roman history to the very origins of the Lupercalia – and to the prehistoric inhabitants of the seven hills, who invented the ritual (so Roman myths claimed) generations before Romulus arrived on the scene to found *Rome* itself. Gelasius may have publicly set himself against the traditions and mythologies of his pagan predecessors; but he knew his enemy and confidently appealed to the history of the institution he was attacking, spanning the centuries between Christian Rome and the earliest years of

1 Gelasius, *Letter against the Lupercalia*; extract (ch.16) = *Religions of Rome* 2, **5.2e**; Hopkins (1991); and below, p. 388.
2 Throughout this book we have used the word 'pagan' or 'paganism' to refer to traditional Roman religion. We do this fully aware that it has been derided by some historians as a loaded term, in origin a specifically Christian way of describing its enemy (below, p. 312). No doubt an ideologically neutral term would be preferable; but we have found 'traditional civic polytheism' (and similar alternatives suggested) more cumbersome and no less – if differently – loaded.

traditional Roman paganism. These are precisely the centuries that we explore in this book: the millennium or more that takes Rome from a primitive village to world empire and finally to Christian capital.

The history of Roman religion (our history, Gelasius' history...) is a history of extraordinary change; it is nothing less than the story of the origin and development of those attitudes and assumptions that still underlie most forms of contemporary religious life in the West and most contemporary religions. This is not just a question of the growth of Christianity. In fact, as we shall emphasize at many points in what follows, early Christianity was a very different religion from its modern descendant – much less familiar in its doctrines, morality or organisation than we might prefer to imagine. Nonetheless in the religious debates and conflicts of the fourth and fifth centuries A.D. we are in a world that is broadly recognisable to us: we can see, for example, issues of religious *belief* being discussed by both pagans and Christians; we can observe religious *communities*, with their own hierarchy and officials, representing a focus of loyalty and commitment quite separate from the political institutions of the state; we can see the range of religious *choices* available (between different communities or different beliefs), and how those choices might have an impact on an individual's sense of identity, on their ambitions, and their view of their place in the world.

So far as we can tell, the religious world of the earliest periods of Roman history was quite different, and much less recognisable in our own contemporary terms. Of course, a lot hangs on '*so far as we can tell*'. Before the third century B.C. (already centuries after the origins of some of the city's most important religious institutions) no Roman literature of any sort survives – let alone any direct comments on the gods or the city's rituals. We have to reconstruct early Roman religion from discussions in much later authors and from a variety of archaeological traces: temple remains, offerings made to the gods, occasionally texts inscribed on bronze or stone recording such dedications. It is a tantalizing, tricky and often inconclusive procedure. But one thing does seem clear enough: that many of our familiar categories for thinking about religion and religious experience simply cannot be usefully applied here; we shall see, for example, how even the idea of 'personal *belief*' (to us, a self-evident part of religious experience) provides a strikingly *in*appropriate model for understanding the religious experience of early Rome. Part of the fascination of these early phases of Roman religion is their sheer difference from our own world and its assumptions.

The importance of this *difference* is one thing that lies behind our decision not to provide any formal definition of 'religion' at this (or any) point in the book: what we have written is the product of a necessary compromise between our own preconceptions, our readings in cross-cultural theory and the impact of the Romans' own (changing) representations of religion and

religious life, their own debates about what religion was and how it operated. We have not worked with a single definition of religion in mind; we
have worked rather to understand what might count as 'religion' in Rome
and how that might make a difference to our own understanding of our
own religious world.[3]

The book focusses on the changes in religious life at Rome over the millennium that separates the origins of the Lupercalia from Gelasius' spirited
(and learned) attack. It is not a matter of tracing a linear development, from
primitive religious simplicity in the early city to something approaching
modern sophistication a thousand years later. In fact our reconstructions
will suggest that, as far back as we can trace it, traditional Roman paganism
was strikingly complex – in its priestly organisation, in its range of divinities
and in its relations with the religious systems of its neighbours. It is a question much more of exploring how religious change could be generated in
Rome. How was religion affected by the political revolutions that defined
Roman history? Could religion be untouched by the transition from
monarchy to (quasi-democratic) 'republic' around the beginning of the
sixth century B.C.? Or untouched again by the civil wars that brought
autocracy back, first under Julius Caesar, finally under his adopted son, the
first emperor Augustus? How again was it affected by the enormous expansion of Rome's empire? What happens to the religious institutions of a small
city state, when that city state grows (as Rome did) to control most of the
known world? And what happens to the religion of the conquered territories under the impact of Roman imperialism? How far did the cultural revolution of the first centuries B.C. and A.D. prompt specifically religious
changes? When philosophy, science, history, poetry and visual imagery
were all offering radically new ways of conceptualizing the individual's
place in the cosmos, was religion to be left behind telling the same old story?

But these questions inevitably raise the bigger question of what *constitutes*
religious change and how we can recognise it. When Gelasius reprimands
his fellow Christians for continuing to support the Lupercalia, in what
sense should we understand the festival of the late fifth century A.D. as the
same as the Lupercalia that was being celebrated back when Rome was a
primitive village? To judge from Gelasius' description, many of the ritual
details were pretty much identical to those we can attest at least five hundred years before: the whipping, for example, and the running about the
town. But what of the significance, the 'meaning'? As we will discover, the
Lupercalia was and is one of the most *disputed* festivals in the Roman calendar: Roman writers argued about its aims (a ritual of purification? of fertility?); they disagreed even about the exact course taken by the runners (was
it *up and down*, or *round and round* the city?).[4] But one thing is certain: no

3 For this 'open textured' approach, Poole (1986).
4 A number of different ancient accounts are collected at *Religions of Rome* 2, 5.2.

ritual could mean the same when it was performed in a Christian capital, under a Christian emperor and the shadow of disapproval of a Christian bishop, as it had five hundred or a thousand years before – whether in the great imperial capital of the Roman empire or in the (as yet) small hamlet by the Tiber. And the claim to which Gelasius particularly objected – that the safety of Rome depended on the gods' rituals being properly performed – was inevitably different, even more loaded perhaps, when uttered in a world in which there was a choice of *god(s)* in which to believe. The paradox is that some of the biggest changes in Roman religion lurk behind the most striking examples of outward continuity, behind exactly the same phrases repeated in wildly different contexts. Throughout this book we shall be alive to just this kind of problem: how to write a history of Roman religion that is not merely a history of outward form.

This book starts with Romulus, the legendary founder of Rome, in chapter 1 and ends with Bishop Gelasius himself in chapter 8; the chapters in between tell the story of religious change through the growth of the city of Rome and the expansion of its empire; through the political changes from monarchy to democracy and back to monarchy (for that is effectively what the rule of the Roman emperors, the so-called 'principate', was). It is a history written in dialogue with ancient writers, most of whom were as partisan as Gelasius in his *Letter against the Lupercalia* (if less openly so): no one, after all, writes objectively about religion; and no literature is written simply to be a 'source' for later historians. Some of these writers were even engaged in a project similar in certain respects to our own: the reconstruction of the earliest phases of Roman religion and the history of its development. As we shall see in Chapter 1, our own understanding of the religious changes that coincided with the expulsion of the early kings of Rome is inextricably bound up with the analysis of Livy – who (five hundred years after the events) was posing exactly the same question as we shall pose: what difference did the fall of the monarchy make to the religious institutions of Rome? Writing the history of Roman religion, in other words, is to join a tradition that stretches back to the ancient world itself.

The history we have written in this volume depends on the ancient texts that are signalled in its footnotes. Though they are rarely quoted here at length, a large number of the passages we refer to are to be found in our companion volume, *Religions of Rome 2: A sourcebook* (from here on, all cross-references to Volume 2 are given by number in bold type, e.g. **4.3a**). This sourcebook is concerned with the same thousand years of Roman history, but it focusses specifically on ancient documents (extracts from literary texts, inscriptions, coins, sculpture and painting); and these are arranged not to tell a chronological story (as in this volume), but thematically across the centuries – to highlight some of the ideas and institutions that serve to unify Roman religion through its long history. It also includes some reference material (a glossary of Roman religious terms, a list of epithets given to Roman deities) that is directly relevant to this book also.

Each of these volumes can be used independently. But we hope that the reader will explore them together. Some of the many voices of the *Religions of Rome* are to be heard best in the dialogue between the two.

Conventions and abbreviations

Conventions

Italics have been used for Greek or Latin words, which are either
explained where they occur or in the glossary at the end of Vol. 2.
Figures in **bold type** (e.g. **1.4b**) refer to texts in Vol. 2.

Abbreviations

With the exception of the following works, we have used a fairly full form
of abbreviation; any doubts about the complete version of periodical
titles will be solved with reference to *L'année philologique*.

AE	*L'année épigraphique* (Paris, 1888–)
ANRW	*Aufstieg und Niedergang der römischen Welt*, edd. H. Temporini & W. Haase (Berlin, 1972–)
BCACR	*Bullettino della Commissione Archeologica Comunale di Roma*
BEFAR	Bibliothèque des Ecoles françaises d'Athènes et de Rome
B. M. Coins	*Coins of the Roman Empire in the British Museum*, H. M. Mattingly et al. (London, 1923–)
CAH	*Cambridge Ancient History*
CIL	*Corpus Inscriptionum Latinarum* (Berlin, 1863–)
CIMRM	*Corpus Inscriptionum et Monumentorum Religionis Mithrae*, ed. M. J. Vermaseren (Leiden, 1956)
CSEL	*Corpus Scriptorum Ecclesiasticorum Latinorum*
CTh	*Codex Theodosianus* (Berlin, 1905)
EPRO	Etudes préliminaires sur les religions orientales dans l'empire romain (Leiden, 1961–)
FGH	*Die Fragmente der griechischen Historiker*, F. Jacoby (Berlin and Leiden, 1923–58)
FIRA	*Fragmenta Iuris Romani Anteiustiniani*, edd. S. Riccobono et al., 2nd edn (Florence, 1968)
IG	*Inscriptiones Graecae* (Berlin, 1895–)
IGR	*Inscriptiones Graecae ad res Romanas pertinentes*, ed. R. Cagnat (Paris, 1906–27)

IGUR	*Inscriptiones Graecae Urbis Romae*, ed. L. Moretti (Rome, 1968–)
ILAfr	*Inscriptions latines d'Afrique*, edd. R. Cagnat et al. (Paris, 1923)
ILCV	*Inscriptiones Latinae Christianae Veteres*, ed. E. Diehl (Berlin, 1925–31)
ILLRP	*Inscriptiones Latinae Liberae Reipublicae*, ed. A. Degrassi (Florence, 1957–63)
ILS	*Inscriptiones Latinae Selectae*, ed. H. Dessau (Berlin, 1892–1916)
JRS	*Journal of Roman Studies*
MEFR(A)	*Mélanges de l'Ecole française de Rome (: Antiquité)*
MRR	*The Magistrates of the Roman Republic*, T. R. S. Broughton, 4 vols (New York, 1951–86)
PdP	*Parola del Passato*
RE	*Paulys Real-Encyclopädie der classischen Altertumswissenschaft*, edd. G. Wissowa, E. Kroll et al. (Berlin & Stuttgart, 1893–78)
RIB	*The Roman Inscriptions of Britain* I, edd. R. G. Collingwood and R. P. Wright (Oxford 1965, repr. Stroud, Glos. 1995)
RIC	*The Roman Imperial Coinage*, edd. H. Mattingly et al. (London, 1926–)
ROL	*Remains of Old Latin*, ed. E. H. Warmington (Loeb Classical Library, Cambridge MA and London, 1935–46)
SIG³	*Sylloge Inscriptionum Graecarum*, 3rd edn, ed. W. Dittenberger (Leipzig, 1915–24)
ZPE	*Zeitschrift für Papyrologie und Epigraphik*

Map 1

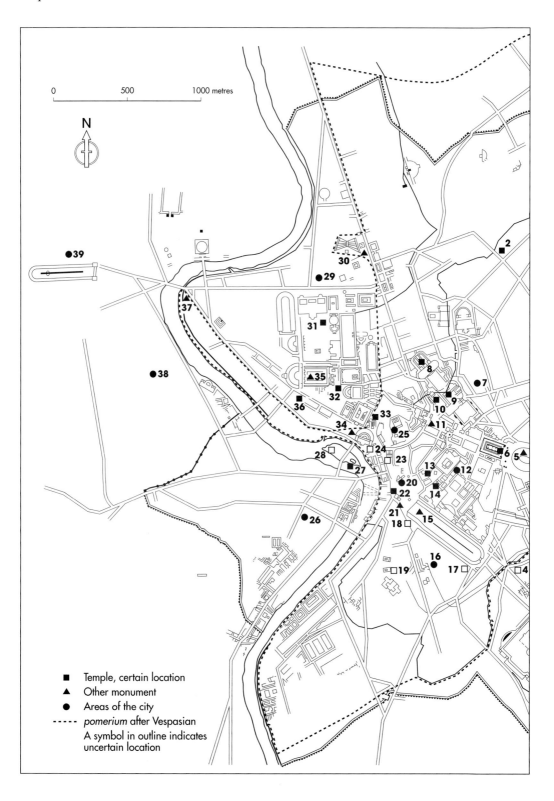

0   500   1000 metres

N

- ■ Temple, certain location
- ▲ Other monument
- ● Areas of the city
- ‑ ‑ ‑ ‑ *pomerium* after Vespasian
- A symbol in outline indicates uncertain location

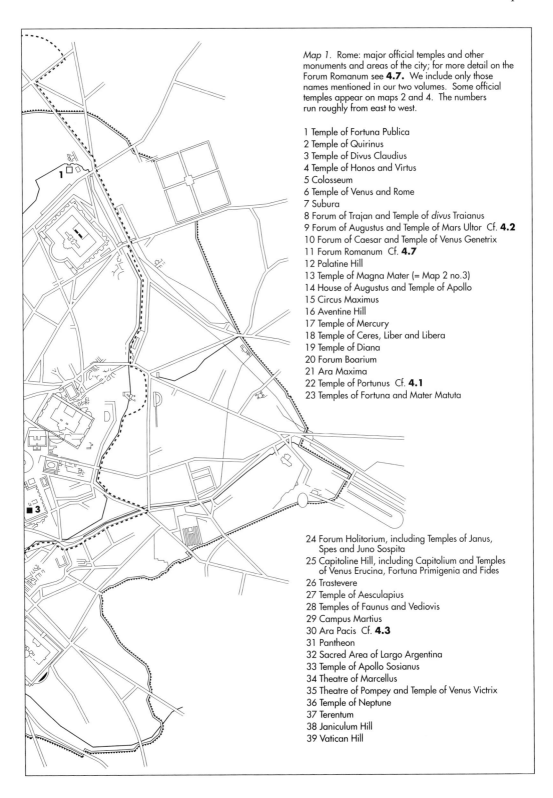

Map 1

Map 1. Rome: major official temples and other monuments and areas of the city; for more detail on the Forum Romanum see **4.7.** We include only those names mentioned in our two volumes. Some official temples appear on maps 2 and 4. The numbers run roughly from east to west.

1 Temple of Fortuna Publica
2 Temple of Quirinus
3 Temple of Divus Claudius
4 Temple of Honos and Virtus
5 Colosseum
6 Temple of Venus and Rome
7 Subura
8 Forum of Trajan and Temple of *divus* Traianus
9 Forum of Augustus and Temple of Mars Ultor Cf. **4.2**
10 Forum of Caesar and Temple of Venus Genetrix
11 Forum Romanum Cf. **4.7**
12 Palatine Hill
13 Temple of Magna Mater (= Map 2 no.3)
14 House of Augustus and Temple of Apollo
15 Circus Maximus
16 Aventine Hill
17 Temple of Mercury
18 Temple of Ceres, Liber and Libera
19 Temple of Diana
20 Forum Boarium
21 Ara Maxima
22 Temple of Portunus Cf. **4.1**
23 Temples of Fortuna and Mater Matuta

24 Forum Holitorium, including Temples of Janus, Spes and Juno Sospita
25 Capitoline Hill, including Capitolium and Temples of Venus Erucina, Fortuna Primigenia and Fides
26 Trastevere
27 Temple of Aesculapius
28 Temples of Faunus and Vediovis
29 Campus Martius
30 Ara Pacis Cf. **4.3**
31 Pantheon
32 Sacred Area of Largo Argentina
33 Temple of Apollo Sosianus
34 Theatre of Marcellus
35 Theatre of Pompey and Temple of Venus Victrix
36 Temple of Neptune
37 Terentum
38 Janiculum Hill
39 Vatican Hill

Map 2

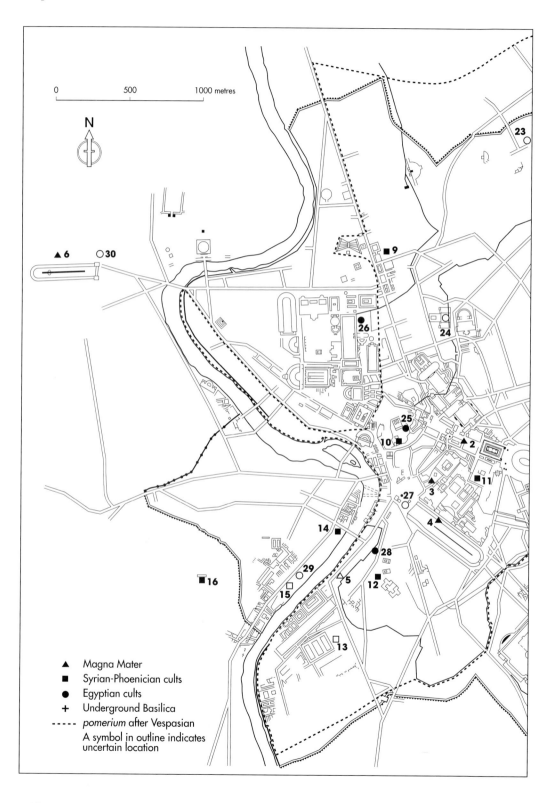

Legend:

- ▲ Magna Mater
- ■ Syrian-Phoenician cults
- ● Egyptian cults
- + Underground Basilica
- - - - - *pomerium* after Vespasian

A symbol in outline indicates uncertain location

Map 2

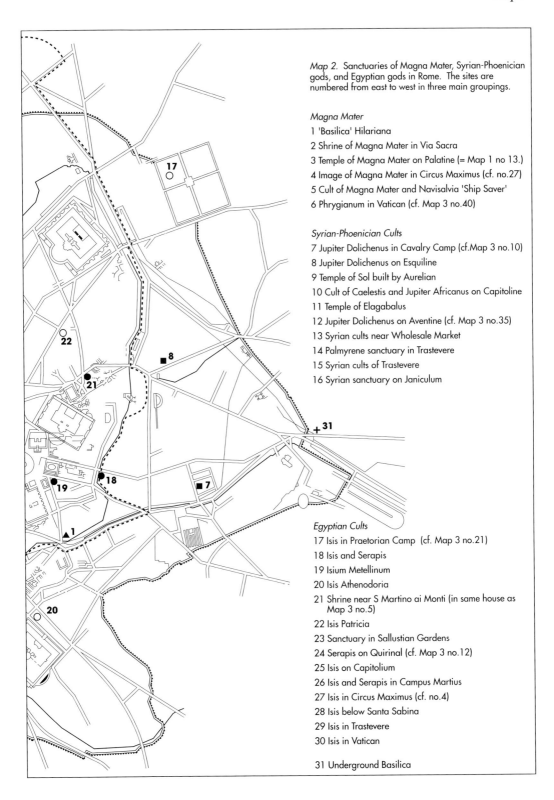

Map 2. Sanctuaries of Magna Mater, Syrian-Phoenician gods, and Egyptian gods in Rome. The sites are numbered from east to west in three main groupings.

Magna Mater
1 'Basilica' Hilariana
2 Shrine of Magna Mater in Via Sacra
3 Temple of Magna Mater on Palatine (= Map 1 no 13.)
4 Image of Magna Mater in Circus Maximus (cf. no.27)
5 Cult of Magna Mater and Navisalvia 'Ship Saver'
6 Phrygianum in Vatican (cf. Map 3 no.40)

Syrian-Phoenician Cults
7 Jupiter Dolichenus in Cavalry Camp (cf.Map 3 no.10)
8 Jupiter Dolichenus on Esquiline
9 Temple of Sol built by Aurelian
10 Cult of Caelestis and Jupiter Africanus on Capitoline
11 Temple of Elagabalus
12 Jupiter Dolichenus on Aventine (cf. Map 3 no.35)
13 Syrian cults near Wholesale Market
14 Palmyrene sanctuary in Trastevere
15 Syrian cults of Trastevere
16 Syrian sanctuary on Janiculum

Egyptian Cults
17 Isis in Praetorian Camp (cf. Map 3 no.21)
18 Isis and Serapis
19 Isium Metellinum
20 Isis Athenodoria
21 Shrine near S Martino ai Monti (in same house as Map 3 no.5)
22 Isis Patricia
23 Sanctuary in Sallustian Gardens
24 Serapis on Quirinal (cf. Map 3 no.12)
25 Isis on Capitolium
26 Isis and Serapis in Campus Martius
27 Isis in Circus Maximus (cf. no.4)
28 Isis below Santa Sabina
29 Isis in Trastevere
30 Isis in Vatican

31 Underground Basilica

Map 3

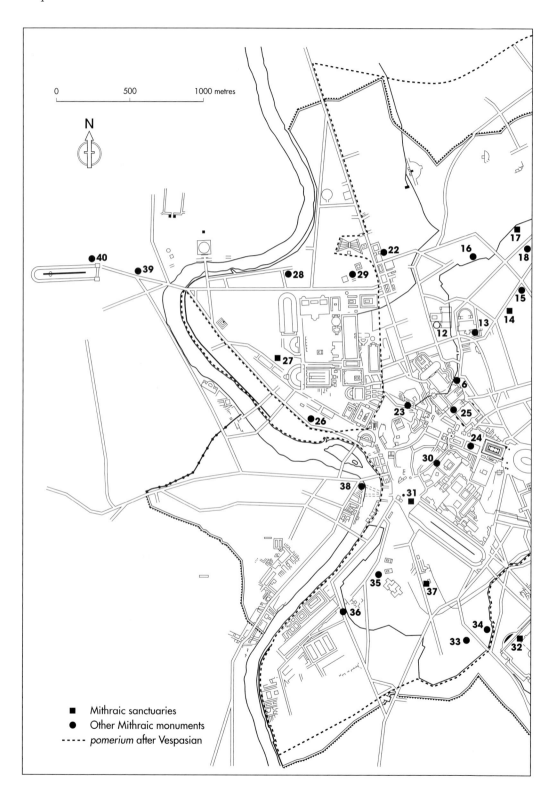

0   500   1000 metres

N

■ Mithraic sanctuaries
● Other Mithraic monuments
- - - - *pomerium* after Vespasian

Map 3

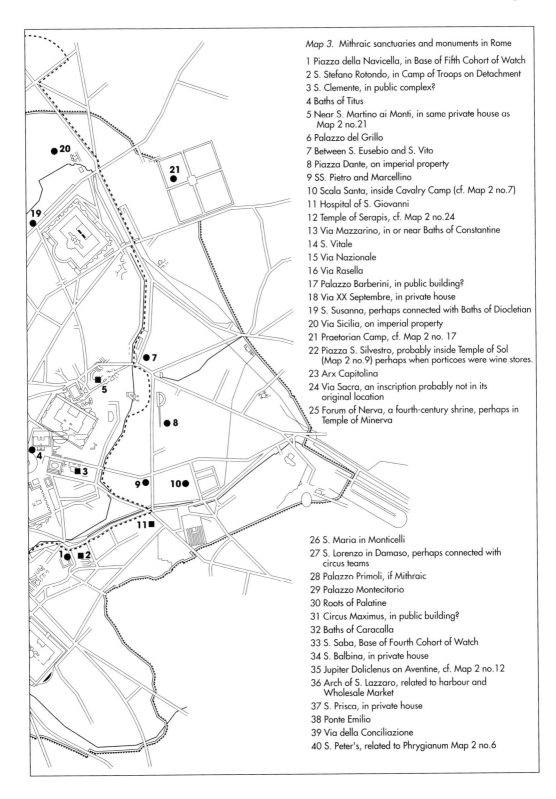

Map 3. Mithraic sanctuaries and monuments in Rome

1 Piazza della Navicella, in Base of Fifth Cohort of Watch
2 S. Stefano Rotondo, in Camp of Troops on Detachment
3 S. Clemente, in public complex?
4 Baths of Titus
5 Near S. Martino ai Monti, in same private house as Map 2 no.21
6 Palazzo del Grillo
7 Between S. Eusebio and S. Vito
8 Piazza Dante, on imperial property
9 SS. Pietro and Marcellino
10 Scala Santa, inside Cavalry Camp (cf. Map 2 no.7)
11 Hospital of S. Giovanni
12 Temple of Serapis, cf. Map 2 no.24
13 Via Mazzarino, in or near Baths of Constantine
14 S. Vitale
15 Via Nazionale
16 Via Rasella
17 Palazzo Barberini, in public building?
18 Via XX Septembre, in private house
19 S. Susanna, perhaps connected with Baths of Diocletian
20 Via Sicilia, on imperial property
21 Praetorian Camp, cf. Map 2 no. 17
22 Piazza S. Silvestro, probably inside Temple of Sol (Map 2 no.9) perhaps when porticoes were wine stores.
23 Arx Capitolina
24 Via Sacra, an inscription probably not in its original location
25 Forum of Nerva, a fourth-century shrine, perhaps in Temple of Minerva

26 S. Maria in Monticelli
27 S. Lorenzo in Damaso, perhaps connected with circus teams
28 Palazzo Primoli, if Mithraic
29 Palazzo Montecitorio
30 Roots of Palatine
31 Circus Maximus, in public building?
32 Baths of Caracalla
33 S. Saba, Base of Fourth Cohort of Watch
34 S. Balbina, in private house
35 Jupiter Doliclenus on Aventine, cf. Map 2 no.12
36 Arch of S. Lazzaro, related to harbour and Wholesale Market
37 S. Prisca, in private house
38 Ponte Emilio
39 Via della Conciliazione
40 S. Peter's, related to Phrygianum Map 2 no.6

Map 4

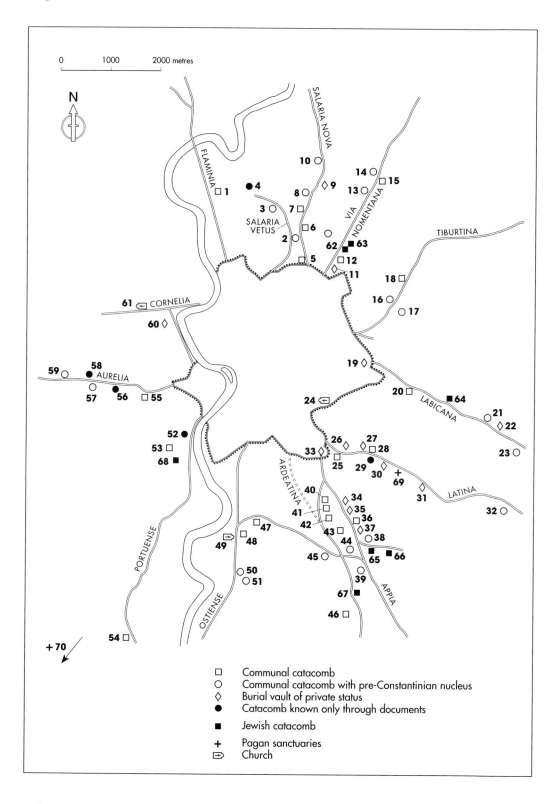

0   1000   2000 metres

N

FLAMINIA

SALARIA NOVA

10 ○

14 ○
13 ○   15 □

8 ○   ♢ 9

3 ○   7 □
SALARIA
VETUS
2 ○   6 □

● 4   1 □

VIA NOMENTANA

TIBURTINA

62 □ ■ 63
12 □
5 □
11 □

18 □
16 ○   17 ○

61 ⇦ CORNELIA

60 ♢

19 ♢

20 □   LABICANA   ■ 64

24 ⇦

21 ○
22 ♢

23 ○

59 ○
58 ● AURELIA
57 ○   56 ●   55 □

52 ●
53 □
68 ■

ARDEATINA

33 ♢
26 ♢   27 ♢
25 □   28 □
29 ●
30
+ 69

31 ♢   LATINA

32 ○

40 □
41 □
42 □
34 ♢
35 ♢
36 □
37 □
43 □   44 □
38 ○

65 ■   66 ■

45 ○

47 □
49 ⇨   48 □

50 ○
51 ○

39 ○

67 ■

46 □

APPIA

PORTUENSE

OSTIENSE

54 □

+ 70 ↘

□   Communal catacomb
○   Communal catacomb with pre-Constantinian nucleus
♢   Burial vault of private status
●   Catacomb known only through documents

■   Jewish catacomb

+   Pagan sanctuaries
⇨   Church

Map 4

Map 4. Jewish and Christian catacombs round Rome (early fourth century A.D.), with St Peter's (61), St John Lateran (24), St Paul's Basilica (49) and two 'pagan' sanctuaries. The sites are numbered along each road clockwise from the north.

Christian catacombs

1 S. Valentino
2 Pamphilus
3 Bassilla
4 Ad clivum cucumeris 'Cucumber Slope'
5 Anonymous
6 Maximus (Felicity)
7 Thrason
8 Jordani
9 Anonymous
10 Priscilla
11 Burial vault of Nicomedes
12 Nicomedes
13 Agnes
14 Nomentana Maius ('Greater')
15 Nomentana Minus ('Lesser')
16 Novatian
17 Cyriaca (S. Lawrence)
18 Hippolytus
19 Burial vault of the Aurelii
20 Castulus
21 Ad duas lauros 'At the Two Laurels'
   (SS Pietro & Marcellino)
22 Villa Celere
23 Zoticus
24 Basilica Constantiniana (S. John Lateran)
25 Gordian & Epimachus
26 Burial vault of the Old Man
27 Trebius Justus
28 Apronianus
29 Tertullinus
30 Via Dino Campagni (Via Latina)
31 Cava della Rossa
32 ad Decimum 'At Tenth Milestone'
33 G.P.Campana
34 Hunters
35 Vibia
36 S. Croce

37 Burial vault Schneider
38 Praetextatus
39 Ad Catacumbas 'At the Catacombs'
   (S. Sebastiano). Memorial of Peter and Paul
40 Basileus
41 Balbina
42 Anonymous
43 Damasus
44 Callistus
45 Domitilla
46 Nunziatella
47 Comodilla
48 Timothy
49 S. Paul
50 Thecla
51 Burial vault of Unknown Martyr
52 S. Felice (= Ad Insalsatos?)
53 Pontian
54 Generosa
55 Ottavilla
56 Processus & Martinian
57 Anonymous Villa Pamphili
58 Duo Felices 'Two Happy Ones'
59 Calepodius
60 Anonymous S. Onofrio
61 S. Peter's

Jewish catacombs
62 Villa Torlonia a
63 Villa Torlonia b
64 Via Labicana
65 Appia Pignatelli
66 Vigna Randanini
67 Vigna Cimarra
68 Monteverde

Pagan sanctuaries
69 Temple of Fortuna Muliebris
70 Sanctuary of Dea Dia

Map 5

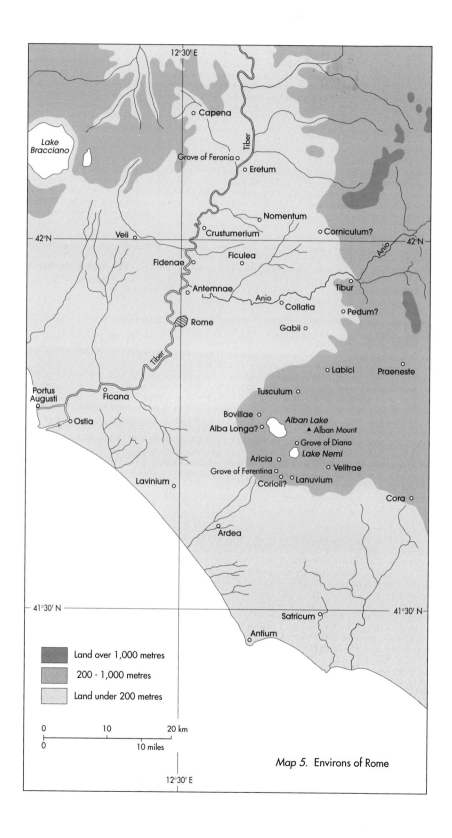

Map 5. Environs of Rome

1 Early Rome

1. Finding the religion of the early Romans

The origins of Roman religion lay in the earliest days of the city of Rome itself. That, at least, was the view held by the Romans – who would have been very puzzled that we should now have any doubt about where, when or how most of their priesthoods, their festivals, their distinctive rituals were established. Roman writers, from poets to philosophers, gave detailed accounts of the founding of Rome by the first king Romulus (the date they came to agree was – on our system of reckoning – 753 B.C.): he consulted the gods for divine approval of the new foundation, carefully laying out the sacred boundary (the *pomerium*) around the city; he built the very first temple in the city (to Jupiter Feretrius, where he dedicated the spoils of his military victories); and he established some of the major festivals that were still being celebrated a thousand years later (it was at his new ritual of the Consualia, for example, with its characteristic horse races and other festivities, that the first Romans carried off the women of the neighbouring Sabine tribes who had come to watch – the so-called 'Rape of the Sabines').[1]

But it was in the reign of the second king Numa that they found even more religious material. For it was Numa, they said, who established most of the priesthoods and the other familiar religious institutions of the city: he was credited with the invention of, among others, the priests of the gods Jupiter, Mars and Quirinus (the three *flamines*), of the *pontifices*, the Vestal Virgins and the Salii (the priests who danced through the city twice a year carrying their special sacred shields – one of which had fallen from the sky as a gift from Jupiter); and he instituted yet more new festivals, which he organized into the first systematic Roman ritual calendar. Henceforth some days of the year were marked down as religious, others as days for public business. Appropriately enough, this peaceable character founded the temple of Janus, whose doors were to be shut whenever the city was not at war. Numa was the first to close its doors; 700 years later

---

1 Roman accounts of early Roman history: Miles (1995); Fox (1996). Among many ancient versions of the stories, note, for example, Plutarch, *Romulus* 11.1–4 = **4.8a** (*pomerium*); Livy I.9 (Sabines); I.10. 5–7 (the first temple). Connections also between Jupiter Feretrius, Numa and the dedication of spoils: Festus p.204L = **1.3**.

Fig. 1.1 Terracotta statuette of Aeneas carrying his father Anchises, one of several found in a votive deposit in Veii, fourth century B.C. Aeneas' escape from burning Troy symbolizes the birth of a new Troy in Italy, a myth widely known in archaic Latium and Etruria – and not at that time restricted to Rome. (Height 0.21m.)

the emperor Augustus proudly followed suit – but it was a rare event in Rome's history.[2]

Roman writers recognized that their religion was based on traditions that went back earlier than the foundation of the city itself. Long before Romulus came on the scene, the site of Rome had been occupied by an exile from Arcadia in Greece, King Evander, who had brought to Italy a variety of Greek religious customs: he had established, for example, rites in honour of Hercules at what was called the 'Greatest Altar' (Ara Maxima) and it was because of this, so Romans explained, that rites at the Ara Maxima were always carried out in a recognizably Greek style (*Graeco ritu*).[3] Evander was also believed to have entertained the Trojan hero

2 Note, for example, Livy I.19.6 – 20.7 = **1.2** (Numa's reforms); Plutarch, *Numa* 10 = **8.4a** (Vestal Virgins); Macrobius, *Saturnalia* I.16.2–6 = **3.1** (calendar). Augustus's closure of the temple of Janus: Augustus, *Achievements* 13.

3 Ara Maxima and Evander: below, pp. 173–4. Other religious foundations of Evander: Plutarch, *Romulus* 21.3–8 = **5.2a** (Lupercalia). The Greek style of ritual was most clearly marked by the dress of the officiant at sacrifice: in Roman style the toga was drawn over the head; in Greek style the head was left bare. Scheid (1996) emphasizes the 'Romanness' of even this so-called 'Greek style'.

Aeneas, who had fled the destruction of his own city and sought safety (and a new site to re-establish the Trojan race) in Italy. (Fig 1.1) This story found its definitive version in Virgil's great national epic, the *Aeneid* – which includes a memorable account of the guided tour that Evander gave Aeneas around the site of the city that was to become Rome. Aeneas himself had a major part to play in the foundation of the Roman race, bringing with him the household gods (Penates) of his native land to a new home and renewed worship among the Romans. But he did not found the city itself; he and his son established 'proto-Romes' at Lavinium and Alba Longa. Only later was the statue of the goddess Pallas Athena that Aeneas had rescued from Troy (the Palladium) moved to the temple of Vesta in the Roman Forum, to be tended by the Vestal Virgins throughout Roman time.[4]

The kings that followed Numa also contributed – though in a less dramatic way – to the religious traditions of Rome. The rituals of the fetial priests, for example, which accompanied the making of treaties and the declaration of war (part of these involved a priest going to the boundaries of enemy territory and hurling a sacred spear across) were devised under the third and fourth rulers, Tullus Hostilius and Ancus Marcius; the fifth king, Tarquin the Elder, an immigrant to Rome from the Etruscan city of Tarquinii, laid the foundations of the temple of Jupiter, Juno and Minerva on the Capitoline hill (a temple that became a symbol of Roman religion, and hundreds of years later was widely imitated across the whole of the Roman empire); the sixth, Servius Tullius, marked the new city's growing dominance over its Latin neighbours by establishing the great 'federal' sanctuary of Diana on the Aventine hill, for all the members of the 'Latin League'. By the time the last king, Tarquin the Proud, was deposed (traditionally in 510 B.C.), and the new republican regime with its succession of annually elected magistrates established, the structure of Roman religion was essentially in place. Of course, all kinds of particular changes were to follow – new rituals, new priesthoods, new temples, new gods; but (in the view of the Romans themselves) the basic religious framework was pretty well fixed by the end of the sixth century B.C.[5]

---

4 Guided tour of Rome: *Aeneid* VIII.306–58 (with pp. 171–4 below, for the religious importance of the site of Rome). Alba and Lavinium: **1.5**; Map 5. Images of Aeneas' flight and arrival in Italy: **9.2b(i)** (coin of 47/6 B.C., showing Aeneas with the Palladium); **4.3c** (sculptured panel from Augustus' Ara Pacis, showing his landing in Italy). Palladium in the temple of Vesta: Dionysius of Halicarnassus, *Roman Antiquities* II.66.5–6 (though Dionysius admits to some uncertainty about the precise contents of the temple).
5 The *fetiales*: Livy I.24 and I.32.6–14 = **1.4a**. The Capitolium: Livy I.55.1 = **1.9b**; for Capitolia outside Rome (from Cosa in Italy and Sufetula in N. Africa), see **10.2c**. Servius Tullius and the sanctuary of Diana: Livy I.45 = **1.5d**; Map 1 no. 19. Cornell (1995) 156–9 and 165–8 discusses how far ancient writers saw the Tarquins as a specifically *Etruscan* dynasty.

There is, then, no shortage of 'evidence' about the earliest phases of Roman religion; the Greek historian of Rome, Dionysius of Halicarnassus, for example, devotes four whole books of his history (much of it concerned with religious institutions) to the period before the Republic was established, the first two covering only to the end of Numa's reign.[6] The problem is not lack of written material, but how we should interpret and make sense of that material. For all the accounts we have of Rome's earliest history are found in writers (Dionysius amongst them) who lived in the first century B.C. or later – more than 600 years after the dates usually given to the reigns of Romulus and Numa. None of our sources is contemporary with the events they describe. Nor could their authors have read any such contemporary accounts on which to base their own: so far as we know, there were no writers in earliest, regal Rome; there was no account left by Numa, say, of his religious foundations. Even for the earliest phases of the Republic (in the fifth and fourth centuries B.C.), it is very hard to know what kind of information (or how reliable) was available to historians writing three or four centuries later.[7]

Judged by our own standards of historical 'accuracy', these ancient accounts of early Rome and its religion are inadequate and misleading; they construct an image of a relatively sophisticated society, more like the city of the first century B.C. than the hamlet of the eighth century. Projections of the contemporary world back into the distant past, they are more myth than history. It is certain that primitive Rome was under the control of men the Romans called *reges* (which we translate as 'kings', though 'chieftains' might be a better term). But many modern historians would now be very doubtful whether at least the two earliest of them – Romulus and Numa – existed at all, let alone whether they carried out the reforms ascribed to them. That, of course, is precisely the point. The writers we are referring to (historians such as Dionysius or Livy; poets such as Virgil or Ovid) set little store by 'accuracy' in our narrow sense. For them, the stories of early Rome, which they told, retold and (sometimes no doubt) invented, were 'true' in quite a different way or, better, were doing a different kind of job: they were using the theme of the city's origins as a way of discussing Roman culture and religion much more generally, of defining and classifying it, of debating its problems and peculiarities. These stories were a way in which the Romans (or, in the case of Dionysius and others, the Greek inhabitants of the Roman empire) explained their own religious system to themselves; and as such they were inevitably embedded in the religious concerns and debates of their writers' own times. As we shall see, for example, stories of the apotheosis of Romulus (into the god Quirinus) were told with particular emphasis, elaborated (some might say *invented*), around the time of Julius Caesar's deification in the 40s B.C. Romulus' ascent to heaven

6 Gabba (1991).   7 Cornell (1995) 1–30.

offered, in other words, a way of understanding, justifying or attacking the recent (and contested) elevation of the dead dictator.[8]

These images of early Rome are central to the way the Romans made sense of their own religion; and so too they are central to our understanding and discussion of Roman religion. It would be nonsense to ignore the figure of 'Numa', the father of the Roman priesthood and founder of the calendar, just because we decided that King Numa (715–672 B.C.) was a figment of the Roman mythic imagination. We shall return to this early history at many points through this book – using (for example) Ovid's explanations of the origins of particular festivals as a way of rethinking their significance in the Rome of Ovid's own day, or exploring the way the myths of Aeneas and Romulus were used to define the position of the first emperor Augustus (and were themselves re-told in the process). But this earliest period will not bulk particularly large in this first chapter on the religion of early Rome.[9]

This chapter is concerned with what we can know about the religion of Rome before the second century B.C., when for the first time contemporary writing survives in some quantity. This was the period in which the distinctive institutions of later periods must have taken shape. But how can we construct an (in our terms) 'historical' account of that religious world, when there are no contemporary written records beyond a few brief, and often enigmatic, inscriptions on stone, metal or pot? This first section concentrates on that question of method: reviewing particular documents and literary traditions which have been claimed to give a privileged access to accurate information on the earliest phases of Rome's religion; exploring some of the recent archaeological discoveries from Rome and elsewhere which have changed the way we can talk of particular aspects of that religion; and discussing various theories that have been used to reconstruct its fundamental character.

One group of documents that has often been given a special place in reconstructions of early Roman religion is a group known (collectively) as 'the calendar'. More than 40 copies (some of them, admittedly, very fragmentary) of a ritual calendar of Roman festivals, inscribed or painted on walls, survive from Rome and the surrounding areas of Italy, mostly dating to the age of Augustus (31 B.C. to A.D.14) or soon after.[10] No two of these calendars are exactly the same: the lists of festivals are slightly different in each

---

8 One version of the story is given in Livy I.16 = **2.8a.** Earlier roots of the cult of Romulus and other 'founders': Liou-Gille (1980); Capdeville (1995).

9 Below, pp. 171–6 and ch. 4 *passim.*

10 The inscriptions are collected in Degrassi (1963), who also gives (388–546) a selection of other important sources for each festival, with bibliography and notes. Discussion and additional fragments in Rüpke (1995) 39–188. The most accessible account in English is Scullard (1981). The calendar itself is discussed, with a selection of extracts at **3.1–3.**

case; and the additional information on the festivals that is regularly included ranges from terse notes on the god or temple involved to more extended entries of several lines, apparently drawn from antiquarian commentators, describing or explaining the rituals. None the less the calendars are all recognizably variations on the same theme, selecting from the same broad group of festivals. We shall be referring to these calendars in many contexts through the chapters that follow. For the moment, we want to stress one small but significant feature in their layout that they all have in common: some of the festival entries are inscribed in capital letters while others are in small letters. The capital-letter festivals are essentially the same group from calendar to calendar, roughly 40 in all – and including, for example, the Lupercalia, the Parilia, the Consualia, the Saturnalia. It seems virtually certain that they form an ancient list of festivals, preserved within the later documents.[11]

But how ancient? We do not know when the characteristic form of time-keeping that underlies these calendars was introduced at Rome – maybe in the course of the republican period, maybe earlier; nor do we know whether its introduction coincided with the fixing of this particular group of capital-letter festivals, or not. It is hard to forget completely the mythic 'Calendar of Numa': certainly some of these festivals contain strange-seeming rituals and have often been interpreted as reflecting archaic social conditions; besides, though some of these festivals (such as those we mentioned above) were still very prominent in the first century B.C., some were totally obscure at the time the calendars were being inscribed; and in no case can it be proved that a capital-letter festival was introduced later than the regal period.[12] On the other hand the idea of the 'Calendar of Numa' (that is, of a very early canonical group of festivals) could be misleading. Even accepting, as is likely, that the capital-letter festivals do represent some ancient list, the purpose of that list remains quite uncertain: not necessarily the oldest festivals of all; perhaps, the most important at some specific date; perhaps even the most important to some individual on some specific occasion, that has somehow become embedded in the tradition.[13] We certainly cannot assume that any festival not in capitals must be a 'later' introduction into the calendar.

A list of the names of early festivals on its own, however, tells us little – without some idea of their content and significance. Here we must turn to a variety of later sources which offer details of the rituals of these festivals and of the stories, traditions and explanations associated with them. By far the richest source of all is Ovid's *Fasti*, a witty verse account of the first six months of the Roman calendar and its rituals.[14] Ovid, however, was writing

11 Mommsen in *CIL* I.1, 2nd edn. (1893), 283–304.
12 Michels (1967) 93–144.
13 Michels (1967) 13–44; radical scepticism in Rüpke (1995) 245–88, esp. 283–6.
14 Below, pp. 174–6; 207–8.

in the reign of Augustus and much of what he has to offer does not consist of traditional Roman stories at all, but of imported Greek ones. So, for example, explaining the odd rituals of the festival of the goddess Vesta (one of our capital-letter group), which involved hanging loaves of bread around asses' necks, he brings in a farcical tale of the Greek god Priapus: once upon a time, he says, at a picnic of the gods, this grotesque and crude rapist crept up on Vesta as she sprawled, unsuspecting, on the grass; but an ass's bray alerted her to his approach – and ever after, on her festal day, asses take a holiday and wear 'necklaces of loaves in memory of his services'.[15] Some of these stories were no doubt introduced by Ovid himself, in the interests of variety or for fun; some may already have been, before his day, incorporated into educated Roman speculation (or joking) about the rituals. But either way it is certain that Ovid's stories do not all date back into the early history of Rome, even if some elements may do. As a source of the religious ideas of his own time Ovid is invaluable; as a source for the remote past, he is hard to trust.

It is not just a question, though, of Ovid being peculiarly unreliable; and the answer does not lie simply in looking for other ancient commentators on the calendar who have not 'polluted' their accounts with anachronistic explanations. The fact is that the rituals prescribed by the calendar of festivals were not handed down with their own original 'official' myth or explanation permanently attached to them. They were constantly re-interpreted and re-explained by their participants. This process of re-interpretation, found in almost every culture, including our own (the annual British ritual of 'Bonfire Night' means something quite different today from three hundred years ago),[16] is precisely the strength of any ritual system: it enables rituals that claim to be unchanging to adopt different social meanings as society evolves new needs and new ideas over the course of time; and it means, for example, that a festival originating within a small community whose main interests were farming can still be relevant maybe 600 years later to a cosmopolitan urban culture, as it is gradually (and often imperceptibly to its participants) refocussed onto new concerns and circumstances.[17] But at the same time it means that the interpretation of the 'original' significance of a festival, especially in a society that has left no written documents, is not just difficult, but close to impossible. The fact that we can trace the same names (Lupercalia, Vinalia etc.) over hundreds of years, or even the fact that the ceremonies may have been carried out in

---

15 *Fasti* VI.319–48 = **2.5** (cf. I.337–53 = **6.4a**).

16 Of course, the conspiracy to blow up the Houses of Parliament, whose detection is celebrated on 5 November, construes in many ways: from a dastardly plot against the crown by Catholic traitors to a popular uprising against the ruling class. Compare the varied significances of Christmas, discussed in Miller (1993).

17 We examine the Roman festival of the Parilia in this light below, pp. 174–6; see also **5.1**.

a similar fashion throughout that time, does not allow us to trace back the same significance from the first century B.C. to the seventh.

The calendar is a prime example of how tantalizing much of the evidence for the religion of early Rome is. Again, it is not that there is no evidence at all. Here we have a remarkable survival: fossilized within later traditions of calendar design, traces of a list of festivals whose origins lie centuries earlier; traces, in other words, of an early Roman document itself, not a first-century B.C. reconstruction of early Roman society. The problem is how to interpret such traces, fragmentary and entirely isolated from their original context.

Other documents and direct evidence from the early Republic, and even the regal period, are almost certainly preserved in the scholarly and anti-quarian tradition of historical writing at Rome in the late Republic and early empire. For the Romans, the greatest of their antiquarians was the first-century Varro, who compiled a vast encyclopaedia of Roman religion with the express purpose, he said, of preserving the ancient religious traditions that were being forgotten or neglected by his contemporaries. This extraordinary polymath would certainly have been able to consult many documents (inscriptions recording temple foundations, for example, religious regula-tions, dedications) no longer available to us and he would no doubt have quoted many in his work. It is hard not to regret the loss of Varro and the fact that his religious encyclopaedia survives only in fragments, quoted as brief dictionary entries or in the accounts of later Christian writers who plun-dered his work and that of other antiquarians solely in order to show how absurd, valueless and obscene was the religion of the classical world that they were seeking to destroy and replace. On the other hand, some of these quo-tations are quite extensive, and the substance of Varro's work may also be preserved in many other authors who do not refer to him directly by name. The loss may not, after all, be as great as we imagine.[18]

Thirty-five books of Livy's *History* do, however, survive – out of the orig-inal 142, which covered the history of Rome from its origins to the reign of the emperor Augustus. Livy's *History* is in many respects preoccupied (as we have already seen) with the issues and concerns of first-century B.C. Rome; and more generally the picture we derive from his writing may be very much an artificial historiographic construction, expressing an 'official

---

18 The fragments of Varro's *Divine Antiquities* are collected (with a commentary) in Cardauns (1976); see also Cardauns (1978). Many are drawn from the Christian writ-ers Augustine (particularly from *The City of God*) and Arnobius (*Against the Gentiles*). It is clear that both authors exploit Varro's material without any concern (or maybe capacity) to be fair to the pagan author – the last thing on their minds; for examples of Augustine's use of Varro, see *The City of God* IV.31 = **1.1a**; VI.5 = **13.9**. Other works of Varro do survive more fully: 6 books out of an original 25 *On the Latin Language*; a complete work *On Agriculture*, in 3 books. Among other antiquarian writers, the dic-tionary of Festus (ed. Lindsay, 1913) preserves some of the Augustan antiquarian Verrius Flaccus (on whom Dihle (1958); Frier (1979) 35–7), whose work underlies the notes in the calendar from Praeneste (Degrassi (1963) 107–45; extract = **3.3b**).

religion' which reflected little of the religious life of the community, or perhaps only that of the élite. On the other hand, Livy does claim to know
many individual 'facts' about religious history going back at least to the early
Republic, sometimes even quoting ancient documents or formulae. How
accurate can this information have been?

Some of the documents (for example, his quotation of the particular
religious formulae used in the declaration of war) are almost certainly fictional reconstructions or inventions, which may have little in common
with the formulae actually used in early Rome.[19] But many of the other
brief records (of vows, special games, the introduction of new cults, innovations in religious procedure, the consultation of religious advisers and so
on) are not likely to be inventions. The pieces of information they contain
are not obviously part of an ideological story of early religion; and many of
them appear (from the form in which they are recorded, or the precise
details they record) to preserve material from the early Republic, if not earlier. Perhaps the clearest example of this comes not from Livy himself, but
from the elder Pliny. In his *Natural History* (written in the middle of the
first century A.D.), Pliny notes the precise year in which the standard procedure for examining the entrails of sacrificial animals ('extispicy') was
amended to take account of the heart in addition to other vital organs.[20]
This information almost certainly comes from some early source: not only
does there seem to be no reason for such an odd piece of 'information' to
have been invented, but it is also dated in a unique way – which it is very
unlikely that Pliny would have made up. The date of the change is given by
the year of the reign of the *rex sacrorum*, that is the 'king of rites' or the
priest who carried on the king's religious duties when kingship itself was
abolished; this makes no sense unless this system of dating continued in
use in priestly records even though it was abandoned for every other purpose when the Republic was founded; if so Pliny (or his source) must have
found this 'nugget' in some priestly context.

This gives us one hint on how information of this type might have been
preserved and transmitted from the earliest period of Rome's history to the
time when the literary tradition of history writing started. Priests in Rome
had traditionally kept records to which they could refer to establish points
of law; and (as we shall discuss later in this chapter) the *pontifices*, in particular, were said to have kept an annual record of events, including, but not
confined to, the sphere of religion. Writing down and recording was a significant part of the function of priests.[21] It is certainly possible that Livy,

19 The formula of the *fetiales* at the beginning of war: Livy I.32.6–14 = **1.4a**; see Ogilvie
    (1965) 127–9, for strong suspicions that it is based on later antiquarian reconstruc-
    tions.
20 *Natural History* XI.186.
21 Moatti (forthcoming). The various records of the *pontifices* in particular: Wissowa
    (1912) 513; Rohde (1936); Frier (1979); below, pp. 25–6.

Pliny and other writers (or the sources on which they drew; there was after all a two-hundred year tradition of history writing at Rome before Livy, mostly lost to us) had access to priestly records with information stretching back centuries. If so (and many modern historians have hoped or assumed that this was the case) then many of their points of fact about religious changes, decisions or developments in early Rome may be more authentic than we would otherwise imagine.

On the other hand, priestly record keeping had (for our purposes) its own limitations. Only changes, not continuities, would have been recorded; and then, presumably, only changes of a particular kind, the ones the priestly authorities noticed and chose to record in their collegiate books. Many other changes will have happened over the course of years without record – through mistakes, neglect, forgetfulness, unobserved social evolution, the unconscious re-building of outmoded conceptions; many of these would never even have been noticed, let alone written down. So even if we could gather together these occasional recorded facts (the foundation of a new temple, the introduction of a new god) and arrange them into some sort of chronological account, it would make a very strange sort of 'history'. A history of religion is, after all, more than a series of religious decisions or changes. Once again, it is not a question of having no 'authentic' information stretching back to the early period; it is a question of having very little context and background against which to interpret the pieces of information that we have.[22]

If evidence of this kind offers only glimpses of the earliest religious history of Rome, modern scholars have tried to construct a broader view by setting the evidence against different theories (or sometimes just different a priori assumptions) about the character of early religions in general and early Roman religion in particular, and about how such religions develop.[23] These theories vary considerably in detail, but they have over all a similar structure and deploy similar methods. First, the earliest Roman religion is uncovered by stripping away all the 'foreign', non-Roman elements that are clearly visible in the religion of (say) the late Republic. Even in that period, some characteristics of Roman religion must strike us as quite distinct from the traditions of the Greeks, Etruscans and even of other Italic peoples that we know of. The Roman gods, for example, even the greatest of them, seem

22 So, for example, without such a context we can make little sense of the change in the ritual of extispicy noted by Pliny: it could be an indication of a major shift in Roman conceptions of the internal organs of the body; equally a sign of some technical and long running priestly dispute; or both. For further discussion of early documents preserved by later writers, see below, pp. 32–4.

23 Among the most influential versions are Warde Fowler (1911); Rose (1926); Latte (1960a); for criticisms of various of these, Dumézil (1970); for their place in the history of the study of Roman religion, Scheid (1987); Durand and Scheid (1994). A quite different approach to the character of the religion and its history is taken by Scheid (1985a) 17–57.

not to have had a marked personal development and character; while a whole range of 'lesser' gods are attested who were essentially a divine aspect of some natural, social or agricultural process (such as Vervactor, the god of 'turning over fallow land', or Imporcitor, the god of 'ploughing with wide furrows'[24]); there were few 'native' myths attaching even to the most prominent rituals; the system offered no eschatology, no explanation of creation or man's relation to it; there was no tradition of prophets or holy men; a surviving fragment of Varro's encyclopaedia of religion even reports that the earliest Romans, for 170 years after the foundation of their city, had no representations of their gods.[25] These characteristics have been interpreted in all kinds of different ways. Some modern scholars have seen them as simple primitive piety – which seems, in fact, to have been the line taken by Varro (who claimed that the worship of the gods would have been more reverently performed, if the Romans had continued to avoid divine images). But at the same time, the temptation is seldom resisted to summarize all this by saying that the Romans were artless, unimaginative and supremely practical folk, and hence that everything involving art, literary imagination, philosophic awareness or spirituality had to be borrowed from outside – whether from Greeks, Etruscans or other Italians.[26]

The second strand of the argument treats the 'development' of Roman religion as effectively a 'deterioration': the 'healthy' period of 'true' Roman religion is retrojected into the remote past; the late Republic is treated as a period when religion was virtually dead; the early Republic then provides a transitional period in which the forces of deterioration gathered strength, while the simplicities of the early native religious experience were progressively lost. Among the mechanisms of this deterioration that have been proposed are: (a) the contamination of the native tradition by foreign, especially Greek, influences; (b) the sterilization of true religiosity by the growth of excessive priestly ritualism; (c) the alienation of an increasingly sophisticated urban population from a religious tradition that had once been a religion of the farm and countryside and failed to evolve. In the case of (c), it is hard to believe that any ancient city lost its involvement with, and dependence on, the seasonal cycle of the agricultural year, let alone the relatively small-town Rome of the third century B.C. The other two suggestions are harder to refute, but no less arbitrary. A different approach will be taken in what follows, but we can point out at once that neither foreign influences nor priestly ritualism necessarily cause the deterioration of a religious

---

24 Note the list of such deities in Servius, *On Virgil's Georgics* I.21; cf, Augustine, *The City of God* VI.9 = **2.2c**. We cannot be certain that these 'godlets' represent a survival of the most primitive Roman conception of divinity; they could equally well be a much later priestly (or antiquarian) construction. For different views, Bayet (1950); Dumézil (1970) 35–8.

25 Varro in Augustine, *The City of God* IV.31 = **1.1a**; in Tertullian, *Apology* 25.12 = fr. 38 (Cardauns).

26 For instance, in relation to extispicy, Schilling (1962)

system; and we will argue too (especially in chapter 3) that it is much harder than many modern writers have assumed to decide what is to count as the 'decline' of a religion.[27]

But there is an even more fundamental challenge to this simple scheme of development. Recent work, particularly in archaeology, has cast doubt on the idea of an early, uncontaminated, native strand of genuine Roman religion; and it has suggested that, rather than seeing pure Roman traditions gradually polluted from outside, Roman religion was an amalgam of different traditions from at least as far back as we can hope to go. Leaving aside its mythical prehistory, Roman religion was always already multicultural.

Archaeological evidence from the sixth century B.C., for example, has shown that (whatever the political relations of Rome and Etruria may have been)[28] in cultural and religious terms Rome was part of a civilization dominated by Etruscans and receptive to the influence of Greeks and possibly of Carthaginians too. A dedication to the divine twins Castor and Pollux found at Lavinium, which uses a version of their Greek title 'Dioskouroi', shows unmistakably that we have to reckon with Greek contacts;[29] some of these contacts may have been mediated through the Etruscans, others coming directly from Greece itself – while it is perfectly possible that there were connections too with Greek settlements in South Italy. Even more striking Greek elements have been revealed by a recent study of the earliest levels of the Roman forum. From this it has become possible to identify almost certainly the early sanctuary of the god Vulcan (the Volcanal); and in the votive deposit from this sanctuary, dating from the second quarter of the sixth century B.C., was an Athenian black-figure vase with a representation of the Greek god Hephaestus. In other words, there was already in the early sixth century some identification of Roman Vulcan and the Greek Hephaestus, and the Greek image of the god had already penetrated to his holy place in the centre of Rome.[30]   In a different way, the discovery of a religious phenomenon widespread throughout central Italy has similar disturbing implications for the conventional image of early Roman religion. Several sites have now produced substantial deposits of votive offerings dating back to at least the fourth century B.C., which consist primarily of small terracotta models of parts of the human body (Fig 1.2);[31] this suggests that there were a number of sanctuaries soon after the beginning of the

27 Discussion of innovation and foreign influence in religion: North (1976).
28 Whether or not, that is, Rome was ever under the direct political ascendancy of Etruria. Some scholars have seen such direct Etruscan control lying behind (among other things) the stories of the Etruscan origin of Tarquin the Elder. Cornell (1995) 151–72 reviews the question.
29 Inscription: *ILLRP* 1271a = **1.7b**. Discussion: Weinstock (1960) 112–14; Castagnoli (1983); Holloway (1994) 130–4.
30 Coarelli (1977b); for a reconstruction of the shrine and the fragment of pottery, **1.7c**; for the Volcanal, Capdeville (1995).
31 Maule and Smith (1959); Fenelli (1975); Comella (1981); and below, n. 221.

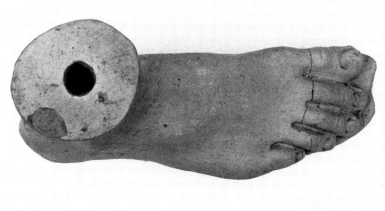

Fig. 1.2 Votive terracottas from Ponte di Nona, 15km to the east of Rome. They were made in the third or second centuries B.C. for a sanctuary on the site abandoned in the late Republic, but were buried together during building operations in the fifth century A.D. This particular deposit included a majority of feet and eyes, perhaps reflecting the sanctuary's curative specialities. (Foot, length 0.3m.; eyes, width 0.05m.)

Republic to which individuals went when seeking cures for their diseases: at these sanctuaries they presumably dedicated terracottas of the afflicted part. This implies not only a cult not mentioned in any surviving ancient account, but also a type of religiosity which the accepted model of early Roman religion seems to exclude: for it implies that individuals turned to the gods directly in search of support with their everyday problems of health and disease. On the accepted model, they would have looked for and expected no such help, practical or spiritual. Another study has suggested that inscriptions discovered at Tor Tignosa near to Lavinium come from a cult in which incubation was practised: that is to say, people came to sleep in the sanctuary in the hope of receiving advice or revelation from the deity in a dream.[32] In this case both Virgil and Ovid describe the use of such a technique in early – or rather mythical – Italy;[33] but their evidence was always thought suspect on the grounds that divine communication through dreams was a characteristically Greek practice, not compatible with the religious life of the early Romans and found in Italy only later when specifically Greek incubation-cults were introduced.[34]

This much more complex picture of early Roman religion undermines some of those narrative accounts of Roman religious history that have been most influential over the last hundred years. So, for example, it is hard to sustain the once popular and powerful idea – influenced by early twentieth century anthropology – that Roman religion gradually evolved from a primitive phase of 'animism' (where divine power was spread widely through all kinds of natural phenomena) to a stage where it had developed

32 Palmer (1974) 79–171; Map 5.
33 Virgil, *Aeneid* VII. 81–106 = **4.11**; Ovid, *Fasti* IV.649–72.
34 It is worth noting how the Roman myths (with which we started this chapter) themselves stressed the 'foreign' elements that made up 'Roman' traditions – the Greek Evander, the Trojan Aeneas etc.; see below, pp. 171–4.

13

'proper' gods and goddesses;[35] if we abandon the idea of an original core of essential Romanness, then we must abandon also any attempt to discover a single linear progression in the history of Roman religion. In this spirit, rather than trying to extract a small kernel of primitive 'Roman' characteristics from the varied evidence of the first century B.C., a different strategy has been to define the central characteristics of early Roman religion *comparatively* – that is by comparison with societies with a similar history. In the rest of this section, we shall look in greater detail at the most influential of these comparative approaches, its main claims and its problems.

The lifetime's project of the historian Georges Dumézil (1898–1986) was to combine evidence from many different Indo-European societies and traditions in order to discover the internal structure of the systems of mythology that were, he claimed, the common inheritance of all these peoples. His theories were based on the much broader and older idea that the societies which speak languages belonging to the 'Indo-European' family (including Greek, Latin, most of the languages of modern Europe, as well as Sanskrit, the old language of North India, and Old Persian) shared more than language; that they had, albeit in the far distant past, a common social and cultural origin.

Dumézil believed that the mythological structure of the Romans and of other Indo-Europeans was derived ultimately from the social divisions of the original Indo-European people themselves, and that these divisions gave rise to a 'tri-functional ideology' – which caused all deities, myths and related human activities to fall into three distinct categories: 1. Religion and Law; 2. War; 3. Production, especially agricultural production. This was an enormously ambitious claim, and at first Dumézil's theories drew very little acceptance. But in time he convinced some other scholars that this tri-partite structure could be detected both in the most archaic Roman religious institutions and in the mythology of the kings, especially in that of the first four.[36] On his view, Romulus and Numa were the symbols of the first function (one a ruler, one a priest); Tullus Hostilius, the third king, and Ancus Marcius, his successor, represented the second and third functions respectively (the inventors of war and of peaceful production).[37]

In Dumézil's perspective, the earliest gods also reflected these three functions – as gods of law and authority, gods of war, gods of production and

---

35 Warde Fowler (1911); Rose (1926); further discussion at **1.1**.

36 Dumézil himself wrote copiously on Rome from the 1930s onwards and provoked more discussion as time went on – some hostile, some supportive. Dumézil (1941–5) is an early statement; (1974) his fullest account of Roman religion – (1970) is the English translation of the first edition; (1968–73) gives the latest version of the mythology of the Roman kings. Discussion: Momigliano (1983); Scheid (1983); (1985a) 74–94; Belier (1991).

37 Tullus as a great warrior: for example, Livy I.23–9; Ancus, at least by inclination, as a more peaceful ruler: for example, Livy I.30 (though see, I.32.6–14 = **1.4a**). Above, pp. 1–4.

agriculture. The familiar deities of the Capitoline triad (Jupiter, Juno and Minerva) failed to fit the model; but he found his three functions in the gods of the 'old triad' – Jupiter, Mars, Quirinus. Although this group was of no particular prominence through most of the history of Roman religion, they were the gods to whom the three important priests of early Rome (the *flamen Dialis* (of Jupiter), *flamen Martialis* and *flamen Quirinalis*) were dedicated – and Dumézil found other traces of evidence to suggest that these three had preceded the Capitoline deities as the central gods of the Roman pantheon. They appeared to fit his three functions perfectly: Jupiter as the king of the gods; Mars the war-god; Quirinus the god of the ordinary citizens, the farmers.[38]

Dumézil's work has prompted much useful discussion about individual festivals or areas of worship at Rome.[39] There are, however, several major problems with his Indo-European scheme overall. If Dumézil were right, that would mean (quite implausibly) that early Roman religion and myth encoded a social organization divided between kings, warriors and producers fundamentally opposed to the 'actual' social organization of republican Rome (even probably regal Rome) itself. For everything we know about early Roman society specifically excludes a division of functions according to Dumézil's model. It was, in fact, one of the defining characteristics of republican Rome (and a principle on which many of its political institutions were based) that the warriors were the peasants, and that the voters were 'warrior-peasants'; not that the warriors and the peasant agriculturalists were separate groups with a separate position in society and separate interests as Dumézil's mythic scheme demands. In order to follow Dumézil, one would need to accept not only that the religious and mythic life of a primitive community could be organized differently from its social life, but that the two could be glaringly incompatible.

This point is reinforced by the character of the gods in the old triad. Even supposing Dumézil were right about their very earliest significance, all three soon developed into the supposed domains of at least one and possibly both of the others. Jupiter, the god of the highest city authority, also received the war-vows of the departing general and provided the centre of the triumphal procession on his return; but he also presided over the harvest in the vineyards.[40] Mars, the god of war, protected the crops and was hence very prominent in the prayers and rituals of the farmer.[41] Quirinus, who was anyway far less prominent in republican times, was certainly connected

---

38 Further discussion at **1.3**.
39 Dumézil (1975) is itself a notable attempt to investigate some of the least understood Roman festivals.
40 Jupiter and the triumph: Versnel (1970) 56–93; Jupiter and the vines: Montanari (1988) 137–62; below, p. 45.
41 It is essential to Dumézil's whole position to interpret Mars as the War God, the God of the second function: Dumézil (1970) 205–45. But a good deal of evidence will not

with the mass of the population and with production, but also appears as a war god like Mars; while his appearance as the divine aspect of Romulus puts him also into the first (kingly) function.[42] Outside this triad even apparently ancient deities do not readily fall into one of Dumézil's three categories. Juno, for example, who is sometimes very much a political goddess in Rome and the surrounding area, is also a warrior goddess and the goddess of women and childbirth. It is well established in studies of Greek polytheism that the spheres of interest of individual deities within the pantheon were more complicated than a one to one correlation (Venus/Aphrodite = goddess of love) would suggest; and that the spheres of deities were shifting, multiple and often defined not in isolation, but in a series of relationships with other gods and goddesses. It may well be, in other words, that Dumézil's attempt to pin down particular divine functions so precisely was itself misconceived.[43] But, even if that were not the case, it is hard to find any of the main deities at Rome that does not cross some or all of Dumézil's most important boundaries.

Dumézil's theorizing shows us once more how powerful in accounts of early Roman religion is the mystique of origins and schemata. But in the end we are confronted with an imaginary Roman tradition of the history of their early religion; with individual pieces of information preserved in later writing either randomly or (in the case of priestly record keeping) by a process of selection we can hardly guess at; with glimpses of different kinds of information and different kinds of religious experience; and with a variety of theories that attempt to explain the information we have. This is both too little and too much. Probably most important for our understanding of Roman religion is the mythic tradition, with its tales of Romulus and Numa, the origins of customs and rituals, that was one of the most powerful ways of thinking about religion that the Romans devised. But, as we have seen, it was not a 'history' of religion in our terms.

We have adopted a quite different approach for exploring the history of Roman religion. We have not followed the method, so often tried before, of seeking the 'real' religion of Rome by stripping away the allegedly later accretions, but rather have used precisely the opposite method. The next three sections (2–5) of this chapter analyse the central structural characteristics of Roman republican religion, very largely based on evidence that refers to the last three centuries of that period. In doing so we have not

fit this view: for example, Cato, *On Agriculture* 141 = **6.3a**, where Mars is clearly protecting farmers; see also on the October Horse, below, pp. 47–8. Different interpretations: Warde Fowler (1911) 131–4; De Sanctis (1907–64) IV.2.149–52; Latte (1960a) 114–16; Scholz (1970); Rüpke (1990) 22–8.

42 Latte (1960a) 113–14; Koch (1960) 17–39; (1963); Brelich (1960); Gagé (1966); Dumézil (1970) 246–72; Liou-Gille (1980) 135–207.

43 For an introduction to studies of Greek polytheism, R. L. Gordon (1981) 1–42; note also the classic study of the relationship of Hestia and Hermes, Vernant (1983) 127–75.

restricted ourselves to the contemporary first-century B.C. material of Cicero and Varro, but have drawn on the account of Livy (writing after the end of the Republic) for the third and second centuries B.C. We do this on the principle that the structural features of any religion change only slowly, and that the third-century system as described by Livy is recognizably similar to the first-century world we know from contemporary sources. In other words we claim that (for all the early imperial interpretation he cast on his material) Livy understood well enough the functioning of the republican religious system to represent it in its broad outlines.

We also accept, however, that the further back in time we attempt to project this picture, the more risk there is that it will be seriously misleading. It is virtually certain that some of the features of republican religion that we identify (for example, some of the priesthoods and priestly colleges) stretched back, in some form, into the earliest period of Rome's history; and that more could be traced back at least to the very earliest period of the Republic itself. On the other hand it is also certain that an overall picture valid for the third century B.C. would be quite invalid for the period of the kings, and in some respects for the early Republic too. There were major breaks in the history of Rome not only at the time of the 'fall of the kings' (traditionally put in the late sixth century B.C.) but also in the last decades of the fourth century, when we can detect radical changes in the nature of the Roman state. It may well be, in fact, that the developed institutions of the Republic (which we and the Romans tend to push back to the years immediately following the end of the monarchy) largely took their distinctive shape at that time.

The risks of assuming too much continuity (religious and political) from the very beginning of the Republic can be well illustrated by considering the tradition about patricians and plebeians. In the late Republic the patricians were a closed caste of ancient clans, while the plebeians were all the other Romans. At that date the patricians had very few political privileges, but some particular priesthoods were restricted to them alone; and in chapter two we shall see how the division applied in the main priestly colleges where places had to be held in certain numbers by patricians and plebeians. It is certainly the case that conflict between patricians and plebeians (and the plebeians' claim to a share in the privileges of patricians) was a major feature of the late fifth and early fourth centuries B.C. And both ancient and modern historians have tended to assume that the distinction applied in an even stronger form in earlier periods: that in the first years of the Republic and even under the monarchy, all the rich, noble, office-holding families were patrician; all the others plebeian. In fact this assumption is very flimsy: it is very possible that there were more than two status groups in the fifth century B.C.; and quite certain that power was not limited to patricians – for example the recorded names of some of the early magistrates are not patrician; and in fact the kings all have non-patrician names.

17

It seems fairly clear that there were radical changes in Roman society between 500 and 300 B.C., marked in part by the increasing rigidity of the patrician/plebeian distinction; we must reckon with the possibility that religious authority changed radically in its character too.[44]

Our argument is that by starting with the developed republican structure we are providing an introduction to the ideas and institutions that will recur throughout this book. At the same time, we are defining a framework within (and against) which to interpret the evidence about earlier Rome, by beginning to assess how similar or different the earliest conditions may have been. Accordingly sections 5 and 6 of this chapter will return to consider the transition from monarchy to Republic, and the character of religious change in the early republican years.

2. The priests and religious authority

In the late Republic, one of the most distinctive features of the Roman religious system was its priestly organization, consisting of a number of 'colleges' and other small groups of priests, each with a particular area of religious duty or expertise. Two underlying principles stand out: first, the sharp differentiation of priestly tasks (priests were specialists, carrying out the particular responsibilities assigned to their college or group); second, collegiality (priests did not operate as individuals, but as a part or as a representative of the group – there was no specific ritual programme for any individual, while any member of the college could properly perform the rituals). This is the basic structure that Roman writers ascribed (mythically) to Numa; and they assumed that it operated in the early republican period too – where, we are told, there were three major colleges of priests: the pontiffs (*pontifices*) the augurs (*augures*) and the 'two men for sacred actions' (*duoviri*, later increased to the 'ten men' *decemviri sacris faciundis*);[45] a fourth college, the fetials (*fetiales*), was perhaps of comparable importance. These four colleges, whose members normally held office for life, were consulted as experts by the senate within their own area of responsibility, and on those issues the senate would defer to their authority. Other groups of priests had ritual duties, on particular occasions or in relation to particular cults, but were not, so far as we know, officially consulted on points of religious law.[46]

44 Historical development in general: Cornell (1995) 242–71.
45 The changing number and title of this priesthood causes problems of terminology: technically they were *duoviri* until they became *decemviri* in 367 B.C. (below, p. 64); they were increased to fifteen (*quindecimviri*) by 51 B.C. – and they retained that title thereafter, even when their numbers were further increased. Broadly following this chronology, we normally call them *duoviri* in chapter 1, *decemviri* in chapter 2 and *quindecimviri* in the rest of the book.
46 Roman priesthood in general: Scheid (1984); (1985a) 36–51; Beard (1990); Scheid (1993).

Fig. 1.3 Heads of two *flamines*, from the south frieze of the Ara Pacis, Rome (**4.3**); their religious importance is marked by their leading the procession of priests (behind Augustus as *pontifex maximus*, but ahead of all the other priests) and they are distinguished by their head-gear, a bonnet with a projecting baton of olive-wood (*apex*). (Height, c. 0.2m.)

This general view of the colleges needs some qualification in particular cases. First, the college of *pontifices* had a far more complex structure than the others. They had a recognized leader (the *pontifex maximus*), who, from the third century B.C. onwards, was elected publicly from the existing *pontifices*, not, as before, chosen by his colleagues. The college also contained a number of other priestly officials: as full members, the *rex sacrorum* and the *flamines* of the gods Jupiter, Mars and Quirinus; and in some sense associated with the college, even if not 'members', the Vestal Virgins, the scribes of the *pontifices*, and the twelve lesser *flamines*.[47] The fifteen *flamines*, through the very nature of their priesthood, suggest a different principle of religious organization: each had his own god to whom he was devoted; he had his ritual programme which he himself, individually, had to fulfil; and he was to a greater or lesser degree restricted in his movements and behaviour. It is a reasonable guess that this represents a very old system of priestly office holding; that the *flamines* had once been independent of the colleges, but were later subordinated to the *pontifices*.[48]

The *haruspices* (diviners) were a second set of priests whose activity diverged from the standard collegiate pattern. One of their main areas of expertise was the interpretation of prodigies. Prodigies were events, reported from Rome or in its territories, which the Romans regarded as 'unnatural' and took as dangerous signs or warnings – monstrous births, rains of blood, even strokes of lightning. These had to be considered by the

47   The structure of the pontifical college: Wissowa (1912) 501–23; De Sanctis (1907–64) IV.2.353–61; Latte (1960a) 195–212, 401–2.
48   The *flamines*: Vanggard (1988); the *flamen Dialis*: Simón (1996); below, pp. 28–9.

senate, who took priestly advice and recommended action to avert the danger.[49] The history of this priestly group is complicated by the fact that ancient writers refer to '*haruspices*' fulfilling a wide variety of functions quite apart from the interpretation of prodigies; and it is far from clear whether we are dealing with a variety of religious officials (all going under the same name) or a single category.[50] It is clear, however, that there was no such thing as a haruspical college until the end of the Republic[51] – although this did not prevent their being consulted by the senate much earlier. In fact, some of the reports of such consultations in the early Republic describe them as being specifically summoned to Rome from Etruria to give advice on prodigies.[52] If those reports imply that the *haruspices* were literally foreigners, outside experts in a particularly Etruscan variety of religious interpretation, that would of course explain their lack of a Roman-style collegiate organization. But so also would the possibility (as may well have been the case later) that these officials were not literally foreign themselves, but were seen as 'foreign' in the sense that they were the representatives of a foreign religious skill. For even if modern archaeology has increasingly come to argue that Etruria and Rome were part of a shared common culture in the sixth century B.C. and even later, Roman imagination in the centuries that followed did not see it that way: for them Etruscan religious traditions were different and alien, and sometimes powerful for that very reason. In this case, a different priestly organization might have been one way of defining and marking as different the religious traditions those priests represented. The 'Etruscan-ness' of the *haruspices* might, in other words, count as the first of several instances we shall discuss in this book where Roman religion constructively used the idea of foreignness as a way of differentiating various sorts of religious power, skill and authority; the first instance of 'foreignness' as a religious metaphor, reflected here in priestly organization.[53]

These various priestly groups at Rome were not ranked in a strict hierarchy of religious authority. The basic rule, even for those that we think of as the more 'important' colleges, was that each group had their own area of concern and of expertise, within which sphere the others never interfered.

49 Bloch (1963) 77–86, 112–57; **7.3**; and below, pp. 37–9.
50 *Haruspices* in general: Thulin (1910); Wissowa (1912) 543–9; Bloch (1960) 43–76; Latte (1960a) 157–60; MacBain (1982) 43–59. Several haruspical activities are illustrated at **7.4** (including the examination of entrails of sacrificial victims; **7.4a** is a reconstruction of the text of a haruspical response); for apparently low-level, 'street-corner' *haruspices*, see (for example) Plautus, *Little Carthaginian* 449–66 = **6.3b**.
51 Torelli (1975) 119–21 argues for a middle republican date for the creation of the *ordo* of *haruspices*; but see MacBain (1982) 47–50; North (1990) 67. Second-century developments, below, p. 113.
52 For example, Livy XXVII.37.6.
53 Below, pp. 245–7 (for foreignness as a metaphor in so-called 'Oriental cults' in the Roman empire). A Roman attack on haruspical skill as foreign and therefore *barbarous*: Cicero, *On the Nature of the Gods* II.10–12 = **7.2** (but the point of this anecdote is, in the end, to confirm the power of haruspicy).

Fig. 1.4 Bronze mirror from Vulci, late fourth B.C., with the name Kalchas inscribed next to the figure. Kalchas is the Greek prophet of the *Iliad,* but is here shown as an Etruscan diviner and – surprisingly – winged: he examines a liver (see **7.4b**); other entrails are on the altar. The iconography suggests that Etruscans, as well as Romans, were using foreignness to define their own religious traditions. (Height, 0.18m.)

The *pontifex maximus* had some limited disciplinary powers, but mostly in relation to the priests and priestesses of his own college – the Vestals, the *rex* and the *flamines;* in the Republic he had no authority over the whole of the priestly structure of the city, let alone control more generally over the relations between the Romans and their gods.[54] But this raises the question of where such authority did lie, and how priestly power was defined and exercised. In the rest of this section we will show that the capacity for religious action and for religious decision-making was widely diffused among different Roman authorities (not only priests); that there was no single central power that controlled (or even claimed to control) Roman relations with their gods; and that the position of the priests can only be understood in the context of the rest of the constitutional and political system of the city. The first step will be to examine the work of the major colleges.

The *augures* were the experts in a variety of techniques used to establish the will of the gods, known as 'taking of the auspices' (*auspicia*).[55] The best-known and probably the earliest of these techniques involved observing the

54 Wissowa (1912) 509–11; Bleicken (1957a); Guizzi (1968) 141–58.
55 *Augures* in general: Warde Fowler (1911) 292–313; Wissowa (1912) 523–34; Dumézil (1970) 594–610; Catalano (1960); (1978); Linderski (1986).

flight and activity of particular species of birds, but the augurs also dealt
with the interpretation of thunder and lightning, the behaviour of certain
animals and so on (one way of discovering divine will was by feeding some
special sacred chickens and seeing if they would eat).[56] They were not, however, concerned with every kind of communication with the gods: the
augurs were not consulted about the interpretation of prodigies; and seem
to have had nothing at all to do with the reading of entrails at sacrifices,
which was the business of officials known (again) as *haruspices*. The *augures*
did not themselves normally take the auspices. It was usually the city magistrates who carried out the ceremonies and the observations required in
their roles as war-leaders or as political or legal officials; and they passed on
the right to take the auspices year by year to their successors.[57] In normal
cases, an *augur* would be present as adviser, perhaps as witness; and after
the event, the augural college would be the source of judgement on the
legality of what had been done or not done.

   These procedures were integrally bound up with the definition of religious boundaries and religious space – one of the most technical and complex areas of Roman religious 'science'. Occasionally signs from the gods
might come unasked, in any place and on any occasion;[58] but normally the
human magistrate would initiate the communication, specifically seeking
the view of the gods on a particular course of action or a particular question. On these occasions the place of consultation and the direction from
which the sign came were crucially important. The taker of the auspices
defined a *templum* in the heavens, a rectangle in which he specified left,
right, front and back; the meaning of the sign depended on its spatial relationship to these defined points. These celestial rectangles had a series of
equivalents on earth to which the same term was applied. Confusingly, a
'temple' in our sense of the word might or might not be a *templum* in this
sense: the 'temple' of Vesta, for instance, was strictly speaking an *aedes* (a
'building', a house for the deity) not a *templum*; while some places that we
would never think to call 'temples' were *templa* in this technical sense –
such as the senate-house, the *comitium* (the open assembly area in the
forum in front of the senate house), and the augurs' own centre for taking
auspices, the *auguraculum*.[59] All these earthly temples were 'inaugurated'
by the augurs, after which they were said (obscurely to us and probably to
many Romans too) to have been 'defined and freed' (*effatum et liberatum*).

56 Wissowa (1912) 231–2; Linderski (1986) 2226–41; for examples of conflicts over the
    sacred chickens, Livy X.40–1; Cicero, *On Divination* I.29.

57 If for any reason there was a gap in the succession of magistrates, the auspices were said
    to have 'returned to the *patres*', that is to the patrician members of the senate, who held
    them in turn until the proper succession was restored. Magdelain (1964).

58 These are now often referred to as *signa oblativa* (though the term is not attested in sur-
    viving Latin sources before the fourth century A.D.).

59 Weinstock (1934); Linderski (1986) 2256–96; the form of words used by the *augures*
    in creating a *templum* is recorded by Varro, *On the Latin Language* VII.8–10 = **4.4**.

Augural expertise, therefore, concerned not just the interpretation of signs but the demarcation of religious space and its boundaries. They operated as a system of categorizing space both within the city and between the outside world and Rome itself; this categorization in turn corresponded to the different types of auspices. One of their most important lines of division was the *pomerium*, the sacred and augural boundary of the city; it was only within this boundary that the 'urban auspices' (*auspicia urbana*) were valid; and magistrates had to be careful to take the auspices again if they crossed the *pomerium* in order to re-establish correct relations with the gods.[60]

The realm of the *augures* provides one of the clearest examples of the convergence of the sacred and the political. All public action in Rome took place within space and according to rituals falling within the province of the augurs. The passing of laws, the holding of elections, discussion in the senate – all took place within spaces defined by the application of augural ritual (the senate, for example, could only meet in a *templum*); each individual meeting was preceded by the taking of the auspices by the magistrates responsible. It followed that the validity of public decisions was seen as dependent on the correct performance of the rituals and on the application of a network of religious rules, whose maintenance was the augurs' concern; and in the constitutional crises of the late republican period, their right to examine whether a religious fault (*vitium*) had occurred in any proceeding of the assemblies gave them a critical role in public controversies. All these augural processes were central to the relations between the city and the gods, and to the legitimacy of public transactions. This is why the augurs were so important politically.

We get a glimpse, however, of a strikingly different image of the augurs in one of the stories told about Rome's earliest history. If the records of augural activity through the Republic stress the technical, sometimes legalistic, skill of the augurs, embedded at the heart of the political process, a story told by Livy of the early augur Attus Navius and his conflict with King Tarquin presents the priest as a miracle worker *in conflict with* the political power of the state (here represented by the monarch).[61] Challenging the power of the king, so the story goes, Navius claimed that he would carry out whatever Tarquin had in his mind; Tarquin triumphantly retorted that he was thinking of cutting a whetstone in half with a razor – which Navius promptly and miraculously did. A commemorative statue of Navius apparently stood in the forum (in the centre of Roman political and religious space) through most of the Republic.[62] There are many ways to interpret this story and the

---

60 The *pomerium*: below pp. 177–81, with evidence collected at **4.8**. The consequences of failing to re-take the auspices on crossing the *pomerium* are illustrated by Cicero, *On the Nature of the Gods* II.10–12 = **7.2**.

61 Livy I.36.2–6 = **7.1a**; Beard (1989).

62 Livy I.36.3 (with Ogilvie (1965) 151).

vested interests that may have lain behind its telling (that it is, for example, a reflection of later conflicts between augurs and a dominant political group; or that it is a surviving hint of a very different type of early priestly activity; and so on); but on almost any interpretation, it is a strong reminder that recorded details of priestly action do not account for the whole of the priestly story; that the historical tradition (in our sense) has its limitations. Priests had a role in Roman myth and imagination, which also determined the way they were seen and operated in the city. In this case, it is not just a question of stories told, or read in Livy. When the republican *augur* went about his priestly business in the Forum, he did so under the shadow of a statue of his mythical, miracle-working predecessor.

The *pontifices* had a wider range of functions and responsibilities than the augurs, less easily defined in simple terms. As a starting point, we might say that their religious duties covered everything that did not fall specifically within the activities of the *augures*, the *fetiales* and the *duoviri*. Like these other colleges, they were treated as experts on problems of sacred law and procedure within their province – such matters as the games, sacrifices and vows, the *sacra* connected with Vesta and the Vestals, tombs and burial law, the inheritance of sacred obligations. Their powers of adjudication do not seem at first sight to lie in areas as politically charged as those dealt with by the augurs; but these issues were, as we shall see, of central importance to public and private life at Rome and the *pontifices* continued throughout the Republic to be as distinguished as the *augures* in membership.[63]

The *pontifices* were unlike other priestly colleges in several respects. We have already seen that their collegiate structure was rather different from the others; they also differed in having functions that took them right outside the limits of religious action – 'religious', that is, in our sense. At its grandest, the role envisaged for them by Roman writers is as the repository of all law, human or divine; Livy suggests that, down to 304 B.C., the formulae, the precise form of words without which no legal action could begin, were secrets known only to the *pontifices*.[64] The significance and history of their legal role is a difficult problem. It is certainly possible that there was a specific 'religious' origin here; that *pontifices* were the earliest source of legal advice for the citizen, essentially on matters of religious procedure, such as the rules of burial – but that, since religious and non-religious law overlapped extensively, the range of advice they offered and the area of their expertise gradually widened.[65] More certainly, the *pontifices*

---

63 See the lists in Szemler (1972) 101–78.

64 Livy IX.46.5.

65 Livy I.20.6–7 leaves no doubt that the *pontifex* was expected to be available to advise the individual citizen; see also Pomponius in Justinian, *Digest* I.2.2.6, which suggests that one in particular was nominated each year for this purpose, at least in the fourth century B.C.; see Watson (1992). Their role in regulating burial at a later period: Pliny, *Letters* X.68 & 69 = **10.4d(iii)** & **(iv)**; *ILS* 8380 = **8.3**.

were responsible for the calendar; for the supervision of adoptions and some other matters of family law; and for the keeping of an annual record of events.

Their control of the calendar goes beyond interest merely in the annual festivals, although that would have been part of their task; the calendar also determined the character of individual days – whether the courts could sit, whether the senate or the *comitia* (assemblies) could meet. The priests were responsible, amongst other things, for 'intercalation'. All systems of time-keeping face the problem of keeping their yearly cycle in step with the 365 days 5 hours 48 minutes 46.43 seconds (more or less) that it actually takes for the earth to circle the sun. Modern Western calendars solve this problem by adding an extra day to their 365 day calendar once every four years (in a leap year).[66] The Roman republican calendar of 355 days needed to add ('intercalate') a whole month at intervals that were determined by the *pontifices*. The college also fixed the celebration of some of the important festivals which had no set date; and the sacred king (*rex sacrorum*), a member of the college, had the task of announcing the beginning of each month (perhaps a survival from an earlier form of the calendar when months began when the new moon was observed). The everyday organization of public time was pontifical business.[67]

The *pontifices'* concern with adoptions, wills and inheritances inevitably involved some elements of strictly religious interest – since each of these areas affected a family's religious obligations (*sacra familiaria*) and raised problems about who would maintain them into the next generation. The college's duties in this area would very likely have drawn them into wider issues of the continuity of family traditions and the control of property, where conflicts would have demanded adjudication between families or between clans (*gentes*).[68] The most (to us) unexpected of pontifical duties was, perhaps, the recording of events. A fragment preserved from the history of Cato the Elder (written in the first half of the second century B.C.) states that they were responsible at that time for 'publishing' the great events of the day on a whitened board, displayed in public;[69] these public reports, according to other writers, formed the basis of a permanent annual record, known to Cicero and, at least allegedly, going back to the earliest times.[70] We do not know exactly what this record contained, or when it was

66 This leap-year system derives from the calendar reforms of Julius Caesar at the very end of the Republic; Bickerman (1980) 47–51.

67 Degrassi (1963) 314–16; Michels (1967) 3–89; Scullard (1981) 41–8; R. L. Gordon (1990a) 184–9; a surviving copy of a republican calendar, from Antium: **3.2**.

68 Cicero discusses at length in *On the Laws* II.47–53 the conflict that could arise for a pontifical lawyer between the rules over the inheritance of *sacra* in pontifical law and the ordinary rules of civil law.

69 *Origins* fr. 77 (Peter) = fr. IV.1 (Chassignet) = Aulus Gellius, *Attic Nights* II.28.6.

70 Cicero, *Orator* II.52; Servius Danielis, *On Virgil's Aeneid* I.373. Discussion, Frier (1979); Cornell (1995) 13–15.

first kept. Roman writers seem to refer to it, however, as one of the college's traditional duties.

We are faced then with a range of what we should call 'secular' functions, as well as the 'religious' ones. One possibility is that the pontiffs were not an exclusively religious body in early Rome; but, rather than imagine that the 'priests' were not wholly 'religious', it is more helpful to think that what counted as 'religion' was differently defined. In almost all cultures the boundary between what is sacred and what is secular is contested and unstable. One of the themes underlying the chapters of this book will, precisely, be the gradual differentiation of these two spheres and the development, for example, of a religious professionalism at Rome that tried to distinguish itself sharply from other areas of human activity. But for the pontiffs of the very early period, there is no reason to assume that some of their tasks seemed more or less 'religious' than others, more or less 'priestly business'.

What, however, of the apparently wide diffusion of their responsibilities, from burial to record-keeping, and beyond? Is there any possible coherence in these different tasks? A central focus of interest? Of course, coherence very much depends on who is searching for it. Different *pontifices*, different Romans, at different periods may have made sense of their combined responsibilities in quite different ways. But one guess is that there was a closer connection than we have so far stressed between their interest in family continuity and their practice of record-keeping; and that many of their functions shared a concern with the preservation, from past time to future, of status and rights within families, within *gentes* and within the community as a whole – and so also with the transmission of ancestral rites into the future. This gave the calendar too a central role, with its organization of the year's time into its destined functions, and its emphasis on past ritual practice as the model for the future. The *pontifices*, in short, linked the past with the future by law, remembrance and recording.

Two other colleges have duties which bring them close to the central workings of the city. The fetials (*fetiales*) controlled and performed the rituals through which alone a war could be started properly; to ensure that the war should both be, and be seen to be, a 'just war' (*bellum iustum*).[71] The most detailed accounts of their activities date from a period when much of their ritual must have been modified or discontinued; but, if Livy is to be believed at all,[72] they were in early times responsible both for ritual action and for what we should call diplomatic action – conveying messages and

---

71 The *fetiales*: Samter (1909) 2259; Wissowa (1912) 550–4; Bayet (1935); Latte (1960a) 121–4; Rüpke (1990) 97–117. Their mythical origins, above pp. 3; 9, drawing on Livy I.24 and I.32.6–14 = **1.4a**. Later changes: below. pp. 132–3, with Servius, *On Virgil's Aeneid* IX.52 = **5.5d**, 194 n. 98.

72 Above, pp. 8–9.

demanding reparations. Later on, they could still be called upon by the senate, to give their view on the correct procedures for the declaration of hostilities.[73] The *duoviri sacris faciundis* were the guardians of the Sibylline Books.[74] The Books themselves will be discussed in a later section,[75] but it is clear enough that the prophetic verses which they contained, and which the college kept and consulted on the senate's instructions, were believed to be of great antiquity. When prodigies were reported, one of the options before the senate, instead of consulting the *haruspices*, was to seek recommendations from the Books. These recommendations repeatedly led to the foundation or introduction of foreign cults, normally Greek and celebrated according to the so-called 'Greek rite' (*Graeco ritu*).[76] In these cases the priests may have had some continuing responsibility for the new cult; but there is no evidence that the *duoviri* exercised any general supervision over Greek cults – to match the supervision that the *pontifices* came to exercise over Roman ones. Both *fetiales* and *duoviri* kept within closely defined areas of action.

All the priests we have looked at exercised their authority within a set of procedures that involved non-priests as well as priests, the 'political' as well as the 'religious' institutions of the city. Priests themselves were not part of an independent or self-sufficient religious structure; nor do they seem ever to have formed a separate caste, or to have acted as a group of specialist professionals, defined by their priestly role. From the third century onwards, the historical record preserves the names of a good proportion of *augures* and *pontifices*; from this it is clear that priests were drawn from among the leading senators – that is, they were the same men who dominated politics and the law, fought the battles, celebrated triumphs and made great fortunes on overseas commands.[77] Although they were in principle the guardians of religious, even of secret, lore, they were not specially trained or selected on any criterion other than family or political status. The holders of the less prominent priesthoods (such as the Salii or Arval Brothers) are less well known to us; but there is little, if any, sign that they were chosen as religious specialists. That is not to say that priests, or some of them, did not become experts in the traditions and records of their colleges; some of them vaunted the technicalities of their discipline and by the late Republic (as we shall see in Chapter 3) proclaimed themselves expert in the history, procedures and religious law of their colleges. But they were always (and arguably by definition) men with a bigger stake in Rome than narrowly 'religious'

73 For example, Livy XXXI.8.3.
74 The general role of this priesthood: Wissowa (1912) 524–43; Gagé (1955) 121–9, 146–54, 199–204, 442–4, 465–7; Radke (1963); Parke (1988) 136–51.
75 Below, pp. 62–3.
76 Above, n. 3.
77 The most famous examples are such men as Caesar, Pompey and Antony, but the lists in Szemler (1972) show how widespread was the practice of combining major political and religious office.

expertise. Cicero regarded this situation as one of the characteristic and important features of the tradition of Rome and as a source of special strength: that (as he put it) 'worship of the gods and the highest interests of the state were in the hands of the same men.'[78]

There is no doubt that by the middle Republic, the priest-politician was an established figure; whether this situation goes right back to the beginnings of the Republic must be more open to debate – though it is usually assumed that it does. The names of some very early priests of the Republic are handed down in the historical tradition; but we cannot be certain that these names are accurately recorded, let alone whether the men concerned were consuls, or other leading magistrates, as well. (It is only later that we can make such confident identifications of individuals.) In some particular respects, the early republican situation must have been different from the later one: the number of priests in the major colleges was far smaller – two or three, as compared to eight or nine after 300 B.C.; and again, they were almost certainly all members of patrician families – plebeians seem to have become members of the *duoviri* when they were increased to ten in 367 B.C., and of the *pontifices* and *augures* only in 300 B.C.[79]

But might there have been an entirely different model of priesthood in the earliest Republic (and so also in the regal period)? Might there have been an earlier pattern of office-holding which sharply divided religious from political duties? Even in the later period, some priests were prevented by traditional rules from entering other areas of public life. The sacred king (*rex sacrorum*) was prevented from holding any office; but – insofar as he was thought to have taken over the religious functions of the deposed king – he is a very special case (to which we shall return in Section 5 of this chapter). The major *flamines* were sometimes prevented by their duties or by the regulations of their priesthoods from holding or exercising all the duties of magistrates; the *flamen Dialis*, for example, was forbidden by these rules to be absent from his own bed for more than two consecutive nights – so obviously could not command an army on campaign.[80] Such restrictions were, step by step, relaxed in the later Republic, until the *flamines* came to play the normal role of an aristocrat in public life. One speculation is that all the other priests too had originally been excluded from public life and from warfare; but that they had followed the same route as the *flamines* (towards a mixed, religious-political career) at a much earlier date. On this view, the very early colleges would have represented much more specialized religious institutions; but as time went on the priestly offices (which unlike the short-term elected magistracies gave their holder a public position for life) might have become tempting prizes for the aristocratic leaders of the day – who gradually brought priesthoods within the sphere of a political career.

78 Cicero, *On his House* 1 = **8.2a**; below, pp. 114–15.
79 Below, pp. 68–9.
80 Below, pp. 105–8.

It would be difficult to disprove this theory; but on balance the view that the priestly colleges had always been part of political life seems more likely to be right. The fundamental difference between the colleges of priests and the *flamines* might not, in any case, be best defined by their political activity. The crucial distinction lies rather in their numbers. The *flamines*, as we have seen, essentially acted as individuals: the *flamen Dialis*, especially, had a ritual programme that only he could perform – so rules to keep him in the city had a particular point (quite apart from preventing a military or political career). It is a central characteristic of the *augures* and the *pontifices*, on the other hand, that they were full colleagues – one could always act instead of another, so that limitations on their movements as individuals would never have been so necessary. If the *flamines* represent (as they most likely do) some very early pattern of priestly office-holding, that model is distinguished from the later one by its non-collegiality; and the political differences follow from that.[81]

The authority exercised by the priestly colleges can only be understood in relation to the authority of magistrates and senate. In general, the initiative in religious action lay with the magistrates: it was they who consulted the gods by taking the auspices before meetings or battles; it was they who performed the dedication of temples to the gods; it was they who conducted censuses and the associated ceremonies; it was they who made public vows and held the games or sacrifices needed to fulfil the vows. The priest's role was to dictate or prescribe the prayers and formulae,[82] to offer advice on the procedures or simply to attend. Again, when it came to religious decision-making, it was not with the priests, but with the senate that the effective power of decision lay. To take one example: when a piece of legislation had been passed by the assemblies, but by some questionable procedure, the priests might be asked by the senate to comment on whether a fault (*vitium*) had taken place; but, subject to the ruling the priests offered, it would be the senate not the priests who would declare the law invalid on religious grounds.[83] The procedure for dealing with the annual prodigy-reports suggests much the same relationship; the senate heard the reports and decided to which groups of priests, if any, they should be referred; the priests replied to the senate; the senate ordered the appropriate actions to take place; it was often the magistrates who carried out the ceremonials on the city's behalf.[84]

To the modern observer, this procedure makes the priests look rather

81 Relations between *pontifices* and other priests: Wissowa (1912) 505–8; Rohde (1936) 112–13. Changes in the latest phase of the Republic (and a striking example of the interchangeability of *flamen* and *pontifices*): below, pp. 130–2.

82 For example, Livy VIII.9.1–10 = **6.6a**.

83 For example, Asconius, *Commentary on Cicero's On Behalf of Cornelius* p. 68C; the character of these incidents is discussed further below, pp. 105–8.

84 For example, Livy XXXI.12.8–9, where the final action is clearly the magistrate's responsibility; procedures in handling prodigies are discussed below, pp. 37–9.

like a constitutional sub-committee of the senate, but this may be a mis-leading analogy. It is true that the priests lacked power of action, but on the other hand they were accepted as supreme authorities on the sacred law in their area. Once the senate had consulted them, it seems inconceivable that their advice would have been ignored. And when smaller issues were at stake – such matters as the precise drafting of vows, the right procedure for the consecration of buildings, the control of the calendar – the priests themselves must in practice have had freedom of decision. This follows the pattern we have already seen at several points in this chapter of the close convergence of religion and politics: religious authority in the general sense has to be located in the interaction (according to particular rules and con-ventions) of magistrates, senate and priests, each college in its own sphere. This implies that, even if they were not sole arbiters, the priests must from a very early period have occupied a critical position in Roman political life, and they must often have been at the centre of controversy over points of ritual and religious procedure with all the political consequences that were entailed. So too, priests must always have been liable to the charge that they were prejudiced in favour of friends and against enemies, that personal or 'political' interests were determining their 'religious' decisions. The idea that Roman priests had once been quite innocent of politics is only a romanticizing fiction about an archaic society.

3. Gods and goddesses in the life of Rome

The first characteristic of Roman gods and goddesses to strike us must be the wide range of different types, all accepted and worshipped. At one extreme, there were the great gods – Mars, Jupiter, Juno and others – each having a variety of major functions, traditions, stories and myths; some of these sto-ries originated in the Greek world, but when told, re-told and adapted in a Roman context they became a central part of a specifically Roman view of their gods. At the other extreme were deities who performed one narrowly defined function or who appeared only in one narrowly defined ritual con-text. As we have seen, even parts of a natural or agricultural process (such as ploughing) could have their own presiding deity;[85] and the possibility of still further unnamed or unknown gods and goddesses was sometimes admitted and allowed for in ritual formulae: for example, an inscription on a republi-can altar found on the Palatine hill in Rome runs, 'To whichever god or god-dess sacred, Gaius Sextius Calvinus, praetor, restored it by decree of the senate.'[86] The time-honoured way of dealing with this variety in the Romans' conception of their gods has been to claim that the gods had become 'frozen' at different points in their evolution: the functional deities

85 Above, p. 11.
86 *ILS* 4015 = *ILLRP* 291. The formula: Appel (1909) 80–2.

represent an early stage of development, when primitive man worshipped powers residing in the natural world, but did not yet see those powers as 'personalities';[87] it was only later that the fully-blown, characterful gods and goddesses emerged as well. But whether or not that evolutionary scheme helps to explain the varieties of divine powers we find at Rome, the important fact is that throughout the republican period, all the types seem to have co-existed with no sign of uneasiness – any more than there seems to be any uneasiness about adding to the pantheon by introducing new deities from outside Rome or recognizing new divine powers at home. It may be that the priests did attempt to list and classify the gods; but, if so, this does not seem to have produced any general convergence of the different types or to have produced (as was sometimes the case in the Greek theological tradition) elaborate genealogies of the different 'generations' of gods to explain the differences between them.

There are only a few traces of intermediate categories (like 'heroes' in Greece) that lay between gods and men. It may be that the dead should be seen as such a category, since they did (as we shall see) receive cult at the festivals of the Parentalia and Lemuria – not as individuals but as a generalized group, under the title of the *di Manes* or *divi parentes* (literally, 'the gods Manes' or 'the deified ancestors').[88] And, with the exception of the founders – Aeneas, Romulus and perhaps Latinus (the mythical king of the Latins) – men did not become gods, either when alive or after death;[89] even these three exceptions are equivocal, because it is not clear how far they themselves became gods, or how far they became identified with gods which already existed (Aeneas with Indiges, Romulus with Quirinus, Latinus with Jupiter Latiaris).[90] Dramatic interaction, however, between humans and gods did occasionally take place: Mars had sexual intercourse with the virgin Rhea Silvia and so begot Romulus; Numa negotiated banteringly with Jupiter and slept with the nymph Egeria; Faunus or Inuus seized and raped women in the wild woods; Castor and Pollux appeared in moments of peril.[91] But these mythical or exceptional transactions apart, Roman writers represent communication between men and gods primarily through the medium of ritualized exchange and the interpretation of signs – not

---

87 This early phase of religion is sometimes termed 'animism'; the divine 'powers' have been given the title *numen* (pl. *numina*) – as in Ovid's description of Terminus, the god of boundary stones, which has been thought, by many scholars, to be a classic case of the survival of such a divine power: *Fasti* II.639–46 = **1.1b**; see Piccaluga (1974). For a critique of these views: **1.1**.

88 Wissowa (1912) 238–40; De Sanctis (1907–64) IV.2.2.43–5; Latte (1960a) 98; Weinstock (1971) 291–6; J. M. C. Toynbee (1971) 34–9; and below, p. 50.

89 Though see below, pp. 44–5; 143, for the 'impersonation' of Jupiter by the Roman general in the ceremony of triumph.

90 Liou-Gille (1980).

91 Rhea Silvia: Dionysius of Halicarnassus, *Roman Antiquities* I.76–9; Livy I.3–4. Egeria: Livy I.21.3. Inuus: Livy I.5.2. Castor and Pollux: Livy II.20.10–13; Dionysius of Halicarnassus, *Roman Antiquities* VI.13.

through intervention, inspiration or incubation. We have already seen that evidence from archaeology can suggest a rather wider picture;[92] but for most of this section we shall be concentrating on written material (prayers, vows and formulae), and on the distinctive characteristics of communication between Romans and their gods.

The Roman historical record preserves a considerable body of texts which claim to be direct quotations of words spoken on particular religious occasions. Though very little survives from the earliest period of the Republic (and what does may largely be later antiquarian invention), there is enough from the third century B.C. on to give us some grasp of the conceptions of divinity and divine behaviour that they embody. Of course, some of these quotations too may be historical fictions or forgeries. But there are nevertheless strong reasons to believe that from this period the accurate formulae of prayers and vows could and sometimes did enter historical accounts. Roman religion placed a great deal of emphasis on the most meticulous repetition of the correct formulae; supposedly, the slightest error in performance, even a single wrong word, led to the repetition of the whole ritual.[93] It also emphasized (as we have seen) the keeping of priestly records and the preservation of ancient writings and traditions. If the spoken word was important, it was presumably also written down with care and accuracy. In what follows we have assumed that the quotations and formulae that we find (mostly) in Livy do derive ultimately from this form of priestly record keeping; and that even if they are not exactly what they claim to be (not, that is, the exact words spoken on the particular occasion described) they are at least a more or less accurate version of words used on occasions of that kind. But there are difficulties too. We discussed in the first section of this chapter the problem of using such 'nuggets' of information or texts from early Rome out of context. In this case, the preserved texts were originally part of a complex of ritual action, which we can only sketchily recreate and which would almost certainly have modified the meaning of the words in use. Imagine trying to reconstruct the action, atmosphere and significance of any contemporary religious ritual simply on the basis of a text of the words spoken.

Some of these quotations preserve public vows, which make very precise undertakings to named gods, explaining the help or benefit asked of the god, laying down the conditions under which the vow will be counted as fulfilled and specifying the gift or ritual action with which the help of the god will be rewarded; these rewards take the form of offerings, sacrifices, special games, the building of temples and so on. Vows could be made in special circumstances or crises (asking for help in war, for example); but there were also regular annual vows for the well-being of the state (*res*

---

92 Above pp. 12–14.
93 For example, Pliny, *Natural History* XXVIII.10–11 = **5.5a**; Köves-Zulauf (1972) 21–34; North (1976).

Fig. 1.5 A selection of coins of the third century B.C., showing some of the earliest surviving representations of Roman deities:
(a) Mars (didrachm, 280–276 B.C.);
(b) Minerva (litra, c. 269 B.C.);
(c) Apollo (as, 275–270 B.C.);
(d) Jupiter, in a four-horse chariot driven by Victory (didrachm, 225-214 B.C.) (e) Janus (as, 225–217 B.C.);
(f) Sol (uncia, 217–215 B.C.).

publica), taken by the year's consul. The most elaborate example we have dates from the early years of the Hannibalic War (217 B.C.), though its wording reflects far earlier traditions.[94] It is highly unusual in the reward it promises to the gods, but it nevertheless illustrates very clearly one of the characteristic ways the Romans conceptualized the relationship of the

94   The text is from Livy XXII.10 = **6.5**. Discussion: Eisenhut (1955); Heurgon (1957) 36–51; North (1976) 5–6; below, p. 80.

divine to their human worshippers. The vow promises the celebration of a so-called 'Sacred Spring' (*ver sacrum*), that is the sacrifice to the gods, in this case Jupiter, of the whole product of a single spring – all the pigs, sheep, goats and cattle that were born. This extraordinary offer (which we otherwise know only from mythical accounts of early Italy) was made subject to a series of reservations: the people were to lay down the dates which would constitute the 'spring'; if there were to be any error or irregularity in the sacrificial procedure the sacrifice would nevertheless count as properly conducted; if any intended victim were to be stolen, the blame should fall on others than the Roman people or the owner. There is to be no doubt about what will, or will not, count as fulfilment of the vow. The formula also specifies exactly what is asked of the gods: that the Roman people should be kept safe for five years in their war both with the Carthaginians and with the Gauls of North Italy, who had joined Hannibal.

The precise and apparently legalistic formulae of this and other vows has often given the impression that Roman vows were 'contractual' in the sense that the gods were seen as laid under an obligation by the mere fact of the taking of the vow. Whatever the individual worshipper may have hoped, in this case (and in general) that is not what the words state or imply. The Romans offered honour and worship in return for divine benevolence; the gods were free to be benevolent or not; if they were not, no obligation arose on either side; no rewards were given. There was, of course, a reciprocity, as in many other religious transactions. If all went well, the humans received the worldly benefits they desired. The gods too benefited in the way that was carefully defined in the original formula: they were bound only in one sense, that is that they would accept as sufficient exactly what they were offered – no more, no less. There are clear analogies here with Roman behaviour outside religion: the Greek historian Polybius, for example, writing in the second century B.C. states that a Roman expected to be paid his debt on the agreed day, not a day later – but not a day earlier either.[95] Roman gods, whether or not anthropomorphic in form, were given mentality and behaviour that mirrored those of their worshippers on a larger scale. There is no sense in which the gods should be seen as all-powerful or irresponsible, with humans as their helpless slaves. But nor could they be reliably controlled or predicted. They could, on the other hand, be negotiated with; they were indeed bound to the human community by a network of obligations, traditions, rules, within which the skill of the priests, magistrates and senate could keep them on the side of the city.

Various forms of vow were used in a wide range of transactions.[96] In the case of war, the gods of the enemy could be seduced by *evocatio*, a vow offering them continuance of cult or possibly even a temple in Rome, if they withdrew their protection from their native city. The first known

95   XXXI.27, especially 10–11.
96   Vows in a variety of private contexts: (for example) *ILS* 3411 & 3513 = **9.5a & b.**

example of this was the evocation of Juno of the Etruscan city of Veii in 396
B.C., who was installed in a temple on the Aventine hill in Rome under the
title Juno Regina.[97] In the course of the war the general might also pray for
aid to any god or goddess and vow a temple, not necessarily a warlike one,
in return for the deity's help. In the most extreme case, in face of a disaster
in battle, the general even could dedicate himself and the legions of the
enemy to the gods of the dead and to the Earth, in a ceremony known as
devotio. In effect, he made himself sacred, the property of the gods (*sacer*),
rather like a sacrificial victim;[98] he then had to mount a horse and rush pre-
cipitately to his death on the enemies' spears. This is first reported as having happened in 340 B.C., when the consul Decius Mus offered his own
life; some accounts have his son and grandson follow his example a generation and two generations later.[99] Here the consul's death obviously
counted as the fulfilment of the vow, though in that respect the sequence of
events was different from usual – since the vow had to be fulfilled before the
gods had had the opportunity to do their part. If the consul failed to die,
according to Livy, an over-life-size image was buried in the earth, evidently
as an attempt to fulfil the unsatisfied vow.[100]

Vows and prayers were regularly recorded in Roman historical writing,
manageable to the historian, precisely because they were verbal and hence
transmittable. But there were other ways in which important communication took place between men and gods. Livy's story of Decius in 340, in
fact, contains two direct messages from gods to men. The first is almost
unique in Livy's narrative, in that it consists of a dream, warning Decius of
what is to come; the second is a type of communication that is reported
much more frequently in the literary tradition:

Before leading their men into battle, the Roman consuls offered sacrifice. It is
said that the *haruspex* pointed out to Decius that the lobe of the liver was
damaged where it referred to his own fortunes, but that in other respects the
victim was acceptable to the gods; Manlius' sacrifice, though, had been perfectly
successful (*egregie litasse*). 'All is well,' replied Decius 'if my colleague has
obtained favourable omens.'[101]

97 Juno of Veii: Livy V.21.1–7 = **2.6a**; a version of the formula is preserved by
    Macrobius, *Saturnalia* III.9.7–8 (see below, pp. 111 and 132–4, with **10.3b** – a late
    republican inscription, probably documenting a new form of the ritual in the first cen-
    tury B.C.). General discussion: Wissowa (1912) 383–4; Dumézil (1970) 424–31; Le
    Gall (1976).
98 We say '*like* a sacrificial victim' advisedly; the general was not literally immolated and
    made part of a ritual sacrificial meal (see below, pp. 36–7). The ceremony of *devotio*
    was reminiscent of animal sacrifice, but not an identical ritual.
99 Livy VIII.9–11.1, part = **6.6a** (the fullest account, 340 B.C.); X.28.12–29.7 (295 B.C.);
    Cicero, *On the Ends of Goods and Evils* II.61; *Tusculan Disputations* I.89; Cassius Dio
    X in Zonaras VIII.5 (279 B.C.); full analysis of the major text: Versnel (1981b).
100 Livy VIII.10.12.
101 Livy VIII.9.1 = **6.6a**.

The crucial word here is *'litare'* (as a noun *'litatio'*); it can be used simply to mean 'sacrifice', but it normally involves the successful completion and acceptance of the victim by the gods. In this case, Decius already knew that he was destined to die for the legions and hence that it did not matter that it should be only his colleague who achieved *litatio*; in other circumstances, his own failure to do so would have been a disastrously bad sign.

Animal sacrifice was the central ritual of many religious occasions; we know enough about it from both literary and archaeological evidence to understand its main stages.[102] In structure, though not in detail, the ritual was closely related to the Greek ritual of sacrifice. The victim was tested and checked to make sure it was suitable; precise rules controlled the choice of sex, age, colour and type of victim, in relation to the deity and the occasion. After a procession to the altar and preparatory rites, a prayer was said in which the divine recipient was named; then the victim was made 'sacred' by the placing of wine and meal on its head and it was at this moment (so it was believed) that the signs (if any) appeared in the entrails that would imply the gods' rejection of the offering.[103] The victim had to be killed by a single blow; its *exta* (entrails) were examined by the *haruspices*;[104] assuming that they were acceptable, the animal was then butchered, cooked and eventually eaten by the worshippers. If the *exta* showed unacceptable signs, further victims could be sacrificed until one was accepted and *litatio* achieved. The whole process was evidently bound by rules and by traditional lore; any error or misfortune – the victim escaping or struggling, the *exta* slipping when offered up at the altar – would have been very inauspicious.[105] Even the butchering seems to have involved special knowledge, with a technical sacred vocabulary for the many different kinds of cuts (and sausages) that were offered to the god.[106] The clear separation of the meat between those parts of the animal offered to the worshippers on the one hand and those

---

102 See the images collected at **6.1**; for various records of animal sacrifice (including some republican examples), **6.2 & 3**. Further images from sculptured reliefs (mostly of imperial date) are collected in Ryberg (1955); Torelli (1982). The literary evidence for sacrifice is plentiful, but extremely scattered; the only coherent accounts are the attack on sacrifice by the Christian Arnobius, in *Against the Gentiles* VII (see, for example, VII.9 = **6.8a**) and the comparison of Greek and Roman practices in Dionysius of Halicarnassus, *Roman Antiquities* VII.72.15–18. Modern discussion: Warde Fowler (1911) 176–85; Wissowa (1912) 409–32; Dumézil (1970) 557–9; Scholz (1981); Scheid (1990b) 421–676.

103 Cicero, *On Divination* II.37 = **13.2b**.

104 For a model liver, presumably a guide to the interpretation of the victim's organ, see **7.4b** (the 'Piacenza Liver'); for a sculptured relief, showing the examination of entrails, **7.4d**. Also above, fig. 1.4. Among many literary references, note Livy XLI.14.7 and 15.1–4 = **7.4c**; Plautus, *Little Carthaginian* 449–66 = **6.3b**.

105 Servius, *On Virgil's Aeneid* II.104; Festus (epitome) p. 351L; Suetonius, *Julius Caesar* 59 (where Caesar ignores the omen).

106 We have to rely on a very hostile (and hilarious) account by Arnobius, *Against the Gentiles* VII.24.

offered to gods on the other is reminiscent of Greek sacrificial ritual; it implies (to draw on conceptions that have been elaborately developed in the study of Greek religion)[107] that one of the functions of the ritual was to represent the division between gods and men by means of the rules and codes of eating and consumption – men being prohibited from consuming the parts designated for the gods. But the ritual offered opportunities for the exchange of messages – prayers from men to gods, warnings and messages of acceptance from gods to men encoded in the entrails.

Warnings also came uninvited, from outside the ritual process. These warnings were in the form of prodigies, whose interpretation by the *haruspices* we have already noticed. They were for the most part what we would call natural events and there are relatively few that seem miraculous or supernatural in our terms; mostly they appear to have been events which defied Roman conceptions of normality – in modern anthropological terms, 'objects out of place', transgressing cultural boundaries, mixing the categories that nature was supposed to hold apart (such as wild animals penetrating the city's space).[108] The lists of these prodigies that Livy preserves in the middle years of his history provides us with one of our best indications of the style of Roman religious activity.[109]

Roman writers do not generally regard such prodigies as the result of a direct intervention by the gods (it was not self-evidently the case that a god, for example, directly caused the monstrous birth); rather they see them as an implication that something relating to the gods had gone seriously wrong. Here, then, more than anywhere else, we find a divine irruption into human lives, demanding a response. That response, for the observer of such an event, was report the prodigy to the senate in Rome; the senate either accepted the prodigy (that is, formally accepted that the event indicated some kind of rupture in the proper relationship of Rome to its gods and hence called for religious action), or it could rule that it had no public significance.[110] Once accepted, it could be referred to the *duoviri* or (as we have seen) to the *haruspices* for advice, and the appropriate actions (*remedia*) to be taken by priests, magistrates or even the people as a whole, were determined. The effect of this action was neutralization of the warning. The signs were not taken to indicate fated or irreversible processes; nor were they taken as the opportunity for formal divination of the gods' will, since traditionally all prodigies were implicitly bad signs – with large numbers, according to

---

107 For example, Detienne and Vernant (1989).

108 This type of boundary crossing is the major theme of Douglas (1966).

109 Bloch (1963) 77–86, 112–57; MacBain (1982). An example of a list of prodigies and their handling (217 B.C.): Livy XXII.1. 8–20 = **7.3a**.

110 The senate ruled in 169 B.C. that certain of the prodigies reported to it that year were not acceptable for public purposes, according to Livy XLIII.13; this is the only time that such a decision is mentioned in our sources, but presumably represents the regular procedure (discussed in MacBain (1982) 25–33). For a Roman officer persuading his soldiers not to see an eclipse as a prodigy, Livy XLIV.37.5–9 = **7.3c**.

Livy, being reported at times of grave danger to the city.[111] The crucial thing was that the resources of senatorial and priestly skill and wisdom were used to avert the dangers, even though there was no absolute guarantee of success. From a functional and political point of view, the system has been interpreted as a means of coping with crises, by focussing fears into an area within which the ruling class could claim special inherited expertise; while the *remedia* might offer an opportunity for holding elaborate ceremonies, sometimes including new festivals or new entertainments, so boosting public morale by civic display.[112]

The overwhelming bulk of the evidence for this system of dealing with the prodigies comes from the later republican period, so the problem once again is whether we are justified in assuming that these practices date back at least to the early period of the Republic. There obviously must have been developments and modifications over the period; if nothing else, as Roman power expanded over Italy, prodigies were recognized throughout the whole peninsula, not just in the immediate area of Rome itself – and this geographical extension alone must have affected the way prodigies were reported, investigated and handled. On the other hand, there is some evidence that has been used to suggest a drastic change in procedures in the mid third century B.C. The evidence comes from the lists of prodigies included by Livy. The first ten books of his history mention occasional prodigies but have none of the regular lists that become common later. The second ten books no longer survive; but Julius Obsequens, who made a collection of Livy's prodigy-lists in the fourth century A.D., began with the list for the year 249 B.C., from Livy's nineteenth book.[113] Obsequens' chosen starting point may well indicate that Livy provided no regular lists until that point. But what kind of change would that imply? It could have been a major change in procedure, that resulted in the lists being publicly available for the first time; but it could have been a change in practices of recording (or even just the chance preservation of a set of documents) that enabled Livy to include that kind of information. Certainly there is no

---

111 Livy's attitudes and principles of selection: Levene (1993) 17–37. He argues that Livy was using prodigies in particular as a literary device, placing his accounts of these events at dramatic moments, when he wanted to heighten the tension or evoke a mysterious dangerous atmosphere. Against this view we might note that Livy's lists are generally spare and factual in style, and strikingly *not* elaborated into the horror stories that they could have been. It certainly remains possible that Livy incorporated material from ancient records relatively unchanged, even if, as Levene proves, the *placing* in his account is manipulated. The origin of Livy's material on prodigies: Rawson (1971); for a different view, North (1986) 255.

112 This function of prodigies and divination is stressed by Liebeschuetz (1979) 7–29 – though it is probably much less specific an argument than it appears. After all almost *anything* that a community does together at a time of crisis can have the effect of boosting morale.

113 The date comes from the title in the first printed edition; a translation of Obsequens is available in the Loeb Classical Library, *Livy* vol. XIV.

Fig. 1.6 Model of the triple temple of Jupiter Optimus Maximus, Juno and Minerva on the Capitoline Hill overlooking the forum of Rome. The plan, with twenty-four columns in all and eighteen in the grand portico, was supposed never to have been changed from republican times onwards.

statement in any of our historical accounts that prodigies played a fundamentally different role in the early Republic.

We have concentrated so far, unavoidably, on particular transactions between humans and gods which have left a mark in the historical record; but the gods, or at least reminders of them in the form of statues and other images, were a constant presence in Roman public and private space. It is not easy to have any very precise idea of the impact of such a presence on a society whose physical environment and experience are known to us only so fragmentarily, but some features still stand out. The early republican city must have been dominated by the great temple of the Capitoline triad, Jupiter, Juno and Minerva, which (as we can judge even from its few surviving traces) seems to have been built on a far greater scale than any of the subsequent republican sacred buildings (Fig. 1.6).[114] Other temples throughout the Republic were much smaller; and many of the buildings that later became great temples will have been in the early period simply altars or holy places. None the less, the city's public centre, the forum, was first laid out and paved as a civic centre before the end of the monarchy and quickly developed so that by the early Republic a series of sacred buildings bounded its southern side – the temples of Saturn, Castor, Vesta and also the Regia, the religious centre of the *rex sacrorum* and the *pontifices*.[115]

114 Dionysius of Halicarnassus, *Roman Antiquities* IV.61; Livy I.55.1 = **1.9b**; *Grande Roma* (1990) 7–9; Cornell (1995) 96 and n. 48, *contra* Castagnoli (1979) 7–9; Map 1 no. 25; and above, p. 3.
115 Coarelli (1983–5) I; Cornell (1995) 108–9, 239–41; Steinby (1993–) II. 313–36, **4.7**, for the Roman forum.

We can assume that, by this time, where there were temples there were also cult images;[116] we have no way of telling how far these images would have been disseminated, whether there would have been terracotta reproductions, whether private houses would then, as they did later, have contained their own images of the household gods.[117] By the end of the Republic these images of the gods were omnipresent and had their own ceremonial: they appeared before the temples on special couches (*pulvinaria*) so that offerings could be given them;[118] they were carried in procession on special litters and their symbols in carriages (*tensae*); at the games (*ludi*) they had their own places from which they watched the racing in the circus; and at the heart of the oldest sets of *ludi* (the Roman and the Plebeian Games), there was also a ceremony called the *epulum Iovis*, 'the feast of Jupiter', which was presumably the offering or sharing of a meal in the presence of the image of Jupiter from the Capitol.[119] There is clear evidence to suggest that all this must have been happening by the third century B.C.; although it is much harder to be sure how much of it goes back to the fifth century, or earlier.

Dionysius of Halicarnassus, writing at the beginning of the empire, gives what he claims to be a description of a fifth-century procession from the Capitoline temple to the Circus Maximus which took place before the *ludi Romani* (Roman Games).[120] Dionysius states that he found this account in the history of Fabius Pictor, a Roman senator who was writing in Greek around 200 B.C.[121] If Dionysius is reliably reporting his source, it seems that Fabius himself either claimed or really believed that he was using a fifth-century document or record as the basis of his description. There are good reasons now to doubt that that could have been the case; however, it certainly implies that the ceremonial was well established by Fabius' own time in the late third century.[122] In Dionysius' words:

At the very end of the procession came the statues of all the gods, carried on men's shoulders – with much the same appearance as statues made by the Greeks, with the same costume, the same symbols and the same gifts, which according to tradition each of them invented and bestowed on humankind.[123]

---

116 Even Varro in Augustine, *The City of God* IV.31 (fr. 18 (Cardauns)) = **1.1a** only claims that the gods went without images for the first one hundred and seventy years of the city's history. Images from the third century, see above, fig. 1.5.
117 (Later) images of the Lares: see **2.2a**.
118 A pair of goddesses on a *pulvinar* are illustrated, **5.5c**.
119 The ritual of the *ludi*: below, pp. 66–7. The *epulum Iovis*: p.63; Warde Fowler (1899) 216–34; Wissowa (1912) 127, 423, 453–4; Degrassi (1963) 509, 530; Scullard (1981) 186–7.
120 *Roman Antiquities* VII.70–2, part = **5.7a**.
121 Fabius Pictor: Frier (1979) 255–84; Momigliano (1990) 80–108.
122 Piganiol (1923) 15–31, 81.
123 *Roman Antiquities* VII.72.13 = **5.7a**. Part of Dionysius' aim here, and throughout his work, is to show that Rome was in origin a Greek city.

Fig. 1.7 Bowl made in Rome or Latium, with the inscription: 'Belolai pocolom' = 'Bellona's dish'. The figure on the bowl could be Bellona herself, but it is quite different from later representations (where the goddess is normally portrayed in armour, not – as here – with dishevelled hair). This is one of a series of bowls bearing the name of deities prominent in Rome in the third century B.C. (other deities named include Aesculapius, Minerva, Venus etc.). To judge from their find-spots, they were not dedications (which would have been found in the particular temple of the deity), but may have functioned as temple souvenirs (taken away from the temple, and so found widely dispersed). The exact find-spot of this particular bowl is not known.

The history of the *ludi* is itself a matter of great controversy; we can do little more than guess which parts (if any) of the ceremonial go back to the early Republic, and so whether this procession of the images was amongst the original elements. We can however say that already by the third century B.C. it was treated as a traditional part of the ritual; that such images of gods were believed to have had a long history of appearance in Roman public ritual.

Much of the evidence for the early history of the Roman gods remains tantalizing. But it is possible to offer a rough outline of their place in the life of Rome: closely involved in the political and military activity of the city, they are seen as forces outside the human community with whom the man of learning and skill, knowing the rules, traditions and rituals, can negotiate and communicate (and if necessary assuage); the activities of the city's leaders on the city's behalf could hardly be conceived except in the context of such a procedure of negotiation and joint action; divine benevolence (secured by human effort) was essential to the success of the state; Rome's history in other words was determined by the actions of men and gods together.

4. Religion and action

Much of the vocabulary used by the Romans in discussing their own religion seems to translate into words comfortably similar to those used in religious contexts today – 'prayer', 'sacrifice', 'vows', 'sacred'; in fact some of our own religious words derive directly from Latin. But translation is always elusive; and this apparent familiarity may be deceptive. It is in considering the relationship between religion and the social organization of republican Rome that the differences become most obvious. The sharpest difference of all is that, at least until the middle Republic, there is no sign in Rome of any specifically religious groups: groups, that is, of men or women who had decided to join together principally on grounds of religious choice. Of course, there were all kinds of groups in which religion played a part: from an early republican date, for example, various associations (*collegia*), such as burial or dining clubs, associated themselves with a divine patron, and were even called after the deity.[124] So too individual citizens might act together with others in carrying out religious duties and ritual – their family, their *gens*, their fellow craftsmen or senators; but these were communities formed on the basis of birth, occupation, domicile or rank, not through any specifically religious conviction. In fact, to put it the other way round, it is hard to know what religious conviction might mean in a world where no religious affiliation resulted from it.

This difference has important implications for the character of religious life at both the social and the individual level. At the social level, it means that there were no autonomous religious groups, with their own special value-systems, ideas or beliefs to defend or advocate; hence there was little chance that religion in itself would ever represent a force for advocating change or reform. At the individual level, it means that men and women were not faced with the need to make (or even the opportunity of making) acts of religious commitment; that in turn implies that they had no religious biographies, no moments of profound new experience or revelation such as to determine the course of their future lives. That, of course, is a much stronger claim. We do not want to suggest that religion was not important to any individual in republican Rome: there must have been many who were profoundly grateful to the gods for recovery from illness, others who were deeply impressed by a divine vision; conversely, at every period in Rome's history, there must have been some who professed themselves thoroughly sceptical about the gods and their supposed activities. In some ways, that is just like today. The crucial difference is that these experiences, beliefs and disbeliefs had no particularly privileged role in defining an individual's actions, behaviour or sense of identity. We have the notion,

---

124   The inscribed regulations for a later burial club, the 'society of Diana and Antinous', *ILS* 7212 = **12.2** and below, 272; 287. In general, see Kloppenborg and Wilson (1996).

which they did not, of an individual having a 'religious identity' that can be distinguished from his or her identity as a citizen or as a family member. If asked what we *are*, we can say 'a Catholic', 'a Moslem', 'an atheist'. It is only in a religious context where beliefs determine choices, that believing as such becomes a central element in the system. Religious 'experiences', 'feelings' or 'beliefs' must all have had quite different significances and resonances in early republican Rome.

When we look, therefore, at the way in which religion and society interacted, we do not find special institutions and activities, set aside from everyday life and designed to pursue religious objectives; but rather a situation in which religion and its associated rituals were embedded in all institutions and activities. As we have already seen, the whole of the political and constitutional system was conducted within an elaborate network of religious ceremonial and regulation which had the effect of bringing the time, space and hence the validity of political action into the divine sphere. It may be true that this area of decision-taking, of elections and of legislation was the one in which (as our historical sources would have us believe) the gods were most interested; but in fact, all important areas of life, public or private, had some religious correlates. In this section we shall explore some of those other areas: notably warfare, agriculture and family life.

Warfare was already sanctified by the rituals of the old calendar of festivals. In March – which had originally been the first month of the year – there was an interconnected set of festivals, mostly directed towards the god Mars (after whom the month was, and still is, named); and there was a corresponding set in October, somewhat less elaborate.[125] On both occasions a central role was played by the priesthood of Salii, founded according to Roman myth by Numa to guard the sacred shields – the *ancilia*. The priests were all patricians, formed into two groups, of Mars and Quirinus respectively; on their festal days they danced through the streets, dressed in the distinctive armour of archaic foot-soldiers.[126] Whatever these ceremonies originally meant (and on this there is considerable argument), there can be little doubt that, at least by the fifth century B.C., they represented a celebration of the annual rhythm of war-making: marking the preparation for a new season of war in March; and in October marking the end of the season, and the putting aside of arms for the winter. In early Rome (when Rome's enemies were still conveniently close at hand) warfare was the summertime activity of a part-time citizen army, fighting under their annual magistrates.

The actual conduct of warfare was also set within a religious context.

125 Warde Fowler (1911) 96–7; Wissowa (1912) 144–6; Degrassi (1963) 417–19; Scullard (1981) 85–7, 193–5.
126 Wissowa (1912) 555–9; Latte (1960a) 114–19; Ogilvie (1965) 98–9; Rüpke (1990) 23–7. The rituals and costume of the Salii: Dionysius of Halicarnassus, *Roman Antiquities* II.70.1–5 = **5.4a**. Their hymn: Quintilian, *Education of an Orator* I.6.40–1 = **5.4c**; the *ancilia* are illustrated on a gemstone, **5.4b**.

Fighting was always preceded by consultation of the gods and by sacrifices, whose rejection by the gods would imply a warning not to join battle.[127] Essentially, the participants in the warfare would seek advantage by establishing a better relationship with the gods and greater claims to divine favour. Sacrifices were held, even in expectation of war, in order to obtain confirmation of the divine attitude; at the opening of the campaign, the ritual of the fetial priests was (as we have seen) intended to ensure that the war was acceptable to the gods as a 'just war'; even in the midst of battle, vows were taken to induce the gods to look favourably or to desert the enemy.[128] By the end of the third century, the religious part of the whole process had become sufficiently familiar to be parodied by the playwright Plautus:

> The generals of both sides, ours and theirs,
> Take vows to Jupiter and exhort the troops.[129]

But if religion and religious ritual penetrated the area of warfare, warfare and its consequences could penetrate the religious sphere of the city. The vows taken by generals could lead to spectacular war-memorials in the form of temples in the city; and the spoils of war might either find their way into the temples by way of dedications, or finance the building of monuments commemorating the generals' achievements.[130] Less permanent, though perhaps even more spectacular, was the triumph, the ancient processional ritual, in which the victorious, returning war-leader paraded through the city's streets at the head of his troops presenting his spoils and his prisoners to the cheering Roman people.[131] He entered the city by a special gateway, the Triumphal Gate, splendidly dressed and riding in a chariot drawn by four horses; his procession made its way to the heart of the city by a special route leading eventually to the temple of Jupiter Capitolinus, where he laid wreaths of laurel in the statue's lap.[132] He himself was dressed in red and his face painted red, exactly like the statue of Jupiter (though in fact Jupiter's dress was itself believed to be that of the ancient Roman kings). The name of the *triumphator* was then added to the special triumphal *fasti*; the supreme ambition of a Roman noble was achieved. In some sense, the triumphing general had been deified for the day and hence (true or not) we have the story of the slave, who stood at his shoulder and whispered:

127 There was a special type of military auspices taken by the consuls as generals on campaign.
128 A vivid account of various religious proceedings taken in expectation of war (in 191 B.C.): Livy XXXVI.1–3.
129 *Amphitryo* 231–2.
130 Harris (1979) 20–1, 261–2; Pietilä-Castrén (1987).
131 The triumph in general, see Ehlers (1948); Versnel (1970); Weinstock (1971) 60–79; Scullard (1981) 213–18; Künzl (1988); Rüpke (1990) 225–34. A description of a lavish triumph: Plutarch, *Aemilius Paullus* 32–4 = **5.8a**. Images of a triumphal procession on a silver cup: **5.8b**.
132 The route: Coarelli (1983–5) I.11–118, (1988) 363–437.

'Remember you are a man.'[133] In any case, much of the ceremonial involved the temporary reversal of the usual forms; the general and his army were never otherwise allowed inside the city and the troops were licensed for this one day to shout abuse and obscenities at their general. Dressed as the god, no doubt in the symbolic terms of the ritual he was the god. But at the grand sacrifice of white oxen, with which the procession ended, it was the *triumphator* who sacrificed, Jupiter who received the victims.

Agriculture, unlike warfare, was not the direct responsibility of the state. Nonetheless, the religious institutions of Rome were much concerned with agricultural success – on which, inevitably, the security and prosperity of the city rested. The calendar of festivals contains rituals connected with grain-crops, with wine-production and with animal husbandry.[134] Some of these festivals have a clear focus. Thus, for instance, the central element of the Robigalia of 25 April was a sacrifice to protect the growing crops from blight.[135] Most of the other rituals connected with grain seem clear enough too: festivals marking the sowing of the seed (Sementivae) at the end of January – though sowing would have been taking place from autumn onwards; a cluster of festivals in April (in addition to the Robigalia) accompanying the period of the growing crops – the Fordicidia, which involved the sacrifice of a pregnant cow to Earth (Tellus), and a festival of Ceres, the goddess of corn;[136] festivals of high summer celebrating the harvesting, storing and protecting of the crops against various dangers.[137] Others are much less easy to explain; and in some cases their fixed timing in the calendar is hard to relate directly to agricultural activity. The two vine festivals (Vinalia), for example, held on 23 April and 19 August – originally, it was said, in honour of Jupiter[138] – do not coincide with any likely date for harvesting the grapes; the first was probably connected instead with the tasting of the previous year's vintage.[139] The Parilia (21 April), the feast of shepherds, the clearest occasion on which the care of animals was the objective, raises another issue: by the end of the Republic this same festival was also interpreted as the celebration

---

133 Epictetus, *Discourses* III.24.85; Tertullian, *Apology* 33.4.
134 Olive growing (which was introduced from Greece to Italy in the sixth century B.C.) did not find any place in the calendar of festivals. This may be an indication that the central series of rituals was fixed before that time; but it still remains puzzling (given the general flexibility of the calendar) why nothing on this theme was added later.
135 Latte (1960a) 67–8; Degrassi (1963) 448–9; Scullard (1981) 108–9; for calendar entries, see **3.3a & b**; with Ovid, *Fasti* IV.905–32 = **2.2b**.
136 Sementivae (late January, but not fixed): Wissowa (1912) 193; Bayet (1950); Scullard (1981) 68. Fordicidia (15 April): Latte (1960a) 68–9; Degrassi (1963) 440–2; Dumézil (1970) 371–4; Scullard (1981) 102. Cerealia (19 April): Le Bonniec (1958) 108–40; Latte (1960a) 68; Dumézil (1970) 374–7; Scullard (1981) 102. Calendar entries referring to April festivals: **3.3a & b**.
137 Dumézil (1975) 59–107.
138 Varro, *On the Latin Language* VI.16; above, p. 15.
139 Wissowa (1912) 115–16, 289–90; Schilling (1954) 98–155; Latte (1960a) 75–6, 184; Degrassi (1963) 446–7, 497–9; Scullard (1981) 106–8, 177; **3.3a & b**.

of the birthday of the city of Rome.[140] Festivals did not have just a single meaning.

Much modern discussion of this cycle of festivals has been under-pinned by the assumption that by the third century B.C. at the latest all these festivals were well on their way to becoming antiquarian survivals having no significance for contemporary, urban-dwelling Romans. It is no doubt true that in Roman religious practice, as in many others, rituals were maintained from year to year out of a general sense of scrupulousness, even where their original significance was long forgotten; it is also true that by the last years of the Republic, antiquarian writers occasionally note elements in these festivals that they cannot explain. By their time, it might be argued, Rome had grown so much and its largely immigrant population become so urbanized and so attached to imported religions, that there would have been little meaning left in the old agricultural rituals. This would be a controversial claim even under the empire; for there was probably never a time when the city of Rome ceased to think of agricultural concerns as central to its way of life. For the third century B.C., however, it is clearly misleading. Rome then was still very much open to the countryside; many of its residents would have owned farms or at least worked on them intermittently, others would have had relations who did; and they would all have been totally dependent on the produce of the local agricultural economy for their food-supply.[141]

It is probably equally misleading to suggest that the simple fact that the festivals had fixed dates in a calendar made those festivals, or at least some of them, meaningless: for a festival intended to celebrate, say, the harvest would sometimes be late, sometimes early, only occasionally coincide exactly. This argument is often reinforced by reference to the Roman practice of intercalation. The insertion of a whole month every few years would have made the fit between the festival and the natural seasons fairly loose in any case. But when the *pontifices* neglected (as we know they sometimes did) the proper cycle of intercalation, the festival calendar would have been grotesquely out of step with the agricultural year; so grotesquely that the festival of the harvest could have been taking place before the seed had even sprouted. All this argument rests on misunderstandings. So far as we know, the early Roman calendar worked accurately enough; there is certainly no evidence that anything went seriously wrong with the cycle of intercalations before some mysterious aberrations at the end of the third century B.C. (presumably caused somehow by the troubles of the period of the

---

140 Wissowa (1912) 199; Latte (1960a) 87–8; Degrassi (1963) 443–5; Dumézil (1975) 188–203; Scullard (1981) 103–5; Beard (1987); below, pp. 174–6. Different ancient interpretations: Ovid, *Fasti* IV.721–806 = **5.1a**; Plutarch, *Romulus* 12.1 = **5.1b**; Athenaeus, *Table-talk* VIII.361 e–f = **5.1c**; note also Propertius IV.4.73–80; Tibullus II.5.87–90.
141 North (1995).

Hannibalic War).[142] Meanwhile, the whole case depends on the assumption that the Romans were very simple-minded in their conception of the relation between religious act and agricultural process; that, for example, a festival designed to ensure divine protection against mildew would be meaningless, unless *at that very moment* the crop was being damaged. In fact, it is partly the point of a communal, ritual calendar that it should transcend such particular, individual moments, offering a ritual structure that can represent and protect (say) the processes of the agricultural year without being constantly tied to the varied and unpredictable conditions of real-life farming. The Romans would have expected that the gods would stay favourable provided the ritual was properly performed at the time prescribed by the priests, following tradition and rule.

A more fundamental question, however, concerns those festivals whose meaning appears to have been disputed even by the Romans themselves. We have already seen, in relation to Ovid's *Fasti*, how interpretations of individual festivals inevitably changed over time. Nevertheless it has remained a convenient modern assumption that, at least at any one moment, each festival had an unambiguous meaning and a single point of reference; or that (to use the categories we have so far used in the section) a festival can be classified as 'agricultural' or 'military'. The Robigalia provides the model here, for our sources connect it with mildew on the corn and with nothing else. In fact, even this case is questionable: it may well be that the Robigalia appears a simple ritual with a unitary meaning largely because we have so few sources that discuss it, and those we have happen to agree. But in many other festivals we are confronted with a profusion of different interpretations, or clearly perceived ambiguities in the ritual and its meaning. In the case of the Lupercalia, for example, at which a group of near naked youths ran round the city, striking those they met with a goat thong, some sources imply that it was a fertility ritual, others that it was a ritual of purification;[143] for the ritual of the October Horse (*equus October*), which involved the sacrifice of a horse to Mars, we read in one ancient writer that it was intended to make the crops prosper, in another that it was a war-ritual, connected with other October ceremonies concerned with the return of the army from its year's campaigning.[144] How are we to deal with these discrepancies?

142 Michels (1967) 145–72; on the state calendar in the middle republican period, Briscoe (1981) 17–26.
143 Modern interpretations of the Lupercalia: Harmon (1978) 1441–6; Scholz (1981); Ulf (1982) (with survey of earlier views, 83–9); Hopkins (1991); Wiseman (1995) 77–88. Ancient interpretations: Plutarch, *Romulus* 21.3–8 = **5.2a**; Varro, *On the Latin Language* VI.34 = **5.2c**; Augustine, *The City of God* XVIII.12 = **5.2d**; for Julius Caesar and his supporters, it could evidently be re-perceived as a coronation ritual, Plutarch, *Julius Caesar* 61.3–4 = **5.2b** (with Dumézil (1970) 349–50).
144 The problem of the October Horse: Warde Fowler (1899) 241–50; Latte (1960a) 119–20; Degrassi (1963) 521; Bayet (1969) 82–3; Scholz (1970); Dumézil (1975)

One answer would stress that it is characteristic of rituals not only that their meanings change over time, but also that they are always liable to be interpreted in different ways by different people, or, for that matter, by the same people on different occasions. Rituals gather significance; though there will always be dominant interpretations, there is no such thing as a single ritual meaning. If only we knew more about the simple Robigalia, we would be bound to find a whole range of different, perhaps idiosyncratic, interpretations clustering around the idea of divine protection for the corn. We should, in fact, expect – rather than be surprised – that different writers explain the same festival in slightly (or significantly) different ways. This plurality of ritual meaning is a feature of almost any ritual system.

There are, however, other specifically Roman issues at stake – as we can see clearly in the (contested) division between military and agricultural festivals. Our own system of classification rigidly separates those two areas of activity. But, as we have seen, in early Rome agriculture and military activity were closely bound up, in the sense that the Roman farmer was also a soldier (and a voter as well); and many of the most important Roman gods and goddesses reflected the life of the human community, with functions that cross these simple categories. It would then seem particularly unlikely that the festivals and their significance should have remained fixed within categories that applied neither to the gods nor to the worshippers. In the case of the October Horse, for example, we should not be trying to decide whether it is either a military, or an agricultural festival; but see it rather as one of the ways in which the convergence of farming and warfare (or more accurately of farmers and fighters) might be expressed.

Our final topic in this section concerns the role of the individual citizen in these rituals, and the relationship of public, state religion to private and domestic life. For the most part, the festivals were conducted on their city's behalf by dignitaries – priests, occasionally priestesses, and magistrates. The only obligation which was generally supposed to fall on the individual citizen was simply to abstain from work while the ceremonies were going on. How far this was obeyed in practice, we do not know. There was certainly some debate, reminiscent of rabbinical debate about the Sabbath, as to what exactly would count as work and what not for this purpose.[145] But on no interpretation does the extent of the citizen's necessary involvement in public ritual go any further. This might in turn imply that these public performances were something quite apart from the individual's life, offering no personal involvement or satisfaction, only the remote awareness that somebody somewhere was protecting the city's relationship with the gods. And from that argument it would be a short next step to say that the religion of individuals did not lie in the state cults at all, but in the cults of the

145–56; Scullard (1981) 193–4. Ancient discussions: Polybius, *History* XII.41.1; Festus p.190L; Plutarch, *Roman Questions* 97.
145 Scullard (1981) 39–40.

family, house or farm to which they did attend personally. The *paterfamilias* was responsible for maintaining the traditional rites of his family, the worship of the Lares and Penates and the other *sacra* inherited from his ancestors and destined to be passed on to his descendants (the *sacra familiae*);[146] while on the country estate, as we learn from the agricultural handbook of Cato the Elder, the whole household (*familia*) including the slaves, would gather together for ceremonies to purify the fields and to pray to the gods for protection and for the fertility of crops and herds.[147] Within the family also the stages of life were marked by religious rituals (*rites de passage*): the acceptance of the baby into the family, the admission of the child into adulthood, marriage, death and burial all fell within the sphere of family religious responsibility, even if (as we have seen) the *pontifices* were responsible for some legal aspects of family life and relationships.[148]

It is possible that for some Romans these private cults would have afforded a separate religious world within which they might have found the personal experience of superhuman beings, the sense of community and of their place in it, which the remoteness of the official cult denied them. Certainly a good deal of poetry of the first centuries B.C. and A.D. celebrates the depth of commitment that must sometimes have been felt towards the religion of the home.[149] And, as we saw earlier, the terracotta votives dedicated in healing cults may give us cause to doubt whether the individual's religious experience was in fact as narrowly bounded as some literary sources have been thought to imply.[150] On the other hand, it is clear that historians have tended to project into this area, about which we really know so little, the elements that they postulate as essential to any religion – personal prayer and contact with the divine, deep feelings and beliefs about man's relation to universal forces – that seem to be missing from the religious life of the Romans. The argument in its simplest terms goes something like this: Roman religion must have involved some forms of deep personal commitment; there is little or no sign of that in public cult; therefore it must have been found in the 'private' religion of home and family. Of course, that is possible. But the argument as it stands rests on the assumption that we challenged at the very beginning of this section: that Roman religion is a relatively familiar set of institutions, obeying roughly the same rules and fulfilling the same human needs as our own. If we accept that the Romans' religious experience might be profoundly different from our own, then we do not necessarily have to search out a context for the personal expression of individual piety; we do not, in other words, have to

146 Statuettes of the Lares, see **2.2a**; a household shrine from Pompeii is illustrated at **4.12**.
147 *On Agriculture* 141 = **6.3a**.
148 Above, pp. 24–6. For a general discussion of the role of private religion, Dorcey (1992) esp. 2–6.
149 For example, Horace, *Odes* III.8; IV.11; Tibullus II.2.
150 Above, pp. 12–13.

find a context in which to imagine the Romans being 'religious' according to our own preconceptions of religiosity. But there are other reasons too for questioning the centrality of private as against public cults.

The separation between city cult and family or farm cult should not be exaggerated. In some festivals, a central ceremony performed in the city was accompanied by rites conducted in families or in the countryside; in others, the only acts reported took place in the family, though it is likely that there was also some corresponding public ritual; other festivals again were celebrated by particular groups of the Roman people – such as the *curiae*, the 30 divisions of Roman citizens that probably stretched back well into regal times.[151] The festivals for the dead (the Parentalia in February and the Lemuria in May) were, for example, essentially domestic festivals focussed on family ancestors, though there was also a public element when, on the first day of the Parentalia, a Vestal Virgin performed the rituals for the dead;[152] at the Parilia in April, our descriptions of what took place clearly refer to individual farms, with the shepherd and even the sheep leaping over bonfires;[153] at the Saturnalia in December, there were sacrifices at the temple of Saturn to open the festivities, but the feasting, exchanging of roles between masters and slaves, merrymaking and present-giving evidently all took place in the households.[154] There were also quite specifically rural festivals, outside the civic structure of the city – the Ambarvalia (lustration of the fields), the Sementivae (festival of sowing) and the Compitalia (celebration at the crossroads both in Rome and in the countryside); these do not have fixed dates in the calendars, though they were a regular part of the ritual year.[155] On still other occasions, a public festival provided the context and occasion for a family event: so at the Liberalia (17 March) boys who had reached the age of puberty took their *toga virilis*, the mark of their admission to the adult community.[156] Sometimes the relationship of public and private elements is particularly complicated: at the Matralia (11 June) the public ceremonial took place at the temple of Mater Matuta in the Forum Boarium; at this festival, we are told, the matrons

---

151 The role of the *curiae* at (for example) the Fornacalia: Ovid, *Fasti* II.527–32; Dionysius of Halicarnassus, *Roman Antiquities* II.23; with Latte (1960a) 143; Scullard (1981) 73.

152 Parentalia (13–21 February): Latte (1960a) 98; Degrassi (1963) 408–9; Scullard (1981) 74–5. Lemuria (9, 11 and 13 May): Latte (1960a) 99; Degrassi (1963) 454–5; Scullard (1981) 118–19.

153 Above, pp. 45–6 with pp. 174–6, below.

154 Latte (1960a) 255; Degrassi (1963) 539; Scullard (1981) 205–7; Versnel (1993) 136–227. Private aspects of the festival: Macrobius, *Saturnalia* I.24.22–3 = **5.3a**; Pliny, *Letters* II.17.23–4 = **5.3c**; and the illustration from a fourth-century A.D. calendar, **5.3b**. For the public rituals, see Livy XXII.1.20 = **7.3a**.

155 Sementivae: above, p. 45. Compitalia (December/January): Latte (1960a) 90–3; Scullard (1981) 58–60; see also below, pp. 184–6. Ambarvalia (May): Latte (1960a) 41–2; Scullard (1981) 124–5.

156 Ovid, *Fasti* III.771–90.

prayed for their nephews and nieces first, not their own children – a prayer, it seems likely, that was repeated by women throughout the city, not just those present at the temple.[157] This range of festivals that bring together ritual in the public and private sphere, shows more than the simple fact that a good deal of private ritual accompanied public events; it suggests that one of the functions of the festival calendar was precisely to link public ritual with private domestic worship – to calibrate the concerns of the community as a whole onto those of the family, and vice versa.

The ritual activities of the Vestal Virgins, the only major female priesthood at Rome, illustrate another aspect of the connections between public and private religion. The Vestals were clearly set apart from the other priestly groups.[158] Six priestesses, chosen in childhood, they lived in a special house next to the temple of Vesta. They had all kinds of privileges, including (unlike other women) the right of making a will without the compliance of a guardian (*tutor*). They also had unique religious responsibilities and were subject to unique penalties if they failed, either by letting the sacred fire go out or by losing their virginity: unchaste Vestals were buried alive.[159] We know a good deal more about their ritual programme than about that of any other priestly group in Rome; and that is probably not a mere accident in the transmission of information, but reflects the high importance of (and ancient interest in) what they did for Rome. There is also good reason for thinking that they were one of the most ancient religious organizations of the city, embedded in the religious structure of the earliest Latin communities of central Italy; certainly, similar priesthoods under the same name were found in the ancient towns nearby, suggesting that they go back to the very earliest history of this whole group of communities.[160]

The Vestals' activities included a good deal of what might be called household work: they were responsible for tending the sacred fire, on the sacred hearth of their temple; they guarded their storehouse (*penus*) and they ritually cleaned it out and expelled the dirt; they gathered the first ears

157 Warde Fowler (1899) 154–7; Latte (1960a) 97; Degrassi (1963) 468–9; Dumézil (1970) 50–5 (introducing parallels from Vedic India) . The sixth-century B.C. temples of Mater Matuta and Fortuna: Castagnoli (1979); Cornell (1995) 147–8; Steinby (1993-) II.281–5; Map 1 no. 23 (with statues surviving from the temple of Fortuna, **1.7a(ii)**). The temple of Mater Matuta at Satricum: **1.6b**.

158 In general, Wissowa (1912) 507–12; Koch (1958) 1732–53; (1960) 1–16; Latte (1960a) 108–11; Ampolo (1971); Pomeroy (1976) 210–14; Radke (1981b); Scheid (1992b) 381–4. The myth of the origin of the Vestals: Plutarch, *Numa* 10 = **8.4a**. Inscriptions in honour of leading Vestals: **8.4b**.

159 Plutarch, *Numa* 10 = **8.4a** emphasizes the punishment of Vestals; see also Plutarch, *Roman Questions* 96; Dionysius of Halicarnassus, *Roman Antiquities* II.67.4; with Koch (1960) 1–16; Guizzi (1968) 141–58; Cornell (1981).

160 Vestal priestesses at Alba Longa and Lavinium: Wissowa (1912) 520–1; Weinstock (1937b) 428–40; Alföldi (1965) 250–65; Dury-Moyaers (1981) 220–6; Radke (1981b); below, pp. 57–9, 323.

of corn from the harvest, ground and baked them to provide the sacred salted meal (*mola salsa*) that was used to sanctify the victim at sacrifices.[161] There is an obvious parallel between Vesta, the hearth of the city, and the hearths of the houses of individual families – the priestesses of the state apparently representing the women of the household. But which women exactly?

The simplest hypothesis that has been used to explain their activity takes us right back to regal Rome, with the suggestion that the life of the Vestals was the life of the ancient regal household and that they themselves originated from (and later symbolically represented) the women of the king's family. The problem is that they do not, in fact, fit the role of either the wives or the daughters of the early kings at all well. The insistence on their virginity makes them very unlikely candidates as wives; while daughters provide an equally unlikely model for a group of priestesses whose legal privileges were utterly different from those of a dependent child (and who in any case wore, as their priestly costume, some of the distinctive clothes of the bride or married woman).[162] Even the links with the king's household are doubtful: for in terms of ritual, their connections are with the *pontifex maximus*, not with the *rex sacrorum* (the priestly successor, as we shall see, of the early kings).[163]

It may be that the key to the Vestals' sacred status lies precisely in its ambiguity: they are paraded as sharing the characteristics of both matrons and virgins, with even some characteristics (such as specific legal rights in the making of wills) of men too.[164] It is a pattern observed in many societies that people and animals deemed 'interstitial', those who fall between the categories into which the world is usually divided, are often also regarded as sacred, powerful or holy.[165] Here it seems plausible that the intermediate sexual status assigned to the priestesses served to mark their separateness and their sacredness. But they were ambiguous or marginal in other ways too: they mediated the realms of public and private, by carrying on private duties in the public sphere; and their ritual programme involved them in all major aspects of Roman life, so linking parts of life often regarded as separate. The Vestals represented a peculiarly extreme version of the connection between the religious life of the home and of the community: if anything went wrong in their house, the threat was to the whole *salus* (safety) of the Roman people – not just of the city, but including the health and fertility of the whole community, its animals and its farms.[166] So too their

161 Latte (1960a) 108–10.
162 The Vestals' legal condition and privileges are the subject of Guizzi (1968).
163 The different suggestions and their problems are reviewed by Beard (1980). For the relations between Vestals and *pontifex maximus*, below, pp. 57–8.
164 Beard (1980) – with critique in Beard (1995).
165 See Douglas (1966); this is another aspect of the 'boundary crossing' we discussed in the context of prodigies, above, p. 37.
166 Koch (1960) 11–16.

unchastity was not just a domestic offence, it occasioned public prodigies requiring extraordinary measures of expiation.[167]

The rituals in which the Vestals were involved emphasize these links. At the Fordicidia, after the pregnant cow had been sacrificed to Tellus (Earth), the unborn calf was taken and burned by the senior Vestal: the calf too was an ambiguous being – living but not born, sacrificed but not capable of being a proper victim; its ashes were then preserved by the Vestals and used, mixed with the dried blood of the previous October's 'October horse', to sprinkle on the bonfires of the Parilia, for the purification of the shepherd and the sheep.[168] The precise implications of this cycle of symbolic acts may not be recoverable; but it does make clear the importance of the Vestals in connecting the fertility of the earth, the health and safety of the flocks, and the city's security in the military sense; it reminds us too of the links underlying the different rituals of the calendar, symbolized by the recycling, from one ritual to another, of the sacrificial ashes. Human fertility was also involved in the Vestals' sphere; and here, for once, we have the help of myths which fit with and clarify a set of rituals. The story is told of various founders or heroes of towns in the region of Latium, around Rome, that they were born of a virgin impregnated either by a spark from the hearth or by a phallus which sprang from the hearth.[169] The Roman Vestals were not only responsible for guarding the hearth, the undying flame, but also for keeping a phallus in their temple. The significance of the flame on their hearth must therefore, in at least one of its aspects, lie in its link with the foundation, generation and continuation of the race. The goddess Vesta herself encapsulated all the elements; she was the flame itself, she was the virgin, she was Vesta the Mother.[170]

The Vestal Virgins were themselves withdrawn from all the ordinary activities of life – living together as priestesses, separately from their families, in one of the most public spots of the whole city (at the east end of the forum); but at the same time they linked, at a ritual level, all the different areas of that life. That connection makes it easier to see why there was so powerful an association between them and the survival of Rome as a whole. And it is no coincidence that they provided the home for the various talismans of that survival – as ancient, it was said, as the sacred objects brought by Aeneas from Troy.[171] In a real crisis, it was these talismans in their care that had to be saved at any cost, even the cost of one's own family – a truth

167 Cornell (1981) 31–3.
168 For example, Ovid, *Fasti* IV.731–4 = **5.1a** (for the purificatory material used at the Parilia).
169 Romulus: Plutarch, *Romulus* 2.3–5. Caeculus of Praeneste: Servius, *On Virgil's Aeneid* VII.678. Servius Tullius: Dionysius of Halicarnassus, *Roman Antiquities* IV.2; Pliny, *Natural History* XXXVI. 204; Ovid, *Fasti* VI.627–36; Plutarch, *Fortune of the Romans* 10; on all these traditions, Capdeville (1995) 1–154.
170 Ovid's interpretation of the goddess: *Fasti* VI.249–348, part = **2.5**.
171 Above, pp. 2–3.

vividly captured by Livy in his story of a plebeian who (when Rome was facing attack by the Gauls in 390 B.C.) made his own wife and children get out of the wagon that was taking them to safety so that he could rescue the Vestals and their sacred objects.[172] Throughout the history of pagan Rome, any suggestion of an irregularity involving the Vestals or their rituals implied a threat to the city itself[173] – even more profoundly than interruptions to any of the other rituals we have discussed in this section.

5. Adjusting to the new Republic

The three preceding sections of this chapter have given a synoptic analysis of the religion of the Romans as we believe it to have been under the developed republican system. We have already expressed our doubts about the value of narrative accounts which have traditionally been based on a combination of guesswork and a priori assumptions. We do, however, think that it is possible to identify some moments of change and to make some progress towards establishing the stages by which religion came to be as we have described it. The first of these stages is the replacement of the kingship by the republican regime, dated in our sources to the end of the sixth century B.C., after the expulsion of the last king, Tarquin the Proud. The story of the expulsion is complicated by the fact that Tarquin appears not just as a villain but as an alien villain, of a family originating in the Etruscan city of Tarquinii and later receiving from his Etruscan kinsmen support against the regime that had expelled him.

Our argument throughout this chapter has been that the religion of later republican Rome reflected closely the ideas and institutions characteristic of the whole republican order. That implies that, despite the Romans' own belief that the origin of most of their central religious institutions lay with the kings, and despite an undoubted continuity in many particular priesthoods, rituals and sacred sites, there must have been a great deal of change to create the developed republican system after the fall of the monarchy. It is tempting to make the periods of religious history fit neatly with the conventional periods of political change; if so, there should have been radical changes when the kings were overthrown and the Republic began. It is, however, very controversial whether or not this was so. As we stressed earlier in this chapter, it is not at all clear whether the institutions of Rome in the fifth and fourth centuries were yet recognizably 'republican'; but even on the assumption that they were, there may have been a considerable delay before religion began to reflect the new political order.

The first problem the founders of the Republic must have had to face was the replacement of the kingship itself. Abolishing kings and replacing

172 Livy V.40.7–10; with Ogilvie (1965) 723–5.
173 For example, Cicero, *On Behalf of Fonteius* 46–8.

them by elected officials was a revolutionary step in its religious implications as well as its political ones, because kings must have taken a leading (if not the leading) role in the religion of the state. Who was to perform their duties, if there was no king any more? and how would the gods react to the new situation? Later Romans, and most modern writers as well, have seen the solution in simple terms. There had still to be one individual who was called the *rex* (king) and would carry out the religious role. But he would now be quite separate from anyone who held the king's other powers. So the new king was named the 'king of rites' (*rex sacrorum*); he had to be a patrician, he became a member of the college of *pontifices* and he was excluded from those who could be elected to positions of power.[174] Clearly it would have been a difficult and delicate task to define the position of the new 'king' in relation to the old priests, and especially within the college of which he would now be a member.

Here as so often, the only accounts of this situation come from the late republican period and later. By that time, the *rex* had become an obscure member of the college, with a largely forgotten range of ritual duties; meanwhile the *pontifex maximus*, the elected leader of the *pontifices*, had become the most powerful of the great political priests. The implication in Livy's account of the foundation of the Republic in Book II of his *History* is that the subordination of the *rex* to the *pontifex maximus* dates back to a deliberate decision taken by the founders.[175] This, then, would be the solution to the problem: the king's potential threat was neutralized by making him a priest subordinate to the *pontifex*. But how anachronistic were such accounts? It has been argued that, like the founding myths of regal Rome itself, this story is another retrojection into the fifth century B.C. of reality as it was known to historians writing in the first century B.C. On this view, the king would originally have kept his authority as head of religion and only slowly in the centuries that followed would the *pontifex maximus* have emerged as the more powerful figure.[176] There can be no certain answer to this question, and the issues take us into the technical details of the college's organization. But the effort is worth making for two reasons: first, it takes us into the prehistory of the office of the *pontifex maximus*, who was to become, as we shall see in later chapters, more and more important over the centuries, until he was effectively the 'high priest' of Rome; second, the

---

174 Wissowa (1912) 504–8; De Sanctis (1907–64) IV.2.355–7; Latte (1960a) 195–6; Dumézil (1970) 576–93; Momigliano (1971); cf. Ampolo (1971) and, for a different view, Cornell (1995) 232–8. The known *reges* are listed by Szemler (1972) 68, 174–5. None of them is known to have achieved any political distinction; below, pp. 106–7.

175 II.2.1.

176 The argument is most fully developed by Latte (1960a) 195–212. The most interesting piece of evidence is a list of the order of priests preserved by Festus p.299L: first the *rex*, then – in second to fourth place – the three *flamines*, fifth the *pontifex maximus*. This order must reflect some archaic 'reality'; but what kind of reality and whether it is early republican rather than regal is quite obscure.

debate about the original power of these two offices provides a good example of how scholars have tried to deploy tiny scraps of evidence to throw some light on the development of Roman religion in this early period.

The *rex sacrorum* was subject to two sets of limitations, which are always assumed to go back to the beginning of the Republic and which give the best indication of the intentions of the founders. First, he was absolutely excluded from playing any part in political life – he could not hold political office of any kind and he did not sit in the senate.[177] This puts him in a different category from the major *flamines*, who seem not to have been specifically excluded from political life, but only limited in what they were allowed to do without violation of their sacred duties and taboos.[178] Evidently, the *rex* was quite deliberately barred from this sphere. The second limitation was that of collegiality: whatever the king's previous relations with the priests had been, he had almost certainly been set apart from them, perhaps using the different groups of priests as advisers in his active role; now as *rex sacrorum*, he was to become a member of one college and not of the others, having a share in religious decision-making, but only in the pontifical sphere and only as one member among others, like the *flamines* and the *pontifices* themselves.[179] He did, however, retain his own ritual programme of action on certain fixed days: he held a sacrifice on the Kalends (the first day) of each month, announced the dates of the festivals of the month on each Nones (the fifth or seventh day), appeared in the Comitium on certain fixed dates (24 March and 24 May) and sacrificed there.[180]

One way of understanding this whole reform is to see the Romans as making a deliberate separation between religious and political areas of the king's duties. At the very least, they were taking a step towards having a religious sphere distinct from political power. But, if this is what they were trying to do, they were doing it very partially. The sacred king was stripped of his power to act in everyday life, but he was far from taking over all the religious tasks of the old king. He had, for instance, no part in taking the auspices before political or military action; these were performed by the new elected magistrates (while oversight of them lay with the college of *augures* of which the *rex sacro-*

---

177 This emerges quite clearly from Livy XL.42.8–10, reporting a conflict in the second century B.C. between a potential *rex sacrorum* and the *pontifex maximus* of the time, who wanted him to abdicate a junior magistracy that he was then holding. The outcome was that he kept his magistracy and did not become *rex*.

178 See, for example, Livy XXXI.50.7; the point was established by C. Valerius Flaccus who had become *flamen* against his will (Livy XXVII.8.4 = **8.2d**); he later rose to be praetor in 183 B.C. See also below, p. 106.

179 Cicero, *On the Response of the Haruspices* 12 gives a list of the members of the college of *pontifices* present at a particular meeting of the college; the *rex sacrorum* of the time is listed like the others, that is, in order of co-optation into the college.

180 His ritual programme: Degrassi (1963) 327–30 (Kalends and Nones); 415–16 (24 February); 430 (24 March); also 538 (15 December); Weinstock (1937a); Momigliano (1971).

rum was not a member). Yet on almost any view, the taking of the auspices must have been one of the old king's key functions. Again, it must be reasonably certain that the original king would have had some general authority over religion as over other aspects of life; but if so, that authority was not passed to the new *rex* at all, but to the various priests and other officials.

A possible view here (and one that has been argued) is that the simple account of the relatively restricted religious powers of the sacred king (an account based largely on Livy) is after all quite wrong: that the new *rex* was originally set up to be the religious head of Rome, carrying on all the religious responsibility and authority of the real king; but that he later lost that position of dominance to the *pontifices* and especially the *pontifex maximus*. In which case our later sources, in giving the *rex* a subordinate role from the very beginning, are reading back into the remote past a situation with which they were familiar in their own time, for lack of any real understanding of fifth-century B.C. conditions. On this argument, it is a lesser issue whether the *rex* or the *pontifex maximus* was originally the designated head of the pontifical college or how exactly the transition from *rex* to *pontifex maximus* was made. The more central point is that the seniority of the *rex* would inevitably have been eroded; that the senior *pontifex* would sooner or later have emerged as the more important figure, irrespective of anyone's plans or intentions, simply because he had access to more of the areas into which religious authority was disseminated, especially to the senate. So even if the *rex* was the senior figure at the start of the Republic, it is inconceivable that he should have maintained that authority, given the disadvantages of his exclusion from the political sphere. On the other hand, if (as this argument supposes) the religious system was quite different in the very earliest phases of the Republic, it would be possible to imagine the original *rex sacrorum* as a powerful religious leader, quite isolated from political life. This view, then, puts at the minimum the amount of religious authority that was removed from the new king compared to the real king on his first appointment.

There is, however, one particular area which has been claimed to prove that the religious power of the *rex* was restricted from the very moment the monarchy fell; this concerns the relationship of the *rex* and *pontifex maximus* to the Vestals and their cult. It was, in all the evidence that we have, the *pontifex* who performed the ceremony of the induction of a new Vestal, using an ancient form of words; he alone, apart from the Vestals themselves, had the right of access to their holiest places of cult; he had the right to whip them when they failed in their obligations and conducted the trial with the college if they were accused of losing their virginity; he also acted ritually together with them on certain occasions.[181] In doing all this, the *pontifex* was exercising power in the most sensitive of all areas of ritual

---

181 Appointment of new Vestals (and *flamines*): Guizzi (1968) 100–5; Dumézil (1970) 582–3, 587–8. Aulus Gellius, *Attic Nights* I.12.10–14.

communication between men and gods. What is more, this is the only area in which the *pontifex* does have special religious authority of his own. In general he acts on behalf of, or as agent of, or simply as one member of the college of *pontifices*; he had no elaborate programme of rituals that he alone could carry out, as for instance did the *flamines*. If the *pontifices* replaced the *rex* in any area at all from the very beginning of the Republic, then their relation with (and control over) the Vestals seems the promising one: for if the Vestals were really the daughters of the royal household, then they must surely have been within the authority of the king in the regal period and it is hard to imagine any occasion on which the authority could have been transferred other than when the monarchy fell.

This whole construction is, however, extremely flimsy. As we have seen, there is little or no reason for regarding the Vestals as in any sense the daughters of the king and his special connexion with them is no more than a guess based on a guess.[182] More importantly still for the present argument, the idea of a transfer from *rex* to *pontifex* in this respect seems to make nonsense of the whole tradition of the origins of the *rex sacrorum*. The theory of the reform is supposed to be that some of the king's ritual performances were so specific to that role and so holy that the gods would only accept them from a *rex*; the name and position of the king had therefore to be preserved; but if the king had immemorial links with the Vestals, as his sometime daughters, and yet his association with them could be instantly handed over to the *pontifex maximus*, even though the *rex sacrorum* was available, the supposed reason for preserving that position collapses completely. The simplest view is that the *pontifex* had his special connexion with the Vestals because he had always had such a connexion, even in the days when the kings were really kings.

In the face of the complex and shifting arguments and counter arguments, it is possible to take a still more radical view: that there was no transfer of authority or any remarkable change at this stage: the *rex sacrorum*, it can be argued, was not a new invention of the Republic at all, but simply the continuation of a priesthood that had already existed in the regal period. So there had originally been two kings, one concerned with the world of action and war, one with matters of religion and cult. According to this argument, at the end of the monarchy, the *rex sacrorum* simply continued to do what he had always done.[183]

There are two conclusions to this discussion. The first is to stress how tantalizing, but elusive, the evidence for this period of Roman history is; it

---

182 The only evidence that gives colour to a special family/religious relationship between the Vestals and the *rex* is the formula quoted by Servius, *On Virgil's Aeneid* X.228: 'vigilasne, rex? vigila.' ('Are you on the watch, King? Be on the watch.') But this shows the Vestals in their role as the defenders of the safety of Rome; it is not necessary to explain it as a survival of their primitive family life.

183 Cornell (1995) 235–6.

is clear, for example, that within the regulations for the Vestals and their relations with other members of the pontifical college, there are preserved some hints of the earliest powers of the different priests in Rome – but it is extremely controversial how we should extract from those hints any clear story of those early conditions or their change and development. Secondly, Livy's version, though the subject of much criticism, does seem as plausible as any of the alternatives on offer. This is perhaps not as paradoxical as it might seem. For, after all, Livy was engaged in exactly the same arguments as we are today, knowing no more than we do – or not much – and seeking, just as we do, to find an explanation that makes sense both of the few secure bits of information and of the later institutions still in existence in his own day.

On any of these views, the purpose underlying the detailed arrangements was that whoever bore the title *rex* should never again be in a position to threaten the city with tyranny. There was also a religious penalty established in the early law code against any aspirant to tyranny: he could be declared *sacer*, that is to say dedicated to the gods, meaning that he could be killed without the killer incurring retribution.[184] In many other respects though, the continuities between regal and republican Rome seem more surprising than the immediate changes. The most striking continuity of all concerns Jupiter Capitolinus and his grandiose new temple. The tradition is that the temple was built by the last Tarquin, finished by the time of his fall, dedicated by the very first college of magistrates of the Republic.[185] However unlikely this story may seem to us now, it does at least encapsulate the ambivalent standing of the cult between monarchy and Republic. The position of Jupiter within the triad, the dominant position and scale of the building, the nature of the cult-practice, all suggest that the king had designed the temple as a grandiose expression of his power and that of his régime. It would perhaps have been going too far to expect that the temple would have been razed to the ground when the Tarquins fell; but it is still surprising that what happened was the precise opposite – the cult became central to the new republican era. It was the focus of the religious activity of the annual magistrates; the god was accepted as the fount of the auspices upon which the relationship of the city with the gods rested; the victorious generals of Rome returned to Rome to lay their laurels at the feet of Jupiter Capitolinus. The ceremonial of the triumph and the related ceremonial of the procession before the games (*pompa circensis*) illustrate the point vividly; the celebrator in each case was actually dressed up – and made up – in the guise of the statue of Jupiter, as he appeared in the Capitoline temple, which was (as we have seen) also the guise of the king. This can hardly

---

184 Livy II.8.2.
185 The tradition of dedication in republican times: Livy II.8 (cf. I.55.1 = **1.9b**); Cicero, *On his House* 139; Dionysius of Halicarnassus, *Roman Antiquities* V.35.3; Tacitus, *Histories* III.72; above, p. 3.

be understood except as the retention of consciously regal ceremonial under the new régime.

This is not the only example of the survival into the Republic of symbols of power belonging to ancient monarchic practice, though it is perhaps the most dramatic one.[186] It seems comprehensible only on the assumption that what is now thought of as *royal* ceremonial was perceived by the Romans, first and foremost, as *Roman*, certainly not as an arbitrary imposition upon them – whether monarchical or Etruscan. For another factor that might have played a part in the religious conflicts of this period is the apparently 'foreign' Etruscan origins of the last kings and the religious institutions associated with them. In fact it was probably as difficult then as it is now to define the boundaries between Etruscan and Roman elements in religion. Although some particular practices (such as haruspicy) would forever remain linked to Etruscan roots, the 'Roman' religious world had become saturated with influences from their Etruscan neighbours which had merged with and transformed the Latin culture of their ancestors. Jupiter was, after all, an ancient Latin deity with an ancient Latin name – and at the same time the focus of what we may choose to classify as (in part at least) Etruscan religious forms (such as the ceremonial of triumph or the Capitoline temple). Meanwhile, there was no alternative high culture, or vocabulary of ceremonial to which Romans could turn. It is unlikely that the early republicans ever conceived of isolating, let alone outlawing, the 'Etruscan' religion in their midst.[187]

There is a different sense also in which the tradition about the changeover from monarchy to Republic is surprisingly muted. As we have seen, the tradition is that most of the major features of the constitution and the religion of Rome were devised and put into effect by the kings, who are presented in our first-century sources as successive founders of the different areas of public life.[188] Little credit is given to the leaders of the republican period. In the form in which we have this tradition, it is a literary construction put together in the late republican period. It incorporates far earlier myths, legends and conceptions about the deeds of the founders and the early kings, but it would be very hazardous to assume that its general message would have been recognizable to Romans of the fifth century B.C. All the same, there does seem to be a shortage of information and storytelling of this kind that refers to the early Republic; and unless all these traditions about the contributions of the monarchs are to be written off as sheer invention of a later period, they must at least have been transmitted *through* the early Republic. If the early republicans were themselves deeply hostile to any suggestion of monarchy or of monarchic practice, it is very

186 Dionysius of Halicarnassus, *Roman Antiquities* III.61–2; for a vigorous statement of the case, Alföldi (1965) 200–2.
187 The 'myth' of Etruscan Rome: Cornell (1995) 151–72; above, pp. 54–5.
188 Above, pp. 2–3.

hard to see how that could have happened. Again, we seem to have to reckon with strong continuities as well as a sharp disruption, if sense is to be made of the tradition which has come down to us.

The overall result of the events that we have considered in this section might be called the 'republican religious order'. We have seen earlier that one of the most remarkable characteristics of this order was that authority over religious matters was widely diffused. The result was that no individual or family could construct a monopoly of religious, any more than of political, power. It can hardly be altogether an accident that the religious and political aspects of the system should reflect one another in this respect. But the situation is not one of straightforward imitation: priests were not, like magistrates, officials elected for one year only; they were chosen by the surviving members of the college for life; besides, the differentiation of the priestly groups, which is one of the most remarkable features of Roman religious organization, almost certainly (as the tradition implies) goes back to the time of the kings – it pre-dates, that is, the republican organization of which it becomes a part. The similarity between the political and the religious institutions of the state must then have resulted, not from the same decisions being taken at the same time, but by similar overall objectives being aimed at. If it is assumed that the king in the regal period acted as the central religious authority co-ordinating the advice of the different colleges, then his subordination, whether by planning or not, would have produced a diffusion of authority; if that is the right way to look at it, then the steps considered in this section – hazy though they now are to us – were indeed the first moves towards a *republican* type of religion.

6. Innovation and change

In the early centuries of the republican period (fifth century to third century B.C.) there were many changes and innovations – new temples and cults, new or revised ceremonies, changes of procedure or decisions about the rules concerning membership of the priestly colleges; there was another type of change too that we might infer or guess at, not special moments of decision, but long-term shifts – for one of the implications of the system we have outlined was that social, political or economic changes, or changes in Rome's relations with other states, would all have had religious repercussions. This second type of change is likely to have had profounder effects in the long run, but it is the first type that our sources tell us about, the ones that are noticed by contemporary recorders. The most serious distinction (which may but does not necessarily correspond to the two types of change) is between changes that could be assimilated to the overall structure and those that threatened to transform it.

Innovation in one form or another is certainly a central feature of

Roman religion and the new gods, goddesses and rituals were for the most part assimilated without difficulty to the existing complex of old cults. Sometimes, they were definitely recognized as non-Roman, but accepted through *evocatio*, through the vows of generals or through the recommendations found in the Sibylline Books.[189] More and more as time passed, and especially in the third century B.C., new deities came in the form of personifications – for the most part personifications of desirable qualities or virtues, such as Concord, Victory, Hope, Faith, Honour and Virtue.[190] In some cases, it may be that such an abstraction gradually took on a more specific personality; it has even been suggested that the Roman goddess Venus started out as an abstraction and only later came to be identified with the Greek Aphrodite.[191] But whatever the detailed history of these developments, the third century saw an intensification of the process of innovation, as Rome's frontiers and contacts widened and as her military successes brought in new resources to be invested in building projects.

Many innovations were inspired by the Sibylline Books, the collections of oracles, kept and consulted by the *duoviri sacris faciundis*, which served both to initiate change and to provide legitimation for what might otherwise have been seen as deviations from the ancestral tradition. The story of the purchase of these Books dates their arrival to the late regal period, when King Tarquin the Elder bought them from an old woman who offered him nine for a certain price; when he refused to buy, she destroyed three of them and offered him the remaining six for the same price; he refused again, so she destroyed three more and offered him the last three, still for the same price. Impressed at last, he paid the price and these three were the books kept by the college.[192] In other accounts, and regularly in the later tradition, the books are called Sibylline and connected with the Sibyl of Cumae; they were believed to contain the destiny of the Romans.[193] The anecdote and the connection with the Sibyl of Cumae may all be late accretions to the tradition; but it is clear enough that the Romans did have a set of oracles in Greek verse, that they regarded as of early origin, though not so early as the foundation of the main institutions in the time of King Numa. The many

189 Above, p. 35; note especially the *evocatio* of Juno of Veii, Livy V.21.1–7 = **2.6a**.

190 Axtell (1907); De Sanctis (1907–64) IV.2.295–303; Latte (1960a) 233–42; Weinstock (1971) 168–9 (Fides = 'Faith'); 260 (Concordia = 'Concord'); 230–3 (Honos/Virtus = 'Honour'/'Virtue'); on these below pp. 88n.55; 105. The special case of Victoria (Victory): below, p. 69. Note also the coin illustrating Honos and Virtus, shown at **2.3b**; and Cicero's explanation of these abstractions, *On the Nature of the Gods* II.60–2 = **2.3a**. Map 1 no. 4 (Honos/Virtus); no. 25 (Fides).

191 Schilling (1954) 87.

192 The story of Tarquin: Dionysius of Halicarnassus, *Roman Antiquities* IV.62 = **1.8**. The Books themselves: Diels (1890); Hoffmann (1933); Gagé (1955) 24–38, 196–204, 432–61, 542–55, 677–82; Latte (1960a) 160–1; Radke (1963) 1115–28; Parke (1988) 190–215. An extract from the books is apparently preserved in Phlegon of Tralles, *On Wonders* 10 = **7.5a**.

193 The origins of the connection, Radke (1963) 1138–9.

consultations of the Books recorded in Roman writers suggest that they mainly contained sets of *remedia*, rituals through which the threatened harm implied by the prodigies might be averted. It was in this context that the Books suggested new cults and rituals, legitimating innovation by their very antiquity – while suggesting too that the Romans saw the Greeks as sources of inspiration and wisdom. Our evidence does not suggest that they contained very much that we should call 'prophetic'; but the silence may be misleading, since this may very well be a case where the nature of our evidence and the preoccupations of the Roman writers on whom we depend are effectively 'censoring' our information and obscuring the variety of religious life in the period. It is certain that a tradition of prophetic skill survived amongst the Etruscans and that they still possessed it in the late republican period.

All kinds of agents were involved in the process of innovation, in different relations to the senate. But whatever the particular role of the senate's various advisers, there is no doubt that the introduction of new deities and forms continued throughout the period. This is not just a phenomenon of religious life. At the same time, the Romans were establishing their practice of admitting new citizens from the surrounding area into their community as full citizens; these open boundaries at the human level are surely inseparable from open boundaries to foreign gods.[194]

To say that innovation was a normal model of the functioning of this religious system, and hence supportive of it, not threatening to it, is not to say that successive introductions did not bring with them new attitudes or ideas, enshrined in the new cults. The problem is to assess which were the new attitudes or ideas, given that we have such an inadequate grasp on what religious forms were available to the early Romans. Thus, the *lectisternium* ritual celebrated for the first time in 399 B.C. has often been seen as a great turning-point: not only did this involve bringing out statues of deities and offering them a meal (an apparent step on the road to seeing the gods and goddesses as sharing human forms and appetites) but the gods and goddesses chosen for the ritual (including, for example, Apollo and his mother Latona) demonstrate clear Greek influence. However it is unclear how radically new this was. Greek influence, we now know, goes back to the sixth century B.C.; and even the meal seems likely to have had a precedent in the *epulum Iovis*, celebrated at the games in September and November, where Jupiter himself was offered a share in the feast.[195]

The obvious direction to look for religious change of deep significance would be the area of social conflict, more particularly to the conflicts that

194 North (1976) 11.
195 The *lectisternium* of 399 B.C.: Livy V.13 = **5.5b** (with the statues of goddesses as if being brought out for a banquet or procession, **5.5c**). See Warde Fowler (1911) 261–5; Bayet (1926) 260–3; Gagé (1955) 168–79; Latte (1960a) 242–4; Ogilvie (1965) 655–7. The *epulum Iovis*: above, p. 40; below, pp. 66–7.

produced the oligarchy of the third century B.C., composed of the dominant plebeian as well as the traditional patrician families. This compromise followed a long series of conflicts, reported by Livy and our other sources, in which the great clans of patricians sought to defend the inherited privileges of their class. It is implicit in the conception of religious life proposed in this chapter that any such long-standing division in society would eventually find some religious expression, since any kind of continuing, coherent action would have had to be put into some relation with the gods and their involvement in Roman life. To a limited extent, it may be possible to detect the lines along which this might have happened, both in the great struggle between the plebeians and the patricians and in the even more obscure struggle between the power and influence of the great clans (*gentes*) and the interest of the city as a whole. The recorded information about plebeian religion and the religion of the *gentes* is, however, very limited; and since, particularly in the early stages, we have only the haziest idea of events or their significance in the history of Rome, any reconstruction of the religious effects of the conflict must be even more tentative.

It seems to be beyond dispute that the patrician families claimed special authority in relation to the community's religious life. The strong form of that claim – that only patricians could communicate with the gods through the auspices[196] – can never have been established, since there were apparently non-patrician senior magistrates at least intermittently in every period and these men must have taken the auspices in order to fulfil their offices; but the patricians did control the priesthoods, or at least the most important ones, as they easily could through the system of collegiate co-option. The tradition is that plebeians attained priesthoods only when specially reserved places were created for them in the colleges: this is reported in 367 B.C. for the *duoviri* (at that point increased to ten), and in 300 B.C. for the *augures* and *pontifices*, increased to eight or nine.[197] Other priestly places, including reserved places in the major colleges, continued to be a patrician preserve. To this extent, the religion of the city in the fifth century B.C. was controlled by the patricians.

It is an important question how far the plebeians developed their own religion, distinct from state religion, in the fifth century B.C. They certainly adopted the temple of Ceres, Liber and Libera (founded in 496 B.C.) as their religious centre and as the storehouse of their records. The plebeian aediles (*aediles*), who probably took their title from the temple (the *aedes*)[198] may possibly have acted as the priests of the plebeian organization, though there is no clear evidence; certainly later on they, like the plebeian tribunes,

196   Livy IV.2.
197   367 B.C.: Livy VI.37.12; 42.2; Wissowa (1912) 534–5. 300 B.C. (*Lex Ogulnia*): Livy X.6–9; Wissowa (1912) 492; Hölkeskamp (1988).
198   De Sanctis (1907–64) IV.2.194–5; Le Bonniec (1958) 348.

Fig. 1.8 Female terracotta figure seated on a throne, near life-size, from Aricia in Latium; almost certainly the goddess Ceres. Dated to c. 300 B.C., the figure is reconstructed from several fragments. (Height, 0.94m.)

became established as magistrates of the Republic.[199] The plebeian associations of Ceres, Liber and Libera suggest also contacts between the Roman plebeians and the Greeks of South Italy, where the corresponding Greek cult (of Demeter, Dionysus and Kore) was strong.[200] It is also possible that other

199 Sabbatucci (1954); J.-C. Richard (1978) 580–4. Of course, this uncertainty raises the question of what would count as a 'priest' in early Roman society, particularly among a group of plebeians outside the central structures of the state.

200 Ceres, Liber and Libera: Dionysius of Halicarnassus, *Roman Antiquities* VI.17 (who gives the tradition that the temple was founded on the recommendation of the Sibylline

temples too show both the influence of Greeks and the effect of plebeian initiatives; for instance, Mercury, corresponding to Greek Hermes, was said to have had his temple dedicated by a plebeian and had strong associations with trade and traders.[201] The temple of the Dioscuri (Castor and Pollux) is another, but more problematic, case: we know that the cult of the Dioscuri in thoroughly Greek form existed at Lavinium, which had such close links with Rome; but the Roman cult shows its own very characteristic forms, especially its emphasis on Castor to the exclusion of Pollux.[202] However we interpret this particular example, it is possible that there was (for whatever reason) a regular connection between South Italian religious influence and a specifically plebeian religious life. We should remember, though, that for any knowledge of this we depend ultimately on information preserved in the priestly, that is, patrician tradition. If plebeian cults did begin as part of a political enterprise in opposition to the patricians, it seems unlikely that we should hear about their existence earlier than their acceptance in the state religion. Perhaps most interesting of all is the strong suggestion that even in the fifth century B.C., when Roman power was at a low ebb,[203] there was such a variety of religious influences at work.

There are other areas in which it is at least a possibility that the plebeians made a distinctive contribution. One of the most famous and characteristic institutions of later Rome were the *ludi*, the Games, which were days, or series of days, of entertainments and competitions, held in honour of and in the presence of particular gods or goddesses, preceded by a great religious procession. They included racing in the circus from an early date and later animal fighting and dramatic performances of various kinds.[204] The festivals of the early calendar do not include whole days of specially marked *ludi*, though various competitions and races do feature in other festivals. One of the very early sets of games was called the 'Plebeian Games' and indeed Cicero calls these the oldest of all; they have at their heart one of the two celebrations of the *epulum Iovis* (feast of Jupiter), the other being at the

Books). Discussion: Le Bonniec (1958) 236–42; Latte (1960a) 161–2; Steinby (1993–) I.260–1. For the suggestion of South Italian connections, see Momigliano (1967) 310–11; with discussion of J.-C. Richard (1978) 503–12. Map 1 no 18.

201 Livy II.27.5–6. See Ogilvie (1965) 303–4; J.-C. Richard (1978) 513–19; Combet-Farnoux (1980) 18–35; J.-C. Richard (1982).

202 Livy II.42.5 (location, 4.7). The problems of the origins of the cult: Latte (1960a) 173–6; Ogilvie (1965) 288–9, 347; J.-C. Richard (1978) 510–11; the Roman character of the cult is discussed by Schilling (1960). In the Greek world the Dioscuri were traditionally patrons of the cavalry: at Rome the cavalry was not specially associated with the patricians – but it was not apparently specially plebeian either (J.-C. Richard (1978) 484–7).

203 Cornell (1995) 293–313.

204 The ritual of the *ludi*: Wissowa (1912) 449–67; Piganiol (1923); Piccaluga (1965); Versnel (1970) 258–70; Weinstock (1971) 282–6; above, pp. 40–1; below, pp. 262–3.

'Roman' games (the other claimant as the oldest set).[205] It is a distinct possibility that days of Games were another plebeian element later adopted by the Roman state.[206]

Finally, on the view of the close connection between religion and politics argued in this chapter, it is inevitable that there was a religious element to some of the political activities of the plebeians in this period: they were, for example, holding their own assemblies, passing their own laws (*plebiscita*) and electing their own magistrates on the model of the city's procedures – but excluding the patricians. It seems inconceivable that they should have done these things without involving the gods in their decision-making. If little reflection of this survives, this must mean their procedures were rejected as invalid by the rules of the patrician priests and never properly recorded. We know at least that later republican tribunes of the *plebs* claimed powers to report omens and to perform consecration and impose curses;[207] there were also oaths that guaranteed the position of these tribunes as plebeian representatives.[208] All these rights must once have been resisted and subsequently accepted by the priestly colleges.

In some ways, the religion of the great Roman *gentes* presents an even more acute problem of interpretation. These were families or groups of families (clans), sharing a common name, whether patrician or plebeian, such as the Claudii, the Cornelii or the Caecilii. We do not hear of cults maintained in such *gentes* until the late Republic, most famously that of the Julii (from which Julius Caesar and, by adoption, Augustus were descended) who maintained a cult of the god Vediovis outside Rome.[209] Of other such gentile cults, however, we hear little or nothing, though the clans in question remained powerful and in other ways preserved their traditions and identities. Even the cult of the Julii we know of only through the chance find of a single inscription. One theory of the early history of republican Rome suggests that at first the central power of the state was very weak and that power in the Latin area lay with clans based on great families and their clients, with only a loose attachment to any particular city. A glimpse of this different social and religious organization is perhaps offered by an inscription from Satricum in southern Latium, about 50

---

205 Cicero, *Against Verres* II.5.36; Le Bonniec (1958) 350–7; J.-C. Richard (1978) 118–24. The *epulum Iovis,* above p. 63.

206 The argument would be that, although we have no dated record of a performance of the Plebeian Games earlier than the earliest known performance of the Roman Games, Cicero was in fact right to give priority to the Plebeian Games; we have no early dated record precisely because such plebeian rituals were not recognized by the 'official' institutions of state religion and so did not enter the traditions of recording associated with the priestly colleges.

207 Bayet (1960).

208 Festus p.422L.

209 *ILS* 2988 = *ILLRP* 270 = **1.6a**; Weinstock (1971) 8–12 and below, p. 89.

kilometres south-east of Rome.[210] This text records a number of clients of a member of the clan Valeria (a man called, in archaic Latin, Poplios Valesios), making a dedication to the god Mars – though we do not know how clearly defined or permanent this group of clients was, or how characteristic this religious activity was. In some ways the lack of information about the cults of the *gentes* is surprising. Perhaps we should think that the growth of the power of the state between 500 and 300 B.C. involved the breaking down of the power of these great clans, and that the disappearance of their own religious traditions was not accidental but a deliberate policy of the priestly colleges.[211]

Some of these issues might have been raised and resolved in the last few years of the fourth century, where our tradition offers at least hints of conflict. The censorship of Appius Claudius Caecus in 312 B.C. saw the control of a major cult – that of Hercules at the Ara Maxima – transferred from the gens Potitia to the state; this is the only record of the removal of gentile control of a cult, but it may not have been so isolated as it now seems.[212] The same period is said to have seen two separate conflicts between Appius' freedman Cn. Flavius and the college of *pontifices* over the publication of some of their secrets and also over the correct procedure for dedication of temples.[213] Then in 300 B.C., as we saw, the plebeians gained access to the two major colleges under the Lex Ogulnia; finally it is probably in the early decades of the third century that the very important but unreported reform was carried which transferred the choice of the *pontifex maximus* from the members of the college to a specially devised form of popular election.[214] There seems to be enough here to make it quite certain that major religious issues were under debate. It is not so easy to see the trend of events or their significance. One element is the attack on the patrician monopoly; another is the limitation of the power and independence of the priestly colleges; a third is the centralization of religious control in the state institutions. This may all help to explain the succession of authoritative priestly figures, several of them plebeians, which characterizes the third and second centuries B.C. If there is any substance in the speculation that early priests might have been more isolated from public life, this would be the point where the priest-politician emerged as a characteristic figure. Whether or not that view is right, we are certainly witnessing here a *development* of priestly roles within the political sphere; which would suggest that in or around the late fourth century, social conflict was having a marked influence on the character of the Roman religious tradition itself.[215]

210   *AE* (1979) 136 = **1.6b**; Versnel in Stibbe *et al* (1980); (1982).
211   Momigliano (1967) 305–12; Versnel in Stibbe *et al* (1980) 112–21.
212   Livy IX.29.9–11 = **1.6c**. The cult: Bayet (1926); Latte (1960a) 213–21. A different view of the events of 312 is given by Palmer (1965). Map 1 no. 21.
213   Livy IX.46.
214   Below, pp. 135–6.
215   Above, pp. 27–30 (where we expressed considerable doubt about any clear split between religious and other public roles, even in early Rome). The first influential

It may be that even more profound changes were being brought in by the stream of new cults so characteristic of the period. In at least one case we can plausibly trace the impact of events outside the Roman area, because the cult of Victoria, not an old Roman cult, was apparently derived from an awareness of Greek Victory cults in the late fourth century and especially of the conquests and the far-famed invincibility of Alexander the Great. Victoria received a temple in 294 B.C.; at the same period other Roman war gods began to attract the title Victor or Invictus. Before long, as the early Roman issues of coinage show, the new goddess was playing a prominent role in the Roman imagery of war.[216]

The coming of Aesculapius is the next example. Livy's story is that the god was introduced direct from Epidaurus in the Peloponnese, the most famous centre of the cult, after the Sibylline Books had been consulted in 293 B.C. as the result of an epidemic.[217] Legates were sent to Greece and returned with a manifestation of the god in the form of a sacred snake which had willingly migrated and now willingly went to the new site of the cult on the island in the Tiber.[218] The epidemic promptly ceased and a new temple was duly dedicated in 291 B.C. The cult certainly acquired some of the features present in the Epidaurian cult, including the custom of incubation and the keeping of snakes and dogs by the priests;[219] there is therefore no doubt that these events did represent the arrival of an avowedly Greek cult.

It is not so easy (here as in other contexts) to establish at all precisely what would have been new to the Romans about the cult. We have already seen that the resort to sanctuaries for help in illness was a long-established tradition in Central Italy;[220] sure enough, a very large deposit of such terracottas of republican date was found in the bed of the Tiber, presumably associated with Aesculapius' temple-site.[221] Again, there is good reason to think that the practice of incubation was not entirely new either.[222] Finally,

---

pontifex maximus known to us was Ti. Coruncanius (Münzer and Jörs (1901)), who was also the first plebeian to hold the office (Livy, *Summaries* XVIII), probably by the 250s B.C. It seems likely, but not certain, that election had been introduced earlier than this.

216 Weinstock (1958) 2504–6; (1971) 91–3; above, p. 62.
217 Livy X.47.6–7 = **2.6c**; Valerius Maximus, *Memorable Deeds and Sayings* I.8.2; <Aurelius Victor>, *On Famous Men* 22; Orosius III.22.5; Besnier (1902); E. Simon (1990) 19–26; Ziolkowski (1992) 17–18; Steinby (1993-) I. 21–2.
218 Map 1 no 27. The snake: Ovid, *Metamorphoses* XV. 736–44; Pliny, *Natural History* XXIX.16; 72; Plutarch, *Roman Questions* 94.
219 Livy, *Summaries* XI; Valerius Maximus, *Memorable Deeds and Sayings* I.8.2; Ovid, *Metamorphoses* XV.622–744; Latte (1960a) 225–7. Incubation: Palmer (1974a) 145–9. The Greek cult of Asklepios: Edelstein and Edelstein (1945); Latte (1960a) 226–7; Nilsson (1961-7) I.805–8; Zaidman and Schmitt Pantel (1992) 128–32.
220 Above, pp. 12–13.
221 Besnier (1902) 229–38; Pensabene et al. (1980). Other collections of republican votives: *Mysteries of Diana* (1983) 46–53; Gatti lo Guzzo (1978) with Häuber (1990) 54–9; above, n.31.
222 Above, p. 13.

the Latin form of the god's name may well have been established before the 290s B.C., or at least it derives from an older form of the Greek name;[223] given the extent of Roman contacts with Greece in the archaic period, this may suggest that the god, as well as the rituals associated with him, was known to the Romans already. So the picture seems to be that the temple to Aesculapius was indeed a gesture of recognition towards the Hellenistic culture that the Romans were now meeting in the south of Italy (and it is interesting that it pre-dates the arrival of the first Greek doctor in Rome);[224] but the innovation is mediated not only by the Sibylline prophecy, but also by previous experience and the religious traditions in central Italy.

Such mediation is frequently associated with Roman 'innovations'. Narrative accounts deriving from literary sources can easily suggest that some radical break in religious life has occurred, but in the ancient world all religious changes had to be negotiated carefully; the idea of openly abandoning the practice of the ancestors or of changing what they had regarded as adequate was scarcely to be tolerated. In some cases that meant finding or emphasizing mythical connections, or situating the new cult amongst associated cults; perhaps sometimes it involves reconstructing the past or re-interpreting rituals.

In some cases, however, the innovation explicitly took the form of developing an ancient cult. At some time in the middle of the third century, the ancient Italian goddess Ceres, who had had a home in Rome at least since the fifth century and who had been specially associated with the *plebs,* was offered what seems to have been a separate cult, known to the Romans as the 'Greek rites' of Ceres.[225] To make the situation still more confusing, it is clear that the character of the older Ceres had in fact been influenced by knowledge of the Greek Demeter, as had Ceres in other parts of Italy[226] but it is possible to distinguish some new elements that belong to the third-century rites. A series of priestesses was regularly brought in from the south of Italy and there were rituals in which women played a particularly prominent part. So, we hear for the first time of groups of matrons and of girls taking part in processions and singing and bringing gifts in honour of Ceres and Proserpina, the mother and the maiden.[227]

223 Radke (1987) 38–41.
224 219 B.C.: Cassius Hemina fr. 26P = Pliny, *Natural History* XXIX.12 (a doctor from the Peloponnese).
225 Arnobius, *Against the Gentiles* II.78, dates the introduction of the cult 'just before' that of Magna Mater in 205 B.C.; Le Bonniec (1958) 381–400; J.-C. Richard (1978) 504–6; for the older form of the cult, above, pp. 64–6.
226 Le Bonniec (1958) 248–53.
227 Livy XXVII.11.1–16; XXVII.37.4–15; Obsequens 34, 36, 43, 46, 53; Diels (1890) 54–6; A. Boyce (1937); MacBain (1982) 127–32; Spaeth (1996) 103–13. The Greek cult is very clearly reflected in the Sibylline oracle of 125 B.C.: Phlegon of Tralles, *On Wonders* 10 = 7.5a.

In this case, what seems at first sight a development of old practices turns out to have been a real change in the religious life of Rome. Apart from the Vestals, who seem to have been an exception to most rules of Roman life, women of any class seem to have played only a limited role in the ancient Roman public cult. All the priests and religious officials, as well as all the magistrates who took part in rituals, were invariably men. The leading role in family religious action was always the *paterfamilias*. There were specific ancient festivals in which women played a central role, certain cults which focussed on childbirth, and of course women may have been present as members of families at almost any city, family and rural ritual.[228] But the presence of separate groups of women in festivals, normal practice in Greek civic festivals, seems not to have been the normal Roman way at any date. It is only in this period that we begin to find such processions and the fact that the Sibylline Books were so prominently connected with the innovation strongly supports the idea that it was Greek influence that lay behind the change.

Proserpina occurs again in what is perhaps a related development, since it involves Dis Pater who is the third member of the fatal mythic triangle: Proserpina is the Daughter; Dis Pater, the King of the Underworld who snatched her away to his Kingdom; Ceres, the Mother who searched for her.[229] This was the introduction of a new set of games called – at least from the time of Augustus, when they were celebrated very elaborately – the 'Saecular' Games.[230] It is not certain what this name meant originally, but it came to imply that the games should be celebrated once every century (the Latin word is *saeculum*).[231] Later antiquarians made up sequences of hundred-years in order to justify holding these games in particular years in which the current emperor wished to have a celebration. There are, however, rather good reasons to think that only two of the reported republican games ever in fact happened – once in the 140s (as we shall see in the next chapter) and once in 249 B.C., which on this view was the start of the series. Varro's notice of the games of 249 B.C. connects them, by implication, with the First Punic War, then in its bitterest phase; the sacrifice was to the underworld powers (Dis Pater and Proserpina) as the black victims imply and was celebrated at an altar in the Campus Martius called the Terentum.[232] The games of the imperial period seem to retain some elements at least from the republican ones, including sacrifices to the ancient Italian fates – the Parcae – and perhaps also the choirs of boys and girls,

228 Scheid (1992b); below, pp. 95–6, 296–7.
229 The Roman explication of the myth: Le Bonniec (1958) 404–23.
230 Below, pp. 201–6.
231 Weinstock (1932).
232 Varro in Censorinus 17.8. Map 1 no 37. Nilsson (1920) outlines the issues; cf. Taylor (1934) 108–10.

which are very likely to be connected with the groups of the Ceres cult discussed above; but the underworld character of the republican rituals seems to have been almost totally transformed. The *ludi Saeculares* of 17 B.C. that we shall discuss in chapter 4 are yet another example – on a massive scale – of the Augustan reinvention of early Roman religion.[233]

233 Below, pp. 201–6.

2 Imperial triumph and religious change

1. The interpretation of change

The most profound transformation of relations between the Romans and the rest of the Mediterranean world took place between the middle of the third and the middle of the second century B.C. – even though that was not the period in which the Roman Empire grew fastest in terms of conquest and territorial control. In 241 B.C., at the end of the first Punic War with Carthage, Roman overseas expansion had only just begun, with the addition of Sicily to their established rule over southern Italy. As victors in the long sea-war against the Carthaginians, they had just established themselves as the major force in the western Mediterranean; but they had shown little or no interest in the Hellenistic kingdoms that dominated the Eastern world of the time and had even found the greatest difficulty in the 270s B.C. in beating off the attacks of Pyrrhus, King of Epirus (in northern Greece), whose invading armies came very close to Rome itself. Meanwhile in the West, the north of what we today call Italy was under the independent control of many different tribes, who had many years of independence and resistance before they too came under Roman control; and the Romans had not yet even established a foothold in Spain, Gaul or North Africa.

A hundred years later the situation had become radically different: the Romans had, whether through deliberate planning or through a series of opportunities and accidents, established extensive, if informal, control over much of the Mediterranean world, though they had proved reluctant to acquire overseas territory under their direct control. The growth of Roman power cannot therefore be assessed by counting new provinces; even so the fact is that the military strength of Rome's major rivals was destroyed in a series of wars between 218 and 187 B.C. and that from those years onwards a steady flow of embassies from all the kingdoms and cities of the Mediterranean world brought their problems and conflicts to the senate at Rome for arbitration and resolution. The authority of the Romans was established: they had no need of permanent garrisons or administrative mechanisms; the fear of potential Roman armed intervention was enough to sustain their influence and to make sure that no undesirable rival power-structures had any chance to establish themselves. The result of these activities was a steady flow of resources and influences from the East into Rome and Roman Italy, despite the fact that the conquerors were curiously slow to establish any system of taxation over their new areas of influence. Successful warfare itself provided the most obvious opportunities for both public and private enrichment; but both Romans and Italians, in both peace and war, found many ways of bringing treasure, profits from trading slaves and works of art to their home towns, with profound effects on their societies and economies.[1]

The result of these spectacular successes was, of course, that Rome, in this period above all, became in ancient eyes the most famous example of a triumphant city. Enemy after enemy had failed before her military strength; the greatest of contemporary kings, the successors of Alexander the Great, had had to humble themselves before this community without kings, as it acquired wealth, glory and manpower beyond the reach of any known rival. The senate, once a town council with limited advisory powers, had come to take decisions affecting the whole of the Mediterranean world. The historian Polybius, originally a Greek statesman, who lived in Rome as a hostage for many years, built his whole history around the problem of this extraordinary transformation of the power balance between the East and the West.[2] Given the assumptions of city-state life in the ancient world, such a succession of triumphs by a single city had profound implications at a religious as well as at a political level: the gods and goddesses of an ancient city were, as we have seen, members of the city's community in much the same sense as were the human citizens.[3] The city's activities required the involvement of humans and deities alike, the performance of rituals playing a critical role in maintaining communication and good faith between them. It follows that a great sequence of triumphs for the city implied both a triumph for the gods and goddesses and also a vindication of the religious system operated by the human members of the community.

Rome's success was the gods' success. In these particular years, therefore, it makes very little sense to think in terms of Roman religion or the Roman deities as 'failing' or 'declining'; or of the Romans 'failing' their gods.[4] And it would be an anachronistic misunderstanding to detach the gods from their involvement with the city's triumphs and hence to suggest that they might be failing the Romans on some deeper, moral level. All the same, the social and cultural developments of the century after 241 B.C. mean that this chapter will be dealing with a society changing from decade to decade, and not only because of the increasing prosperity brought by military successes.

1 For these developments, Gabba (1989).
2 F.W.Walbank (1972); Derow (1979); Ferrary (1988) 265–348.
3 Above, pp. 30–41; Scheid (1985a) 51–7.
4 This is the assumption that lies behind much modern work in this area; it is raised explicitly by Bayet (1957) 149–55; Dumézil (1970) 457–89 opposes the notion of religious crisis at this date. The problems associated with the 'decline' of Roman religion (at any period – and in the late Republic in particular) are discussed below, pp. 117–19 and ch. 3 *passim*.

In the first place, the cultural influence of the Greeks on the Romans and their neighbours (going far beyond the traces of contact with the Greek world that we identified in the last chapter) was firmly established in the course of the third century – some time before Roman military intervention in the East from the second century B.C., and so before Roman conquerors brought many of the greatest cultural prizes of Greece back home as war booty. And it was not just influence from Greece itself: Romans of this period were finding Greek civilization also in the Western centres of Greek culture (such as Naples and Syracuse) that were now under their own influence. All this is quite clearly evidenced in the archaeological record of the period, in art and architecture;[5] it is also clear from the development of a Roman literary tradition explicitly based on Greek models, in both epic and drama, that Roman writers and artists were looking deliberately to the Greeks in their desire to develop their own cultural traditions.[6] The surviving plays of Plautus (who died in the early second century B.C.) are the only direct witnesses of this early literature to have been preserved more or less complete; but in fact these comedies, aimed at a popular audience, are the best possible evidence to show how Greek prototypes were borrowed and adapted for the new Roman audiences. It is not surprising that these influences came, as we shall see, to have consequences and reflections in religion as well.[7]

Secondly, the nature of the Roman population changed dramatically in the course of this period, so that it becomes progressively more difficult to define what it meant to be a Roman, or to assess what the religious traditions of Rome meant to the inhabitants of the city and of Roman Italy. Two long-term processes are involved here: first, throughout the third century, the Romans pursued their long-established tradition of extending their own citizenship to other Italian communities, so that more and more of central Italy became formally incorporated in Rome; secondly, and again following established practice, slaves freed by Roman citizens became Roman citizens themselves.[8] One of the functions of religion in this situation may have been 'acculturation': its processions, festivals and celebrations were one of the ways of educating these new citizens in the meaning of Roman life and history, providing a map of Roman-ness for those who had not inherited this knowledge.[9] But at the same time the rate of incorporation of outsiders must have caused tensions and dangers and, as we seek to interpret the surviving record, it is essential to remember how rapid the pace of change and adaptation must have been.

The rapidity of change both in Rome's external power and her internal

---

5 Boëthius (1978) 136–215; Morel (1989).
6 Gratwick (1982); Jocelyn (1990); Gruen (1993) 183–222.
7 Below, pp. 79–87.
8 Sherwin-White (1973); Beard and Crawford (1985) 78–82.
9 Beard (1989).

social organization would present a formidable challenge for religious historians, even if they had a far better understanding than is actually possible about the religious life of earlier periods. On the other hand, however, the nature of the historical record surviving from these years (and particularly the central years of the period) presents an important opportunity of understanding religious life at Rome. The years from 218 B.C. to 167 B.C., including the second Punic War, against Hannibal, and Rome's great victories in the East, are known to us through twenty-five surviving books of Livy (Books XXI–XLV). We discussed Livy's evidence for the earliest period of Roman history in the last chapter, his retrospective construction of the primitive religious system and his preservation of occasional 'nuggets' of very ancient material. The character of his religious record for this later period is very different. It may strike the modern reader as in many ways odd and unappealing, consisting as it does mostly of short notices of vows, the consultations of priests, the consultation of the Sibylline Books and so on; but the value of these notices lies in their consistency and the detail they offer on regular religious procedures. This kind of information is not available at any other period. The evidence we have for the late Republic and early empire is in many ways far richer, far closer to the events described and has much more chance of reflecting contemporary religious ideas and attitudes. But it does not include the regular factual notices that we find only in Livy. As we shall see in the next chapter, the different type of information surviving from these different periods makes direct comparison between the two very difficult. It remains a problem to assess how far religious life had changed in a profound way between the second and first centuries B.C. and how far the apparent differences result from disparities in the nature of information that has survived.

The detailed religious information Livy preserves in this form probably derives from earlier historians, writing year-by-year ('annalistic') accounts of Roman history in the last third of the second century B.C. or the earlier part of the first. Livy himself seems to have made little effort to check the detail of his reports, so their reliability depends on the care with which these earlier lost writers set about their task and the value of the sources of information they had available to them. There is no possible way of checking the details of particular notices, and there have been many challenges to Livy's credibility.[10] But on the whole there is good reason to think that, even if there may be error and confusion quite frequently, the general picture is solidly based. In one case – the Bacchanalia crisis which we shall discuss later – we have both an inscribed text of a senatorial decree and Livy's version of it: he survives this test creditably, though not impeccably: his summary of the decree shows that definite knowledge of the main lines has come through in the tradition, but on the details of a very difficult text

10   Most radically, Gelzer (1935); (1936); Klotz (1940–1). Briscoe (1973) 1–12 and Luce (1977) especially 139–84 stress the variety, and value, of Livy's sources.

Livy's summary alone would be distinctly misleading.[11] At the same time, he set the events in an elaborate framework, which may have been constructed on some knowledge of the historical situation, but which is more of an indication of attitudes to the Bacchic cult in Livy's own time.

Very much the same considerations apply to the great bulk of Livy's notices of religious matters: it would be far too sceptical to reject the lists of priests, the reports of senatorial action over prodigies, the details of the procedures adopted in the event of a war-vote and so on, in so far as they provide us with a general picture of the forms, procedures and preoccupations of Roman public religion in this period; but it would also be quite wrong to treat these second- or third-hand records as though they were completely reliable. Livy undoubtedly shapes and controls his material for the purposes of literary presentation; it would be quite hazardous therefore to assume that his placing of the material or his concentration on particular years necessarily respects the tradition he received, let alone the exact details of the original events and decisions.[12] Livy was also writing his history of the middle Republic with an underlying conception of Roman religious history that was very much the product of the experiences of his own time and the political assumptions of the régime under which he lived.[13] For him, as no doubt for many others, the piety and scrupulousness of the ancestors was a vital ingredient of their success in peace and war. Whether consciously as a propagandist or unconsciously as a contemporary witness, he was writing in the shadow of the 'revival' of religion under the emperor Augustus; and that was based on the assumption that the political failure of the late republicans was intimately connected with their failure (as it was perceived) to maintain their traditions of piety. Livy's whole conception of the third/second century B.C. was coloured by this assumption. Ideally we would like some control from the period itself, either to support or weaken Livy's version. The sections that follow will show how far this is possible in individual instances; but it has to be admitted that the control is limited.

The best control at the moment is perhaps provided by coin-types: these are firmly dated in an unbroken sequence through the whole period[14] and they show us a whole range of images of deities, rituals and religious symbols. They show dramatically how in early periods the state itself was the focus of coin designs; later, coins became the vehicles of self-advertisement by the great Roman families; finally we find the rapidly changing types (including numerous 'religious' references) of the first century, reflecting

---

11 Below, pp. 92–6.
12 Above, pp. 8–10.
13 Livy's views on religion: Stübler (1941); Kajanto (1957); Liebeschuetz (1967); (1979) 4–11; Levene (1993) 16–33.
14 Crawford (1974) established the dates of coin-issues almost always to an exact year, enabling the evolution of designs (or 'types') to be accurately followed.

the competition between individuals and eventually the glorification of the great dynastic leaders.[15]

By this period, and increasingly as we move into the second century B.C., there are also contemporary literary texts that spasmodically throw light on individual issues or give us an indication of the religious possibilities open to Romans of this period. So, for example, fragments survive of Ennius, the first Roman epic poet (writing in the early second century B.C.) which give us a surprising picture of his own religious ideas; substantial fragments also survive of his re-statement or translation of the work of Euhemerus, a Greek author of a century or more earlier than his time, who wrote an account of the Greek gods treating them as human beings of ancient times who had only become the recipients of worship after their deaths.[16] Cato the Elder, too, who wrote both on agriculture and a historical account of Rome and Italy down to his own time (the *Origins*), not only preserves evidence of a number of traditions and rituals that would otherwise have been lost, but also occasionally reveals his own assumptions about religious matters.[17] But perhaps most valuable of all are the surviving plays of Plautus and, a generation later, of Terence: largely translations of, or adaptations from, earlier Greek comedies, they still give us direct evidence of drama that would have been seen by Roman audiences at the time.[18]

All the same, for this period, just as for the period discussed in chapter 1, the evidence that survives does not allow us the same kind of religious history that we can write for the first centuries B.C. and A.D. – not to mention the fourth, or fourteenth or eighteenth centuries A.D.: we can scarcely know anything at all about the religious experience or thoughts of any single individual of the period; even amongst the élite, our picture is oblique and inferential; about the religious perspective of the poor we can hardly even guess. All we know well are formal acts in the public arena, such as the taking or fulfilling of a vow by a private individual; or actions on behalf of the city taken by public officials as part of their State duties. It is true that we know far more about the second than we do about the seventh century B.C.; but what kind of analysis can we offer on the basis of this data and in the absence of any access to the religious experience of individuals?

---

15 For example, the coins of Sulla illustrated at **9.1b (ii)** & **(iii)**; and Julius Caesar, **9.2b (i)**. Discussion: Mattingly (1960) 71–86; Crawford (1974) 725–54.

16 Translation of Ennius' epic on Roman history, the *Annals*: *ROL* I. 3–215; of his *Euhemerus*: *ROL* I.415–31 (for Christian critique of 'Euhemerism', see, for example, Lactantius, *Divine Institutes* I.11.44 = **2.8d**). Discussion: Gratwick (1982) 60–76, 157–8; Skutsch (1985); Gruen (1990) 108–23.

17 Cato's *On Agriculture* survives complete. Of the *Origins*, we have only fragments, best edited with a French translation by Chassignet (1986); one fragment (28, Chassignet) is cited at **1.5c(i)**. A particularly valuable passage of Cato is discussed by North (1990) 58–60.

18 Discussion: Chalmers (1965); Konstan (1983); Gruen (1990) 124–57. Note the citations from Plautus: *Amphitryo* 1–25 = **2.1c**; *Little Carthaginian* 449–66 = **6.3b**.

In our view, it is possible to create a comprehensible picture of religious life in this period. It is perfectly true that the material we have sets limits to the kind of understanding that can be reached. But as we implied in chapter 1, the character of the religious record we have is to some extent a function of the religious life of the society in question. The absences in that record are not entirely random: the lack, for example, of private religious biographies is probably not so much a sad loss for the historian to lament, as an indication of a society in which this particular form of religious discourse had no (or only a very limited) place.[19] Meanwhile, with the material we have, much progress can be made towards understanding the social importance of religion and its part in political life – without the witness of individual experience. Later chapters of this book will trace the development of personal experience and individual self-expression in the religious sphere. The purpose of this chapter is to see what relationship can be established between religious change in Roman society and the wider historical processes that were transforming that society itself in this period.

2. The later third century B.C.: innovation and tradition

The third century emerges as the high point of religious innovation for the Romans. The earlier years of the century, as we have seen, give a striking picture of a community quite prepared to accept foreign cults and practices in their midst and showing no sign of any fear that they might be diluting the Roman-ness of Roman religion. The fullest record exists, however, for the years of the Hannibalic threat to Rome, 218–201 B.C., when there seems to have been a dramatic increase in the rate of these innovations, both in ritual practice and in the acceptance of 'new' deities. This has often been interpreted as a panic reaction or crisis, in the years that saw the great invasions of Italy – by the Gauls in the 220s B.C. and then by the Carthaginians after 218 B.C.[20] But there is no need to see this as an exceptional situation in which the Romans were driven to extreme measures by their terror over their failure to control the Carthaginian invasions. Moments of panic there may have been; but by and large the priests, the senate and the magistrates were continuing to react as they had done throughout the century, even if the dramatic military disasters of the 210s B.C. must have placed them under greater pressure than they were used to. On the other hand, it can be argued that the years after 200 B.C. saw a reaction against the third century's tradition of experimentalism, when at least some of the ruling élite became suspicious of the influence of Greeks and

---

19 Above, pp. 42–3. The evolution of religious autobiography: Baslez (1993), and especially Quet (1993).
20 The argument of, for example, Warde Fowler (1911) 314–31; Latte (1960a) 251–8; A. Toynbee (1965) II.374–415; for a different approach, Wardman (1982) 33–41.

Asiatics on their own customs.[21] This in turn raises the question of how simple or unproblematic the whole process of innovation was: the fact that a 'new' cult or a 'Greek' cult received a temple or festival does not show us how the Romans themselves understood this 'newness' or 'Greekness'; or answer the question of what exactly was new and how the newness was accommodated to previous practice. If the last third of the century was a turning point in the religious life of the Romans, that must partly be connected with the rush of innovations which (even in the relatively open society of Rome) raised problems about the nature of the tradition and its relation to foreign religions.

Once again Livy's narratives of most of these innovations are centred on a series of reports of prodigies and of the ways these prodigies were handled – new temples or cults (as we saw in chapter 1) being a regular part of the Roman response to the upset in relations between humans and gods that such events were held to signal. In this period we can see fairly clearly that Livy's treatment often has a political bias: his narrative of prodigies repeatedly emphasizes the place of the senate at the centre of events and shows it as organizing the city's response to the reports that come in from all over Italy – controlling religious and political response to such crises. This was almost certainly an over-simplified, not to say heavily loaded, account of events; and it may well give us a much more controlled and purposive impression of the action taken after prodigies than was really the case.

The list of innovations is very impressive: it includes new sets of games and the reform of the older festival of the Saturnalia;[22] the revival (or perhaps introduction to Rome) of the very ancient Italian practice of vowing the *ver sacrum*, that is the dedicating of the whole year's increase of the flocks to Jupiter;[23] the introduction of two foreign goddesses, Venus of Eryx (in Sicily) and Magna Mater (or Cybele), from Asia Minor, one at the beginning and the other towards the end of the war;[24] the introduction of a new sequence of rituals to deal with the evil prodigy of the birth of a hermaphrodite;[25] the extension of 'Roman' ritual action outside Rome itself to other towns in central Italy.[26]

Perhaps the most startling innovation of all was a form of human offering carried out by the Romans – so far as we know entirely new to their experience. These human offerings consisted of the burying alive of a pair

21 Below, pp. 87–98.
22 Livy XXII.1.20 = **7.3a**; Le Glay (1966) 467–78; Guittard (1976).
23 Livy XXII.10 = **6.5**; XXXIII.44.1; XXXIV.44.1–3; 6; Heurgon (1957) 36–51; above, p. 34. Elsewhere in Italy, the dedication was often to Mars not to Jupiter; on the Italian *ver sacrum,* Dench (1995).
24 Below, pp. 83; 96–8.
25 Livy XXVII.27 (207 B.C.); see Diels (1890); A.Boyce (1937). There are many recorded instances of the expiation of the birth of hermaphrodites in the late second and early first centuries B.C. listed in MacBain (1982) 127–35; below, p. 82; **7.5a**.
26 MacBain (1982) 25–33.

of Greeks and a pair of Gauls in the heart of Rome – in the forum Boarium ('Cattle Market').[27] This was done in 228 B.C., in face of a Gallic invasion; after the battle of Cannae in 216 B.C., where the Romans were defeated by Gauls and Carthaginians; and again in 113 B.C., when a Gallic invasion was again being prepared.[28] On two, and perhaps on three, of these occasions there was at the same time an accusation of unchastity against the Vestals and a Vestal trial.[29] The link between Vestal accusation and human offering could be seen in very general terms: both accusation and offering being reactions to the same threat to the safety of Rome by Gallic conquest, while the security of the city was assured above all by the Vestals' preservation of their ritual purity. A much closer link, however, between the two events is suggested by the fact that both the Greeks and Gauls and also the condemned Vestals were buried alive – though in strikingly different locations: the Vestals were buried at the very limit of the city in the *campus sceleratus*, the Greeks and Gauls in its market-place, the forum Boarium.

The significance of this ritual has been much debated. In neither case are we dealing with sacrifice in terms of the normal Roman ritual; so far as we know there was no immolation of the victims, no act of killing, no return of *exta* to the gods. It was not therefore strictly inconsistent of the Romans to have forbidden human sacrifice, as they did later on; for according to the formal religious rules this killing was not a sacrifice.[30] The pairs may have symbolized the peoples from which they came; and so their occupation of a tomb, in a place where the dead were not normally buried, could have been intended to avert the possibility of a real occupation of the city by the enemy. On the other hand, the precise identity of the victims has been thought a problem, because there is no particular historical moment when both Gauls and Greeks simultaneously threatened the security of Rome; and there are equally plausible candidates for Rome's enemies at almost any point (Samnites or Etruscans, for example). Maybe the answer is that the cer-

27 Schwenn (1915) 148–54; Cichorius (1922); Bémont (1960); Latte (1960a) 256–8; Briquel (1981); Fraschetti (1981).

28 228 B.C.: Cassius Dio fr. 47 (= Tzetzes on Lycophron, *Alexandra* 602); Plutarch, *Marcellus* 3; Orosius IV.13.3. 216 B.C.: Livy XXII.57.4. 114/13 B.C.: Plutarch, *Roman Questions* 83 = **6.6b**.

29 Clearly in 216 B.C. (Livy XXII.57.1–6); and in 113 B.C. (Plutarch, *Roman Questions* 83 = **6.6b**; Asconius, *Commentary on Cicero's Speech On behalf of Milo* 45–6C; Livy, *Summaries* LXIII); less so in 225 B.C. when the date of the Vestal trial is best attested as earlier (c. 228 B.C.) than the interment, though the chronology is far from certain. For the incident, see Livy, *Summaries* XX; for the date, Münzer, *RE* 7A.768–70. On the incident of 113, see further below, p. 137.

30 Though (whatever the formal rules) there was obviously an uncertain boundary between what did and what did not constitute a sacrifice; Plutarch, for example, *Roman Questions* 83 = **6.6b**, puts the Roman action into the same category as human sacrifice. For Roman prohibition of human sacrifice, see Pliny, *Natural History* XXX.1.2 = **11.3** (referring to 97 B.C.); but the context makes it clear that this was sacrifice by magicians not state priests.

emony was fixed by an old prophecy in the Sibylline collection, as our sources hint, and the Greeks and Gauls must have been generally the most fearsome peoples when the prophecy originated and symbolized Rome's most threatening enemies.[31] Certainly the Gauls continued to be a real threat to Rome's security even up to the first century B.C.; and *their* killing at any rate makes some sort of sense in connection with the punishment of the Vestals, whose virginity (as we have seen) stood for the safety of the state.[32]

Another reaction to the war, also perhaps an attempt to avert danger by ritual means, is suggested by the very heavy emphasis on Juno in the course of the Hannibalic War. This is repeatedly in evidence (for example, in the attention given to the Juno who was patron deity of Lanuvium),[33] but it becomes most spectacular in the procession of 207 B.C. to the temple of Juno Regina on the Aventine Hill in Rome:

From the temple of Apollo through the Carmental Gate two white cows were led into the city; behind them were carried two cypress-wood statues of Juno Regina; then came twenty-seven maidens in long gowns who sang the hymn to Juno Regina. <Various other rituals then took place in the Forum.> Thence by way of the Vicus Tuscus and the Velabrum through the Forum Boarium, they climbed the street of Publicius and reached the temple of Juno Regina. The *decemviri* immolated the victims and the cypress wood statues were carried into the temple.[34]

This is one of the occasions on which women are found taking on their major ritual roles, in the way we have seen to be a distinctive new feature of third-century B.C. Roman life.[35] This stress on Juno may also be connected with the fact that Astarte, the protective goddess of Rome's enemy Carthage, was seen as the equivalent of Roman Juno. Astarte was not, we are told, actually 'summoned out' (*evocata*) of Carthage during the war; but she was apparently somehow 'placated' (*exorata*).[36] This special attention to Juno on the Aventine, who was herself a 'foreign' Juno (having been 'evoked' from Veii),[37] may be a way of representing the supreme goddess of Carthage in a ritual form short of offering a new cult to her.

Whether this is true or not, two other foreign goddesses were explicitly

---

31 This is implied by Cassius Dio (fr. 47), who quotes the prophecy as saying 'Greeks and Gauls shall occupy the city'. Discussion: R. Bloch (1963) 101–3; Fraschetti (1981) 59–66.

32 Greece did not however continue to be a military danger to Rome throughout this period. Most explanations tend to leave the presence of the Greek pair unexplained, except as a survival of the original oracular text and the time of its composition. For Vestals and the security of the state, above, pp. 52–4.

33 Livy XXI.62.4 (218 B.C.); XXIV.10.6 (215 B.C.). Statue-head: Fig. 2.1.

34 Livy XXVII.37. The 27 maidens reappear later in connection with Ceres and Proserpina, above p. 70 (see Phlegon of Tralles, *On Wonders* 10 = 7.5a).

35 Above, pp. 70–1.

36 This distinction is made by Servius, *On Virgil's Aeneid* XII.841; he implies that Juno was not 'evoked' until 146 B.C. (see below, p. 111). See also Palmer (1974) 48–9.

Fig. 2.1 Marble head of statue of Juno Sospita, from Lanuvium, possibly the cult image from the temple. Two holes on either side of the head would have provided the fixings for the goddess's head-dress; the back of the head is unworked. It was discovered in Lanuvium in the 1920s, but its current whereabouts are not known. The date must be middle-late republican, but it is hard to date more closely until the head can be re-examined. (Height, 0.56m.)

invited into Rome, one at the beginning and one at the end of this war. The remarkable thing is that both were brought right into the very centre of the city, not kept outside the sacred boundary (*pomerium*) as was commonly the case with foreign deities: Venus of Eryx in Sicily was given a temple on the Capitol in 217 B.C. after the Roman defeat at Trasimene;[38] Cybele, the Magna Mater (to whom we shall return below), was vowed a temple in 205 B.C., in the last years of the war; the temple was built on the Palatine after the end of the war.[39] In both cases, the cults turned out to have aspects the

37   Above, pp. 34–5 (for Juno and the whole ritual of *evocatio*).
38   Livy XXII.9.7; 10.10; XXII.30.13; Schilling (1954) 233–54; Galinsky (1969) 174–6; Weinstock (1971) 15–17. Map 1 no. 25.
39   Below, pp. 96–7. Map 1 no. 13.

Romans perhaps had not expected (with Magna Mater, wild, Eastern, self-castrated priests); but in both cases, one powerful reason for their introduction may have been the goddesses' mythic connection with the Trojans, the adventures of Aeneas and the foundation legends of the city.[40] So despite their apparent strangeness, these goddesses could also be seen as central parts of the Roman inheritance, not new at all, and so really at home in their new temples. As so often at Rome, the startling innovation represented by these deities turns out to be perceived more as a return to the past than as a revolutionary change. On the other hand, even the emphasis on the Trojan tradition itself may have been something of a departure, for we have little evidence of serious attention to their Trojan inheritance in the Rome of the fourth or third centuries B.C.[41]

We are suggesting then that, while the third century may be the high-point of innovation, there is no reason to think that the successive importations of cults would have been seen by the Romans themselves as necessarily leading to any radical disturbance of the old order. Still less do they seem to have been panic measures in dangerous situations. It may be that beneath the surface of events, there were developments to cause concern to the authorities: and perhaps some of the innovations may be interpreted as reactions by the senate to developments within society as a whole which caused them anxiety. The next section will return to this important question.

In the case of one very public man, however, the evidence we have suggests a rather different picture, and a clearer break with tradition. The victor of the war against Hannibal, Scipio Africanus (236–184/3 B.C.), seems to have left a religious image profoundly different from that of his contemporaries. The problem is to assess how far this image derived from his own activities, how far from the speculations of later historians. The most surprising evidence of all comes from writers under the early principate who may, of course, have been re-interpreting Scipio in the light of late republican experience.[42] They report stories that imply that Scipio was deliberately imitating Alexander the Great: a story, for instance, that his mother was visited by a snake at the time of his conception, just like Alexander's mother Olympias – implying (in both cases) that the child was begotten by a god, not a human father. They also report that he was so familiar a visitor to Jupiter's temple on the Capitoline that the temple dogs knew him and did not bark. This close connection with the gods would be quite unlike anything known about other leading Romans of the period.

That at least part of this tradition goes back to the second century B.C. is

---

40 Venus: Galinsky (1969); Aeneas legends and Magna Mater: below, pp. 197–8.
41 Gruen (1993) 11–21 (arguing that it was familiar through much of the the third century).
42 For example, Aulus Gellius, *Attic Nights* VI.1.1–6 = **9.1a**; Livy XXVI.19; F. W. Walbank (1967).

Fig. 2.2 Bronze statue of the early second century B.C. It was found in Rome and presumably represents a leading figure of the period, shown in Greek style, in heroic nudity. If it is the portrait of a Roman, it reflects a surprising Roman acceptance of Greek conventions in portraying and symbolizing power (certainly not common later). It may, however, be a portrait of a Hellenistic prince brought to Rome as booty from the Greek world. (Height, 2.22m.)

supported by Polybius, who gives a long account, perhaps derived from Scipio family tradition.[43] Although what he says is different from the later writers, he too suggests an individual religious stance quite unlike that of any other Roman leader before Marius and Sulla (whom we shall be considering

43 Polybius X.2.20; for Polybius' association with the Cornelii Scipiones, Astin (1967) 12–34; F.W.Walbank (1972) 1–19.

85

in the next chapter).[44] The notable thing about Polybius is that he was evidently uncomfortable with the stories he found, because they implied that Scipio had actually been assisted in his successes by dreams and revelations from the gods. Polybius saw this as detracting from his successes and sought to defend him by showing that he had only pretended to receive divine guidance, while his actions were all really determined by rational calculation. Greek and Roman ideas are in conflict here: Polybius interprets the evidence in the light of the familiar Greek assumption that luck detracts from merit; while the tradition he is criticizing was making the Roman assumption that help from the gods implied *felicitas,* 'divinely inspired good luck',[45] that itself demonstrated the merit of the general. This emphasis on *felicitas* (and the parade of a close relationship with the gods that it implied) is familiar to us from the age of Sulla and his successors; according to these later sources at least, Scipio was already playing the part of the *felix* more than a hundred years earlier.[46]

That Scipio was indeed ahead of his time in both his methods and ambitions (and in his claims to divine favour) would fit well enough with the stories of how he later became the victim of attacks from some of his peers.[47] Notoriously, the facts about these disputes and the issues at stake in them are hopelessly confused in our sources; but there must have been reasons for the unpopularity, and the stories of his particular familiarity with the divine would make it all the more understandable. There is also a wider pattern to which this would all conform. The tense years of the Hannibalic War gave opportunities of glory and exceptional careers to several of the leading Romans of the day; magistracies awarded before the regular age, repeated consulships and triumphs, even the supreme emergency office the Romans called 'dictatorships' were part of the resorts of these years. All these were factors, as we shall see, in the last period of the Republic that went hand in hand with the special religious status that attached to individual politicians, exceptional political power being inextricably linked with the gods and their favour and protection. But, after Scipio, the next decade or two in the second century B.C. saw a reaction against this kind of exceptional power, including legislation to enforce the regular rules of the normal aristocratic career pattern;[48] hence too, perhaps, the reaction against Scipio's claims to religious pre-eminence.

The next section will consider the possibility that a similar reaction against experimentalism affected still more areas of Roman religious life. Whether the stories of Scipio should be seen as truth or as historical

---

44 Below, pp. 143–4.
45 For a definition of *felicitas,* Cicero, *On the Command of Pompey* 47 = **9.1c.**
46 Erkell (1952) 43–128; Fugier (1963) 31–44; J.-C. Richard (1965); Weinstock (1971) 112–14; Champeaux (1982–7) II.216–18.
47 Scipio trials: Fraccaro (1911); Astin (1978) 60–2; Gruen (1990) 135–7.
48 The *Lex Villia Annalis*: Livy XL.44.1; *MRR* I.388; Astin (1958).

fiction, their tone of disapproval may well be connected in some way to the phase of re-imposed discipline that marks the beginning of the second century.

3.   Reactions to change

The central theme of this section will be the reaction of the Romans towards religious activity outside their direct control, and especially towards cults that they saw as foreign. To give a context for this, however, we shall start by considering an area over which they did have control: the building of temples in the city of Rome itself. The history of temple building not only gives some idea of religious trends and attitudes in these years; it also shows how we can begin to draw broad conclusions from apparently small and disconnected pieces of antiquarian information.

Roman temples were not independent centres of power, influence or riches in the republican period; they did not, with rare exceptions, have priestly personnel attached to them and they did not therefore provide a power base for the priests as opposed to other groups of society. Priests and priestesses operated independently from particular temples and the temples did not represent a concentration of economic power; we do not know exactly how temples were funded, but there is no sign that they were regularly thought of as major landowners.[49] They were essentially houses for the cult-statues of the deities and the altars in front of them provided the location where victims were offered.[50]

As Rome grew in population, size and wealth, so the number of temples increased, either by the building of new temples for old deities, or for new deities that had been introduced or recognized for the first time. For the most part, each god or goddess had a single temple or perhaps two, though major ones (Jupiter or Juno, for example) could appear with different defining names and functions; and we know that some cults had small shrines in many places through the city.[51] Our information on the overall progress of temple-building is quite full for the years for which Livy is extant, because he records temple foundations as a regular part of his narrative. For the following period, our information is much patchier; and we shall see in the next chapter how difficult this makes it to draw any detailed comparisons of temple-building across the last centuries of the Republic.

---

49   For some evidence on temple lands in Roman Italy, Frontinus (?) in Agennius Urbicus, *Disputes over Land* (ed. C. Thulin, *Corpus Agrimensorum* 48.3–25); Carlsen (1994); for lands owned by priestly colleges, see Hyginus, *Statuses of Lands* (ed. Thulin 80.7–13); we discuss in Chapter 7 (pp. 340–2) Roman reactions to quite different models of temple organization that they found in their imperial territories,

50   The basic plan of a Roman temple: **4.1** (the temple of Portunus at Rome).

51   There is a list of some of the most important divine epithets in Vol. 2. 369–70.

But even after the surviving books of Livy end, the record can be partly restored by casual reference in historians, by the mention of temples in the State Calendars or from the archaeological record, which enables us to establish the location of most though not all republican temples. So the development can in broad terms be traced through the whole Republic.[52]

Between the middle of the third and the middle of the second centuries B.C., temple-building was closely involved with successful warfare and (apart from the cases where the Sibylline Books were involved) for the most part resulted from vows made by commanders in the field.[53] The building costs were normally met by the booty and profits of the campaign. However, the religious authorities could control or limit the commander's wishes if they were seen as in conflict with the rules of the sacred law; the priests, the senate and the censors were all likely to be involved and the final public action of dedicating the temple to the god or goddess was carefully controlled by rules, including a requirement for a vote of the people autho-rizing the act of dedication.[54] The objective of the vower was presumably to keep as much control of this as possible and sometimes one man, or one man and his immediate relations, would act successively as vower, builder and dedicator. In any case the family connection with a particular temple could carry on in subsequent generations, providing an abiding memorial of the victory.[55] So, from the general's point of view, this was a priceless opportunity to use the public space as a permanent memorial of his achievements; from the city's point of view, it was a parade of its triumphs and its spoils over the centuries; from the gods' point of view, it was a demonstration of their continuous involvement in the progress of Roman expansion.

It is clear that in these circumstances, while the choice of deities to receive temples must have responded in a general way to the ideas and tastes of the period, there can be no question of looking for any religious policy as such: neither senate nor priests can have been in a position to maintain any consistency, even if they could exercise restraint by advice and non-co-oper-ation. All the same, it is also extremely clear that the list of temples built in the second century has a distinctly less adventurous character than the list

52   See below, pp. 88–91,122–4 and Map 1, for the major temples. At all periods there are of course still problems about the identification of particular sites; see, for example, the extended debates about the identity of temples in the Largo Argentina at Rome, Coarelli et al. (1981) 37–49.

53   Above, pp. 34–5.

54   Cicero, *On his House* 36.

55   So, for example, the temple of Honos et Virtus (Honour and Virtue) at the Porta Capena was vowed by Marcus Claudius Marcellus (consul 222 B.C. etc), dedicated by his son (consul 194 B.C.) and embellished by his grandson (consul 166 B.C. etc). See Asco-nius, *Commentary on Cicero's Speech against Piso* p12C; Strabo, *Geography* III.4.13; Cicero, *On the Nature of the Gods* II. 61 = **2.3a**. For problems over the vow, below, p. 105.

for those of the third. The only explicitly foreign temple built was the temple to the Magna Mater that we have already mentioned; if there were any more cults imported from overseas, they were thoroughly disguised behind an appearance of local tradition.[56] Meanwhile, the long sequence of divinized personifications is reduced to an erratic trickle.

The very first decade of the century brings a sharp statement of the new attitude. The temples built are to Vediovis, to Faunus, to Fortuna Primigenia and to Juno Sospita;[57] all four of these are notably local Latin deities and the latter two the chief goddesses of leading Latin communities. Fortuna Primigenia is the goddess of the oracular temple at Praeneste, which was to be so lavishly rebuilt at the end of the century;[58] Juno Sospita the great goddess of Lanuvium, who had received marked attention in the previous war.[59] Vediovis raises more complicated problems, partly because of confusion in the sources as to what was built and where, partly because there are few good clues as to his character, other than that he was in some way 'opposite' to Jupiter ('Iovis' is formed from the root of 'Jupiter'; and the 've-' prefix implies either 'not-Jupiter' or 'little-Jupiter'). In one guise he was the patron god of the *gens Julia*, as we learn from an inscription from Bovillae, dedicated as it tells us by the 'law of Alba Longa';[60] so a possible theory is that he was the young Jupiter, the divine form of Iulus, son of Aeneas, founder of Alba Longa and ancestor of the Julii.[61] In the case of his Roman cult, however, he received two temples and the general who took the vows on both occasions was a Furius Purpurio, not a Julius; and on both occasions he was fighting against Gauls.[62] This has led to the suggestion that Vediovis was chosen as the Latin version of a Gaulish power, making the vow similar to an evocation.[63] However, the fact that the temple was built in such a central position in the city and under the name of a Latin deity makes it certain that the cult was seen by Romans as basically their own.

Later in the century, there is little temple-building that conflicts with this trend; the list is basically a very conservative one, in the sense that it

---

56 As we suggested above (p. 82), Astarte might be lurking behind the Roman Juno; see also some of the claims about Vediovis, below, n. 63.

57 Vediovis and Faunus: Map 1 no. 28. Fortuna: Map 1 no. 25. Juno: Map 1 no. 24.

58 Illustration of Praeneste: **4.9**. Cult and temple: Champeaux (1982–7) I.1–147 (Praeneste); II.1–35 (Rome). The date of re-building: Fasolo and Gullini (1953) 301–24; Degrassi (1969); Champeaux (1982–7) II.235–6.

59 Juno Sospita (alternatively Sispes): A.E. Gordon (1938) 24–37; Palmer (1974e) 30–2; Chiarucci (1983) 56–79. Juno in the Hannibalic war: above, pp. 82–3.

60 *ILS* 2988 = *ILLRP* 270 = **1.6a**; above, p. 67.

61 As suggested by Weinstock (1971) 8–12; also Liou-Gille (1980) especially 85–134, 179–207, who argues that Latin founders after death became gods under a different name (above, p. 31).

62 One temple (dedicated in 193 B.C.) was on the Tiber island (Livy XXI.21.12; XXXIV.53.7); the other (191 B.C.) on the Capitoline (Livy XXXV.41.8). There is a good deal of confusion in these notices; on which, Radke (1979) 306–10.

63 Palmer (1974) 153–71.

limits itself to well-established local deities. The only real innovations are two new personifications: Pietas ('Piety'), next door to Juno Sospita, was vowed by Manius Acilius Glabrio before battle against King Antiochus in 191 B.C. and dedicated by his son in 181 B.C.;[64] Felicitas was built by Licinius Lucullus from the booty of his Spanish campaign in 151–150 B.C.[65] In both cases it is interesting that these qualities receive divine status so late in the sequence of personifications, perhaps because they effectively deify the qualities of the general himself – and so represent something close to a claim to divine status.[66] Apart from these cases, the list keeps to a remarkably traditional group – Juno, Diana, Fortuna, Jupiter, Mars.[67]

By this time, however, there appears to be a contrast between the conservative list of deities and the innovative appearance of the temples themselves. It should be remembered that throughout the republican period, the development of Rome did not attempt to compete with the great contemporary Hellenistic cities: there were no grandiose schemes of civic development and not before the first emperor Augustus did marble become the accepted guise of public buildings;[68] even plans for stone theatres were resisted until the time of Pompey, in the mid-first century B.C.[69] All the same, there was clear development in the course of the second century. In particular the 140s and 130s B.C. saw a spate of building in the wake of the military successes of the period in Greece, Africa and Spain; the deities to whom they are dedicated are still very traditional – Jupiter, Mars, Hercules, Virtus – but the dedicators are notably sympathetic to Greek culture and the temples are strikingly more advanced in terms of art and architecture, employing leading Greek artists and techniques.[70] Velleius Paterculus, for example, in the early first century A.D., writes of the statues by Lysippus, originally commissioned for Alexander the Great, that were the 'chief ornament' of the temple of Jupiter Stator; and it is this same temple, so Velleius implies, that was the first marble temple in the city of Rome.[71] In some

64 Livy XL.34.4.

65 Strabo, *Geography* VIII.381; Cicero, *Against Verres* II.4.4; Cassius Dio, fr. 75.2. For the sense of *Felicitas*, above, p. 86.

66 In this respect they follow the precedent of Honos and Virtus; above, p. 88 n. 55.

67 Fortuna Equestris (Equestrian) vowed by Quintus Fabius Flaccus in 180 B.C., dedicated in 179 B.C. (Livy XL.40.10; 44.9); Juno and Diana, both dedicated by Marcus Aemilius Lepidus in 179 B.C. (Livy XL.52).

68 Zanker (1988) 18–25; below, pp. 196–201.

69 North (1992).

70 Jupiter Stator (c. 146 B.C.): Platner and Ashby (1929) 304–5; Velleius Paterculus, *History of Rome* I.11.3–5; Vitruvius, *On Architecture* III.2.5. Hercules (c. 146 B.C.): Platner and Ashby (1929) 256–7; *ILLRP* 122; Plutarch, *Precepts* 20. Mars in Campo (138–7 B.C.?): Platner and Ashby (1929) 328; Nepos, quoted by Priscian, *Institutes* VIII.17; Scholiast (p.179 Stangl) on Cicero, *On Behalf of Archias* 27; Valerius Maximus, *Memorable Deeds and Sayings* VIII.14.2; Pliny, *Natural History* XXXVI.26. Virtus (133 B.C.): Platner and Ashby (1929) 582; Plutarch, *On the Fortune of Rome* 5. General developments: Boëthius (1978) 156–78.

71 Velleius Paterculus, *History of Rome* I.11.3–5.

Fig. 2.3 Round marble temple in the Forum Boarium, Rome, probably dedicated to Hercules Victor and known as 'Olivarius'. The temple is dated archaeologically to the last decade of the second century B.C. Still more or less complete, it is the earliest surviving building to reflect the Greek taste and architectural traditions that can be traced back to the temple foundations of the 140s B.C. (Height 18m.)

ways the technical innovations of their form make the conservatism of the Roman choice of deities for these temples all the more striking.

The causes of this apparent conservatism were not simple. But, if we are right to identify a sharp change between the third and second centuries in the type of gods for whom new temples were built in Rome, then this may express growing reservations about 'non-Roman' religions; or at least it may illustrate the growing importance of the boundary (defined much more sharply than we can attest before) between what was Roman and what was not. In fact the late third and second centuries saw a series of incidents in which the Roman ruling class took restrictive action against certain forms of religious activity; and it is these that we must now explore further.

The main incidents in the story of caution take us back to the last few years of the third century. During the Hannibalic War, Livy reports an action by a *praetor* against some form of 'undesirable' religious practice by the women of Rome. As we have seen, women do not figure prominently in accounts of republican religion, and that makes the report the more striking. Livy is frustratingly unspecific about the activities of which the *praetor* disapproved; but it seems highly likely that cult groups of the god Bacchus – which were to be ruthlessly destroyed in 186 B.C. – were the targets in this case as well.[72] Then, towards the end of the war, as mentioned already, a vow

72 Livy XXV.1.6–12; *MRR* I.263; Warde Fowler (1911) 324–5 identifies totally with the good sense of the Roman authorities. Enquiries into various forms of religion in the following year: Livy XXV.12.3 = 7.5c.

was taken which resulted in the bringing to Rome of the cult of Cybele, whom the Romans called Magna Mater – the Great Mother. There is some reason to think of this, not just as an élite initiative, but as a response to popular pressure. In any case, the cult when it arrived was subject to unprecedented controls. Finally, in 186 B.C. the cult of Bacchus was ferociously suppressed in circumstances about which we know enough to establish the main lines of the senate's policy. These three actions may seem at first sight not to have very much in common. Certainly, the treatment of the Magna Mater could hardly be more different from that of Bacchus: the one established as a city goddess in the very heart of Rome (albeit under certain restrictions), the other persecuted and expelled. But the principles determining action turn out to have more consistency than might appear. It is persecution of the Bacchus cult about which we have the best information and that will provide the best starting point.

Livy provides us with a long account of the events of 186 B.C., but it has always been clear that the information he gives, while crucial evidence for the attitudes to the Bacchic cult of his own day, has a much more problematic relationship to the events of the second century B.C.[73] In the first place – though some elements are more sober – much of his account takes the form of a little drama about the son of a good family, his wicked step-father and his freed-woman mistress with a heart of gold, a plot reminiscent of the plays written in Greece in the Hellenistic period and imitated by Plautus. Here the young Aebutius is persuaded to join the Bacchists by his mother, who wishes to find a way to blackmail him into not revealing his step-father's misdeeds; but his mistress, Hispala, who had been initiated earlier warns him of the danger and his aunt takes the whole story to the consuls.[74] It seems likely that in Livy's narrative we are dealing with a major literary re-working of his source material. We do however have a check on Livy's account, because of the preservation of an inscribed copy of the senatorial decree which was the result of the scandal and laid down the regulations for the cult in the future. Comparison between this surviving text and Livy's version of it suggests that, for all the literary colour he imposed, he had good contemporary sources.[75]

The aspect of Livy's story that requires the most fundamental revision lies deep in his dramatic narrative. The narrative point of this story is to explain how the consul, with detective work and persistence, uncovered the secret plot of the Bacchus worshippers. As soon as he knows the terrible truth, he goes straight to the senate and the people and launches a savage

73 Livy XXXIX.8–19, part = **12.1a**; cf 29.8–10; 41.6–7; XL.19.9–10; *ILS* 18 = *ILLRP* 511 = **12.1b**. Discussion: Gelzer (1936); Méautis (1940); Tierney (1947); Bruhl (1953) 82–116; Festugière (1954); Van Son (1960); Gallini (1970) 11–96; Turcan (1972); North (1979); Pailler (1988) (with full bibliographical discussion); Montanari (1988) 103–31; Gruen (1990) 34–78.
74 Livy XXXIX. 9–14, part = **12.1a**; 19. 3–6.
75 The text is *ILS* 18 = *ILLRP* 511 = **12.1b**. See above, pp. 76–7.

investigation through Rome and its territory, soon to be extended to the whole of Italy. Only the courage of Aebutius and Hispala allows all this to happen and the danger to be averted. Some of the details of this story come close to admitting its absurdity. Thus the consul is made to tell the people of Rome that they have long heard strange music and strange cries in the night and that matrons bearing torches have been seen racing through the city; but nobody realized what all this meant until Hispala revealed the truth.[76]

In fact, it has always been clear from Plautus' explicit references[77] that the Bacchic cult itself was established years before 186 B.C., since it is treated in his plays as something exotic, but familiar. We now have the confirmation of archaeological discoveries in Etruria that a cult-grotto (including a ceremonial throne decorated with images of the cult – see Fig. 2.4) was built in the third century in what was virtually a public part of the city of Volsinii and that this was destroyed at the time of the senate's action in 186 B.C.[78] This can leave little doubt that Livy's narrative of a sudden discovery is a fiction. The best guess is that the senate in 186 B.C. did not discover a new, unacceptable cult, but rather decided to repress a well-established cult, whose development it had previously tolerated. The moment was convenient, because it was the first year of many in which there were no pressing military problems. Perhaps, too, the senate would have found it salutary to be parading the dangers of meddling with foreign religions, just after Rome's victorious armies had returned from the East. But even if the details of the tale Livy tells may be fiction, it is not necessarily a fiction created by historians. The Roman authorities in 186 B.C. were taking a dangerous course of action and they may well have felt the need to create a sense of emergency to justify what they were doing: some of the fiction may well go back to the second century itself.

The scale of the problem the senate faced can be assessed from the different types of evidence we have. The Bacchic cult was evidently very widespread in Italy, north and south as well as in the Roman area itself.[79] It was to be found not just in Roman and Latin communities, but allied ones as well.[80] It cut across all the usual boundaries between social groups, for we

---

76 Livy XXXIX.15.6–7.

77 *Amphitryo* 703–4; *The Pot of Gold* 408, 411a; *The Braggart Warrior* 854–8, 1016; *The Two Bacchises* 53, 371–2; *Casina* 978–82; the references are the more impressive because they are casual mentions which imply prior knowledge in the audience. Discussion: Pailler (1988) 229–38; Gruen (1990) 150–2.

78 Pailler (1976); (1983); for a good general survey of the Italian evidence, Bruhl (1953) 58–81.

79 Distribution: Pailler (1988) 275–303.

80 The senatorial decree itself (*ILS* 18 = *ILLRP* 511 = **12.1b**) mentions both Roman and Latin individuals and is addressed to allied communities ('those who were bound <to Rome> by treaty'); for a different view of this, Galsterer (1976) 169. Livy's account (XXXIX.17–19) also makes it clear that Roman punitive action took place throughout Italy.

Fig. 2.4 Dionysiac terracotta throne, from Bolsena (Roman Volsinii), reconstructed from small fragments found in an underground chamber, which dates from the third century B.C. and was deliberately destroyed early in the second. The throne's decoration – crouching panther and *putto* – probably refer to the myths about Dionysus' early life and the chamber may well be a cult meeting place, (perhaps) destroyed in the course of the persecution. (Height 0.82m.)

know of devotees amongst slaves and free, among Romans, Latins and allies, men and women, country people and city-dwellers, rich and poor.[81] The fact that the cult in this form had established itself so widely is itself remarkable; for Italy was still a very diverse area in languages, culture and traditions. Paradoxically enough, given its repression, it is the spread of the Bacchic movement that provides the clearest evidence that the process of

81 Country/town and rich/poor are both implied throughout Livy's account. All the other categories of people are mentioned in the decree itself, which regulates differentially their access to the Bacchic groups and their roles within them.

cultural unification in Italy was well advanced; the very presence of what seems to be a similar cult in so many places throughout Italy itself implies a degree of cultural convergence. On the other hand the suppression of the Bacchic groups by the senate throughout Italy must have set a precedent and tested the loyalty of the allies to the very limit, since Roman authority in allied Italy rested, at least formally, on treaties with the individual cities and tribes, treaties which gave the Romans no right to interfere in their internal affairs.

Can we then explain why the senate felt compelled to make its attempt to destroy the Bacchic cult, despite what must have been formidable dangers and the fact that they had no tradition of such action? The primary evidence, derived from the text of the decree the senate passed at the time, shows that their ruling was not that Bacchic practice as such should become illegal, but that apart from traditional practices, it should be kept to a very small scale and, in particular, that the groups or cells of Bacchists should not be allowed to retain their internal organization – no leadership, no fund-keeping, no oaths and so on: 'No man shall be a priest... None of them shall seek to have money in common. No one shall seek to appoint either man or woman as master or acting master, or seek henceforth to exchange mutual oaths, vows, pledges or promises.'[82] This tells us two things: first that the cult had previously been based on a highly structured group basis – which would otherwise have been unknown to us; secondly, that this was the threat the senate wished above all to destroy. However much the ritual activity of the groups may have seemed unacceptable in itself (the cult's emphasis on drunkenness and violence – even if, in the Bacchists' own terms, a means of achieving ecstasy and union with the god[83] – cannot have appealed to the Roman authorities), it was the form and structure within which that ritual took place that they sought to control.[84]

It must have been the power over individuals obtained by the group's leaders that would have seemed so radically new and dangerous to the Roman élite. They had been accustomed to control religious life; now they faced a movement in some sense in opposition to the traditions of state religious life, generated by the personal commitment of individuals.[85] Worse still was the threat raised to the authority of the family, as emerges clearly

---

82 Lines 10–14 (= **12.1b**). The most acute discussion of the clauses of the decree is Tierney (1947).

83 Méautis (1940) and Festugière (1954) show how Livy's account may be re-interpreted to produce the Bacchic version.

84 Gruen (1990) 65–78 attempts, by contrast, to interpret the suppression of the cult as (among other things) a gesture against Hellenism. For further discussion of our view, that a growing cult whose structure was unfamiliar to the Roman authorities was genuinely seen as threatening to the social order, see North (1979).

85 We discussed above, pp. 42–3, the absence from traditional state cult of 'personal commitment' in modern terms.

from Livy's narrative, full as it is of family tensions.[86] The Roman family was firmly based on the authority of the father over all his descendants, who formed a religious as well as a worldly community. It would have been disturbing and quite unacceptable that a man, or still worse a woman or child, of this community should take action that transferred their obedience to new and unauthorized groups, such as the Bacchists. This was a religious phenomenon of which Roman tradition, so far as we know, had no experience at all.[87] The position of women within the cult may also have been a particularly sensitive issue at this time. We certainly hear of the involvement of women in the groups, though the hostility of our sources seems to be directed more against the addition of men to what had been thought to be a female cult, than against the women as such; certainly the final regulations allow the continuation of female priests while banning male ones, and attendance at the cult's meetings seems to be referred to as 'being present among the <female> Bacchants', as though that is the primary form of the cult.[88]

The sources that happen to survive thus give us a brief flash of enlightenment about the religious situation of Roman Italy at this one moment, but leave us with problems about both the past and the future of these very important developments. So far as the past is concerned, we have already suggested that the disciplinary action taken by the praetor during the Second Punic War was somehow connected with the activities at that time of the Bacchic groups; the senate presumably already knew what was happening, at least to some extent, but preferred to take careful and restrained action rather than to precipitate the conflict as they did eventually in 186 B.C. It is important too that the earlier action was specifically concerned with the position of women. As for the future, we hear no more about Bacchic groups, but are left to decide whether that means that the suppression succeeded, or that the authorities lost interest after the 180s B.C.

Meanwhile, the senate's treatment of the cult of Magna Mater when it duly arrived suggests the same kind of suspicion of independent religious activity. This cult was originally brought over with every sign of Roman enthusiasm and commitment. It was invited on the suggestion of the Sibylline books; Delphi was consulted; the goddess's symbol, a black stone, was shipped over from Pergamum and greeted by an appropriate miracle; after the end of the war, a new temple was built in a prominent position on the Palatine hill in Rome and new games started to be celebrated once the

---

86 Not only in the story of Aebutius himself, but in the reference to possible divisions within families when the news reaches the senate, Livy XXXIX.14.4 = **12.1a**.
87 Gallini (1970) 20–5; North (1979).
88 Male membership of the cult was envisaged, if duly sanctioned; the point is that (both in symbol and legislation) the cult could be presented as if it was *essentially* female. Instead of 'being present among the <female> Bacchants', we might translate: 'going to the Bacchic women'.

dedication had taken place, and possibly earlier.[89] So far, we have the normal pattern of an invitation to a new deity in a war-crisis, followed by the offering of temple, worship and so on.

It was during this second phase that various restraints and controls on the cult and various unusual characteristics become apparent. There seems to have been a specific law passed in relation to this cult, known to us from Dionysius of Halicarnassus: that 'no native-born Roman walks through the city dressed in bright clothes, begging for alms or accompanied by flute-players, nor worships the goddess with wild Phrygian ceremonies.'[90] We do not know the date of this legislation, but it seems most likely that it was part of the early regulations for the cult in the second century B.C. Certainly the cult was carefully controlled: the Phrygian priest and priestess who came with the cult were segregated and inaccessible to the Romans, their cultic activities were confined to the temple and to a single procession from which Roman citizens were excluded. Meanwhile amongst themselves the noble Romans set up new 'companionships' (*sodalitates*) to dine in the goddess's honour; of these the only members were the leading nobles themselves.[91] No Roman citizens, and perhaps not even their slaves, were allowed to become priests.[92] The new games associated with the cult (the Megalesian Games) also had special rules attached to them: slaves were excluded and, for the first time, senators were separated from non-senators in the audience.[93]

One possible explanation of these unusual regulations is that the Romans discovered the undesirable features of the cult only when the black stone and its accompanying priests arrived. Until that point they had never heard of the self-castrated priests, the wild music and chanting, the dancing to ecstasy, or the dying god Attis, all of which were characteristic of the cult in Asia Minor. The regulations followed as they discovered all these (undesirable) things about the cult; the delay between the arrival of the black stone in 204 B.C. and the real launching of temple and games in 194

89 The main sources: Livy XXIX.10.4–11.8; 14.5 = **2.7a**; Ovid, *Fasti* IV.247–348. General discussion and the introduction of the cult: Graillot (1912); Lambrechts (1951); (1952); Bömer (1964); Thomas (1984) 1525–8; Vermaseren (1977); Turcan (1989) 42–6; Beard (1994); Borgeaud (1996) 89–130. The introduction specifically: Bremmer in Bremmer and Horsfall (1987) 105–11; Gruen (1990) 5–33. Temple: Map 1 no. 13.

90 *Roman Antiquities* II.19 = **8.7a**. This regulation (banning native Romans from distinctively Eastern aspects of the cult) is puzzling in some respects – not least in its reference to 'native-born Romans', not (in those terms at any rate) a recognised category in Roman legislation.

91 Cicero, *On Old Age* 45; Aulus Gellius, *Attic Nights* II.24.2; see also the entry in the calendar of Praeneste (4 April) = **3.3b**. Discussion: Versnel (1980) 108–11.

92 Dionysius of Halicarnassus, *Roman Antiquities* II.19 = **8.7a**; for the prohibition on slaves, Graillot (1912) 76 (an inference from a story at Obsequens 44a).

93 The Megalesian Games: Wiseman (1974) 159–69. The later development of this tendency towards the structured presentation of the citizens: Rawson (1987).

B.C. could thus be explained by their hesitation as they found out the awful truth of a cult that was wildly too foreign to fit into even the most expansive definition of what was Roman.[94] This may seem to imply too simple-minded a picture of the senate's role; and of course we are well-informed neither about the Romans' expectations of the cult nor about the reality they found. In one respect, however, archaeological evidence from the temple suggests that there is something in the view that the new cult brought with it elements the senate had not anticipated. Under the level of the original platform the excavators found a cache of simple terracottas of the Magna Mater's companion – or companion god – Attis.[95] This was a surprising find, because on the basis of the other evidence the importance of Attis in Rome originated in the first century A.D. and his presence under the Republic, let alone from the very beginning, would not otherwise have been known.[96] Secondly, the poor quality of the terracottas suggests not an official offering but a group of poor devotees of the cult. Once again, we seem to find here the hint of a religious life in Rome far more various than the official record allows us to see.

Whatever should be the interpretation of any of these events, it is the aftermath of the Bacchanalia that sets the most difficult problems. Of the fate of the Bacchic groups after 180 B.C., we have no information at all; it seems impossible that the Romans should have unintentionally eliminated the cult, but it certainly ceased to be a problem for them. Perhaps, it went underground for a time and then became less aggressive and more acceptable within traditional structures; perhaps, in any case the religious authorities came to accept such forms of religion more readily. It seems to be characteristic of the worship of Bacchus to fluctuate between periods of enthusiastic renewal and periods of domestication. It is certainly a tamed version of the cult that we meet again in the imperial period. But an important part of the argument we have presented suggests that, by the first decade of the second century, this form of group cult, at odds with traditional modes of behaviour, was well established and widespread in Italy. As we shall show, it was the group cult, depending on voluntary adherence, that was in the end to bring the most radical changes to Roman religious life. The Bacchic groups of Italy were the first example of the problems that could arise; later groups were to become more and more independent, to develop their own ideas and value-systems, to be more and more deeply in conflict with the established social and family structures.

---

94 First games 194 B.C.: Livy XXXIV.54 (alternatively, following Livy XXXVI.36, in 191 B.C.); for a sculptured relief depicting the arrival, **2.7b**.
95 Main publication: Romanelli (1963); some of the terracottas are illustrated, **2.7d**. The correct chronology of the development of the temple: Coarelli (1977a) 11–13; (1982) 39–41.
96 Lambrechts (1962); Vermaseren (1977) 43.

4.   **Priests in politics**

By the last century of the Republic, the membership and activities of the
priestly colleges had unmistakeably become controversial 'political' issues,
much more directly than the traditional connection between politics and
religion in Roman public life would imply. The series of laws that regulated
the system of selecting the priests would make that clear by itself. We shall
discuss these in greater detail in the next chapter.[97] But the proposal that
new priests should be chosen by popular election (replacing the old system
of co-optation by the college) first arose to our knowledge in 145 B.C.;[98]
and we need to consider at this point whether the highly political character
of the republican priesthoods was a radically new development in the late
Republic, or a gradual development and exaggeration of mid-republican
conditions, or whether it quite simply reflects the traditional conditions of
Roman public religion, made apparent for the first time, through the better and more direct quality of the sources available for the lifetime and
memory span of Cicero and his contemporaries. Were the priesthoods
monopolized by members of the élite? If so, how? Were the priests therefore
entirely political in their activities and importance? In this section these
questions will be considered in relation to the situation of the third and second centuries; the next section will analyse the particular religious atmosphere of the years before the radical changes in political life that date from
the 130s B.C., particularly associated with the attempted reforms of the two
brothers Tiberius and Gaius Gracchus.[99]

   In the third century B.C., the character and activities of the Roman
priestly colleges were still, in general, as they had been since the foundation of the Republic; only their membership had been changed to admit
the plebeians and expand the number of places in the colleges (according
to the terms of a law (*lex Ogulnia*) passed in 300 B.C.).[100] At some date, as
we have seen, probably in the course of the third century itself, a form of
election was adopted as a means of selection of the *pontifex maximus*;[101] we
have no way of knowing exactly how the selection had been made before
this reform was passed, whether by vote of the members of the college or
just by seniority, as seems very likely for the early republican period, when
the college had been so much smaller. In any case, it seems highly probable
that the reform should be connected with the *lex Ogulnia*, since the choice
between possible plebeian and patrician candidates will automatically have
arisen as a result of the new law and must have raised sensitive political

---

 97   Below, pp. 135–7.
 98   Cicero, *On Friendship* 96; cf. *Brutus* 83; *On the Nature of the Gods* III. 5; *On the State*
      VI.2. *MRR* I.469, 470.
 99   For the period of change 133–79 B.C., Brunt (1971) 74–111.
 100 Above, pp. 64, 68.
 101 Above, p. 68. The first reported election is that in 212 B.C. (see n.104, below).

issues. The electoral system adopted was known as voting by the 'lesser part of the people' (*minor pars populi*): that is to say, only seventeen out of the thirty-five voting 'tribes', chosen by lot on each occasion, voted;[102] in explicitly not giving the power of decision to the people as a whole, this voting system suggests some compunction or perhaps some opposition about the idea of popular election for a religious office. It is certain that the candidates had already to be *pontifices* before they could stand and that they had to be nominated by existing members; this ensured that any new *pontifex maximus* would be acceptable to the existing ones, but the reform also made it possible for the less senior members of the college to compete in an election. The result may well have been to make the *pontifex maximus* a more important figure than he had been before: at least we hear of prominent plebeian *pontifices maximi* in the years that follow;[103] and before the end of the century we first meet the phenomenon of a young noble being elected over the heads of older competitors and so promoting his career in a way later associated with the rise of Julius Caesar, who was elected *pontifex maximus* in 63 B.C. immediately before his spectacular emergence as a political force in the following years.[104] So whether or not the cause of this change was political, the eventual consequences certainly were; it is at least possible that this was an important step towards the politicization of the colleges.

In the early years of the second century Livy reports very briefly another reform that may also reflect political issues, though once again our knowledge of it is very limited.[105] We are dealing with a major political and religious event, in this case nothing less than the creation of a complete new college of priests, one of the four 'major colleges' (along with the *pontifices, augures* and *decemviri*) as they were later called. It was a reform that was presumably enacted by a vote of the people, though there is no way of knowing whether the senate or other priests in particular proposed or supported the bill. At first, this new priesthood consisted of only three members, later seven. Their duties were connected quite specifically with the rituals of the games and their title (*triumviri epulones*) with the feast of Jupiter (*epulum Iovis* – see Fig. 2.5) which was a feature of the Roman and the Plebeian Games, the oldest and most important.[106] The duties they took on had presumably been the responsibility of the *pontifices* themselves in earlier years;[107] and the institution must at

---

102 This is clear from Cicero, *On the Agrarian Law* II.16. Voting procedures: Taylor (1966) 59–83 (82 on election of *pontifex maximus*).

103 The succession from Tiberius Coruncanius (mid-third century) onwards: J.-C. Richard (1968); Szemler (1972) 78–9.

104 The young noble was Publius Licinius Crassus, in the first reported election to the office in 212 B.C.: Livy XXV.5.2–4; *MRR* I.271; Szemler (1972) 30, 105–7. Caesar: Taylor (1942).

105 Livy XXXIII.42.1; *MRR* I.336.

106 Above, p. 40.

107 That is the implication of Cicero (*Orator* III.73). The fact that they became one of the

Fig. 2.5 Coin issued by Caius Coelius Caldus in 51 B.C., the year before he was *quaestor* to Cicero. The central element is a figure placing food on a table, which bears the inscription 'L. Caldus VIIvir epu(lo)'. This is presumably a representation of the moneyer's father, Lucius Coelius Caldus, who was a member of the *epulones*. It is the only known portrayal of the preparation of the *epulum Iovis*.

one level reflect the growth of the games in the third century and hence the complexity of the rituals connected with them. However, it was not priests, whether *pontifices* or *epulones*, but magistrates who actually administered the games. The priests will have had a role in the rituals, but essentially provided a source of expert advice about ritual procedure and problems. The most tempting explanation is that the intended function of the college was to act as a check on the activities of the magistrates who actually held the games. A profitable career could be built at this period by using conspicuous expenditure on the games as one of the first rungs (the aedileship) of the political ladder: this lavish display was supposed to ensure rapid election to the higher ranks (praetorship and consulship), at which serious warfare and serious profits would follow. In the years preceding this bill, the plebeian aediles in particular had been very successful in being elected to the praetorship during the year of their aedileship, in fact within a short period of their holding these games.[108]

It is possible that one other structural change was made to the priestly order in the second century B.C. The *haruspices*, as we saw in chapter 1, had originally been (in some sense) outside the Roman religious order – 'called in' from Etruria for advice about points of ritual, especially in the case of prodigies.[109] By the early Empire it seems quite clear that, while not becoming a college in the proper sense, they had been formed into a unity for Roman purposes, with a fixed approved list of sixty members.[110] Cicero reports that the senate once passed a decree to encourage the maintenance of the art of haruspicy within the leading families of the Etruscan cities.[111] He gives no date,[112] but if this decree was passed in the middle of the second century, as seems most likely, then we might look for signs of revival of their

four senior colleges of Rome suggests that they could be consulted on points of law and authority; see Cicero, *On the Response of the Haruspices* 21.
108 Scullard (1973) 24–5; on the games and politics, Morgan (1990).
109 Above, pp. 19–20.
110 Thulin (1906–09); above, p. 20.
111 Cicero, *On Divination* I.92; Valerius Maximus, *Memorable Deeds and Sayings* I.1.3; cf. Tacitus, *Annals* XI.15; below, p. 113.
112 Or at least only the vaguest indication: 'at the time when the empire was flourishing' (Cicero, *On Divination* I. 92).

Fig. 2.6 Coins (silver denarii) issued by Marcus Volteius in 78 B.C.: (a) the Capitoline temple (on the reverse, Jupiter); (b) Erymanthian Boar, as one of Hercules' labours (rev. Hercules); (c) Ceres in chariot drawn by snakes, holding torches (rev. Liber); (d) Cybele (Magna Mater) in chariot drawn by lions (rev. ?Attis); (e) Tripod (rev. Apollo). Four of the five types refer to the deities connected with the main sets of annual games (the Roman Games (a); the Games of Ceres (c); of Magna Mater (d); of Apollo (e)). Hercules must here represent the Plebeian Games, though these are usually connected rather with Jupiter.

influence. For these years Livy's record gives the *haruspices* a major and growing role: not only do reports of their responses become more regular in the second century B.C., but they seem increasingly willing to depart from the Roman tradition in offering not just ritual recommendations, but also interpretations and prophecies.[113] At the same time there are signs of a revival of interest in Etruscan records and traditions.[114]

The membership of the three most senior priestly colleges is better known for the late third and early second centuries than for any other period of the Republic; the names of many priests are also known in the late republican period, but only the surviving books of Livy provide us with methodical information by reporting the deaths and successions in the different colleges. Throughout this period new priests were always chosen (co-opted) by the existing members of the college. Livy's record means that we can in principle identify all, or almost all, the priests who would have been

113 The response quoted by Cicero in *On the Response of the Haruspices* (= 7.4a) gives an idea of the kind of response Livy must be reporting from a century earlier.
114 Etruscan prophecy: Heurgon (1959); cf. Turcan (1976).

members of a college at the time of a particular co-optation, and would have taken part in the selection of the new priest. Information of this quality comes only from the years covered by Livy's Books XXI–XLV; that is the years 218–167 B.C. For the *augures* and the *pontifices*, there are full lists for much of the time (and it is these priesthoods that will form the basis of our discussion); but the record preserved of the *decemviri sacris faciundis* seems for some reason to have omitted half the ten places in the college; for the *epulones*, we know the names of the very first members, but cannot know whether Livy reports all the changes thereafter; for other less prominent priests, as we have noted before, we have no methodical record at all; even for important groups such as the *fetiales* or the *haruspices*, we know no single name. Even given these limitations it is possible to reach some firm conclusions about Roman priestly colleges and their methods of recruitment.[115]

It is quite clear that, at least in the colleges for which full lists survive, the priesthoods were virtually monopolized by members of the best established, élite families. Leading figures almost always held priesthoods, sometimes when quite young;[116] and the priestly lists co-incide to a striking degree with lists of the most successful and powerful generals and politicians of the day.[117] Just occasionally, a less predictable name turns up; and there are occasions when selection to a priesthood comes late in a man's career, even following his consulship – but this is usually the case only for those of less distinguished ancestry.[118] From the point of view of the élite as a group, this is all perfectly predictable and corresponds, as we mentioned in chapter 1, to Cicero's description of one of the striking characteristics of the Roman religious system, that the same men hold both priesthoods and political offices.[119]

This monopoly has another characteristic, equally typical of the Roman republican order. Priesthoods were not just kept within a limited group of families but also shared amongst these families according to what seem to be accepted but unwritten principles; there were occasional exceptions, but as a general rule:

(a) no *gens* (clan) holds more than one place in any college at the same time;

(b) no individual holds more than one priesthood, or at least not more than one in the colleges to which our lists apply.[120]

This is a striking example of the sharing of power, honour and responsibility

---

115 Szemler (1972) 157–62.

116 North (1990) 533.

117 The lists in Szemler (1972) 182–8 give a useful overview of career patterns, though not reliable in detail.

118 Most of the known cases fall in the 190s and 180s B.C.: Szemler (1972) 182–8. Most notable are the succession of *pontifices* nos. 15–19 (Szemler); this must imply that the college was deliberately co-opting more senior men at this period.

119 *On his House* 1 = **8.2a**.

120 North (1990).

widely through the élite that characterized the republican system. And it is all the more striking because, at least in principle, the system of co-optation should have provided the opportunity for the concentration of continuing control of the college in the hands of some dominant group of political allies. Once any group had a voting majority in a college of nine members, it should have been simplicity itself to establish permanent control and this would become detectable in the record. Yet so far as we can judge, all the leading families maintain a share in the colleges and none ever establishes an impressive concentration. Another striking feature is that families move from one college to another over the generations and do not seem to establish an inherited preference for one college rather than another.[121] This seems to fit the same pattern: if a priest's son was able to reach his own priesthood before his father's death that would have to mean seeking a place in a college other than his father's (because of the rule against two members of the same *gens* simultaneously being members of the same priesthood). Sons do sometimes succeed fathers in the same priesthood after their death, but this is not a regular pattern.[122]

The evidence of membership leaves no doubt that the senior priestly colleges were an important perquisite of the members of the ruling class and that they took a great deal of trouble to make sure that the places were properly allocated, like other sources of honour and power, amongst themselves. Precisely because the members were the great successful politicians of the period, it has been assumed that their motives for wanting religious office must also have been political not religious: hence the widespread assumption that the actions of the colleges and their members were entirely motivated by politics.

The reports we have about the priestly colleges in this period do not in fact explicitly reveal the use, or abuse, of their authority for narrowly political purposes. No doubt, all kinds of interests were canvassed (or, at least, in the background) when decisions or co-optations were discussed in the meetings of the priestly colleges – from the high-minded to the blatantly self-interested. But when Livy reports their actions, as he does on many occasions, he virtually never gives substantial grounds for thinking that their decisions were politically motivated or that conflict between rival groups found expression through religious interpretations or rulings. Here as so often, however, it is possible that Livy, or the sources he was using, deliberately imposed a particular view on the evidence: because he saw religious conflict for political reasons as part of the deterioration of behaviour associated with the very last years of the Republic, he therefore eliminated any trace of it in his accounts of earlier generations – or simply failed to

---

121 North (1990) 532–4.

122 For example, *pontifices* 16 and 20 (Szemler): *decemviri sacris faciundis* 4, 5 and 13 (Szemler). For the puzzling case of the two Scipios (Scipio Nasica Corculum and Scipio Nasica Serapio), North (1990) 533–4.

recognize it. Modern political historians have given themselves a generous licence to exploit this gap (as they see it) in Livy's account and have in consequence sought to interpret all religious conflict in this earlier period as rooted in political opposition. All the incidents discussed over the next few pages have been interpreted as attempts by one group to gain advantage against another through the completely cynical manipulation of the sacred law (*ius divinum*).[123]

We are concerned with a series of incidents in which conflict arises between priests or between priests and magistrates. The style of these incidents itself repays attention. Characteristically, they turn on points of religious law, with the priests (or one group of priests) resisting some practical or innovative proposal on the grounds that it is against custom and rule (*ius*). Thus, for instance the *pontifices* in 222 B.C. prevented Marcus Claudius Marcellus from adding the cult of Virtus to an existing temple of Honos, on the grounds that it was essential for each of the deities to have their own chapel (*cella*) – so that, it was argued, in the event of a lightning stroke it would be clear who was the offended deity to whom the appropriate sacrifices should be made.[124] Or again, in 200 B.C., the *pontifex maximus* protested against a proposal that a vow should not include the specification of a fund through which the gods would be repaid for their co-operation if the terms of the vow were fulfilled.[125] Similarly, in 176 B.C. there was a debate involving the 'experts in the sacred law' (*ius divinum*) as to whether an irregularity had occurred in the religious proceedings of a defeated general.[126] All these incidents involve disputed points of law, on which different views could be, and no doubt were, taken.

Obviously, these disputes did have a political aspect; the figures involved are either leading politicians and generals or have ambitions to become such. The conflict is about points of religious propriety, almost of etiquette, and perhaps it is helpful to think of the losers as losing public face rather than any specific political advantage. Marcellus, for instance, had to bow to the decision of the *pontifices* and build his temple to their plan not to his own; Honos and Virtus had their separate chapels. All the same, public face was very important in a politician's career, a substantial part in the construction of his *auctoritas* ('authority'). Marcellus must have hoped that his friends in the college would support his case and that they would carry the vote.

---

123 For example, Münzer (1920) 261–3; Scullard (1973) 87–8 (and n. 3); 166–7 (and n.3).
124 Livy XXV.40.1–3; XXVII.25.7–9; cf. Cicero, *Against Verres* II.4.120–23; *On the Nature of the Gods* II.1; *On the State* I.21; Asconius, *Commentary on Cicero's Speech against Piso* 12C.
125 Livy XXXI.9.5–10.
126 Livy XLI.15.1–4; 18.7–8; 18.14–16; Valeton (1895) 61–4; Linderski (1986) 2173–5, 2184–6; Rosenstein (1990) 88–90.

But the strictly 'political' interpretation would have to go much further than this: it would need to assume that it was only the political considerations that were relevant, while the legal-religious issues mattered not at all. This hypothesis is about as improbable as could be. It involves assuming, without any justification, that Romans of a century or more before Cicero's time were far more radically sceptical than he ever was (a man who repeatedly emphasized in public pronouncements and 'private' letters, as we shall see, the importance of maintaining forms and proprieties in public behaviour). In the absence of any clear evidence at all, the only way of defending this purely political analysis is to take it as referring not to public argument or parade, but to secret motives undisclosed at the time. Of course, we can always speculate about secret motives; but there is not much to distinguish such speculation from sheer fantasy.

The issues of this debate are best considered in the context of a particular sequence of conflicts between 242 B.C. and 131 B.C. in which successive *pontifices maximi* sought to prevent colleagues from taking actions which would allegedly have violated their sacred obligations.[127] The details of these incidents differ, but their background and structure is much the same. As we saw in chapter 1, within the college of *pontifices* both the *rex sacrorum* and the three major *flamines* were subject to limitations on their political activities. The *rex* was not allowed to hold any magistracy at all; he was bound by the very principle on which the Republic was founded – that the king should never hold political authority. The *flamen Dialis* had a whole battery of restrictions and taboos, in addition to his ritual duties, that would have made it impossible for him to have carried out the duties of a magistrate in command of armies and provinces.[128] Even the office of a magistrate at Rome itself would raise the problem that the *flamen* could not bind himself by an oath (as magistrates might be required to do) and the *flamen Dialis* was for many years regarded as ineligible for any office. It is not known how many of these regulations applied to the *flamines* of Mars and Quirinus; though we know that they had at least some rituals to be performed at specific times in Rome, requiring their presence in the city.[129] It is these restrictions on political action that the *pontifex maximus* repeatedly acted to maintain – in the face of priests who repeatedly wished to assume another public office or military command.

The procedure we are dealing with was quite consistent. The *pontifex* imposed his fine (*multa*) on the priest he wished to restrain; the legal basis of this action is not known, but he could use a fine not only against priests

---

127 A thorough summary and analysis of the evidence: Bleicken (1957a); (1957b).
128 Above, pp. 28–9.
129 The *flamen Quirinalis* had to be in Rome for the Robigalia (25 April), Scullard (1981) 108; the Consualia (15 December), Scullard (1981) 177; and, no doubt, the Quirinalia (17 February) – since it was the festival of his own god. For the patchiness of our knowledge, Rohde (1936) 100–7.

of his own college, but against magistrates who were not priests and even a private man whom he intended to inaugurate as a priest. The *multa* was, however, subject to appeal; and the pattern was for a hearing to take place, through the agency of a tribune of the *plebs*, before the Roman people who had the final power of decision. Even on this issue, where the legal rules of the college of *pontifices* were at issue, the decision was not left to the priests alone. On the other hand, the priestly viewpoint regularly won in the end: in every case we know where a decision was reached in this way, the *flamen* was instructed to obey the *pontifex maximus*, and only when he did so was the threat of the fine withdrawn.[130]

There is no reason to deny that factional and political issues will have been at stake in some of these conflicts; in 131 B.C., the *pontifex maximus* was himself one of the rival candidates for the particular command which he forbade the *flamen* to undertake, so he can hardly be said to have had no interest.[131] We also have one explicit reference in the historian Tacitus (writing in the early second century A.D.) to these very incidents, in which he implies that it was hatred not principle that caused the trouble.[132] However, this allegation is not Tacitus' own comment, but put in the mouth of a priest who wanted to discredit these ancient precedents of enforcing the rules and restrictions; the text confirms that personal or political rivalry was one possible ancient interpretation of what happened, but not that it was the only possible interpretation. Two issues have been neglected unduly in the discussion. First, there was a real and important religious issue at stake in the series of conflicts. The priests in question wished to pursue their ambitions, but the priesthoods they held constituted an impediment. As we saw in the last chapter, this arose partly because there was a difference between their position and that of other members of the various colleges: in that the *rex* and the *flamines* were unique priests whose obligations could not properly be fulfilled by other members of the pontifical college.[133] In the view of successive *pontifices maximi*, there was no alternative to their being in Rome at the time of the rituals to which they were tied.

The second point that has been neglected is the normal result of these conflicts. The debates were very public, leading to a popular vote, which was held to settle the matter. In every case, the popular vote supported the *pontifex maximus* in his defence of the sacred law and forced the would-be general to

---

130 All the evidence is collected by Bleicken (1957b). Examples: Livy XXVII.8.4–10 = **8.2d**; XL.42.8–11.

131 Cicero, *Philippics* XI.18. The consul Licinius Crassus Mucianus, in his capacity as *pontifex maximus*, restrained his colleague in the consulship, Lucius Valerius Flaccus (who was also *flamen Martialis*); he then won the vote and the military command, against Scipio Aemilianus. Discussion: Astin (1967) 234–5.

132 The case is that of Servius Maluginensis: Tacitus, *Annals* III.58; below, p. 193.

133 Below, pp. 131–2, for the functions of the *flamen Dialis* carried out by the *pontifices*, while the flaminate remained unfilled.

moderate his ambitions. So, even if one part of the truth in these cases is that animosities were let loose, another part of the truth is that an important principle of the sacred law was attacked, defended and publicly vindicated. So far as the period here discussed is concerned, the result was victory not defeat for the religious authorities of Rome and their traditional rules.

5. The religious situation of the mid-second century

For the middle years of the century our information is quite different in character: after the end of the surviving text of Livy, we have only brief summaries of his books made in late antiquity and there is a general gap in our literary record of Roman life until the 130s B.C.[134] On the other hand, we have for the very first time an analysis of the religion of Rome by a contemporary observer, the Greek Polybius.[135] He is no mean witness, since he was well-informed and well-placed to make his observations. The son of a leading Greek politician of the 160s B.C., he was brought to Italy as a hostage and (as we saw) lived in Rome for many years and came to have close contacts with members of the Roman élite.[136] His history aimed to explain Rome's rise to power and its victory over the Greeks to a Greek (or Greek-speaking) audience.[137] Polybius' is not at all a casual discussion of Roman religion: it comes at a critical point in his analysis of Rome's strengths, which is itself central to his whole explanation of her success. He argues that the strength of the Romans, as against that of the Greeks, derived to a significant extent from their religious customs. It is clear that he had been impressed by the care and scrupulousness with which he saw these matters being handled in Rome. The theory he offers is that religion should be seen as a means by which the ruling élite manipulated and disciplined their people; the Greek weakness lay in the decline of popular belief, which had in turn led to a weakening of the social order. Characteristically, however, Polybius managed to contradict his own theories by his own observations. He implies that in Rome as in Greece there was a gap between élite and popular attitudes – and that it was by élite manipulation of those popular religious attitudes that social order was maintained. But the example he gives to illustrate Roman piety is the behaviour of the magistrates, not the common people: Roman magistrates, unlike Greek ones, can be relied upon to keep the sacred oaths that they take. In other words, by focussing on the religious scrupulosity of the *élite*, he immediately contradicts the gap in attitudes implied by his own theory.

134   There are no *Lives* of Plutarch for this period; Appian's narrative of the Civil Wars starts with the Gracchi; the relevant books of Cassius Dio are lost.
135   Polybius VI.56 = **13.1b.**
136   Roman friends of Polybius: Astin (1967) 14–20; F.W. Walbank (1972) 8–13.
137   Above, p. 74.

What is most interesting about Polybius' discussion is not so much his own ideas as the context in which they must have arisen and the discussion they would have provoked. His remarks could hardly have arisen in isolation and they therefore suggest that religion in Rome was becoming a matter for discussion and debate, at least so far as Polybius' noble Roman friends were concerned. It is certainly worth considering whether there are other signs of increasing self-consciousness about their religious traditions. In fact, it is a striking feature of the mid-second century that, in a period for which all the continuous narrative sources fail us, a quite surprising amount of what we do know concerns religious matters; and a good deal of it suggests an atmosphere of controversy and reflection, but not yet of bitter conflict.

In the first place there are indications that political conflict was getting far more closely involved with religious institutions – as is most obvious in evidence of legislation or attempted legislation. In 145 B.C. there was an attempt by a tribune, Caius Licinius, to introduce some form of election for priests instead of the traditional co-optation within the colleges themselves. The proposal was eventually rejected or abandoned and it is only known because of a famous speech attacking the proposal by the friend of Scipio Aemilianus, Caius Laelius. Only small fragments of the speech survive, but they suggest that he defended the priests' control over their own membership by emphasizing the arcane vocabulary and traditions of the colleges.[138] That kind of defence was perhaps to be expected; but the reasons for the proposal are not so easy to see. It would be natural to expect such a proposal at a time when the membership of the colleges and their activities could be perceived as standing in the way of popular legislation. If so, we should assume, though we do not know of, controversial decisions by the priests in the 150s or early 140s B.C. It certainly is true that the augural college of the 130s B.C., about which we know a good deal from Cicero, contained a formidable block of supporters and relations of Aemilianus (of whom Laelius was one) – the first time, in fact, that we can detect one dominant group within a priestly college. If this was true already by the 140s B.C., then it would be an economical hypothesis to suggest that Laelius was defending the position of a dominant priestly group, which would have been precisely Licinius' target.[139] The guess cannot be confirmed.

A second law, the *lex Aelia Fufia*, this time passed successfully, also seems

---

138 Fragments of the speech: Malcovati (1955) 117–18, especially fr. 15 & 16 = Cicero, *On the Nature of the Gods* III.43; *On the State* VI.2.2.

139 North (1990) 536–7 and n. 31. The idea of Licinius' proposal as a challenge to the authority of the traditional élite is supported by another reform associated with his name: he was reported to have been the first to challenge senatorial authority by turning his back on the senate house when speaking on the rostra, facing the people in the open space of the forum (a more than symbolic gesture also attributed to Gaius Gracchus); Cicero, *On Friendship* 96.

to belong to some time around the 140s B.C. Again we owe our information to Cicero,[140] but on this occasion not in a mood of refined antiquarianism, but of raw political hostility, the mood in which his evidence is least to be trusted. While attacking the legislation of his enemy Clodius, he implies that it had destroyed the provisions of the *lex Aelia Fufia* on the procedure for *obnuntiatio*, that is, the announcement of signs from the gods that would prevent the conduct of assemblies or other business. He claims that this law was one of the great bastions of resistance to the revolutionary schemes of later tribunes: that it was, in other words, a law that provided the legal mechanism for the senatorial traditionalists (the '*optimates*') when they sought to cancel popular laws, from the 130s B.C. onwards.[141] The problem is that, though Cicero mentions the law often enough, he never gives any explicit information about its provisions; nor does any other source.[142] But unless we are to think that he was simply inventing this legislation, it has to be accepted that *obnuntiatio* in the first century rested, or partly rested, on this legislation, not simply on the *ius* (the sacred law) of the *augures*; the law must therefore have been an intervention into that *ius*. That such laws as those of Licinius and Aelius should have been proposed after the clashes between radical and conservative that particularly characterized the period after 133 B.C. would be unsurprising; as it is, there is a strong suggestion here that priests and politics were in the realm of controversy much earlier than we should otherwise have expected; that the kind of political-cum-religious battles started much earlier than our surviving sources tell us.[143]

This suggestion of controversy applies not only to political aspects but to a series of unusual ritual actions in these same decades. It is tempting to speak here of a tendency to revivalism: for, although that might be too simple a term to describe what was happening, rites were repeatedly respected that might well have been neglected or forgotten; and it seems likely that this reflects the ideas of leading priests such as Aemilius Paullus and his natural son, Cornelius Scipio Aemilianus,[144] both of whom were *augures*.

First, there was probably a celebration in 160 B.C. of the very infrequent 'augury of safety' (*augurium salutis*),[145] in which Aemilius Paullus was

140 Cicero mentions these laws in his speeches *Against Piso* 9, 10; *Against Vatinius* 5, 18, 23, 37; *On Behalf of Sestius* 33, 114; *On the Response of the Haruspices* 58; *After his Return, in the Senate* 11; *On the Consular Provinces* 46. The only clue to date is provided by *Against Piso* 10, where he speaks of the laws being 'about 100 years' ('*centum prope annos*') before 58 B.C.

141 Cicero, *Against Vatinius* 18: 'these laws frequently weakened and repressed the outrages of the tribunes.'

142 Hence the many theories on the subject (and Clodius' reform): Weinstock (1937c); Balsdon (1957); Sumner (1963); Astin (1964); Weinrib (1970); T. Mitchell (1986).

143 Taylor (1962) offers other arguments for seeing the political conflicts associated with the Gracchi stretching further back into the second century B.C.

144 He had been adopted by Publius Scipio.

145 Plutarch, *Aemilius Paullus* 39. The nature of the ceremony mentioned, but not identified, by Plutarch is very likely to have been the *augurium salutis*; the date is hard to fix

involved just before his death. Then, in 149 B.C., on the eve of the major wars in Africa and Greece, the games for Dis and Proserpina at the Terentum were celebrated for the second time. The first revival of these games is likely to be the time when they were recognized as regular centennial games, again suggesting conscious decisions, presumably this time on the initiative of the *decemviri sacris faciundis*.[146] The war against Carthage (the Third Punic War, 149–146 B.C.) brings more evidence: Aemilianus seems to have performed two archaic ceremonies: the 'devotion' of Carthage to the gods of the underworld[147] and the 'evocation' of the Juno of Carthage.[148] In both cases, the formulae used have come down to us in Macrobius' *Saturnalia* (written soon after A.D. 431), where they are said to have been recorded in the work of a certain 'Furius', who is probably Aemilianus' friend Lucius Furius Philus, consul in 136 B.C.[149] The genuineness of these two documents has been questioned,[150] but there is no strong reason to doubt that these were the formulae used in the 140s B.C.; if so, it is very significant that the same group of nobles were reviving them, using them, and recording them in their writings.

The 130s B.C. saw the sequence continue and it becomes easier to judge what was happening. During the Spanish wars of these years, several commanders found themselves in acute military difficulties and one of them, Hostilius Mancinus, the consul of 137 B.C., made a treaty on his own authority with the Numantines after his army was trapped. The senate refused to endorse his treaty. Following ancient precedents the renunciation of the treaty was marked by handing over the commander to the enemy. Mancinus was duly surrendered to the Numantines by the *fetiales*, naked and bound.[151] The Numantines refused to accept him, but the treaty was still regarded by the Romans as null and void.[152] Both Furius and Aemilianus were involved in these events; but whether or not the religious device by which the treaty was renounced was their doing, there seems to be an inescapable connection between the actions of the 130s and the historical

---

precisely but there were few occasions when the Romans were not involved in major warfare (a requirement for the fulfilment of the ritual). The significance of the *augurium salutis*: below, p. 188. Discussion: Liegle (1942).

146 Saecular Games: above, pp. 71–2; below, pp. 201–6.

147 This ceremony is clearly related to the *devotio* of the Roman general (above, pp. 35–6), but concerns the whole (enemy) town, not the individual commander: Versnel (1976).

148 Above, p. 82 (for the earlier 'placating' of the goddess).

149 Macrobius, *Saturnalia* III.9.6–11. Furius' writings are not otherwise known.

150 Wissowa (1907); Latte (1960a) 125 and n.2. Rawson (1973) 168–72 reviews the evidence. It has been thought decisive that there is no evidence for a temple of Juno of Carthage in Rome; but as we see below (pp. 132–4), some later forms of *evocatio* involved a new temple erected on provincial territory.

151 Cicero, *On Duties* III.109. Other sources: *MRR* I.484–5.

152 Discussion: Astin (1967) 132–3; Crawford (1973); Rosenstein (1990) 136–7, 148–50.

precedent of the Battle of the Caudine Forks in the Samnite Wars (321 B.C.), after which the treaty was said to have been renounced in the same way.[153] It is possible either that the Caudine Forks provided the example for the handing over of Mancinus or that the history of the battle was reconstructed to reflect the second-century events. Either way the link between the two seems inescapable. We have a clear case of religious action and antiquarian research re-inforcing one another.

These individual incidents may not, on their own, prove very much. But it seems hard not to see connections between these various conscious exploitations of the past as a model for present action: the speech of Laelius, the revival of the *ludi* at the Terentum, the rituals at Carthage, the handing over of Mancinus. All suggest that, at least within a group of aristocratic allies, there was a self-conscious awareness of the religious tradition of the past and the need to preserve it. It is not therefore very surprising to find that the same years saw the first attempts to write about the religious customs of Rome. These attempts are best attested by the works that deal directly with religious antiquities, such as the book ascribed to Fabius Pictor (probably not Fabius Pictor the Roman historian writing in Greek in the late third century B.C., but an antiquarian of the mid-second century B.C.). The few surviving fragments show us at least one of the concerns of this work: that is the detailed recording of the regulations, dress and practices of some of the oldest priesthoods.[154] Most famous and extensive are the details of the taboos of the *flamen Dialis*, preserved for us by the later antiquarian Aulus Gellius, but taken from Fabius' work.[155] Much the same preoccupations are strongly suggested by the antiquarian elements in the

153 Crawford (1973).
154 Fragments: Peter (1906–14) I.114–16 (with clxxiv–vi).
155 *Attic Nights* X.15 = **8.1b**.

Fig. 2.7 Altar from
Rome, the so-called
'Altar of Domitius
Ahenobarbus'. The
side illustrated (now
in Paris) originally
formed one of four;
the other three (now
in Munich) show
the marriage of
Neptune, probably
implying that the
altar derived from a
temple of Neptune.
In the centre, at an
altar, a magistrate,
with attendant,
waits to sacrifice; the
victims (ox, pig and
sheep) approach
from the right, in
procession with
soldiers; on the left,
a group of Romans
wearing togas (i.e.
not in military dress)
surround a man
with a writing tablet.
The most likely
interpretation is that
the scene depicts the
duties of a *censor*:
recording the census
of citizens (left); and
performing the
'lustral' sacrifice
(*suovetaurilia*),
which marked the
period of the census.
The sacrificer is
possibly (though not
certainly) Domitius
Ahenobarbus, *censor*
in 115 B.C. (Height,
0.82m., length
5.66m.)

writing of the very first Latin-writing historians – Cato, Gellius and Piso,
writing in the mid second century.[156] In all of them, religious notices of one
kind or another are strikingly prominent.

The best indication that there is some connection between a policy of
defending and restoring 'native' practices and suspecting and rejecting 'foreign' ones, comes from two senatorial decrees, one of which certainly
belongs to this period, the other very probably. The first is dated to 139 B.C.
and provided for the expulsion of astrologers amongst others from Rome
because they were exploiting a bogus art for profit.[157] The second, as we
have seen, provided for the encouragement of the discipline of the *haruspices* among the aristocratic families of Etruria 'in case such a great art
should through the weakness of men lose its true religious authority and be
subordinated to trade and profit'.[158] Nervousness about the paid diviner
and the power he might generate is of course common to both actions and
no doubt did provide a large part of the motivation. But the key difference
is evidently that the art of the *haruspices* was now established as part of the
senate's armoury for coping with problems and must therefore be revived
and defended as part of the 'Roman' tradition.[159]

The rituals and festivals of Rome provided for Romans and non-
Romans at all periods a demonstration of what was most traditional and
typical about the history and life of Rome; a demonstration of what
counted as *Roman*. Rome in the second century B.C. was a quite different
city from the Rome that we explored in the first chapter. By this period
Romans were (and knew themselves to be) a world power; the small city-
state on the Tiber was already well on the way to being the multicultural
cosmopolis that will form the subject of the rest of the book. The ancient
religious traditions of the city – Rome's relations with its divine citizens –
explained Rome's rise to power, represented its success and ensured its continuance for the future. The constructive revival of old, half-forgotten rituals played a key role in the extension of Roman horizons. It was an assertion
that the religious traditions of early Rome ordered the imperial universe.
But in the next chapter we shall see how fragile that assertion could sometimes seem in the political life of the late republican city – where the stakes
were nothing less than world rule for the Roman people and (close to)
absolute power for their political leaders.

156   Latte (1960b); Rawson (1976).
157   Valerius Maximus, *Memorable Deeds and Sayings* I.3.2. There is no doubt about the
       expulsion of *Chaldaei* (Chaldaeans), that is astrologers; the identity of a second group
       referred to, probably Jews, is less certain. Expulsions in general: below, pp. 231–2.
158   Cicero, *On Divination* I.92.
159   Paraded revival of haruspicy under the emperor Claudius: Tacitus, *Annals* XI.15;
       below, pp. 210; 228.

3 Religion in the late Republic

On 29 September 57 B.C. the pontifical college met in Rome to decide the fate of Cicero's house. Cicero's savage repression of the conspiracy of Catiline in 63 B.C. (a dastardly revolutionary plot, or a storm in a tea-cup, depending on your point of view) had rebounded on him. Publius Clodius Pulcher, his personal and political enemy, had taken advantage of Cicero's illegal execution of Roman citizens among the conspirators without even the semblance of a trial; and in 58 B.C. – with his old enemy clearly in mind – had passed a law condemning to exile anyone who had failed to adopt the proper legal procedures in putting a citizen to death. Cicero was forced to leave the city, while Clodius promptly celebrated his victory with the destruction of Cicero's house and by consecrating on part of its site a shrine to the goddess Liberty, *Libertas* (a devastatingly loaded, or intentionally irritating, choice of deity, no doubt – for it was the principles of *libertas* that Cicero was charged with violating). But, in the switchback politics of the 50s, the tables soon turned once more. By 57 Cicero had been recalled, and the senate, faced with the problem of his property, referred to the *pontifices* the question of whether or not the consecration of the site had been valid; whether or not, in other words, Cicero could have his land back. After hearing representatives from both sides, the college decided that, as the consecration had been carried out without the authorization of the Roman people (and so was invalid), the site could be returned to Cicero. The senate confirmed the decision – and Cicero set about re-building.[1]

What sets this incident apart from any of the religious events we have touched on in earlier chapters is the survival of the speech that Cicero delivered to the *pontifices* on the occasion of the hearing. We do not, in other words, come to this piece of priestly business through the formal record of problem and decision, in the few sentences (at most) that Livy would normally choose to allot to such matters; we do not meet it as part of *history*, business done and decided. Cicero's speech (even though altered or embellished, no doubt, after delivery for written circulation) takes us right into the uncertain process of religious decision making, into the heart of the contest. It does not reflect or record the discourse of religion; it *is* that discourse.

Of course, *we* know (as did ancient readers) that Cicero won the case.

---

1 The background to this incident: Rawson (1975) 60–145; T. Mitchell (1991) 98–203.

And so his words inevitably enlist us as admiring witnesses to the winning arguments in priestly debate, the successful repartee of religious conflict, the clever flattery directed to the priests by this pleader in the pontifical court. For example, when Cicero opens with the impressive lines:

> Among the many things, gentlemen of the pontifical college, that our ancestors created and established under divine inspiration, nothing is more renowned than their decision to entrust the worship of the gods and the highest interests of the state to the same men – so that the most eminent and illustrious citizens might ensure the maintenance of religion by the proper administration of the state, and the maintenance of the state by the prudent interpretation of religion,[2]

we should not forget that this is not only an astute analysis of the overlap of political and religious officials in the late Republic, the interplay of religion and politics. It is also an expert orator's estimation of how a group of Roman priests would *wish* to hear their roles defined; as well as, no doubt, a reflection of what a wider readership (of the 'published' version of the speech) would be expected to think an appropriate opening in a speech given to the *pontifices*... All these issues are the subject of this chapter; the formal adjudication of the religious status of Cicero's property is only one aspect of the religion of the late Republic; equally important is how that adjudication is presented and discussed at every level.

Cicero's speech *On his House* is not an isolated survival, a lucky 'one-off' for the historian of late republican religion. A leading political figure of his day, the most famous Roman orator ever, and prolific author – Cicero's writing takes the reader time and again into the immediacy of religious debate and the day-to-day operations of religious business. Another surviving speech, originally delivered to the senate in 56 B.C., deals directly and at length with the response given by the *haruspices* to a strange rumbling noise that had been heard outside Rome, and attempts (once more in conflict with Clodius) to settle a 'correct' interpretation on the enigmatic words of the diviners.[3] And in many others, religious arguments (and arguments about religion) play a crucial part, even if not as the main focus of the speech: Cicero's notorious opponent Verres (one time Roman governor of Sicily, on trial for extortion) is, for example, stridently attacked for fiddling the accounts during a restoration of the temple of Castor in the Roman forum;[4] Pompey, on the other hand, gets Cicero's full backing for a new military command on the grounds that he is particularly favoured by the gods.[5] Outside the public arena of forum or senate-house, Cicero's surviving correspondence (particularly the hundreds of letters to his friend Atticus) gives at some periods an almost daily

2 Cicero, *On his House* 1 = **8.2a**.
3 Below, pp. 137–8.
4 *Against Verres* II. 1.129–54; Steinby (1993–) I.242–5.
5 For example, *On the Command of Pompey* 33 and 36 (Pompey's *divina virtus*, 'god-like or god-given virtue'); 47 (= **9.1c**) and 48 (the benefits from the gods bestowed on Pompey).

115

commentary on all manner of 'religious' news: from the discovery of a case of sacrilege and its upshots, to Cicero's despair at the death of his daughter Tullia and his elaborate plans to build her a 'shrine' (*fanum*) and to achieve her *apotheosis*.[6]

We shall look in more detail in the following sections at many of these examples; but we shall look too at Cicero's theoretical analysis of the religion of his own time. For he was not only a major actor on the political scene and a vivid reporter of day-to-day events (in religion, politics or whatever sphere); he was also the leading philosopher, theologian and theorist of his generation – which was itself the first generation at Rome to develop an analytical critique of Roman customs and traditions. Of course, many Romans from as far back as the foundation of their city must have wondered about the existence or character of the gods, or the reasons for their worship; but it was the late Republic that saw the transformation of that speculation (partly through the influence of Greek philosophy) into written, intellectual *analysis*. Cicero himself wrote carefully argued treatises *On the Nature of the Gods* and *On Divination* (where he put all kinds of Roman divinatory practice, from prodigies to dream interpretation, under a sceptical microscope); and in his book *On the Laws* (inspired by Plato's work of the same name) he even devised an elaborate code of religious rules for an ideal city – not so very different from an idealized Rome. This new tradition of explicit self-reflection is another factor that sets the history of late republican religion apart from earlier centuries.[7]

Cicero's writing dominates the late Republic, and inevitably focusses our attention onto the years from the late 80s to the mid 40s, the period of his surviving speeches, letters and treatises. In most of his arguments (such as that over his house, or on the response of the *haruspices*) the view of 'the other side' is lost to us, except as it is represented (or mis-represented) by Cicero himself. There is, for example, no surviving trace of Clodius' speech to the *pontifices* in which he must have made his counter-claims in favour of the shrine of Liberty; and we have only Cicero's allusions to Clodius' rival interpretation of the haruspical response. So, in what follows, we shall on occasion be prompted to wonder what these religious debates as a whole might have looked like, not just Cicero's side of the argument.

But Cicero, though dominant, is not the only surviving witness of late republican religion; not the only surviving author of the period to define, debate and *write* late republican religion for us. Even without Cicero, the list of relevant contemporary material far outstrips anything we have found in earlier chapters of this book: from Lucretius' philosophical poem *On the Nature of Things* (which attempts to remove death's sting with a materialist

6 Discovery of sacrilege: below, pp. 129–30; the death and shrine of Tullia: (for example) *Letters to Atticus* XII. 12, 18, 19, 20, 36, 41; with Shackleton Bailey (1965–70) Vol. v, 404–13.
7 Below, pp. 150–1.

theory of incessant flux)[8] to Catullus' poem on the self-castration of Attis, the mythical consort of the goddess Magna Mater (whose introduction to Rome was discussed in chapter 2);[9] from the surviving fragments, quoted in later writers, of Varro's great encyclopaedia of the gods and religious institutions of the city (the work of a polymath who outbid even Cicero in antiquarian learning)[10] to two long autobiographical accounts from the pen of the *pontifex maximus* himself (better known as Julius Caesar's *Gallic War* and *Civil War*).[11] It is in all this writing that we can glimpse for the first (and arguably the only) time in Roman history something of the complexity of religion and its representations, the different perspectives, interests, practices and discourses that constitute the religion of Rome.

In the light of this apparent prominence of religious concerns in the writing of the first century B.C., it may come as a surprise that the religion of this period has so often appeared to modern observers to be a classic case of religion 'in decline', neglected or manipulated for 'purely political' ends. If (as we have already seen) intimations of decline have been an undercurrent in the modern accounts of almost every period of republican religious history, here in the first century B.C. those intimations are horribly fulfilled; here the scenario offered us is not merely that of a few sacred chickens unceremoniously dumped overboard, but of whole temples falling down, priesthoods left unfilled, omens and oracles cynically invented for political advantage...[12]

Many factors have worked together to make this grim picture seem plausible. In part, religion has been conscripted into a narrative of *political* decline in the last century of the Republic: over the hundred years of (more or less) civil war from the Gracchi to the assassination of Julius Caesar in 44 B.C., in which rival Roman generals battled it out for control of most of the known world, the traditions of the (free) Republic sank into autocracy; and religion, predictably, sank with the best of them.[13] But there is more underlying the view of religious decline than simply a convenient model of the collapse of republican Rome. One of the reasons that *decline* has entered

---

8   Clay (1983).
9   Catullus 63; below, pp. 164–6.
10   The survival of Varro's encyclopaedia is discussed above, p. 8; also below, pp. 151–2.
11   Little of either of these accounts is concerned with specifically religious issues; but note the *pontifex maximus'* analysis of Gallic religion, *Gallic War* VI.17 = **2.9a.**
12   Sacred chickens as a means of divination: above, p. 22 and n.56. They were the centre of a classic case of religious transgression in 249 B.C., when Publius Claudius Pulcher, exasperated that they would not produce favourable omens, cast them overboard his ship and engaged in a naval battle with the enemy; the moral of the story was, of course, that he lost the battle (Cicero, *On Divination* I.29; *On the Nature of the Gods* II.7; Suetonius, *Tiberius* 2.2). Modern accounts stress the failure of late republican religion: for example, Nock (1934) 468–9; Taylor (1949) 76–97; Dumézil (1970) 526–50.
13   Detailed coverage of the major personalities and events of this period: *CAH* IX²; more briefly, Brunt (1971) 74–147; more briefly still, Beard and Crawford (1985).

the analysis is precisely because several ancient writers themselves chose to characterize the religion of the period in this way. The poet Horace, like other authors writing under the first emperor Augustus, looked back to the final decades of the Republic as an era of religious desolation – at the same time, urging the new generation to restore the temples and, by implication, the religious traditions:

You will expiate the sins of your ancestors, though you do not deserve to, citizen of Rome, until you have rebuilt the temples and the ruined shrines of the gods and the images fouled with black smoke.[14]

And this view of neglect is apparently borne out not only by Augustus' own claim (in his *Achievements*) that he had restored 82 temples in his sixth consulship (28 B.C.) alone, but also by various observations in late republican authors themselves. Varro, for example, explained his religious encyclopaedia as a necessary attempt to rescue from oblivion the most ancient strands of Roman religious tradition – offering a baroque (and grossly self-flattering) comparison of his project with Aeneas' rescue of his household gods from the burning ruins of Troy.[15]

The first two sections of this chapter will explore further the apparent contrast between these two images of Roman religion in the late Republic: on the one hand, its centrality within a wide range of ancient writing, its generation of new, explicitly religious forms of expression in Roman theology and philosophy; on the other, its decline and neglect, as witnessed and lamented by Romans themselves. We will consider, in particular, what kind of comparison is possible between the religious life of the late Republic and earlier (or later) periods; and how we can ever evaluate claims that this (or any) religion is in decline, what it would mean, for example, to *know* that a religious system was demonstrably 'failing' – then or now.

In the second part of the chapter, we will turn to other aspects of the religion of the period: from the involvement of religious practice and conflicts in the political battles of the end of the Republic, through the deification of Julius Caesar, to the changing relations of Roman religion with the growing Roman empire. But through all these discussions we shall attempt to highlight the particular importance of contemporary religious discourse and debate, and the new ways of representing religion that were characteristic of the Ciceronian generation. To be sure, we do not imagine the urban poor or the rural peasants (who made up the vast majority of the Roman citizens at this, as at every, date) participating in the kind of theoretical discussions staged for us by Cicero; those discussions were the pastime of a very few, even among the élite. But it was a pastime that was to change forever the way Roman religion could be understood and discussed by

---

14   *Odes* III.6.1–4; below, p. 181.
15   Augustus, *Achievements* 20.4; Varro, *Divine Antiquities*, fr. 2a (Cardauns), from Augustine, *City of God* VI.2.

Romans themselves. For the revolution of the late Republic was as much intellectual as it was political, as much a revolution of the mind as of the sword; and religion was part of that revolution of the mind.

1. Comparative history?

The controversy around Cicero's house, with which we opened this chapter, reveals some of the problems that face anyone trying to compare the status and 'strength' of religion between, say, the middle and late Republic (between, that is, the periods discussed in this and the last chapter). As we saw, Cicero's speech before the *pontifices* took us right into the middle of religious conflict, into a world of religious rules that were not fixed (or at least were open to challenge), into the inextricable mixture of religious, political and personal enmity. It is a totally different kind of representation of religious business from the brief, ordered, retrospective account of a historian such as Livy, on whom we depend for almost all we think we know of religion in the middle Republic.

The modern observer is faced with (at least) two quite separate possibilities in comparing the Ciceronian-style account of the first century with the Livian style of the third or early second centuries. The first is that in religious terms these two periods really were worlds apart; that by the late Republic the ordered rules of religious practice that typified the earlier years, and are reflected in Livy, had irrevocably broken down into the conflict and dissent of which Cicero's speeches, on this and other occasions, are a significant part. The second is that the apparent difference between the two periods lies essentially in the mode of representation: the difference, in other words, is between the contribution of an engaged participant (Cicero) and the narrative of a distanced annalistic historian (Livy). On this model, if we still had Livy's account of the argument over the consecration of Cicero's house, it would be hard to distinguish from those earlier disputes (between *pontifex maximus* and *flamen*, for example), where Livy gives us just the bare bones of the conflict, the final decision and very little more. And so, conversely, if we still had the words spoken by the different parties in the disputes so tersely related by Livy they would look just as charged, just as personally loaded, just as challenging to the idea of religious consensus as anything spoken by Cicero. Livy himself hints as much when – in recounting the argument of 189 B.C. between the *pontifex maximus* and the *flamen Quirinalis* (who wished to take command of a province, against the will of the *pontifex*) – he briefly mentions 'the vigorous quarrels' in the senate and assembly, 'appeals to the tribunes', the 'anger' of the losing party.[16] Scratch the surface of the Livian narrative, in

16   189 B.C.: Livy XXXVII. 51; cf. a similar dispute in 209 B.C., Livy XXVII.8.4–10 = **8.2d**. The significance of such conflicts is discussed above, with further references: pp. 106–8.

119

other words, and you would find a whole series of speeches very like Cicero's.

Neither of these views is particularly convincing, at least not in an extreme form. Although there clearly is a difference of reporting, and a wholly different *purpose* in the different accounts, we are not dealing simply with a different rhetorical style. It is hard to believe that there was no difference in the character and importance of religious arguments in the two periods; hard to believe that while the Republic lurched to its collapse, it was business as usual in the religious department. If nothing else, the simple fact of the circulation of such speeches as Cicero's, the fact that this kind of religious argument was available to be read outside the meeting at which it was originally delivered, speaks to some difference in religious atmosphere in the last years of the Republic.[17] The problem is, *what* difference? And *how* are we to characterize the complex of similarities and differences that mark the late republican changes?

Some of the same issues are at stake when we come to explore the contrasts between the last decades of the Republic and the early imperial period; and to explore the repeated claims in Augustan literature that the new emperor brought a new religious deal, after the impious neglect that had marked the previous era. It is obviously important to recognize that the Augustan régime was inevitably committed to that view of religious decline and restoration; that, if the traditional axiom that proper piety towards the gods brought Roman success still meant *anything*, then the disasters of the civil wars that finally destroyed the Republic (and Rome too – almost) could only signify impiety and neglect of the gods; and that this predetermined logic of decline says a lot about Augustan self-imaging, but little perhaps about the 'actual' conditions of the late Republic. It is also the case that many of the nostalgic remarks of Cicero and Varro, that appear to confirm the sad state of religion in their own day, may be just that – nostalgia; and nostalgia, as a state of mind, can flourish under the healthiest of régimes. On the other hand, none of these considerations is sufficient to prove the republican decline of religion *merely* an Augustan fiction, or *just* intellectual nostalgia. Varro, for example, supplied a great deal of information about cults and practices that had lapsed by his own time, which he identified (nostalgically maybe) as evidence of decline. Besides, it may be that the nostalgia of the late Republic, the pervading sense (whatever the truth) that religion was somehow in better shape in the past, is one of the most important characteristics that we should be investigating.

The problems in trying to judge this period of religious history against its neighbours, to calibrate its religious strengths and weaknesses, are

17 The custom for leading public figures to preserve and circulate their speeches was established by the end of the second century B.C. Although the ancestor of this tradition was the elder Cato, writing in the early second century B.C., it is a characteristically late republican phenomenon.

almost insurmountable. And it is probably not worth the effort; after all, what would it mean to say, of our own time, that the twentieth century was *less* or *more* pious, *less* or *more* religious, *less* or *more* concerned with theology, than the nineteenth?[18] There is, however, one area where we can test the difference in levels of piety that is proclaimed between the late Republic and what preceded and followed it: temple foundation and repair. We saw in chapter 2 how temple building could be a useful indicator of changing religious preferences among the Roman élite; we now take that discussion of the material setting of religion forward into the late second and first centuries B.C., with some rather different questions in mind. At the same time, we shall be able to see one of the contributions that archaeology can make to our understanding of religious history even in a period that is so well documented by literary texts.

The questions we will be looking to answer are these: what happened to the religious buildings of the city during the late Republic? were ancient temples duly tended and repaired? were new temples founded? how different was the late republican pattern from what had gone before? Once again comparison between Livy and Cicero is central to the issue. Livy records, as we have seen, an impressive series of temple buildings and dedications up to the mid second century B.C. (where his surviving text breaks off).[19] Cicero, from time to time, focusses on a particular crisis surrounding a temple: Verres' supposedly fraudulent restoration of the Temple of Castor, for example, or the accidental destruction of the temple of the Nymphs in street riots in 57 B.C.[20] Otherwise temples only feature prominently again in the Augustan literature that claims the restoration of the dilapidations of the previous generation and vaunts its own lavish temple building schemes (some of which still survive).[21] It is clear from this bald summary how modern observers have come to conclude that the late Republic was a particularly low point in care for the religious buildings of the city – which is itself seen as a significant index for respect for religion more generally. It is also clear, from what we have already said, that there can be no simple comparison between Livy's text on the one hand (with its regular inclusion of information on major religious dedications) and Cicero's writing on the other (where temple matters intrude only when out of the ordinary or

---

18 These problems have not, however, prevented scholars of many periods from attempting such comparisons; a 'classic' study of this kind is Vovelle (1973). But even some of the 'clearest' evidence for religious change allows wildly different interpretations. If, to take a modern example, church attendance falls dramatically over a hundred year period, that could indicate a 'decline' in religion; but it could equally well signal a growing emphasis on private spirituality (outside the formal institutional framework of the church).

19 Above, pp. 69–70; 87–90.

20 Castor: n.4; Nymphs: *On behalf of Milo* 73; *Stoic Paradoxes* 31.

21 Below, pp. 196–201. The remains of Augustus' temple of Mars Ultor and the Ara Pacis: **4.2** and **3**.

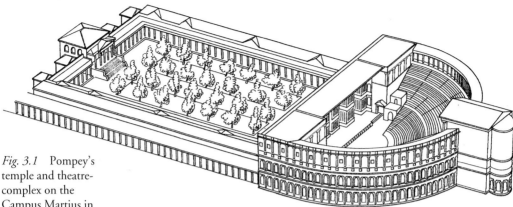

Fig. 3.1 Pompey's temple and theatre-complex on the Campus Martius in Rome (dedicated 55 B.C.), according to one of the many possible reconstructions. The temple of Venus Victrix is on the far right, approached by the stepped auditorium of the theatre; beyond the stage, to the left, a garden surrounded by colonnades. (Map 1 no. 35) (Overall length of the theatre and garden, c. 260m.)

relevant to some oratorical purpose at hand); or between Cicero and the pietistic boasts found in some Augustan writers.[22] But can we go further than that, to show (for example) that the Augustan representation of late republican temple dilapidation – however crucial to Augustan *self*-representation – is, in late republican terms, a *mis*-representation?

For once, we believe that we can – up to a point. A careful search through the casual references (often in later writers) to religious building projects of the period, combined with the surviving evidence of archaeology, can produce a clear enough picture of the regular founding of new temples and the continued maintenance of the old through the last years of the Republic. The great generals of the first century B.C. seem to have followed the pattern of their predecessors in founding (presumably out of the spoils of their victories) new temples in the city.

Pompey (to take just one of these generals) can be credited with at least three foundations: a temple of Hercules (briefly alluded to in Vitruvius' handbook *On Architecture* and Pliny's *Natural History*);[23] a temple of Minerva (also known from a brief discussion by Pliny);[24] and a much more famous temple of Venus Victrix, 'Giver of Victory' (Fig. 3.1).[25] This temple of Venus has often been underrated as a religious building because it was part of a lavish scheme, closely associated with a theatre – as if its real purpose was (or so many modern observers, and ancient Christian polemicists,

22 We are not considering here that even more tricky period between the end of the surviving text of Livy (in 167 B.C.) and the start of the period covered by Cicero's writing. This is well analysed by Coarelli (1977a); though Coarelli does not emphasize the crucial differences between the testimony of Livy and Cicero, and he treats the final period of the Republic as if it were as methodically documented as the period covered by Livy.
23 *On Architecture* III.3.5 (referring to the ornamentation of its pediment); *Natural History* XXXIV. 57 (on a statue of Hercules kept inside it).
24 *Natural History* VII. 97 (explicitly stated to be funded from the spoils of war).
25 For example, Aulus Gellius, *Attic Nights* X.1.6–7; Pliny, *Natural History* VIII.20. Map 1 no. 35.

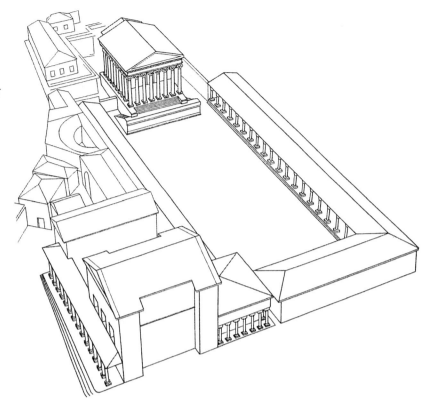

Fig. 3.2 Caesar's Forum (a possible reconstruction). The temple of Venus Genetrix stands at one end of the open piazza. (Map 1 no. 10) (Overall length of temple and forum, c.133m.)

have thought)[26] *merely* to give respectability to a place of popular entertainment. In fact, whatever Pompey's real motives, it fits into a long Italian tradition of just such 'theatre-temples' and is not a smart new invention at all.[27] Caesar too was involved in major religious building. His new forum was centred around a temple of Venus Genetrix ('the Ancestor' – both of the Romans and his own family, the Julii), dedicated in 46 B.C. (Fig. 3.2); and he planned (though did not live to complete) a huge new temple of Mars, which (according to Suetonius) was to be the biggest temple anywhere in the world.[28]

Even outside the circle of the most powerful figures of the period, other foundations by less prominent members of the élite can also be traced. There are, for example, three inscriptions surviving from Rome that mention

26 The classic discussion here is Tertullian, *On the Spectacles* 10.5–6 (below, p. 262); followed by many more recent writers – for example, Veyne (1976) 435. L. Richardson (1992) regards the temple dedication as 'playful' (p.411).

27 See Hanson (1959) (Pompey's theatre: pp. 43–55). The scheme of this whole Pompeian development has been the subject of a number of (imaginative) studies: for example, Coarelli (1971–2); Sauron (1987). For a different reconstruction, L. Richardson (1987). For the temple-cum-theatre at Praeneste, **4.9**.

28 Venus Genetrix: Weinstock (1971) 80–7; Amici (1991); Steinby (1993–) II.306–7; Map 1 no. 10. Mars: Suetonius, *Julius Caesar* 44; Weinstock (1971) 128–32 (discussing the relationship of these plans with Augustan dedications to Mars).

a 'caretaker' (*aedituus*) of the temple of Diana *Planciana*. It seems very likely that the name 'Planciana' refers to the founder of the temple, probably Cnaeus Plancius, who issued coins bearing symbols of Diana in 55 B.C. Plancius was not a leading figure in late-republican Rome; though he was important enough to be elected *aedile* in the mid-50s B.C. and was defended by Cicero (in his speech *For Plancius*) against a charge of electoral corruption.[29]

A very similar picture emerges if we consider the restoration of existing temple buildings. The repair and upkeep of the Capitoline temple of Jupiter Optimus Maximus was clearly prestigious enough to be the object of competition between leading magistrates: for example, in 62 B.C. Julius Caesar as *praetor* tried to remove responsibility for the upkeep from Quintus Lutatius Catulus (and give it to Pompey) on the grounds that he was taking too long over restoration.[30] But other, less illustrious, temples had facelifts too. Cicero, for example, refers in his letters to his own embellishment of the temple of Tellus (Earth);[31] and one of the few thoroughly excavated temples in the city, the temple of Juturna (Temple A, in the site known as the Largo Argentina), appears from the surviving remains to have been extensively refaced in the middle years of the first century B.C.[32]

We have more than enough material then to undermine any strident claims (whether made by ancient or modern authors) that the religious environment of the late Republic was in a state of complete neglect or collapse. We can be confident, at the very least, that those claims are seriously exaggerated; they may even be quite 'wrong'. But this is not the end of our problem. Unless we are to convict the Augustan authors of wilful deception, we shall still be faced with wondering in what sense, *for them,* the claims of religious dilapidation were 'true'. One possibility is that they were (in a limited sense) literally true, but only at the very end of the Republic as a result of the sustained and vicious bout of civil war which followed Caesar's assassination in 44 B.C. It is also possible, however, that they were true only in the sense of the traditional symbolic logic of Roman piety: the proper worship of the gods leads to Roman success; Roman failure stems from the neglect of the gods; the temples of the city must have been

---

29 The inscriptions: *CIL* VI.2210 (=*ILS* 4999); *AE* (1971) 31–2; the coin: Crawford (1974) 455 no. 432 (though Crawford interprets the female head as Macedonia, not Diana, and the symbols of the hunt as a reference to the hunting lands of Crete – both regions where Plancius had held office). For the association of the temple with Plancius (and possible archaeological traces), Panciera (1970–1); (1987) – against C. P. Jones (1976) who would associate it with an early imperial Plancius. Steinby (1993–) II.15.

30 Suetonius, *Julius Caesar* 15. The temple had been destroyed by fire in 83 B.C. There is no reason to suppose (as has sometimes been done – for example, in Nock (1934) 468) that the repairs were seriously unfinished over twenty years later. The temple had, after all, been re-dedicated in 69 B.C. (Livy, *Summaries* XCVIII); and already in 76 B.C. it had apparently been used to house Sibylline Oracles (Lactantius, *On Anger* 22.6, quoting Fenestella) – implying, at the very least, four walls and a roof.

31 Cicero, *To his Brother Quintus* III.1.14.

32 Iacopi (1968–9); Coarelli et al. (1981) 16–18; Map 1 no. 32.

neglected during a period of Roman political failure. But even (or especially) if that is the case, those claims – false or not by other criteria – remain *religious* claims that demand our attention, not dismissal.

Besides, there may be a large gap between the fabric of the religious buildings of the city of Rome and the religious ideology, attitudes and devotion of its citizens. We are well aware from our own experience that there sometimes is, and sometimes is not, a connection between the upkeep of religious buildings and the upkeep of 'faith'; and the connection is equally hazardous for Rome. We can never know what any Roman 'felt', at any period, when he decided to use his wealth to build a temple to a particular god; still less how Romans might have felt when entering, walking past or simply gazing at the religious monuments of their city. If the continued upkeep of temple buildings is, in other words, an index of continuity of *expenditure* on religious display, it is not necessarily an index of continuity of attitude, feeling or experience. As we move on through this chapter to look at different areas of the Roman religious world, we shall keep in mind *what might count* as an index of that experience.

2. Disruption and neglect?

Many of the contemporary, or near contemporary, accounts of religious conflict in the late Republic do suggest extraordinary disruptions in the religious life of the city. Irrespective of any model of development or decline; irrespective, that is, of any suggestion that the situation was *worse* then than in the periods that immediately preceded or followed it; irrespective of the political turmoil that almost inevitably implicated the religious institutions of the state... irrespective of all such considerations, religion in the last decades of the Republic was conspicuously failing, neglected, abused, manipulated, flouted. That at least (as we have already noted) has been the view of many modern commentators.

This section examines two of the major incidents, the *causes célèbres*, of late republican religious 'abuse'. It reveals a set of religious rules, a religious 'system', that is often disrupted during this period; sometimes unable to adapt to all the strange and unprecedented circumstances that it faced; occasionally pushed to the limit of what political advantage might be extracted from it;[33] overloaded, certainly, by the enormous political stakes that were now entailed in almost every public conflict (it was, after all, control of the whole world that Caesar and Pompey fought out in the civil war of the 40s B.C.). But, crucially, neither of these incidents, nor any of the others we might have chosen to highlight, attest an atmosphere in which religious traditions were *simply* violated: we find, for example, no case

33   This is North's formulation: North (1990) 528.

where the formal decision of a college of priests was blithely contravened; no clear case where the proper religious procedures (however problematically defined) were *simply* ignored.

At the same time, this section will pose the question of what constitutes religious *neglect*, as it explores two particular cases of religious traditions that changed or died out during the period. Here we shall meet again the challenge of different points of view, different judgements passed on the same events. So, for example, some observers (ancient or modern) will interpret the disappearance of a particular priesthood, or the neglect of a particular tradition, as an indication of the strength of the religious system overall; it is, after all, only a dead system, a religious fossil, that preserves *all* its traditions, no matter how far circumstances have changed; any living religion discards some of the old, while bringing on the new; in short, it *adapts*. But for other observers the same disappearance, of a ritual (say) carried out for centuries, or of a priesthood that (however quaintly old-fashioned) evoked some of the most hallowed traditions of the city, will mark a crucial stage in Rome's disregard for its gods, its collective amnesia about their worship. The point is, as we shall see, that 'neglect' is always a matter of interpretation; and accusations of neglect almost inevitably appear hand in hand with boasts of adaptation and updating. Both sides of the coin have to be taken seriously.

Bibulus watches the heavens

As consul in 59 B.C., Julius Caesar introduced into the assembly a notoriously controversial piece of legislation to redistribute land to veteran soldiers; the bill was implacably opposed by his colleague in the consulship, Marcus Calpurnius Bibulus. The precise details of the conflict are far from clear. But it seems that at the beginning of the year Bibulus offered objection to Caesar's proposals in the traditional way: he appeared in the Forum and declared to the presiding magistrate that he had seen (or that he would be watching for) evil omens, preventing the progress of legislation.[34] We, of course, do not know what exactly these omens were, or what it would have meant for Bibulus to claim to have *seen* them. But the logic of this kind of procedure (which has an established place in Roman voting and legislation)[35] is clear enough: if the gods support and promote the Roman state

---

34 This is the implication of a rather muddled passage of Suetonius: *Julius Caesar* 20; for the events of Caesar's consulship, see Meier (1995) 204–23.

35 The procedure Bibulus used (or attempted to use), known as *obnuntiatio*, was regulated by the *lex Aelia et Fufia*. For the debate about the exact terms of these laws, and about their reform by Clodius in 58 B.C., above, pp. 109–10. The procedure itself is also obscure in a number of respects: in particular the uncertain boundary between, on the one hand, claiming that you had seen ill omens and, on the other, announcing that you would be watching for them; both seem to have had the effect (in theory, at least) of halting proceedings.

(as they do), then they will make known their opposition to legislation that is against the interests of the state. The snag, of course, is that there could be vastly different views on what legislation is in fact 'good for Rome'.

As the year went on, however, there was more and more rioting and civil disturbance. And Bibulus himself became the object of such violent assaults from partisans of Caesar that he took refuge in his own house; too frightened to go out, perhaps, he simply issued messages that he was watching the sky for omens (*de caelo spectare*). The assemblies went ahead despite these objections and the land bill and other controversial legislation were passed.[36] These laws were to prove vulnerable to all kinds of challenge, on the grounds that their passing had violated religious rules. On one occasion in 58 B.C., according to Cicero, Clodius himself arranged a public meeting (*contio*) with Bibulus and a group of augurs. This was not a formal session of the priestly college, followed by a formal priestly ruling on the problem, but a chance, it seems, for Clodius to put the hypothetical question to the priests: if you *were* to be asked, as priests, if it was legal to conduct an assembly while Bibulus was watching the heavens, what would you say? Cicero claims (but he would...) that the augurs replied that such an assembly would not be legal.[37] In fact, however, no such question was ever formally put to them as a college; and Caesar's legislation remained challenged, but in force.[38]

One way of looking at this incident is as a flagrant example of the heedless flouting of religious rules in the last phase of the Republic: Bibulus had followed traditional procedures (validated by the augurs in their discussion with Clodius), but Caesar and his friends had simply ridden roughshod over them all. Cicero presumably reasoned that way, as have many modern observers – who have seen in this incident a clear case of the absolute domination of religious concerns by factional politics; and blatant disregard for religious obligations where they conflicted with secular ambitions. But this is only one side of the story. Through all the partisan ranting of Cicero in favour of Bibulus' objections, one thing is clear: that the status of Caesar's legislation was, and remained, controversial. Caesar (the *pontifex maximus*) did not, in other words, simply *get away with* total disregard for religious propriety. We need to try to get closer to what might lie at the centre of the controversy.

36 Cicero, *Letters to Atticus* II.16.2; 19.2; 20.4; 21.3–5; with a detailed chronology by Taylor (1951); Shackleton Bailey (1965–70) I. 406–8.

37 *On his House* 39–41. Clodius was particularly implicated in this question, because he (born a patrician) had been adopted into a plebeian family in an assembly chaired by Caesar, while Bibulus was watching the heavens. His election to the tribunate of 58 (and so also all the legislation that he had carried then, including the law that led to Cicero's banishment) would be invalid if his adoption was invalid; for plebeian status was a prerequisite for holding the office of tribune.

38 For other attacks, Cicero, *On the Response of the Haruspices* 48; *On the Consular Provinces* 45–6.

It seems very likely that a question mark hung over the effective status of Bibulus' own actions. He claimed through much of his consulship to be 'watching the heavens', but he did not – as was, we assume, the traditional practice – declare this in person to the presiding magistrate before the assembly took place; instead, he sent a series of runners carrying messages of what he was doing...! Such a procedure could have been seen in at least two completely different ways. On the one hand it must have been argued that, once Bibulus had incarcerated himself at home and started simply to send messages that he was 'watching the heavens', his objections had no validity; for ill omens only constituted proper obstruction to public business if announced in person, on the spot.[39] On the other, it must also have been arguable that, since violence made it impossible for Bibulus to attend the assemblies and follow the standard procedures, the religious objections should stand, however procedurally incorrect. And even some of Caesar's own supporters seem to have taken the line (or so, again, Cicero would have us believe) that the legislation should be re-submitted, this time with all the proper observances.[40]

It is now (and almost certainly would have been then) hard to resolve those two opposing views. That is of course the point. We have no precise idea of the terms that governed the declaration of ill omens, but it seems very likely that, while they may have *assumed* the presence of the objector at the assembly concerned, they did not directly stipulate it.[41] For the conventions of this religious practice had taken shape over a period when the effects of the prolonged urban violence of the last decades of the Republic could hardly have been foreseen; earlier generations, in other words, would not have thought to legislate for an objector who was too scared to go out. If so, it would not have been the case in 59 of not following the religious rules, but of not knowing what were the rules to follow.

All kinds of factors come together to make Bibulus' objections to Caesar's legislation in 59 such a *cause célèbre*. Beyond the accusations and counter-accusations over the uncertainty of the religious rules themselves, there was also the fact that an enormous amount was at stake in any decision; if Bibulus' objections were valid, then the whole legislative programme of Caesar's consulship would have to be annulled (as well as all the legislation passed by Clodius as tribune).[42] It may well have been the republican tradition to *improvise* the religious rules as was necessary, but too

39 Linderski (1965) 425–6; Lintott (1968) 144–5 (with criticisms of his detailed interpretation, Linderski (1986) 2165).

40 *On the Consular Provinces* 46.

41 T. Mitchell (1986) suggests that Clodius' reform of the legislation governing *obnuntiatio* in 58 B.C. amounted to the introduction of a clear statement that the presence of the objector was required at the assembly concerned. Most modern scholars have realised that, despite Cicero's claims, Clodius' legislation did not involve the wholesale abolition of *obnuntiatio*.

42 Above, n. 37.

much was at stake here for that improvisation to work smoothly: the legislative and constitutional chaos that would have followed the annulment of all decisions made in the face of Bibulus' objection is unthinkable. The sheer scale of political business (and its implications) presumably *was* a distinctive feature of the political and religious world of the late Republic. Whether or not it amounts to a proof of a failing religious system depends on your point of view.

The trial of Clodius

A slightly earlier incident of religious conflict provides a second example of these difficulties in *applying* the traditional rules. This was the controversy of 62–61 B.C., after the invasion of ceremonies of the Bona Dea (traditionally restricted to women only) by Cicero's adversary – so it was believed – Publius Clodius Pulcher. This incident was apparently followed immediately by faultlessly correct action: the Vestal Virgins repeated the ritual; the senate asked the Vestals and *pontifices* to investigate, and they judged it to count as sacrilege; the consuls were instructed to frame a bill to institute a formal trial; Julius Caesar (in whose house the ceremonies had taken place) even divorced his wife as a direct result of the scandal.[43] So far, so good; but some of the quarrels and disagreements that were to surround the trial itself again suggest uncertainty in how such a process should be handled, and in the eyes of some, no doubt, a breakdown in the city's ability to control religious disorder.

We should recognize straight away that the act of sacrilege on its own (however outrageous to contemporary observers) is not particularly important for *our* view of late republican religion. It is hard to imagine that there had not *always* been this kind of isolated, high-spirited attack on the traditional conventions of ritual; for no religion anywhere has succeeded in getting everyone to obey all the rules all the time, and most religions (we suspect) have not particularly sought to.[44] Nor is the fact that Clodius was eventually acquitted itself a strong signal of religious failure. For despite the fulminations of Cicero (who, predictably, attributed the acquittal to

---

43 Especially, Cicero, *Letters to Atticus* I.13.3 (= **8.2b**); 14.1–5; 15.1–6. The famous line (quoted by Plutarch, *Caesar* 10.6) that Caesar divorced his wife on the grounds that she 'must be above suspicion' refers to allegations that she had been having an affair with Clodius – hence the prank. Modern debates on the politics of this incident: Balsdon (1951); Tatum (1990). The ritual itself: Versnel (1993) 228–88. The cult of the goddess in general: Brouwer (1989). Note Juvenal's satiric treatment of the women's rites of the Bona Dea: *Satires* 6. 314–41 = **13.4**.

44 In fact (as we implied in the case of the drowning of the sacred chickens, above p. 117, n. 12) telling the story of a few religious misdemeanours (and the dire consequences that normally followed) could be an important weapon in the armoury of religious traditionalism; religious traditions in other words needed to parade a few exemplary rule-breakers and their punishment.

bribery of the jury), very few people could have known – and *we* and Cicero are certainly not among them – whether Clodius was guilty or not. The problems are much more to be located in the squabbles over whether there should be a formal trial at all, and how the jury was to be composed.

Throughout his account of these events in his letters to Atticus, Cicero huffs and puffs – deriding (as he had to[45]) almost every aspect of the procedure, from the mistaken tactics of his own allies to the failure at one stage in the voting proceedings to produce any ballot papers with the option 'yes' on them. At the same time, though, he makes it absolutely clear that the handling of the sacrilege was high on the public agenda, a major focus of debate. Part of this debate may well have been prompted by all kinds of personal enmities and loyalties, by the interests of factional politics; for a conviction on such a charge would certainly have put Clodius' whole career in jeopardy. But this is not at all to suggest that there was widespread acceptance of behaviour that appeared to flout traditional, religious rules; quite the reverse, in fact, if we imagine that Clodius' career really was in danger. The problems lie, rather, in formulating the details of the judicial action, in establishing a procedure for dealing with this particular religious crime – in the context of such ruinously high stakes. Cicero, we should remember, reports no claim that the disruption of the festival didn't matter, or that such religious business was the concern only of a few old grey-beards.

The *flamen Dialis*

For more than seventy years, from 87 or 86 B.C. to 11 B.C., the office of *flamen Dialis*, the ancient priesthood of Jupiter, was left unfilled.[46] Not surprisingly, this has been seen as a classic example of religious neglect. Some ancient authors write in approval of Augustus' appointment of a new priest after the long gap, as one component of his 'revival' of traditional religion.[47] For many modern writers, the lapse in the office has been one of the clearest signs of the Roman élite's lack of interest in religion at this period or, at least, of their shifting priorities: they were, in other words, no longer willing to countenance the inconvenient taboos of this venerable office (particularly when those taboos, as we have seen, could obstruct a full political and military career). All this is true, so far as it goes. Augustus very likely did vaunt his re-appointment of a *flamen Dialis*, as a sign of a new religious deal after decades of neglect; and so it might well have appeared to many observers at

45 His final letter to Atticus on the subject (I.16), written after the trial had taken place, and only in response to a query from Atticus himself (had Cicero shamefacedly kept mum?), is particularly strongly defensive – in ascribing his own side's defeat in a case they should have won to the appalling bribery practised by the opponents.

46 Tacitus, *Annals* III.58. Below, p. 193.

47 For example, Suetonius, *Augustus* 31. As soon as Augustus had taken over the office of *pontifex maximus*, and so had the traditional authority to make a nomination to the post, he seems to have appointed a new *flamen*. For a different view, Bowersock (1990).

the time. No doubt also there were some members of the Roman aristocracy (as we know already from centuries earlier) who found the archaic restrictions on this particular priest more than irksome.[48] None the less, if we examine the circumstances that lie behind the first vacancy in the priesthood in the 80s, we shall find them to be rather more complicated than simple unwillingness to undertake the office; and we shall find the degree of neglect of the *rituals* normally undertaken by the priest much less than is often assumed. In the case of the *flamen Dialis* we can glimpse some of the complex stories that might lie behind any instance of apparent neglect of traditional ritual.

The story starts in the civil wars in the 80s B.C. When Rome was under the control of Cinna and Marius, in 87 or in early 86, the young Julius Caesar was designated as *flamen Dialis*, in succession to Lucius Cornelius Merula, who had committed suicide after the Marian takeover of the city. But before Caesar had been formally inaugurated into the office, Rome had fallen once more to Sulla, who annulled all the enactments and appointments made by his enemies.[49] It is impossible now to reconstruct how the Roman élite viewed the vacant flaminate, or Caesar's status in relation to the priestly office that arguably he already filled. It is impossible to know whether or not Caesar himself was privately relieved to find a convenient way out of a priesthood that would, in due course, almost certainly have conflicted with his political ambitions. But we can see that it was Sulla's action in dismissing Caesar, in the confusion of civil war, that represented the first step in the suspension of the priesthood; not, that is, some general agreement that the office no longer mattered.

The crucial decision, of course, was what should happen to the various rituals usually carried out by the *flamen*: the absence of a priest was one thing, the failure to fulfil the proper rituals of the state was quite another. We have already seen that the peculiar position of the *flamines* as individual priests of their deity could be seen to demand that the rituals assigned to them were carried out by them alone, outside the collegiate structure of the pontifical college (which would normally imply the interchangeability of one priest with another). On the other hand, if you chose to think of the *flamines* as regular members of the pontifical college, it would be clear enough that, in the absence of a *flamen*, his duties could fall to the other *pontifices*. This is, in fact, precisely what Tacitus states, when he puts into the mouth of the *flamen Dialis* of A.D. 22 the claim that, over the long years when the priesthood was unoccupied, the *pontifices* performed the rituals: 'the ceremonies continued without interruption' and even though the office was vacant 'there was no detriment to the rites'.[50] Of course, this particular

---

48 Above, pp. 106–8; the taboos and restrictions are collected by Aulus Gellius, *Attic Nights* X.15.1–25 = **8.1b**.

49 Taylor (1941) 113–16; Leone (1976).

50 *Annals* III.58. We may be dealing here with a historical development by which the independent status of the *flamines* within the pontifical college was gradually weakened;

priest has an axe to grind himself; for these are his arguments in support of his own claim to be allowed out of Italy to hold the governorship of the province of Asia. But, even so, he gives us a further clue as to how the long vacancy in the office *might* have developed. Suppose there was a brief period when there was widespread uncertainty about who was (or was not) the *flamen Dialis;* suppose then (as we have seen was almost certainly the case) the *pontifices* took over the rituals of the vacant priesthood; and suppose this situation carried on, as a temporary measure, for a whole year, for the complete annual cycle of ceremonies normally performed by the *flamen...* Is that not already the makings of a new *system?* Has it not already habituated the Roman élite to a change of roles amongst the priestly hierarchy? Has not the lapse in the tenure of the flaminate been effectively masked?

Yes and no. For some Romans, the performance of the rituals was probably what really counted, the absence of an archaic priest, with a strange pointed hat, much less. For others, the vacancy in an office which (as its odd taboos underlined) represented the most ancient traditions of Roman piety, stretching back as far as you could trace into the mythical origins of the city, must have seemed a clear sign that Rome was disastrously failing in its obligations to the gods. Still others (presumably the vast majority) would never even have noticed the absence.[51] For *us*, however, the circumstances surrounding the lapse in this office (more than the simple fact of the lapse itself) highlight the close interrelationship between the disturbances of civil war and the apparent 'neglect' of religion; as well as the various tactics of *change* and *adaptation* (in this case a growth in the ritual obligations of the *pontifices*) that might accompany such lapses.

The changing ceremony of *evocatio*

Our next example focusses even more strongly on these changes. The geographical expansion of Roman imperial power underlies several of the most striking losses and adaptations in the religious traditions of Rome during the late Republic. Various rituals of war, for example, that originated in the now distant days when Rome was fighting her Italian neighbours were no longer appropriate (and in some cases almost impossible to carry out) when Rome's expansion was far overseas. One of the clearest instances of this is the ritual of the fetial priests on the declaration of war. It had been traditional fetial practice to proceed to the border of Rome's territory and to hurl a ritual spear across into the enemy's land: a first symbolic mark of the

---

so that they became (like the other *pontifices*) increasingly interchangeable in their priestly duties.

51 We should more correctly say that all of these attitudes could be (and no doubt were) held by one and the same individual: sometimes they regretted the absence of a *flamen Dialis,* sometimes they entirely accepted the pontifical role in the ritual duties – but mostly they didn't give much thought to it.

coming war. But when Rome's enemies were no longer her neighbours, but lived hundreds of miles away overseas, that particular ritual became practically impossible to carry out – short of packing the priests off on a boat, and waiting maybe months for them to make the journey. Instead the ritual was retained in a new form: a piece of land in Rome itself, near the temple of Bellona, was designated (by legal fiction) 'enemy ground' and it was into this that the priests threw their spears. Whether this was a case of lazy sophistry, conscientious adaptation to new circumstances or imaginative creativity, the ritual continued to be carried out – but in a new form.[52]

The ritual of *evocatio* undergoes a similar, but more complex, change. As we have seen, the tradition here was that the Roman commander should press home his advantage in war by offering to the patron deity of the enemy a better temple and better worship in Rome, if he or she were to desert their home city and come over onto the Roman side. The best recorded occasion of this practice was the *evocatio* of the goddess Juno, patron of Veii, who deserted the Veians for the Romans in 396 (thus ensuring Rome's victory), and who was worshipped thereafter at Rome with a famous temple on the Aventine Hill.[53] It has often been thought that this practice had entirely died out at Rome by the late Republic. For the temple of Vortumnus (founded in 264 B.C.) is the last temple in the city clearly to owe its origin to this particular ritual; for whatever happened at the evocation of Juno from Carthage in 146 B.C. (even if we do not bracket it off as an antiquarian fantasy), there is no evidence that it resulted in the building of a new temple for the goddess in Rome.[54] But an inscription discovered in Asia Minor suggests that the practice did not die out; rather, it was performed differently.

This inscription was discovered, on a building block, at the site of the city of Isaura Vetus, taken by the Romans in 75 B.C. It refers to the defeat of the city and to the fulfilment of a 'vow' of the Roman commander, echoing in its language some of the formulae used (as other, literary, accounts suggest) in the ceremony of *evocatio*. The most plausible explanation is that this inscribed stone comes from a temple dedicated by the Roman general to the patron deity of Isaura Vetus, who had been 'called out' of the town in the traditional way; but that on this occasion the temple offered to the deity was not in Rome itself, but on provincial territory.[55]

This is just one piece of evidence, fragmentary at that. But it may allow us to construct a different account of the late republican history of this ritual: not

---

52 Servius, *On Virgil's Aeneid* IX.52 = **5.5d**. The precise chronology of the changes, disuse and revival of the fetial rituals is unclear; Rich (1976) 56–60, 104–7. For a more sceptical view, suggesting that this reform of the ritual was an invented piece of archaism on the part of Octavian (in the civil wars following the assassination of Julius Caesar), Rüpke (1990) 105–7, below, p. 194 n. 98. Early fetial rituals: above, pp. 26–7.

53 Livy V.21.1–7 = **2.6a**; above, pp. 34–5.

54 Above, p. 111.

55 *AE* (1977) 816 = **10.3b**; see A. Hall (1973); Le Gall (1976).

that it entirely died out, but that the location of the promised temple changed. If this is the case, it could be seen as a relaxation, a 'watering down', of the traditional religious obligations of the ritual. But it could also be seen in the context of changing definitions of 'Roman-ness', of what counted as 'Roman'. Whereas in the early Republic to offer a rival deity a *Roman* home meant precisely offering a temple in the city itself, at the end of the Republic by contrast, imperial expansion, and the changing Roman horizons that went with it, meant that provincial territory could now be deemed *Roman* enough to stand for Rome. We may be dealing then with one feature (of which we shall see more later) of Roman religious adaptation to a vastly expanded empire.

The disruption of religion in the late Republic will continue to baffle its modern observers, as (no doubt) it baffled ancient observers too. It is not difficult to spot all kinds of 'impieties' and 'failures', or to be struck by the outrage of Cicero at some of the events he witnessed, by the irresolvable conflicts that threatened those whose business it was to handle Roman relations with the gods smoothly. But, not surprisingly (and appropriately enough), it is far less easy to *evaluate* or *generalize*. We have already emphasised, in discussing the four incidents that we have chosen in this section, how different interpretations follow from different points of view, and different starting points; how the same incident can be seen as outright neglect *and* constructive adaptation, cynical self-seeking *and* uncertain fumbling after the proper religious course of action. The same would be true if we were to look in any detail at any of the other particular *causes célèbres* we have not examined here: from accusations of forging oracles to priestly 'manipulation' of the calendar.[56]

Paradoxically, though, one thing does seem to be clear through this extraordinary array of different views, interpretations and debates: namely that religion remained throughout this period a central concern of the Roman governing class, even if principally as a focus of their conflicts. There was, in other words, a consensus that religion belonged high up on the public agenda. In the next section we shall explore this consensus further, as we look more closely at the role of religion within public, political debate from the late second century onwards.

3. The politics of religion

As part of Roman public life, religion was (and always had been) a part of the political struggles and disagreements in the city. Disputes that were, in our terms, concerned with political power and control, were in Rome necessarily associated with rival claims to religious expertise and with rival claims to privileged access to the gods. That was the view of Livy, for example, who –

---

56 Accusation of forgery: Cicero, *Letters to Friends* I.4.2. Cicero's own attempt to influence the decision of the *pontifices* on intercalation: *Letters to Atticus* V.9.2.

from his early imperial standpoint – perceived the political struggles of the early Republic partly in terms of struggles against patrician monopoly of religious knowledge and of access to the divine. In the final stages of his account of 'The Struggle of the Orders', he gives a vivid picture of the passing of the *lex Ogulnia* in 300 B.C., the law which gave plebeians designated places in the pontifical and augural colleges. The patricians, according to Livy, saw such a law as a contamination of religious rites, and so liable to bring disaster on the state; the plebeians regarded it as the necessary culmination of the inroads they had already made into magisterial and military office-holding.[57] It would have made no sense in Roman terms to have claimed rights to political power without also claiming rights to religious authority and expertise.

The struggles of the late Republic and the ever intensifying political competition provide even clearer testimony of the inevitable religious dimension within political controversy at Rome. It was not just a question of arguments being framed (as we shall see clearly later) in terms of the will of the gods, or of divine approval manifest for this or that course of action. As political debate came to focus, in part at least, on the opposition between *optimates* and *populares* – on the clash, that is, between those who voiced the interests of the traditional governing class and those who claimed to speak for, and were in turn backed by, the people at large – religious debate too seems to have become increasingly concerned with issues of control between aristocracy and people: with attacks on the stranglehold of the *optimates* over priestly office-holding and with attempts to locate religious (along with political) authority more firmly in the hands of the people as a whole. The historian Sallust, for example, who interprets the conflicts of the late Republic very much in these terms, puts into the mouth of Caius Memmius (tribune 111 B.C.) a virulent attack on the dominance of the nobles, who

walk in grandeur before the eyes <of the people>, some flaunting their priesthoods and consulships, others their triumphs, just as if these were honours and not stolen goods.[58]

The juxtaposition of 'priesthoods' and 'consulships' here is not an accident. Those who resented what they saw as the illicit monopoly of power by a narrow group of nobles would necessarily assert the people's right of control over both religious and political office, over dealings with the gods as well as with men.

One of the clearest cases of the assertion (and rejection) of popular control over religion is found in the series of laws governing the choice of priests for the four major priestly colleges. As we have seen in earlier chapters, the traditional means of recruiting priests to most of the colleges was

---

57 Livy X.6.1 – 9.2; above, pp. 64, 68, 99. Patrician monopoly had never been quite so clear cut as the later tradition tries to make it; above, pp. 63–7.
58 *Jugurthine War* 31.10.

co-optation: on the death of a serving priest, his colleagues in the college themselves selected his replacement (on what principles, we do not know). It was only in the case of the choice of the *pontifex maximus* from among the members of the pontifical college that a limited form of popular election had been practised, since the third century B.C.[59] The process of co-optation had been first formally challenged (so far as we know) in 145 B.C., when Caius Licinius Crassus introduced a bill to replace the traditional system with popular election.[60] That bill, as we saw in chapter 2, was defeated; but a similar proposal introduced in 104 B.C. by Cnaeus Domitius Ahenobarbus (consul 96) succeeded: the priests of the four major colleges (*pontifices, augures, decemviri* and *triumviri*) retained the right to nominate candidates for their priesthoods, but the choice between the candidates nominated was put in the hands of a special popular assembly, formed by 17 out of the 35 Roman voting tribes – the method of election already used for the *pontifex maximus*. The priests themselves no longer had complete control over the membership of their colleges.

Roman writers offer various interpretations of this measure. Suetonius, in particular, stresses the personal motives of Domitius: having himself failed to be co-opted into the pontifical college, he proceeded out of pique to reform the method of entry.[61] We cannot judge the truth of such allegations; and, indeed, all kinds of personal or narrowly political motives may have lain behind Domitius' proposal. But the details of the law itself suggest that a delicate compromise between the interests of the people and the traditional priestly groups may have been at work here. On the one hand, the electoral assembly was (as we have noted) already used in a priestly context; while the definition of that body as being just less than half of the normal popular assembly (seventeen out of the thirty-five tribes) suggests that here, as with the election of the *pontifex maximus,* there might have been some compunction about asserting outright popular control over priestly business. It was also the case that the college could exclude any candidate of whom they did not, for whatever reason, approve. On the other hand, the requirement that each member of the college should make a nomination for election, and that no more than two priests could nominate the same candidate, looks like an attempt to ensure that the assembly had a *real* choice, that the college could not fix the election in advance. However guarded, this reform clearly represents a political and religious challenge to the dominance of the traditional élite, a claim for popular control over the full range of state offices.[62]

59 See above, p. 68, where we connect the introduction of this electoral process with the roughly contemporary *lex Ogulnia*.
60 Above, p. 109.
61 *Nero* 1.1; in a similar vein, Asconius, *Commentary on Cicero's On Behalf of Scaurus* p.21 (Clark), with Scheid (1981) 124–5, 168–71.
62 For the challenge to élite dominance and full background to the reforms, Rawson (1974); North (1990).

The regulations for priestly elections remained a live issue for years. Domitius' law was repealed by the dictator Sulla, as part of his re-assertion of traditional senatorial control; but it was later re-enacted in 63 B.C. by the tribune Labienus – in the last of the series of laws which undid the various controversial aspects of Sulla's reforms, after his retirement. Labienus was a well-known radical and at that time a friend of Julius Caesar; support for the 'popular cause' inevitably involved support for popular control of human relations with the gods.[63]

Another challenge to traditional religious authority can be detected in the events of 114–113 B.C., when a number of Vestal Virgins were declared guilty of unchastity and put to death (as was the rule) by burial alive in an underground chamber. The story starts in 114, when the daughter of a Roman equestrian had been struck dead by lightning, while riding on horseback; she was found with her tongue out and her dress pulled up to her waist. This was declared a prodigy and interpreted by the Etruscan *haruspices* as an indication of a scandal involving virgins and knights. As a result, in December 114, according to traditional practice, three Vestal Virgins were tried for unchastity before the pontifical college; one of them was found guilty and sentenced to death. In reaction to the acquittal of the other two Vestals, Sextus Peducaeus, tribune of 113 B.C., carried a bill through the popular assembly to institute a new trial – this time with jurors of equestrian rank and a specially appointed prosecutor, the ex-consul Lucius Cassius Longinus. This new trial resulted in a death sentence for the other two Vestals.[64] The traditional competence of the *pontifices* to preserve correct relations with the gods had been called into question, while the power of the people to control the behaviour of public religious officials had been asserted.

On other occasions rival claims by individual politicians to privileged access to the gods provided the focus of political debate: a man could demonstrate the correctness of his own political stance by showing that he, rather than his political opponent, was acting in accordance with divine will. This was clearly the case in 56 B.C., when Cicero and Clodius engaged in public debate over the interpretation of a prodigy – Cicero's speech *On the Response of the Haruspices* (as we have already mentioned) representing one side of the argument. The haruspical response to the strange noise that had been heard on lands outside Rome had alluded to various causes of divine anger with the city: the pollution of games (*ludi*); the profanation of

63 Cassius Dio XXXVII.37.1–2. For an example of the role of influence, favour and patronage in the nomination and election of new priests, see Cicero, *Letters to Brutus* I.7 = **8.2c** (Cicero as *augur* being urged to nominate the stepson of a friend to a vacant position in the college).

64 Livy, *Summaries* 63; Obsequens 37; Asconius, *Commentary on Cicero's On behalf of Milo* pp. 45–6 (Clark); Plutarch, *Roman Questions* 83 = **6.6b**; see also Rawson (1974) 207–8; Cornell (1981) 28; Fraschetti (1984). This incident was also linked with the burial alive of a pair of Gauls and Greeks; above, pp. 80–2.

sacred places; the killing of orators; neglected oaths; ancient and secret rituals performed improperly.[65] Yet (no doubt following the traditional pattern of such responses) much still remained unclear and unspecific, in need of further interpretation and debate.

In the arguments that followed Clodius and Cicero offered their own quite different interpretations of what the *haruspices* had actually meant, item by item. Clodius, for example, claimed (rather convincingly, we are tempted to suggest – despite Cicero's scorn) that the 'profanation of sacred places' was a reference to Cicero's destruction of the shrine of Liberty. Cicero himself, on the other hand, in his surviving speech, related 'the pollution of games' to Clodius' disruption of the Megalesian Games (held in honour of Magna Mater) and claimed that the 'ancient and secret rituals performed improperly' were the rituals of the Bona Dea, reputedly invaded by Clodius a few years earlier.[66] Much of this debate was clearly a series of opportunistic appeals to a conveniently vague haruspical response; a crafty exploitation of religious forms at the (political) expense of a rival. But at the centre of the argument – what they were arguing *about* – was a priestly interpretation of a sign sent by the gods. When both Clodius and Cicero claimed as correct their own, partisan, interpretation of the prodigy, each was effectively attempting to establish his own position as the privileged interpreter of the will of the gods. Divine allegiance was important for the Roman politician. In the turbulent politics of the mid 50s, it must inevitably have been less clear than ever before where that allegiance lay. Connections with the gods (as well as the alienation of the divine from one's rivals) had to be constantly paraded and re-paraded.

Underlying these apparently deep divisions over the control of religion and access to the favour of the gods, there was (as we noted at the end of the last section) a striking *consensus* of religious ideology. Cicero's speeches offer a clear instance of this. Loaded, partisan, aggressively one-sided – they were the most successful works of political rhetoric that the Roman world had ever known, constantly admired and imitated. In speech after speech, Cicero enlists the support of his listeners (and later his readers) with appeals to the gods and to the shared traditions of Roman religion and myth. In the first of his speeches against Catiline, for example, delivered in 63 B.C. to the senate (meeting in the temple of Jupiter Stator on the lower slopes of the Palatine), part of his persuasion of the wavering senators draws on the traditions of the particular temple in which they are assembled. He not only evokes Jupiter 'the Stayer' ('who holds the Romans firm in battle' – or 'who stops them from running for it...'), but interweaves allusions to the mythi-

65 Cicero, *On the Response of the Haruspices*, with a reconstructed text of the response itself, 7.4a. For the *haruspices* in general, see above, pp. 19–20; on the particular circumstances of this speech, Lenaghan (1969).

66 *On the Response of the Haruspices* 9, 22–29, 37–39. The exaggeration of Cicero's claims: Lenaghan (1969) 114–17; Wiseman (1974) 159–69.

cal foundation of the temple, vowed by Romulus in the heat of his battles with the Sabines. He offers, in other words, a mythical model for the kind of threat he claims the city faces from Catiline, and by implication presents himself as a new founder of Rome. Privately, many senators may have been irritated, disbelieving or amused by these claims; but it seems clear enough that Roman *public* discourse found one of its strongest rallying cries in such appeals to the city's religious traditions.[67]

But this public religious consensus is important too in the conflicts and disagreements of late republican politics; it is not just a feature of grand Ciceronian appeals to 'unity' in the state. Crucially, there is no sign in any Roman political debate that any public figure ever openly rejected the traditional framework for understanding the gods' relations with humankind. Political argument consisted in large part of accusations that 'the other side' had neglected their proper duty to the gods, or had flouted divine law. It was a competition (in our terms) about how, and by whom, access to the gods was to be controlled — not about rival claims on the importance or existence of the divine. So far as we can tell, no radical political stance brought with it a fundamental challenge to the traditional assumptions of how the gods operated in the world. There were, to be sure, as there always had been, individual cults and individual deities that were invested (for various reasons) with a particular popular resonance. The temple of Ceres, for example, as we have seen, had special 'plebeian' associations from the early Republic; likewise the cult of the Lares Compitales (at local shrines throughout the regions (*vici*) of the city) was a centre of religious and social life for, particularly, slaves and poor (and was later to be developed by Augustus precisely for its popular associations); while Clodius' dedication of his shrine to Liberty on the site of Cicero's house no doubt had, as must have been the intention, a popular appeal.[68] There were always likely to be choices and preferences of this kind in any polytheism. But if these cults did act as a focus for an entirely different view of man's relations with gods, no evidence has survived to suggest it.

The particular quarrels between Clodius and Cicero well illustrate the religious consensus that operated even (or especially) in disagreement.

---

67 For example, *Against Catiline* I. 11, 33; Vasaly (1993) 40–87. In choosing this *senatorial* speech as an example of religious rhetoric, we are effectively questioning the common view that, while Cicero loads his speeches to the (easily impressed and superstitious) people with divine appeals, in speaking to the (sophisticated and sceptical) senate he keeps the gods off the agenda. As Vasaly shows, this is simply wrong. For further discussion of the importance of place and location in Roman religion, below, pp. 173–4 and ch. 4 *passim*.

68 Ceres: above, pp. 65–6. Clodius and Libertas: Allen (1944); Gallini (1962) 267–9. The popular character of the Compitalia and the local Lares, and the relations between these associations and professional *collegia*: Accame (1942); Lintott (1968) 77–83; Flambard (1977); and (for specifically Augustan developments) below, pp. 184–6, and **8.6a** (an altar of the Lares Augusti).

These battles are known, as we have already remarked, almost entirely from the side of Cicero, who constantly characterized Clodius as 'the enemy of the gods' – whether for the invasion of the rites of the Bona Dea, or the 'destruction' of the auspices (in his reforms of the rules for *obnuntiatio* in 58 B.C.). The truth that may lie behind any of these allegations is now impossible to assess (and in many cases always was). More important is the fact that Clodius appears to have returned in kind what were, after all, quite traditional accusations of divine disfavour. As we have seen from Cicero's defence in his speech *On the Response of the Haruspices,* Clodius did not disregard or even ridicule Cicero's religious rhetoric; he did not stand outside the system and laugh at its silly conventions. He turned the tables, and within the same religious framework as his opponent, he claimed the allegiance of the gods for himself, and their enmity for Cicero. It was similar with other radical politicians. Saturninus (tribune in 103 and 100 B.C.), for example, protected his contentious legislation by demanding an oath of observance (*sanctio*) sworn by the central civic deities of Jupiter and the Penates in front of the temple of Castor in the Forum;[69] and Catiline kept a silver eagle in a shrine in his house, as if taking over for his uprising the symbolic protection of the eagle traditionally kept in the official shrine of a legionary camp.[70] The question, then, was not *whether* the gods were perceived to co-operate with the political leaders of Rome; but with *which* political leaders was their favour placed?

But this raises yet another question, which we will turn to consider in the next section: quite how *close* is the co-operation of men and gods, quite how easy is it to draw a distinction between the divine and the human?

4. Divus Julius: becoming a god?

The honours granted to Julius Caesar immediately before his assassination suggest that he had been accorded the status of a god – or something very like it: he had, for example, the right to have a priest (*flamen*) of his cult, to adorn his house with a pediment (as if it were a temple) and to place his own image in formal processions of images of the gods. Shortly after his death, he was given other marks of divine status: altars, sacrifices, a temple and in 42 B.C. a formal decree of deification, making him *divus* Julius. Ever since the moment they were granted, these honours – particularly those

---

69 Appian, *Civil Wars* I.29–31 refers in general terms to an oath applied to Saturninus' land law. *FIRA* I.6 (the *Lex Latina Tabulae Bantinae*) is a fragmentary inscribed text of what is almost certainly one of Saturninus' laws, with the oath in front of the temple of Castor prescribed in section 3; Crawford (1996) I.193–208 (with text and translation of all that survives).

70 Cicero, *Against Catiline* I.9.24. This eagle was, in fact, even more symbolically loaded: it had been one of the legionary standards on Marius' campaign against the Germans (Sallust, *The War against Catiline* 59.3).

granted before his death – have been the focus of debate. If you ask the question 'Had Caesar officially become a Roman god, or not, before his death? Was he, or was he not, a deity?' you will not find a clear answer. Predictably, both Roman writers and modern scholars offer different and often contradictory views.[71] Some speak stridently for, some stridently against, his manifest divinity; taken together they attest only the impossibility of fixing a precise category for Caesar, whether divine or human.[72]

It is, nevertheless, certain enough that the honours granted to him before the Ides of March 44 B.C. likened him in various respects to the gods, assimilated him to divine status. That assimilation itself could be understood in different ways: both as an outrageously new, foreign, element within the political and religious horizons of the Roman élite, and as a form of honour which had strong traditional roots in Roman conceptions of deity and of relations between political leaders and the gods. On the one hand, that is, particular inspiration for various of Caesar's divine symbols may well have been drawn from the East, and the cult repertoire of the Hellenistic kings; the public celebrations on Caesar's birthday, for example, and the renaming of a calendar month and an electoral tribe in his honour have clear precedents in the honours paid to certain Hellenistic monarchs.[73] On the other hand, some aspects of Caesar's divine status are comprehensible as the developments of existing trends in Roman religious ideology and practice. The boundary between gods and men was never as rigidly defined in Roman paganism as it is supposed to be in modern Judaeo-Christian traditions. Even if, as we have seen, the mythic world of Rome was more sparsely populated than its Greek equivalent with such intermediate categories between gods and men as 'nymphs' and 'heroes', it did incorporate men, such as Romulus, who *became* gods; the Roman ritual of triumph involved the impersonation of a god by the successful general; and in the Roman cult of the dead, past members of the community shared in some degree of divinity.[74] There was no sharp polarity, but a spectrum between the human and the divine. Throughout the late Republic the

71 How could they not? you might ask. What would it *mean* to be certain on such an issue – before, or for that matter after, Caesar's death? Contemporary invective against Caesar's honours: Cicero, *Philippic* II.110–11 = **9.2a** (delivered in 44 B.C.); this speech, with its apparently detailed knowledge of Caesar's cult, suggests that the 'programme' for deification was well worked out and well known months before the formal decree in 42 B.C. For coins of Octavian (the future emperor Augustus) illustrating his descent from *divus* Julius, **9.2b (iii)** and **(iv)**.

72 The classic study here is Weinstock (1971) – which should be read with North (1975); note also Taylor (1931) 58–77; Vogt (1953); Ehrenberg (1964); Gesche (1968), with full earlier bibliography in Dobesch (1966).

73 Cassius Dio XLIV.4.4 (with Weinstock (1971) 206–9); XLIV.5.2 (with Weinstock (1971) 152–62). Some scholars have also seen the traditions of Etruscan/Roman kingship in the honours paid to Caesar, for example Kraft (1952–3).

74 Romulus and other mythic examples of deification: above, p. 31; the triumph: pp. 44–5; the cult of the dead: p. 31.

status of the successful politician veered increasingly towards the divine end of that spectrum. Caesar, in some senses, represented a culmination of this trend.

Rome's political and military leaders had always enjoyed close relations with the gods. The logic of much of the display and debate discussed in earlier sections of this chapter (and in earlier chapters) was that magistrates and gods worked in cooperation to ensure the well-being of Rome; that the success of the state depended on the common purpose of its human and divine leaders. But there is another side to that logic: successful action, political or military, necessarily brought men into close association with the gods. So, as we have seen, in the ceremony of triumph the victorious general literally put on the clothes of Jupiter Optimus Maximus: in celebration of the victories that had been won through his cooperation with the gods, he slipped into the god's shoes.[75]

But it was not as simple as that bare summary might suggest. The parade of any *association* between gods and men inevitably raised all kinds of questions: just how close was the association, for example, and how permanent? quite how literally was it to be taken? The story of the slave at the triumph constantly reminding the general *that he was a man* (not a god), offers its own clear antidote to the outright *identification* of man and god that might be implied by some of the ceremony itself: for those who chose to hear them, the slave's words effectively stated that this was a general *dressed up as* Jupiter, acting, playing a part, not a general *to be identified with,* indistinguishable from, his divine model. Besides, even if for some the identification of man and god went closer than that, the triumph was by definition a temporary state; if the general stepped into Jupiter's shoes, it was just for a day.[76] Much the same was true for office-holding itself in the practice of the early and middle Republic. Magistracies and military commands were, by definition, temporary – held according to traditional practice for just a year at a time; if they brought their holders into proximity with the gods (even if not the extreme proximity reserved for the triumph), that proximity did not last long.

The late Republic set a new pattern of dominance, breaking with those earlier conventions. As the great political leaders of the age increasingly managed, by the repetition and extension of offices and by series of special commands, to exercise power at Rome for long periods, in some cases almost continuously, so they came to claim *long term* association with the gods. Sometimes adopting the symbolism of the triumph, sometimes using other marks of proximity to the divine, they displayed themselves (or were treated by others) as favourites of the gods, as *like* the gods, or ultimately as gods outright. So, at least, one version of the background to Caesar's deification would run.

75 Above, pp. 44–5.
76 And in any case it was on the way to being faced down on the Capitol by the real thing.

Already by the late third or early second century B.C. there are clear hints of the divine elevation of powerful political and military figures. We have already seen, for example, the close association that Scipio Africanus claimed (or was accused of claiming) with Jupiter Optimus Maximus.[77] A little later Aemilius Paullus, after his victory over the Macedonian king Perseus at Pydna in 168 B.C., is said to have been granted not only a triumph, but also the right to wear triumphal dress at all Circus games.[78] We should think very carefully about what this honour was, and what it might signify. Paullus was allowed to dress in the costume of Jupiter, with purple cloak and crown, and reddened face just like the statue – and so to appear at these regular public (and religious) gatherings of huge numbers of the Roman people. Maybe the fancy dress would have gone unnoticed; or maybe many of the participants would have been struck (impressed, outraged...) by the presence of their general-as-Jupiter. But, however it was perceived, this honour for Paullus must represent an important break with the temporary honorific status conferred by the traditional triumphal ceremony – extending its association of man and god beyond the moment of the ceremony itself. It was to be an honour granted again to Pompey in 63 B.C.[79] and later, with even further extensions, to Caesar: the dictator was allowed to wear such costume on all public occasions.[80]

The leading political figures of the last decades of the Republic displayed (or were popularly granted) other marks of assimilation to the gods. This never amounted to a 'formal' decree of recognition *as a god* (like that granted to Caesar after his death, when he became officially *divus* Julius); but nevertheless the distinctions between some of the leading figures in the state and the gods were increasingly blurred. The political dominance of Marius, for example, seven times consul and triumphant victor over the renegade African king, Jugurtha, and over the Germans, was matched by his religious elevation. Not only did he go so far as to enter the senate in his triumphal dress – a display of religious and political dominance amongst other members of the élite from which he was forced to draw back; but after his victory over the German invaders he was promised, by the grateful people so it is said, offerings of food and libations *along with the gods*.[81] This kind of outburst of popular support for a favoured political

---

77 See above, pp. 84–6.
78 <Aurelius Victor> *On Famous Men* 56.5. A tenuous precedent for the extension of one element of triumphal honours may be found in the example of Caius Duilius (consul 260 B.C.), who (it was reputed), following a great naval victory, was granted the privilege of returning home after all public banquets accompanied by music and torchlight, as after a triumph; see <Aurelius Victor> *On Famous Men* 38.4; Valerius Maximus, *Memorable Deeds and Sayings* III.6.4; Florus I.18.10.
79 Cassius Dio XXXVII.21.4; Velleius Paterculus, *History of Rome* II.40.4 (stating that he only used the honour once); Cicero, *Letters to Atticus* I.18.6.
80 Cassius Dio XLIII.43.1; Appian, *Civil Wars* II.106.442.
81 Plutarch, *Marius* 27.9; Valerius Maximus, *Memorable Deeds and Sayings* VIII.15.7.

leader was no doubt temporary and informal (to the extent that it was sanctioned by no official law or decree); it also had earlier precedents – in, for example, the brothers Gracchi, who had received some sort of cult after their deaths at the places where each had been killed.[82] But Marius seems to have set a pattern of cult for the living. Fifteen years later, in 86 B.C., the *praetor* Marius Gratidianus issued a popular edict, reasserting the traditional value of the Roman *denarius*, and was rewarded 'with statues erected in every street, before which incense and candles were burned'. It may be significant that Cicero connects these divine honours with the independent action of Gratidianus in issuing the edict in his own name, without reference to his colleagues – so directly linking divine status with (claims to) political dominance.[83]

Association with the gods could also be seen in the form of the protection or favour that a politician might claim from an individual deity. Venus, in particular, ancestor of the family of Aeneas (and so by extension of the whole Roman people) became prominent in the careers of several leading men of the first century B.C. Such divine protection was in itself a relatively modest claim (compared with some of the honours we have just been considering). But this parade of divine favour developed, particularly in the hands of Pompey and Caesar, into a competitive display of ever closer connections with the goddess.

At the beginning of the first century B.C. Sulla, the dictator, claimed the protection of Venus in Italy and of her Greek 'equivalent', Aphrodite, in the East. He advertised this association not only on coins minted under his authority, but also in his temple foundations and in his dedication of an axe at Aphrodite's great sanctuary at Aphrodisias in Asia Minor – apparently following the goddess' appearance to him in a dream. But Sulla's titles too incorporated his claims to her divine favour. In the Greek world he was regularly styled Lucius Cornelius Sulla *Epaphroditus*, and in the West he took the name *Felix* as an extra *cognomen* – a title which indicated good fortune brought by the gods, in this case almost certainly by Venus.[84]

Pompey followed suit – as it seems from the coins bearing images of Venus issued by his supporters, and from the dedications of his own lavish building schemes. As we have seen, his enormous theatre-temple in Rome was centred on a shrine of Venus Victrix (through whose aid, we are to assume, Pompey had won his victories); and a slightly later shrine in the same building complex was dedicated to Felicitas, a clear echo of Sulla's title

82 Plutarch, *Caius Gracchus* 18.2.
83 Cicero, *On Duties* III.80; also Pliny, *Natural History* XXXIII.132. The cult of Gratidianus was presumably at the local shrines of the *vici*; above, p. 139, below, p. 185.
84 Plutarch, *Sulla* 19.9; 34.4–5 = **9.1b (i)**; Appian, *Civil War* I.97 – with Schilling (1954) 272–95; Champeaux (1982–87) II.216–36. For a discordant view (that Sulla's associations were with the Greek Aphrodite rather than the Roman Venus) and a bibliography of earlier work, Balsdon (1951).

Felix. It is as if Pompey was taking over from the memory of Sulla the particular patronage of Venus, divine ancestress of the Roman race. The degree of outright rivalry between the two men that is implied by this is glimpsed in an anecdote from early in Pompey's career, still in the period of the dominance of Sulla. Pompey is said to have wanted to ride into Rome for his triumph on a chariot drawn by four elephants; as this was a vehicle particularly associated with Venus, it was effectively an attempt to upstage Sulla and his divine associations.[85]

Caesar, of course, could outbid both Sulla and Pompey. For him, Venus was more than a patron goddess; she was the ancestress of the family of Aeneas, from which his own family of the Julii traced their line. Caesar, in other words, could claim to be a direct descendant of the goddess herself. He himself made a point of this already in 68 B.C., in his funeral oration for his aunt Julia, celebrating her divine ancestry from Venus. And later, as we have seen, when he embarked on the grand development of a new and lavish forum (no doubt itself a calculated bid to rival the building schemes of Pompey), he dedicated *his* temple to Venus *Genetrix* (the ancestor). The significance of this would have been clear for those who chose to think of it: while Pompey and others could claim the support of Venus as the forbear of the Roman race as a whole, Caesar could and did parade her as the particular ancestress of his own family.[86] It is a significance highlighted in another anecdote told of Pompey – this time dreaming, before his final battle with Caesar at Pharsalus, of spoils decorating his temple of Venus Victrix. According to Plutarch, 'on some accounts he was encouraged, but on others depressed, by the dream. He feared lest the race of Caesar, which went back to Venus, was to receive glory and splendour through him.'[87]

But even before Caesar himself had drawn directly on the repertoire of divine honours granted to Hellenistic kings in the Greek world, Rome's expansion in the Eastern Mediterranean brought with it another context in which leading Romans became closely associated with the gods. From at least the second century B.C., there is a small body of evidence to show individual Roman generals and governors receiving various forms of divine honours from Eastern cities – presumably on the pattern of the honours they had granted their pre-Roman rulers. From the point of view of the cities concerned, this practice may well have been part of their strategy of

---

85 Coins: Crawford (1974) p. 448 no. 424; p. 449 no. 426.3. Theatre-temple: above pp. 122–3, with (for *Felicitas*) Degrassi (1963) 191 (*Fasti Amiternini*, 12 Aug.) and Weinstock (1971) 93 and 114; note also Cicero's stress on *felicitas* in his speech *On the Command of Pompey* (for example, 47 = **9.1c**), Champeaux (1982–7) II.236–59. The triumph: Plutarch, *Pompey* 14 – in fact, the team of elephants proved too big to get through the city gates, so the plan had to be dropped.

86 Funeral speech: Suetonius, *Julius Caesar* 6. Coins celebrating his connections with Venus: **9.2b(i)** – **(iii)**. The scheme as a whole, above, p. 123.

87 Plutarch, *Pompey* 68.2–3.

Fig. 3.3 A fragment of a frieze from the temple of Venus Genetrix showing Cupids playing with a washing bowl, a scabbard and a shield. The armour alludes to the god Mars and to the story of his love affair with Venus. Like most of the visible remains of this temple, the frieze dates from a restoration of the early second century A.D. – though the original decoration must also have featured the goddess and her myth. (Height of block, 1.45m.; length, 1.92m.)

'fitting the Romans in' to their own familiar system of power and honours.[88] From the point of view of the generals thus honoured, the granting of such divine status might have seemed either an outrageous form of impious flattery from a conquered people, to be tolerated only in the interests of provincial control; or, on the other hand, a confirmation of the traditional Roman association between political leadership and the divine – as well as an opportunity to explore more lavish and explicit forms of cult away from the gaze of their peers in Rome. Probably their reaction took in all three.

The earliest and one of the most vivid examples concerns honours given to Titus Quinctius Flamininus (the consul of 198 B.C. and upholder of the 'freedom' of Greece against the claims of Philip V of Macedon). Plutarch describes the rituals at Chalcis in his honour that were still performed three hundred years later – sacrifices, libations, a hymn of praise, as well as the appointment of his own priest. He even quotes the last lines of the hymn: '...we revere the trusty Romans, cherished by our solemn vows. Sing, maidens, to Zeus the great, to Rome and Titus, with the trusty Romans. Hail Paean Apollo. Hail Titus our saviour.'[89] And we can find evidence for other such honours later in the Republic, even if they were not always so long-lasting: a priest and sacrifices for Manius Aquilius, who established the

88 Price (1984) 42–7,
89 Plutarch, *Flamininus* 16.3–4. On some occasions these lines must have been sung, by some participants at least, with as much irony as reverence; the 'trusty Romans' scarcely able to avoid becoming a joke. For other honours to Flamininus, in other cities, Weinstock (1971) 289; inscriptions translated in Sherk (1984) no. 6.

Roman organization of the province of Asia in the 120s B.C.;[90] a festival (the *Mucia*) in honour of Quintus Mucius Scaevola, *proconsul* of Asia in 97 B.C.;[91] temples voted to Cicero (though refused by him) on more than one occasion in the East.[92]

By far the most striking array of divine honours, however, were those offered to Pompey during his major commands in the East. A month was renamed after him at Mytilene; he had a cult on the island of Delos, with cult officials, *Pompeiastai*, recorded in inscriptions; he was honoured as 'saviour' at Samos and Mytilene; it is also possible that temples were actually built to house his cult.[93] Plutarch also suggests that his divinity was part of the street-talk of Greek graffiti, quoting a line scratched on an Athenian wall, apparently addressed to Pompey: 'The more you know you're a man, the more you become a god'. Plutarch hazards no guess at how Pompey took this message, when he saw it; but we will surely spot its double edge, as well as its allusion to the language of the triumphal ceremony: 'remember you're a man'.[94]

These honours for Pompey far outstrip, in their closeness to specifically religious cult, any that we know he was offered (or claimed) at Rome. Whatever these eastern honours entailed, with whatever enthusiasm, or sense of obligation, they were performed (and the bare references in inscriptions give us almost no clue on that), they contrast markedly with the *relatively* traditionalist image Pompey seems to have had in Italy itself. How important that distinction was, between West and East, is much less clear to determine. It would, for example, be impossibly neat to imagine that Pompey's divine status, enjoyed and exploited in Greece, was shed instantly he touched Italian soil. All the same, one way of understanding the novelty of Caesar's divine status is as a novelty of place: Caesar, that is, finally brought *to Rome* a degree of outright identification with the gods that his rival had attained (or dared to assume, perhaps) only in the East – out of range of the constraining gaze of his peers.[95]

90 *IGR* IV.293. col. ii, 20–6; with Magie (1950) 153–4, 157–8.
91 Cicero, *Against Verres* II.2.51; W. Dittenberger- K. Purgold, *Die Inschriften von Olympia* (1896) no. 327; *IGR* IV 188 (trans. Sherk (1984) no. 58); Magie (1950) 173–4, 1064.
92 *Letters to his Brother Quintus* I.1.26; *Letters to Atticus* V.21.7. But note the honorific statues, in their own *exedra*, given to various members of Cicero's family at Samos: Dörner and Gruber (1953).
93 The month at Mytilene: *IG* XII.2.589 (l. 18); Robert (1969) 49, n.8. *Pompeiastai*: *SIG*³ 749A. 'Saviour': *SIG*³ 749B, 751 (trans. Sherk (1984) no. 75). The only evidence for temples comes from the line allegedly uttered over (or perhaps inscribed on) Pompey's tomb by the emperor Hadrian: 'how mean a tomb for one so overladen with temples!' (Appian, *Civil War* II.86; Cassius Dio LXIX.11.1). See also Tuchelt (1979) 105–12 and Price (1984) 46, who argue against there being cult places for Roman magistrates.
94 Plutarch, *Pompey* 27.
95 Weinstock (1971) explores throughout the Pompeian precedents for Caesar's divine honours; the model of Caesar as 'Pompey in Rome' is also clearly suggested by Crawford (1976).

Every narrative of Roman apotheosis tells, at the same time, a story of uncertainty, challenge, debate and mixed motives. It would be naive to suppose that leading Romans saw divine honours simply and solely as a reflection and extension of the traditional links between gods and magistrates. Many, or most, must have enjoyed the prospect of being treated like a god (at the same time, no doubt, as feeling uncomfortable about such a display of excess); many must have perceived the advantage over their rivals that divine honours would bring, and have planned (or solicited) yet further marks of divine status. It would be likewise naive to imagine that those offering divine honours did not on some occasions calculate that the offer would redound to their own benefit. There was an advantage in *your* community (rather than the town thirty miles down the road) being the one that presented the Roman governor with a series of sacrifices and a grandiose temple. Nor should we imagine that, even in the Greek world, there were no objections to offers of divine honours to Roman generals. The very fact that the evidence for these divine honours is so patchy, particularly in the decades immediately following Flamininus, in the early and mid second century, may suggest that such honours were not actually common. And that, in turn, may suggest that it was not at first generally accepted that these temporary Roman commanders, turning up for a short-term stint of power, *did* fit into the model of the earlier Hellenistic kings and their divine power.[96]

Deification is not, then, just *our* problem. Roman religion, as we have seen, constructed the boundary between humans and the gods very differently from most modern world religions; and that must have made a difference to the ways most people would have understood (or accepted) what seems to us an extraordinary, impossible status transition: *becoming* a god. On the other hand, many of the puzzlements and problems we find were shared by Romans too: did honours equal to those given to the gods mean that the recipient was no different from a god like Jupiter or Mars? what actually happened at the moment of deification? and so on.[97]

These debates and conflicts are highlighted for us clearly in the different versions told in the first century B.C., and later, of the myth of Romulus' death and apotheosis. Romulus could provide a mythic model for the final, and official, deification of Caesar, as *divus* Julius, after his assassination in 44 B.C. Rome's founder, so one version of the story went, simply disappeared at

---

96 Nor may the granting of divine honours to individual Romans have been generally acceptable to the senate; below, p. 160.

97 For explicit recognition of these and many other bafflements of apotheosis, Seneca's *Pumpkinification of Claudius* (almost certainly written just after – and in reaction to – the deification of the emperor Claudius) is the classic text; for a satiric treatment of the mechanisms of decision-making that lay behind apotheosis, for example, see *Pumpkinification* 9 = **9.2c**. But Cicero's theology also broaches some of these issues; for example, *On the Nature of the Gods* III.49–50, where the problem of the status of a god who started life as a human is explicitly raised.

his death: he vanished in a cloud. Then, shortly after, he made known to the world his new divine status, as the god Quirinus – appearing to announce the fact to a Roman called (appropriately enough) Proculus *Julius*. Rome's founder, so the myth says, joined the gods, witnessed by an ancestor of the very next man who would receive official apotheosis, temple and cult in Rome: a story spread wide by partisans of Caesar. But significantly, almost every time that this story is told by Roman writers, it is challenged by dis-cordant versions that are told along with it: Proculus Julius may just have been 'put up' by the senators, who wished to deflect any suggestion that they had murdered the king; or indeed the king really was murdered, and 'disappeared' by being cut up into tiny pieces and hidden in the senators' togas...[98] These mythic variants are not just a cunning subversion of Caesar's divinity, reasserting his bloody death over any claims to godhead. More generally, the telling and re-telling of this complicated and conflicting *set* of myths opens up each time the uncertainty of any human claim to be, or to have become, a god – or, for that matter to have witnessed that 'becoming'. It asserts deifi-cation as a process that involves fraud *and* piety, tradition *and* contrived nov-elty, political advantage *and* religious truth: for the Romans, as for us.

5. Religious differentiation: scepticism, expertise and magic

One of the ways to understand the varied and complex processes of change that characterized the late Republic, in almost every sphere of life, is to think in terms of 'structural *differentiation*'. As Roman society became more complex, many areas of activity that had previously remained unde-fined (or at least deeply embedded in traditional social and family groups) developed – for the first time as far as we can tell – a separate identity, with specific rules, claiming relative autonomy from other activities and institu-tions. Rhetoric, for example, became a specialized skill, professionally taught, not an accomplishment picked up at home or by practice in the Forum; likewise the institutions of criminal and civil law witnessed the development of legal experts, men who had made themselves knowledge-able in the law and carefully distinguished their skill from that of advocates and orators.[99] The stages and causes of these developments are complex to reconstruct. The relative impact of the internal changes within Rome itself, versus the effect of growing Roman contact with the already highly differ-entiated world of some of the Greek states, is hard to evaluate. The conse-quences are nevertheless clear: by the end of the Republic a range of new and specialized activities existed; and, with those activities, new forms of discourse and intellectual expertise.

98 Cicero, *On the State* II.20; Livy I.16 = **2.8a**; Dionysius of Halicarnassus, *Roman Antiquities* II.56; Plutarch, *Romulus* 27–8.
99 Hopkins (1978) 76–80; Rawson (1985) 143–55.

Religion is the area in which this particular model of change is most helpful. Traditionally religion was deeply embedded in the political institutions of Rome: the political élite were at the same time those who controlled human relations with the gods; the senate, more than any other single institution, was the central locus of 'religious' and 'political' power. In many respects this remained as true at the end of the Republic as it had been two or three centuries earlier. But, at the same time, we can trace – at least over the last century B.C. – the beginning of a progression towards the isolation of 'religion' as an autonomous area of human activity, with its own rules, its own technical and professional discourse. In this section, we shall look at two particular aspects of this process: first, the development of a theoretical (sometimes sceptical) discourse of religion, together with the emergence of religious experts and enthusiasts; and second, the development of more sharply defined boundaries between different types of religious experience: between the licit and the illicit, between religion and magic.

The philosophical treatises of Cicero are (as we noted at the very beginning of this chapter) the earliest surviving works in Latin to develop theoretical arguments, sceptical of the established traditions of Roman religion. One of the most engaging of these treatises is the dialogue *On Divination*, written during 44 and 43 B.C., whose second book includes an extended attack (in the mouth of Cicero the augur himself) on the validity of Roman augury, the significance of portents and dreams, and the agreed interpretation of oracles. In a spirited, and sometimes witty, attack, all manner of ridicule is poured on the gullible – who believe, for example, that cocks crowing before a battle may portend victory for one side or the other; or that if a sacrificial victim is found to have no heart, disaster inevitably looms. The 'rational' philosopher in Cicero has good sport, arguing that cocks crow too often for it to be significant of anything at all; or that it would be simply impossible for any animal ever to have lived without a heart.[100] No element of Roman divination escapes this ruthless scrutiny.

The fact that Cicero could construct these sceptical arguments does not necessarily indicate that he himself held such views; nor that they were common among the Roman élite of his day. In fact, the second sceptical book of *On Divination* is preceded and balanced by a first book, which draws on Greek Stoic philosophy to present the arguments (put into the mouth of Cicero's brother Quintus) *in favour* of traditional practices of divination.[101] But even if Cicero himself *was* personally committed to an out and out sceptical position, it is not the most important aspect of this or any of his other theological studies. Much more significant is the fact that this

---

100 For example, *On Divination* II.36–7 = **13.2b** (the impossibility of an animal living without a heart); II.56 (the insignificance of cocks crowing).
101 For example, I.118–19 = **13.2a** (the absence of a heart signalling disaster); I.74 (the significance of cocks crowing).

kind of theoretical argument about traditional practice had begun to be framed *at all.* The philosophical definition and *defence* of traditional Roman piety that we see throughout Cicero's work are just as important in the history of Roman religious ideas as the development of a particular strand of *sceptical* inquiry, which has often been given more attention. Both developments indicate a religion that was becoming an area of interest, identifiable as separate and thus the object of scrutiny, of scepticism and defence.[102]

This differentiation of religion was certainly associated with increasing Roman familiarity with Greek philosophy. Contact with the philosophical traditions of the Greek world did, as we saw in chapter 2, stretch back considerably further than the mid first century B.C. As early as the beginning of the second century, Ennius, the great epic poet of the Republic, had produced a Latin translation of Euhemerus' work on the human origins of the gods, of which a few paragraphs from a prose version survive; and we have reference to (though no surviving trace of) a number of treatises from the end of the second century B.C. and later, which were probably expositions in Latin of Greek philosophical doctrines.[103] It is, of course, impossible to judge writing that no longer survives. But from Cicero's claims, at least, it would seem that his own treatises (and the philosophical work of his contemporaries) were crucially different in kind from their predecessors; and that it was only at the very end of the Republic that Greek theory came to be deployed on specifically *Roman* problems and practice, defining and differentiating new areas of recognizably *Roman* discourse. This was the first period, in other words, that Roman philosophy was more than translation from the Greek; the first period to define 'religion' through (and as part of) such intellectual theorizing.[104]

Antiquarian enquiry and the emergence of specifically religious historians is another aspect of the process of differentiation. Even if this material

---

102   Beard (1986); Schofield (1986). For a different perspective, stressing the outright scepticism of *On Divination,* Linderski (1982); Momigliano (1984); Timpanaro (1988).

103   Roman philosophical experts: for example, Spurius Mummius (mid second century B.C.): Cicero, *Brutus* 94; Publius Rutilius Rufus (consul 105 B.C.): *Brutus* 114; *On the Orator* I.227; Titus Albucius (*praetor* c.105 B.C.): *Brutus* 131. For Latin treatises, note the work of Amafinius (? early first century B.C.): *Tusculan Disputations* IV.6; Rabirius: *Academica* (second edition) I.5; Catius: *Letters to Friends* XV.16.1; 19.1. Though perhaps Cicero had a tendency to exaggerate the extent of earlier Roman philosophical activity, in order to give a pedigree to his own work (which some contemporaries clearly saw as un-Roman activity). For Ennius, above, p. 78.

104   The point is that the development of theory and the definition of 'religion' are integral parts of the same process; they go hand in hand; one does not precede the other; Beard (1986) 36–41. One possible earlier case of a Roman philosophical writer explicitly considering Roman practice is Mucius Scaevola (consul 95 B.C.) whose remarks on state religion are quoted by Augustine (*The City of God* IV.27; the theme is continued at VI.5 = **13.9**). It seems likely, however, that Augustine is quoting the words not of

now survives only in 'fragments' quoted by later Roman writers, there is enough to highlight the cultural investment in religious expertise and religious curiosity that distinguished the late Republic from earlier periods of Roman history. By far the most comprehensive of the antiquarian treatises on Roman religion was Varro's great encyclopaedia, *Divine and Human Antiquities*, which devoted sixteen (of its forty-one) volumes to the gods and religious institutions of the city. From the quotations that are preserved (notably in Augustine's *The City of God*) we can gain some idea of its structure and content. It was clearly a work of rigorous *classification*, dividing its subject into five principal sections (priesthoods, holy places, festivals, rites and gods) and offering within those sections yet finer distinctions on types of deity and institution: shrines (*sacella*), for example, were treated separately from temples (*aedes sacrae*); gods specifically concerned with human beings (presiding over birth or marriage) were placed in a separate category from those concerned with food or clothing. But the *Antiquities* was also a work of *compilation*, assembling often recondite information on traditional Roman religion: the reason for the particular type of headdress worn by the *flamen Dialis;* the significance of the festival of the Lupercalia; the precise difference in responsibility between the god Liber and the goddess Ceres.[105]

Other works along these lines are known, although they do not now survive even to the extent of Varro's, nor did they originally reach such vast lengths. Nigidius Figulus (*praetor* in 58 B.C.) was perhaps Varro's closest precursor, with a work *On the Gods* in at least nineteen books, as well as treatises on divination and haruspicy, dreams and astrology.[106] But among other writers were Granius Flaccus who dedicated to Julius Caesar a work *De Indigitamentis* (*On Forms of Address*), which discussed the formulae used by the *pontifices* in addressing the gods; and Aulus Caecina, another contemporary of Cicero and Caesar, and a man with distinguished Etruscan forebears, produced a Latin version of the Etruscan science of thunderbolts and their religious interpretation.[107] There was also apparently something of an industry in writing on augury and the augural college. Cicero himself wrote one such treatise (in addition to his *On Divination*), and another was dedicated to him. This was written by Appius Claudius Pulcher, the consul of 54 B.C., who was such a passionate defender of augury that he was nicknamed

the 'real' Scaevola, but of Scaevola as a character in a dialogue of Cicero's contemporary Varro; Cardauns (1960). Others, however, have felt more inclined to accept the quoted words as words of the 'real' man (see Rawson (1985) 299–300). Different views on the character and significance of this early Roman philosophy: Rawson (1985) 282–316; Brunt (1989).

105 Cardauns (1976). Antiquarian information: fr. 51 (headdress), from Aulus Gellius *Attic Nights* X.15.32; fr. 76 (Lupercalia), from Varro, *On the Latin Language* VI.13; fr. 260 (Liber and Ceres), from Augustine, *City of God* VII.16.

106 Rawson (1985) 309–12. Surviving fragments of his work are edited in a collection by A. Swoboda (1889, repr. 1964); with a brilliant parody in Lucan (I.639–72).

107 The surviving fragments of Granius: Funaioli (1907) 429–35. Caecina: Rawson (1985) 304–5.

the 'Pisidian' (after the people of Pisidia in Asia Minor, renowned for their own devotion to augury). Appius Claudius was also representative of the new breed of religious 'enthusiast'; not only was he an augur himself, but he also endowed new building works at the famous Greek sanctuary at Eleusis, as well as making a point of going to consult the Delphic oracle.[108]

These works are almost certainly a new phenomenon of the latest phase of the Republic. Of course, we have seen that writing had long been associated with Roman religion: the *pontifices* and *augures* had, for example, long kept records within their own colleges of ritual prescriptions and various aspects of religious law; we have also noted the constructive 'revivals' of religious rituals in the mid second century, apparently based on priestly antiquarian enquiry.[109] The late republican works were, however, quite different from writing of that kind; for (even when written by priests themselves) they were not part of internal priestly discourse *within* religion or directly related to ritual performance; they were commentaries *on* religion from an external standpoint. Unlike the so-called 'priestly books' of rules, formulae and precedents, they existed at a distance from traditional religious practice, defining religion as an object of scholarly interest, an object of *knowledge*. This is not to suggest that what Varro, and the others, wrote was not itself 'religious'. To construct religion as the object of scholarly curiosity, whose traditions and rules could be investigated and preserved by a process of scholarly enquiry, was inevitably to change the way religion could be perceived and understood. Varro was himself contributing to the history of religious thought as much as he was commenting on that history. And in fact his great encyclopaedia was to become, almost from the moment he wrote it, a work of even greater symbolic authority than the priests' own books – 'as Varro says' being a legitimating Roman catchphrase for almost any claim (bogus or not) about the history, traditions and theology of state religion.[110]

One of the religious 'interests' of Appius Claudius Pulcher was, supposedly, necromancy; according to Cicero, he called up the spirits of the dead, presumably (given his enthusiasms) to entice prophecy out of them.[111] Another of his contemporaries, Nigidius Figulus, was even more renowned for his devotion to magic and astrology, alongside (as we have seen) an

108 Late republican works on augury in general: Rawson (1985) 302. Appius Claudius: Cicero, *On Divination* I.105; *Letters to Atticus* VI.1.26; 6.2; Valerius Maximus, *Memorable Deeds and Sayings* I.10; *ILLRP* 401. Appius Claudius was by no means the only Roman to explore traditional Greek religion: late republican Roman initiates at Eleusis include Sulla (Plutarch, *Sulla* 26.1); also Clinton (1989). Inscriptions commemorating the initiations of Romans into the mysteries of Samothrace: Fraser (1960) nos. 28a, 30, 32 (translations in Sherk (1984) no. 27); but Roman interest in the Samothracian gods (sometimes said to be the ancestors of the Roman Penates) may be a very special case (see Price (1998) ch. 8).

109 Above, pp. 9–10; 25–6; 110–13. Below, p. 181 on the imperial period.

110 For example, Seneca, *Pumpkinification of Claudius* 8.

111 *On Divination* I.132; *Tusculan Disputations* I.37.

equally enthusiastic commitment to traditional divination, both Roman and Etruscan.[112] This takes us into another area of differentiation of religion in the late Republic: that is, the construction of increasingly sharp boundaries between different types of religious activity, between 'proper' religion and its illicit (or marginal) variants. In part the development of these boundaries reflects the growing diversity of religious practice, the increasingly wide range of options in human relations with the gods, that came to be distinguished more clearly one from another over the late decades of the Republic; but to an equal, if not greater, extent, it was a consequence of a new desire to categorize, ever more subtly, the varieties of religious experience that had long been part of the Roman world. In the late Republic, in other words, we begin for the first time to hear of practices designated as 'magical'. Many of these practices had, in fact, been part of religious activity at Rome as far back as you could trace; what was new was precisely their designation as 'magical', and the definition of magic as a separate category.[113]

Definitions of 'magic' have always been debated. There have been many ambitious modern attempts to offer a definition that applies equally well across all cultures and all historical periods; we shall discuss some of these in chapter 5. But it is worth emphasizing now that many of these attempted definitions miss the point. It is not just a question of different societies understanding magical practice in all kinds of different ways, offering different explanations and theories of how magic originated and developed, and disagreeing about what in their own world is to count as 'magical', rather than (say) 'religious'. It is rather that (despite modern attempts to generalize across cultures and despite the claims of some self-styled 'magicians' to be deploying a universal skill) 'magic' is not a single category at all; but a term applied to a set of operations whose rules conflict with the prevailing rules of religion, science or logic of the society concerned. And so, for the historian, the interest of what we may choose to call 'magic' lies in how that conflict is defined, what particular practices are perceived as breaking the rules, and how that perception changes over time.

The development of the concept of magic (or 'the magical arts') at Rome is, in detail, very obscure; but we can trace some broad outlines. From the early and middle Republic there is plenty of evidence for what *we* would understand as magical practice – and for its prohibition. Cato's treatise *On Agriculture*, for example, written around 160 B.C., includes a clear example of what is in our terms a magical remedy for healing sprains and fractures: 'Whatever the fracture, it will be cured with this charm: Take a green reed four or five foot long and split it down the middle, and have two men hold it on your hips. Start to chant, *motas vaeta daries dardares astataries dissunapiter...*';[114] and the fifth-century B.C. legal code, *The*

---

112 Servius, *On Virgil's Aeneid* X.175; Rawson (1985) 309–10.
113 A general overview: Garosi (1976); North (1980); Graf (1994); below, pp. 233–6.
114 *On Agriculture* 160. As usual with such charms, all kinds of half-sense are buried in this

Twelve Tables, contains the clause that 'no one should enchant another man's crops'.[115] But it is much less clear that, in contemporary Roman terms, we are dealing here with the specific category of 'magic' or with prohibitions directed at 'magical' practices as such. Cato appears to have seen the healing charm no differently from other remedies (that we might call 'practical' or 'scientific') suggested in his work; and the legal prohibition in *The Twelve Tables* seems to have been directed principally at the results of the action (that is, damage to another man's property), rather than against the method by which that damage was brought about. It was not until the late Republic (and then only tentatively) that magic began to be defined as a particular and perverted form of religion.

The earliest extended Roman account of the magical arts that survives is part of the Elder Pliny's *Natural History*, his vast encyclopaedia of the whole natural world, finished in the 70s A.D. Here he attempts to trace the spread of magical practice (originating in Persia and moving through Greece and Italy) and to define magic in relation to science and religion. He refers, for example, to the bestial quality of magic (men sacrificing men, or drinking human blood) and to its characteristic use of spells, charms and incantations – consistently opposing magic to the 'normal' rules of human behaviour and the traditions of Roman religion.[116] We shall consider Pliny's account in greater detail in a later chapter.[117] At this point we want to ask only how far it is possible to trace any such attempts at a formal definition of 'magic' back into the late Republic.

There is no surviving work from a late republican author that attempts, like Pliny's *Natural History*, a synoptic account of magic.[118] Yet there are allusions that do seem to foreshadow some of the elements of Pliny's theories in a range of writers of the mid first century B.C. Catullus, for example, abuses one of his favourite targets, Gellius, by saying that a magician (*magus*) will be the result of his incest with his mother, alluding at the same time to the Persian origin of magic.[119] Cicero, likewise abusing his opponent Vatinius, charges him with just the kind of activities characterized by Pliny as 'magical'. Under the cloak of so-called 'Pythagoreanism', Cicero claims, Vatinius indulged in calling up spirits and sacrificing young human victims to the gods below: a sign of the flouting of traditional religious norms that Cicero makes parallel to Vatinius' disregard for augury and the

---

nonsense formula. The final word, for example, is reminiscent both of *Jupiter* and of any compound of *dis –* (splitting) *apart.*

115 Pliny, *Natural History* XXVIII.17–18; Seneca, *Natural Enquiries* IV.7.2; Crawford (1996) II.682–84.

116 Pliny's account of the historical development of magic: *Natural History* XXX.1–18 (part = **11.3**); but magic is an important theme throughout Books XXVIII and XXX (see, for example, XXVIII.4–5; 19–21). See also Köves-Zulauf (1978) 256–66.

117 See below, p. 219.

118 The most likely candidate to have written one is Nigidius Figulus.

119 Catullus 90.

auspices.[120] This is, of course, all very different from any systematic account of magical practice; and its abusive rhetoric tells us almost nothing about the actual behaviour of its targets, or how they themselves would have defined their actions. All the same, the overlaps with Pliny are striking – and they suggest that the late Republic did witness the beginning of the process that was to define magic quite specifically as something outside, or in opposition to, the proper religious norms of Rome. That 'magic' could be used as a cliché of abuse is an important piece of evidence in any attempt to chart the history of that category.

All kinds of factors no doubt contributed to the development of a formal category of magic. Foreign influences, as in philosophy and theology, no doubt played some part. In particular, the convenient view that the origin of magic lay somehow outside the civilized world (in barbarian Persia) may well have derived from Greek definitions of magic and Greek polemic against the Persians.[121] But as with the other themes discussed in this section, the underlying context lies in Roman society itself and increasing complexity of Roman culture and intellectual life. The same processes, in other words, that fostered a definition of 'religion' as an autonomous area of human activity also fostered a definition of religion's 'anti-types'.

6.   Rome and the outside world

Almost every section of this chapter has touched on the religious consequences of the growth of Rome's empire: the change in the traditional fetial ritual for declaring war; religious honour paid to Roman generals in the East; the effect of growing contact with Greek philosophy on the development of religious discourse at Rome. This final section will consider directly two aspects of religious change in the context of the expanding empire: first, Rome's export of some of its own religious forms to the outside world; second, the place of 'foreign' religions in Rome itself, in this last period of the Republic. The chapter will close by looking at a painting and a poem from that period, both of which throw light on the complexity of (and the complexity of our interpretations of) the religious world of the first century, its 'foreign' cults, and its cult groups.

Roman religion belonged in Rome. As we shall emphasize in the following chapters, it was closely tied by its rituals and myths to the city itself; and its deities, priests and ceremonies were not systematically exported to conquered territories (just as, for the most part, 'native' religious traditions continued under Roman domination).[122] Nonetheless Roman power influenced the religion of Italian and provincial territories, while Roman

120   *Against Vatinius* 14.
121   Pliny, *Natural History* XXX.3–11, with Garosi (1976) 30–1; see also the extracts at **11.3**.
122   Below, pp. 339–48.

imperialism was in part expressed through the development of religious institutions in the provinces. In this sense, by the late Republic, religion that was recognizably 'Roman' in some senses could be found elsewhere than in Rome itself.

The clearest instance of the direct export of Roman religious forms can be seen in the establishment and regulation of religious practices in the *coloniae* of Roman citizens, founded for the settlement of military veterans and the poor in Italy and sometimes (at least from the late second century B.C.) in provincial territory. We shall consider the religious life of *coloniae* more fully in chapter 7; for the moment it is enough to stress that these communities, in theory at least, mirrored the religious institutions of Rome itself. Not only were they founded according to a religious ritual modelled on that which Romulus was supposed to have used in the foundation of Rome: the auspices were taken and the founder ploughed a furrow round the site to mark its sacred boundary (replicating the *pomerium* of Rome).[123] But also some central features of their religious organization were copied directly from that of the parent city. This is well illustrated by the charter of foundation that survives for Julius Caesar's *colonia* at Urso in Southern Spain, laying out in detail the constitution of the new city.[124] Several clauses in this charter make regulations for the selection and service of the civic priests, *pontifices* and *augures*; these clearly drew on the rules and privileges of the Roman priests of the same name, and even directly referred to the religious practice of Rome in framing some of their terms: 'Let these *pontifices* and *augures*...be guaranteed freedom from military service and compulsory obligations in the same way as a *pontifex* is and shall be in Rome.'[125] Rome's export of a new community, in other words, might involve a self-conscious replication of Roman religious forms outside Rome.

But the export of Roman religious practice, especially to the Greek world, often entailed a more complex process than the deliberate and direct replication of Roman cult abroad. The spread of Roman dominance led provincial communities – directly encouraged by Rome or not – to adopt (or adapt) various 'Roman' rites and religious institutions. Some of these were drawn directly from Roman religion itself; others were significantly different from anything found at Rome, but were nevertheless defined explicitly in terms of Roman power.

Various developments show the cities of the Greek world using for the first time elements of specifically Roman religious and mythic symbolism. An inscription from the island of Chios, for example, provides an unusually clear illustration of how Roman myth might be incorporated into a

---

123 Below, pp. 328–9.
124 The charter is known from a late first century A.D. copy of the original regulations. The significance of this copy and other aspects of the regulations: below, p. 328.
125 *ILS* 6087, section 66 (= **10.2a**); for a discussion and translation of the whole document, Crawford (1996) I.393–454.

Greek religious context. It records the establishment, probably in the early second century B.C., of a procession, sacrifice and games honouring Rome; but it also records the dedication of some kind of representation (whether a visual image, a written account, or both, is not clear) of the story of Romulus and Remus and their suckling by the wolf. That is, one Roman mythic version of the foundation of their city is here put on display in a Greek cultic context.[126]

In other cases Eastern cities paraded their allegiance to Rome in the religious centre of Rome itself. So, for example, a series of inscriptions from the Capitoline hill recording dedications by various Eastern communities in gratitude for Roman benefactions or assistance shows another side of Greek assimilation of Roman religious forms. The exact date of many of these dedications is disputed; this is partly because some of the earliest texts of the group are preserved only in *re*-inscriptions of the early first century B.C. and others have been lost and survive only in manuscript copies from the Renaissance. Nonetheless it seems certain enough that this series of offerings had started at least by the late second century B.C.[127] It includes a dedication by the Lycians of a statue of 'Roma' to Capitoline Jupiter and the Roman People: 'in recognition of their goodness, benevolence and favour towards the Lycians'.[128] And there are too, among others, dedications by a man surnamed 'Philopator and Philadelphus' (a King of Pontus, or member of its royal house, of the late second or first century B.C.) and Ariobarzanes of Cappadocia (early first century B.C.), presumably also to the Capitoline god.[129] In other words, as Roman power spread, so also Roman religion, its cults and deities, began to have a significance further and further afield. The gods of the city of Rome, in the city of Rome, received offerings and dedications from an ever widening group of 'foreigners'.

But one of the most striking developments in the eastern Mediterranean was not, in fact, a replication of any cult or deity that was found at Rome at all. From the early second century on, there spread through the Greek world cults centred on the deified personification of Rome – *Dea Roma*, 'Goddess Rome' – or such variants as 'The People of Rome' or 'Rome and the Roman Benefactors'.[130] A few communities in the East dedicated temples to Roma – notably Smyrna from as early as 195 B.C., Alabanda in Caria

---

126 *Supplementum Epigraphicum Graecum* XXX 1073; Moretti (1980); Derow and Forrest (1982), with arguments for a date around 190–188 B.C. The religious foundations are focussed on the goddess 'Roma'; see below, pp. 159–60.

127 The dossier of republican texts, see *ILLRP* 174–81 (selections in *ILS* 30–4); for discussion and controversy over the precise dating, the form of the monument to which the texts were affixed and the circumstances of the dedications, Degrassi (1951–2); Mellor (1975) 203–6; Lintott (1978).

128 *ILS* 31 = *ILLRP* 174

129 *ILS* 30 = *ILLRP* 180; *ILLRP* 181

130 For example, the representation of Romulus and Remus at Chios was dedicated to Roma, and in the context of a festival of Roma (n. 126); a statue of Roma was dedicated by the Lycians on the Capitol (n. 128); note also the terms of the hymn to

Fig. 3.4 This seemingly anonymous statue is, in fact, one of the earliest surviving statues – perhaps *the* earliest – of the Goddess Rome (late second century B.C.). Found on the island of Delos, it is identified by an inscription which records that it is a dedication to the goddess (in thanks for her 'good will') by an association known as the 'Poseidoniasts'; this was a group of traders from Berytus (Beirut) named after, and presumably under the protection of, the god Poseidon. (Height, as preserved, 1.54m.)

and Miletus (all in Asia Minor). A particularly vivid inscription from the temple at Miletus details the regulations for the priesthood of Roma, the festival of the Romaia, as well as the regular sacrifices to be performed for the goddess. It shows that, at Miletus at least, these sacrifices were not only made on occasions specific to the cult of Roma herself, but that the regular turning points of civic life (such as the entry into office of new magistrates) were also marked by sacrifices to 'Rome and its People'.[131]

It is not clear overall (or in any particular case, for that matter) what prompted the establishment of the cult of Roma in the cities of the Greek

Flamininus, quoted above p. 146. The cult of Roma in general: Mellor (1975); Fayer (1976); Price (1984) 40–3.

131 Sokolowski (1955) no. 49 = **10.3a**; for Smyrna: Tacitus, *Annals* IV.56; Alabanda: Livy XLIII.6.5.

world. No similar cult is known from Rome itself until the reign of Hadrian;[132] so we cannot be dealing here with Greek emulation of contemporary Roman practice. It may be that for some citizens of the erstwhile independent Greek communities, the cult of some abstract conception of 'Rome' was a good deal more acceptable than the granting of divine honours to individual Romans; that Dea Roma provided a way of recognizing (celebrating, if need be) Roman power without treating the rapid turn-over of local governors as divine. It may also be that it was leading Romans themselves – as individuals or in the senate – who let their Greek clients know that they took exception to the granting of divine honours to individual members of their class. We simply do not know. What *is* certain is that a religious representation of Rome developed in the Greek East side by side with Roman dominance; that the Eastern cities gradually incorporated Roman power into their own religious and cultural world.

But to return finally to the city of Rome itself. In the last chapter, we looked in detail at the introduction of the goddess Magna Mater in 205 B.C., and at the ambivalence of Roman reactions to her cult: apparent distaste for the flamboyantly 'foreign' elements of the cult (in particular, the self-castrated, self-flagellating, wild Phrygian priests, the *galli*) at the same time as official incorporation within the cults of the state.[133] Magna Mater, as we observed, marked the last of the great third-century series, starting with Aesculapius, of new deities and cults introduced from the Greek world into Rome by vote of senate and people. Religious imports by no means entirely died out in the last period of the Republic (they never did at Rome). We can point, for example, to new cults of Isis and Sarapis, coming ultimately from Egypt (though almost certainly strongly Hellenized by the time they reached Rome). But they were not 'voted in' by the state authorities, as Magna Mater had been; nor were they the result of a consultation of the Sibylline Books, which had prompted so many of the earlier arrivals.

At this period, however, the surviving evidence draws our attention not so much to the first arrival of the new cults, but to the ways – once they had arrived – such recognizably 'foreign' cults operated within the society, culture and religion of Rome and Italy.[134] Part of that operation is a story of tension and conflict. Although we have no case so well documented as the crisis over the worship of Bacchus in the early second century,[135] it is clear

---

132 Beaujeu (1955) 128–36; Mellor (1975) 201; below, pp. 257–8.

133 Above, pp. 96–8.

134 It all depends, of course, on what you mean by 'foreign'. The inverted commas here are crucial. They refer to the conventional Roman *representation* of those cults as foreign – which has no necessary connection with the political or ethnic origin of those involved in the cults. To put it at its simplest: the cult of Magna Mater was insistently paraded by Roman writers as a 'foreign' cult; the majority of those participating in its rituals were no doubt as 'Roman' as anyone in Rome in the first century B.C., and on. See further below, pp. 164–6.

135 See above, pp. 91–6.

that attempts at the control of some cults and practices continued through the first century B.C. We have almost no evidence at all for the circumstances that led to the destruction of the shrines of Isis in (probably) 59, 58, 53, 50 and again in 48 B.C.; nor, for that matter, for those that led to the expulsion of the astrologers (*Chaldaei*) from Rome in 139 B.C.[136] But we can make a plausible guess at one or two factors that might have lain behind such action. The cult of Isis, with its independent priesthood and its devotion to a personal and caring deity could represent (like the Bacchic cult) a potentially dangerous alternative society, out of the control of the traditional political élite.[137] Likewise astrology, with its specialized form of religious knowledge in the hands of a set of religious experts outside the priestly groups of the city, necessarily constituted a separate (and perhaps rival) focus of religious power. Although it did not offer a *social* alternative in the sense of group membership, it represented (as we have seen in other areas before) a form of religious differentiation which threatened the undifferentiated politico-religious amalgam of traditional Roman practice.[138]

But the role and significance of 'foreign' cults at Rome was much more wide-ranging and complex than any such simple narrative of acceptance and incorporation versus control and expulsion might suggest. To conclude this chapter we shall look at two late republican representations of these cults (a painting representing the cult of Bacchus/Dionysus and a poem on the self-castration of Attis, the mythic 'ancestor' of the self-castrating priests of Magna Mater) – to explore further some of the ways these cults had, by the first century B.C., entered the visual, cultural and intellectual repertoire of the Roman world.

The best known Roman painting of all that survive from the ancient world depicts the god Dionysus, with a female companion, probably Ariadne – in a composition that includes other scenes which seem to represent various elements of the god's cult. It was painted towards the end of the period we have been considering in this chapter, probably between 60 and 50 B.C., in a villa just outside the town of Pompeii, the so-called 'Villa of the Mysteries' (taking its modern name from the ostensible subject of the painting).[139]

---

136 Shrines of Isis: Tertullian, *To the Gentiles* I.10.17–18 (quoting Varro); Cassius Dio XL.47.3–4; XLII.26.2; Valerius Maximus, *Memorable Deeds and Sayings* I.3.4 (with Malaise (1972b) 362–77). Astrologers: Valerius Maximus, *Memorable Deeds and Sayings* I.3.3: Livy, *Summaries* LIV; with Cramer (1951). As we shall emphasize below, pp. 230–1, we have no idea how, or how effectively, or by whom such expulsions were put into force.

137 The potential of the cult of Isis to develop into an independent focus of loyalty is illustrated by the account of the cult in Apuleius, *Metamorphoses* (for example, XI.21–5; (21 = **8.8**). Below, pp. 287–8.

138 Below, pp. 231–3.

139 Full documentation: Maiuri (1931). Discussion, different approaches and extensive bibliography: Seaford (1981); Ling (1991) 101–4; Henderson (1996).

This painting (the 'Villa of the Mysteries *frieze'*) runs all round one room of the villa (over 20 metres in total length) (Fig. 3.5), and shows a series of figures on almost human scale, set against a rich red background: men, women, gods, mythical creatures... At the centre of one of the short sides (the other is largely taken up with a wide entrance-way) Dionysus reclines in a woman's lap; and the couple are flanked on the left by a group of three mythical figures (a Silenus holds up a bowl into which two satyrs peer intently, one of them holding up a Silenus mask, over the Silenus' head); and on the right by a near naked woman, who kneels down to draw back a veil from what may be a giant phallus – while next to her, at the corner of the room, a winged female figure wields a large whip. She seems to be whipping a woman in a state of ecstasy or trance at the end of the adjacent long side of the room, who kneels down to expose her naked back, her head resting in the lap of another (clothed) female figure. A naked female dancer twirls behind. Almost all the rest of this long side is occupied by a window; but on the long side opposite, there is a series of figures who point us in the direction of Dionysus. Moving from the far end (after a small doorway) we pass from a scene where a naked boy reads from a scroll, through a series of women (one carrying a tray of (perhaps) cakes, a group gathered around a table) up to a Silenus playing a lyre, two young satyrs (one of whom is suckling a goat) and finally (next to the short wall that carries the tableau of Dionysus) another female figure starting backwards – as if in fright at something she has seen on the end wall.

The interpretation of these extraordinary images is extremely difficult. Most art historians have agreed that the painting as a whole depicts aspects of the Bacchic/Dionysiac cult – intermingled, according to some, with the initiatory rites of a marriage; but there is almost no agreement about how it works in detail. So, for example, some have it that the satyrs and Silenus on the end wall are practising a form of divination (lecanomancy – where images are read out of a cup of liquid); others that they are witnessing a Dionysiac miracle, as the bowl fills spontaneously with wine.[140] Some see the winged figure with the whip as an agent of initiation, flagellating the kneeling girl as a mark of her entry into the cult; while others would deny that she is whipping the kneeling figure at all, but rather turning in aversion from the (cultic) revelation of the phallus behind her – a demonic figure, not an agent of the cult at all.[141] Such detailed problems of interpretation are connected to the broader issue of how the frieze is to be *read*. One view suggests that we are following the initiatory progress of a single woman (whether into the cult of Bacchus, or into marriage), who re-appears in different scenes through the frieze; that it is in other words a visual *narrative* of initiation. Others argue, by contrast, that it is an impressionistic montage of discrete images, that have no narrative connection one with

140 Mudie Cooke (1913) 167–9; Zuntz (1963) 184–6; Sauron (1984) 171.
141 J.Toynbee (1929) 77–86; Lehmann (1962); Turcan (1969).

Fig. 3.5 A section of the 'Villa of the Mysteries frieze', Pompeii c.60–50 B.C. (height, 3.31m.). On the short wall (right): (i) Dionysus reclining in a woman's lap, probably Ariadne; (ii) Silenus and satyrs. On the long wall, from the left: (iii) women around a table; (iv) Silenus playing a lyre; (v) two satyrs; (vi) 'frightened woman'.

another; or even that it shows the simultaneous initiation of several women into the cult of Bacchus.[142]

There is equally fierce disagreement about the purpose of the room decorated by these images and the history of the paintings themselves. It could be a Dionysiac cult room, with the images on the walls closely reflecting the activity that took place within those walls. Or that at least might have been the origin of the scheme, when the villa was in the hands (let's imagine...) of a devotee of the cult. Years later the images could have remained as 'just decoration', or a quaint reminder of some ancestor's religious enthusiasms. They might, on the other hand, have been 'just decoration' all along: a version, perhaps, of some famous Greek painting, chosen by the villa's owner out of the local painter's book of patterns, a testament to his enthusiasm for Greek art rather than religion. Expensive wallpaper, in other words.[143]

It will obviously make a difference to how we understand these images

142 Maiuri (1931) 128, for example, sees it as a montage of simultaneous events; J.Toynbee (1929) reads it as a narrative of initiation into marriage; Clarke (1991) 94–111 argues against any attempt to 'pin down the meaning(s) of the frieze'.

143 Different views of the room's function and the 'originality' of the frieze: Little (1972) 3–5, 9–10, 13–16; Grant (1971) 103 (the painter as a 'devotee' of the cult); McKay (1977) 148 ('the festival hall...designed for Dionysiac feastings').

whether we choose to think of them as the specifically religious icons of a specifically religious room or as an extravagant attempt to replicate an old Greek masterpiece on Italian soil. But those differences should not obscure a much more important (and certain) point that this painting raises for any history of the religious world of Rome and Italy in the first century B.C. Even (or especially) if we do choose to classify the frieze as 'decorative', it attests to an entirely new range of possibilities in the religious experience of this period: the visual repertoire of the Dionysiac cult, that is, has recognizably entered the repertoire of even domestic decoration; and with it, of course, the representation of an emphatically personal kind of religious commitment. The images that people saw around them, even in their homes, now included the visual icons of a cult that a hundred years earlier had been rigorously controlled by the Roman authorities. The boundaries of what was recognizable and acceptable as religious were widening – as we shall see too in our final example.

Among the poems of Catullus is a poem of almost a hundred lines that takes as its central theme the self-castration of Attis.[144] Attis was, as we have already seen, the mythic 'consort' of the goddess Magna Mater and the mythic 'ancestor' of her castrated priests, the *galli*. Attis, it was told, had been the favourite of Magna Mater, but when she suspected his love for another, she drove him into a frenzy in which he castrated himself. In Rome, this story and the priests who were said to follow his example represented the wildest and most 'foreign' aspect of Magna Mater's cult.[145]

The poem tells the story of this castration, from its mad exultant beginning:

> Having sailed the sea-deeps in a swift vessel,
> Attis arrived, ardently he entered
> The Phrygian forest, set feverish foot
> In the dark, dense-leaved demesne of the Goddess,
> And there moved by madness, bemused in his mind,
> Lopped off the load of his loins with a sharp flint.[146]

through Attis' first exultant reaction and his rousing calls to his fellow worshippers – to his later, unfrenzied, horror at his own action:

> "............ Female now,
> But born boy, I became bearded, then as man
> Was admired among athletes, ace among wrestlers;
> My front door frequented, foot-warmed my threshold,
> My doorposts decked with dewy garlands,
> I bounded from bed at the break of each day.

144 *Poem* 63, with the important analyses by Rubino (1974) and Skinner (1993).
145 Above, p. 98, with the images of Attis, **2.7d** *Galli*: Beard (1994); note also the image of the *gallus* on a tomb of Roman imperial date, **8.7c**; and Juvenal's satiric account, *Satires* 6.511–21 = **8.7b**.
146 Lines 1–5 (trans. Michie).

> A slave now of Cybele, must I serve her sisterhood?
> Be a maenad, a moiety of myself, a man-corpse?" [147]

Finally (after the goddess herself has driven Attis once more into frenzy) the last lines of the poem are spoken as if in the voice of the poet himself:

> Great Goddess, Goddess who guards Mount Dindymus,
> May your furies all fall far from my house.
> Make other men mad, but have mercy on me![148]

Arguments about the context and purpose of this poem are similar, in some respects, to the arguments about the Villa of the Mysteries frieze we have just explored. On the one hand, there are those who would see this poem as a hymn written by Catullus for ritual performance at the goddess's festival of the Megalesia.[149] The Megalesia, it is generally believed, was the focus of the more 'Roman' side of the cult; and this hymn, with its emphasis on the power of Magna Mater, but at the same time on the unacceptability of the self-castrating frenzy that was supposed to characterize its wilder, 'Phrygian' elements, might fit in well with that festival. On the other, the poem has been seen as very much the product of the *study*, not of the temple or ritual theatre, desktop versifying, drawing heavily on, maybe even translating from, some lost Greek model from the repertoire of Hellenistic poetry: the product of Catullus' passion for Greek poetry, not his engagement with the cult of the goddess.[150] Again, as with the Villa of the Mysteries, it would make a difference if we could certainly decide between these different positions; if, for example, we knew that we could take this poem (in origin at least) as part of the cult's own internal discourse, as one of the ways this cult talked to itself, about itself. But, of course, we cannot; and, again, there are other more important points to raise.

Catullus' Attis poem goes right to the heart of Roman society and values, questioning the very nature of the 'Romanness' that those values entail. This is not only a poem about castration; it is a poem that questions the whole definition of gender, directly asking what it is that constitutes a *man*, setting social norms against biological nature (and its mutilations). It is a poem that forever prompts questions about madness and frenzy, about what it is to know that you are, or that anyone else is, sane – or mad; as well as about the limits of power that may be exercised by one being over another, in slavery, for example, or in passion. In short, it is a poem that confronts and questions every notion of the subject, and of subjectivity. It is possible that some Romans had *always* asked themselves such questions in some form or other, right from the city's very beginnings. But Catullus' formulations of these

147 Lines 62–9.
148 Lines 90–2.
149 Wiseman (1985) 198–206.
150 Fordyce (1961) 262 ('its spirit is so Greek ...that it seems certain that Catullus was translating or adapting a Greek original'.).

issues are radically new and terrifyingly pointed; there is no trace of anything like them in any earlier Latin literature that survives.

The crucial point is that all these issues are discussed in this poem within the frame of religion. We are not dealing here with dilemmas of incorporation or expulsion of 'foreign' cults; we are dealing with those cults, and their repertoire of rituals and myths, as established *ways of thinking* at Rome about the most central human values. If some Romans were in this period establishing a tradition of questioning and wondering about all aspects of their own culture, if they were explicitly challenging, dissecting and reconstructing embedded notions of what it was to be, and act like, a Roman – they were doing that, in part, within the discourse of religion. Religion was, and remained, good to think with.

4 The place of religion: Rome in the early Empire

Roman religion continued under the empire to be a key set of practices which permitted reflections and debates on Roman identity. In part these reflections picked up earlier preoccupations. Roman religion, as we have seen with the building of temples at Rome, had always been closely linked with the city of Rome and its boundaries.[1] In part the reflections respond to new political imperatives. Under the first emperor, Augustus, the restructuring of a number of religious institutions resulted in changes within Rome, and, more widely, in the empire. It is these that we explore in this chapter, focussing at the same time on the new social and political régime of the end of the first century B.C., when Rome returned to the government of an autocracy: a monarchy in all but name. The assassination of Julius Caesar in 44 B.C. had been followed by a series of civil wars in which the supporters of Caesar first defeated the party of his murderers (led by Brutus and Cassius), then turned on each other. Finally in 31 B.C. Octavian (Caesar's nephew and adoptive son) defeated his former ally Antony at the battle of Actium and secured what they had all been fighting for – control of Rome and, with it, the Mediterranean world. The reign of Octavian (under the title of 'Augustus' that he used from 27 B.C.) was a crucial political turning point in Rome's history. Although it would later be remembered by some as the reign that witnessed the birth of Jesus (son of God, prophet or common criminal – as different people would see him), for most Romans it was the period when Rome reverted to one man rule. Most of the political institutions of the Republic remained intact (the senate continued to meet and to be of crucial importance; the old republican offices – consul, praetor and so on – were still keenly sought); Augustus' own watchword was 'restoration' not 'revolution'; but all the same there could be no doubt that Rome was now controlled by the emperor. How then did Augustus' new deal impact on the traditional religion of Rome?[2]

The importance of the *religion of place* during this period is illustrated by an episode from Livy's *History*, written in the early 20s B.C. After the sack of Rome by the Gauls in 390 B.C., there was a proposal that the Romans should migrate to the newly conquered town of Veii, rather than rebuild

---

1 Above, pp. 87–91. Studies of place, boundaries and identity: J. Z. Smith (1978), (1987); Mol (1976), (1985).
2 The politics of the reign of Augustus: Wells (1992) 49–78; Crook (1996).

Rome. Livy put in the mouth of the Roman general Camillus a striking rejection of this proposal, which emphasized the religious foundation of the city, the necessity for the ancient cults to be located in Rome within its sacred boundary: 'We have a city founded by the auspices and augury; there is not a corner of it that is not full of our cults and our gods; our regular rituals have not only their appointed places, but also their appointed times.'[3] This speech articulated issues of contemporary significance for Augustan Rome.[4] There had been fear that Caesar would move the capital from Rome to the East, a fear that was revived by Antony's alliance with Cleopatra. Augustus, however, was to promote Rome as the heart of the empire. Camillus' re-establishment of the ancestral rites is here made neatly to foreshadow the religious activity of Augustus himself and his argument about the indissoluble ties between Rome and its cults encapsulates the preoccupation of the imperial age with *place*. This stress was not an innovation of the Augustan age, but it was particularly emphasized in the writing of the period. Indeed the new political order was conceived and imagined by the Romans within the physical and symbolic setting of *the city of Rome*.

This chapter will explore some of the religious implications of that preoccupation, from the emphasis on the sacred boundary of the city (the *pomerium*) to the reconstruction of many religious buildings in the city under Augustus and to religious rituals centred on the history and mythology of Rome itself. It will focus largely on the Augustan period, though the subsequent history of various key institutions will illustrate how the new system provided a framework for the rest of the imperial period.[5] The chapters that follow will emphasize later periods, extending our investigation of the Augustan system to consider: the religious self-definition of the Roman élite, the significance of official cults in the life of the city of Rome, the 'popular' and 'oriental' religions of Rome, and the relationship of Rome to the outside world.

The Augustan restructuring of the earlier republican system was represented at the time as 'restoration': just as Augustus had 'restored the *res publica*', so also he had 'restored traditional cults' – reviving the rituals that had faded away, rebuilding the temples that had fallen down, filling the priesthoods that were vacant. Modern scholars have often held that this view was indeed broadly correct. They have diverged from the Augustan perspective mainly to argue that, since the decline was real, the Augustan revival could only be artificial; meaningful religious energies – so that argument goes – were located in other contexts ('Oriental cults' or, later, Christianity).[6]

---

3 V.52.2; cf. above, pp. 53–4 (the rescue of the Vestals' *sacra* from the Gallic sack).
4 Liebeschuetz (1967). Livy's perspective in general: Levene (1993); above, pp. 8–9; 76–7. Map 5 for Veii.
5 Augustan religion: Nock (1934); Liebeschuetz (1979) 55–100; Kienast (1982) 185–214.
6 Warde Fowler (1911) 428–51; Latte (1960a) 294–311; but see Scheid (1990b) 677–732.

This orthodoxy now seems very fragile – for the early empire as much as for the late Republic. If, as we have argued, a simple model of 'decline' is misleading for the age of Cicero, then so too is a simple model of 'revival' for the age of Augustus, for it tends to obscure the extent of change and restructuring in the system. On the other hand, like 'decline', the Augustan stress on 'restoration' need not be treated merely as a cunning obfuscation; rather it was a highly loaded religious term, offering a crucial way of relating the Augustan present to its republican past.

One important aspect of the religious changes of the early principate was the development of rituals which focussed more directly on the emperor himself, especially after his death. These are normally described in modern accounts as 'the imperial cult', treated as a striking innovation, and placed in a separate category from 'the restoration of religion'. But, as we shall show, these imperial rituals can more helpfully be seen as part of the general 'restructuring' of religion at the time – drawing on the longstanding traditions of Rome, though increasingly focussing on the person of the emperor himself. In fact, as we have already seen in the last chapter (and will return to below), even the apotheosis of the dead emperor was as much rooted in 'tradition' as it was a radical innovation of autocratic rule – and inevitably problematic for that reason.

The sources for this chapter are rich and diverse. For the Augustan period there is an abundance of contemporary writing. In addition to the great poets whose perspectives have always figured in discussion of Roman religion (Virgil, Horace and Propertius), there are three major writers whose works are more rarely exploited – at least, as a means of throwing light on this period of religious history. Livy published the first five books of his *History of Rome* (covering the period from the origin of the city to its sack by the Gauls in 390 B.C.) in the early 20s B.C., at the beginning of the Augustan principate. We have already seen, in exploring the earliest history of Roman religion, how the concerns of Livy's own day influence his treatment of the distant past.[7] In this chapter we shall focus explicitly (as we did briefly with the speech of Camillus) on those topical concerns which inform his narrative. Likewise Dionysius of Halicarnassus' *Roman Antiquities* lays great emphasis, in its first two books, on the founding of rites which continued from the time of Hercules, Romulus or Numa down to the author's own day. Dionysius lived in Rome from 30 B.C., and published Book I of his *Antiquities* in 7 B.C. Whatever the value of the work as a factual record of early Rome, as a repository of Roman myths it is invaluable evidence for an Augustan perspective on the past – all the more interesting because of the particular standpoint of Dionysius himself. Not only was he a Greek from Asia Minor, writing in Greek to explain Roman history and culture to a Greek audience, but he was also trying to argue that

7 Above, pp. 77; 119–20.

Rome was by origin a Greek city, and that it had preserved many of the best aspects of Greek culture that had been lost by his own degenerate contemporaries: a vivid illustration of the complex 'multicultural' debates that characterized the Graeco-Roman world at this time.[8] Thirdly Ovid's *Fasti*, a poem composed perhaps between A.D. 4 and 8, though revised subsequently, is a dazzling, often witty, account of the calendar and festivals of the first six months of the Roman year (the second half of the year and of the poem is missing). The *Fasti* presents a huge array of stories that tell of the origins of the various festivals, a welter of explanations for the different ceremonies: it is a unique reflection on the religious practices and mythology of the Augustan age.[9]

Among later authors, important information is found in Suetonius' biographies of emperors (written in the 120s A.D.), and in the surviving parts of Cassius Dio's vast *Roman History* (written in the early third century A.D.).[10] Yet just as Livy's account of early Rome sheds as much light on the period in which it was written as on the historical period that is its subject, so with these later writers we constantly face the possibility of anachronism: in referring to the Augustan period, they inevitably reflect the concerns of their own day. In fact Dio sometimes slips into the present tense when discussing religious changes of the Augustan principate (as well as more strictly constitutional reforms); and he highlights festivals and ceremonies (for example, the Augustalia in honour of the emperor himself, or the sacrifices established at the altar of Rome and Augustus at Lyons) that are still practised in his own day.

Alongside all these very different books, texts survive inscribed on bronze or stone, that once stood on religious buildings or that offered public, official records of religious events and ceremonies. Augustus' account of his *Achievements* (which includes his record of temple restoration) is such a document – one copy (now lost) was inscribed on bronze pillars outside Augustus' Mausoleum in Rome; the main text we have was found inscribed on a wall of the temple of Rome and Augustus in Ankara. Another (which we discuss below) contains an elaborate record of the ceremonies of the Saecular Games that took place in 17 B.C., including details of the animals sacrificed and the words of the prayers spoken on the occasion by Augustus and the other participants. Not only is this valuable evidence for religious

---

8 Gabba (1991). In contrast with Polybius, who had argued for the difference between Romans and Greeks, Dionysius has a new question: who are the Greeks or Romans? Roman institutions as originally Greek: for example, *Roman Antiquities* VII.72.1–13 = 5.7a (above, p. 40).

9 It is not certain whether Ovid never wrote about the remaining six months of the year, or whether the books have not survived; for a review of the problem, Newlands (1995) 3–6. The *Fasti* and Roman religion: Schilling (1969); Miller (1991); Phillips (1992); Scheid (1992a), with Feeney (1991) 188–249 on his *Metamorphoses*. The *Fasti* as a 'subversive' poem: for example, Hinds (1992); but see Feeney (1992).

10 Suetonius: Wallace–Hadrill (1983). Cassius Dio: Rich (1990) 1–20.

activity; the public display of such documents is itself an important part of religious ideology. Inscriptions are, in fact, one distinctive part of the material and archaeological evidence for religion at Rome – from temples and altars to coins and dedications. None of the main Augustan temples has been preserved complete (and we rely on a combination of archaeological and literary evidence to fill out our conception of them). But what survives of the religious monuments of the Augustan city offers, as we shall see, an unrivalled opportunity to explore the physical fabric of religious cult and ideology.[11]

1. Myths and place

Roman mythology never existed – or so it has often been claimed. We have already discussed in chapter 1 the theory that in the earliest period of Rome there were no *gods* as such, only primitive powers undifferentiated by personal attributes. This is closely related to the theory of Rome as a 'myth-less' society; for if there were no gods, then it follows that there could be no stories about their deeds and adventures, or their dealings with humans – the stock-in-trade of what we think of as 'myth'. Only gradually, so the argument goes, as these powers were replaced by anthropomorphic gods, did Rome acquire some sort of mythology in the last centuries B.C., largely under the influence of Greece with its huge repertoire of myths.[12]

Other theories hold that Rome's native mythological tradition was somehow 'lost', or 'forgotten'. So, for example, we have seen it to be a central tenet of Georges Dumézil's work on early Roman religion that there once had been a Roman mythology, parallel to that of other Indo-European peoples. The corollary of this is that it was swamped by the influx of Greek mythology in the middle Republic.[13] Others have suggested that the native traditions of Roman myth did survive in the popular culture – plays, songs and folktales – of Rome and Italy right up to the imperial period; but that it is now almost entirely hidden from our view, being marginal to the élite writing (with its roots specifically in Greek literature and Greek cultural models) that survives from Rome.[14]

There are many complicated issues involved here: not least, the very

11 For the social and physical context of the changes in Rome, below, pp. 245–312; Zanker (1988).

12 Wissowa (1912) 9; Latte (1926); Rose (1950) 281: 'It is as certain as any negative historical proposition can ever be that Rome had no myths, at least none of a kind which could possibly associate themselves with cult.' Horsfall in Bremmer and Horsfall (1987) 1–11 and Graf (1993) discuss generally the 'absence' of Roman myths. See above, pp. 10–11.

13 Briefly Dumézil (1970) 47–59 (with pp. 14–16 above); also Koch (1937) (with review by Syme (1939)).

14 Wiseman (1989).

definition of Roman mythology, what counts as a 'myth' in any culture, and how far we can ever think of any system of myth as just an 'alien import'. But even without entering into such theoretical questions, the modern denial of Roman mythology does seem almost perverse. After all, the public imagery of late republican and Augustan Rome was largely mythological; the early books of Livy and Dionysius of Halicarnassus are full of mythological stories about early Rome; Ovid's *Fasti* consists very largely of descriptions of festivals and their associated myths. These writers would have been perplexed to be told (as is implied in much modern work on the subject) that their myths were either trivial or merely foreign imports, and so of little significance for Roman culture and religion.[15]

Like all of Roman culture, Roman mythology was inevitably a complicated amalgam: it included adaptations or borrowings from Greek myth as well as 'native' Italic traditions. It is fruitless to attempt to distinguish precisely between these different strands; and it would be to miss the point of the complex cultural interactions that had characterized Roman culture from its earliest history to suggest that simply because the origin of a particular story can be traced to Greece, that story could somehow not count also as Roman. On the other hand, ancient writers themselves did sometimes choose to stress the difference between Greek and Roman myths current in the early empire. It is a crucial fact that Roman mythology, however strongly influenced it may have been by the Greek repertoire, could be portrayed as distinctively different from its Greek counterpart.

So Dionysius of Halicarnassus commends Romulus, whom he holds responsible for the establishment of Roman religion, for following 'the best customs in use among the Greeks', while rejecting 'all the traditional <Greek> myths concerning the gods, which contain blasphemies and calumnies against them'.[16] Dionysius implies that Rome lacked three standard Greek contexts which might have perpetuated such improper stories: theogonies, with their accounts of gods fighting for sovereignty (as when Zeus overthrows and imprisons his father Kronos); an epic and theatrical tradition which could show gods involved in warfare with mortals or bound in subjection to them (as when Apollo in Homer's *Iliad* serves as herdsman to king Laomedon); and ritual contexts involving dying gods or the promiscuous participation of men and women (such as the mysteries of Persephone or Dionysus). Even when new cults were officially introduced to Rome from Greece and elsewhere, he says, the Romans did not take over the 'mythical clap-trap' associated with them.

When Dionysius praises Romulus, and Roman religion of his own day,

---

15 Grant (1973) is the best introduction. For more radical views, see Beard (1993) and Feeney (1998) ch. 2. Habinek (1992) argues the crippling of Roman studies by the romanticizing of things Greek; as here by the stress on the primacy of Greek myth.

16 Dionysius of Halicarnassus, *Roman Antiquities* II.18–20 = **8.7a**. He may here be following Varro. Cf. Gabba (1991) 118–38; Borgeaud (1993).

he is writing in the context of a longstanding debate in Greece about the propriety, or impropriety, of mythology. He is not offering an objective analysis of the character of Roman myth; he is drawing a loaded opposition between Roman and contemporary Greek culture, suggesting (paradoxically to us) that it is now the Romans who are the true and proper Greeks – representing Greek culture stripped of its degenerate aspects. All the same, it is important to note that an educated Greek *could* portray Roman mythology as quite different from the traditional Greek stories about their gods. This stands in sharp contrast to modern theories about the profound Hellenization of Roman religion in the middle and late Republic; and to modern claims that Roman mythology was nothing other than a set of translations from the Greek.

Roman myths were in essence myths of place. Greek myths too related to specific cities and territories, but at the same time they were regularly linked to wider Greek, or Panhellenic, mythology. In general Roman myths do not have such a wider context. Rather, the sites and monuments of the city of Rome dominate Roman mythology – from the grandeur of the Capitoline Hill to the ancient hut of Romulus still lovingly preserved on the Palatine into the imperial period.[17] These myths recounted the history of the area of Rome itself, from earliest times to the Augustan age; as in Virgil's *Aeneid*, when Aeneas, guided around the future site of the city, visits so many landmarks that were to memorialize key moments in the growth of Rome through the centuries.[18] In fact, vivid tokens of this history were incorporated in the cults of Rome: the mysterious shields of the Salian priests, for example, included a shield that was said to have dropped to Rome from heaven in the reign of Numa.[19]

Dionysius devotes the whole of his first book to the earliest populations of the area around the site of Rome, especially the Arcadians, who were themselves (significantly for Dionysius's multi-cultural tale) Greeks by origin. The Arcadians were responsible for consecrating 'many precincts, altars and images of the gods and instituted purifications and sacrifices according to the custom of their own country, which continued to be performed in the same manner down to my day'.[20] The most striking of these was the cult of Hercules, who passed through the area on one of his labours and throttled a local bandit, Cacus. Evander, king of the Arcadians, wanted to offer divine honours to Hercules, knowing that he was destined for immortality. Hercules himself performed the initial rites and asked the Arcadians to perpetuate the honours by sacrificing at the very spot each year with 'Greek rites'. The altar at which Hercules sacrificed 'is called by the Romans the Greatest Altar [Ara Maxima]. It stands near the place they

---

17 Dionysius of Halicarnassus, *Roman Antiquities* I.79.
18 *Aeneid* VIII.18–369.
19 Above, p. 1; Salian shields carved on a gem stone: **5.4b.**
20 Dionysius of Halicarnassus, *Roman Antiquities* I.33.3.

call the Cattle Market [Forum Boarium] and is held in great veneration by the inhabitants.'[21]

The ritual of this altar was, and is, the subject of learned debate. The Greek nature of the sacrifices practised there was a puzzle. For Dionysius, it was telling evidence for his theory that Rome was originally a Greek city – neatly illustrated by the story of Evander and Hercules. But the further peculiarity, that women were barred from the altar, attracted a host of explanations in its own right. A Roman historian of the second century B.C. explained the ban through a story that the mother of Evander and her women were late for sacrifice.[22] Varro, on the other hand, told that the priestess of the Bona Dea (whose shrine lay near the Ara Maxima) refused to allow Hercules to drink from the goddess's spring, and so Hercules banned women from his altar.[23] These accounts show how wide-ranging the implications of *place* could be. When the antiquarians, historians and poets of the late Republic and early Empire speculated on the myth and ritual of this particular cult site at the Ara Maxima, more was involved than the simple physical *location* of the cult. In this case, ideas of *place* lead straight to demarcations of *gender*, that is to rival claims about the religious *place* of women.[24] Stories of Rome *situated* the Roman system of cultural norms and practices.

The Parilia

Many Roman myths refer to the founding and early years of Rome. One myth, which is worth considering at some length, linked the festival of the Parilia to the founding of the city and the creation of its sacred boundary, the *pomerium*. Ovid devotes over a hundred lines of the *Fasti* to this ancient rural festival, designed to purify the sheep and cattle by calling on the god (or goddess – the sex of the deity was uncertain) Pales.[25] He starts by assuring the reader of his personal credentials: 'I have often myself borne along, with loaded hands, the ashes of the calf and the beanstalks, the sacred materials of purification. To be sure, I have myself leapt over the fires arranged

21 Ibid. I.40. Cf. Wissowa (1912) 273–5, Steinby (1993–) III.15–17. Winter (1910) and Bayet (1926) 127–54 elucidate the different versions of the story; Coarelli (1988) 61–77 notes the Greek design of the altar (Map 1 no. 21). Virgil too incorporated this story into his 'history': *Aeneid* VIII.267–79, as did Ovid (Fantham (1992)).

22 *Origin of the Roman Race* 6.7, from Cassius Hemina; cf. Plutarch, *Roman Questions* 60.

23 Macrobius, *Saturnalia* I.12.28. Propertius IV.9 follows Varro's account, not without a sense of humour.

24 This perspective persisted through the imperial period. An inscription of the early third century, probably put up near the altar, commemorates the offering of the solemn sacrifice which Hercules had established at the time of Evander: *ILS* 3402.

25 Deity: Ovid, *Fasti* IV.820; Plutarch, *Romulus* 12. Testimonia on the Parilia: Degrassi (1963) 443–5; **5.1a.** The name of the festival Parilia/Palilia, was supposed to be derived from the name of the deity Pales. Dionysius of Halicarnassus, *Roman Antiquities* I.88.3 is uncertain whether it predated the foundation of the city.

three in a row, and the moist laurel has sprinkled its drops of water over me.'[26] The long description that follows seems to fall into two parts. First, the urban festival (whose details pick up the rituals in which Ovid claims to have participated): 'Go, people, and bring from the virgin's altar the materials of purification. Vesta will provide them; by Vesta's generosity you will be pure. The blood of a horse will make up those materials, together with the ashes of a calf; the third ingredient will be the empty stalk of a hard bean.'[27] Next, Ovid moves on to the rural festival of purification of sheep and cattle: 'Shepherd, purify your well-fed sheep as dusk first falls. First sprinkle the ground with water and sweep it with a broom' and so on. If we are right to distinguish these two versions of the festival in Ovid's account, it is still hard to compare the two since the description of the rural festival is much fuller than his account of the urban one. Yet it is interesting that in drawing this distinction Ovid may be reflecting the religious theories and categories of Varro, who insisted on the distinction between the public and private festivals – a distinction which may largely overlap with that between the urban and the rural.[28]

Ovid goes on to discuss the origins, and hence significance, of the festival. The Parilia, like any Roman festival, permitted a multitude of competing explanations.[29] Ovid offers no fewer than seven: (i) fire is a natural purifier; (ii) fire and water were used together because everything is composed out of opposing elements; (iii) fire and water contain the source of life, as in the symbolism of exile and marriage; (iv) the festival alludes to Phaethon and Deucalion's flood, an explanation Ovid doubts; (v) shepherds once accidentally ignited straw; (vi) Aeneas' piety allowed him to pass through flames unscathed; (vii) when Rome was founded, orders were given to transfer to new houses; the country folk set fire to the old houses and leaped with their cattle through the flames. Ovid appears to favour the last interpretation ('Is it not nearer the truth...?' he writes), stressing that the ritual still happens ('it continues even now, on your birthday, Rome').

Ovid develops his favoured interpretation by recounting the story of Romulus and the city's foundation, a story to which we shall return in the context of Augustus. Romulus chose the time of the celebration of the Parilia to found Rome. He marked out the lines of the wall of the new city with a furrow, praying to Jupiter, Mars and Vesta; Jupiter responded with a favourable augury. Romulus then instructed one Celer to kill anyone who crossed the walls or the furrow, but Remus, his twin brother, in ignorance of the ban, leaped across them and was struck down by Celer. In this version, the Parilia,

---

26 Ovid, *Fasti* IV.725–8 = **5.1a**.
27 *Fasti* IV.731–4 = **5.1a**.
28 Rural festival: *Fasti* 735–82 = part **5.1a**. Public and private: Varro, quoted by scholiast on Persius I.72.
29 Cf. above, pp. 50; 53; Beard (1987).

the founding of Rome, the creation of the *pomerium* and the killing of Remus all interconnect.[30]

In backing this interpretation Ovid was in good company. Though modern scholars have in general been happy to treat the Parilia as a genuinely primitive pastoral ritual which survived into the metropolitan world of imperial Rome,[31] most of the ancient evidence we have associates the festival with the birth of Rome. The earliest surviving Roman calendar (dating from the last years of the Republic) marks against the entry for the Parilia 'Rome founded', and this association appears to become even stronger as time goes on. When news of Julius Caesar's decisive victory in the Civil Wars at Munda in 45 B.C. arrived in Rome at the time of the Parilia, the coincidence was exploited in favour of Caesar, the new Romulus: games were added to the festival, at which people wore crowns in Caesar's honour.[32] And the Romulan theme became dominant in A.D. 121 when Hadrian chose the date of the Parilia to found his new temple of Venus and Roma; the festival continued to have lively celebrations, but was now known as the Romaea: the Festival of Rome.[33]

The Parilia provides a vivid example of the productivity of interpretations of Roman festivals. Ovid revels in the many ways the festival could be seen: in terms of natural science (fire as a natural purifier); philosophy (fire and water as opposing elements); Greek myths (Phaethon and Deucalion); accident (chance fire caused by shepherds); Roman myth (Aeneas and Troy). But it is much harder to plot how the favoured interpretation may have changed over time, or to show that (or when) any particular view of the origin and meaning of the festival faded or dropped away. Ovid's privileging of a historicizing interpretation of the Parilia, which at the same time links the festival with the site of Rome, is strongly characteristic of the late Republic and early Empire – as we have seen in the contemporary accounts of Hercules and the Ara Maxima. And it is clear enough, in broad terms, that this connection of the festival with Rome's foundation became more emphatic. But such an association may itself incorporate old ideas of the purification of herds, or re-workings of those ideas. So for Ovid, the ancient festival which marks the foundation of Rome also evokes a primitive pastoral golden age lodged at the very origins of the imperial city.

---

30 *Fasti* IV.833–48. There was another version of the killing of Remus: Livy I.7.2; Dionysius of Halicarnassus, *Roman Antiquities* I.87.2. The myth: Bremmer in Bremmer and Horsfall (1987) ch. 3; Wiseman (1995); Hinds (1992) 113–49 argues for ambivalence in Ovid's presentation.

31 Wissowa (1912) 199–201; Scullard (1981) 103–5. This view fails to exploit the differences between the urban and the rural festivals. Dumézil (1969) 283–7 and (1970) 380–5 uses the festival to illuminate a cognate Indian deity.

32 Weinstock (1971) 184–6. Propertius IV.1.19–20 notes that the ritual had become more elaborate.

33 Athenaeus VIII.361 ef = **5.1c**; Beaujeu (1955) 128–33; below, pp. 257–8.

The *pomerium*

The *pomerium* is another important aspect of the Roman myth of place. The story of the twin brothers, Romulus and Remus, concerns not only the creation of the city but also that of its sacred boundary, the cause of fateful conflict between the twins. When they disputed which of them was to found the new city, the issue was settled by augury: Remus on the Aventine hill saw six vultures; but Romulus on the Palatine saw twelve. The myth insisted on the exclusion of the Aventine from the boundary of the *pomerium* , emphasizing that it was a place apart from Rome proper, even if closely related to the city's sacred enclosure. And at the end of this episode, the killing of Remus underlined the sanctity of the city's boundary, dearer than any brother. The myth presents a *definition* of Rome.[34]

The *pomerium* had a physical presence too. In the imperial period it was clearly marked by massive blocks of stone, 2 m. tall and 1 m. square.[35] Placed wherever the line of the *pomerium* changed direction, the precise distance in Roman feet between each marker stone was indicated on the stone itself and all the stones were numbered in sequence along the line of the *pomerium*. These huge markers embody the self-aggrandizement of the emperors who set them up; the republican *pomerium* had been precisely defined along its route, though not so aggressively, and no markers of any kind survive before the imperial period. The stones also ensured that there was no uncertainty about the line of the boundary, as well as allowing it to be *re-placed* from time to time, changed and extended.

There had been three alterations during the Republic to what was supposedly the original *pomerium* of Romulus; and in the imperial period extensions were carried out by Claudius and Vespasian. These took the area enclosed by the *pomerium* up from 325 hectares to 665 (under Claudius) and 745 hectares (under Vespasian). So too, when a dyke was built to control the Tiber floods, Hadrian ensured that new boundary stones were erected directly above the old ones; and in A.D. 271–5 Aurelian built the walls then necessary for Rome's defence closely following, it seems, the line of the *pomerium*. Such extensions are not primarily the result of the physical growth of Rome's population and the material need for more urban space. For most of Rome's history the *pomerium* was a sacred boundary,

34 The execution of those who damaged city walls was justified in Roman law by the story of Remus: Justinian's *Digest* I.8.11 (Pomponius). Introduction: Andreussi (1988); Liou-Gille (1993); Plutarch, *Romulus* 11.1–4 = **4.8a**; Lugli (1952–69) I.116–31. Roman preoccupation with space: Rykwert (1976); Meslin (1978) ch. 2; Grandazzi (1993). Cosmological models for towns (in Nepal and India): Pieper (1977); Barré et al. (1981); Gutschow (1982). Until the time of Claudius the Aventine hill was outside the *pomerium*.

35 Extent of *pomerium*: Maps 1–3; Labrousse (1937); Poe (1984); Boatwright (1987) 64–71. Illustration of marker: **4.8c.** The area enclosed by the *pomerium* was almost exactly that covered by the early third century A.D. official map of Rome, though the *pomerium* itself was not marked.

which did not even claim to mark the edge of the built-up area of the city. The extensions were linked rather to the connection between the boundary of the city of Rome and the boundary of Roman territory as a whole. Thus the historian Tacitus refers to an 'ancient custom' which allowed those who had extended the empire also to extend the *pomerium*; and the marker stones of Claudius (conqueror of southern Britain) and Vespasian (conqueror of more of Britain and part of Germany) include the formula: 'having increased the boundaries of the Roman people, he increased and defined the *pomerium*'. The right to extend the *pomerium* was sufficiently important to be listed specifically in the powers granted to Vespasian at his accession – parading a connection between the power of the emperor, military success and Rome's sacred space.[36]

The boundary was also reinforced at time of crisis. Following dire portents, the *pontifices* purified the city with solemn lustrations, moving round the circuit of the *pomerium*. For example, in A.D. 43 the discovery inside a temple on the Capitol of a horned owl, a bird considered to be particularly inauspicious, led to the lustration of the city.[37] The significance of such lustrations is vividly depicted in Lucan's epic on the civil wars at the end of the Republic, written in the mid-first century A.D. He describes at length a lustration of the city ordered by an Etruscan prophet after Caesar's crossing of the Rubicon, as the city waited in panic for him to march on Rome. 'He orders a procession of the frightened citizens all around Rome: the *pontifices*, to whom the rite was entrusted, purify the city-walls with solemn ceremony, and move around the furthest limits of the long *pomerium*. Behind them comes the lesser throng ...'[38] This particular occasion may well be a poetic invention, but it remains a vivid reflection of the religious ideology of the imperial period. Rome could never allow another Remus to cross the *pomerium*; at times of threat the boundary had to be purified and strengthened.

The *pomerium* continued in the early empire (as we have seen in the republican period) to be a significant dividing line between different types of human activity and between different types of human relations with the gods – though some of the rules were adapted to accommodate the emperor and the new régime of politics. Civil authority had traditionally been defined and limited by this sacred boundary. So, for example, in the Republic the powers of a tribune of the people had been restricted to the

---

36   Extensions: Tacitus, *Annals* XII.23–4 = **4.8b**; Aulus Gellius, *Attic Nights* XIII.14.3; **4.8c**. The *Augustan History* claims that Augustus, Nero, Trajan and Aurelian extended the *pomerium*, but see Syme (1978b); Boatwright (1986). *ILS* 244.14–16 (trans. Braund (1985) 110–11), citing Claudius as precedent.

37   Pliny, *Natural History* X.35; owl as an omen: X.34 = **7.3b(ii)**. Cf. Tacitus, *Annals* XIII.24, *Histories* I.87.1, IV.53, with Wissowa (1912) 391. Such lustrations may be the origin of the alleged festival of the Amburbium: Wissowa (1912) 142 and n. 14; Scullard (1981) 82–3.

38   Lucan I.584–604, quotation from 592–6. Propertius IV.4.73 describes a threat to the boundary (by Tarpeia) at the Parilia, 'the day the city first got its walls'.

area within the *pomerium*; when in 30 B.C. Octavian was given some of the powers of a tribune (particularly to aid those who appealed to him), these powers were likewise restricted to the area within the sacred boundary. Even then, however, an extra mile outside the *pomerium* was added to his patch; and soon, when he was given full 'tribunician power' in 23 B.C., the spatial restriction was entirely dropped. All emperors who followed him enjoyed the same power, unrestricted by the *pomerium*.[39]

In the Republic, the *pomerium* had been a crucial dividing line between different types of political activity. One of the main assemblies, the so-called 'tribal assembly' of the Roman people, had been able to meet only within the *pomerium*. The formal reason for this was religious: it was only within the sacred boundary of the city that the *auspicia* – the favourable signs from the gods that were necessary before any assembly – could be received by civil magistrates. The other main assembly, the 'centuriate assembly', which had been defined in military terms, had only been able to meet outside it.[40] These popular assemblies lost ground in the first century A.D., with the shift in executive power towards the senate and emperor; but their meetings were still bound by the old rules of place. This aspect of Roman self-definition was retained – or embalmed. Augury and the science of *auspicia*, meanwhile, continued to be important under the empire: a list of auguries between the years A.D. 1 and 17 survives on stone, and *augures*, who were the priests responsible for the interpretation of the auspices, as well as for maintaining the *pomerium* itself, were appointed until the end of the fourth century A.D.[41]

Military authority at Rome, as the rules about the holding of assemblies show, was also traditionally defined in terms of the *pomerium*. The basic rule was that this authority lapsed when a commander crossed the *pomerium*: civil and military power were entirely separate; the area within the sacred boundary was so outside the sphere of military power that a general could not even enter it without laying that power down. The only regular exception to this was the ceremony of triumph – though it was only on the very day of his triumph that the general could enter the city, waiting outside the city with his army until that moment. In celebrating their triumphs emperors sometimes made a show of following these ancient rules. When Vespasian, for example, celebrated his victory over the Jews he spent the night before the triumph outside the *pomerium*, so as to start the triumph by crossing it at the Triumphal Gate.[42] Here a sense

---

39 Cassius Dio LI.19.6. Cf. Suetonius, *Tiberius* 11.3.
40 Taylor (1966) 5–6; Magdelain (1968) 57–67; Magdelain (1977); Catalano (1978) 422–5, 479–91; Rüpke (1990) 29–57.
41 Auguries: *CIL* VI 36841 (trans. in part, Braund (1985) no.774). *Pomerium*: Wissowa (1912) 534 n. 2; Labrousse (1937) 170 n. 1. For what might be an *augur* dealing with an Augustan *comitium*, Torelli (1975) 111–16, 131–2.
42 Josephus, *Jewish War* VII.123. For the Younger Drusus, Tacitus, *Annals* III.11.1, 19.4; for Trajan, the relief from Arch of Beneventum, Hassel (1966) 19–20 and pls. 15, 17.

of traditional propriety blends with a self-conscious, propagandist display of religious scrupulosity.[43] Such a gesture of respect for the old sacred boundary is akin to Augustus himself banning Egyptian rites within the *pomerium* – so 'restoring' (or maybe 'inventing') a principle that the worship of foreign gods should not occur within the sacred boundary of Rome.[44]

Inevitably, however, the emperor's power altered the conceptual distinction between the 'civil' and the 'military' spheres: unlike republican magistrates, emperors exercised authority in both those spheres simultaneously. Under Augustus, complex constitutional arrangements were worked out to parade the legitimacy of this new state of affairs. From 23–19 B.C. he held so-called 'proconsular *imperium*' which (exceptionally) was deemed *not* to lapse when he crossed the *pomerium*, and from 19 B.C. Augustus, and later emperors, held in addition 'consular *imperium*', which meant that they now had formal power applicable both inside and outside Rome. This creative combination of traditional republican categories of power legalized the emperor's command of troops inside Rome – though the camp of the Praetorian Guard was located, tactfully (or mock traditionally, some might argue), just outside the *pomerium*. Some emperors even appeared in the city in military dress.[45] The consequences of this extended beyond the political sphere. The combination of civil and military power in the hands of the emperor meant that the *pomerium*, as a religious boundary, ceased to exclude the military. Thus in 2 B.C. the god Mars received for the first time a temple within the *pomerium*.[46]

In one area, however, even emperors proved no exception to the traditional rules of the *pomerium*. The ancient prohibition on burial within the *pomerium* was reaffirmed on several occasions up to the fourth century A.D., and seems to have been generally observed by emperors themselves. Julius Caesar had been voted in advance the special privilege of a tomb inside the *pomerium*, but in the end his ashes were buried in his family tomb. Other imperial cremations and burials in the Campus Martius seem to have been sited deliberately outside the *pomerium*. Trajan's burial was an exceptional case. He had died in the East after conquering Parthia, and his ashes were brought into Rome in triumphal procession and placed in the base of his column – which stood within the *pomerium*. But this

43 Vespasian was, of course, hardly following the traditional rules to the letter; he had already entered the city when returning from campaign – he went out only to spend the night before his triumph outside the *pomerium*.

44 Most scholars believe that the principle existed throughout the republican period, but it was at least enhanced under Augustus: Nock (1952) 213; Ziolkowski (1992) 265–96. Egyptian rites: below, p. 230.

45 Alföldi (1935) 5–8, 47–9.

46 Below, pp. 199–20. There was already within the *pomerium* a temple to Quirinus, who was associated with Mars, and Varro 'recorded' a primitive cult of Mars on the Capitol. Cf. Scholz (1970) 18–33.

anomaly was explained and (plausibly or implausibly) justified by an allegedly traditional right of those who held triumphs to be buried within the city.[47]

2.   The re-placing of Roman religion

Much of the writing of the early empire emphasizes the importance of maintaining Roman religious traditions. This concern for the proper performance of religious rites is highlighted by Valerius Maximus' *Memorable Deeds and Sayings*, a compilation of stories and anecdotes drawn from republican history, dedicated to the emperor Tiberius. The first chapter deals with religion, quoting cases of religious practices being maintained even in the face of severe difficulties, of punishment meted out to those who ignored the claims of religion, and of the correct response to instances of 'superstition'. So, for example, he briefly tells the story of a Vestal Virgin who allowed the sacred flame to go out, thus raising suspicions of her own unchastity; she was cleared by the aid of the goddess herself and a miraculous rekindling of the flame.[48]

Another index of the energy put into the organization of religion in the early Empire is the production of books on religious law. Traditionally, sacred law had been the special preserve of the priestly colleges. But from the second century B.C. various priests published books on the subject; and in the second half of the first century B.C. those who were not themselves priests – antiquarians, jurisconsults and various religious experts – wrote further treatises.[49] This activity quickened in the early Empire. Antistius Labeo wrote *On Pontifical Law* in at least fifteen books; Ateius Capito *On Pontifical Law* in at least six books, *On Law of Sacrifices* and *On Augural Law;* Veranius *On Auspices* and *Pontifical Questions.*[50] These treatises codified the basic framework of sacred law – and became themselves a venerated part of Roman religious tradition. This venerable status may account for the fact that, as far as we know, no further books were written on the subject, despite the fact that leading jurists were often members of priestly colleges.

Poets too emphasize the need to pay particular attention to religion. As we saw in the last chapter, Horace, writing in the early 20s B.C., associated the recent travails of Rome with religious neglect.[51] This is a typical Augustan perspective on recent history, closely paralleled in Livy's writing

47   J.-C. Richard (1966).
48   I.1.6.
49   Above, pp. 112–13, 153.
50   Schulz (1946) 40–1, 80–1, 89–90, 138.
51   Horace, *Odes* III.6, with Jal (1962). Temples had been neglected by the rich in favour of their private luxury: *Odes* II.15.17–20; *Satires* II.2.103–4. Against the decline thesis see above, pp. 11–12; 117–19 and ch. 3 *passim.*

on early Rome. Both writers ascribe Roman disaster to neglect of religious tradition;[52] but equally the Augustan poets present Rome's future as lying in the hands of one man, with new and unprecedented power in the city.[53] It is to his revolutionary position, and to the religious innovations and adaptations brought about through him, that we turn in the rest of this chapter – starting with the implications of the name he assumed in 27 B.C.: *Augustus*.

Augustus – or new Romulus?

Victory against Antony gave Octavian such dominance over Rome that his official Roman name, Imperator Caesar, seemed no longer adequate to represent his exceptional status: some people proposed that he be called Romulus, as if to style him the second founder of Rome.[54] Others thought that this was too regal a name, as well as carrying the taint of fratricide in the story of Romulus' murder of his brother Remus. There was, besides, the uncomfortable tradition (as we have seen) that Romulus had been murdered by the senators – a story which had particular resonances with the death of Julius Caesar, Octavian's forerunner, adoptive father and closest role-model. An alternative proposal won the day. From 27 B.C., he was officially re-titled Imperator Caesar *Augustus*. Like 'Romulus', the name 'Augustus' indicated that the bearer was uniquely favoured by the gods for the service of Rome. The story was told that when Octavian was campaigning for his first consulship in 43 B.C. six vultures appeared, and when he was elected six more appeared; this auspicy, with its echo of the myth of Romulus, indicated that he too, like Romulus, would (re)found the city of Rome.[55] This theme was maintained in the invention of the name 'Augustus', a word previously known only as an epithet (used particularly of places) with the meaning 'consecrated by *augures*'. As a name it evoked not only the favour of the gods, but also the auspicy that marked the founding of Rome. Yet 'Augustus' in no way proclaimed regal status, and as a new name had no unfortunate past.[56] In other respects, however, Romulus featured prominently in the religious imagery of Augustus, who in 16 B.C. rebuilt the temple of Quirinus – a god identified since the late Republic

52 Compare Virgil, *Georgics* I.501–2. Horace parallels the fate of Troy with that of Rome: *Odes* III.3.
53 Virgil, *Georgics* I.498–501. Horace, *Odes* I.2 with Bickerman (1961) and Nisbet and Hubbard (1970) 34–6.
54 Suetonius, *Augustus* 7.2 and Cassius Dio LIII.16.7–8, with Scott (1925).
55 Obsequens 69; Cassius Dio XLVI.46.1–3 gives six plus twelve. Suetonius, *Augustus* 95 and Appian, *Civil Wars* III.94 give twelve only and treat them as a different type of auspicy.
56 Suetonius, *Augustus* 7.2, drawing on the Augustan writer Verrius Flaccus, also used by Festus, p. 2 L; Ovid, *Fasti* I.608–16. Cf. Gagé (1930); Erkell (1952) 9–39; Dumézil (1957).

with the deified Romulus. The original decoration of this temple no longer
survives, but a fragment of a later relief depicts the pediment of the temple
(Fig. 4.1).[57] The whole composition is focussed on the taking of augury. At
the centre is a lattice-work door, which probably alludes to the entrance
into the *auguraculum,* the rectangular space within which augury was carried out. To the left of the door are Victory, Mars, Jupiter, and a female god
with cornucopia, perhaps Pales, the deity after whom the Palatine was
named. To the right are Mercury, a female deity (Bona Dea?), Hercules,
and another female figure (?Murcia, associated with the Aventine). This
fine collection of deities is impressive enough, but the important point is
that these gods are connected with Romulus and Remus. At either end of
the pediment they sit as *augures,* watching for a sign from heaven. In the
top centre and to the left are the vultures seen at the founding of Rome. All
but the deity on the far right look towards the seated Romulus on the left,
and the birds are flying in his direction. Though divine favour was to point
towards Romulus, the twins are shown acting together.

There may be a conscious attempt here to depict Romulus and Remus
in fraternal harmony; just as, in the *Aeneid,* Virgil has Jupiter prophesy that
'Quirinus with his brother Remus' will give laws to Rome.[58] But no representation of this pair, however united, could repress the stories of fratricide
and Romulus' assassination by his senators. Horace writing in the late 30s
B.C., condemning the likely renewal of bloodshed in the civil wars, turns
the murder of Remus explicitly into the origin of civil strife – so making the

57   Map 1 no. 2; Hommel (1954) 9–22; Koeppel (1984) 51–3; Wiseman (1995) 144–50.
In the original temple the senate had erected in 45 B.C. a statue of Caesar: Cicero, *Letters
to Atticus* XII.45.3, XIII.28.3. On the Forum of Augustus, below, pp. 199–201.
58   *Aeneid* I.292–3 (cf. *Georgics* II.533). This fraternal harmony was a way of evoking the
end of civil war that had marked Rome from the beginning. Weinstock (1971) 261 on
this repeated 'concord' theme.

violence of citizen against citizen as old as the city itself, and defining Rome as a doomed cycle of fratricide: 'A bitter fate pursues the Romans, and the crime of a brother's murder, ever since blameless Remus' blood was spilt upon the ground, to be a curse upon posterity.' Ovid, by contrast, suggestively exposes the impossibility of reconciling the different interpretations of the role of Romulus. In his account of the Parilia, he appears to exonerate the founder. He makes Romulus say to Remus, pacifically: 'There is no need for strife. Great faith is put in augury; let us try the birds' (i.e. augury); and, as we have seen, he blames the death of Remus on his ignorance of Romulus' prohibition and on the action of a henchman, Celer. But this version is also neatly undercut by Ovid himself, with his appeal to the god Quirinus to help with the telling of the tale – so making it clear that this is a partisan version of events, Romulus' side of the story, derived from the deified Romulus himself.[59] Different readers would have found this problem reflecting on Augustus in different ways, as he tried to be a new 'improved' Romulus, with the embarrassing stains laundered away. But however precisely interpreted, the poets show how Roman myth remained an important medium for the conduct of Roman politics and religion.

Restructuring the city

Augustus also 'revived' traditions associated with another king of Rome, Servius Tullius (the sixth king), in reorganizing the structure of the city. In doing so, he created a series of analogues, on a small local scale, to the reformed religious organization of the state as a whole. In the system that was originally created (according to Roman tradition) by Servius Tullius, the city had been divided into four *regiones* (districts) – each subdivided into a number of *vici* (wards); and, within the *vici*, at every crossroads there were shrines to the Lares, where annual sacrifices were offered. In the late Republic the colleges responsible for the cults at crossroads in the city had become a focus for political protest and Julius Caesar had attempted to suppress them; but Octavian gave theatrical performances in every ward of the city in 29 B.C. to celebrate his triple triumph, and on other occasions. Meanwhile the cults themselves seem to have continued in the early Augustan period.[60]

In 7 B.C. Augustus divided Rome into fourteen districts and 265 wards.[61] This reorganization transformed the cults of the wards: from 7 B.C.

---

59 Horace, *Epodes* 7; Ovid, *Fasti* IV.813–14. Cf. on Romulus, Wagenvoort (1956b); Koch (1960) 142–75; Weinstock (1971) 175–99; Grant (1973) 101–47. Harries (1989) 170–1 and Hinds (1992) 142–8 detect equivocation in Ovid's account. Elsewhere, Ovid is very critical of Romulus.

60 Above, p. 139. Boyancé (1950); Dionysius of Halicarnassus, *Roman Antiquities* IV.14.4; Degrassi (1965) 269–71.

61 Wissowa (1912) 167–73; Alföldi (1973) 18–36; Liebeschuetz (1979) 69–71; Kienast (1982) 164–6; Fraschetti (1990) 204–73.

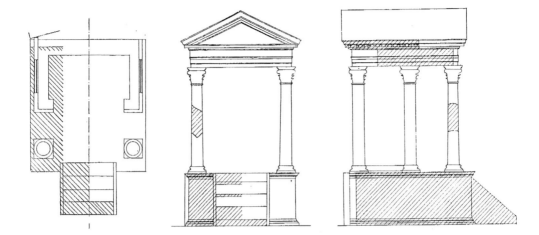

Fig. 4.2 A reconstruction of the shrine of the Lares at Compitum Acili, Rome.

onwards they became cults of the Lares Augusti and the Genius Augusti. Their traditional celebrations were also changed. To the old festival of the Lares on 1 May was added a new celebration on 1 August, when the magistrates took up office, probably in honour of the Genius Augusti.[62] The significance of these new cults is clear enough in outline, if not in detail. The Lares (usually translated, all too automatically, as 'household gods') were ancient but obscure deities, seen by some ancient writers as the deified spirits of the dead.[63] On this interpretation, the Lares Augusti would be the emperor's ancestors, and the Genius Augusti, the Spirit of Augustus himself. In other words, the public ward cults now consisted of cults that had previously been the private cults of Augustus and his family, located within his own house.[64]

The new cults involved building a shrine at the crossroads in each ward. The best known example is a modest monument in marble, just 2.80m. by 2.38m., with a flight of five steps running up to the shrine, which sheltered images of the Lares Augusti and the Genius Augusti. In front of it stood a small altar (54 cm. high) (Fig. 4.2).[65] The sculptured reliefs on some of the other extant altars attempt to display the connections of past and present, city and ward. Thus the most elaborately carved example shows, on the two smaller sides, a sacrifice performed by the ward magistrates, and the scene

62 Ovid, *Fasti* V.129, 147–8; Suetonius, *Augustus* 31.4; Niebling (1956) 324–5. Three *vici* seem to have been reorganized not in 7 B.C., but in 12, 9 and 6 B.C.

63 Festus p. 108 L; Arnobius, *Against the Gentiles* III.41 (= Varro fr. 209 (Cardauns)); statuettes, **2.2a**.

64 The only precedent for the Lares Augusti is a solitary dedication from Gallia Cisalpina (*ILLRP* 200, 59 B.C.), but the popular veneration of the Gracchi and Marius Gratidianus seems to have taken place at the neighbourhood shrines (above, p. 144). For the relation between these cults and Augustus' cult of Vesta see below, pp. 189–91. Whatever the exact reasoning the political conclusion seems inevitable.

65 E. Nash (1968) I.290–1; Steinby (1993–) I.314–15. Full publication: Colini (1961–2); Tamassia (1961–2). Further details: Dondin-Payre (1987). Cf. Holland (1937); Hänlein-Schäfer (1996) 74–81. Another altar with inscription: *ILS* 9520 = **8.6a**.

(made famous by Virgil's epic) of Aeneas' discovery of a sow on his arrival in Italy; and on the two larger sides, Victory with the shield of Virtue awarded to Augustus and the apotheosis of Caesar (Fig. 4.3). These reliefs are clearly similar in some respects to the iconography of 'official' Augustan art; but the (often crude) style of their carving, and the wide range of scenes chosen to decorate the altars, are distinctive. They suggest that, though Augustus devised the cults of the Lares Augusti and of his Genius for the wards, and presented statues of the gods to them,[66] the specific arrangements and the designs of the altars were the responsibility of the local officials.[67]

The Augustan reorganization of the ward cults gave the emperor a place throughout the city of Rome. The shrines continued to be repaired (and used) through the third century and still feature in the catalogues of Roman monuments compiled in the fourth century.[68] The cults were not a transient Augustan phenomenon, but played their part in permanently re-orienting Roman religion under the Empire. The creation of the new wards took the emphasis on *place* to every corner of the city; here we see the emperor inserted within a religious framework that incorporated the whole city, by creating an opportunity for local participation in the creation of imperial Rome's new mythology.

Priesthoods and the emperor

Augustus held priesthoods only at Rome itself. So far as we know he took no religious office outside the capital; but there he gradually accumulated membership of all the major priestly colleges, becoming *pontifex* in 48 B.C., *augur* in 41–40 B.C., *quindecimvir sacris faciundis* in c.37 B.C., and *septemvir epulonum* by 16 B.C. To mark this cumulation of priestly offices a coin was issued in 16 B.C. featuring the symbols of each of the four priesthoods.[69] In addition, Augustus was made a member of three of the lesser priesthoods: *frater Arvalis, sodalis Titius* and *fetialis*. Portraits of the emperor, both on coins and on statues, frequently showed him veiled in a toga, in the stance of sacrifice. In fact, from this period on, virtually no one else is depicted on a Roman public monument conducting sacrifice: Roman religion was becoming tied to a particular person as well as to a particular place.

66 Degrassi (1963) 96; Ovid, *Fasti* V.145–6; Palmer (1990) 17.
67 Zanker (1969); (1970–71); Panciera (1987) 73–8; Zanker (1988) 129–135. For example, one altar (the 'Belvedere Altar') seems to have combined the figure of 'Victory' and the honorific 'Shield of Virtue' (both in the senate house and both characteristic parts of 'official' Augustan iconography) to create the figure of Victory bringing a purely military shield.
68 Panciera (1970) 138–51; (1980); (1987) 61–73. *AE* (1975) 14: an attempt to avoid the duties of *vici magister,* which involved games with *venatio* (hunting displays). Fourth century catalogues: below, p. 382.
69 *RIC* I².69, nos. 367–8. Cf. *RIC* I².73, no. 410, 13 B.C. Gagé (1931); also Bayet (1955). Zanker (1988) 126–8 and R. L. Gordon (1990b) stress the emperor as the archetypal sacrificer.

Fig. 4.3 The Belvedere altar, Rome, 12–2 B.C. (a) Sacrifice at ward altar, by ward magistrate (on right); an attendant (on left) proffers two images of the Lares Augusti as recipients of the cult; (b) Aeneas' discovery of the sow which portended the successful foundation of Alba Longa – the city which the Romans regarded as the precursor of the city of Rome itself. The figure on the left may be a prophet. The story was told by Virgil (*Aeneid* III.389–93, VIII.42–8, 81–5), and is also featured on the Ara Pacis (**4.3c**); (c) Victory with the honorific shield awarded to Augustus in 27 B.C. The inscription reads: 'The senate and people of Rome to Emperor Caesar Augustus, son of *divus* (Julius), *pontifex maximus*, hailed *imperator* <gap> times, *consul* <gap> times, with tribunician power for <gap> years'. The altar was put up many years after the award of the shield and those who commissioned it never completed (or did not know) the details of Augustus' titles at the time. (d) The apotheosis of Caesar (?), observed by Augustus on left and by Venus (?) and Augustus' heirs on right. (Height 0.95m., width 0.97m., depth 0.67m.)

In the Republic it had been extremely unusual for anyone to hold more than one major priesthood. Julius Caesar had been both *pontifex* and *augur*, but Augustus went way beyond even Caesar's precedent; and his management of the imperial family established the cumulation of priestly offices as a privilege of emperors and their heirs only.[70] When Nero was adopted by Claudius in A.D. 50, coins were issued with the same four symbols as had appeared on Augustus' coins and a legend indicating that Nero had been co-opted as an extra, supernumerary, member of the four major priestly colleges, by decree of the senate.[71] This co-optation into four colleges simultaneously was an innovation, and it marked Nero out as Claudius' chosen heir, setting a precedent for the future as a way of designating the emperor's successor. But at the same time the emperor and his heir were staking a claim to embrace all religious activity in Rome.

The first two of Augustus' offices, *augur* and *pontifex*, are worth considering here; we shall return to the *quindecimviri sacris faciundis* later. The *lituus*, the *augures'* ceremonial staff that had become the symbol of the priesthood, was regularly featured on the coinage of Octavian in the 30s B.C.[72] This was one of the ways in which Octavian, like other republican leaders, emphasized that his military authority was properly founded on religious observance. But after his victory at Actium he stressed the peaceful overtones of the office of *augur*. In 29 B.C. Octavian took the so-called '*augurium salutis*'. This was an augural ceremony that could be carried out only at a time when no Roman forces were fighting – to ascertain whether it was propitious for the consuls even to ask the gods to grant safety to the state. It was, in the extravagant words of an official inscribed record, the 'greatest augury by which the safety of the Roman people is sought'. In fact, we know of only two occasions when it was attempted before 29 B.C. – in about 160 B.C. and during Cicero's consulship in 63 B.C. But it is treated by ancient writers as a venerable tradition *revived* by the emperor, another aspect of the 'restoration' of religion at the beginning of the principate. It was at least a 'tradition' that was maintained: an inscription records seven performances between A.D. 1 and 17; and Tacitus notes another occasion under Claudius in A.D. 49.[73]

The key priestly office was that of *pontifex maximus*. Augustus had been a member of the pontifical college since 48 B.C., but in 44 B.C., on the assassination of Caesar, it was Lepidus (then in alliance with Octavian and Mark Antony, in the so-called 'second triumvirate') who was appointed head of

70 Weinstock (1971) 28–34; Lewis (1955) 23, 94–101. The rules of republican priestly office-holding: above, pp. 103–5.

71 *RIC* I².125, nos. 76–7 (= **8.5a(ii)**), 129, no. 107 (A.D. 50–54). For the history of this type see *B. M. Coins* III.xl–xliii.

72 Gagé (1930).

73 Revival: Suetonius, *Augustus* 31.4; Cassius Dio LI.20.4. Repeated: *CIL* VI 36841 (trans., in part, Braund (1985) no. 774); Tacitus, *Annals* XII.23.1. Performed in 160s B.C.: above, pp. 110–11. The semantic link with 'Augustus': above, p. 182.

the college. Augustus did not remove Lepidus from office, even when he was disgraced. But with a dramatic display of restraint, in the name of the traditional proprieties of priestly office, he waited until the death of Lepidus in 13 B.C. before being elected *pontifex maximus* in 12 B.C. In his own account of his *Achievements,* he laid great emphasis on the popularity of his election: 'such crowds poured in from the whole of Italy for my election as are never recorded at Rome before'. The date on which the election occurred was even celebrated by an annual festival, and it is noted in Ovid's *Fasti.*[74] Augustus' election to this office (and also, as we shall see, his transformation of it) proved to be of central importance in the restructuring of Roman religion.

The *pontifex maximus* was traditionally obliged to live in an official house, which stood in the Forum adjacent to the precinct of the Vestal Virgins; even Julius Caesar conformed to this rule. Augustus, on the other hand, was unwilling to give up his own house on the Palatine, though he found ways to recognise the obligation that he should live in a public, official residence. Initially, he made a part of his own house public property; but subsequently (A.D. 3), after a fire destroyed the house, he rebuilt it and made it all public property.[75] This was more than a technical evasion of (or genuflection towards) an inconvenient regulation. It signalled an important step in the redefinition of the office of *pontifex maximus,* as well as a new alignment between that priestly office and the goddess Vesta.

Far from leaving the cult of Vesta behind, Augustus' displacement of the residence of the *pontifex maximus* to the Palatine reaffirmed, and even intensified, the connection with the goddess. Just under two months after Augustus became *pontifex maximus* there was dedicated 'an image and [shrine] of Vesta in the house of Imperator Caesar Augustus *pontifex maximus*'.[76] The old shrine which contained the sacred flame and an array of secret objects remained in the Forum, but the new shrine inside Augustus' house on the Palatine had radical implications for his position as *pontifex maximus.* The closeness of the relationship between Augustus and Vesta was stressed by contemporary writers. They told, for example, that it was Aeneas who had brought the fire of Vesta with him from Troy to Italy, and Romulus (himself the son of a Vestal, by the god Mars) who had transferred the cult from Alba Longa to Rome – so linking the origin of the cult with the mythical forebears of Augustus.[77] They sometimes claim actual kinship

---

74 Augustus, *Achievements* 10.2 = **8.5b**; Degrassi (1963) 420; Ovid, *Fasti* III.415–28.

75 Possible Caesarian rebuilding in the vicinity of the temple of Vesta: R. T. Scott (1993) 169–74 (Map: **4.7**). Augustus: Cassius Dio LIV.27.3; LV.12.4–5. In 36 B.C. Octavian had been voted a house at public expense: Cassius Dio XLIX.15.5. Cf. Weinstock (1971) 276–81.

76 Map 1 no. 14. Degrassi (1963) 452. The restoration of the word 'shrine' on the inscription is controversial, but see Guarducci (1971). There was already a ramp linking the old temple of Vesta to the Palatine: Steinby (1993). See also Fig. 4.4.

77 Aeneas: Virgil, *Aeneid* II.296, 567; Ovid, *Fasti* I.527–8, III.29, VI.227; *Metamorphoses* XV.730–1; Propertius IV.4.69; Dionysius of Halicarnassus, *Roman Antiquities* II.65.2.

Fig. 4.4 A relief on a base now in Sorrento represents the cult of Vesta, perhaps in its new location on the Palatine. On the right, Vesta enthroned, pouring a libation, flanked by two female figures – possibly other goddesses. She is approached by a group of five Vestals, headed no doubt (in the lost central section) by the sixth Vestal and perhaps by Augustus as *pontifex maximus*. Beyond the curtains (which indicate that this is an indoor scene) is visible, on the right, the round shrine of Vesta in the Forum, with the Palladium within – showing that the main scene is not taking place there; also visible are statues of a bull and a ram; and, on the left, columns of an Ionic temple, maybe that of Apollo on the Palatine. There are three other scenes not illustrated here. On the right side of the base are Apollo, Latona and Diana, modelled on the cult images in the temple of Apollo. On the left side, in front of the house of Augustus, Mars led by Cupid and (probably) Venus approaching perhaps the numen of Augustus. On the rear, Magna Mater. (Height 1.17m., max. width 1.90m., max. depth 1.20m.)

between Vesta and Augustus, as when Ovid prays, 'Gods of ancient Troy, the worthiest prize to him who bore you, you whose weight saved Aeneas from the foe, a priest descended from Aeneas handles divinities related to him; Vesta, you must guard his person related to you.'[78] Augustus was thus connected to Vesta both by blood and by the deeds of his ancestors.

The creation of the shrine on the Palatine was an important stage in the formation of a peculiarly imperial residence, with particular religious resonances.

Romulus: Plutarch, *Romulus* 22; Dionysius II.64.5–69 argues at length for the alternative that Numa established the cult in Rome.
78 *Fasti* III.423–6. Cf. Fraschetti (1990) 331–60; Feeney (1991) 205–24.

Though in some ways Augustus' house continued to be just one among many aristocratic residences on the Palatine, it was also now transformed into a palace – a palace shared between the emperor, Vesta and (as we shall see below) Apollo. So Ovid again writes, 'Vesta has been received into the house of her kinsman; so have the senators rightly decreed. Apollo has part of the house; another part has been given up to Vesta; what remains is occupied by Augustus himself ... A single house holds three eternal gods.'[79] But there were further implications. Not only could the *pontifex maximus* now be called 'priest of Vesta';[80] not only had Vesta now been relocated in a new imperial setting; but even more crucially the public hearth of the state, with its associations of the success of the Roman empire, had been fused with the private hearth of Augustus. The emperor (and the emperor's house) could now be claimed to stand for the state.

The new relationship with Vesta is just one aspect of the transformation of the office of *pontifex maximus*. It is striking that in his biography of Augustus, Suetonius groups his major religious reforms under the heading of the emperor's role as *pontifex maximus,* – even though some are demonstrably earlier than his assumption of that office.[81] But, even if inaccurate in detail, Suetonius was in essence correct. For Augustus had established a new conception of the office of *pontifex maximus*, which did give it an overall religious authority in the state and a preeminent capacity to introduce religious reform.[82]

The *pontifices* were, if with the *augures*, the most prestigious priestly college of the Republic. The *pontifex maximus* enjoyed considerable prestige, and the office was keenly fought for; but he was technically (and in practice) merely head of one of the priestly colleges, with no general authority over any other college or over 'religion' more generally.[83] This situation, however, was already beginning to change with the emergence of dynasts in the late Republic and (particularly clearly) in the dictatorship of Julius Caesar. In 44 B.C., for example, it was decreed that Caesar's son or adopted son should become *pontifex maximus* after him – suggesting that it was being seen not just as 'chairmanship' of a priestly college but as a (hereditary) part of Caesar's autocratic power.[84] That certainly is how it developed

---

79 Ovid, *Fasti* IV.949–54. Cf. Wiseman (1987).

80 Ovid, *Fasti* III.699, V.573; *Metamorphoses* XV.778, retrospectively applied to Julius Caesar. In the third and fourth centuries the *pontifices* were also known as *pontifices Vestae: RE* VIII.A.2, 1760.

81 *Augustus* 31. Modern scholars sometimes say that in 12 B.C. Augustus became 'head' of Roman religion, a pagan equivalent of Archbishop of Canterbury, Chief Rabbi or Pope; and so they are inclined to date his religious reforms to the period after 12 B.C. Wissowa (1912) 74; Wilhelm (1915); Liebeschuetz (1979) 70.

82 The political implications of the charge are clear in the debate in A.D. 22 about the office of *flamen Dialis:* below, p. 193.

83 Beard (1990); above, pp. 20–1; 54–6.

84 Cassius Dio XLIV.5.3.

with Augustus. After his election to the office, it was impossible for anyone but the emperor living on the Palatine to be *pontifex maximus*. All subsequent emperors took up the position soon after their accession and regularly featured it among their official titles. In short, it became a keystone of the religious system. So Dio stresses in his account of the reign of Augustus (in the middle of a series of reflections on the nature of the emperor's power that clearly also draws on circumstances of the third century A.D.): 'From the fact that they are enrolled in all the priesthoods and moreover can grant most of the priesthoods to others, and that one of them, even if two or three emperors are ruling jointly, is *pontifex maximus,* they control all sacred and religious matters'.[85] From 12 B.C. onwards, for the first time, Roman religion had a head.

Priesthoods and the senatorial élite

The traditional senatorial priesthoods retained their prestige during the early Empire, and the prestige of some was actually increased by Augustus.[86] Partly no doubt because these priesthoods, unlike magistracies, were held for life, they were eagerly sought; partly too because the number of positions available meant that (even though in the first two centuries of the Empire it was not possible for a senator to be a member of more than one of the four main colleges) only a quarter to a third of senators, and a half of all consuls, could become priests. The younger Pliny published among his correspondence a letter proudly responding to a friend's congratulations on his appointment to the college of *augures*: 'the priesthood is an ancient and religious office, which has an especial sanctity in that it is held for life';[87] and some senators saw membership of one of the priestly colleges as the pinnacle of their career, ranking higher than being praetor or consul.

Appointment to a priesthood, however, now depended in part on the patronage of the emperor. Cassius Dio says that in 29 B.C. Octavian was allowed to appoint priests even beyond the regular number, a principle which continued (he writes) to his own day.[88] Not that such appointments were necessarily overtly autocratic. Augustus and later emperors were members of all four priestly colleges, and could exercise their patronage through influence on traditional priestly elections. All the same, there was little doubt in whose gift priestly office ultimately lay. In an earlier letter addressed to Trajan, Pliny explicitly asks the emperor for the grant of a

---

85 Cassius Dio LIII.17.8. From the mid second century onwards emperors sometimes shared their political powers with prospective heirs.
86 Below, p. 194 (revival of Arval Brothers).
87 Pliny, *Letters* IV.8.
88 Cassius Dio LI.20.3. Augustus, *Achievements* 25.3 notes that of the 700 senators who supported his rise to power about 170 were, or became, priests. Scheid (1978), (1990b) 201–14; Millar (1977) 357 n. 15 on first cumulation of major priesthoods. The four colleges were paraded on the Ara Pacis: **4.3b**; above, Fig. 1.3 (*flamines*); Zanker (1988) 120–3.

priesthood, 'the office either of *augur* or of *septemvir*, both of which are now vacant'.[89]

Nevertheless, despite keen competition for most priesthoods, two offices caused particular problems. The office of *flamen Dialis* had been vacant since 87 B.C., until Augustus as *pontifex maximus* had the post filled in 11 B.C.[90] It remained subject to unique restrictions and taboos, many of which must have made the priesthood unattractive to potential holders – and which (as we have seen) had caused conflict between *flamines* and *pontifex maximus* more than a hundred years earlier. It may have been in response to the unattractiveness of the office that Augustus made certain changes to the rules, or (as Tacitus has his successor Tiberius put it) 'altered certain relics of a primitive antiquity to the modern spirit'.[91] The full details of the changes are lost to us, but the priest was now allowed to spend more nights outside Rome (the previous rule had prevented him spending more than two nights away) and there seem also to have been changes in the status of his wife.[92] The debates over the restrictions continued beyond Augustus' reign. In A.D. 22, one *flamen Dialis* argued that he should be allowed to leave Rome to govern a province; earlier bans imposed by *pontifices maximi* had been the result of private feuds, while now that the *pontifex maximus* was also the supreme person, he was above such motives. Tiberius, however, as *pontifex maximus* ruled against such a radical change (using, according to Tacitus, the earlier minor reforms of Augustus as an argument against any such major departure from precedent). When this *flamen* died, Tiberius argued that the restriction of the office to those married by the archaic, and now rare, ceremony of *confarreatio* should be lifted. The senate, to whom the matter was referred, decided that no change was necessary, and the son of the old *flamen* was chosen to replace his father. Tiberius himself, meanwhile, introduced a law to remove more of the legal restrictions on the *flamen*'s wife.[93]

Augustus also attempted to solve problems over the appointment of Vestal Virgins. On one occasion when a Vestal had died, he found senators were reluctant to put their daughters forward as candidates (girls were normally chosen for this priesthood between the ages of six and ten). According to Suetonius, Augustus swore that if any of his granddaughters had been of the appropriate age, he would have proposed them. But he also increased the privileges of the Vestals, including special seats in the theatre;

---

89 Pliny, *Letters* X.13.

90 This 'gap' in the flaminate: above, pp. 130–1.

91 Aulus Gellius, *Attic Nights* XI.15.14 (= **8.1b**). Tacitus, *Annals* IV.16.3. Cf. Rohde (1936) 136–7.

92 Tacitus, *Annals* III.71.3; Gaius, *Institutes* I.136, fragmentary. Cf. Aulus Gellius, *Attic Nights* X.15.14 and 17 (= **8.1b**) for other changes.

93 Tacitus, *Annals* III.58–59.1, 71 (A.D. 22); IV.16 (A.D. 24). Cf. Domitian's permission for a *flamen Dialis* to divorce his wife: Plutarch, *Roman Questions* 50. Earlier arguments about the selection of the *flamen Dialis*: Livy XXVII.8.4–10 = **8.2d**; above, pp. 106–8.

later, distinguished imperial women sat among the Vestals in the theatre.[94] We do not know how successful such official encouragement was; nor is it clear how the closer links between the imperial house and the cult of Vesta affected the priesthood and its popularity. But Tacitus writes that under Tiberius two senators vied with each other to have their daughters chosen as Vestal Virgins; and the office remained in high prestige through the third into the fourth century.[95]

The Vestals, in fact, accumulated new, imperial functions in addition to their traditional ones. In the Republic they had been present with the other priests at the grand funeral of Sulla and it was voted that with the *pontifices* they should every five years offer up prayers for Caesar's safety.[96] After the battle of Actium the Vestals headed the procession which greeted the returning Octavian; they were present too at the dedication of the Ara Pacis, and with the magistrates and priests were responsible for the annual sacrifices there. (They are represented on the small, inner frieze on the altar itself.) The Vestals were even put in charge of the cult of the deified Livia.[97] So, while Vesta gained a new shrine on the Palatine, the Vestals gained a concern for the emperor and his family – still further linking the emperor to the hearth of Rome, and to the favour of the gods for Rome which that hearth symbolized.

The history of the Arval Brothers illustrates the extent and nature of changes in priesthoods in the imperial period in all its complexity. We know almost nothing about the Arvals' activities during the Republic. Although their sanctuary on the outskirts of Rome is attested archaeologically from the third century B.C., the only literary reference to them before the imperial period is in Varro's work *On the Latin Language*. There he explains that they perform rites to make the crops grow and that their name (*fratres Arvales*) comes either from sowing (*ferendo*) and fields (*arvis*), or from the Greek *fratria* or brotherhood. Octavian became a member of the college and, perhaps in 29 B.C., placed the body on a new footing.[98] Significantly, in the imperial period the name was explained differently. The nurse of Romulus had twelve sons, but one died and Romulus himself took his place, calling himself and the others 'Arval Brothers'.[99] This myth entirely suited a college which included Augustus, the new Romulus.

94 Suetonius, *Augustus* 31.3, 44.3. Tacitus, *Annals* IV.16.4; Cassius Dio LIX.3, 4, LX.22.2. In fact no imperial daughters were ever appointed as Vestal Virgins.

95 Tacitus, *Annals* II.86. Cf. IV.16.4: a grant of two million sesterces to a new Vestal, presumably in addition to the traditional salary. Nock (1930), though he cannot prove an increase in prestige in the third century; **8.4b** (inscriptions honouring Vestals).

96 Appian, *Civil Wars* I.106; II.106.

97 Ara Pacis: Ryberg (1955) 41, 43, 51–2, 71–4 (cf. **4.3a** n. 1); Cassius Dio LI.19.2; Augustus, *Achievements* 11–12. Livia: Cassius Dio LX.5.2. Part of the inner frieze is illustrated: **6.1a**.

98 Map 4 no. 70; Varro, *On the Latin Language* V.85 (= **8.1a**). Scheid (1990b) 679–732. Cf. Saulnier (1980) and Wiedemann (1986) for reorganization of the *fetiales*; above, p. 133.

99 Pliny, *Natural History* XVIII.6; Aulus Gellius, *Attic Nights* VII.7.8, quoting Masurius Sabinus (*floruit* Tiberius-Nero) who drew on earlier historians.

The revived college inscribed a record on stone of its membership and of the ceremonies it carried out year by year (notably its three-day festival held in May in honour of Dea Dia, an obscure deity known only from these inscriptions). The extensive fragments that have been discovered in their sanctuary run from 21 B.C. to A.D. 304, and are the fullest extant record of any of the priesthoods of Rome.[100] The lists of Arval members that we can reconstruct from the inscribed record allow us to explore in detail the changing patterns of recruitment to the priesthood. So, for example, from its first Augustan appointments to the end of Nero's reign, the college was of considerable distinction, with members drawn from the most prominent members of the senate. Thereafter it went through a series of changes. At times (under Vespasian, Marcus Aurelius and Caracalla) those recruited to the college were no less distinguished than those elected to the four major colleges, while at other times the Arvals seem to have been drawn from the middle ranks of the senate which could not expect consulships or major priesthoods.[101] The detailed records of the Arvals allow us to detect (more fully than for any other priesthood) a complex and changing history of patronage and recruitment to the college, which may be related to the needs of the emperor to conciliate opponents and honour allies.

The inscribed records of the Arval ceremonies also demonstrate the extent to which the ancient (or allegedly ancient) cults of Rome were re-structured round the figure of the emperor. The main festival of Dea Dia herself was never adapted to include any sacrifices or rituals specifically focussed on the emperor (even if he was sometimes present in his capacity as priest), but he and his family did become the focus of a range of quite separate 'imperial rituals' performed by the college. Throughout the Julio-Claudian period, the Arval Brothers made annual vows and carried out sac-rifices 'for the emperor's safety', and they offered sacrifices to mark imperial birthdays, accessions, deaths and deifications – or sometimes to celebrate the suppression of a conspiracy against the emperor, or his safe return to Rome from abroad. Their sanctuary of Dea Dia also included a Caesareum, a 'shrine of the Caesars' containing imperial statues. In general, however, the sacrifices they performed for the emperor did not take place in the sanc-tuary of Dea Dia, nor (at least from the mid first century A.D.) did they involve sacrifices to her. Their 'dynastic' sacrifices in the Julio-Claudian period took place mainly on the Capitol or at the temple of the deified Augustus, and from the Flavian period onwards exclusively on the Capitol. The deities involved were the Capitoline triad, Jupiter, Juno and Minerva,

---

100 A new edition of the inscriptions is forthcoming (ed. Scheid); extracts, **4.5**, **6.2**; Lewis and Reinhold (1990) II.516–19. For the fluidity of the record, Beard (1985), with comments of Scheid (1990b) 66–72, 431, 617, 732–40. The record inscribed on stone was presumably based on archival documents kept on paper by the priests .

101 Scheid (1975); Syme (1980); Scheid (1990a).

Salus publica, and deified members of the imperial house, as well as the Genius of the living emperor and the Juno of the empress.

After A.D. 69, at the end of the Julio-Claudian dynasty, there were changes in the rituals of the Arvals. The annual vows for the emperor's safety remained a regular element in their ritual calendar throughout their history, but from the late first century their records show no more regular sacrifices to the *divi*;[102] imperial birthdays were no longer celebrated; and sacrifices for occasional events (such as the discovery of plots or the commemoration of imperial victories) became much less common. In fact, the proportion of the recorded Arval rituals with a direct imperial reference dropped from two thirds or even three quarters under the Julio-Claudians to a quarter or even less in the second and third centuries A.D. Again we do not know exactly how to explain this change (nor, for that matter, can we be certain that the inscribed records of the priesthood are an accurate record of all the rituals that were actually carried out); but we can glimpse here something of the process by which traditional priests became involved also in 'imperial rituals', and the changing patterns of those rituals over time. Suetonius' apparently simple reference to Augustus' 'restoration of ancient cults which had gradually fallen into disuse'[103] should not blind us to the fact that 'restoration' entailed a radical shift in focus.

Temples

The building or rebuilding of temples is another aspect of the restructuring of the religious system around the person of the emperor. As we have seen, Augustus himself records in his *Achievements* that he repaired eighty-two temples in 28 B.C. alone; and he names fourteen other temples in Rome that he built or restored during his reign. This account of temple-building is interspersed with references to his work on other, secular buildings, such as the senate-house, theatres, the water supply and a road[104] – as if this temple construction was to be seen simply as part of the republican tradition of victorious generals and other senators carrying out building works in the city. There was, however, a profound difference. While senators continued to erect some *secular* buildings during the reign of Augustus, after 33 B.C. only Augustus and members of his family built *temples* in Rome. This may have been a generous shouldering of responsibility for temples in Rome on the part of the emperor. But, even if so, it had clear political and religious consequences. On the one hand, senators (now excluded from their traditional

---

102 This change might be connected with a development in the function of the *sodales Augustales* and other imperial priesthoods in Rome itself, who may have taken over sacrifices to the *divi* previously carried out by the Arvals.

103 Suetonius, *Augustus* 31.4.

104 *Achievements* 19–21. Cf. Eck (1984) 136–42. Wissowa (1912) 596–7 lists the new temples, though that to Neptune was probably a restoration; in general: Gros (1976); Zanker (1988) 65–71, 102–18, 135–56; Purcell (1996).

opportunity for display in the capital) increased their munificence to their native cities in Italy and elsewhere. On the other, temple building placed the emperor and his family in a unique relationship with the gods, increasing the importance of the emperor and permitting a novel prominence to his female relatives (who were also associated with these building schemes).[105]

The reign of Augustus is a crucial period for temple building; in contrast to the following fifty years, when only two new state temples were built. Moreover all the state temples built in Rome in the Augustan period, or immediately afterwards, refer directly or indirectly to the emperor. Two were dedicated to a deified member of the imperial house (*divus* Julius, *divus* Augustus). Three relate to victories on the part of the emperor (Apollo, Neptune, Mars Ultor). Two stress imperial virtues (Concordia, Iustitia). One (Jupiter Tonans) was dedicated by Augustus in thanks for his narrow escape from a thunderbolt. In addition some of the old temples rebuilt by Augustus gained new, imperial, associations. Three temples built or rebuilt by Augustus may be taken as exemplary of this new focus: Magna Mater, Apollo and Mars Ultor.

The temple of the Magna Mater on the Palatine was a well-known peculiarity in the late Republic. It had been built originally shortly after introduction of the cult of the goddess from Phrygia in 204 B.C., and was rebuilt by Augustus around 2 B.C., and probably restored again following a fire in A.D. 3.[106] We have already seen some of the ambivalences of this cult: an element of 'foreign' barbaric exoticism within the city, at the same time as it held an established position within the 'official' cults of the city. These ambivalences remain. The cult retained all kinds of 'Phrygian' peculiarities, not only in its flamboyant priesthood, but also in religious claims and mythical traditions: Ovid, for example, refers to Magna Mater holding precedence over the other gods (who were her children), and describes the offering to her of herbs, which the earth once grew without human labour – so apparently sacralizing the most primitive stage of human existence before the Greek Ceres introduced cereal cultivation.[107] But in the Augustan period the specifically Roman, even imperial, aspects of the goddess became increasingly emphasized. Her Phrygian homeland was strongly associated with the Trojan origins of Rome: according to Ovid again (telling the story

---

105 All temples 'would have fallen into complete ruins, without the far-seeing care of our sacred leader, under whom the shrines feel not the touch of age; and not content with doing favours to humankind he does them to the gods. O holy one, who builds and rebuilds the temples, I pray the powers above may take such care of you as you of them': Ovid, *Fasti* II.59–64. Cf. I.13–14, Livy IV.20.7, Suetonius, *Augustus* 29–30; above, pp. 121–5. Temple building by Livia: Purcell (1986) 88–9; below, p. 297. Temple building by later emperors: below, pp. 253–9.

106 Map 1 no. 13. The arrival of the goddess: above, pp. 96–8. Date of repair: Syme (1978a) 30. See generally Lambrechts (1951); Boyancé (1954); Bömer (1964); Wiseman (1984).

107 Ovid, *Fasti* IV.367–72 with Brelich (1965).

of the goddess's arrival at Rome during the Hannibalic War), she had almost followed Aeneas from neighbouring Troy to Italy but 'realized that Fate did not yet require her power for Latium', so waited five hundred years till she was summoned by a Sibylline Oracle; and in Virgil's *Aeneid* Magna Mater appears as a protectress of Aeneas on his journeys. When Augustus rebuilt the temple, he made a particular show of the venerable antiquity of the cult of the goddess: he built the temple not in marble (the material of almost all his new building projects) but in traditional tufa – blocks of coarse local stone and the material of most of the earliest temples at Rome.[108]

Near the temple of the Magna Mater on the Palatine, and directly adjacent to his own house, Augustus built a temple of Apollo on what had been his own land. The site had been struck by lightning in 36 B.C., a sign (or so at least it was interpeted by some religious experts) that the god himself had chosen this particular spot. Augustus promptly made it public property, conse-crated it to Apollo, finally dedicating the temple itself in 28 B.C. The temple was one of the grandest in the city with lavish sculptural decoration: statues of Danaus and his fifty daughters, the Danaids, between the columns of the portico in front of the temple; ivory carvings on the door, showing (on one side) the killing of Niobe's children by Apollo and his sister Diana, and (on the other) the expulsion of the Gauls from Delphi; inside the temple, statues of Apollo, Diana and their mother Latona, works (originally brought to Rome as booty) by three of the finest Greek sculptors of the fourth century B.C.[109] It quickly became a major religious focus. The ancient Sibylline Books were transferred there from the temple of Jupiter, probably in 23–19 B.C. (it was, after all, under inspiration from Apollo that the Sibyl herself was said to prophesy).[110] And it was one of the settings for the rituals of the Saecular Games, held in 17 B.C., to which we shall return below.

The location of the temple is very striking. The earlier temple of Apollo was in the Circus Flaminius, outside the *pomerium*. Augustus not only moved his cult inside the sacred boundary of the city; but he brought the god effectively into his own house – as Ovid aptly recalled with his refer-ence to 'a single house <that> holds three eternal gods'. This complex of divine and human residence (emperor's palace, shrine of Vesta and temple of Apollo) was without precedent in Rome, and clearly evoked the divine associations of Augustus.[111]

---

108 *Fasti* IV.251–4, 272. Virgil, *Aeneid* II.693–7, IX.77–9, X.252–5.

109 Map 1 no. 14; Steinby (1993–) I.54–7. The archaeological remains have not yet been properly published. Lightning: Suetonius, *Augustus* 29.3; Cassius Dio XLIX.15.5. Grandeur: Propertius II.31; Pliny, *Natural History* XXXVI.24, 25, 32. Very little of this sculpture now survives; but there are several ancient descriptions of it, as well as representations (on later sculpture panels and on coins) of some of the individual pieces. For representation on the so-called 'Sorrento base': above, Fig. 4.4.

110 Gagé (1931) 99–101; (1955) 542–55.

111 However, the excavator's claim that a private ramp linked Augustus' house to the terrace of the temple is implausible: the difference in levels is too great. Ovid: above, p. 191.

This temple also signified a shift in the character of Apollo at Rome. Previously his main role had been as a healing god, of no particular prominence; now he was to be central to Augustus' new Rome. The iconography of the sanctuary prompted all kinds of connections between Apollo and the new imperial régime.[112] So, for example, the statues of the Danaids recalled not only their righteous action in killing the impious sons of Aegyptus, but also the dedication of a temple to Apollo by Danaus after he won the throne of Argos (an analogy perhaps with the establishment of Augustan monarchy). Similarly the doors of the temple, in highlighting the punishments meted out by Apollo to those who disobeyed him (Niobe, the Gauls), evoked the role of Apollo at the battle of Actium in 31 B.C., where it was said he had helped Augustus to defeat (and punish) Antony and Cleopatra. Significantly Augustus also founded a temple of Apollo on the outskirts of his new city of Nikopolis ('Victory City', near Actium), with a prestigious Panhellenic four-yearly festival of Actian Apollo, which was still being celebrated over 250 years later.[113]

The third major Augustan temple, which was later described by Pliny the Elder as among the most beautiful buildings in the world, is a classic example of the complex interrelationship between innovation and tradition, restructuring and continuity, that characterizes most of the religious developments of the early principate. The temple of Mars Ultor (as we have already seen, the first temple to the god of war within the *pomerium*) formed the centrepiece of Augustus' new forum, built next to the forum of Caesar and dedicated in 2 B.C.[114] Plans for the temple originated in a vow Augustus allegedly took in 42 B.C., when he defeated the murderers of his father. But the emphasis on Mars as the 'Avenger' also evoked Augustus' vengeance on the Parthians in 20 B.C.; the standards lost by Crassus in his defeat at the hands of the Parthians were recovered and placed in the innermost shrine of the temple. This allusion to contemporary achievements against foreign foes was reinforced by the military functions prescribed for the temple from its foundation. Military commanders were to set off from the temple, the senate was to meet in it to vote triumphs, and victorious generals were to dedicate to Mars the symbols of their triumphs.[115] Military glory was to be displayed in a setting which explicitly evoked the emperor's authority.

The design of the forum and temple articulates the relationship between Augustus, the gods and Rome. Augustus was referred to overtly only by the

---

112 Liebeschuetz (1979) 82–5; Zanker (1983); Kellum (1985); Zanker (1988) 65–9, 85–9, 240–5; Lefèvre (1989). The alleged restoration of the earlier temple by Sosius in 34–32 B.C. (Map 1 no. 33) in fact took place under Augustus: Gros (1976) 211–29; Steinby (1993–) I.49–54.

113 Gagé (1936a); Sarikakis (1965).

114 Map 1 no. 9. Described in Ovid, *Fasti* V.545–98; Pliny, *Natural History* XXXVI.102. Location within *pomerium*: above, p. 180.

115 Suetonius, *Augustus* 29 (= **4.2c**); Cassius Dio LV.10.2–3. Cf. Bonnefond (1987).

prominent dedicatory inscription with his name on the architrave, and by a statue which stood in the chariot in the centre of the forum; but his presence lay behind (and helps to make sense of) the iconography of the whole complex. The cult statue of Mars Ultor stood, next to the recovered standards, on a podium in the apse at the far end of the temple – a figure which alluded both to Augustus' piety in avenging Caesar and to his military success against the Parthians. There was also, almost certainly, a statue of Venus (perhaps standing on the podium next to Mars Ultor, or more likely in the main part of the temple) – recalling Augustus', and Caesar's, descent from the goddess herself. Many scholars have believed (though the evidence for this is much less clear) that there was a statue of *divus* Julius too, a further parade of Augustus' divine forebears.[116] On the pediment were Mars, Venus and Fortune; Romulus as *augur* and the personification of victorious Roma flanked them, and on either side were representations of the Palatine, the site of Romulus' augury, and the river Tiber (Fig. 4.5). All these figures could be seen as mythical analogues for Augustus' own victories and restorations of Rome. In the porticoes on either side of the temple stood a balancing series of statues depicting Augustus' dual ancestry. On one side was Aeneas, the descendant of Venus, dutifully carrying his father from the flames of Troy (echoing Augustus' own filial piety), and flanked by his descendants, the kings of Alba Longa and the Julii (Augustus' family line). Facing this series was a statue of Romulus, the son of Mars, victoriously bearing the armour of an enemy king whom he had slain in battle, and round him other figures of Roman republican history, celebrated mainly for their military prowess. In all there were about 108 statues, each with a brief inscription itemizing their distinctions. To these famous predecessors and ancestors, stretching back to Aeneas, Romulus and through them to Venus and Mars, Augustus was here proclaimed as the heir.

These new religious images were, of course, much less straightforward than such a brief description might suggest. We have already noted the potential ambivalence of the figure of Romulus in Augustan image-making. Here again the stress (for example) on divine descent that is so evident in the sculptural programme might itself have raised some uncomfortable questions for a cynical viewer: Romulus was, after all, the son of Mars by a *Vestal Virgin*, who was bound on pain of death by a vow of chastity... Besides, more generally, the obvious innovations in Augustan religion might sometimes seem to conflict with the claims about the restoration of ancestral practice. The new temples of Apollo and of Mars Ultor did actually take over functions that had

---

116 Plan and reconstruction: **4.2**; Zanker (n.d); Koeppel (1983) 98–101; J. C. Anderson (1984) 65–100; *Kaiser Augustus* (1988) 149–200; Zanker (1988) 183–215, 256–7; Alföldy (1991) 289, 293–7; Fishwick (1992b) 335–6; Steinby (1993–) II.289–95. Romulus: Degrassi (1939). A relief from Carthage has been used to argue that there were *three* cult statues in the temple (Mars, Venus and *divus* Julius); for discussion of this possibility, see below, p. 333 fig 7.2 (caption).

Fig. 4.5 The pediment of the temple of Mars Ultor on a relief of the mid first century A.D. The temple is seen in the background of the main subject of the relief, which is a state sacrifice. (Width 1.22m.)

traditionally been part of the cult of Jupiter Optimus Maximus: the Sibylline Books were moved to the Palatine, and some military functions to the Forum Augustum. And Suetonius' biography of Augustus describes a dream in which Jupiter Optimus Maximus complained to Augustus that worshippers were being diverted from his own temple by the emperor's new shrine of Jupiter Tonans nearby.[117] The story goes that Augustus deferentially pointed out that Jupiter Tonans was merely the doorkeeper of Jupiter Optimus Maximus. Such a line of argument would at least be consistent with his various displays of devotion to the traditional Capitoline cult: he rebuilt the temple of Jupiter Optimus Maximus after it had been destroyed by fire; he made lavish offerings there to Jupiter; and the annual vows for the emperor's safety were always performed on the Capitol. It is impossible now to judge overall how awkwardly, or how smoothly, the new temples were integrated into the religious life of Rome.

The Saecular Games

One of the main events of Augustus' reign was the celebration of the Saecular Games in 17 B.C.[118] This occasion is uniquely well documented in a variety of surviving sources: ranging from the Sibylline oracle ordaining the procedures to the inscribed record of the games, and the hymn of Horace sung at the festival. From this material we can reconstruct in some detail the programme of events at the festival, and detect some of the ways

117 Suetonius, *Augustus* 91.2.
118 Above, pp. 71–2; 111. Pighi (1965) reprints the sources; **5.7b** is the Augustan inscription. There are two new fragments of the inscription in Moretti (1982–84). La Rocca (1984) 3–55 speculatively discusses the Terentum (Map 1 no. 37); Manzano (1984) gives the numismatic evidence.

in which this traditional republican festival (whose earliest celebrations we discussed in chapters 1 and 2) was both preserved and transformed under Augustus and his successors.

The games were, as we have already seen, tied to one particular spot in the city, in the north-west Campus Martius beside the Tiber at an altar known as the Tarentum (or Terentum); and it was here that the inscribed records of the ceremonies were later set up. From at least the first century B.C. onwards, this location was explained by the story – set in Italy's mythic past – of a man called Valesius, who lived in Sabine territory near to Rome, and of his efforts to obtain a cure for his children who had fallen grievously sick. He was told by the gods to take them to Tarentum and to give them water from the Tiber to drink, heated up on the altar of Dis Pater and Proserpina, the gods of the underworld. He took this to mean that he should go to the Greek colony called Tarentum, in the 'instep' of Italy; so he set out on what was to be a long journey – putting in for the night by the river Tiber on the Campus Martius and drawing water from the river (which he heated on a makeshift hearth) for his thirsty children; and they woke up the next morning miraculously cured. It turned out that this spot on the Campus Martius was also called Tarentum and that there was an altar of Dis Pater and Proserpina lying buried under the place where he had built his hearth. In thanks for the cure Valesius established three nights of sacrifices and games.[119]

The Saecular Games of Augustus were tied to this same traditional place; but in other respects they differed substantially from their republican predecessors, notably in their focus on the emperor himself and his son-in-law and heir, Agrippa. Although, as we have seen, the details of the early celebrations of this ritual are hard to reconstruct, it seems clear enough that the priesthood of the *quindecimviri* were in overall charge of proceedings. Formally that arrangement continued in 17 B.C. Augustus and Agrippa were themselves members of this college, and they played their traditional roles within it; Augustus, for example, initiated the celebrations by writing to the board of priests in his capacity as one of its four 'presidents'. But in the festival itself they almost seem to have taken control, beyond that of any other priest. Agrippa himself was just an ordinary member of the board, but the other three 'presidents' stood aside in his favour. Together, Augustus and Agrippa seem to have led the ritual, the emperor alone offering the nocturnal prayers, and his heir joining in those spoken by day. He also seems to have ended each prayer with a petition 'for me, my house and my household'. This was a traditional prayer formula,[120] but in Augustus'

---

119 Zosimus II.1–3 (and Valerius Maximus, *Memorable Deeds and Sayings* II.4.5). Versnel (1982) 217–28 discusses the relation of the story to the Roman family of the Valerii.

120 This formula, a restoration in the inscription, appears in Cato, *On Agriculture* 134, 139, 141. It is used by the matrons: Augustan *acta* line 130 (restored) = **5.7b**; Severan *acta* IV.12 = Pighi (1965) 157.

mouth the old words acquired a new dynastic resonance. Besides, the hymn specially composed by the poet Horace for the celebrations, and sung on the third day by a choir of twenty seven boys and twenty seven girls, stressed the central importance of Augustus: 'May the illustrious descendant of Anchises and Venus obtain the help of you gods whom he worships with white oxen, superior to the enemy, merciful to the prostrate foe.' The Saecular Games had acquired a new focus.

It seems very likely that the rituals themselves were also transformed. Even if our ideas of republican proceedings are in large part conjectural, some elements of the ceremonies recorded on the inscription appear distinctively Augustan. The preliminary distribution of torches, sulphur and asphalt to (it is claimed) the entire free population of Rome is reminiscent of the attempt to create widespread participation that we saw in the cult of the Lares Augusti. There may well also be a conscious link here with rituals of purification in the festival of the Parilia: just as that festival was connected with the original founding of Rome, so the Saecular Games marked the regular *rebirth* of the city. The incorporation of the new temple of Apollo on the Palatine is also striking: this was one of the locations where the *quindecimviri* took in offerings of crops and gave out the materials for purification, and where on the third day sacrifice and prayer were offered to Apollo and Diana and the saecular hymn was first sung.

There was also a significant change in the deities associated with the festival. The fragment of Varro which refers to the foundation of the Games mentions only Dis Pater and Proserpina. There is, however, no mention of these particular gods in the inscribed record of the Augustan festival – where they seem to have been replaced by the Fates, the Goddesses of Childbirth (Ilythiae) and Terra Mater (Mother Earth) in the night-time celebrations, and in the day-time celebrations by Jupiter, Juno, Apollo and Diana. It is these deities too who form the focus of Horace's hymn. That is to say, instead of an emphasis on the gloomy gods of the Underworld, marking the passing of an era, the Augustan games marked the birth of a new age. And the fertility of Mother Earth (one of the prominent images also on the Augustan Ara Pacis – see Fig.4.6) can be understood to be guarded by the Fates and the Goddesses of Childbirth.[121]

The theatrical displays of the festival (the *ludi* proper) also help reveal the different layers of tradition and innovation that made up the celebrations.[122] There were two quite different sorts of these 'games'. The first is described as follows: 'when the sacrifice was completed, games were celebrated by night on a stage without the additional construction of a theatre and without the erection of seating.' This continued into the following day, but there were in addition 'Latin games in a wooden theatre which had been erected on the Campus Martius next to the Tiber'. This second type

121 Varro in Censorinus, *Birthday* 17.8 (= Pighi (1965) 37–8).
122 Erkell (1969). Theatres: Map 1 nos. 34–35.

Fig. 4.6 'Earth' on a relief from the Ara Pacis, Rome (much restored in the sixteenth century). In the centre, a female figure with two children and pomegranates, grapes and nuts on her lap; in front of her a cow and a sheep. On the left, a female figure flying aloft on a swan (?), and on the right, another female figure on the back of a sea creature. The central figure clearly represents notions of fertility (human and agricultural), set between images of sky and sea. The iconography is much debated; but – as this relief forms one of a pair (of which the other is certainly a personification of Rome) – it seems very likely that we are dealing with 'earth' or 'fertility' in the sense of *Italy*. For the design of the Ara Pacis see **4.3c**, and fig.7.2b for a provincial adaptation of this relief. (Height 1.55m., width 2.44m.)

of games reappeared in the seven days of games that followed (and closed) the festival. These took three forms and were held in three locations: those held in the theatre in the Campus Martius; the Greek shows in the Theatre of Pompey and Greek stage plays in the theatre in the Circus Flaminius. The first type of games, without theatre and without seats, was avowedly primitive (and maybe unpopular; at least, they were not repeated in the seven days at the end of the festival). But they recall one version of the origin of the festival as a whole. Varro's remarks on the foundation of this ritual are, in fact, drawn from his work (now lost) on the origin of theatrical performances in Rome, which he associated with the introduction of what he calls the *ludi Tarentini* (that is the Saecular Games). Those who had read their Varro knew that quaint games of this type had to be incorporated into the new structure.

More generally, appeals to religious tradition served to legitimate the rituals and organization of these, distinctively Augustan, Games. The inscription records the consultation of 'ancient books', perhaps the archives of the *quindecimviri*, for details on how to finance the Games (though it also records that no such information was found); and advice on the performance of the rituals was sought from the jurist and expert in religious law, Ateius Capito.[123] And the main shape of the rituals was provided by a Sibylline oracle, still preserved among the fragments of Phlegon, a Greek historian writing in the second century A.D. Shortly before the Augustan celebration the Sibylline oracles were purged of spurious items and deposited beneath the statue of Apollo in the new temple on the Palatine, and perhaps in the process this oracular text, enjoining quite new rituals, was 'discovered' or 're-discovered'. It could be an ancient text but the fact that it appears to recommend so conveniently the specifically Augustan form of ritual has suggested that it was an antiquarian product of the Augustan age, incorporating or imitating earlier material; so, for example, the hopes expressed in the oracle, as well as in the prayers delivered at the celebrations themselves, for the obedience of the Latins to Rome made little sense under the empire (centuries after any hostility between Latins and Romans) – and were probably drawn from earlier republican material, or consciously mimicking it, to give an antique flavour to the text.[124] The 'ancient books', legal expertise and the Sibylline oracle combined to create and sanction the new rites.

The timing of the celebrations also received due authority combined with a fictitious tradition. We have already seen in chapters 1 and 2 that the only surely attested republican celebrations took place in 249 and 146 B.C. How far there was an established regular cycle of Games at that period is quite unclear; but those dates would suggest (if anything) a normal interval of about a hundred years.[125] In the Augustan period, however, following the Sibylline oracle (and Varro), a cycle of 110 years was accepted as authentic; and a sequence of earlier republican games was 'established', beginning in 456 B.C. These were added after 17 B.C. to the official Calendar inscribed in the Roman Forum, creating a new history of the Games which ignored the two earlier attested celebrations. Even so, some puzzles remain. The cycle of 110 years would have authorized games in 16 B.C. rather than 17 B.C. and there is no really satisfactory explanation for the discrepancy.[126]

123 Ancient books: Moretti (1982–4). Ateius Capito: Zosimus II.4.2.
124 Phlegon, *On the Long-lived* 5.2 = *FGH* 257 F 37 = Pighi (1965) 56–7 (trans. Braund (1985) 296–7); Zosimus II.6 also quotes the oracle. Diels (1890) 13–15; Gagé (1933a) 177–83; Momigliano (1938) 625, (1941) 165.
125 Above, pp. 71–2; 111.
126 For earlier plans to celebrate games in 23 B.C., Virgil, *Aeneid* VI.65–70, 791–4, with Merkelbach (1961) 91–9. One explanation of the discrepancy is that it was the result of disagreement over the precise year of the foundation of Rome.

The Augustan games formed the model for all subsequent celebrations. Claudius celebrated games in A.D. 47, receiving censure from modern scholars for his self-interested and politically convenient choice of date, which does not fit the Augustan cycle. In fact the choice of A.D. 47 may have been justified by the fact that it was 800 years from the foundation of Rome; and a cycle of 100 years was a legitimate alternative (indeed the surviving Greek text of Augustus' *Achievements* (wrongly) translates *saecularis* as 'every hundred years'). Thereafter Domitian celebrated the games in A.D. 88 (six years ahead of the Augustan cycle) and Septimius Severus in A.D. 204 (back on the Augustan calculations). Both Domitian's and Severus' games followed the Augustan procedure extremely closely. There were of course some changes (a new hymn was written for 204, when the emperor and his family were also somewhat more prominent), but the basic structure of events was unaltered.

To add to the complexity, a second cycle of games was also established under the Empire.[127] Taking its lead from Claudius' celebration of Saecular Games 800 years after the foundation of Rome, games were also held in the following two centuries (A.D. 148 and 248). These were not counted in the official numbered sequence of Saecular Games and, in A.D. 148 and 248 at least, the ritual was quite different. The Tarentum seems to have been displaced in favour of rites in front of the temple of Rome and Venus, known as the Temple of the City, and the date was probably changed to 21 April, the birthday of Rome. These anniversary celebrations, which developed from the Augustan framework, mark the emergence of a new consciousness of the importance of the city of Rome – and of the importance of the emperor within it.

Imperial rituals

The religious position of the Roman emperor was dominant within the city; his authority was pervasive, but also strikingly diffuse. There was no one major ceremony, such as a coronation or new year's festival, at which the emperor himself was – as emperor – the leading actor; nor did any one religious ritual sum up his religious status and role.[128] Rather, a range of rituals developed which clearly associated the emperor with the gods or linked him with religious institutions and ceremonies; in a variety of different ways he became *incorporated* within the religious framework of the city (in much the same way as he had been associated with the cult and sanctuary of Vesta). From 30 B.C. games were celebrated every five years by one of the colleges of priests, or by the consuls, in fulfilment of vows to the gods that had been taken for Augustus' health. In 13, 8 and 7 B.C. special votive games were held in thanks for his safe return to Rome. In 28 B.C.

---

127 Gagé (1933b), (1936b). Non-performance in A.D. 314, below, p. 372.
128 For such ceremonies elsewhere, Cannadine and Price (1987).

Augustus' name was inscribed in the hymn of the Salii by a decree of the senate; this ancient hymn (by the late Republic almost incomprehensible even to the priests themselves) continued to be sung in the twice yearly Salian rituals, but now the name of Augustus must have rung out to listeners clear as a bell amongst the arcane and venerable mumbo-jumbo.[129] Even in private, libations might be offered to Augustus at banquets, while images of Augustus and members of his family stood in household shrines, sometimes tended by associations of 'worshippers of Augustus'.[130]

The *numen*, or divine power, of Augustus also received public honours in Rome. Although, strictly speaking, there was no official public cult in the city of the living Augustus as a god, Tiberius did dedicate (probably in A.D. 6) an altar on the Palatine next to the house of Augustus, at which the four main priestly colleges sacrificed to his *numen*.[131] *Numen* was not shared by ordinary people, and (unlike the Lares Augusti) had no resonances in traditional family cult of ancestors. The establishment of its official cult signalled that the emperor himself, in person, was not actually receiving cult due to the gods – and, at the same time, signalled that of course there was very little that separated Augustus from the gods. There must have been, in other words, all the difference (and yet almost none at all) between worshipping Augustus himself and worshipping his *numen*.

Ovid's *Fasti* neatly encapsulates the presence of the emperor throughout religious ritual, cult and myth. Interspersed with accounts of traditional festivals (such as the Parilia), Ovid mentioned every official festival of Augustan significance, such as the founding of the Ara Pacis or the establishment of the cult of the Lares Augusti.[132] The poet has often been accused of flattery, or (alternatively) of subversive irony at the emperor's expense. But nonetheless his preoccupations closely reflect the emphases of the developing state calendar. Augustus, in fact, recurs in all kinds of religious contexts through the *Fasti*: the mother of the Arcadian king Evander prophesies the rule of Augustus and his family; battles of Caesar and Augustus are recorded on otherwise blank dates as well as the closing of the temple of Janus that followed on the establishment of the Augustan peace; the disappearance of one temple leads to mention of Augustus' programme of temple restoration. The emperor's presence is even signalled,

---

129 Cassius Dio LI.19.7 with Weinstock (1971) 217–19; Augustus, *Achievements* 9.1; Palmer (1990) 14–17. Salii: Augustus, *Achievements* 10.1; Cassius Dio LI.20.1; Quintilian, *Education of an Orator* I.6.40–1 = **5.4c**. The same honour posthumously for members of the imperial family: Crawford (1996) I.37 and *AE* (1984) 508 IIc (trans. Sherk (1988) 63–72); Tacitus, *Annals* II.83, IV.9.

130 Cassius Dio LI.19.7; Petronius, *Satyricon* 60; Ovid, *Fasti* II.637–8; cf. Horace, *Odes* IV.5.31–2; Ovid, *Letters from Pontus* IV.9.105–110; Tacitus, *Annals* I.73.2. Cf. Santero (1983).

131 Map 1 no. 14. Degrassi (1963) 401, restored with dating of Alföldi (1973) 42–4. Location: Wiseman (1991) 55, 57, 109. For examples from outside Rome see below pp. 354–5. See Fishwick (1969) for the distinction between *genius* and *numen*.

132 I.709–22; V.129–46.

paradoxically, by absences and omissions. At the introduction to the sixth book, Ovid offers three explanations of the etymology of the month of 'June' and pleads his inability to decide between them; but he makes no mention of the 'obvious' etymology, from Junius Brutus, the liberator of Rome from the kings and ancestor of that other Brutus who had killed Julius Caesar. The suspicious reader might well imagine here that Ovid is using such a glaring omission precisely to draw attention to the story he does not mention. But even if so (and we cannot know how ancient readers took it), it is yet another indication of how, and in how many different ways, the emperor and his achievements were a constant presence throughout the poem – just as they were in the ritual calendar itself.[133]

Emperors after death were seen in sharper divine focus.[134] The official cult of Caesar offered one obvious model for Augustus and subsequent emperors. Though some honours, as we have seen, were probably voted for Caesar in his lifetime, it was their consolidation after his death that became decisive for subsequent practice. In 42 B.C. the senate passed the official consecration of Caesar, including the building of a temple; in 40 B.C. Antony was inaugurated as the first *flamen divi Julii* (an office to which he had been appointed in 44 B.C.), and Augustus began to call himself *divi filius*. Finally, in 29 B.C. Augustus appointed a new *flamen* in place of Antony and dedicated the temple to Caesar, an event celebrated by lavish contests. The temple dominated the south side of the Forum Romanum and formed the backdrop for public speakers using the new tribunal in front of it.[135] The posthumous status of Caesar was thus assured. Valerius Maximus, writing under Tiberius, told the story of *divus* Julius appearing to Cassius, one of his murderers, at the battle of Philippi, to tell the 'tyrannicide' that he had not actually killed Caesar because his 'divinity' could never be extinguished; and elsewhere Valerius prayed by Caesar's altars and temples that his divinity would favour and protect the human race.[136]

After his death Augustus was promoted to the divine status long held by Caesar – a transition that was, inevitably, as predictable and smoothly managed as it was (in the usual paradox of apotheosis) outrageously unbelievable. The expectation was expressed in his lifetime that he would ascend to his rightful place in heaven, and immediately after his death Augustus was duly made a *divus*. His funeral, cremation and burial in the Mausoleum were grand versions of the traditional funeral of the Roman nobility; but afterwards a senior senator (who was said to have been handsomely rewarded for his pains, to the tune of a million sesterces, by Augustus'

---

133 Prophecy: I.529–36. Battles: IV.377–84, 627–8. Janus: I.281–8. Temples: II.55–66. June: VI.1–100; Macrobius, *Saturnalia* I.12.31.

134 Price (1987); Arce (1988); Fraschetti (1990) 42–120; above, pp. 140–9 on Caesar; **9.3**; **4.7** for Roman Forum. For Romulus as precedent cf. above pp. 4–5; 141–2; 182–4 and **2.8a**.

135 Weinstock (1971) 385–401.

136 *Memorable Deeds and Sayings* I.8.8; 6.13.

widow Livia) declared on oath to the senate that he had actually seen Augustus ascending to heaven. As a result, in the words of the official state calendar, 'on that day heavenly honours were decreed by the senate to the divine Augustus'. The main 'heavenly honours' were a temple built between the Capitol and the Palatine, a *flamen*, who was to be a member of Augustus' own family, and a priestly college of *sodales Augustales,* comprising leading members of the senatorial order. Augustus, like his ancestor Romulus, went to join the gods.[137]

In this area too the practices of the Augustan age established the basic framework which prevailed for the rest of the imperial period. Emperors and members of their families were given divine honours by vote of the senate only after their death and then only in recognition of the fact (so the official version went) that they had, by their merits, actually become gods. The Augustan system marks a change from the tone of the period of the civil wars after the death of Caesar when Octavian was commonly thought to have held a dinner party of the Twelve Gods, himself appearing as Apollo – dangerously straddling the border between fancy-dress and blasphemy. In addition, official coins from the mint of Rome of the early 20s B.C. showed Octavian as Apollo, Jupiter and Neptune, and the original plan for the great new temple of the Pantheon ('All the gods') was that it should be named after Augustus and have his statue inside it.[138]

After 27 B.C., Augustus no longer employed such imagery; and accounts of the reigns of his successors suggest that those norms remained in place. In most cases it is impossible now to reconstruct exactly how any individual emperor negotiated the delicate boundary between (god-like) humanity and outright divinity; but Roman historians regularly use accusations (right, wrong – or, no doubt, often exaggerated) that an emperor was claiming the status of a god as a symbol of his utter transgression of all the rules of proper behaviour. So it was recounted that Gaius Caligula, after a popular start to his reign, began to make assertions of his own personal divinity: he is said to have sat between the statues of Castor and Pollux in the temple in the Forum, showing himself to be worshipped by those who entered; he wore the clothing or attributes of a wide range of deities, and established a temple to his own godhead.[139] For his biographer all this demonstrated that Gaius was no longer emperor or even king, but monster; and stories of Gaius' reign (however exaggerated) survived as a warning to subsequent emperors not to destroy the Augustan norms. Thus Claudius,

137 Witness: Suetonius, *Augustus* 100.4; Cassius Dio LVI.46.2. Calendar: Degrassi (1963) 510. Temple: Fishwick (1992a); Steinby (1993–) I.145–6. *Sodales*: Price (1987) 78–9. Below, pp. 348–62, on the provinces.

138 Suetonius, *Augustus* 70. Coins: Burnett (1983) discussing Sutherland and Carson, *RIC* I² nos. 270–272; cf. Zanker (1988) 40–2. Pantheon: Cassius Dio LIII.27.3 with Coarelli (1983b) and Fishwick (1992b); below, p. 257.

139 **4.7** (map of Forum); Suetonius, *Caligula* 22, 52. Cf. Philo, *Embassy* 78–113, Cassius Dio LIX.26–8.

Gaius' successor, seems to have made a show of reverting to the maintenance of ancestral Roman customs. According to his biographer, 'he corrected various abuses, revived some old customs or even established some new ones'. For example, he always offered a supplication when a bird of ill omen was seen on the Capitol, and in making treaties he recited the ancient formula of the *fetiales*.[140] But even he became the subject of a witty (and cruel) satire, mocking the ludicrous process of his apotheosis.[141]

This basic pattern of paraded transgression and reassertion of the Augustan norm seems to have repeated itself from the first century A.D. into the third century. After the excesses of Nero, who sought to rival various gods, came the down-to-earth Vespasian, who on his deathbed (so it was said) made a joke about his own apotheosis.[142] His younger son, Domitian, on the other hand, (though in many respects he was a strong traditionalist) is said to have demanded to be addressed as *dominus et deus noster*, 'our master and god'.[143] And a century later Commodus identified himself so closely with Hercules that he had Hercules' lion-skin and club carried before him in the street and converted the great Colossus (an enormous statue, originally erected by Nero, and later giving its name to the nearby 'Colosseum') into a statue of himself as Hercules. All this is reported with horror by the eyewitness senatorial historian Cassius Dio.[144] Throughout the imperial period, the religious norms established under the first emperor continued to provide a framework within which religious action or transgression might be defined and judged – as we shall see further, both inside and outside the city of Rome, in the next chapter.

140 Suetonius, *Claudius* 22, 25.5. Cf. Tacitus, *Annals* XI.15 on *haruspices*; below, p. 228.
141 Seneca, *Apocolocyntosis* (9 = **9.2c**).
142 Nero did not seek lifetime deification in Rome: Griffin (1984) 215–19; though as we shall see several times in the course of this book, the boundary between being *like* a god and outright divinity is very hard to draw. Vespasian: Suetonius, *Vespasian* 23.4.
143 Suetonius, *Domitian* 13.2; Pliny, *Panegyric* 2.3, 52.2.
144 Statue: **2.8c**; Cassius Dio LXXIII.15–22. Cf. Beaujeu (1955) 400–9. Elagabalus, below, pp. 255–6.

5 *The boundaries of Roman religion*

The restructuring of the religious system of Rome under Augustus introduced our account of Roman religion in the imperial period, from Augustus to Constantine (A.D. 306–337).[1] In the next three chapters we focus on particular themes over these three centuries: the construction and transgression of religious boundaries; the development of official religion in Rome itself, and the proliferation of alternatives to those traditional cults; the role of religion outside the capital in the relations between Rome and the rest of the empire. The final chapter will turn briefly to the period from Constantine onwards, examining the religious transformations of the fourth century during the reigns of the first Christian emperors.

In each of these chapters the role of the city of Rome as the metropolis of a vast empire will be a crucial factor in understanding the history of Roman religion. In this chapter we shall show how the Roman élite defined 'proper' and 'improper' religious activity (as part of the process of defining their own position in the state), and how they took legal steps to defend the Roman system against real or imaginary enemies of religion; but we shall also see how the scope of these definitions and actions changed over time, extending a preoccupation with Rome in particular in the late Republic and early first century A.D. to concern for the whole empire. Chapter 6 focusses explicitly on the religious life of the city of Rome, continuing the theme of the earlier chapters of this book; but at the same time it examines many of the new religions with their roots in more distant parts of the empire, that flourished in the capital over this period (from the cults of Jupiter Dolichenus or Mithras to Judaism and Christianity). Chapter 7 returns to the empire at large, to trace Rome's impact on the religious life of the provinces.

Our aim is to investigate the history of imperial religion over the period as a whole. Many histories of Roman religion effectively stop with Augustus himself, as if from that point on (in Rome at least) the religious concepts and institutions of the imperial period were largely unchanging and without particular interest. It is assumed that the civic cults of the Greek world remained important throughout the imperial period, vital in the life of their cities. The so-called 'Oriental religions' too have been the

---

1 For the history of this period, see Wells (1992); Averil Cameron (1993a) 1–46.

subject of many studies, partly no doubt because they have been seen not just as dynamically 'new', but also as the precursors or even rivals of Christianity. But scholars have tended to neglect the official cults of the centre of the empire through most of the three centuries of the principate. In fact, the standard framework for understanding the religious developments of the period is normally found not in the history of traditional cults at all, but in the rise of Christianity. In these chapters we mean to focus attention back onto those traditional cults.

We shall stress too, in this chapter in particular, that traditional Roman paganism was not, as has been claimed, 'completely tolerant, in heaven as on earth'.[2] The fact that there was a plurality of gods did not necessarily mean that religion had no limits, or that (apart, of course, from Christianity) 'anything went'. Polytheistic systems can be as resistant as monotheism to innovation and foreign influence. And, although Roman religion was marked throughout its history by religious innovation of all kinds, there were, at the same time, clear and repeated signs of concern about the influence of foreign cults; there were also specifically 'religious crimes', categories of religious transgression liable (as in the case of the unchastity of Vestals) to public punishment.[3] Rome was never a religious 'free for all'.

The Roman élite undoubtedly conceived of its own religious system as superior to the cults of its conquered subjects. No Roman propounded the view that Rome should respect the religious liberty of other peoples.[4] This does not mean that the Romans were therefore *in*tolerant (indeed, the concept of 'toleration' is distinctively modern and does not apply at this period). The issue is rather the degree of *exclusivity* of the Roman system, how it operated and how it changed – particularly as the empire prompted new ways of defining what was 'Roman', new ways of thinking about what was to count as 'Roman' and what was not. The shift in Roman concern from the purity of the capital alone to the maintenance of correct practices throughout the empire is directly connected to changing views of 'Roman-ness'.

In setting boundaries between the legitimate and the illegitimate, between 'us' and 'them', the Roman élite identified a set of transgressive religious stereotypes (from horrendous witches to monstrous Christians) against whom they waged war, with the stylus and with the sword – or with wild beasts in the arena: 'Christians to the lions' was a powerful slogan. Work on witch hunts in later history has shown how such invention of enemies is one way in which particular communities (or subsections of them)

---

2   MacMullen (1981) 2; cf. Bowersock (1990) 6: 'Polytheism is by definition tolerant and accommodating.' This view goes back to David Hume's *Natural History of Religion* (1757) ch. 9.

3   Mommsen (1890); Guterman (1951); *contra*, Scheid (1981). Above, pp. 51–3; 81; 137.

4   Garnsey (1984). Modern religious pluralism: Hamnett (1990). Fourth century A.D.: below, pp. 365–75.

define and re-define their own identities; groups reassert a sense of their own cohesion by fighting off enemies who are often quite imaginary.[5] But it is much less clear why some societies act in this way and others do not. There are many ways of defining cultural identity, besides inventing demons: why do some societies hunt witches and others not?[6]

One explanation links the construction of dangerous outsiders with the creation of a strong centralized political system and with the sometimes difficult moves towards the integration of the state.[7] So, for example, the witch hunt in Scotland has been related to the growth of central, national authorities which were concerned to extend and legitimize their powers; 'idolatry' (that is, indigenous religions) in parts of the Spanish New World was actively repressed in the sixteenth and seventeenth centuries, when *laissez faire* administration was being replaced by increased control by the central government; or again, the political 'witch hunts' of the modern world correlate closely with the existence of single-party states, and are concerned to extirpate the enemy within.[8] In other words, so this argument runs, it is the attempt to maintain a unified political centre that leads to the invention of political subversives.

The role of women is often crucial in this process. In many societies the explicit exclusion of women from the political order (or, at least, their marginalization from the centres of power) makes their 'integration' into the state peculiarly problematic. Hence the frequency, it is argued, of *female* demons and subversives: witches are (and were) stereotypically women.

Such theorizing is very suggestive for Rome. We have already noted the emphasis on *female* subversion in the story of the Bacchic cult in the second century B.C.[9] As the Roman empire expanded, it faced ever sharper problems of identity and cohesion – particularly as it moved in the first century A.D. from a conquest model, in which Rome and Italy simply administered ever-growing conquered territories, to a more complex model of incorporation and integration, with Roman citizenship extended throughout the empire and local élites incorporated into the service of Rome. This is precisely the kind of move towards integration that could encourage the construction of

5 Europe: Cohn (1975). Salem: Erikson (1966).
6 K. Thomas (1971) 535–69, 581–2; also Macfarlane (1970), a point already made by the anthropologist Max Marwick. Cf. Boyer and Nissenbaum (1974) on Salem. McCarthyism too has been explained in terms of the status anxieties of the US middle class, but it also needs to be set in a broader international and domestic context: Caute (1978).
7 Weber (1951) 213–19 on China; Weinstein (1987) 114–36 on the suppression of Buddhism A.D. 840–846; Hansen (1990) 79–104 on award of government titles to gods; Kuhn (1990) on actions against sorcery.
8 Scotland: Larner (1981); cf. generally Ankarloo and Henningsen (1990). New World: Duviols (1971) on Peru, with different perspective in MacCormack (1991); Greenleaf (1969) on Mexico. Modern witch hunts: Bergesen (1977). Medieval persecution of Jews, heretics and lepers: Moore (1987); and the Spanish inquisition: Monter (1990).
9 Above, pp. 92–6.

subversives, demons and witches. It offers a striking contrast with the small-scale Greek city-states of the classical period: there, political and religious identities were defined relatively unproblematically through the rules for access to sacrifice, and there were few if any legal worries about magicians or other religious subversives.[10]

Religion was, in short, a major aspect of the changing relationship between Rome and her empire. The classic statement of the importance of central religious policy, and of the links between religious subversion and political danger and disintegration, was framed by the historian Cassius Dio, writing in the early third century A.D. It is presented in an imaginary speech put into the mouth of Maecenas, counselling his friend Octavian in 29 B.C.:

> If you truly desire to become immortal, do as I advise. In addition, not only must you yourself worship the divine everywhere and in every way according to ancestral custom and force everyone else to honour it; but you must also reject and punish those who make some foreign innovation in its worship, not only for the sake of the gods (since anyone despising them will not honour anyone else), but also because such people who introduce new deities persuade many people to change their ways, leading to conspiracies, revolts and factions, which are most unsuitable for a monarchy. So you must not allow anyone to be godless or a sorcerer. The art of divination is necessary, and you should certainly appoint some as diviners from entrails and birds, to whom those wishing a consultation will go. But magicians should be absolutely banned, for such people, by speaking far more lies than truths, often cause many disturbances.[11]

This forceful interpretation of strong imperial control of Roman religion encapsulates the themes of this chapter, definitions of religion and their practical consequences in the construction of the 'imagined community' of the Roman empire.[12]

1. Defining the acceptable

We have seen that distinctions between proper and improper religious activity were one means by which different social groups in the Roman empire constructed their identities. These distinctions had, no doubt, always been debated. But in the early history of the city of Rome, and in other states in the ancient world, where political identity was defined by

---

10 Plato's *Laws* (XI 932e–933e) treats magic as a type of poisoning, as did Roman law (below, p. 233), but there is no sign that this was normal (Saunders (1991) 318–23). Note also the regulation of Dionysiac cult in Ptolemaic Egypt: *Select Papyri* (Loeb edn.) no. 208 with Nilsson (1957).
11 Cassius Dio LII.36.1–3.
12 We borrow the term from Anderson (1983). The Roman empire combines aspects of Anderson's 'religious community', 'dynastic realm' and 'nationalism' (or 'imagined community').

descent and where access to religious rites was coextensive with political rights, the drawing of such distinctions will have been much less problematic than in the Roman empire – where there could be no such simple certainties. The Roman empire raised in a particularly acute form the question of 'Roman-ness': What did it mean in this vast multicultural territory to *be* Roman, or to *feel* Roman?

The answer varied according to the standing, ethnic origin and gender of the individual; but for men, at least, an important part of the answer was religious. For many ordinary Roman citizens in Italy participation in the official festivals (or in the patterns of behaviour, the alternating rhythms of festal and 'everyday' activities, ordained by the official ritual calendar) may have sufficed; in the east, where Roman citizenship was relatively rare in the early empire, special religious affirmations of Roman identity on the part of Roman citizens are sometimes found – in the form of cults of a specifically Roman type.[13] In general, though, we are left to guess at the perspectives of the common people.

We are much better informed on the debates that surrounded the religious self-definition of the Roman élite. For them, the very fluidity of the élite group made that definition a particularly pressing issue. Membership of the senate may have been a clear enough indication of status; but the equestrian order was much more amorphous, and both were constantly open to new members not only from Italy, but also from the provinces, first western and then eastern. There was also the question of their status in relation to the rest of the populace – a relationship which was now inevitably affected by the role of the emperor himself. How, then, was the discourse of religion (and religious enmity) incorporated into the self-definition of these men, as a social, political and cultural élite? In what senses were the boundaries of the élite negotiated through religious boundaries?

A pair of Roman terms, *religio* and *superstitio*, provides a starting point: two key terms with which the Romans debated the nature of correct religious behaviour. As we shall see, *religio* was regularly an aspect of a Roman's *self*-description; while *superstitio* was always a slur against others; but they do not denote simple, or easily definable, opposites. 'Proper' and 'improper' religion are loaded, shifting terms, whose precise definitions were as much a matter of dispute between Romans as between modern historians; they were discursive categories which framed religious arguments, as well as being labels of approval or disapproval.[14]

Our own words 'religion' and 'superstition' may be misleading here. So too might be the way in which Christian writers drew the distinction

13 Below, pp. 240; 322–3; 336–7.
14 *Religio*: Kätzler (1952–3); Michels (1976). *Superstitio*: Grodzynski (1974a), an excellent study; Janssen (1979). Cf. Scheid (1985b) and Sachot (1991). Though scholars sometimes undertake studies of either one word or the other, it is essential to consider the two words in relation to each other.

between the two words: '*religio* is worship of the true god, *superstitio* of a false', as the Christian Lactantius remarked in the early fourth century A.D. – so asserting that alien practices and gods were not merely inferior to his own, but actually bogus.[15] The traditional Roman distinction seems to have made no such assumption about truth and falsehood; when Romans in the early empire debated the nature of *religio* and *superstitio* they were discussing instead different *forms* of human relations with the gods. This is captured in Seneca's formulation that '*religio* honours the gods, *superstitio* wrongs them.'[16]

Religio regularly refers to the traditional honours paid to the gods by the state. The official records of the Augustan Saecular Games, for example, observed that the games were celebrated 'because of *religio*' and Pliny the Younger, praising the emperor Trajan in the senate in A.D. 100, describes the Roman state as 'devoted to *religiones* and always earning by piety the favour of the gods'.[17] Similarly, the first chapter of Valerius Maximus' *Memorable Deeds and Sayings* collects republican anecdotes to illustrate the preservation or neglect of *religio,* in the context of the Roman state. For example, a *praetor* who was a Salian priest and could have been excused from the dance of the Salii because of his magistracy went through the dance, at the order of his father, the chief Salian. 'Our state has always considered that *religio* takes precedence over everything else, even when it wished the privileges of its chief officers to be evident.'[18] The focus of the term was on public, communal behaviour towards the gods of the state. *Religio* was displayed by individuals – from the emperor to members of local élites – primarily within this public context. Good emperors displayed 'outstanding care and *religio* towards public rituals'; bad ones were defined as those who ignored gods or *religiones* – and were criticized for their impiety.[19] The budding senator who is the imagined recipient of Quintilian's treatise on oratory was advised that 'there are questions concerned with auguries, responses and all sorts of *religio*, all of them the subject of major debates in the senate, on which the senator will have to discourse if he is to be the public figure (*vir civilis*) we would have him be.'[20] Individual Vestal Virgins were commended for being extremely holy and *religiosae*; private individuals in Rome and elsewhere were proud to record that they had established rites (*religio*) or were *religiosi*. For example, in the Roman *colonia* of Timgad in North Africa a member of the local élite

15 Lactantius, *Divine Institutes* IV.28.11.
16 Seneca, *On Mercy* II.5.1.
17 *CIL* VI 32323 lines 54 and 56 (Pighi (1965) 111) = **5.7b,** and also the Severan records I.30, III.5, IV.8 (Pighi (1965) 143, 149, 157). Pliny, *Panegyric* 74.5.
18 I.1.9; above, p. 18. Cf. R. L. Gordon (1990c) 235–8.
19 *ILS* 341, Antoninus Pius. Bad emperors: Suetonius, *Julius Caesar* 59, *Tiberius* 69, *Nero* 56, *Otho* 8.
20 Quintilian, *Education of an Orator* XII.2.21. The term recurs in *Declamations* by Seneca, Quintilian and pseudo-Quintilian.

dedicated at his own expense a statue of the Goddess of the City 'for the celebration of public *religio* and the embellishment of his noble city'.[21] And Apuleius, defending himself on a charge of magic (to which we shall return), stressed that his public speech in honour of Aesculapius had found favour with the *religiosi* inhabitants of a town in North Africa; his prosecutor in contrast completely ignored religious matters.[22] Members of the élite in Rome and the provinces were keen to make a display of *religio*.

A dictionary compiled in the Augustan period defines 'religious people' as 'those who have a taste for carrying out or omitting ritual in accordance with the custom of the state and are not involved in superstitions'.[23] The major threat to *religio* was not here perceived (as we might expect) to be the systematic neglect of the gods, or actual denial of their existence; such anxieties are not prominent in the writing of the early empire. More often the counterpart of *religio* was *superstitio*. This was ambiguous between two meanings: excessive forms of behaviour, that is 'irregular' religious practices ('not following the customs of the state') and excessive commitment, an excessive commitment to the gods. As a policing tool, either meaning could be useful: behaviour could be monitored by others; commitment was more slippery (what was to count?), and ensured that the concept was internalized for personal monitoring (anyone could be vulnerable to the charge). In either case, the term *superstitio* was used initially to categorize the improper behaviour of individuals rather than groups, and was focussed on internal irregularities in Rome itself rather than Italy and the provinces. Anyone could become addicted, but women were thought particularly likely to lose their self-control: the obituary of an Augustan lady noted among her virtues '*religio* without *superstitio*'.[24] *Superstitio*, in other words, differed from *religio* in its excessive devotion towards ritual and the gods, which was often seen to be motivated by an inappropriate desire for knowledge. Though it might be condemned as fraudulent, it could not be entirely dismissed. Indeed, *superstitio*, far from being a false religion, could be seen as an extremely powerful and dangerous practice which might threaten the stability of *religio* and the state.

Seneca devoted an entire treatise, *On Superstition,* to this important and problematic concept. This work is now known to us almost exclusively through quotations in St Augustine's *City of God,* and there is no guarantee, or even likelihood, that Augustine presents a balanced picture of its contents – he, after all, was using it as a weapon against traditional Roman cult, delighting in what he chose to interpret as an attack on aspects of paganism

---

21   *ILS* 3535, 4167–70, 4930–2, 4936–7, *CIL* X 1894; Timgad: *AE* (1987) 1078 (A.D. 214–15), with pp. 338–9 below; the phrase *cultus religionis* is found already in Valerius Maximus, *Memorable Deeds and Sayings* I.6.13, II.4.4, V.2.1.

22   *Apology* 55.11, 56.3–4.

23   Festus, p. 366 L.

24   *ILS* 8393.30–31 of 'Turia' (trans. Braund (1985) 268).

by a leading pagan writer.[25] Besides, the fact that the work was originally in dialogue form, with different views being presented, debated and no doubt overturned makes it even more difficult to reconstruct, from short quotations, the overall argument of the work.[26] But it seems fairly clear that Seneca, writing as a Stoic philosopher, criticized some of the mythology and practices of the Roman state (the incestuous marriages ascribed to the gods, for example);[27] as well as condemning various rites of foreign origin (self-mutilation, the displays of grief at the death of Osiris, various Jewish practices)[28] and popular excesses in relation to the Roman gods. In a particularly memorable quotation he ridicules the various forms of worship in the Capitoline sanctuary in Rome: 'Go to the Capitoline and you will be ashamed of the madness on display...One servant informs Jupiter of the name of those who visit him, another tells him the time; one is his bather, another his anointer – at least he makes an empty gesture with his arms to imitate anointing...An expert mime-actor, now a crippled old man, used to act a mime each day in the Capitol, as if the gods would enjoy watching a player when men had ceased to.'[29]

This critique of certain aspects of even the most traditional Roman practices shows how wide the scope of *superstitio* might be. Here it is in fact extended, in a philosophical argument, to include what might in other contexts be counted as *religio* – the myths and cult, for example, of the major gods of the state in the city of Rome itself. Seneca's other targets include a variety of popular forms of worship, as well as the rituals of foreign gods practised in Rome. Almost certainly, as we have suggested, this criticism of popular excesses in divine worship would have served to define more sharply the position of the élite in Rome: the élite were not 'superstitious' and took no part in such forms of 'superstitious' ritual. But at the same time, as we shall see, increased worries about bizarre 'foreign' cults in the city of Rome itself in turn affected how Romans viewed those cults in their original locations.

As Seneca's treatise itself helps to illustrate, the use of the term *superstitio* seems to have widened over the first century A.D., both conceptually and geographically. The most striking development, however, was that the concept of magic emerged as the ultimate *superstitio*, a system whose principles

---

25 Augustine, *The City of God* VI.10 (*On Superstition*, frr. 35–7 (Haase)) = **9.5d**. The treatise: Lausberg (1970) 197–227. Seneca's religious position: Mazzoli (1984); Hutchinson (1993) 222–39. The Epicurean Lucretius had identified *religio* and *superstitio* (e.g. I.62–5).

26 The problem of dealing with any dialogue in fragmentary form is that we cannot be sure whether the views expressed in the fragment were subsequently rejected, queried or even ridiculed in the context of the work as a whole; see our comments on Augustine, *City of God* VI.5 = **13.9**.

27 Fr. 39 (Haase); also 33.

28 Fr. 34, 35 (= **9.5d**), 41–3 (Haase).

29 Fr. 36 (Haase) = **9.5d**.

were parodic of and in opposition to true *religio*. The definition of magic is famously contentious and debated. In the nineteenth century and earlier part of the twentieth many theorists (most notoriously Sir James Frazer, the author of *The Golden Bough*) defined 'magic' as an inferior and prior form of religion: whereas religion had a complex cognitive significance, magical actions were purely instrumental, believed to have a direct causal effect on the world (as when sticking pins in a model of one's enemy is thought to cause that person pain); or, in an alternative formulation, the magician *coerced* the deities, whereas the priest of religion *entreated* them in prayer and sacrifice. Such theories still underlie widely held conceptions of magic. But this grand developmental scheme, in which magic is seen as the precursor of 'true religion', has become increasingly discredited, along with the nineteenth-century evolutionary views of human society and development of which it is a part. Besides, the definition of magic as coercive and instrumental as against the (essentially Christian and partisan) view of 'real' religion as non-instrumental and non-coercive does not often match (or help us to classify) the varieties of ritual, worship or religious officials we find in the ancient world. A better starting point, as we saw in chapter 3, is the discussions of magic (and its relation to religion) in the writing of Romans themselves.[30]

According to the encyclopaedia of the Elder Pliny, magic was a heady combination of medicine, religion and astrology, originating in Persia, and meeting human desires for health, control of the gods and knowledge of the future. The system was in his view, totally fraudulent. He recounts, for example, how the emperor Nero ('whose passion for magic was no less than his passion for the lyre and tragic song') lavished massive resources on magical arts wanting to give orders to the gods – but dropped them when they failed to work: 'that the craft is a fraud there could be no greater or more indisputable proof.' And he frequently points to the mendacious claims concerning the magical properties of particular animals and plants made by the 'Magi' (the title of Persian priests, but extended in the Graeco-Roman world to include all 'magicians'): a cure for toothache, for example, that prescribed burning the head of a dog dead from rabies, before dropping the ash (mixed in cyprus oil) into the ear that was closer to the painful tooth.[31]

The opposition between religion and magic is drawn even more evocatively in Lucan's epic poem on the civil wars between Pompey and Caesar,

---

30 Garosi (1976); Schilling (1979) 204–14; North (1980); above, pp. 153–6. Graeco-Roman magic: Hull (1974), a clear introduction; J. Z. Smith (1978) ch. 9; Segal (1981); R. L. Gordon (1987b); Faraone and Obbink (1991); Versnel (1991); Gager (1992); Graf (1994). Skorupski (1976) 125–59 analyses anthropological theories of magic; Luhrmann (1989) defends the 'rationality' of witchcraft.

31 The history of magical arts: Pliny, *Natural History* XXX.1–18 = **11.3** in part. Toothache: XXX.21. Cf. Beagon (1992) 102–13.

the *Pharsalia*.[32] In the midst of the conflict, shortly before the battle of Pharsalia itself, Lucan focusses on the behaviour of Pompey's son, Sextus Pompeius, desperate to know how events would turn out. But Sextus relies not on such legitimate sources as oracles and divination; instead, 'he knew about the mysteries of cruel magicians which the gods above abominate, and grim altars with funereal rites, proof of the truth that Pluto and the shades below exist; and the wretch was convinced that the gods of heaven know too little'.[33] Accordingly he consulted the Thessalian witch Erichtho, an embodiment of illegitimate power. A foreigner and a female, she could undo the laws of nature – instilling love, for example, against the decrees of destiny ('austere old men blaze with illicit passions') or arresting the rotation of the heavens and the flow of rivers. She inhabited deserted graves, feeding on rotting bodies, 'gleefully scooping out the stiffened eyeballs, and gnawing the yellow nails on the withered hand'; and she foretold the future, not with the proper prayers, hymns or sacrifices to the gods, but by 'necromancy', with revivified corpses. This disgusting abomination was the antithesis of rational and humane religious practices. As one recent analyst has put it: 'Erichtho ... is a vision of ultimate disorder, a nightmare in flesh. By contrast, the world maintained by the dominant order is rational, purposive and coherent...The magician's purposes are entirely anti-social; he destroys decency, custom and law; he offends the gods; but most of all he threatens the hierarchy of the politico-social order.' To destroy the illicit power of magic – whether real or imaginary – was effectively to reassert the dominance of that order.[34]

The relationship of this stereotype to the reality of magical practice is, however, complex. Magic was an important part of the fictional repertoire of Roman writers, but it was not *only* a figment of the imagination of the élite; and its practice may have become more prominent through the principate – a consequence perhaps of it too (like other forms of knowledge) becoming partially professionalized in the hands of literate experts in the imperial period. So, for example, the surviving Latin curses (often scratched on lead tablets, and so preserved) increase greatly in number under the empire, and the Greek magical papyri from Egypt are most common in the third and fourth centuries A.D.[35] Roman anxieties about magic may in part have been triggered by changes in its practices and prominence, as well as by the internal logic of their own world view.

But so too, conversely, Roman anxieties about the power of magic may actually have fostered the very practices that were feared. We do not know exactly how magicians at Rome perceived their magical power, how they

---

32 Lucan, *Pharsalia* VI.413–830, with R. L. Gordon (1987a). Cf. Horace, *Epode* 5 = **11.4** in part.
33 VI.430–4.
34 R. L. Gordon (1990c) 255.
35 Some examples are translated in **11.5**. See also Fig. 5.1.

Fig. 5.1 A scene in stucco from the Underground Basilica at Porta Maggiore, Rome (on which see below, pp. 273–4). It seems to show four participants in magic rites – two men (with pointed hats and wearing only loin cloths) and two women. The focus of attention is a table between the two figures on the right; a water pot and a wine jug stand beside it, two goblets and a cooking pot on top. (Height 0.58m., width 2.45m.)

won followers to their craft, how far they viewed their own activities as subversive. The surviving literature of this period preserves no authentic magician's voice; for our élite authors effectively silenced the magician at the same time as they abominated him (or her). But we may well guess that Roman preoccupations with the dangers of magic offered one access to power, albeit illicit, to those excluded from the hierarchy of the 'politico-social order'. To express a fear, for example, that magic could kill even the emperor was also to expose the emperor's vulnerability – and to expose the existence of a different form of power that could (with the right skill) be tapped. Magical practice and the fear of magic were, no doubt, symbiotic.

By the early second century A.D. we can detect another development in the use of the term *superstitio*: the word began to denote the religious practices of particular foreign peoples. In the late Republic and into the first century A.D. there seems to have been a general assumption at Rome that each foreign race had its own characteristic religious practices; even though they were no doubt thought inferior to Roman practice, the 'native' religions of the provincial populations of the Roman empire were not systematically dismissed or derided. But from the second century at the latest— perhaps as it became more pressing for the Roman élite to define itself in relation to the provinces (and provincial élites) – that position changed. Tacitus, for example, refers to the Druids' prophecy that Rome would fall to the Gauls as 'an empty *superstitio*'.[36] Egyptian and Jewish rituals too were branded with the

36 Tacitus, *Histories* IV.54.4; cf. *Annals* XIV.30; cf. Grodzynski (1974a).

221

same label. According to Tacitus again, the people of Alexandria 'subject to superstitions' worshipped the god Sarapis above all; while his extremely hostile account of Jewish customs observes that this race was 'prone to *superstitio*, and opposed to religious practices'.[37] The polarization of the two categories is here made explicit. At the same time, these foreign cults were seen as potential forces of political subversion: Druids prophesied the downfall of Rome and the Jews actually did revolt against Rome. (Fig. 5.2) Egyptian cults too were often perceived in terms of political opposition to Rome. Although (as we shall see in the next chapter) the cult of Isis in particular came to have a prominent place within the religions of the capital, much of the writing of the Augustan period had presented the emperor's victory over Cleopatra as a victory of Roman over Egyptian gods.

It was not, of course, the case that all 'non-Roman' cults were branded in this way. Not only (as we have seen) did religious practice at Rome often blur the distinction between native Roman and imported 'foreign' cults; but Roman writers could accept, even sometimes admire, striking divergences from strictly 'Roman' practice. In Italy, for example, in a place not far from the capital, a group of families walked unscathed on burning logs at their annual festival of Apollo. For this, according to the Elder Pliny, they were rewarded by the senate with perpetual immunity from military service and from all other obligations to the state. So too the emperor Marcus Aurelius describes in a letter how he came upon a small town south east of Rome.

There we inspected that ancient township [Anagnia], a tiny place indeed but containing many antiquities and buildings, and religious ceremonies beyond number. There was not a corner without its chapel or shrine or temple. Many books too, written on linen, which has a religious significance. Then on the gate, as we came out, we found an inscription twice over to this effect: *flamen sume samentum* [priest put on the fell]. I asked one of the townsmen what the last word meant. He said that it was Hernican for the pelt of the victim, which the priest draws over his peaked cap on entering the city.[38]

The letter gives a vivid picture of the religious life of a small Italian town and of the reactions of at least one leading Roman to its peculiarities; Marcus' remarks are strikingly ambivalent – a mixture of antiquarian curiosity, patronizing benevolence and 'genuine' warmth.

Outside Italy too the single term *superstitio* covered a multitude of sins. Though Judaism might be regarded as a *superstitio*, even Tacitus grudgingly accorded the justification of tradition for at least some of its allegedly

---

37 *Histories* IV.81.2; V.13.1; cf. V.4–5 = **11.8a**. For republican resistance to Isis see above, pp. 160–1; for positive images of these cults, below, pp. 278–91.

38 Fire-walkers in territory of Falisci: Pliny, *Natural History* VII.19; cf. Virgil, *Aeneid* XI.785–90. Anagnia: Marcus Aurelius to Fronto, in Fronto, *Letters* (Loeb edn.) I.175. Local magistrates in charge of religion had been permitted to Anagnia after its subjection in 306 B.C.: Livy IX.43.24. Cf. below, pp. 321–2 for the retention of non-Roman traditions.

Fig. 5.2 The Arch of Titus in Rome celebrating the suppression of the Jewish Revolt of A.D. 66–70 includes a scene commemorating the carrying of spoils from the Temple in Jerusalem in triumphal procession at Rome: the menorah (seven-branched candle-stick); and an offering table, on which stand two incense vessels, and two trumpets. It is striking that this representation should give such prominence to the religious objects of the Jews. (Height 2.02m., width 3.92m.)

bizarre practices: 'These rites, whatever their origins, are sanctioned by their antiquity.'[39] Indeed some Jewish writers even claimed the primacy of Jewish over Greek thought: in the mid first century A.D. Philo assumes through his extensive expositions of the Pentateuch (the first five books of the later Christian Old Testament) that Plato borrowed from Moses; and towards the end of the first century Josephus' *Against Apion* again took for granted that Greek civilization was dependent on the Jews, though inferior to Jewish practices.[40]

In Greece, the Eleusinian mysteries provide a striking example of the negotiable boundary between what was acceptable and unacceptable in Roman terms. These mysteries involved nocturnal and secret rites; but far from condemning them, many Romans, including Augustus and other emperors, were themselves initiated at Eleusis. In addition to the special cultural role of Greece in the Roman empire, the civic nature of this cult, its antiquity and its myths – long familiar at Rome – guaranteed its prestigious position, at least until the fourth century A.D.[41] The Romans even

39 Tacitus, *Histories* V.5 = **11.8a**; Celsus in Origen, *Against Celsus* V.25.
40 Philo does not argue his case at any one point; Josephus, *Against Apion* II.168. Such arguments may be echoed in the second-century Pythagorean Numenius, though his direct knowledge of Jewish writings was probably very limited: M. J. Edwards (1990).
41 Below, p. 374.

223

granted legal privileges to specific sanctuaries in Greece: the Roman jurist Ulpian lists those deities who were, exceptionally, allowed by law to be the beneficiaries of wills and receive bequests – the great majority being the gods of temples in the Greek world.[42]

Greek religion was not, however, exempt from Roman criticism. The Romans sought, for example, to regulate perceived abuses of Greek sanctuaries, particularly the so-called 'right of asylum' – which guaranteed a place of safety to anyone who chose to take refuge there. This right was not unknown in Rome: one of the myths of the city's origins had Romulus establishing an asylum in order to attract men to his newly founded city; and (perhaps as a self-conscious imitation of that precedent) the temple of *divus* Julius in the forum was declared an asylum – while statues of emperors too were often treated 'religiously' as places of safe refuge (where criminals and runaways could find protection). But the right had long been common in Greece; and there were fears among the Roman authorities of widespread abuse of this privilege. Tacitus describes how in the reign of Tiberius the senate carefully scrutinized the claims of numerous Greek sanctuaries to the right of asylum, dismissed some and imposed a limit on their numbers. Inevitably the historian has his own axe to grind in recounting this incident, as part of his analysis of the corrupt and hypocritical régime of Tiberius (in particular we should spot a loaded comparison with another senatorial debate a few chapters earlier, on the abuse in Rome itself of the religious protection offered by statues and other images of the emperor). Even so the account reflects Roman unease with some aspects of Greek religious practice: the sanctuaries, Tacitus claims, had become havens not only for runaway slaves and debtors, but also for those liable to capital punishment; the Greek communities were in practice protecting criminal behaviour along with the worship of the gods.[43]

This raises the question of how far the categories for proper and improper religion employed by the élites of the Greek cities under the empire mapped onto the Roman categories we have been discussing. Certainly there are some themes in Greek writing that seem very similar to Roman preoccupations. For example, Plutarch's essay on marriage advises that the good wife should worship only the gods her husband accepts and shut the door to excessive rituals and foreign 'superstitions'. Magicians as at Rome were abominated; in fact, the hagiographic biography of Apollonius of Tyana denies explicitly that Apollonius, despite his special knowledge of the future, his miraculous cures, and his ability to vanish into thin air, was a 'magician'.[44] On the other hand, though *eusebeia* ('piety') to the gods and

---

42 Ulpian, *Tituli* 22.6 in *FIRA* II.285.
43 Statues: Price (1984) 192–3. Tacitus, *Annals* III.60–3. Cf. below, p. 343.
44 Plutarch, *Advice to Bride and Groom* 140d. Lucian, *Alexander* 21 refers to a treatise attacking magicians by Celsus, an Epicurean philosopher. Philostratus, *Life of Apollonius* I.2, IV.18, V.12, VII.11, 20, 33–4, 39, VIII.5, 7, 19, 30.

emperor was regularly proclaimed by members of Greek élites, there was no one general category, like *superstitio*, for deviations from the norm. *Deisidaimonia* (literally, 'fear of the gods' – the word used by Plutarch in his marital advice) was only a partial analogue. Like *superstitio*, it categorized excessive and demeaning behaviour towards the gods, but it was not generally extended to include magic or the practices of foreign peoples.[45] In Greek translations from Latin, *superstitio* was rendered not by *deisidaimonia* but by an uncomfortable shuffle of terms – from *mataiotes* ('vanity') to *atheotes* ('atheism').[46]

Of course, in the multi-cultural world of the Roman empire, no sharp barrier between Greek and Roman thought or cultural systems could hold; many of the élite were in fact well-versed in both Greek and Latin writing. The linguistic and cultural differences we have pointed to (with the different ways of classifying religious acts and experience that they imply) prove that proper religious behaviour could be pinned to no single definition; that the boundaries between what was licit and what illicit were always there to be re-negotiated.

For the Roman authorities, however, some cases were clearer than others. On Christianity the official Roman position was for centuries undisputably negative. Whereas Greek writers accused the Christians of being *atheoi*, 'godless', Romans did not trouble with the existence of the Christian god, but classified the worship as *superstitio*, rather than *religio*. In the words of Tacitus, 'the deadly *superstitio* was checked for a time [by the execution of Christ], but broke out again, not only in Judaea, the origin of the evil, but even in the capital'. The Younger Pliny too in his investigation of Christianity in Pontus (a province in Asia Minor) concluded that it was 'a degenerate *superstitio* carried to extravagant lengths'.[47] Pliny seems to have expected improprieties, but found nothing out of the ordinary reported (merely hymn-singing, oaths against theft, robbery and adultery – and the consumption of perfectly ordinary food). Immoral actions might be expected to form part of a *superstitio* but in this case their absence did not weaken the classification of Christianity as 'superstitious'.

It is likely that Pliny had heard extravagant accusations about Christian behaviour that he was unable to substantiate. Such accusations at any rate feature prominently in the disputes over Christianity in the later second and early third centuries. Christians were accused, it seems, of holding nocturnal gatherings for magical purposes, and of ritual cannibalism and incest, that is of fundamental breaches of the code of humanity.[48] The origin of

---

45 There are exceptions: e.g. Plutarch, *On Superstition* 169c, 171b–e.

46 E.g. *mataiotes* ('vanity') of the Christians (Eusebius, *Ecclesiastical History* IX.7.3–14 with S. Mitchell (1988) 108, line 4); *atheotes* ('atheism') in Cassius Dio LXVII.14.

47 Christians as 'godless': Harnack (1905); Brox (1966). Tacitus, *Annals* XV.44.5 = **11.11a**; cf. Suetonius, *Nero* 16.2; Pliny, *Letters* X.96.8 = **11.11b**.

48 Magic: Tertullian, *To his Wife* II.5.3; Origen, *Against Celsus* I.6, VI.38–40, VIII.60; *Martyrdom of Perpetua* 16. Crimes: Athenagoras, *Embassy* 3.1, 31–33; Minucius Felix,

these accusations is debated. Some modern writers have argued that they arose from distorted knowledge of Christian ritual practices (eating the body and drinking the blood of Christ; the ritual kiss) or from actual or alleged practices of Christian 'heretical' groups. Others have suggested that they are parodic reversals of actual practice (Christian abstinence from sacrifices, for example, and in some cases from marriage converted into their parodic opposites and projected onto the Christians) or even the powerful, but essentially fictionalizing, stereotypes of illicit, foreign religions – stereotypes traceable in Rome at least as far back as the affair of the Bacchanalia, two centuries before Christ.[49] The accusations probably in part resulted from Christian isolationism exacerbated by active evangelizing as well as the cult's novelty. Certainly some ancient critics stressed that Christianity had abandoned the traditions of Judaism and, in so doing, had abandoned all claims to the authority that derived from such traditions; Christianity had no ancestral legitimacy at all, originating (as Tacitus put it) with Christus, who 'was executed in the principate of Tiberius by the governor Pontius Pilate'.[50] But whatever their origins, such accusations no doubt fuelled fears about the loyalty to Rome of Christians, who often avoided military service and civic office-holding, and refused to sacrifice for the well-being of the emperor. However, by the mid third century the old charges of incest and cannibalism were generally discounted;[51] Greeks continued to accuse Christians of 'godlessness',[52] but Christianity was by now too visible and distinct to be classified with the other superstitions.

Christians themselves rejected the charges laid against them – although they recounted them both zealously, and no doubt exaggeratedly, in their own partisan writings. Thus the most evocative, as well as the most outrageous of the alleged charges survive in Christian literature itself.[53] Some of the earliest followers of Christ claimed that his teaching lay in the Jewish tradition, and was in fact the fulfilment of the Jewish law and the prophets;

Octavius 9.5–6 (= **11.11d**) with Benko (1984) 54–78; M.J. Edwards (1992); Rives (1995b). M. Smith (1978) 45–67 and Benko (1984) 103–39 exaggerate the pre-Constantinian evidence for actual Christian magical practices.

49 Christianity 'barbarian': Justin, *First Apology* 7.3, 46.3, 60.11; Tatian, *Oration* 1.1; Eusebius, *Ecclesiastical History* V.1.63, VI.19.7; Arnobius, *Against the Gentiles* II.66. The issue was exacerbated by the appeal of Christianity to women. The combination of stereotypes of foreign and female, which had been deployed by classical Greeks of eastern women out of control, has always been especially potent. Cf. Said (1978), though the negative stereotype of women is only latent in this work.

50 Novelty: Celsus in Origen, *Against Celsus* I.14, II.4, V.33. Tacitus, *Annals* XV.44 = **11.11a**.

51 Origen, *Against Celsus* VI.27, 40.

52 Note, however, that Greek accusations of 'godlessness' continued (*Tituli Asiae Minoris* II.3, 785 = *Inschriften von Arykanda* 12, petition to Maximinus of A.D. 312 (trans. Lewis and Reinhold (1990) II.570–1)). Constantine's treatment of the Christians: below, ch. 8.

53 Above, n. 48. Christians in the second and third centuries wrote a series of defences of their faith: below, pp. 309–10.

though later, in the second century A.D., Justin argued that Christianity was rather the fulfilment of Greek, specifically Platonic, thought – so formulating for the first time what was to become a perennial debate about the relationship of Christianity to 'secular' wisdom.[54]

The boundary between Christianity and magic was a particularly sensitive area. Jews in second-century Palestine were formally barred from practising magic or consulting soothsayers, but their religious leaders treated the matters as natural temptations in the world around them, posing no conceptual problem for Judaism.[55] By contrast, because of Christian claims about Christ's miracles, Justin and other writers did face a conceptual challenge from magic. According to Justin, any accusations of magic against the Christians were the fault of demons who, after Christ's ascension, had brought forward people who claimed to be gods and performed magical acts. The most notorious of these was a certain Simon, who combined a profession of Christianity with magical powers. The Acts of the Apostles sought to marginalize him and other 'impostors' (Paul, for example, calls on the power of God to blind a magician); while they defended the miracles of Christ and the apostles against the charge of magic. This attempt to draw a clear distinction between magic and miracle, and to reject any notion of Christ as a 'magician', is also an important theme in Origen's defence of Christianity – in answer to the charges of the pagan Celsus.[56] But the issue of magic remained a sensitive issue in church practice. In the third century A.D. a Christian refutation of 'heresies' included a section on magicians as a 'heresy'; and a set of official rules, which probably refer to the church at Rome, specifically forbade magicians to be considered for membership.[57]

Eventually, however, it was the Christians who managed to place their stamp on the terms *religio* and *superstitio*. Their positive claim at least by the early third century was that Christianity itself was 'the true *religio* of the true god'; it was paganism that was mere *superstitio*.[58] The implication is that some Christians at least accepted the words of the traditional argument, but modified the meaning of *religio* to include *their* truth, neatly reversing the terms on their opponents. This was a reversal which, as we shall see in chapter 8, began to have considerable practical importance in the fourth century A.D.

---

54   Chadwick (1966).
55   *The Mishnah, Sanhedrin* 7.7, 7.11, *Kerithoth* (*'Extirpation'*) 1.1.
56   Justin, *First Apology* 26 = **12.7a(i)**; Acts of the Apostles 13.6–12; *Acts of Peter* 4–32, with Poupon (1981) and Remus (1983). Origen, *Against Celsus* I.6, 28, 68; IV.33; VI.38–41; VIII.37, with Gallagher (1982).
57   Hippolytus, *Refutation* IV.28–42; *Apostolic Tradition* of Hippolytus XVI.21–2. For 'orthodox' accusations of immorality against 'heretics' see Irenaeus, *Against Heresies* I.6.2–3 (= **12.7e(ii)**).
58   Tertullian, *Apology* 24.2; Minucius Felix, *Octavius* 1.5, 24.10, 38.7, reversing the anti-Christian argument of 13.5. Cf. Koep (1962); Michels (1976) 66–72.

2. Patrolling the unacceptable

The Roman élite invested large amounts of their cultural energy in evaluating religious activities, in prising apart proper and improper forms of religion. This was not merely a matter of intellectual satisfaction, nor of constructing a secure identity for the Roman élite in Rome and the empire. Formulated definitions were accompanied by a series of administrative and judicial measures of gradually increasing scope, radiating from Rome to the whole empire, to regulate religious practice. The connections between the ideological evaluations that we have discussed so far in this chapter and the practical regulations that form the subject of what follows are many and various. We have already noted the symbiosis between fear of magic and magical practice. There are similar overlaps here. Practical regulations do not simply follow from some prior evaluation or definition; rather, a prohibition on a particular activity often ensures that it is defined and perceived as illicit or improper; regulations may, in other words, be responsible for evaluation, as much as they are a consequence of it. Behind the narrative of practical steps taken to suppress and stigmatize various kinds of religious behaviour that follows in the rest of this chapter lies a complex series of interactions between the ideological, symbolic and practical aspects of religious culture in the Roman empire.

The first stage in the sequence of actions against *superstitio* was the attempt to maintain the purity of the centre, at Rome, irrespective of practices elsewhere in the empire. The lead was set from the top. Both Augustus and Hadrian are reported by their biographers to have despised foreign cults; and Suetonius also notes that, when in Egypt, Augustus declined to visit the sacred Apis bull, and highly commended his grandson Gaius for not offering prayers to Jehovah in Jerusalem. Pliny likewise characterized the good emperor as one who did not have 'the ministrants of a foreign superstition' at his dinner table (an implied comparison between Trajan, the emperor reigning at the time, and his predecessor Domitian, whose posthumous demonization stressed, among other immoralities, his enthusiasm for foreign cults). In fact, by the mid first century A.D., the growth of 'foreign superstitions' at Rome could be portrayed as a threat to the 'official' Roman system: so, at least in Tacitus' account, the emperor Claudius found the popularity of these alien cults partially responsible for the neglect of the art of haruspicy among the great Etruscan families, and he took steps to revive the art. Even here, however, the definitions were not always quite so simple as they might at first sight seem. It is not just that some emperors ('monsters' or not) were enthusiastic patrons of foreign cults at Rome. Suetonius himself shows how fluid the categories might be: Augustus' scorn for foreign cults was in fact limited to those that were not 'ancient and long standing foreign rites'. Even – or especially – in the case of alien religions, the shifting standard of 'antiquity' (another instance of the religious *authority of tradition*) might always offer a legitimate alibi for their worship.[59]

In Rome the élite continued to police the religious behaviour of its own members – as we can see from anecdotes about individuals who were persuaded or forced to conform to conventional practices. Seneca, for example, tells us that in his youth he was persuaded by Pythagorean arguments and renounced meat. 'Foreign cults were subject to expulsions [i.e., in the Tiberian period], and abstinence from certain meats counted as one of the marks of *superstitio*.' At the request of his father, he returned to a normal, carnivorous diet.[60] A member of the élite could not afford to deviate from Roman dietary norms and become associated either with popular foreign cults or with an excess of philosophy. Pressure to conform could even take legal form. Tacitus records the trial of Pomponia Graecina, wife of a prominent senator, on a charge of foreign *superstitio*. She underwent a preliminary hearing before the senate and was then tried by her husband.[61] Rejection of foreign superstition created a sense of unity for the Roman élite in relation to the empire, though consistency was hardly possible given the expanding nature of the Roman élite.

The publicly paraded religious activity of the Roman élite was predominantly connected with the traditional cults of Rome – so further emphasizing their distance from 'foreign superstition'. Senators continued to serve in the four major priestly colleges until well into the fourth century A.D. and, as we saw in the last chapter, there was often keen competition for the emperor's favour – on which priestly appointments now depended. They also regularly recorded their membership of some of the ancient 'minor colleges': not only the Arval Brothers, but also the *fetiales* (whose ritual was used by the emperor Marcus Aurelius in declaring war in A.D. 179, and who are attested into the third century A.D.) and the Salii (who continued to meet until the fourth century A.D.). Equestrians likewise proudly erected statues of themselves as Luperci – again a priesthood with associations that stretched back to the mythical founding of Rome.[62] The gods honoured in dedications by senators and equestrian officials serving in the provinces also reflect this traditional emphasis: these were predominantly the 'official' gods of Rome, especially Jupiter; while conversely (before the fourth century at least) senators and equestrian officials seem rarely to have been initiated

---

59   Suetonius, *Augustus* 93; *Augustan History, Hadrian* 22.10; Pliny, *Panegyric* 49.8; Tacitus, *Annals* XI.15. According to Philo, *Embassy* 157 (= **12.6c(ii)**) Augustus himself paid for sacrifices at Jerusalem, but this is probably an apologetic fiction.

60   Seneca, *Letters* 108.22. Seneca's text confuses the danger of *superstitio* and philosophy: though his father did not fear legal actions in relation to cult practices, he was particularly opposed to philosophy. Tiberian expulsions: below, pp. 230–1.

61   Tacitus, *Annals* XIII.32 = **11.10**, with Mommsen (1899) 19 (A.D. 57); cf. Cassius Dio LXVII.14 (A.D. 95).

62   Beaujeu (1964); Eck (1989b); above, pp. 192–6. *Fetiales*: Cassius Dio LXXII.33.3; *AE* (1948) 241. *Salii*: Cirilli (1913) 43–6. *Luperci*: Wrede (1983).

into foreign mystery cults. Despite the fact that the élite was drawn increasingly from outside Italy, only exceptionally did its members make dedications (outside their home towns) to their ancestral gods. For the most part those joining the Roman élite displayed their adherence to a public value system, centred on the official cults of Rome.[63]

From the start of the principate a series of direct measures was taken to control the religious activities and associations of those outside the élite. Both Caesar and Augustus banned private societies (*collegia*), fearing their role in social or political disorder – though they made an exception of those founded for certain legitimate purposes, spelled out in a senatorial decree that survives from the Augustan period. Social clubs were banned, but the poor were permitted to pay a monthly contribution to ensure a decent burial for themselves, and to meet once a month; from the mid second century A.D. no one could be a member of more than one club (thus eliminating the spectre of general conspiracy evident in the Bacchanalia affair). Soldiers were also prohibited from forming clubs. However, meetings for the sake of *religio* were permitted (for both soldiers and civilians), so long as the society did not violate the senatorial decree. This decision necessarily entailed judgements about what counted as *religio*. Funeral societies which met under the auspices of a god were included; the Jews in Rome were specifically permitted by Caesar to continue collecting money and meeting together; and soldiers could form societies to worship Jupiter Dolichenus or Mithras. But the Roman authorities, as we shall see, denied the legitimacy of Christian meetings.[64]

An important traditional tactic for maintaining the religious purity of the centre was the expulsion of non-citizens, and their 'foreign' activities, from Rome and Italy. In the late Republic we hear from time to time of actions taken against various groups: rhetors, diviners, Jews, followers of Isis. The expulsion of religious groups continued up to the mid first century A.D. Augustus, for example, banned Egyptian rites within the *pomerium*, a ban later extended to the suburbs of Rome up to one Roman mile from the city.[65] In all such banning orders, in any society, there is always liable to be a gap between the legal ruling and its practical consequences. In this case (and in most others at Rome) we have virtually no idea how the order was put into practice, who (if anyone) was responsible for searching out Isiac rites, or how they decided what exactly was to count as such a ritual within the terms of the ban. Certainly these repeated rulings did not have the effect of clearing Rome of Egyptian cults; and in A.D. 19 a

63 Rarity of initiations, below pp. 291–2. For coexistence of one ancestral cult (Dionysus) see below, p. 271. For (rare) dedications to local gods, see below, p. 328.

64 Suetonius, *Caesar* 42.3, *Augustus* 32.1; *ILS* 4966, 7212 = **12.2**; Josephus, *Jewish Antiquities* XIV.213–6 = **12.6c(i)**; *Digest* XXXVII.22 = **11.9**. Above, pp. 95–6 [Bacchanalia]; Mommsen (1899) 876–7.

65 On late Republic, above, pp. 177–81. Cassius Dio LIII.2.4 (28 B.C.), LIV.6.6 (21 B.C.). On the *pomerium*, above, pp. 160–1.

scandal involving a high-ranking Roman lady brought the religion of Isis again to the emperor's attention. This virtuous married lady was said to have been a particular devotee of the cult – a devotion that was used against her by a suitor whose importunate demands she had rejected: he tricked her into coming to the temple of Isis and sleeping with him, believing him to be the Egyptian god Anubis. When the man taunted her, by revealing the trick, she had the case brought before Tiberius, who destroyed the temple, threw the statue of Isis into the Tiber and crucified the priests (for their complicity in the plot). At the same time, the Jews too suffered from imperial attention because of alleged embezzlement of gifts from another upper-class Roman lady destined for the temple in Jerusalem. A total of 4,000 Jews and Egyptians were sent to Sardinia to serve in the army; the others were to leave Italy unless they gave up their superstitions by a certain date.[66] Though the test for renunciation of the *superstitio* is not stated, the demand for renunciation prefigures the demand later made of Christians.

Astrologers (and magicians) were also formally expelled from Rome and Italy in the first century A.D., as they had been in 139 and 33 B.C.[67] Astrology itself (unlike magic) was not seen by the Roman authorities as intrinsically dangerous. Certain aspects of astrology (such as some personal horoscopes – see Fig. 5.3) were regarded as perfectly acceptable forms of divination: emperors and other members of the Roman élite could consult astrologers without incurring obloquy, and astrology might even support imperial power – regularly predicting, for example, a future emperor's rise or military triumphs. But astrology – like all techniques which claim to offer knowledge of the future – could also be deeply threatening; it could predict an emperor's downfall as much as his success. The emperor Tiberius found it necessary to act against astrologers and magicians in A.D. 16 with the discovery of a conspiracy against himself. Two decrees were passed by the senate, laying down, first, the expulsion of astrologers and magicians from Rome and Italy, and secondly the death penalty for non-Romans and exile for Romans who were still practising these arts in the city.[68] The Tiberian senatorial decree set the precedent, but raised explicitly some of the definitional problems that we have already noted (what was to *count* as astrology within the terms of the law?). Lawyers debated whether mere knowledge of astrology was punishable, or only its actual practice. At first they decided that knowledge was not prohibited, but subsequently their views diverged. In any case, emperors repeated the Tiberian ban seven times during the rest

66 Josephus, *Jewish Antiquities* XVIII.65–84; Tacitus, *Annals* II.85; Suetonius, *Tiberius* 36. There was also a temporary ban on Jewish assemblies under Claudius.
67 Above, pp. 113; 161. Cramer (1954) 233–48; cf. also MacMullen (1966) 95–162.
68 Tacitus, *Annals* II.32; Suetonius, *Tiberius* 36; Cassius Dio LVII.15.8–9; Ulpian in *Comparison of Mosaic and Roman Law* XV.2 = **11.7a**. Mommsen (1899) 640 n. 7 believed that Tacitus and Cassius Dio were incorrect in referring to magicians, but this view depends on the verbatim accuracy of the excerpt from Ulpian. On acceptable astrology see **7.8**.

of the first century A.D. (with one further doubtful case in the later second century A.D.) – so prefiguring Tacitus' neat formulation that astrologers would 'always be banned and always retained' at Rome.[69]

There were in addition legal rules and prohibitions on astrology that referred to both Rome and the empire more generally; these overlap with, but by the late first century A.D. tend to replace, the policy of expulsions – whose aims were more or less restricted to removing this troublesome practice from the heart of the state. Astrology was the subject of a general Augustan edict which forbade consultations that took place in private without witnesses, or any consultations at all about the date of someone's death. The last ban included consultations by slaves about their master's death or by people about themselves or members of their own family, penalties for which were laid down in later legal texts. At the same time, according to Cassius Dio, Augustus published his own horoscope – a sign of his own confidence in his position, as well as a useful tactic to preempt all further astrological activity by others; but he banned all such publications for the future.[70]

69 Tacitus, *Histories* I.22.
70 Mommsen (1899) 861–5; Cramer (1954) 248–81. Augustan edict: Cassius Dio LVI.25.5 (A.D. 11); cf. Suetonius, *Augustus* 94 (= **7.8a**) for Augustus's enthusiasm for astrology. Later jurists: Ulpian in *Comparison* XV.2 = **11.7a**; Paul, *Opinions* V.21 (= *FIRA* II.406–7). Cf. T. Barton (1994) 38–52.

Fig. 5.3 One of a pair of ivory zodiacal tables, from the healing sanctuary of Apollo at Grand (Vosges, France), which were destroyed c. A.D. 170. In the centre: Sun and Moon. Round them are the twelve signs of the zodiac, each marked with Greek letters indicating the 'domain' of the planet, according to the Egyptian system. A large circle shows as Egyptian gods the 36 decans, that is the gods who each influence ten days per zodiacal sign; each is labelled with its name, originally in Egyptian, but transcribed into Greek. In the corners are the four winds. These very Egyptian objects (a startling discovery in a Gallic sanctuary) presumably served to guide the choice of treatments for diseases and also to predict lengths of life and manners of death. Astrologers in Rome and elsewhere used similarly arcane tables. (Height 0.19m., width 0.29m.)

Most fully reported in our sources are the series of trials in Rome which dealt with alleged consultations about the future of the emperor or members of his family. Some fifteen cases involving astrologers or their clients are attested in the first century A.D. and two or three cases in the next hundred or so years. For example, the distinguished Lollia Paulina, once married to the emperor Gaius Caligula and an unsuccessful candidate for the hand of the emperor Claudius, was accused of 'having consulted astrologers, magicians and the oracle of Clarian Apollo (in Asia Minor) about the emperor's marriage' – that is, about whether she herself would be Claudius' next wife. Tacitus portrays this accusation as driven by the personal hatred of Agrippina, who was herself by this time married to the emperor. But, all the same, for 'her pernicious plans against the state' Lollia Paulina was exiled by the senate, and she was later forced to commit suicide.[71]

Anxieties about illicit divination were not limited to Rome. In the provinces astrologers in the second century certainly asked for trouble by offering (illegal) ways of computing death dates from horoscopes, and in turn provincial governors enforced control of illegal divination as at Rome. The jurist Ulpian included in his treatise on the duties of provincial governors a section explaining the regulation of astrologers and soothsayers; a papyrus document survives from Roman Egypt, with a copy of a general ban on divination issued by a governor of the province in the late second century A.D. (on the grounds that it led people astray and brought danger); and at the end of the third century A.D. the emperor Diocletian issued a general ban on astrology.[72] Consultations of diviners which threatened the stability of private families or the life of the emperor himself were obvious targets for punishment.

By the late Republic, magic was brought under an earlier general law on murder and poisoning, the *lex Cornelia de sicariis et veneficiis* of 81 B.C. The category of *venenum*, which included both poisoning and magic, caught the magician who was, in the words of Apuleius, 'popularly believed to hold discourse with the immortal gods and thus to have the power to do everything he wanted by the mysterious force of certain incantations.' The precise wording of the law does not survive, but we have a late third or early fourth century A.D. commentary on it: impious and nocturnal rites indicated magical practices; rites involving human sacrifice were illegal, as were rites that enchanted, bewitched or bound anyone.[73]

Human sacrifice was thought characteristic of magic. In the imperial period such a ritual was regarded as a monstrous perversion of legitimate

---

71 Tacitus, *Annals* XII.22 (A.D. 49).

72 Astrologers: Ptolemy, *Tetrabiblos* III.9, IV.9; Vettius Valens, *Anthology* V.9, 12 (225.3, 237.8 Kroll). Ulpian in *Comparison* XV.2 = **11.7a**; *ZPE* 27 (1977) 151–6 = **11.7b**. Diocletian: *Codex Justinianus* IX.18.2 (A.D. 294). For actions by Christian emperors, see below, p. 372. On the threat of prophecy, Potter (1994) 171–82.

73 Mommsen (1899) 639–43; Massonneau (1934) 159–96. Apuleius, *Apology* 26.6. Paul, *Opinions* V.23.14–19 = **11.2b**.

animal sacrifice, and so utterly 'foreign'; the Roman authorities sought to eradicate it, whether performed by Roman citizens or by others.[74] Their actions against the Druids provide a clear example both of their increasingly stringent moves against human sacrifice, and also of the extension of the category of magic (as it became defined by this particular form of perverted ritual). The first stage, under Augustus, was a prohibition on the cult for Roman citizens; then the cult was proscribed in the Gallic provinces themselves. By the late first century A.D. what the Elder Pliny called this 'magic' flourished only in Britain -

with such grand ritual that it might seem that she gave it to the Persians. So universal was the cult of magic throughout the world, although its nations disagree or are unknown to each other. It is beyond calculation how great is the debt owed to the Romans, who swept away the monstrous rites, in which to kill a man was the highest religious duty and for him to be eaten a passport to health.[75]

Human sacrifice had, in other words, become such a clear diagnostic of magic that what Julius Caesar had once seen as the traditional religion of the Gauls (albeit with the barbarous characteristic of human sacrifice), by the mid first century A.D. was re-categorized as a magical art – with all the political and social dangers this implied.[76]

The enchantment wrought by magic regularly had two major objectives: causing death and instilling love. The classic example of the former is the death of Germanicus (nephew and adopted son of Tiberius) in Syria in A.D. 19. Germanicus himself believed that he had been given *venenum*, a belief that was strengthened by the fact that 'in the floor and walls of his house were found remains of human bodies, spells, curses, lead tablets inscribed with the name 'Germanicus', charred and blood-smeared ashes and other devices of witchcraft by which it is believed that living souls can be devoted to the powers below the earth'.[77] Those who accepted Germanicus' explanation of his fatal illness despatched to Rome a woman who was famous in the province as a magician; she, however, died before reaching Rome. The 'discoveries' illustrate features regularly denounced as elements of magical practices: the use of human bodies, lead curse tablets, the associated finds

74 Livy XXII.57.6 stresses the 'un-Romanness' of human offerings, which had in fact been made in Rome in the second century B.C.; above, pp. 80–2; Plutarch, *Roman Questions* 83 = **6.6b**.

75 Pliny, *Natural History* XXX.13 = **11.3**; Suetonius, *Claudius* 25.5; cf. Pomponius Mela III.18. Pliny and Suetonius disagree about whether the general proscription of the cult was due to Tiberius or Claudius. The earlier intervention may simply be the senatorial decree of A.D. 16 on astrology. Druids: Piggott (1968); D. Nash (1976); Letta (1984); above, pp. 221–2.

76 Caesar, *Gallic War* VI.16. Sacrifice of children to Saturn in North Africa was unacceptable to the Romans (Tertullian, *Apology* 9.2–3 with Rives (1994)) and human sacrifice was apparently banned almost everywhere under Hadrian (Porphyry, *On Abstinence* II.56.3).

77 Tacitus, *Annals* II.69, 74.2, III.7.2, 12–14. Cf. Gager (1992).

and the female professional. At the subsequent trial in Rome of the governor of Syria (who was believed to have been behind Germanicus' death), the charge of magic and poisoning – note the wavering implicit in the term *venenum* – was successfully countered by the defence; and the case against him came to hinge on alleged political and military misdemeanours.[78] But using magic to commit murder remained an offence punishable with the utmost severity.

Causing someone to fall in love by means of magic also carried the death penalty. A surviving speech, supposedly given by Apuleius before the governor of Africa in A.D. 158–9 (though the whole case could be fictional), plays with the range of possible charges and counter-arguments under the *lex Cornelia*.[79] This *Defence on a Charge of Magic* takes us from Rome to a provincial setting, where one strategy for victory in a local dispute was to invoke Roman law. The dispute is supposed to have arisen out of Apuleius' marriage to Pudentilla, a wealthy widow of Oea (modern Tripoli), the second city of Tripolitania. Her late husband's family, who saw a fortune disappearing from them, have charged Apuleius with having captured the affections of Pudentilla by magic. Apuleius' speech of defence argues not that the alleged actions were intrinsically impossible, but that other, innocent interpretations could be placed upon them. He rebuts the accusations with two main arguments: first against the allegations that he was a magician; and secondly against the particular claims that he had bewitched Pudentilla. The defence against general magical practices opens with a burlesque account of the acquisition of a certain type of fish.[80] What could this possibly have to do with magic? Admittedly Apuleius had sought out rare types of fish, but this was simply to satisfy his intellectual and medical interests. We almost forget that the prosecution had alleged that Apuleius used these fish for love magic, a recognized magical practice. Then there was the bewitching of a boy and of a woman so that they fell down in fits; he had not attempted, he retorts, to use these people for divinatory purposes, they were simply epileptics whom he was trying to help.[81] Apuleius is further accused of keeping certain mysterious objects in a household shrine. The objects were indeed secret, but not therefore magical; rather, they were the emblems of religious rites of initiation in Greece.[82] The charge of nocturnal sacrifices, which left bird feathers and soot in the house, might seem serious, but how could he have risked discovery? (In any case the allegation had been made by a disreputable character).[83] Finally,

---

78 The inscribed version of the senatorial decree passed at the end of the trial illuminates only these misdemeanours (tr. *JRS* 87 (1997) 250–3).

79 Valette (1908) is the best introduction; recently, Hijmans (1994); Abt (1908) gives a detailed commentary. The social context: Pavis d'Escurac (1974).

80 Apuleius, *Defence on a Charge of Magic*, sect. 29–41.

81 Sect. 42–52.

82 Sect. 53–6.

83 Sect. 57–60.

there was the manufacture of a statuette from rare wood, in the figure of a corpse, which he called (in Greek) 'king' and used for magical purposes. The statuette, he countered, did not represent a corpse but a god, and was not used in a sinister manner – though Apuleius declines to tell the governor the name of the deity.[84]

After these general charges of magical practices Apuleius turns to the specific case concerning Pudentilla.[85] The prosecution's main evidence was a letter in which Pudentilla confessed to having been bewitched – but Apuleius argues that, of course, such a confession was not necessarily true, and that the passage in any case had been quoted out of context. The long final section of the speech is then devoted to the mundane world of family intrigue, far from the murky practices of magic.

Throughout, the prosecution is supposed to have tried to build up a picture of the young adventurer who bewitched an older widow into marriage during his brief stay in the town; he fitted the conventional expectations of the magician; possessing secret objects in the household shrine and an infernal statuette, he performed nocturnal rites, used fish for love charms and bewitched others to assist in the process. Apuleius argues, in his defence, that he was a philosopher, interested in medicine, who was on the side of religion, not of magic. For all its entertaining and possibly fictional status, the speech shows very clearly the kind of disputes that could arise around the boundary between religion and superstition or magic; that much of the power of magic (and so in the accusations of magic) resided precisely in the fact that it might be detected by some in activities deemed perfectly innocent by others. Magic was something no-one could ever be sure about, in presence or in absence. In Apuleius' *Defence* it is seen as a ready slur to cast at philosophers, always at risk of being misunderstood in the Roman order.

The Christians were also the object of regulations by the Roman authorities. As with the prohibitions on astrology and magic, the Roman response broadened out from Rome to the provinces, first haphazardly and then more systematically. The story is inevitably fragmented, not just because of the variety of Roman attitudes, but also (as we shall see in the next chapter) because of the different things that 'Christianity' itself could mean in this early period; for a variety of sects held competing versions of the faith, and those who claimed to be members of the church showed different degrees of commitment and loyalty.[86] Indeed almost all the details – legal, political, religious, social – of the punishment (or persecution) of the Christians have been hotly and minutely disputed from Roman times until today. In the rest of this chapter we shall attempt to finesse these disputes, by thinking in general terms about official Roman responses to

84 Sect. 61–5.
85 Sect. 66–101.
86 The same must be true of followers of Isis and other gods.

Christianity in the context of their responses to other forms of undesirable behaviour.[87]

Initially, so the author of the Acts of the Apostles skilfully makes out, the Roman authorities had no complaints against the Christians; problems arose only from local troublemakers (Jews and others). But Acts ends with Paul in Rome preaching the faith while awaiting trial. Shortly afterwards, in the aftermath of the disastrous fire that destroyed much of Rome (A.D. 64), Nero seized the Christians of Rome as scapegoats: arrested and condemned to die in the amphitheatre, they were torn to pieces by dogs or burnt on the cross as human torches. Tacitus reports a mixed reaction from the rest of the people to this spectacular series of executions: in part, he implies, it was a popular move, as the Christians were 'hated for their vices'; but his own account is also aimed against Nero's cruelty – and he notes that the Christian victims were pitied by some, not because they were innocent, but because they were destroyed to 'gratify one man's cruelty, rather than serve the public good'.[88]

By the end of the century we can find action taken against Christians in the provinces. No doubt practice varied considerably in different provinces, at different moments, under different governors and in different local circumstances – depending also on the number and prominence of Christians in different areas of the empire. But it seems that there were executions from the late first century A.D. onwards; and it soon became a recognized practice for governors to execute those who admitted that they were Christians, but were not Roman citizens; and to send Roman citizens (who enjoyed the protection of Roman law) to Rome for trial.

Our main (and almost our only) piece of Roman evidence for responses to the Christians at the beginning of the second century comes from the correspondence between Pliny, then governor of Pontus-Bithynia, and the emperor Trajan.[89] Pliny asked for clarification about what constituted guilt: was profession of Christianity alone sufficient, or were associated criminal actions necessary? (The uncertainty parallels the unresolved juristic debate we have noted about whether the knowledge or only the practice of astrology was criminal.) And should those who had renounced their Christian faith also be punished? Pliny said that his practice so far had been to send Roman citizens to Rome for trial and to execute all non-citizens who

---

87 There is now a general scholarly consensus on the Roman legal framework for persecution: de Ste. Croix (1963); Barnes (1968). Christianity is stated by some scholars to have been a *religio illicita,* but as is implied by our earlier discussion of *religio* that expression is quite contradictory in Roman terms, and does not appear in non-Christian writers; Tertullian's usage of *religio licita (Apology* 21.1) does not justify it.

88 Acts of the Apostles 28.30–1 = **12.7b(i)**. Cf. Nock (1938). A memorial to Paul in Rome: **12.7f(iii–iv)**. Nero: Tacitus, *Annals* XV.44 = **11.11a**. Nero's execution of these Christians and of Paul suffices to explain Tertullian's phrase *institutum Neronianum* (*To the Gentiles* I.7.8–9).

89 *Letters* X.96–7 = **11.11b**.

repeatedly claimed to be Christians. ('If they claimed it, I repeated the question a second and third time, threatening them with capital punishment; those who persisted, I ordered to be executed. For I had no hesitation... that that stubbornness and rigid obstinacy should certainly be punished.') Pliny satisfied himself by investigation that the Christians had committed no criminal actions, and thus executed the non-citizens simply for being Christians. But he also raised with Trajan the problem of what to do with the *ex*-Christians, suggesting by implication that they should not be punished. Trajan in his reply agreed that the issue of ex-Christians was complicated and that there was no one course of action ('for no general rule can be laid down to a fixed formula'). He also agreed that ex-Christians should 'obtain acquittal as a result of their repentance'.

Persecution of the Christians was rarely the top of anyone's priorities in the second century A.D. Governors do not appear to have sought out Christians, or other malefactors.[90] The origins of persecutions were local, and diverse. The precise sparks that ignited local pogroms are hidden from us, as our Christian narratives focus on the subsequent trials of Christians before the Roman governors. But we may guess that often (just as the trial of Apuleius grows from a dispute over property) trials of Christians could spring from personal and local enmities.[91] Pliny, in fact, had acted on the basis of anonymous denunciations, but Trajan, in his reply, very firmly and explicitly ruled these out as unacceptable, and it seems to have been the general rule that accusations could be made only in person. This was the normal Roman procedure in all types of cases (the legal system, which had no equivalent of the modern public prosecutor, depended on individuals bringing cases); and it should have prevented such accusations from getting out of hand – with the accuser, appearing in person, himself liable for a charge of malicious prosecution (*calumnia*) if the accusation failed.

This situation changed by the early third century A.D., when a more 'active' and 'systematic' approach was taken to provincial administration in general. By this period governors were expected to search out 'the sacrilegious, brigands, kidnappers and thieves', which must have affected their treatment of Christians; and Christians write as if they assumed that governors could instigate or suppress widespread accusations against them.[92] This is in clear contrast to the pattern of non-initiation by governors prescribed in the exchange between Pliny and Trajan (which we must not assume applied to the later imperial period). It is also one of the first signs of the formulation of general rules for the treatment of Christians. The

90 Tertullian, *Apology* 2.6–9 argued that this was illogical, but it was parallel to the handling of astrology and magic.
91 E.g. Justin, *Second Apology* 2 = **12.7f(i)**.
92 Ulpian in *Digest* I.18.13 pr.; cf. the repression of divination by a governor of Egypt: *ZPE* 27 (1977) 151–6 = **11.7b**. Tertullian, *To Scapula* 5 (= **12.7c(ii)**). The actual martyr acts, however, stress the reluctance of the governor to execute Christians, and the exceptional tenacity of the martyr.

response of Trajan to Pliny had validity only for the specific province to which it was addressed. Christians elsewhere may have cited it in their defence (it was known, for example, to the Christian writer Tertullian),[93] but only from the middle of the second century A.D. were imperial judgements specific to particular provinces generalized to the whole empire by jurists. By the early third century Ulpian includes in his treatise 'On the Functions of the Provincial Governor' the judgements of earlier emperors on the penalties appropriate for Christians.[94] Such attempts to codify the earlier haphazard decisions and so to define Christians as a single category of relevance to governors throughout the empire are in themselves extremely important. Still they need not necessarily have transformed the pattern of day-to-day relations between the Roman authorities and Christians – many governors would only have appealed to the 'rule book' when their habitual practice (whether of inactivity or vigilant action) broke down.

A much more aggressive development in the Roman treatment of the Christians came in late A.D. 249 or early 250. As part of the first case of a *general* persecution of Christians, the emperor Decius ordered the whole population of the empire to offer sacrifices to the gods.[95] This edict was the first central Roman pronouncement to impose on all Christians worldwide behaviour they could only find unacceptable. It is very hard to imagine how it could ever have been enforced – by what mechanisms, that is, the whole population of the empire could have been tracked down and made to demonstrate a sacrifice. But there is evidence, from Spain to Egypt, that some people did perform sacrifice to comply with the demands of the edict. The sacrifice test was similar to that which Pliny and other governors had employed, as a means of testing out suspected Christians, but now people had to declare that they had *always* sacrificed to the gods; in other words, a lapsed Christian could escape only by lying. Afterwards (as exemplified in the Egyptian documents that survive) the sacrificer received an official document, signed by two officials who had witnessed the sacrifice. We should note, however, that Decius did not specify which gods were to be the recipients of the sacrifices – and it would seem that local gods were as acceptable as specifically Roman ones. In this case the demand was not that Christians should worship Roman deities, but that they should participate in the sacrificial system as a whole with its offering of incense, pouring of libations and tasting of sacrificial meat. Sacrifice (not particular gods or festivals) here delimited and paraded the true subjects of Rome.

In general, however, the Christians were seen to be in conflict with the specific traditions of *Roman* religion. Tertullian claims in his *Apology* that

---

93 *Apology* 2.6–7.
94 Lactantius, *Divine Institutes* V.11.
95 Frend (1965) 404–21; Clarke (1984–) I.21–39; Lane Fox (1986) 450–9. Sacrifice test: **6.8c**.

the principal accusation against the Christians was 'slighting especially Roman *religio*', and this point is also made in the context of second century trials of Christians.[96] In the Acts of the Apostles too, one story of local reactions to Paul's activities in Philippi, a Roman *colonia*, suggests there was a feeling that Christians were a threat to *Roman* customs in particular ('Paul and Silas advocate customs which it is not lawful for us Romans to accept or practise.').[97] Such a feeling may well have become more prevalent with the spread of Roman-style cults in the west in the second century A.D.[98] Certainly, Capitolia (shrines of Jupiter, Juno and Minerva, on the Roman model, established in the provinces) feature as the focal point of conflict between traditionalists and Christians. According to Tertullian, Christians refused to take part in the annual vows at them – although (not surprisingly) in the Decian persecution some Christians did go up to the

96 Tertullian, *Apology* 24.1. Trajan in Pliny, *Letters* X.97.2 = **11.11b**; *Acts of the Scillitan Martyrs* 5, 14, in Musurillo (1972) no. 6 and Bastiaensen (1990) 97–105, 405–11. Tertullian's claim is ignored by scholars who argue that Christians were simply obliged to sacrifice to the local gods.
97 Acts of the Apostles 16.19–24, Philippi; below, pp. 328–34 on *coloniae*.
98 Below, pp. 334–6.

Fig. 5.4 A fourth-century painting from the Catacomb of Basileus (otherwise known as that of Marcus and Marcellinus: Map 4 no.40) illustrating an incident from the Book of Daniel (3.12–18): three young men refuse to venerate the image of the Babylonian king Nebuchad-nezzar. Although the young men are portrayed (appropriately) in eastern dress, the bust of the king is like that of a Roman emperor, while the man giving the instructions is also in Roman, military, dress. This version of the Old Testament scene may thus evoke conflicts between Christians and the Roman authorities.

Capitolium at Carthage to sacrifice.[99] Christians sometimes called such apostates '*Capitolini*' and the church council held in Spain after Diocletian's persecution in the early fourth century would word its general prohibition against apostasy in terms of going up to the idols of the Capitolium in order to sacrifice; while Cyprian, the bishop of Carthage, could employ the Capitolium as an image for the enemy of the Christian church.[100]

The dramatic extension of Roman citizenship to almost all the free population of the empire in A.D. 212 may have intensified this sense of opposition between Christians and *Roman* religious traditions. The emperor Caracalla's edict proclaiming the grant explained that he wanted to thank the immortal gods for having preserved him from a conspiracy: 'So I think I can in this way perform a [magnificent and pious] act, worthy of their majesty, by gathering to their rites [as Romans] all the multitude that joins my people.'[101] Whatever the many reasons that lay behind Caracalla's decision to extend Roman citizenship in this way (his own public version was just one of a multitude of factors), the logic of the edict is very striking. The emperor assumes that the new citizens, who in the past had their own cults, will now add special lustre to the worship of gods who are by implication Roman. Increasingly, Christians were set against a religious world that the central authorities at least could define as *Roman*.

After Decius, there were further outbreaks of general persecution; for it was not a continuous process. Imperial regulations during these periods acted even more directly than before against the Christians as a category, and further emphasized the demand to adhere to specifically Roman gods. In A.D. 257 the emperor Valerian ordered 'all those who practise Roman religion to perform Roman rites' – the performance of sacrifice being the crucial test. Christian bishops, presbyters and deacons who failed to do this were exiled; the clergy were prohibited on pain of death from holding Christian gatherings or burials in their cemeteries. The following year those bishops, presbyters and deacons who still refused to sacrifice became liable to execution; in addition, Christian senators, high-ranking officials and equestrians were liable to loss of property and life, their wives to exile; and Christian members of the imperial service were to be sent off to hard labour on imperial estates. One governor, in Africa, who was trying the case of the

99 Tertullian, *On the Crown* 12.3; Cyprian, *On the Lapsed* 8, 24; *Letters* 59.13.3. For martyr acts involving Capitolia see H. Leclercq in *Dictionnaire d'archéologie chrétienne et de liturgie* 2.2 (1925) 2043–8.

100 Pacian, *Letters* 2.3; Council of Elvira, canon 59, *Patrologia Latina* LXXXIV 308 = Martínez Díez and Rodriguez (1984) 261, with dating of Lane Fox (1986) 664–7 (extracts – not this canon – trans. in Stevenson (1987) no. 265); Cyprian, *Letters* 59.18.1.

101 *P. Giessen* 40: the text is uncertain, but the drift is clear. Buraselis (1989) explores the different interpretations. See below, pp. 362–3 for what may be one town's response to the edict.

bishop Cyprian, is made to declare what must have become the 'official' view: 'You have long persisted in your sacrilegious views, and you have joined to yourself many other vicious men in a conspiracy. You have set yourself up as an enemy of the Roman gods and religious rites.'[102]

In the reign of the emperor Diocletian (A.D. 284–305), the next, and almost the last, period of anti-Christian legislation, there seems to have been particular stress on (allegedly) ancestral Roman virtues, and the desirability of imposing those virtues on the empire as a whole. This is partly, no doubt, to be connected with the emperor's aim of consolidating central authority after the chaos and disorder of the previous fifty years; but it played an important role too in attacks on the Christians and, conversely, in the support of traditional religion. So, for example, the preface to an imperial edict affirming the validity of specifically Roman rules on the degrees of kinship permitted in marriage links obedience to Roman laws with divine favour for Rome. Diocletian also ordered the followers of the new Manichaean religion to be executed; ancient religious practices, with their traditional authority, should not be challenged by new-fangled cults of foreign, Persian, origin.[103] He also took a series of measures of increasing severity against the Christians.[104] These began with a demand that all at court and all soldiers were to sacrifice (? A.D. 302); then Christian worship was declared illegal, and all those engaged in lawsuits had to offer sacrifice (A.D. 303); Christian clergy were imprisoned, and released only after sacrificing (A.D. 303); and, finally, the whole population of the empire was ordered to sacrifice (A.D. 304). According to a Christian account of the proceedings, the governor of Africa told one Christian on trial before him 'to sacrifice to all our gods for the welfare of the emperors'; when she refused, he advised her: 'Break with this *superstitio*, and bow your head to the sacred rites of the Roman gods... However devoted you are, we ask that you bow your head in the sacred temples and offer incense to the gods of the Romans... Revere Roman *religio*, which is observed by our lords the unconquerable Caesars as well as ourselves.'[105] The lines were by now drawn with brutal clarity – or so (to judge from such Christian texts) it seemed to the Christians.

How should we understand these periods of general persecution, instigated by the central Roman authorities under Decius, Valerian and Diocletian? Why did general persecutions start at this point after generations of

---

102 *Acts of Cyprian* 1.1, 3.4 in Musurillo (1972) no. 11, with English translation, and Bastiaensen (1990) 193–231. 478–90; Lane Fox (1986) 549–56; Schwarte (1989); below, p. 271. The text of Valerian's order is uncertain: Schwarte (1989) 121–7.

103 *Comparison of Greek and Roman Law* VI.4 in *FIRA* II.558–60 (A.D. 295); *Comparison* XV.3 = **11.12** (A.D. 302, or 297).

104 de Ste. Croix (1954); Frend (1965) 477–535; Lane Fox (1986) 594–608.

105 *Acts of Crispina* 1.3–4, 2.1, 2.4, in Musurillo (1972) no. 24. For the persecution of Maximinus in A.D. 312, see, S. Mitchell (1988) (trans. Lewis and Reinhold (1990) II.571), S. Mitchell (1993) II.64–5.

relative calm for the Christians, or at worst only haphazard attacks? Certainly these years were a time of great difficulties for the empire (political, economic and military); and there must have been some connection between these problems and the extension of persecution. But it is not enough to call the Christians scapegoats for Roman anxiety: the situation had changed in the 200 years since Nero had rounded up his scores of Christians after the fire of Rome.

Another factor that may have lain behind the persecutions is alarm on the part of the emperors and their advisers about the performance of traditional rites. In Rome itself representatives of the people had long supplicated the gods at times of crisis, and earlier emperors had expected that their subjects would sacrifice to the gods on their behalf at the appropriate times.[106] On this view (despite the impression given by our strident Christian sources that they were the intended target) Decius' edict affected the Christians only by implication; he was primarily aiming to revive traditional cult (reacting to problems that had worried Pliny in Pontus).[107] He was certainly honoured in one town as 'the restorer of rites and freedom' and instructed another town to restore a statue of 'the god Neptune';[108] and there is some evidence for the Greek world that (even if some major festivals, such as games in honour of the traditional gods, still flourished) local élites were beginning to lose interest in the traditional routes to civic prestige, which included the financing of civic festivals.[109] According to this model, Decius stands as an advocate of traditional religion first, a persecutor of Christians only second.

On the other hand, there are good reasons why emperors should have seen Christians in particular as a danger, and some evidence that they did. Some fourth-century Christians maintain that those who instigated the persecutions were reacting to an increase in the number of the faithful; by that date certainly Christians not only formed the largest voluntary association in the city of Rome (partly due to their active recruitment of converts), but the church had developed a much stronger organization, with a powerful hierarchy of bishops and other officials.[110] Decius is said to have been more afraid of the election of a new bishop of Rome than of a pretender to

106 E.g. Tacitus, *Annals* XV.44; Halkin (1953); below, p. 320, on vows.
107 Pliny, *Letters* X.96 = **11.11b** (a striking example of concerns about *participation* in traditional cult; though traditional Roman religion was emphatically *not* centred around the kind of congregational worship typical of modern world religions, the role of popular participation has often been under-emphasized: above, pp. 48–52, below, pp. 259–63).
108 *AE* (1973) 235 (Cosa) with Lane Fox (1986) 453; J. B. Brusin, *Inscriptiones Aquileiae* (Udine 1991) no. 326 with Alföldy (1989) 65 (Aquileia). In the 360s Julian was praised in North Africa as 'restorer of freedom and Roman *religiones*' (*ILS* 752 with reading of *MEFR* 14 (1894) 77 no. 130).
109 Local rites: Liebeschuetz (1979) 231–4; Lane Fox (1986) 572–85.
110 Below, pp. 304–5.

the throne,[111] and, as we have seen, Valerian and Diocletian acted specifically against Christian presbyters and bishops – that is against the organizational hierarchy of the church. At the very least Christianity had a much higher profile in the late third and early fourth centuries than a hundred years before.

In the chapters that follow we shall trace many different aspects of Christianity and the other religions that we have briefly introduced here; the next chapter will explore the vitality of some of the activities that we have just seen largely in the negative light of official control and suppression. There is no single narrative in the history of religion. This chapter has shown that, notwithstanding – or possibly *because of* – the structural *openness* of Roman culture and religion stressed in earlier chapters, the story of religion at Rome is also a story of exclusions and prohibitions; and that Roman writers themselves stressed boundary and transgression, as well as import and incorporation.

We have only tantalizing glimpses of how these exclusions operated on the ground; but we have attempted here to offer one framework for understanding the changes and development in patterns of Roman religious control. We have suggested, schematically, a move from the late republican and early imperial practice – when the boundaries were upheld by the relatively haphazard expulsion of undesirables from Rome and Italy – to a much more systematic and empire-wide series of regulations, which became increasingly focussed on Christians, as the most undesirable and dangerous group of all.

Of course, the battle (symbolic and literal) against *superstitio* could never be won; it was a battle to be constantly fought and re-fought, not finished. For it was partly in this contest, with enemies real and imaginary, that true *religio* found its definition – and the Roman élite, as religion's most active defenders, displayed (to themselves as much as to anyone else) their own indispensability to the religious, political and social order they, and their ancestors, had created.

111 Cyprian, *Letters* 55.9.

6 The religions of imperial Rome

This chapter sets religion into the fabric of urban life in the first three centuries A.D. – both the official cults of the state and the unofficial cults that we have so far viewed (in chapter 5) largely through the hostile eyes of members of the Roman élite. We shall explore in particular the proliferation of religious choices that had started already in the Republic, but which came even more strongly to characterize the religious world of the city of Rome during the empire: from the great civic cults and festivals, through private or local associations worshipping state gods (such as Aesculapius and Hygieia), through those 'foreign' cults that remained strongly linked to particular ethnic groups in Rome (the Palmyrenes or Jews, for example), to cults (of Isis, Mithras, or Christianity) that were purely *elective* – entered, that is, not by virtue of race or social position, but through individual choice, with no qualification for their adherents (at least in theory) other than personal religious commitment.

The city of imperial Rome was vast, with a population that may at times have approached one million people. (In Europe, even by the end of the seventeenth century A.D., only London, Paris and Constantinople had populations over 400,000.) The population was also highly diverse, socially, culturally and ethnically. One way of picturing the sharp stratification of Roman society is on the model of a triangle: at the apex was the emperor, with his family and the 600 or so senators (plus their families) – the highest echelon of the élite, and also the principal holders of religious office in the official system; the next level of social status was the much broader equestrian order, numbering some thousands; below them came the far greater number of ordinary Roman citizens, men and women who had little active political role under the empire; below them (and no doubt just as numerous) free non-citizens and slaves. But such a model does not recognize all kinds of other differences that served to distinguish different groups of the population of the city, whether Roman citizens or non-citizens – notably differences of ethnic and cultural origin. A high proportion, perhaps even a majority of the population was originally not from Rome or Italy; one second-century observer described Rome as the microcosm of the world, with people from all the great cities of the Greek East (from Alexandria, for example, Antioch, Nicomedia, Athens) and whole ethnic groups settled there en masse (from Cappadocia, Scythia and Pontus, among others).[1] Many of the foreigners were slaves or ex-slaves (though ex-slaves would have been Roman citizens, if their masters had themselves been Roman citizens and had formally freed them before the appropriate Roman magistrate); others came to Rome voluntarily, and in the early empire lacked any formal *Roman* status – although after the emperor Caracalla's edict in A.D. 212, all the free population of Rome (and the empire) became Roman citizens.

So the question of 'Roman-ness', of what is to count as 'Roman' and what 'foreign' in this multi-cultural atmosphere, will inevitably underlie this chapter too. Focussing principally on the city of Rome itself, we shall be highlighting the links between the official and unofficial cults (against the background of a single city and its inhabitants) as well as exploring further the differences that distinguish them. For this reason, we have chosen to divide the chapter into themes that cut across boundaries of individual cults. We have not, in other words, devoted particular sections of our analysis to particular cults (Isis or Christianity, for example), nor even to a general category of 'Oriental' cults – though for ease of reference discussion of the major cults in each section normally follows the same order: adherents of Isis, Mithras, Jahveh, Christ. The aim is to expose the web of connections that links 'Roman' religion to the seemingly 'unRoman'. The role of religion as *one* way of defining Roman identity in communities outside Rome will be explored further in the next chapter.

Our treatment takes care to avoid the standard term 'Oriental religions' in discussing the new religious options in imperial Rome. This category was first widely used, if not invented, by the Belgian scholar Franz Cumont in the early years of the twentieth century in his pioneering studies of Roman religion: for Cumont, the key to understanding the religious history of the period lay in the influx into Rome of a group of Eastern religions that shared a number of common characteristics setting them apart from traditional civic cults – and paving the way, eventually, for the rise of Christianity. As we shall see, however, these religions cannot be so neatly pigeon-holed as 'Oriental'.[2] Several of the cults did certainly proclaim an eastern 'origin' for their wisdom, but it is often clear that a Roman version of the cult differed substantially from its (notional) eastern ancestor. Above all, the 'Orient' itself was hardly the homogeneous category that we (like the Romans, no doubt) often try to make it: different cults came from quite different religious backgrounds – the religious traditions of the home of

---

1 Athenaeus, *Table-talk* I.20b-c, extant only in a paraphrase; so Polemo in Galen XVIII.1.347 (Kühn); below, p. 271. Cf. La Piana (1927); MacMullen (1993). Greek names, which form a majority of those attested at Rome (c. 57% for the free; c. 67% for slaves), are a cultural phenomenon and do not prove Eastern origins, while 'barbarian' (mainly Semitic) names form only c. 2% of those attested (for example, **12.3a**, a list of initiates of Jupiter Dolichenus): Solin (1971) 146–58; Solin (1996).

2 Cumont (1911). Burkert (1987) also rejects the category 'Oriental cults'; on Mithras, R. L. Gordon (1975); below, pp. 279–80. For a general critique of 'Orientalism', Said (1978).

Mithras in Persia, for example, had little in common with the Egyptian traditions in the worship of Isis and Sarapis.

Overall there is as much to separate these new 'Eastern' cults, as there is to group them together into a single category. Some were defined by their initiation of the worshipper into secret 'mysteries';[3] others (such as Isis and Magna Mater – who, as we have seen, was 'officially' incorporated under the aegis of magistrates and priests) were public cults before they acquired private ceremonies of initiation. These mysteries, even if they proclaimed an eastern origin, were almost certainly descended from earlier Greek initiation cults. Nor is there any clear evidence that all these cults shared a common preoccupation with 'salvation'; it is, in fact, the modern assumption (following Cumont) that the 'Oriental cults' were the precursors of and rivals to Christianity that has encouraged us to construct them in those terms – on directly Christianizing lines.

We must also resist the assumption that new, 'foreign' cults were necessarily particularly attractive to those who had little official role in the traditional Roman civic cults. Was there, after all, a strong opposition between 'official' religion (and its office-holders drawn almost exclusively from the senate) and the 'popular' religious life of the city? Was there a range of religious activities among the ordinary people of Rome that had almost nothing in common with the aristocratic practices of official religion? The answer to such questions may, in part, be yes. But the opposition between 'official' and 'popular' can be deceptive; and official and popular manifestations were most probably different aspects, on different levels, of a *continuum* of religious institutions and practices. There was nothing to stop a cult having significance for both the élite and the mass of the population.[4]

We shall investigate the nature of the choices offered by the new cults always against the background of the civic cults (section 1); indeed, in so far as the new religions were seen either as complements or as alternatives to traditional religion, they cannot be understood except in relation to it. We shall think about these choices in terms of the prominence and visibility of the new cults in the city (section 2), their appeal (section 3) and their membership (section 4). Of course, although we have chosen to concentrate on the city of Rome, these new cults did not exist only there. In Section 5 of this chapter we shall consider their distribution and character across the empire.

The evidence for this subject is extremely rich and diverse. In addition to a wide range of literary texts (from Apuleius' *Metamorphoses*, a novel partly centred on the cult of Isis, to outspoken tracts of Christian polemic

3 A convenient definition of a 'mystery cult' is found in Burkert (1987) 11: 'Mysteries were initiation rituals of a voluntary, personal and secret character that aimed at a change of mind through experience of the sacred.'

4 Price (1984) 108. This is not to say that the significance was necessarily the same for both élite and mass: alternative interpretations can occur within the same symbolic system.

and self-defence),[5] archaeological material survives in the city of Rome both from the major civic temples and from the temples and shrines of the new cults. These remains include some of the very best preserved Roman buildings anywhere in the world (Hadrian's temple of all the gods, the Pantheon, has been in active use as temple or church ever since the second century A.D., even if much restored); but they also include far more poorly preserved monuments, often just as hard to interpret as the remains from earliest Rome.[6] Inscriptions too (as we noted in chapter 4) continue throughout the first three centuries A.D. to be an important source of information on all kinds of cult (except, for reasons we shall see, on Christianity). For example, inscribed dedications or vows, and sometimes the preservation of inscribed membership lists of particular cults, enable us to gauge the social standing or ethnic origin of worshippers; while in the empire at large, such inscriptions are often crucial in tracing the spread of a particular cult.[7]

To consider the empire as a whole, as well as the city of Rome itself, raises the question of how far individual cults were essentially the same in different parts of the world; how far, that is, the cult of the 'same' deity held the same religious, social or political significance in Gaul or Greece as it did in Rome. The problem is particularly clear with Judaism and with Christianity – where later histories of each of these two religions have sought to define and maintain 'orthodoxy', and to represent a single religious tradition, effectively unchanging throughout the empire and imperial history. In fact no Jewish literary texts of this period survive from the west, and we should not simply assume that Judaism was identical in those regions to its form(s) in the east. In the case of Christianity (whose preserved texts now overwhelm those of all the other cults combined) there is plentiful evidence for the many different varieties of faith and worship that could be called 'Christian' during this period – even if particular variants were regarded as 'heresies' by other Christians and later 'orthodox' historians.[8] But the other cults too cannot possibly have been the homogeneous

---

5 Not all of these texts relate specifically to Rome. We have drawn on texts (such as much of Apuleius' *Metamorphoses*) which are focussed on other parts of the empire – where they are relevant and with the justification that they were part of Roman literary culture, read at Rome. We are constantly aware however of the differences that must have been apparent between the religious life of Rome and (say) Corinth.

6 For example, below, p. 258 on the temple of the Sun.

7 They belong mainly to the period between A.D. 100 and 250, as is true of the general epigraphic record of the Latin West; MacMullen (1981) 115–16 notes the time span of the inscriptions. (Cf. below nn. 68–9 for the problem of identifying Christian meeting places.)

8 Reflections on the notion of 'heresy': R. Williams (1989). Christianity and the mysteries: J. Z. Smith (1990). We also hope that our emphasis on the sheer variety of 'Christian' beliefs and practices will free this chapter from the common, crypto-Protestant, scholarly agenda of determining whether the 'core' of Christianity was affected by its Jewish and Graeco-Roman religious environment.

and exclusive entities that they are often taken to be. The cult, for example, of Magna Mater that is well attested in third-century Lyons may have had important things in common with the cult of the goddess in first century Rome, but it will not have been the *same*; nor – for that matter – could the views, understanding or religious commitment even of those who gathered together at the same festival, on the same day, in the same place ever have been identical. Our last section in this chapter does investigate the degrees of religious continuity in these cults traceable across the Roman world. By and large, however, in discussing the religions of the empire we have tried to avoid thinking in terms of uniformity, or in terms of a central core 'orthodox' tradition with its peripheral 'variants'; we have preferred to think rather in terms of different religions as clusters of ideas, people and rituals, sharing some common identity across time and place, but at the same time inevitably invested with different meanings in their different contexts.[9]

1. The landscape of official cults at Rome

The system of official cults of Rome continued – and continued to develop – after the restructuring of the Augustan period. We have already noted, for example, the enduring importance of the *pomerium*, of the ward cults of the Genius Augusti and the Lares Augusti, the continued prominence of senatorial priesthoods and the celebrations of the Saecular Games by the emperors Claudius, Domitian and Septimius Severus;[10] throughout the period too the senate continued to handle numerous items of religious business (albeit under the authority of the emperor), while senatorial magistrates continued to be responsible (as they had been also during the Republic) for putting on the games that formed part of the official festivals.[11] There were also significant changes in the system after Augustus, which we shall trace in this section through the history of temple building in the city. Structural changes in religion are often hard to delineate; by focussing specifically on the religious *landscape* of Rome under the empire, we shall bring out in a vividly concrete register some of the structural changes in Roman religion through our period.

Official Roman religion could not fail to have changed over the three centuries of the principate; in fact, even a ritual in the late third century A.D. celebrated identically as it had been in the late first century B.C. would

---

9 Classification in terms of family or sporadic resemblances, 'polythetic classification': Needham (1975).

10 Above, pp. 177–81; 186; 192–6; 206.

11 Senate: Talbert (1984) 386–91. The praetors, from 22 B.C. onwards, gained increased distinction as the presidents of the games: Salomonson (1956) 34–41, 77–88; for the fourth century A.D., below, p. 383.

inevitably have become a *different* ritual in the course of its preservation.[12] On the other hand, many details of these religious changes remain uncertain, for a whole variety of reasons. One is the pattern of survivals. Throughout this book we have emphasized, for example, the important evidence for religion in civic calendars of festivals, found (inscribed or painted) in Rome and the towns of Italy. We cannot, however, follow this evidence through the later centuries of the principate (and so follow the changes that might, or might not, be revealed) for the simple reason that all but one of the calendars surviving on stone date from the reigns of Augustus and Tiberius – until A.D. 354, when a calendar was recorded in manuscript.[13] This may be a sheer accident of survival; or it may itself be an important indication of change, a move away (for whatever reason) from the permanent public display of the festal cycle.[14] The immediate consequence for us is that we have almost no evidence of the formal calendrical cycle of Roman rituals between the mid first and fourth centuries A.D. By the fourth century it is clear that there had been great changes, but we cannot say precisely when most of them were made.[15]

A striking instance of this uncertainty concerns the festivals of Isis in Rome, partly because of swings and ambiguities in official attitudes – with characteristic tension between exclusion and acceptance, and a series of banning orders, obeyed or ignored by turns. In the late Republic, the cult was formally suppressed, only for the triumvirs to vow a shrine to the goddess in 43 B.C.; and we saw in chapter 5 that official action was taken once more against the cult under Augustus and Tiberius.[16] At some point between then and the fourth century A.D. festivals of Isis entered the official Roman calendar; but when? One guess is that the cult was made official by the emperor Gaius Caligula; but it is only a guess. Certainly after his reign comments on the cult's status are still ambiguous: some authors claim the goddess as 'Roman', others stress her foreign exoticism. A clearer indication perhaps is found in the planning of the main Roman sanctuary of Isis on the Campus Martius: from at least the second century A.D. onwards, this was architecturally related (by an arch) to the east side of the Saepta, or official voting area, and to other public monuments in this area – suggesting, at

12 In the same way, the significance of the Christian Eucharist varies depending on the social, intellectual and theological context; above, pp. xx–xii; 6–8; 47–8, on the fluidity of ritual meaning.

13 Salzman (1990); extract in **3.3d**; below, pp. 378–80; 382–3.

14 This may be because towns came to realize that festivals were liable to change with dynastic events (for control of imperial festivals, below, p. 251), and so replaced stone calendars with painted ones – more practical at the time, but far less likely to endure to the present day. But see Wallace-Hadrill (1987) for calendars as a significantly Augustan phenomenon.

15 Below, pp. 382–3. Cf. **3.3b** and **d**. Hence our uncertainty about when the festivals of Magna Mater and Attis were reformed: Lambrechts (1952); Van Doren (1953); Vermaseren (1977) 113–24.

16 Above, pp. 230–1.

least, its integration into the official landscape of Rome.[17] It was also the only new foreign sanctuary, so far as we can tell from the surviving fragments, to be represented on the third-century A.D. official map of the city of Rome.[18] But if these hints do indicate its 'official' incorporation into state religion, we certainly cannot pinpoint any precise moment for its change of status.

Such uncertainties obviously raise questions about the whole category of 'official cults'; and whether there was any clear boundary between 'official' and 'unofficial' religions at Rome. The position was surely much more nuanced than those single terms suggest; and transition between the status of marginal (even banned) cult and that of 'official' religion must have been a gradual one. All the same the category of 'official cults' can still be a helpful one. They seem, for example, to have shared a number of characteristic rights and privileges: their buildings stood on 'public land' which had been made 'sacred' by an act of the Roman people or the emperor, and whose cult received money from the state.[19] Also, in provincial towns which received Roman charters there was a clear category of official festivals: on festival days certain types of legal business were prohibited.[20] There is also evidence for a striking degree of uniformity (and hence, it follows, central regulation) in the official system. In the early third century A.D., for example, the Arval Brothers in Rome and an auxiliary cohort of the Roman army stationed at Dura Europus on Rome's eastern frontier (whose sacrificial calendar survives on papyrus) sacrificed to exactly the same set of deified emperors and empresses; this clearly suggests that they were both following some official list which prescribed which *divi* should receive sacrifice and (by implication) which should not.[21] This dropping of those who were now out of political favour – as well as the abolition of other rituals (Nerva, among other emperors, scrapped various sacrifices as an economy measure) – was legitimated by the religious authority of the emperor himself.[22]

17 Map 2 no. 26; below, Fig. 6.2. Wissowa (1912) 352–5; Malaise (1972b) 221–8; Castagnoli (1981); Mora (1990) II.72–112; below, n. 59. A festival of Isis appears on one Roman calendar dating A.D. 175–225: Salzman (1990) 170.
18 Carettoni et al. (1960) 31 (reproduced as L. Richardson (1992) fig. 46).
19 Festus p. 284.18–21, 298.22–5, 348.33–350.6, 424.13–30 (ed. Lindsay). Wissowa (1912) 361 and 362 used fourth-century evidence to argue that the temples to Jupiter Dolichenus and Dea Syria were 'official', but it is very dangerous to retroject evidence from the fourth century, when all possible cults were incorporated in the face of Christianity; below, pp. 383–4.
20 *AE* (1986) 333 para. 92 (*lex Irnitana*; trans. *JRS* 76 (1986) 198); below, pp. 315, 356 on these charters.
21 Dura calendar: Fink, Hoey and Snyder (1940) = 3.5 and below, pp. 324–8 on the army. The *lex Irnitana* (above, n. 20) also assumes an official list of festivals in honour of the imperial house.
22 Abolition of festivals: Cassius Dio LX.17.1 (Claudius); Tacitus, *Histories* IV.40 (A.D. 70) (a senatorial commission); Cassius Dio LXVIII.2.3 (Nerva); Cassius Dio LXIX.2.3 (Trajan's Parthian Games abolished); Marcus Aurelius (*Augustan History, Marcus Aurelius* 10.10) limited to 135 the number of festival days on which legal business was banned. Changes by the fourth century A.D.: below, p. 383.

Throughout the empire the emperor was seen as the principal source of innovation and took the lead in promoting new cults.[23] This is one important facet of the religious focus on the emperor, characteristic (as we have seen) of the Augustan restructuring and continued – if anything, intensified – through the principate. The emperor's religious dominance had wide-ranging effects. The traditional systematic reporting of prodigies, for example, had disappeared already in the Augustan period: these seemingly random intrusions of divine displeasure must have appeared incongruous in a system where divine favour flowed through the emperor; such prodigies as were noted generally centred on the births and deaths of emperors.[24] A complementary change was the annual offering of vows (*vota*) on 3 January for the well-being of the emperor, participation in which became nearly obligatory for the Roman élite. The ancient senatorial priesthoods took a leading part in these ceremonies, as we have noted in the case of the Arval Brothers; Pliny writes to Trajan from his province to inform him that the annual vows have been carried out in Pontus-Bithynia; while a letter from Fronto to Marcus Aurelius suggests that they were performed privately too. These imperial vows sum up the official position of the emperor as the focus for human aspirations and the beneficiary of divine support.[25]

In the rest of this section we shall be tracing imperial change and innovation through temples and temple-building. The emperor's role as *pontifex maximus,* as intermediary between Rome and the gods, involved responsibility for the fabric of the official cults of Rome. Emperors were regularly praised for restoring sacred shrines as well as for preserving public rituals.[26] Many of the day-to-day duties would, however, have been delegated, and remained outside the knowledge and practical control of the emperor himself. A pair of senior senatorial officials, for example, was responsible for giving permissions for religious dedications in public places, and for the maintenance of official religious buildings; below them was a vast range of junior officials down to the imperial freedmen who

---

23 Down to the third century B.C. the *decemviri* (later, the *quindecimviri*) had been responsible for the introduction of new cults, through the medium of the Sibylline Books, but their last major innovation was the cult of Magna Mater in 204 B.C. In the late Republic the senate and then individual political leaders, such as Sulla and Caesar, took the lead in promoting new cults. Above, p. 191 on imperial religious authority.

24 A contemporary writer noted with regret that portents were no longer reported publicly or officially recorded: Livy XLIII.13.1. Liebeschuetz (1979) 57–8, 159–61. Above, pp. 37–9 (on republican system).

25 Pliny, *Letters* X.35; Fronto, *Letters* (Loeb edn.) I.228–30. When Pliny petitioned Trajan for a priesthood (*augur* or *septemvir*), he noted that it would enable him to add his official prayers on behalf of the emperor to those he already offered privately: *Letters* X.13. Cf. Scheid (1990b) 298–309. The army and empire: pp. 320; 325–6.

26 *Pontifex maximus:* Pliny, *Panegyric* 83.5, 94.4; Suetonius, *Titus* 9.1; above, pp. 188–92. *ILS* 252 (A.D. 77–8); *ILS* 295 (A.D. 113–14); *ILS* 129 (A.D. 202); *ILS* 255 and 3781 (Severan). 'Restoration' was strongly motivated ideologically: above, pp. 196–7; E. Thomas and Witschel (1992).

often acted as caretakers (*aeditui*) of individual temples.[27] But symbolically (and practically, no doubt, in the case of major decisions and major new foundations) it was the emperor who controlled the temples of official cult.

One of the most striking changes in the landscape of Roman religion under the empire was the impact of the new temples of deified emperors. Almost half the twenty or so new state temples built between the reigns of Augustus and Constantine were dedicated to *divi*, for, at least up to the mid second century A.D., almost all deified emperors had a temple built in their honour (deified empresses generally shared the temple of their husbands; minor deities of the imperial family usually had no specific shrine).[28] These nine new temples followed the precedent set by Octavian, who had consecrated the temple to *divus* Julius in the Roman Forum where Caesar's funeral pyre had stood; although they did not claim to occupy the very site of the imperial pyres, the vowing of a temple, its building and dedication were the culmination of an elaborate process of funeral and official consecration by the Roman senate. Most temples of the *divi* were large and conspicuous. That of *divus* Antoninus and *diva* Faustina (later converted into a church) still towers over the Forum.[29] The colossal temple to the deified Trajan and his wife Plotina (of which very little now survives) seems to have been added on to Trajan's Forum by Hadrian – so completing that vast complex which focussed directly on Trajan's military achievements, burial and apotheosis, and was noted in antiquity as one of the most remarkable sights of Rome.[30] The temples of the *divi* not only reflect the religious dominance of the emperor; they themselves added enormously to the monumental prominence of emperors at Rome.

Other imperial foundations raise much more acute questions about the limits of acceptable innovation at Rome. Just as Augustus had built temples to a particular group of deities closely associated with his régime, so Vespasian promoted the cult of Pax, Domitian that of Minerva – and both these traditional Roman deities were honoured with new temples as centre pieces

27 *Curator aedium sacrarum et operum publicorum:* A. E. Gordon (1952) 279–304; Kolb (1993); fourth century: below, p. 382. Imperial delegation of restoration, of Capitolium: Tacitus, *Histories* IV.53. Outside Rome, local councils gave permission for sites (e.g. **12.5c(v)**) and *aediles* looked after them (*lex Irnitana*: *AE* (1986) 333 paras 19, 79 (trans. *JRS* 76 (1986) 182, 194); Rives (1995a) 28–39).

28 Wissowa (1912) 596–7 has a list, from which we have excluded temples not certainly official (above, n. 19; Caelestis was also a private cult: Rives (1995a) 68–9) or not certainly imperial in date (Jupiter Propugnator, Bellona Pulvinensis). Augustan temple building: above, pp. 196–201. Up to Marcus Aurelius only Nerva and Lucius Verus did not have their own temples; after that only the temple to Divus Romulus of c. A.D. 307 is attested (below, p. 260).

29 Above pp. 197; 208; Price (1987) 77–8; **4.7** for the temples in the Roman Forum.

30 Map 1 no. 8; Zanker (1970); Boatwright (1987) 74–98; Steinby (1993–) II.348–56. For the huge precinct of *divus* Claudius, Map 1 no. 3; E. Nash (1968) I.243–8; Steinby (1993–) I.277–8.

of grand new fora.[31] Particular foreign deities were also honoured in this way. Emperors did not systematically seek to transfer foreign cults from the provinces to the capital; there was no policy to make Rome an official show-case for the religious life of the empire. Individual emperors might import cults (or cult images) to Rome, sometimes as a result of conquest (as in the republican tradition): Aurelian, for example, in A.D. 274 brought the Sun and Belos from Palmyra after its recapture by him.[32] In other cases, as we shall see, the emperor's new foundations reflect his own 'foreign' back-ground: it was a marker of the yet greater religious complexity, the even less certain boundary between the Roman and the foreign, that, from the second century on, emperors themselves were often of provincial origin. What was to count as 'Roman' religion, when the *pontifex maximus* himself, the apex of the official religious structure of Rome, came from Spain or Syria?

Caracalla's temple of Sarapis on the Quirinal hill, attested by an inscrip-tion recording the dedication of a temple by Caracalla to the Egyptian god, was an imperial foundation to an Egyptian god within the sacred boundary of the city.[33] But how Egyptian is 'Egyptian'? The cult of Sarapis at Rome was often associated with Egyptian Isis, with all its paraded marks of alien cult (Egyptian music, shaved heads, bizarre costumes...). At the same time a cult of Sarapis could be seen as more Greek than Egyptian, and hence much more easily brought into the sphere of Roman public cult. There was a tradition that the cult had originally been introduced to the Egyptian coastal city of Alexandria (one of the major Mediterranean centres of Greek culture) not from inland Egypt but from elsewhere in the Greek world; while the priesthood of the cult in Rome, in the nearby port of Ostia, as well as in Alexandria itself, was purely Greek in form. The case of Sarapis shows that not all cults that are Egyptian in name need also be Egyptian in atmosphere, feeling or ritual – so further problematizing the boundary between what is Roman and what is not.

31 Pax: Platner and Ashby (1929) 386–8; J. C. Anderson (1984) 101–18. Minerva: Steinby (1993–) II.309; J. C. Anderson (1984) 129–33. For the continuing impor-tance of Roman cults in the third century A.D., Alföldy (1989).

32 The formal procedures of *evocatio* are not attested under the empire (for their last attested use see above, pp. 132–4). Aurelian: Zosimus I.61.2; *Augustan History, Aurelian* 25.5–6 claims the Roman cult was derived from that at Emesa; below, p. 256.

33 Map 2 no. 24. *ILS* 4387, on a plaque not the architrave of the temple. Valenzani (1991–2). Malaise (1972b) 131–6 on Greekness. This also shows how different archae-ological reconstructions can lead to very different interpretations of the religious history of Rome. The inscription has often been linked to the nearby remains of a massive tem-ple (below, n. 34). If that connection were correct, it would provide powerful evidence for the public prominence of an Egyptian cult within the *pomerium*, under lavish offi-cial imperial patronage, by the early third century A.D. In fact, there is no very strong reason to link the modest inscription with the huge temple; and it is much more plau-sible (especially given how much was being spent on Caracalla's other massive building projects) to think in terms of a much smaller, much less prominent, structure some-where in the area.

Two other temples represent different ways of incorporating the foreign. The first is a massive temple whose remains are on the Quirinal, almost certainly the emperor Septimius Severus' new foundation in honour of Liber and Hercules. It was the second largest temple ever built in Rome (we shall consider the largest shortly), with its central square covering 13,000 square metres, and its columns over 21 metres high; for the contemporary senatorial historian Cassius Dio a prime example of the emperor's useless extravagance. Liber (or Bacchus) and Hercules were gods long familiar at Rome; and although the worship of Bacchus had been on occasion the focus of official Roman control, there was no obvious sense in which Hercules was regularly regarded as dangerously alien. On the other hand, in this particular pairing Liber and Hercules were the ancestral gods of the emperor's birthplace at Lepcis Magna in North Africa. We do not know how Roman or foreign they seemed in this particular temple; besides, their image would have changed with different worshippers or observers, with different backgrounds and in different religious contexts. Nevertheless, if Egyptian Sarapis could claim a Greek pedigree, it is clear too that such apparently 'Roman' gods as Liber and Hercules could also evoke the African homeland of the new emperor.[34]

One emperor in the third century A.D. became particularly associated with the introduction of flagrantly alien cults, incompatible with the traditions of official Roman religion. Marcus Aurelius Antoninus (known posthumously as Elagabalus, after the deity whom he promoted and whose priest he was) is said to have introduced from his native city in Syria the cult of the god Elagabalus. The surviving ancient accounts of the career of this emperor (who was only 18 years old when he came to the throne and ruled for just four years) are flamboyantly extravagant – full of lurid anecdotes about his strange sexual practices (an attempted sex-change, for example) and stories of black humour about his treatment of the élite (a banquet that ended with a shower of rose petals so numerous that they actually smothered the guests...). These accounts in general are much more important for what they can tell us about common Roman fantasies of transgressive behaviour than for any accurate information they may (or more often may not) offer about the history of Elagabalus' reign.[35] But surviving archaeological evidence from Rome does confirm some elements of the religious

34 Marked by Map 2 no. 24. Cassius Dio LXXVII.16.3; E. Nash (1968) II.376–83; Valenzani (1991–2). The similarity to the temple of Sarapis at Alexandria, on a hill with an approach from the rear, is not a decisive argument in favour of this temple also being a Sarapeum.

35 These criticisms are attested only after the overthrow of the emperor. Cassius Dio LXXX.11–12, 21.2; Herodian V.5.6–6.10; *Augustan History, Elagabalus* 8 = **6.6c** for an extreme example. Turcan (1989) 174–80; Baldus (1991); Millar (1993) 306–8. The form of the name 'Heliogabalus' sometimes used today is not found before the fourth century. Elagabalus also brought Caelestis from Carthage (Cassius Dio LXXIX.12; Herodian V.6.4–5).

changes reported by the literary sources. Since this is such a spectacular display of innovation, imagined, debated and stigmatized, we shall consider it in some detail.

The story goes that in A.D. 219 the emperor brought from Emesa to Rome the cult image of the god – which (like the cult image of Magna Mater, introduced in 204 B.C.) took the form not of a statue, but of an unworked stone. In Rome he established two temples for the god: one (referred to by ancient writers) on the outskirts; and another huge one (of which some traces still remain) on the Palatine – probably rebuilding and enlarging the existing temple of Jupiter Ultor.[36] The cult image was apparently carried in procession between the two temples twice a year. In lingering over the disgusting irregularities of the reign, Dio claims that what was most offensive about these religious innovations was not the foreign nature of the deity, nor the strange aspects of the worship (though they were bad enough – ranging from circumcision to human sacrifice; bizarrely too the emperor even 'married off' his deity to the Carthaginian goddess Tanit or Caelestis); worse was the fact that the new god was placed at the head of the Roman pantheon, above Jupiter (and was invoked first in all public sacrifices), and that the emperor paraded his role as priest of this foreign god. Indeed the priesthood was occasionally featured on the emperor's coinage; and the Greek historian Herodian, writing just after Elagabalus' reign, tells how the emperor (before he had arrived in Italy) had sent to the senate a portrait of himself dressed in his eastern priestly costume – with instructions that it should be hung in the senate-house.[37] There could hardly be a more striking reversal of the Augustan association between the emperor and *pontifex maximus;* the fantasy (at least) of a radical overturning of the association between imperial power and official religion. As with other stories of the career of Elagabalus, this anecdote prompts its readers to reflect on the *possibility* that the marginal, 'foreign' religions of the empire might indeed usurp the position of 'official' cult. In the 'official' version of the story, of course, the upshot is the public restoration of traditional order: the god and the emperor were so closely associated that when the emperor fell the god was banished from Rome, and the temple rededicated, fittingly enough, to Jupiter Ultor, the Avenger.

Religious innovation in the principate was not, however, only a matter of the importation of new cults from the provinces of the empire. A number of temple foundations seem to represent new ways of conceptualizing the relationship between *place* and the traditions of Rome – whose importance in the Augustan period we discussed in chapter 4. In particular, three

---

36 Map 2 no. 11; the suburban temple may have been in the sanctuary of Palmyran gods: Map 2 no. 14. E. Nash (1968) I.537–41; Coarelli (1986a) 230–53, (1987) 433–9; excavations in Vigna Barberini (1990) and following years, Chausson (1995), Steinby (1993–) I.14–16, III.10–11.
37 Herodian V.5.5–7 = **8.5c.**

new state temples of the second and third centuries attempted in different and novel ways to relate Rome to the whole cosmic order. First, two Hadrianic temples. The Pantheon, perhaps the most impressive monument to have survived from imperial Rome, replaced an earlier Augustan temple on the same spot, which had already been much restored.[38] Hadrian emphasized his adherence to Augustan ideology in various different ways: he restored the original inscription above the porch, so that the building still emblazoned the name of Agrippa (Augustus' right-hand man) as builder; and he retained the principal deities honoured in the original building, including Mars and Venus, perhaps along with statues of Augustus and Agrippa. But the building itself had a revolutionary new plan: behind the porch, the temple consisted of an enormous rotunda, covered by a dome – with light entering the vast space inside through a circular opening in the centre of the dome. It is one of the most dramatic designs of any Roman building; even today the shafts of light that come through the central aperture, moving with the sun, are spectacular. But it is not *just* spectacle. Dio observes that the form of the whole temple, with its domed roof, resembles the heavens themselves.[39] And although there have been endless theories about the precise interpretation of the architectural symbolism, it is clear that in evoking the vault of heaven with its sun, the building displayed the old deities of Rome in an explicitly cosmic setting.[40]

Hadrian's temple of Venus and Rome, close to the Roman Forum, also expressed a new relationship between Rome and the divine order.[41] This was the largest temple ever built in the city (with a platform 145 by 100 metres and surrounding columns almost 2 metres in diameter). Its plan was quite unlike any other in the city; for, in order to house the statues of the two deities, two chambers (*cellae*) were constructed, back to back – one entered from the colonnade at the front of the temple to the west, the other from the colonnade at the rear. Just as with the Pantheon, there are strong Augustan echoes in this building: the cult of Venus, in particular, alludes in an Augustan manner to the goddess who was the mother of Aeneas. But there are radical innovations too. In this Hadrianic temple, Venus' associations were no longer with the current dynasty (which, in any case, did not claim divine descent), but with Rome as a whole. Even more strikingly the goddess 'Rome' shared the dedication of the temple with Venus. There had long been cults of Rome in the Greek world, so too more recently in the Latin west; even in Rome there was a minor cult of the '*Genius* of the Roman people'. But this was the first

38 Map 1 no. 31; Fig. 6.1. E. Nash (1968) II.170–5; De Fine Licht (1968); W. L. MacDonald (1976); Boatwright (1987) 42–51; above, p. 209.

39 LIII.27.2.

40 The building thus develops the traditional notion of the *templum*, a designated space in a special relationship to the heavens: see **4.4** for more details. It was also a place where the emperor administered justice: Cassius Dio LXIX.7.1.

41 Map 1 no. 6. E. Nash (1968) II.496–9; Beaujeu (1955) 128–61; Boatwright (1987) 101, 119–33; Cassatella and Panella (1990). Cf. above, pp. 160, 176 and below, p. 259.

time that 'Rome' received a cult in the city itself. Here, in what was later known as the 'temple of the city', eternal Roma was represented, enthroned and holding in her right hand the Palladium, symbol of Rome's eternity. This was a revolutionary development in the religion of place, a new expression of the enduring place of Rome in the divine order. It goes closely together with

Fig. 6.1 The
Pantheon, as
depicted in a
nineteenth-century
engraving.

Hadrian's adaptation of the festival of the Parilia. As we have seen, since at
least the first century B.C. the primeval festival of the Parilia had been taken
to commemorate the foundation of the city. It seems that Hadrian dedicated
this new temple during the Parilia, perhaps in A.D. 121, a festival which in
turn was henceforth known as the 'Romaea'.[42]

A temple built more than a century later illustrates even more clearly the
potential ambiguities between tradition and innovation. In A.D. 274 the
emperor Aurelian dedicated a great temple to the Sun (Sol), which was
famed in antiquity for the richness of the offerings and dedications it contained. Though little survives today, its remains were recorded by antiquarians between the sixteenth and eighteenth centuries; and we rely largely on
their reports in attempting to reconstruct its general appearance – an
unusual design (if our reconstructions are right) of one grand precinct, surrounded by a portico, with a temple building in the middle, another
smaller precinct forming an entrance, and perhaps a third precinct off the
other side.[43] The cult of the Sun can have clear associations with eastern
religions: the full title of the god Elagabalus was, in fact, Sol Invictus
Elagabalus – Invincible Sun Elagabalus; and here it is often assumed that
the particular form of the cult derived from the cult of Ba'al at Palmyra in
Syria, after Aurelian's successful campaigns there. Certainly, the building of
this temple has been interpreted by modern and (in all likelihood) ancient
observers as the final triumph of 'Oriental cults' in Rome. At the same
time, however, its significance had Roman roots too. So, for example, a regular sacrifice to Sol is marked on 9 August of several Augustan calendars;
and there had been a longstanding identification in both the Greek and
Roman worlds of the god Apollo with Sol (or Greek Helios). The sanctuary was also located in a place with strong associations with the Augustan
principate: it was opposite the famous Ara Pacis, and near another historic
altar, the Ara Providentiae (the Altar of Providence, founded under the
early empire). Besides, the imagery of the god – at least on the few contemporary coins on which it is shown – is strongly Graeco-Roman, rather
than Oriental (contrast the explicit eastern imagery attached to Elagabalus'
cult); and the priesthood founded to serve the cult was given the very
Roman title of '*pontifices* of the Sun'. A single divine name 'Sun' could
evoke either alien 'Oriental' excess or 'native' traditionalism, or both; the
same cult arrangements – here, for example, the new priesthood – could
suggest both a continuing adherence to traditional religious forms, as well
as an aggressive attempt to outdo those traditions (the invention of a new
set of *pontifices* after nearly a thousand years representing a challenge to, as
much as respect for, the old arrangements).

Such developments continue up to the very last phases of pagan Rome.

42 Athenaeus, *Table-talk* VIII.361e–f = **5.1c**.
43 Map 2 no. 9. Wissowa (1912) 315 n. 3, 367–8; Kähler (1937); Coarelli (1983a) 240–1;
    Torelli (1992). Below, n. 56. Coins: *RIC* V.1, p. 301 (*asses* of mint at Serdica).

Though the emperors of the late third and early fourth centuries (the tetrarchs) did not build major new temples, still there were significant new foundations in the very heart of the traditional city. Diocletian commemorated vows to the gods taken at the twentieth anniversary of his rule (in A.D. 303) with a major monument in the Roman Forum. Maxentius (A.D. 306–312), who restored Hadrian's temple of Venus and Rome after a fire, also built near the Roman Forum in A.D. 307 a small round temple to his deified (and well-named) son Romulus (it was close to the massive basilica he built for judicial business, which still dominates the forum); this temple came to include other *divi* of the dynasty, but was rededicated by Constantine (who defeated Maxentius to take the throne in A.D. 312) to Jupiter Stator. This was no doubt another loaded dedication – the first temple to Jupiter Stator in the city had, it was said, been dedicated by the legendary Romulus, the founder of the city.[44] Even in this last period of the pagan history of Rome, the official cults of the state and official temple foundations still found a powerful symbolism in the most ancient stories and places of Rome.

2. The visibility of religions

In this section we consider the impact of religions on the population of the capital. How conscious of the state festivals would an 'ordinary' inhabitant of the city have been? How noticeable were the new cults – whether in terms of their buildings, their religious activities, or their social prominence? What was the impact of their claims on writers and other intellectuals? We start by exploring popular involvement in the official religions of Rome. As we have seen, there is clear evidence throughout the principate for the religious and priestly activity of the élite in state cult. But how much of that impinged on the rest of the population? The senatorial officials may have performed these rituals anywhere between piously and perfunctorily. But was the rest of the city passionately involved or entirely unmoved by them?[45]

The senatorial élite did not monopolize state cults – whether as office-holders or as participants. The Luperci (as we have already noted) were drawn principally from the *equites* during this period. Minor priesthoods, too, such as the so-called 'lesser' *pontifices* and *flamines* (who are now, admittedly, little more than names to us) were also reserved for the *equites*; as were many of the ancient priesthoods of the Latin cities round Rome.[46] The equestrian order was still of course unquestionably part of the

---

44 Liebeschuetz (1979) 236–7; Coarelli (1986b) 1–35. There were also religious monuments in private houses probably of this date: a three-aisled room, whose apse was decorated with a wolf suckling Romulus and Remus, with a Lupercus on each side; and a shrine on the Esquiline hill containing statues of Egyptian and other gods. Lupercal: *Spätantike* (1983) 279–80; Weiland (1992); Esquiline: Map 2 no. 21; Malaise (1972a) 176–7; Stambaugh (1978) 598. On Constantine, below, pp. 369–75.

45 The use of official religious imagery in the private sphere: Zanker (1988) 265–95.

élite. But more humble Romans also had a variety of parts to play within official religion. In addition to the local cults of the wards that we discussed in chapter 4 (under the charge of four annual magistrates, who were mainly ex-slaves, aided by four slave officials),[47] many cults of the Roman people as a whole gave 'ordinary' citizens official roles. In the cult of Magna Mater during the empire, for example – a religion which always challenges any strict boundary we might try to draw between the Roman and the foreign, between official and 'alternative' religions[48] – the priests and priestesses were mainly ex-slaves, newly enfranchised Roman citizens.[49] (This was a notable change from republican practice when the cult's priestly officials came from the goddess' native Phrygia in Asia Minor, and Roman citizens were banned from serving in the cult.) Likewise ex-slaves (as well as freeborn men from the Italian towns) provided many of the specialist personnel required in all the most central Roman rituals: musicians to play at the rites, men to kill the sacrificial animals, *haruspices*, temple attendants and so forth. Many of these groups of cult 'servants' even proudly formed their own professional associations around their religious duties; these were not just, in other words, positions of menial service, but part of a paraded official religious status open to some of the most lowly inhabitants of Rome.[50]

Official festivals of the state calendar could also have a considerable impact on public life at all levels. Not all festivals, no doubt; it is a fair guess that during the principate some of the minor rituals would have been carried out by a handful of priests, quite properly and routinely but practically unnoticed by anyone else. Many festivals on the other hand did make a difference to the lives of a wide cross-section of the city's population.[51] This could be a matter of active participation: we know that crowds sometimes turned out to watch the Lupercalia (some women no doubt waiting to be struck with the thongs wielded by the Luperci – which were reputed to bring fertility to the childless); some festivals (like the Saturnalia) involved private celebrations at the same time as public sacrifices; and at *supplicationes* everyone, male or female, was supposed to sacrifice wine and incense in public. It is striking too that Athenaeus in the second century A.D., writing a (fictional) scholarly discussion set in Rome, has the calm of his

46   Luperci: Wrede (1983); above, pp. 184–6. 'Lesser' *pontifices* and *flamines* and *tubicines*: Wissowa (1912) 489, 492, 519, 557. Latin priesthoods, below, p. 323.

47   They were responsible for the local festivals, including the local games (*ludi compitalicii*), and the names of the magistrates were inscribed, just like the names of the consuls, on official lists (starting mainly in 7 B.C.). Above, pp. 184–6; **8.6a**. For the parallel associations of *Augustales* outside Rome, below, pp. 323–4.

48   Above, pp. 96–98; 164–6; with the passages collected at **2.7**.

49   Even the *archigalli* found in the second and third centuries A.D. were mainly ex-slaves. Wissowa (1912) 320; Lambrechts (1952) 155–9; Schillinger (1979) 289–97, 360–2. Cf. below, pp. 337–8 for control by the *quindecimviri*.

50   Waltzing (1895–1900) IV.131–5; Purcell (1983); Di Stefano Manzella (1994).

51   Any regulations on participation normally apply specifically to Roman citizens, but participation was not monitored and free non-citizens were presumably not excluded.

intellectual speakers disturbed by the noise of boisterous enjoyment, of music and singing in the streets at the Parilia.[52]

Religious rules also prescribed activities that could *not* take place on festal days. According to the state calendar, the courts did not sit on most major festival days; and sometimes religious celebrations were accompanied by a ban on mourning one's own kin – in the Saecular Games of A.D. 204 the closure of the courts (as well as the prohibition on mourning) lasted, exceptionally, for 30 days. At least in theory (for rules affecting private conduct are always especially hard to enforce), religious festivals made a difference to the lives of the city's inhabitants.

One particular kind of religious ceremonial certainly involved mass participation. The various types of *ludi* (games) – from circus races to theatrical performances or gladiatorial shows – were regularly given as part of the festivals to the gods or deified emperors. Of course, many of those who went to enjoy the races or the plays may not have had 'religion' (in our sense of the word) uppermost in their minds; but there remained strong associations between the games and the gods throughout the principate. Images and symbols of the appropriate deities, for example, were paraded through the streets of Rome to the Circus or theatre, where sacrifices were performed; and the audience is reported, on one occasion at least (in the civil wars at the very end of the Republic), to have been keenly observant of this ritual. In 40 B.C., during the campaign of Octavian and Antony against Sextus Pompey, at the festival of Pompey's patron god Neptune, the statue of Neptune was carried into the Circus and the people showed their support for Pompey by warmly applauding; when Octavian subsequently had it omitted from the procession, there was a riot.[53] Of course, the audience was here putting a strongly 'political' gloss on the ceremonies; but they were certainly not oblivious of these divine preliminaries, merely waiting for the 'entertainment' to start – as Christian critics of the late second and third centuries A.D. confirm when they argue that Christians should avoid all games, not only because of their intrinsic immorality, but also because of their context in the worship of the traditional gods.[54]

The number of days of *ludi* increased under the empire. There were 77

---

52 Lupercalia: Plutarch, *Romulus* 21 = **5.2a**. Saturnalia: Macrobius I.24.22–3 = **5.3a**; Pliny, *Letters* II.17.23–4 = **5.3b**. At the Saecular Games the whole free population of the city was supposed to purify itself. Above, p. 203. Cf. Ovid, *Fasti* III.523–696 for the popular festival of Anna Perenna. Participation: above, pp. 48–52.

53 Cassius Dio XLVIII.31, preferable to Suetonius, *Augustus* 16. The circus (Map 1 no. 15) with its statues of the gods was a widespread motif on mosaics, reliefs and sarcophagi: Humphrey (1986) 175–294. See also below, p. 383 fig. 8.3.

54 Tertullian, *On Shows*; also *On Shows* ascribed to Cyprian, but probably by Novatian and hence written in Rome. *Ludi*: Wissowa (1912) 449–67; Taylor (1935); Balsdon (1969) 244–339; Weismann (1972) on Christians; Hopkins (1983) 1–30; above, pp. 122–3. There is a similar argument as to whether classical Athenian tragedies were 'religious' or merely 'entertaining': Goldhill (1987).

days in Rome in the early first century A.D., 177 days in the mid fourth century A.D.[55] The increase was due partly to the addition of *ludi* to ancient festivals, partly to the creation of new festivals or the building of new temples commemorated by games. So, for example, when Hadrian dedicated the precinct of the temple to Venus and Rome in A.D. 121, he added circus games to the ancient Parilia, which became a festival popular with all the residents of Rome and all visitors to the city. The foundation of Aurelian's temple of the Sun was commemorated with games on a four-year cycle (recorded under a Greek title: 'the *agon* (contest) of the Sun'), and by the fourth century this cult was also associated with annual four-day *ludi*.[56]

Ludi were events for the city as a whole, open not just to Roman citizens, but to foreigners and slaves. When much of the Colosseum was destroyed by lightning in A.D. 217 on the day of the Vulcanalia (the festival of the god Vulcan), this was taken to portend the evils that would afflict the whole Roman empire, whence came the spectators that usually packed the building. And during the major shows put on by Augustus, the streets were said to be so empty that he had to station guards round the city to prevent robbery.[57] This story is told because it celebrated the popularity of the *ludi* presented under the auspices of the emperor and his care for city and citizens; but it gives a good idea of the scale of the games. 150,000 could sit in the Circus Maximus, and the Colosseum (opened in A.D. 80) held 50,000 seated, and another 5,000 standing at the top. This was one way the people as a whole, citizens and others, were collectively involved in the official cults of imperial Rome.

Against this background of the great state temples and public festivals, how visible were the new cults of Rome? We have emphasized throughout this book that 'new' cults were no novelty at Rome – and some of the republican imports were among the most conspicuous in the city. At the festivals of Magna Mater in the late Republic and early empire, for example, eunuchs preceded the goddess through the streets of Rome banging drums and clashing cymbals; these eunuchs, dressed in their bright costume, with heavy jewels and long greased hair, seem even to have had official permission to go round the city 'begging' for funds, at least on the appointed days of the year. But what of the more recent imports? How visible and how distinctive were *their* monuments and buildings? Jews and Christians may not have been instantly identifiable in the streets of Rome by a characteristic costume or style of hair – but was there anything else that made them conspicuous?[58]

---

55 Calendar entries for April (**3.3**) include the Megalesian Games, games of Ceres, of Flora, and 'Public Fortune' – extending over several days.

56 Parilia: Beaujeu (1955) 131–2; Salzman (1990) 155; cf. above, pp. 174–6. *Ludi Solis*: Salzman (1990) 127, 150–1.

57 Vulcanalia: Cassius Dio LXXIX.25–26.1. Augustus: Suetonius, *Augustus* 43.1.

58 Jews: Cohen (1993). Priests of Magna Mater: above, pp. 164–6. There may also have been travelling priests of the Syrian goddess who openly demanded money for their cult: Apuleius, *Metamorphoses* VIII.24–30, XI.4, 8–10 (= **5.6c**).

One of the major new cults in Rome paraded a particularly clear distinctive identity through its public monuments and rituals. The sanctuary of Isis and Sarapis on the Campus Martius differed from normal Graeco-Roman temples in its design and decoration; and much of it (also unlike a traditional civic sanctuary) was not open to non initiates (Fig. 6.2).[59] It seems to have been started in the reigns of Augustus and Gaius, but the sanctuary as we know it dates from the later first century A.D., with some later additions and alterations. Two arches formed the entrance to a large courtyard some 70 metres across, within which was an obelisk honouring the emperor Domitian, who had rebuilt the temple (perhaps on a new plan) after its destruction by fire in A.D. 80. This courtyard was open to passers-by, but two sanctuaries opened off it, accessible only through narrow doorways and probably not evident to the general public. To the south was a sanctuary of Isis: here, at the centre of a great semicircular apse, was a colossal statue of the deity, flanked in other niches by statues of Sarapis and Anubis. Projecting into the water in the middle of the apse were giant statues in Greek style, of Tiber, Nile and Ocean, symbolizing the position of the cult in the Roman world. To the north was a great courtyard, up to 70 metres across and 140 metres long. Its layout and purpose are not wholly clear (as the Severan marble plan largely breaks off at this point and as excavations have been only very partial), but it included at least one (and presumably two) lines of obelisks or trees, perhaps forming a processional route, and at the far end probably shrines for Isis and Sarapis, one (Isis) in Egyptian style, the other (Sarapis) in Greek style. The plan of this northern area was probably modelled on the sanctuary of Sarapis at Saqquara in Egypt. Overall, some of the decoration came directly from Egypt – including several sphinxes and portraits of earlier Egyptian rulers (pharaohs and Ptolemies) and also several of the obelisks that were re-used centuries later to decorate the Renaissance piazzas of Rome. Other items, including baboons and crocodiles, were imitations of genuine Egyptian products but further enhanced the 'Egyptian' atmosphere. In addition, the priests of the cult obeyed bizarre regulations of dress and diet: shaved heads, white robes, a prohibition on the eating of pork and fish and the drinking of wine. Elaborate daily rituals took place in these sanctuaries behind closed doors, but outside the sanctuary individual initiates could be seen performing actions that seemed quite weird to some observers – such as leaping into the river Tiber; and on festival days grand carnival processions passed through the streets of Rome.[60]

59 Map 2 no. 26. Above, n. 17; Malaise (1972a) 187–214; Lembke (1994); Steinby (1993–) III.107–9. For a painting from Herculaneum of an Isis temple, **12.4e**.

60 Priests: Malaise (1972b) 113–43; Illustration: **5.8e**. Rituals: Malaise (1972b) 217–43; Juvenal, *Satires* 6.522–41 = **12.4d**; Apuleius, *Metamorphoses* XI.9–10 = **5.6c** gives a fictional account set in Corinth. See above, pp. 250–1 for the problem of the status of these festivals. Recondite 'Egyptian' books used in initiations: Apuleius, *Metamorphoses* XI.22.

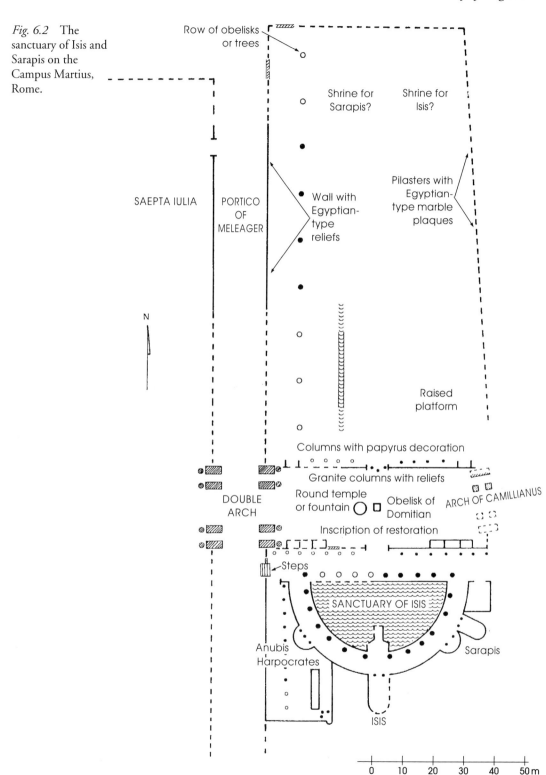

Fig. 6.2 The sanctuary of Isis and Sarapis on the Campus Martius, Rome.

Row of obelisks or trees

Shrine for Sarapis?

Shrine for Isis?

Pilasters with Egyptian-type marble plaques

SAEPTA IULIA

PORTICO OF MELEAGER

Wall with Egyptian-type reliefs

N

Raised platform

Columns with papyrus decoration

Granite columns with reliefs

DOUBLE ARCH

Round temple or fountain

Obelisk of Domitian

ARCH OF CAMILLIANUS

Inscription of restoration

Steps

SANCTUARY OF ISIS

Anubis Harpocrates

Sarapis

ISIS

0   10   20   30   40   50 m

In addition to this major sanctuary of Isis, there is evidence for some thirteen other sites of Egyptian cults in imperial Rome, varying widely in size, character and prominence. One of the fourteen regions into which the city was divided was named, in lists of the fourth century A.D. (detailing the different regions and their buildings), after a sanctuary of Isis and Sarapis. Although we can identify no surviving traces of this sanctuary, it must have been prominent enough by the mid fourth century A.D. for it (rather than, say, the Colosseum which was in the same region) to give its name to this division of the city.[61] Other sanctuaries are, to us at least, obscure – and some were contained within private houses. For example, the series of second-century A.D. Isiac graffiti from a house on the Aventine hill seems to have been written by a small Isiac group which met there.[62]

No other 'foreign' religion in the city was so visible to the casual visitor. The cult of Mithras seems to have been established in Rome by the early second century A.D. and evidence for it remains abundant until the second half of the third century A.D. The classic sanctuaries of the cult (the so-called 'caves') appeared in the middle of the second century.[63] Up to forty of these sanctuaries, dating to the second and third centuries A.D., can be located in Rome – or else fairly certainly conjectured (from inscriptional evidence, for example).[64] They rank among the most elaborately designed and decorated of all religious places in Rome. But they were sited away from the casual eye, inside buildings which had rooms to let, in private houses, or in the various military camps scattered across the city. Similarly in Ostia Mithraic sanctuaries were found in secluded locations, away from the major roads; and only two were entered directly from the street. Mithraic sanctuaries were for the initiates alone and presented no public exterior to the world. This seclusion of its shrines may have been one of the ways in which Mithraism differentiated itself from traditional civic cult: consciously opposing its dark and private places to the public openness of civic temples.

There seems to have been a similar seclusion (though not necessarily for similar reasons) about many of the cult places of Judaism and, in its earliest phases, of Christianity. By the mid first century B.C. there was a substantial Jewish community in Rome, numbering several thousands by the

61 Map 2 no. 18; Coarelli (1982) 59–63. Region III: Malaise (1972a) 171–6; Häuber (1990) 43–54; de Vos (1993); Steinby (1993–) III.110–12.

62 Map 2 no. 28. Darsy (1968) 30–55; Malaise (1972a) 142, 225–7; **12.4f**; below, p. 269. Cf. White (1990) 26–59 for other adaptations of houses.

63 R. L. Gordon (1977–8); Boyce and Grenet (1991) 468–90. General introductions: Vermaseren (1963); Merkelbach (1984), with excellent pictures; Clauss (1990); Beck (1992); Turcan (1993). The evidence peters out when western inscriptions largely disappear: above, n. 7. 'Caves': below, n. 96; photograph in **4.6a**.

64 Map 3. Coarelli (1979). Coarelli's arguments for a total of 700 Mithraic sanctuaries in Rome are very fragile; Clauss (1992) 17–18 is rightly sceptical, particularly on the epigraphic evidence, but fails to account for the evidence of the monuments. Steinby (1993–) III.257–70 catalogues 27 sanctuaries.

Augustan period. Their presence in the city was well known (even though their religious practices did not involve the public displays and processions associated with other cults); and in Ostia a synagogue has been excavated, dating in its earliest phases to the first century A.D., prominently located, even if on the outskirts of the town. However, though literary and epigraphic sources mention about eleven Jewish synagogues in Rome itself during the imperial period, none of them is known archaeologically. This may be a matter of chance survivals and losses; and one of the synagogues was certainly once prominent enough to be mentioned in an inscription as a local landmark.[65] But it may also be that most of these synagogues were simple meeting places in houses, leaving no permanent marks of their religious function.

Evidence of the early Christian church shows how complex and shifting issues of visibility or invisibility might be. Christians certainly seem to have avoided distinctive and recognizable 'churches' in Rome until at least the third century A.D. Christian groups were established in Rome by the late 50s (Paul wrote a letter to the Romans, that is to the Christian community in the city, *c.* A.D. 55, and Christians were executed by Nero in A.D. 64); and Christian adherents in Rome increased, by stages which we cannot trace, until by the mid third century A.D. the church in Rome had about 150 officials and was able to support 1500 widows and poor – suggesting that the whole community was to be numbered in thousands, making it almost certainly the largest 'association' in the city.[66] But Christians met in small groups around Rome, mainly in rooms in private houses; and like Jewish synagogues, none of their pre-Constantinian buildings in Rome has been securely identified. Indeed, the 'house church' at Dura Europus in Syria is the only excavated example of a clearly identified early Christian meeting place from the whole of the empire earlier than the fourth century A.D.[67]

Prudence and fear of persecution no doubt in part lay behind this lack of public display. But some Christians seem also to have felt that specific sanctuaries were inappropriate, since no object or building could or should enclose the majesty of god. But whatever the reasons for the secrecy, it also fuelled hostility to Christians. One Christian writer around A.D. 200 represents his opponents attacking the members of his community as 'a crowd that lurks in hiding places, shunning the light; they are speechless in public but gabble away in corners'.[68] In the third century, however, there was an

---

65 Leon (1960); Schürer (1973–87) III.1, 73–82, 95–102; Solin (1983) 654–725; White (1990) 60–101; **4.14a** (Ostia Synagogue). Local landmark: *CIL* VI.9821 = Noy (1995) no. 602.

66 Eusebius, *Ecclesiastical History* VI.43.11. Modern guesses of the total number range from 10,000 to 30,000 or even 50,000.

67 Dura church (A.D. 240s): **4.15a**.

68 *Martyrdom of Justin* 3 = **12.7f(ii)**. Minucius Felix, *Octavius* 32 = **2.10c**, 8.4 = **11.11d**. Cf. Pietri (1978); Snyder (1985) 67–82; Lampe (1989) 301–45; White (1990) 102–23.

increasing number of purpose-built Christian churches, some, it seems, of considerable grandeur. No archaeological traces survive; but by the mid third century A.D. the Christian meeting places had become sufficiently evident for the emperor Valerian to order the confiscation of church property, and a little later Porphyry could claim in his treatise *Against the Christians* that Christians imitated the construction of temples in building great places for their prayer meetings. All this, of course, is before the reign of Constantine and the end of the main periods of persecution – suggesting that fear of reprisals was not the only reason for the lack of display in the earliest phases of the cult.[69]

As early as the second century there were some Christian landmarks in Rome whose religious significance was evident to members of the church at least – even if not recognized more widely. The Christian historian, Eusebius, quotes a Christian priest at Rome appealing (in an argument with a so-called 'heretic') to monuments to the Apostles Paul on the Ostian Way and Peter on the Vatican Hill. The monument on the Vatican is probably to be identified with a structure built around A.D. 170, and excavated below the apse of the church of Saint Peter's (founded by Constantine) (Fig. 6.3).[70] This unpretentious monument was built in a cemetery consisting of fairly lavish tombs, as well as a number of simple burials, some of which may be Christian. It was fitted carefully into an awkwardly restricted site in such a way as to suggest that the spot itself was felt to be of particular importance; and, although there is no firm evidence (such as an inscription) to link the monument conclusively with the saint, various features which would offer access to pilgrims suggest that those who built the monument believed that it marked the tomb of Peter. To the passing non-Christian, on the other hand, the structure would not stand out from the other tombs in the cemetery. Matters of visibility depend not least on who is looking: although some cults (such as the Isiac religion) may have forced their presence on any one who came in the way of their public rituals, others would have been visible only selectively. The committed Christian may have perceived the city of Rome as a place loaded with Christian associations, marked by the presence of Christian meeting places and monuments whose existence would often have been hidden from, or unnoticed by, the casual passer-by.

But visibility, and the significance of that visibility, also depended on the precise location of a cult or cult building within the city. The *pomerium*

---

69 Third/early fourth-century churches: Porphyry, *Against the Christians* fr. 76 (Harnack); *CSEL* XXVI.186–8 = **4.15b**; Eusebius, *Ecclesiastical History* VIII.1.5. Cf. Laurin (1954); Lane Fox (1986) 587; White (1990) 123–48. Below, pp. 368–9; 376–7, for fourth-century churches in Rome.

70 Eusebius, *Ecclesiastical History* II.25.6–7 = **12.7f(iii)**, A.D. 199–217. Map 4 no. 61; Toynbee and Ward-Perkins (1956); Chadwick (1957); Eck (1987) on social standing of the deceased; Arbeiter (1988) 21–49; Lampe (1989) 82–94. For the third-century memorial of Peter and Paul, Map 4 no. 39: **12.7f(iv)**.

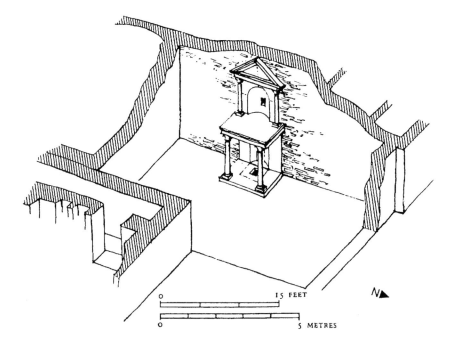

Fig. 6.3
Monument to
Peter, Rome.

remained a significant boundary through the imperial period. Foreign cults which had been 'officially' established might have sanctuaries within the *pomerium*, but even Aurelian's temple of the Sun was sited just outside it, and the only prominent sanctuary of the unofficial cults, that of Isis, was also beyond the *pomerium*.[71] The principal area of Jewish settlement in the Augustan period was also outside the *pomerium*, west of the Tiber, in what is now Trastevere; seven of the known synagogues were probably located here. One synagogue (the local landmark that we have already mentioned) was near the *agger*, that is the line of the *pomerium* – though we do not know on which side; others were in the Campus Martius and in the populous area of the Subura just north of the Fora (the latter of these at least was clearly inside the *pomerium*).[72] The location of Christian meeting places is not known with even that degree of precision, though they were probably scattered throughout the residential areas of the city, perhaps mainly in Trastevere and on the south-east side of the city in the first and second centuries A.D.[73] It seems fairly certain, in any case, that only those foreign sanctuaries that were effectively out of public view, positioned in houses or rooms within public buildings, lay inside the *pomerium*.[74] There were, in

71 *Pomerium*: above, pp. 177–81. Magna Mater: Map 2 no. 3. Sarapeum of Caracalla: Map 2 no. 24. Elagabalus, temporarily: Map 2 no. 11. Sol: Map 2 no. 9.

72 Map 1 nos. 7, 26, 29. Trastevere: Philo, *Embassy* 155 = **12.6c(ii)**. *Agger*: above, n. 65.

73 Lampe (1989) 10–52. The interesting discussion of the distribution of pre-Constantinian churches in Vielliard (1941) sadly falls on evidential grounds; above, n. 62.

74 As for example the Isiac meeting place on the Aventine (Map 2 no. 28; above, n. 62). For Mithraic sanctuaries, Map 3.

other words, no blatant, unofficial 'foreign' sanctuaries in the monumental centre of Rome. If you chose not to look outside that centre, the traditional cults of the Roman state might seem unaffected by the religious developments in the rest of the city.

We are much better informed about the location of Jews and Christians when they were dead – in their communal burial areas known as catacombs. Communal burial arrangements had precedents in Rome and Italy. In the early empire members of professional associations, and the slaves and ex-slaves of the imperial house and of other families, were sometimes buried together in *columbaria* (literally 'dovecotes'), built above ground with niches to hold the individual cremation urns. And elsewhere in Italy members of some religious associations shared burial arrangements; we occasionally find, for example, burial sites of the worshippers of Bona Dea Caelestis, of Hercules, of Jupiter Caelestis, of Isis and for the *dendrophori* ('tree-bearers') of Magna Mater.[75] By the second century A.D. ordinary Romans had started to use not these traditional *columbaria* but (sometimes extensive) underground chambers, or catacombs. Some of these were soon taken over by Christians, and other, specifically Christian, burial sites were established – all located, following the civic rules, well outside the *pomerium*.

Some of these Christian burial areas began as private foundations (like the catacombs of Priscilla, founded by A.D. 190; or those of Praetextatus, in early third century A.D.); but from around A.D. 200 Christians also had their first communal cemetery (Callistus).[76] In total, the Christian catacombs, which were in use through the fourth century A.D., have more than 1000 kilometres of corridors, off which burial chambers themselves were arranged, with space for some 6 million people. As their extent suggests, they were designed for all members of the church, rich and poor alike; charges for cemeteries were kept low and salaries paid to the officials of the cemeteries.[77]

The Jewish community in Rome also had catacombs exclusive to members of their faith. Seven Jewish catacombs have been found, a mile or two outside the city. These date from the early third (or possibly the later second) century A.D. onwards, the earliest in Trastevere. Some of these burial grounds are quite extensive; the catacombs on the Via Nomentana, for example, on the north east of Rome have 3000 feet of galleries.[78]

75 Waltzing (1895–1900) I.277–93, IV.484–95; below, p. 273.
76 Priscilla: Map 4 no. 10. Praetextatus: Map 4 no. 38. Callistus: Map 4 no. 43.
77 Map 4 nos. 1–60. Testini (1966) 83–122; Brandenburg (1984); Pergola (1986); Guyon (1987); Finney (1994) 146–230; introductory, Stevenson (1978) and Snyder (1985) 82–115. Hippolytus, *Apostolic Tradition* 40. Commemoration: Février (1978). Burial of bishops: Map 4 no. 44; Stevenson (1978) 28.
78 Map 4 nos. 62–8. Schürer (1973–87) III.1, 79–81; Vismara (1986); Rutgers (1990), (1992), (1995), 50–99, who argues that the catacombs were not exclusive; Finney (1994) 247–63 on paintings. This dating assumes that the first and second century A.D. brickstamps in the catacombs were reused.

Catacombs now have a romantic image: film and fiction portray them as Christian places of refuge during times of persecution. There is, in fact, no evidence that the cemeteries were ever used in this way; though they were regularly visited by the living to commemorate the dead, formed the focus of the cult of some Christian martyrs and were a noticeable part of the landscape of Rome in the principate. Some catacombs may have had tombs and other associated buildings visible above ground, and they were sufficiently closely identified with Christian activity for the emperor Valerian to have thought it necessary to ban Christians from using them.[79]

A cult may, of course, have had a prominent sanctuary with striking public rituals – but still have made little (religious) impact on the population at large; it may never have seemed a religious option for most of those who passed its doors. Conversely, a cult may largely have remained hidden from public view, but at the same time have been a major focus of popular interest – through, perhaps, the activities of its members in seeking out new adherents. The visibility of foreign cults in Rome, in other words, has a social dimension. The presence of a cult in Rome does not in itself mean that it opened new religious options to the population as a whole.

In this respect, cults centred on individual families were perhaps the least visible. We get a rare glimpse into one such cult (of Dionysus) from an inscription on a statue base honouring one Agrippinilla, a member of a leading senatorial family in the mid-second century A.D; it was found about 10 miles south-east of Rome.[80] On the stone below the name of Agrippinilla herself are listed the names of 420 people in 25 or 26 grades of initiation. At first sight the text gives the impression of a massive influx of Orientals to Rome (many of the names listed have an Eastern ring) – bringing, so it might seem, the cult of Dionysus with them and attracting others to join. In fact, this stone is much more likely to be the commemoration of a particular family cult. Agrippinilla's family traced its ancestry back 200 years to Mytilene on the Greek island of Lesbos, where there was an important local cult of Dionysus. The 420 initiates listed had probably not joined this cult by religious choice; nor were they necessarily of eastern origins (despite the sound of their names). They were the slaves and ex-slaves of this and a related senatorial family; and were initiated into this ancestral familial cult not primarily through religious choice, but by virtue of their membership of the two families.

Of course, many foreigners who moved to Rome did continue to worship their ancestral gods, according to the customs of their original countries; but did not necessarily seek new cult members from the population at large. People flocked to Rome from both the eastern and western parts of the empire. No doubt almost all of them kept to some of the religious tra-

---

79 Above, p. 241. Sixtus, the bishop of Rome, and four deacons, were indeed executed in the cemetery of Callistus under Valerian: Cyprian, *Letters* 80.1.
80 Dionysus: *IGUR* I 160, with Scheid (1986); above, n. 1 on names.

ditions of their homeland. But of civilians it was only groups from the east who actually established sanctuaries of their ancestral cults in Rome. In Trastevere there was a sanctuary to a number of gods from Palmyra in Syria; the dedications were made by immigrants from there to 'their ancestral deities' in a combination of Latin, Greek and Aramaic (the common language of the near east).[81] The Jewish community in Rome too may be seen primarily as an ethnic group. They probably originated mainly in the eastern Mediterranean, some being brought to Rome as slaves after successive captures of Jerusalem in 63 and 37 B.C. and subsequently emancipated.

Other cults, however, were 'elective' – in the sense that they were open either to any individual who chose to join, or at least to those who satisfied some basic qualification for membership (such as a particular profession – or, in the case of the Mithraic cult, were male). The degree of commitment implied by these choices varied greatly from cult to cult. As in the republican period, there were associations which people joined by virtue of their occupation, or to ensure themselves a decent burial. These associations were regularly under the auspices of a god, but it may not have been the cult of that deity as such which attracted members, nor any particular 'religious' conviction.[82] For example, at Lanuvium south-east of Rome a group of men, both slave and free, formed an association of worshippers of Diana and Antinous.[83] Diana was often the patroness of such associations, and Antinous, Hadrian's favourite, had died (and achieved divine status) shortly before the creation of the association; it was on his new temple in the town that the rules of the association were inscribed. This association dined together six times a year, on the birthdays of Diana and of Antinous, and on the birthdays of four high-ranking local figures, when sacrifices of incense and wine were made. Members also paid monthly contributions which ensured that the association would give them a proper burial, even if they died far from home.

How far this and other such societies are seen as 'religious' groups depends on what activities we decide to classify as 'religious'. Even then, it remains clear enough that different participants might have had different priorities, or that a solemn religious feast for one might simply have been a good party for another. The association's rules emphasise what seem to us the non-religious aspects of the association; and no greater weight is apparently given to the birthdays of the two deities than to those of the four local dignitaries. Feasting and funerals have often been taken to be the principal (and worldly) objectives of the association. On the other hand, it was actually

---

81 Map 2 no. 14; Dionysius of Halicarnassus, *Roman Antiquities* II.19.3; *IGUR* I 117–25, with Schneider (1987) and Chausson (1995) 661–718. The exceptional deity of western origin is Epona, who became known in Rome as patron of horses: Wissowa (1912) 86, 377.

82 Waltzing (1895–1900) I.195–255, II.138–9; Ausbüttel (1982) 49–59. For the Republic, above, pp. 42–3; 160–1.

83 Map 5. *ILS* 7212 = **12.2** (A.D. 136). Cf. *ILS* 7213, Aesculapius and Hygieia.

named after two deities – so parading its specifically religious identity to members and non-members alike; while for many members the proper rituals of a funeral and the care of the burial place after death might have been uppermost in their religious priorities.

There is, however, a clear contrast between a group such as the worshippers of Diana and Antinous and the associations (say) attached to the cult of Magna Mater. From the second century A.D. onwards, special groups of 'tree-bearers' (*dendrophori*) and 'reed-bearers' (*cannophori*) played their parts in the cult's ritual (notably at the spring festival, where a pine tree was carried in procession to the goddess's temple, and reeds carried in procession through the streets). And in the cult of Bellona, a deity often closely linked with Magna Mater, there was also in some places another association, of 'bodyguards' (*hastiferi*).[84] Though members of these groups no doubt shared various kinds of 'social' activities, their central defining function was their role in the ritual of the cult. The official sanctioning of the cult was extended to these associations, which offered a model for other elective groups.

Other cult organizations in Rome, outside the official cults of the state, seem to have attracted members through a specifically religious appeal. Two examples from Rome – both attested, though in very different ways, through surviving archaeological material – will illustrate the nature of the religious choices involved. Next to one of the city gates (the modern Porta Maggiore) are the remains of an underground building, some 12 metres long by 9 metres wide, divided into three aisles, with a vaulted ceiling elaborately decorated with stucco panels – which show a variety of figures from Graeco-Roman myth, interspersed with religious scenes and symbols. It is now generally known as 'The Underground Basilica at the Porta Maggiore' and it dates originally to around A.D. 40 (Fig. 6.4).[85] The purpose of the building is much disputed. Some argue that it was designed to house funerary urns, and that the stucco scenes are essentially decorative, not a coherent symbolic programme. Others hold that it was for the meetings of a religious group, and that the stucco scenes amount to an elaborate symbolic code, which made sense in the context of the shared religious or philosophical beliefs of the group's members. The building remains puzzling: but certainly the plan of the building would be very unusual for a burial place and no trace of any funerary urns has ever been found; while

---

84 Magna Mater: Waltzing (1895–1900) I.240–53; Schillinger (1979) 312–32, 398–406. Bellona: Fishwick (1967). Both rituals alluded to the mythology of the cult: Attis had castrated himself at the foot of a pine tree; the reeds allude to the riverbank on which the baby Attis had been exposed, and/or the place where Attis had been unfaithful towards Magna Mater.

85 Map 2 no. 31; E. Nash (1968) I.169–73; Luciani (1984) 214–21. Funerary: Mielsch (1975) 29–33, 118–21. Religious (Pythagorean): Carcopino (1926); Sauron (1994) 604–30. In English, Vermaseren (1977) 55–7, with North (1980) 189. For one scene see fig. 5.1.

Fig. 6.4 The central 'nave' of the Underground Basilica at Porta Maggiore, Rome, looking east to the apse; on each side is an aisle. The vaulted ceiling of the nave and aisles is covered with stucco scenes (for an example from the nave see fig. 5.1).

some of the mythological scenes are so unusual for decoration of this type that it is hard not to imagine that some intricate symbolism underlies it all. It has often been suggested, for example, that the rare depiction of the poetess Sappho throwing herself to her death from a cliff might have been a symbol of the liberation of the soul from the body. If the building did belong to a particular religious association, it offers one image of the essentially private (and, to outsiders, mysterious) world of a cult meeting place, unobtrusive behind closed doors.

The second example, by contrast, concerns a named and relatively well-known cult: the cult of Jupiter Dolichenus, believed to have originated in Doliche in northern Syria. (The name indicates both its place of origin and the Romanization – under the title Jupiter – of the Syrian 'Ba'al'.) This cult was widespread among non-Syrians in the western empire, in both civilian and military contexts. There were three sanctuaries in Rome: one was in or near the camp of the imperial cavalry guard, one was used mainly by soldiers of the watch, and the third, on the Aventine, seems to have been used solely by civilians.[86] The Aventine sanctuary, which is probably the best documented sanctuary of Jupiter Dolichenus in the empire, dates from the mid second century A.D., though it overlies an earlier, probably Augustan building.[87] Inscriptions connected with this sanctuary suggest that its adherents formed a tightly knit group, with a complex hierarchy: a priest who might also be called 'father of candidates', a scribe and 'patrons' who presided over a series of initiates ('brothers'). It seems very unlikely that this organization was visible (let alone comprehensible) to those outside the cult; and we can only guess what difference their cultic role would have made to the initiates when they left the sanctuary and proceeded with their 'ordinary' lives; we can also only guess how new adherents found out about (or decided to join) the cult. There is, to be sure, no evidence that the cult of Jupiter Dolichenus (nor any other of the elective religions) stimulated any adverse attention; but then there is hardly any evidence for its making any public impact at all outside the walls of its sanctuaries and its initiated members. This is a striking contrast to the cult of Isis – which was an exception among these elective cults both in its public prominence and in the violent reactions it provoked.

The attraction of new adherents was more problematic in Judaism and Christianity than in any other of these cults. The Jewish community remained a group largely defined by descent which did not seek actively to gain new members. On the other hand, Jews did recognize a category of converts ('proselytes') to Judaism. Outsiders did become attracted to the Jewish faith: some admired Jewish monotheism and the absence of religious images, others followed part of the Jewish law (for example on the observance of the sabbath or on diet), while a number became fully committed to Judaism and acquired the status of proselytes. Outside Rome, an early third-century Jewish inscription from Aphrodisias in Asia Minor mentions both proselytes (that is, full converts) and 'god-fearers', a term which seems to have referred to gentiles who followed some aspects of Jewish law or practices. And in Rome itself, there is a handful of tombstones (two male and five female)

86 Map 2 nos. 7, 8, 12.
87 Colini (1935); E. Nash (1968) I.521–4; Hörig (1984); Hörig and Schwertheim (1987) 221–35; Turcan (1989) 156–65; Steinby (1993–) III.133–4; Millar (1993) 248–9 on Doliche; **12.3** (a selection of documents of the cult). For the incorporation of local gods into the Roman system, below, pp. 313–19; 339–48.

in which the deceased is specifically designated a proselyte; a small number, maybe – but it is a status that we would not necessarily have expected to be proclaimed on tombstones. However such fringe members were attracted, the process certainly caused adverse comment from some Roman writers: Tacitus, for example, in his lengthy description of Jewish practices that formed part of his account of the emperor Titus' capture of Jerusalem, lays particular stress on the wickedness of Jewish proselytes 'who scorned their ancestral religion'; and the historian Cassius Dio records that in A.D. 95 the emperor Domitian put his own cousin to death and exiled his wife on charges of 'atheism', because 'they had drifted into Judaism'. There was almost certainly a tension here between on the one hand the status of Judaism as the ethnic religion of the Jews (and as such not expected to be seeking to widen its group of adherents) and on the other the increase in its numbers outside the ethnic group through a process (however casually, however unsystematically) of 'proselytizing'.[88]

Christianity lacked the ethnic links of Judaism. Initially it depended for its members entirely on conversion, both from Jews and non-Jews; and the exhortations ascribed to Jesus in the Gospels, and the travels of Paul actively seeking out new converts, define it at its origins as a missionary religion. After Paul there seems to have been no organized or systematic programme of attracting non-believers; but itinerant preachers remained active in different areas of the Roman world – and even if they did not draw attention to themselves in public, conversion was clearly a central aim. One pagan criticism of Christianity focussed on the personal approaches made by Christians to non-Christians; and on the ways they insinuated themselves into private houses and 'corrupted' the women and children with their bizarre ideas. These complaints seem to refer to the kind of low-key evangelizing that must have been prudent given that those offended could seek to have the missionary executed by the Roman authorities. But it also suggests a thoroughly unRoman model of social spread, through vigorous personal diffusion of the cult, transcending the absence of prominent and grand cult centres.[89]

Finally in this section we turn to consider the intellectual impact of these cults. How far did their claims influence Roman writers? How far was there a literary or intellectual response to these new religions? There are, as we saw briefly in the last chapter, a variety of jibes and critiques directed at some of the most prominent of the new cults: from Juvenal's satire on some

---

88 The range of attitudes: Varro in Augustine, *City of God* IV.31 = **1.1a**; Varro in Augustine, *The Harmony of the Evangelists* I.22.30 = **12.6a**; Juvenal 14.96–106 = **11.8b**; Tacitus, *Histories* V.4–5 = **11.8a**. Proselytes: *CIL* VI 29756 = Noy (1995) no. 577 = **12.6d(ii)**; Aphrodisias: Reynolds and Tannenbaum (1987) = **12.6e**. Cf. Goodman (1994a). Punishment: Cassius Dio LXVII.14 (A.D. 95). On the tensions between sects and society in modern Britain, see B. R. Wilson (1990) 46–68.

89 Origen, *Against Celsus* III.55 = **11.11c**; Justin, *Second Apology* 2 = **12.7f(i)**. Cf. Lane Fox (1986) 312–17. Manichaean proselytizing: below, p. 303.

of the rituals of Isis to the Greek writer Lucian's ironic account of the alleged charlatan Peregrinos, who had succeeded in duping simple-minded Christians (along with other gullible Greeks).[90] Christianity, in particular, prompted extended critiques, generating a sequence of pagan theological responses to its claims and practices. The first one known to us is Celsus' *True Doctrine,* written in Greek *c.* A.D. 180, perhaps in Alexandria – though it is not preserved independently, but known only through lengthy quotation in Origen's attempted refutation of it (*Against Celsus,* written in the late 240s A.D.). From these quotations, it seems that Celsus argued that Christianity was an untraditional deviation from Judaism, which was itself a falling away from the original Egyptian cults, and which thus lacked any grounds for credence; it was also totally objectionable for its subversion of the household by conversions of slaves, women and children.[91] A century later the neo-Platonic philosopher Porphyry mounted a much better informed attack on Christianity, which argued (rightly), for example, that the Book of Daniel was in fact written centuries after its purported date of composition; and these objections later formed the basis for a tract by a high-ranking Roman official Hierocles in the early fourth century A.D.[92]

Such criticism, now a commonplace of Christian biblical scholarship, may have been seriously unsettling to Christians at the time; certainly the church historian Eusebius took the trouble to compose detailed refutations of both Porphyry and Hierocles. On the other hand, these high profile intellectual disputes would inevitably have had the effect of drawing more attention to the cult itself; in the process of refuting Christianity pagan writers inevitably gave it the prominence that they feared.

Not all writing was hostile. Various authors commented on Judaism with positive approval or at least sympathetically, and sought to locate it within their own terms of reference. The medical writer and philosopher Galen, for example, stated that Jewish views of the creation were superior to that of the Greek philosopher Epicurus, though Galen himself argued for a different position.[93] The nature of the goddess Isis was the subject of an essay by Plutarch, who used the cult to expound his own Platonic-style philosophy (*On Isis and Osiris*). The most complex case, however, is that of Mithras. In the mid second century A.D. two philosophers Numenius and Cronius, drawing upon earlier treatises on the cult, discussed Mithraism in the context of their own (Platonic and Pythagorean) philosophical views. These discussions have not survived; but they were used by the later

90 Above, pp. 214–25. E.g. Juvenal 6.522–41 = **12.4d**; 14.96–106 = **11.8b**; Lucian, *Perigrinos* with C. P. Jones (1986) 117–32.

91 E.g. Origen, *Against Celsus* I.9, III.55 = **11.11c**. Generally: Labriolle (1934).

92 Porphyry's treatise may date to the early 270s (rather than the early fourth century): Croke (1984–5). Sossianus Hierocles drew analogies between Christ and the pagan holy man Apollonius of Tyana.

93 Galen, *The Usefulness of the Parts of the Body* XI.14 = **12.6b**; cf. Varro cited in n. 88 above; Plutarch, *Table-talk* 4.6.

philosopher Porphyry and are known to us through him. Porphyry advanced arguments in favour both of vegetarianism and of a particular allegorical reading of a passage of Homer's *Odyssey* on the basis of these Mithraic texts. The imagery of the cult of Mithras was evidently extremely suggestive to these philosophers, who deployed it for their own arguments and purposes.

These philosophical readings are almost our only early literary accounts of the Mithraic cult; and it is very hard to know how far they reflect the theology and intellectual style current within the cult itself – or how far they have transformed it for their own philosophical purposes.[94] But this is only a pressing problem if you imagine that there ever was a single 'real' Mithraic message which could, in principle and if you had enough evidence, be disentangled. We suggested earlier in this chapter that it is more helpful to think of these cults in terms of shifting *clusters* of ideas, people and beliefs; and that under the rubric of a single cult title ('Mithraism', for example), we might find quite substantial religious differences (or, at least, different emphases) depending on the context, the place, or for that matter the literary form, in which the cult was represented. On this model the philosophical treatises take their place as one more distinctive way in which the cult (and its representations) spread through the Roman world. Religions were not necessarily hidden by the seclusion of their secret cult places; literary, philosophic, even satiric representations could always give public prominence to a cult whose rituals took place behind closed doors.

3.   The appeal

We have seen the impact that the different new cults in Rome could make on an observer – whether wandering the streets of Rome, or reading in a library. But what was the appeal of these cults, especially in comparison with the traditional cults of Rome? What would make you wish to participate? The new cults had a different focus from the official system: they referred primarily to places other than Rome; some of them also constructed a much more complex symbolic system than traditional cults; they also offered the initiates *change* – both in this life and (sometimes) after death. Can we understand how far these religions would have seemed distinctively different from the civic cults of the city? How far would they have seemed really *new*? Many of the new cults did offer a striking alternative to the 'religion of place' we explored in chapter 4. If the state cult focussed specifically on Rome, other religions evoked different lands, far away. The

94 Porphyry, *On Abstinence from Animal Food* IV.16 = **12.5d**; *On the Cave of the Nymphs in the Odyssey* 5–6, 15–16, 17–18, 24–25 = **4.6c**, **12.5g**. Turcan (1975) argues for complete philosophical transformation; *contra*, Beck (1984) 2055–6, 2078–9; (1988) 73–85.

very name of Jupiter Dolichenus, for example, points to Doliche in north-ern Syria, the original home of the god. And the cult of Isis derived from Egypt and paraded many 'Egyptian' features. It is clear that in practice the cult in the Graeco-Roman world was very different from its Egyptian 'ori-gins'; but nonetheless Isiac sanctuaries in Italy were loaded (as we have seen) with distinctively Egyptian (or pseudo-Egyptian) objects, from obelisks to sphinxes; and when Lucius is initiated in Apuleius' *Metamorphoses* the books used are written in 'unintelligible' – presumably Egyptian – script.[95]

These complex evocations of foreign places are well illustrated in the cult of Mithras, which claimed Persia as its source of wisdom. The Persian sage Zoroaster was said to have founded the cult in the distant past, and numerous aspects of the cult alluded to its Persian 'origins'. Two religious terms used in the rituals (*nama* – 'hail' and *nabarzes* – 'victorious') are of Persian origin – one certainly so, the other probably; and 'Persian' was the title of one of the grades of initiation. The design of Mithraic sanctuaries also evoked a cave in Persia, where – as an act of primordial sacrifice – the god Mithras himself was said to have slain a bull.[96] This sacrifice was regu-larly depicted in sculpture and painting at one end of Mithraic sanctuaries: Mithras on a bull's back forces it to the ground; pulling its head up by the nostrils, he plunges in a knife behind or beside the head. The violence of the scene marks this out as quite alien to the practice of 'normal' Graeco-Roman sacrifice, in which the victim was expected to die willingly; the role of the god in the Mithraic sacrificial ritual is also strikingly different (break-ing the traditional civic norms which firmly separated the roles of humans and gods in sacrifice).[97]

The Persian 'origins' of Mithras cannot, however, be taken at face value: the picture is much more complicated than a simple diffusion of the cult from a Persian homeland to Rome.[98] Mithras was an ancient Persian deity, known to the Greeks from at least the fifth century B.C.; and his cult may indeed have become better known in Asia Minor from the first centuries B.C. and A.D. through the Persian settlements there. However, the form of the cult most familiar to us, the initiatory cult, does not seem to derive from Per-sia at all. It is found first in the west, has no significant resemblance to its sup-posed Persian 'origins', and seems largely to be a western construct. The fact that this new western form of the cult *represents itself* as the wisdom of the

95 Above, n. 59. Differences: Malaise (1972b) 217–21 (Sailing of Isis), 230–8 (initiation), 475; below, n. 110.

96 R. L. Gordon (1989) 64–71; for an actual cave as a Mithraic sanctuary, *CIMRM* 2303–9, near Tirguşor in Moesia Inferior.

97 Turcan (1981), (1991), (1993) 138–45. Animal sacrifice does not seem to have been part of Mithraic practice. For 'normal' sacrifices, Scullard (1981) 22–5; Detienne and Vernant (1989), on Greece; Scheid (1990b) 441–676; above, pp. 36–7; illustrations in **6.1**.

98 Cumont (1896–9), (1903) argued for diffusion.

Persian sage Zoroaster does not mean that it literally *was* a version of Persian Zoroastrianism. The claims of foreign origins must here in part be playing the role of a religious metaphor or symbol, appealing to symbolic authority outside the city of Rome and emphasizing the cult's difference from traditional civic religion.[99]

Judaism too was focussed on another place, Jerusalem. Until the destruction of the temple there by the Romans in A.D. 70 (following the Jewish Revolt) Jews throughout the empire regularly sent money to Jerusalem. These practical ties to Jerusalem were broken at that point (sacrifices were not resumed in Jerusalem after A.D. 70), but Jewish scriptures continued to evoke Judaea. The Jewish historian Josephus, writing in Rome after the destruction of the temple, refers to the temple and its cult in the present tense; and in the second century A.D. Jewish sages in Judaea wrote extensive and elaborate sets of rules about the performance of sacrifices and the maintenance of the sanctuary – just as if it still existed. The real Jerusalem, in other words, was reconstructed as a purely symbolic focus.[100]

The focus of these cults on places other than Rome did not, however, preclude the worship, even in the same sanctuary, of deities from the Graeco-Roman civic pantheon; nor did it necessarily imply rejection of the political order ordained and upheld by civic religion. Consider, for example, the sanctuary of Magna Mater at Ostia: it included not only temples of Magna Mater and her 'consort', Attis, but also a shrine of Bellona, and a series of statues of other gods – Pan, Bacchus, Venus and maybe Ceres.[101] Context inevitably makes a difference to how a deity is perceived and understood; and here the association with Magna Mater and her cult may have prompted viewers to rethink their ideas of Pan or Venus, to reinterpret them in the light of the goddess, her strange rituals and her castrated priests. But at the same time, these other gods and goddesses brought into this sanctuary the associations of their own roles in civic cult, so linking Magna Mater to the concerns of the state. This is a link, in fact, powerfully reinforced in some inscriptions from the sanctuary which record the performance of the cult's characteristic form of sacrifice, the *taurobolium* ('bull killing'): the texts state that the sacrifice was carried out 'for the wellbeing of the emperor'.[102] Of course, Magna Mater (though 'foreign' in all kinds of ways) had been officially introduced to Rome; and it is not therefore surprising, perhaps, to find her so closely associated with the concerns of the Roman state and other deities of the civic pantheon. But we find the same pattern in other cults too, those which had not in any sense been 'officially' incorporated: there were, in fact, many different ways of expressing their

---

99 R. L. Gordon (1975), (1977–8); Beck (1984) 2063–71, (1991), (1994).
100 Money: Schürer (1973–87) II.271–2; Josephus, *Jewish Antiquities* XIV.213–6 = **12.6c(i)**. Josephus, *Against Apion* II.193–8; Neusner (1979–80); below, p. 304.
101 Vermaseren (1977–89) III.107–19.
102 Vermaseren (1977–89) III nos. 405–7, 417. See below, p. 338.

relationship with traditional Roman cults and deities, quite apart from the impression of exclusivity given by the physical layout and position of some of their sanctuaries.

In the sanctuary of Jupiter Dolichenus on the Aventine in Rome[103] an extremely wide range of gods is represented alongside Jupiter (as we saw, a Romanization of the Syrian Ba'al) and other gods of Doliche. These included Graeco-Roman gods of the civic pantheon (a statue of Diana, for example, of Hercules and of Apollo), as well as Mithras and Egyptian deities. One surviving sculptured panel, in fact, shows the Dolichene gods together with representations of Isis and Sarapis. And, as in the Ostian sanctuary of Magna Mater, there are dedications to the apparently foreign deities 'for the well-being' of the emperor. In this case, however, there seems to be an attempt to assert the superiority of 'Jupiter Optimus Maximus Dolichenus' over the whole pantheon, above both the old gods like Minerva and Apollo, and the Egyptian and Persian gods. The main god is described as 'protector of the whole world' – and his title 'Optimus Maximus' brazenly mimics the cult title of Jupiter in his temple on the Capitoline: on the Aventine and elsewhere in the empire, in other words, the cult of Dolichenus borrows the epithets of the Capitoline triad (the title 'Juno Regina' is sometimes given to his female partner) to express the over-arching position of the Dolichene deities – so effectively claiming to usurp that of the state cult itself.[104] In this sort of cosmology, the display and incorporation of other deities could reinforce a strength – even parade the superiority – of an 'alternative' cult.

The cosmology of the cult of Isis, too, often incorporates other cults and deities. Though the goddess was of explicitly Egyptian origin, Isiac hymns (preserved on inscriptions) praised her as responsible for the whole apparatus of the Graeco-Roman pantheon; and her adherents claimed that she was worshipped under many different divine names throughout the world – that she *was* (in other words) the goddess otherwise worshipped under the name of Venus, Minerva or Magna Mater. These ideas may underlie the presence of statuettes of Dionysus and Venus in the Isiac temple at Pompeii. They may also give a very particular gloss to the various links between Isis (as *the* all powerful deity) and the political order: the temple of Isis at Beneventum included a statue of Domitian as Pharaoh; an Isiac festival at Corinth, fictionalized by Apuleius, was explicitly designed to favour Rome (one of the priests prayed before the assembled people for the emperor, the senate, knights and people of the Roman world). But in general the archaeological evidence for the cult of Isis presents a peculiar (and revealing) set of problems. The major temples of Isis in Italy have not yet

103 Map 2 no. 12.
104 Hörig and Schwertheim (1987) 221–35. Well-being of emperor: *ILS* 1707 = Hörig and Schwertheim (1987) no. 372; *AE* (1940) 71 = Hörig and Schwertheim (1987) no. 356; *AE* (1940) 80 = Hörig and Schwertheim (1987) no. 385.

been systematically excavated, but have been reconstructed instead on the basis of casual finds – a process which may give them a much too exclusively 'Egyptian' image.[105] So, for example, the sanctuary at Beneventum (which is known from inscriptions) has had numerous 'Egyptian' finds in the town assigned to it – images of Isis, Apis bulls, Sphinxes, as well as the 'Egyptianizing' Domitian we have just mentioned. For all we know, other 'non-Egyptian' images may once have belonged there too. But in the archaeological record a casual find of a statue of (say) Hermes or Venus is never likely to be assigned to a shrine of Isis. There is, of course, a circular process at work here: if only objects with a strongly Egyptian style are associated with Isiac shrines, then Isiac shrines will inevitably appear exclusively Egyptian. This is another clear example of how archaeological interpretation and archaeological assumptions can affect our understanding of cult practice and ideas.

In the case of the 'Persian' cosmology of the cult of Mithras archaeology has offered particularly important material. Excavations have shown that, in some Mithraic sanctuaries at least, the cult (which literary evidence might have encouraged us to see as rigidly separate from the civic pantheon) did allow a place to a wide range of other deities. For example, in the excavations of the sanctuary of Mithras under the church of S. Prisca in Rome heads of Sarapis, Venus and perhaps Mars were discovered, as well as representations of Hecate, Fortuna, Dionysus and Asclepius.[106] And in that same sanctuary is preserved, painted on the wall, a line of verse: 'fertile earth, through whom Pales procreates everything'.[107] The line, which may be the opening of a Mithraic prayer, celebrates the role of the Roman deity Pales (whose festival, the Parilia, we discussed in chapter 4) in the promotion of fertility – though it is unclear from this single surviving line how that was related to the role of Mithras himself. In addition, as in the other cults we have looked at, dedications were often made to Mithras for the well-being of the emperor. The arcane and astronomical aspects of the cult of Mithras, which have been over-emphasized in some current interpretations, co-existed with the traditional god and the temporal order. There appears nevertheless to be an important difference in the incorporation of

105 Isis: *Inschriften von Kyme* 41 = **12.4a**; Apuleius, *Metamorphoses* XI.5 = **12.4b**. Sanctuaries: Wild (1984); Pompeii: *Alla ricerca di Iside* (1992) 70. Beneventum: Müller (1969); Malaise (1972a) 294–305; Corinth: Apuleius, *Metamorphoses* XI.17. In the western empire only the sanctuary at Sabratha has been dealt with fully; that may have had a statue of Heracles: Pesce (1953) 51.

106 Map 3 no. 37; Vermaseren and van Essen (1965) 134–7, 342 nos. 20–21, 343 no. 24, 383 no. 966, 435 no. 11, 447 nos. 82, 84. Similarly the Walbrook sanctuary in London contained images of Minerva, Sarapis, Mercury, Water-god, Genius, Dioscorus, Bacchus and Mother-god with Rider gods: J. Toynbee (1986). Mithraic reliefs from Gaul and Germany feature at the top an assembly of gods: *CIMRM* 966, Saarburg; 1292, Osterburken. Cf. Clauss (1990) 153–74.

107 Vermaseren and van Essen (1965) 187 = **12.5h(iv)**. On the Parilia see above, pp. 174–6; Alföldy (1989) 93 for (rare) dedications to Pales.

the various deities of the traditional pantheon between the cult of Mithras and the cult of Jupiter Dolichenus. In the cult of Dolichenus there seems to have been some attempt to set the civic pantheon into a new structure, now under the Syrian god; in the cult of Mithras the evidence that we have suggests no more than that individual members of the cult did sometimes feel that particular Graeco-Roman gods had their place in a Mithraic sanctuary, choosing, in other words, to re-locate the traditions of Rome within a new cosmic setting. The overlap and inter-relationship between traditional and alternative cults could take many different forms.

A sanctuary of Syrian gods on the Janiculan hill in Rome shows how complicated such inter-relationships might be.[108] The excavations of the sanctuary offer little secure archaeological evidence for its character before the fourth century A.D., but epigraphic evidence illuminates the cult in the second century A.D. The main deity was Jupiter Optimus Maximus Heliopolitanus, who (like Jupiter Dolichenus) combines the principal deity of Rome with an 'origin' at Heliopolis (Baalbek in Lebanon); and the second-century phase of the sanctuary seems to have been sponsored by a wealthy Syrian living in Rome, one Gaionas. The links with the traditional Roman religious order are much more intricate than the dedications on behalf of the emperor made to the god by Marcus Antonius Gaionas would, on their own, suggest. The eastern 'origin' of the cult itself is complicated by the fact (as we shall see in chapter 7) that Heliopolis in Lebanon was in the territory of the Roman *colonia* of veteran soldiers at Berytus (modern Beirut), and that from the first century A.D. the cult in Heliopolis was itself in part a Roman adaptation, designed for the Roman settlers there. Besides, dedications on the Janiculan linked Syrian deities to the Furrina nymphs, whose ancient grove (and spring of Furrina) was near the Syrian sanctuary and whose festival figured in the official calendars of the Republic and early empire. The new deities were thus tied to the traditions of a specific place in Rome.

The relationship of Christianity to Rome – both as a place and a political power – is articulated rather differently in surviving Christian writing. One strand of thought, going back to the Book of Revelation, identified Rome, 'the whore of Babylon', as a satanic power, and envisaged apocalyptic doom falling on the Roman empire. Many outsiders certainly thought that the Christians were hostile to Rome, either because they had heard of their apocalyptic hopes or simply because of the Christian refusal to participate in religious rituals. In striking contrast with the other cults we have reviewed, early Christianity did not incorporate rituals celebrated for

---

108 Map 2 no. 16. Savage (1940) 29, 35–9, 44–52; Goodhue (1975); Hajjar (1977) 357–80, 523–58; Mele (1982); Calzini Gysens and Duthoy (1992); Steinby (1993–) III.138–43. See below, p. 292 on Gaionas and pp. 384–6 for the fourth-century sanctuary; Varro, *On the Latin Language* V.84 = **8.1a** on Furrina (who became plural under the empire).

the emperor's well-being. A second strand of Christian thinking, however, and one which is more prominent in the surviving texts, sought to counter the fears of non-Christians. Defenders of Christianity cited biblical passages to argue that they recognized the power of the state and did in fact pray in their own terms for the emperor. Some even hoped for the conversion of the emperor to Christianity. But such arguments, which still explicitly rejected the accepted religious underpinning of imperial power, could not persuade traditionalists. Emperors and Roman officials demanded that what *they* regarded as divine blessing be invoked on behalf of the state.[109]

The novelty of many of these alternative cults partly depended on a relationship to texts and to the written word as a generator (or guarantor) of religious meaning that was strikingly different from Roman civic cults. The traditional cults certainly had books of religious formulae, which preserved the proper texts of prayers; there were also numerous priestly collections of religious rules and decisions. But they had no written works which established their tenets and doctrine, or provided explanation (religious *exegesis*) of their rituals or moral prescription for their adherents. Exegesis and prescription *were* offered within traditional civic paganism – but outside any formal religious context, and by men of learning or philosophers, who might, or might not, also be priests. By contrast in the cult of Isis great emphasis was laid on the sacred books, allegedly deriving from Egypt – which, as we have seen, were featured in the initiation of Lucius in Apuleius' novel. Judaism too had a large number of writings long regarded as authoritative and which formed the basis of much of their religious observance; so, for example, over the year in a synagogue the first five books of what Christians came to call the Old Testament were read out, and the members of the community received instruction in their 'ancestral philosophy', that is, the scriptural texts.[110] In the period after the destruction of the temple at Jerusalem, Jewish sages in Palestine, and later Babylon, began to create elaborate exegeses of the scriptures and rules for ordinary living, which were compiled from the late second century A.D. onwards. Christianity also had a wide range of doctrinal texts, on the life of Christ and the lives of the apostles, as well as treatises on theology and pastoral matters. The sheer diversity of these texts became a major factor in debates in the second and third centuries A.D. between those who saw themselves as 'Orthodox' Christians, and those they viewed as 'heretics': 'Orthodox'

109 Apocalyptics: Revelation 13. 17–18; Hippolytus, *Commentary on Daniel* IV.5–8 (*Griechischer christ. Schrift.* I.196–207); *Sibylline Oracles* VIII.1–216. Defences: Justin, *Apology* 17; Tertullian, *Apology* 30–2; Origen, *Against Celsus* VIII.73–5. Cf. Pagels (1988) 32–56; Alexander (1991). For requests for divine favour by emperors in the early fourth century A.D.: Eusebius, *Ecclesiastical History* VII.17.5; Lactantius, *On the Deaths of the Persecutors* 48.2–12 (= **11.13a**).

110 Isis: above, n. 95. Jews: Philo, *Embassy* 156 = **12.6c(ii)**; Schürer (1973–87) II.447–54. Sages: **12.6g**. For the role of writing in traditional religion, above, pp. 9–10; 24–6; 195.

churches based their beliefs and practice on selections from the whole range of Christian texts that were quite different from those chosen by 'heretics'. Only gradually did an agreed canon of authoritative Christian texts emerge.[111]

In the cult of Mithras we know very little about the role, status or content of its various religious books and treatises. On the other hand, from writers such as Porphyry and from the iconography of its cult images and places, we can reconstruct a good deal of what seems to have been a complex and peculiar system of symbols and 'received wisdom'. This was partly structured around the names of the sequence of Mithraic grades of initiation themselves: 'raven', 'male bride', 'soldier', 'lion', 'Persian', 'sun-runner', 'father'. It seems clear that some of these names drew their significance from (and, at the same time, manipulated) the common-knowledge and day-to-day beliefs of the time. Ravens, for example, were commonly believed in the Roman world to be able to talk and to understand signs from the gods; Mithraic 'ravens' were on the boundary between outsiders and full initiates, just as the real bird was on that between animals, humans and the divine. Not all the grades played on 'ordinary' beliefs in this way: the 'male bride', for example, is a deliberate paradox, presumably the subject of complicated exegesis within the cult.[112]

Mithraic temples seem to have had a particular role in the cult's symbolic system. They were not simply replicas of Mithras' cave in Persia; some also had a complex astronomical symbolism which turned the temple into a 'map' of the universe.[113] Roman *templa* also had a cosmic orientation: the Latin word *templum* denoted an area of the heavens; and we have already seen in this chapter how the design of the Hadrianic Pantheon evoked the vault of heaven with the sun. But Mithraic temples were far more explicit and complex in their symbolism: one end, for example, seems regularly to have stood for the dark, the night and the west, the other for the light (of Mithras), the sun and the east – so giving a *religious* 'orientation' to the temple, which might be exactly the opposite of its real-life, *geographical*, orientation; the axis of (religious) north and south might also be marked, as well as the planetary spheres and the signs of the zodiac.

Astronomical learning is also on display in the Mithraic sanctuary – as a way, it seems, of showing the celestial journey of the human soul through the fixed stars. The characteristic scene of the killing of the bull by Mithras, regularly shown at the 'east' end of the temple, provides a clear example of this. These representations often include a striking, and at first sight baffling, set of symbols: a dog, snake and scorpion. But these, together with the bull itself, almost certainly correspond to a set of constellations: Canis

---

111 Below, pp. 304–7. Canon: Campenhausen (1972); J. Barton (1986); Metzger (1987).
112 Below, n. 124; R. L. Gordon (1980a) 48–54; Beck (1984) 2056–63. A collection of Mithraic documents: **4.6; 12.5a.**
113 Porphyry, *On the Cave* 6 = **4.6c**; Beck (1976), (1977–8); R. L. Gordon (1989) 50–60.

Major/Minor, Hydra, Scorpio, Taurus. Mithras himself may be associated with the Sun, and the Sun's main constellation Leo. Above the scene of bull-killing itself, the signs of the zodiac are sometimes shown; while beside it stand two figures known as Cautes (shown with raised torch) and Cautopates (shown with lowered torch), who represented the opposites of *day* and *night*, *growth* and *decay*, and oversaw the soul's entry to and departure from this life.[114]

Many of the new cults, as we have already seen, proclaimed the superiority of one single supreme deity: Jupiter Dolichenus was described in the Aventine sanctuary as 'protector of the whole world'; Isis was believed to be the supreme power in the universe and the origin of civilization; the cult of Mithras focussed on the mediating exploits of Mithras; Judaism and Christianity both stressed the might of one god. How far then should any or all of these cults be seen as monotheistic? Were they, as a group, a reflection of a general trend in the imperial period towards monotheism?

Without a doubt there were some adherents of these alternative cults who recognized no other deity but *their* god (whether Isis, Mithras or the Christian god); adherents who were, in the very strictest sense, monotheists. It seems also fairly clear that such people increased in number over our period. It is much harder, however, to trace any general, unified trend towards monotheism. Not only were the cosmologies of the various cults so different that the single label 'monotheistic' unhelpfully blurs out the profound differences between them: even within Judaism and Christianity (the central cases of monotheistic cults) there were considerable variants – in Judaism god was generally seen as the head of a number of divine beings, who were not always under his control,[115] and in Christianity the supreme god was related, in different ways by different Christian groups, to the Son and the Holy Spirit.[116] But monotheism itself is no single phenomenon. Rather, it occupies part of a spectrum between an extreme form of polytheism (where all of a large number of deities are treated as effectively equal) and an equally extreme position that insists on the existence of only one god; and, in practice, it rarely draws a clear distinction between those who believe that their particular deity is by far the most important and powerful (perhaps, like Isis, incorporating all others) and those who believe that their deity is literally the only one.[117] Of course, within official Roman civic paganism there were well established traditions which claimed the supremacy for one god – whether Jupiter Optimus Maximus, or Elagabalus; and private worship throughout pagan antiquity must always

---

114 **12.5b**; Porphyry, *On the Cave* 24–5 = **12.5g**. Beck (1984) 2079–89; (1988); (1994). Cf. generally R. L. Gordon (1989). Roman *templa*: Varro, *On the Latin Language* VII.8–10 = **4.4**; above, pp. 22–3.

115 Hayman (1991).

116 Kelly (1978) 83–162.

117 The term 'henotheism' is sometimes used to describe personal devotion to one god, without rejection of other gods: Versnel (1990) 35–8.

have left open the possibility for any individual to devote him- or herself exclusively to one deity. The claim to a new supremacy for a particular god may well have been an important part of the appeal of the elective cults; but even this did not necessarily, on its own, mark a complete rupture with the traditional religious practice.[118]

As we have seen over the last few pages, the issue of similarity and difference between traditional and alternative cults depends in many respects (just as it must have done in antiquity) on your standpoint, or on which particular features you decide to stress. For some worshippers or some observers, for example, the cult of Isis could represent a complete rejection of traditional, civic paganism – for others it was part of, or an extension of, traditional religious life. There are nevertheless a few particular features of new cults which serve to mark them out much more strongly from traditional religions than this model would suggest. These features might be grouped under the term 'transformation': for all these new cults claimed to make much more of an impact than traditional religions on the everyday world and on the after-life of their adherents.[119]

In this life, most elective cults offered a new sense of community. As we have seen, the worship of traditional deities could have a social dimension. The association of Diana and Antinous, for example, met six times a year for sacrifice and dinner, and ensured that members had a decent burial. But most new, elective cults offered a much stronger type of membership, which they marked by special initiatory rituals. So, for example, in the cult of Isis, alongside the relatively public rituals, individual initiations became increasingly important from the first century A.D. onwards; members took part in the rituals at the main sanctuaries, or met in private groups, such as the one which (as we have already seen) used a house on the Aventine hill.[120] The most vivid account we have of Isiac initiation concerns Lucius in Apuleius' novel *The Metamorphoses*.[121] Lucius, miraculously transformed by the goddess Isis from a donkey back into a man, sought formal initiation into her cult at Corinth in Greece, through purity, abstinence from unclean foods, and daily service in her temple. After the secrets of the holy books were explained to him by the priest, he underwent an initiation that took him down to the entrance of the underworld and brought him back to life again. Lucius then, at the instruction of the goddess, went to Rome, where he prayed daily in the temple of Isis on the Campus Martius. But, because he was a stranger in that sanctuary, though not to the *religio*, he was told by Isis to undergo two further initiations, one into the mysteries of Osiris her

---

118 On some debates see **2.10**.

119 The difference is often expressed in terms of the offer of 'salvation', which has heavy Christian connotations and tends to set up misleading comparisons between the new cults and Christianity. 'Transformation' seems a much more helpful term.

120 U. Bianchi (1980); Malaise (1981); Burkert (1987) 40–1. Aventine house above, n. 62.

121 Extracts: XI.5–6, 23–5 = **12.4b**.

consort and one again into the mysteries of Isis.[122] Apuleius at several points teases the reader about what he can or will tell (even in a fictional account) about the experience of religious initiation. Much of his point is to explore the tensions of such a religion: how far secrecy is compatible with the retelling of a (fictional) initiation; what is secret, or where the secrets reside, in an initiatory religion; how far such secrecy challenges the structures of Graeco-Roman civic life.

Initiation inevitably meant entry into another (secret) world; and it was particularly associated with those foreign cults which met only privately. In the cult of Mithras individuals probably belonged primarily to one Mithraic sanctuary and its group of worshippers. Inscriptions record lists of initiates, varying from 10 to 36. One inscription, for example, records the 34 members involved in the restoration of a sanctuary in A.D. 183 (of whom 5 died of the plague of A.D. 184), and the subsequent annual initiations between then and A.D. 201 of between one and eight new members.[123] The sequence of seven initiatory grades also defined an individual member's rank within the cult: the first three grades were preparatory, not implying full cult membership; the 'lion' was the crucial pivotal rank, while the 'father' represented the highest degree of perfection. Men progressed up through the grades, passing through fresh rituals of initiation, each with its own complex symbolism.[124] Individuals presumably belonged primarily to one Mithraic sanctuary and its group of worshippers – and moved up the Mithraic ranks within their own particular 'congregation'.

Christians too had a set of procedures for new members, which varied from group to group and over time. One common pattern, at least by the late second century A.D., had a transitional phase leading to baptism; people in this position, which could last for up to three years, were known as 'catechumens'.[125] A community of Christian initiates had a particularly strong sense of group identity. It was only Christians (and Jews) who practised charity towards their own members (the poor, widows, prisoners); and Jews and Christians alone had cemeteries specific to their faiths (no cemeteries in Rome were reserved for initiates of the other cults).

Membership of the new cults affected, in different ways, the everyday life of their members. As we have seen in earlier chapters, the traditional

---

122 The extra two initiations are odd. Winkler (1985) 215–23 treats them as subversive of the first one, but they show at most Lucius' over-enthusiasm.

123 Piccottini (1994), from Virunum. Cf. *CIMRM* 2296 = **12.5c(viii)** (Istros).

124 Vermaseren (1963) 129–53; above, n. 112; Brashear (1992) for initiatory catechism from Egypt (below, p. 303). Porphyry, *On Abstinence* IV.16 = **12.5d**; Tertullian, *On the Soldier's Crown* 15 = **12.5e**; sanctuary of Felicissimus, Ostia = **12.5a**; Porphyry, *On the Cave* 15 = **12.5g**. 'Lion' and 'Father' are the only grades commonly found in inscriptions.

125 On the catechumenate see Hippolytus, *Apostolic Tradition* 15–19. Modern accounts tend to ignore this institution, and present Christian conversion as instantaneous, like Paul's experience on the road to Damascus.

cults of Rome were based on (and, in turn, acted to legitimate) the public status of individuals within the community of the state – whether citizen, matron, or *pontifex*. What was distinctive about the new cults was their drive toward a strong religious identity through strictly controlled rules of behaviour; and they created new statuses and new ways of life that may have started within the walls of the sanctuary, but extended outside those walls too. In theory, just as Apuleius' Lucius was instructed by Isis herself, Isiac initiates were supposed to devote their whole life to the goddess, to obey the rules of her cult, and to practise perfect purity. Mithraic initiates were also expected to obey strong rules of purity and to oppose evil in the world.[126] Jews, to the anger of some non-Jews, kept themselves apart from their neighbours by special dietary rules and by the celebration of their own calendar (resting on the Sabbath). Christians were expected to mark their difference by living a different life, often defined through particular control of sexuality or a particular régime of the body: some Christians, for example, made a public parade of their choice to retain their virginity.[127] In all these religions, though, practice must have varied widely. Individuals and individual communities must have defined their own norms; there were, no doubt, as many who lapsed from the rules (at least in their strictest form) as adhered to them.

In some of the new cults this 'transformation' affected the fate of the initiate after death, as well as in the day-to-day world of this life. Traditional pagan culture offered all kinds of views of death and the after-life: ranging from a terrifying series of punishments for those who had sinned in this life, through a more or less pleasant state of being that followed but was secondary to this life, to uncertainty or denial that any form of after-life was possible (or knowable).[128] The traditional cults of Rome included rituals that honoured, commemorated and made offerings to the dead: the annual festival of the Parentalia, for example, involved feasting at the tombs of relatives and ancestors. But the official state cult did not particularly emphasize the fate of the individual after death, or urge a particular view of the after-life. Some of the new cults, on the other hand, constructed death much more sharply as a 'problem' – and, at the same time, offered a 'solution'.[129] Certainly, not all the new cults promised life after

---

126 Isis: Apuleius, *Metamorphoses* XI.6 (= **12.4b**), 19. Mithras: Porphyry, *On the Cave* 15 = **12.5g**; R. L. Gordon (1975) 241. One question is how far Mithraic initiates felt an exclusive allegiance to their cult; however, despite what some scholars have claimed, Tertullian, *On the Crown* 15 = **12.5e** does not show that Mithraic soldiers were exempted from wearing garlands at military sacrifices.

127 Jews: Tacitus, *Histories* V.4–5 – **11.8a**; Juvenal 14.96–106 = **11.8b**. Christians: Lane Fox (1986) 336–74; Brown (1988).

128 A range of documents on death and the after-life are collected at **9.6**, with Cicero, *On the State* VI.13–16 = **9.1d**.

129 But one should not therefore assume that the pre-Christian world in general was yearning for a new answer to the 'problem' of death.

death; in the case of Jupiter Dolichenus, for example, there is no evidence to suggest that immortality was an issue.[130] And those religions that did make claims about a future life after death presented radically different pictures. When in a dream Isis promised Lucius escape from his ass's body, she said that he would be subject to her for the rest of his life, which she could prolong beyond what the fates appointed, and after death he would find her shining in the darkness of the underworld. His subsequent initiation, as we saw, took him down to the entrance of the underworld and back to life again.[131] The cult of Isis had implications for life and death, but even so more emphasis is placed on extending the span of life than on the after-life – which is pictured in fairly undifferentiated terms. The transformational aspects of the cult of Mithras are more striking, as the initiate ascended through the seven grades. In addition to its cultic title (raven, male bride, etc.), each grade was correlated with a different planet; and the soul of the initiate was probably conceived as rising during his lifetime further and further away from the earth, finally achieving *apogenesis* or birth away from the material world. That is, the progressive transformation of the soul of the initiate in this life, on which much of the cult focussed, was probably conceived as continuing after death.[132] This is a quite different conception from the ideas of immortality or resurrection that developed among some Jews by the first century A.D.,[133] and became particularly associated with Christianity – which offered not only a radically new life here and now, but also the hope of a bodily resurrection and a glorious after-life.

Over the centuries, the Christian model has created a demand for immortality; but, of course, the other cults were not 'failures' because they did not promise this particular kind of life after death. In fact, through the first centuries A.D., Christian writers had to defend the idea of bodily resurrection against general mockery; and it was this very strange notion that prompted the writing of some of the first technical works of Christian theology.[134] Only a Christian perspective finds bodily resurrection self-

---

130 Nor was the cult of Attis concerned with the after-life (Burkert (1987) 25). Cf. generally Burkert (1987) 21–8, 48, 105.

131 Above, p. 287. For control of fate, *Inschriften von Kyme* 41 = **12.4a**. For relief by Osiris in the underworld, Vidman (1969) 459–63 (no. 459 = **9.6c**).

132 Origen, *Against Celsus* VI.22 = **12.5f**; Porphyry, *On the Cave* 6 = **4.6c**. Cf. Turcan (1982); Beck (1988) 77–82 denies Mithraic interest in the after-life; the case depends on the weight given to Celsus and Porphyry. A dipinto in the Santa Prisca sanctuary refers to the pouring of blood, possibly for the benefit of initiates, but the reading is uncertain: **12.5h(xii)**.

133 Schürer (1973–87) II.539–44; Sanders (1992) 298–303; cf. *CIL* VI 39086 = Noy (1995) no. 103 = **12.6d(iii)**.

134 The Christian defence begins with Acts of the Apostles XVII.32 and continues in the various *Apologies*. Pre-Constantinian treatises were written by Justin (?), Athenagoras, Hippolytus, Tertullian, Origen, Peter of Alexandria and Methodius; cf. Origen, *Against Celsus* VIII.49 = **9.6d**.

rior to the different versions of after-life (or not) within tra-
ın thought, or to the Isiac model of immortality, or to the
ion of the soul of the Mithraic initiate.

rs

ıe new cults attract? Did the different 'messages' we have just
ɛal to some sections of the inhabitants of Rome more than to
the poor more commonly to be found among the adherents
? Women more commonly than men? Did these alternative
ιct those who had only a small role to play in the traditional
d the political order that those cults sustained? Were they, in
'religions of disadvantage'?
o simple answer to those questions. We have already discussed
within the population of Rome, which had no single axis
ʻilege and disadvantage: in a society where some of the richest and
ɛd members were to be found outside (were indeed ineligible for)
he élite, it makes no sense to imagine a single category of 'the dis-
advantageɑ . Besides, it is now (and no doubt always was for most outside
observers) very hard to reconstruct accurately the membership of any particular cult; for apparently casual references to a cult's adherents in the writing of the period are often part and parcel of an attack on that cult – deriding
a religion as being, for example, the business of women and slaves. Occasionally membership lists survive, inscribed in stone or on bronze. We shall
exploit these in what follows; but even such inscriptions (which were
inevitably put up for some particular reason on some particular occasion)
may not reveal a typical cross-section of a cult's followers. Christianity is here
a special case. The spotlight cast by the New Testament texts on the earliest
history of the religion provided much fuller information than anything we
have for the spread and social composition of the church over the next two
hundred years.

We shall begin with the question of how far the élite (defined in a variety of ways) were involved in these cults; for the fact that the rich in the
Roman world inscribed their activities on stone or bronze can help us trace
their involvement in and around these alternative cults.

Male members of the senatorial order appear conspicuously absent from
the elective cults. No senators are attested as initiates of Jupiter Dolichenus,
Jupiter Optimus Maximus Heliopolitanus, Isis, Mithras or (probably)
Christianity before the mid third century A.D. Their interest in these cults,
as we shall see in chapter 8, became strong only in the fourth century A.D.
Before then, from Rome and Ostia just two senators are definitely attested

135 *ILS* 6149 = **12.4c**; Malaise (1972b) 79.

as members of the cult of Isis.[135] There were some Christian senators and knights by the mid third century, against whom the emperor Valerian directed particular attention in his ruling against the Christians of A.D. 258, but presumably they were a tiny minority of the Roman élite.[136] The rules of dress and behaviour associated with initiation in the various alternative cults are no doubt a significant factor here: the public parade of 'alternative' religious status was hardly compatible with the civic and religious rituals, and the codes of dress, associated with a public senatorial (or even equestrian) career.

But there is a question of what counts as 'adherence' to a particular cult; for it was obviously possible to favour or support (or be intrigued by) a religion without being an initiate in the strictest sense. Senators and equestrians certainly patronized cults in this way. So, for example, senior army officers, whether senators or equestrians, made dedications to Mithras during their period of command in the provinces. They may have found it politic to encourage a cult that was popular with their men, without becoming initiated themselves or (so far as we can tell) continuing their association with the cult on their return to Rome.[137] But they too may have found a more specifically religious appeal in the cult; while such élite involvement – even if marginal – no doubt made a considerable difference to the standing and public image of the cult.

This pattern of cult *patronage* is found also among those of equestrian status at Rome (a status defined essentially by free birth and wealth); unlike senators, the majority of Roman knights held no specific Roman office. In the sanctuary of Jupiter Dolichenus on the Aventine one man in making a gift to the sanctuary proudly describes himself as a Roman knight; though in this case, from the later third century, the man also claims membership of the cult (as a 'candidate', *candidatus*).[138] On another occasion we can see a wealthy patron displaying his *aspirations* for Roman civic status at the same time as his support of an alternative cult. Gaionas, who paid for the second century phase of the Syrian sanctuary on the Janiculan, stressed in the commemorative inscription his holding of what is probably a (minor) Roman office with responsibility for night-time security and fire patrol.[139] As we have already seen, Gaionas was in fact a wealthy Syrian, who belonged to the middle ranks of the free population of Rome; but here in the context of an apparently 'foreign' cult, he classifies himself as a *Roman* office-holder.

136 Eck (1971), (1979); above, p. 241.
137 Note, however, an *eques Romanus* as a Pater in a military sanctuary of Mithras in Rome (Map 3 no. 2; Lissi Caronna (1986) 31) and the initiation of senatorial tribunes at a sanctuary in the legionary base at Aquincum (Eck (1989b) 48). There was apparently no favour accorded to the cult of Mithras by the emperor until the fourth century A.D.: M. Simon (1979).
138 Map 2 no. 12; *ILS* 4316 = **12.3b**.
139 Map 2 no. 16. Nocturnal office (*cistiber*): *CIL* VI 36793, with Goodhue (1975) 31 n. 90; *ILS* 398 = *IGUR* 166, with *AE* (1980) 38; *ILS* 4294. Above, n. 108.

Outside Rome, members of local élites (those we may define as holding the rank of 'town councillor') were involved in these cults much more widely and fully. The cult of Isis, for example, had a strikingly different profile even in the other towns of Italy. It had been established in Greece since the fourth century B.C., initially as the preserve of immigrants from Egypt; but, from the second century B.C. onwards, local citizens too had held priesthoods of Isis, which seem to have counted much as ordinary civic priesthoods. It was probably as a result of commercial contact with the Greek world that the cult of Isis appeared in Italy in the mid second century B.C. – where it again received the support of the local élites. At Pompeii near Naples town councillors became priests of the cult, and Isiac initiates even signalled their support for people seeking election to civic magistracies.[140] Judaism too was a long established cult in some Greek cities of Asia Minor. At Aphrodisias in the third century A.D. nine non-Jewish members of the town council are attested as 'god-fearers' on a list of donors from the local synagogue.[141]

Not all such cults outside Rome, however, followed this pattern of more widespread élite involvement. The cult of Mithras hardly penetrated local élites at all, remaining a strongly military cult.[142] A very few town councillors are attested in the cult; but the majority of these come from the 'military' provinces, in the Danube area – a region which had a weak local civic tradition, and where many councillors were serving or retired soldiers. Christianity also fitted uneasily with local office holding. Indeed one accusation levelled against Christians was that they scorned magistracies; and it is only rarely before the fourth century A.D. that declared Christians are found holding local offices. Christians are attested, for example, as councillors in one part of Asia Minor in the third century A.D. and a church council held in Spain after A.D. 312 banned from communion Christians who had been magistrates or imperial priests (the length of the ban depending on whether they had sacrificed, given games or only worn the priestly crown).[143] These differences are partly a reflection of different definitions of 'ancestral' religion. Local élites, like the Roman élite, were concerned to maintain their 'ancestral' local cults; but what counted as that varied from place to place. The goddess Isis, for example, might claim longstanding, if not 'ancestral', acceptability in various parts of the Roman world; the god Mithras hardly anywhere.

The mass of support for the new cults in Rome itself must have come

140 Dunand (1980); Malaise (1972b) 75–85; (1984); elections: *ILS* 6419f; 6420b (trans. in Lewis and Reinhold (1990) II.237).
141 Reynolds and Tannenbaum (1987) = **12.6e**. Cf. generally Trebilco (1991).
142 Mithras: R. L. Gordon (1972); Clauss (1992) 266.
143 Origen, *Against Celsus* VIII.75; Minucius Felix, *Octavius* 8.4 (= **11.11d**); Lane Fox (1986) 294–5; Council of Elvira canons 2–4, 55–6 in *Patrologia Latina* LXXXIV 302, 307–8 = Martínez Díez and Rodriguez (1984) 242, 259–60, with dating of Lane Fox (1986) 664–8 (trans. in Stevenson (1987) no. 265).

from those who made up the vast bulk of the 'ordinary' inhabitants of the capital – freeborn citizens, slaves and ex-slaves. But within that vast population, did particular groups dominate membership? We have already seen that some of the new cults in Rome were supported by foreigners in the city, continuing to worship the gods of their native land. But did men and women of eastern origin or descent predominate more generally in these alternative religions? Certainly many of the names recorded in these religions seem on their own to imply eastern origin. In Rome and Italy the priesthood of Isis remained in the hands of immigrants from Egypt, and about half the worshippers of Isis and Sarapis epigraphically attested in Rome have Greek names. Likewise the inscribed list of initiates in the Aventine sanctuary of Jupiter Dolichenus includes a good number with Greek and Semitic names. A variety of languages, in addition to Latin, is also attested in these cults. Greek is the commonest of these: Mithraic dedications were often inscribed in Greek (sometimes as well as Latin); two thirds of the Jewish texts from Rome are written in Greek (the rest in Latin, with a tiny number in Hebrew or Aramaic), and the synagogue services in Rome (as in other Mediterranean diaspora communities) were probably mainly in Greek.[144] Other languages included Egyptian (and pseudo-Egyptian) in the cult of Isis, and Aramaic in the cult of the Palmyrene gods.[145]

It would be misleading, however, to argue simply from these foreign elements within the cults that the majority of the worshippers themselves were eastern in a literal sense. Of course, Greek language can (and certainly sometimes does) indicate a Greek speaking origin. But, as we have noted already, many of the foreign aspects of these cults were part of their symbolic repertoire, their construction of a source of authority outside the city – rather than a clear indication of foreign origin. Besides, names alone can be a very tricky guide to ethnic or cultural origin. It is absolutely clear that many Romans with apparently eastern names had no actual connection (or only the remotest) with the east itself. Such names, for example, were commonly given to slaves born and bred in Rome – not even necessarily of eastern descent – and they were inherited sometimes by their free descendants. They are certainly not enough to prove in general a predominance of easterners within the new cults as a whole.

There is clearer evidence for membership of the cult of Mithras, which had a more specific and restricted appeal than most of the new religions. Here ethnic origin does not seem to be particularly at issue. Mithraic inscriptions suggest that the main adherents of the cult were soldiers, up to the level of centurion, imperial slaves and ex-slaves, and also slaves and ex-slaves of private citizens. Throughout the empire, the classic location for a Mithraic shrine is an army camp; and in Ostia, half of the Mithraists

---

144 Isis: Malaise (1972b) 67–75, 163–70; Jupiter Dolichenus: *AE* (1940) 75 = **12.3a**; *ILS* 4316 = **12.3b**; Jews: Schürer (1973–87) III.1.142–4; Noy (1995) 513–14.
145 Cf. nn. 60, 81.

known from inscriptions were slaves or ex-slaves.[146] The experience common to these groups was that of discipline, hierarchy and the possibility of self-advancement. The structure of the cult mirrored this experience. Those of higher rank (centurions or civilians) tended to fill the higher grades of initiation, and the sequence of grades, with their planetary analogues, offered a parallel 'career' that conformed to and confirmed the everyday world of the participants.

The history and spread of Christianity at Rome in the first and second centuries A.D. offer a more diverse picture than this. The earliest Roman Christians seem to have been predominantly Greek-speaking; Paul's *Letters* to the church at Rome, for example, as to other Christian communities were written in Greek. This use of Greek as a common tongue between different Christian groups is a stronger argument than the language of names alone; and it may well indicate that members of the church were drawn initially from immigrants from the Greek-speaking east. In the course of the second century A.D., however, it is clear that Christians made increasing use of Latin: both the Old and the New Testaments seem to have been translated into Latin in the second century (though these versions do not survive), and so were some other Christian texts originally written in Greek; the liturgy, on the other hand, the most conservative element of ecclesiastical practice, remained in Greek until the third quarter of the fourth century A.D.[147] The growing importance of Latin might then mirror the growing domestication of the Christian church at Rome through the third into the fourth century A.D., and its increasing spread among groups whose native tongue was Latin.

By A.D. 200 Christians were found in Rome at every level of society: some upper class women (and a few men) were, at least by that date, prominent in the Christian community; from the earliest times Christian slaves and ex-slaves had been employed in leading Roman households, including the emperor's;[148] Christians also served in the ranks of the army in the second and third centuries A.D. (though not, it seems, as officers) – most, presumably, managing to fudge the issue of attendance at pagan sacrifices obligatory in military service.[149] More generally, to the distress of a contemporary Christian writer, many second-century Roman Christians were 'absorbed in business affairs, wealth, friendship with pagans, and

---

146 R. L. Gordon (1972); Clauss (1992) tabulates the information. The appeal of Jupiter Dolichenus to soldiers: P. M. Brennan in Horsley (1981–) IV.118–26. The Ostian argument is based largely on the Greek-style nomenclature of the Mithraists, which is normally taken to show servile origins (cf. above, n. 1 for the 'cultural phenomenon" visible here).

147 Bardy (1948) 161–4; Lampe (1989) 117–19; below, p. 376.

148 Paul, Letter to Romans 16.10–11; to Philippians 4.22; *ILS* 1738 = **12.7c(i)**; graffito in **2.10b**. Cf. Countryman (1980) for the importance of the wealth of the minority, and problems it caused; and generally Lampe (1989).

149 Helgeland (1979) lists military martyrs. For the religion of the army, below, pp. 324–8.

many other occupations of this world'. This comment reveals as much about the variety of 'Christian' behaviour (however strict the rules were in theory) as it does about the varied social composition of the Christian community.[150]

A contrasting image stresses the poverty of many professed Christians. In addition to the 1500 widows and poor supported by the church in the mid third century A.D., Christian writers could claim that Christians in Rome had to work hard to stay alive, and that even so the majority suffered from cold and hunger.[151] And those who attacked the Christians readily deployed this point in their polemic: Celsus, for example, assumes that most Christians were ill-educated – humble artisans, or children and women (both slave and free) in more substantial houses; while Minucius Felix has his pagan opponent characterize Christians as the dregs of society.[152] These two different images of Christianity do more than reflect the wide social range from which adherents of this new religion were drawn. Within the discourse of (and about) Christianity, *poverty* was clearly vested with symbolic, religious significance just as *foreignness* was in several of the other cults we already have examined: there was, for example, a heavily loaded clash between a Christian ideal of poverty (as reflected in some of the teaching ascribed to Jesus) and the abomination of the poor and destitute in élite pagan culture; in Christianity the poor were both a metaphor and a reality. Precisely this kind of symbolic re-evaluation of poverty made it a particularly attractive religion to the poor as a group; but it also makes it peculiarly difficult for us to trace accurately the presence of the poor (in strictly economic terms) in early Christian communities.[153]

Gender had always been a factor in the organization of cult. It is important to consider how the appeal of the various cults to different genders determined the membership of new religions. The official civic cults of Rome were principally in the control of men – though there were some exceptions. The tending of the flame of the goddess Vesta was, famously, in the charge of six Vestal Virgins; a few male priests (notably the *flamen Dialis*) were obliged to have a wife to share in some of the rituals; while women in the imperial family might themselves hold priesthoods of deified members of their house. Some cults and festivals too demanded the participation of women: one of the main Roman festivals, of the Bona Dea, in fact excluded men (as we saw in chapter 3); and the ceremonies of the

---

150 Hermas, *Shepherd*, Mandata 10.1.3, ed. R. Joly, Sources Chrétiennes 53, p. 186; cf. Simil. 1.50.1, Joly p. 210; Simil. 8.7.4, Joly p. 278; Simil. 9.22.2, Joly p. 338. Lampe (1989) 71–8.

151 Above, n. 66; Minucius Felix, *Octavius* 12.2.

152 Celsus caricatures, but Origen in his reply to Celsus does not dispute his assumptions: Origen, *Against Celsus* III.55 = **11.11c**. Minucius Felix: *Octavius* 8.4 (= **11.11d**), a charge denied at 31.6. Cf. Lane Fox (1986) 293–312.

153 Countryman (1980). Christians, as also Jews, aided the poor (e.g. Justin, *First Apology* 67 = **12.7d(i)a**).

Saecular Games involved 110 matrons, the number apparently corresponding to the number of years in the *saeculum*. The temple of Fortuna Muliebris, the Fortune of Women, according to tradition had been dedicated by senatorial wives in 493 B.C., four miles from the city of Rome, and served as the focus for their religious activities. In the imperial period it was restored by Augustus' wife Livia (and again by the emperor Septimius Severus, along with his two sons and his wife Julia Domna). Her lavish piety emphasized the importance of the religious role of upper class women.[154] All these roles seem largely restricted to women of senatorial families. But one official festival, marked in the calendar, also explicitly involved women below the senatorial class: the festival of Fortuna Virilis, 'the Fortune of Men', was celebrated by women of both upper and lower rank – with women 'of lower status' (according to one calendar entry) worshipping the deity 'in the baths'.[155]

In general, however, although the *attendance* of women at most religious occasions (including *ludi*) was not prohibited, they had little opportunity to take any active religious role in state cults. So, for example, the occupational or burial associations in the penumbra of the civic cults did not generally include women; only in the purely domestic associations of the great households were women normally members.[156] Much more fundamentally (though the evidence is not entirely clear), they may have been banned – in theory, at any rate – from carrying out animal sacrifice; and so prohibited from any officiating role in *the* central defining ritual of civic religious activity.[157]

These limited roles may have been satisfying to some women; but almost certainly not to all. How far then did women find in the new cults a part to play that was not available to them in civic religions? Upper class male writers regularly portrayed women as particularly liable to succumb to the charms of *superstitio* and feared religious activity by women outside very narrowly defined limits – as is illustrated by the trial of the wife of a senator for her attachment to a foreign *superstitio*, and the strong, negative stereotypes that portrayed the adherents of the cult of Isis, and Christianity, as mainly female.[158] But was there any truth in these male fears? Did women form a particularly significant element in the membership of the new cults as such?

---

154 Cf. Scheid (1992b). Vestals, above, pp. 193–4; Bona Dea, above, pp. 129–30; Saecular Games, above, pp. 201–6; Fortuna Muliebris, Map 4 no. 69, Champeaux (1982–7) I.335–73; Scheid (1992b) 388–90; Livia, above, p. 197.

155 **3.3b**, 1 April. For the various puzzles associated with this festival, Champeaux (1982–7) I.375–95.

156 Waltzing (1895–1900) I.348–9, IV.254–7; Ausbüttel (1982) 42.

157 De Cazanove (1987); Scheid (1992b) 379–80.

158 Above, pp. 213; 226; 229. Bacchanalia: above, pp. 92–6; Livy XXXIX.8–14 = **12.1a**. Isis: Juvenal 6.522–41 = **12.4d**. Christianity: Origen, *Against Celsus* III.55 = **11.11c**; Minucius Felix, *Octavius* 8.4, 9.6 = **11.11d**.

In some cults, definitely not. Women, for example, were not initiated into the cults of Jupiter Dolichenus or Mithras. Indeed the symbolism of the cult of Mithras classified women as noxious hyenas, animals which stood as the antithesis of civilized values – even more aggressively misogynist, it would seem, than the ideology of the official religion. In both cults, however, women are found on the margins, making dedications in the sanctuaries; and in one case having a Mithraic prayer inscribed on stone.[159]

In other cults there were roles for women. They served, for example, as priestesses of Magna Mater and participated in the cult of Dionysus – as they had in the second century B.C., when, so Livy's account runs, the senate had been shocked into imposing controls on the cult in part by the promiscuous mingling of the sexes that was said to characterize it. The Dionysiac cult whose members were recorded on the statue base honouring Agrippinilla included slaves and ex-slaves of both sexes.[160] In the cult of Isis too women were given particular titles and status: 'Bubastiaca', for example – a devotee of the cat goddess Bubastis seen as an aspect of Isis; or 'Memphiana' – an allusion to the major cult of Isis at Memphis in Egypt; and as members of the group of *pastophoroi*, whose job was to open the temple during ceremonies. The ideal of joint participation is represented in a painting of an Isiac sanctuary from Herculaneum: two choruses of male and female initiates, decorously separated, hymned the goddess – who in extant hymns is praised as the founder of marriage and of love between man and woman.[161]

At least outside Palestine, Jewish women held various offices: 'elder', 'leader of the synagogue', and 'mother of the synagogue'.[162] Christianity also attracted many women, who – both rich and poor – had specific roles within the church. Women deacons, for example, had the tasks of instructing female initiates in the faith and of caring for sick women; an 'order' of widows had the tasks of regular prayer and of charity; and women died as martyrs at the hands of the Roman authorities – and were canonized as Christian saints and heroines. Besides, some Christian groups developed a theology in which a female principle was incorporated along with the Son or the Father; and in these groups women became the mouthpiece for prophecies, were teachers and even (it was said) priests and bishops.[163]

159 J. Toynbee (1955–6); R. L. Gordon (1980a); p. 266 above. Hyenas: Porphyry, *On Abstinence* IV.16 = **12.5d**; prayer: Mussies (1982). Note also the portrait bust of an old lady from the Santa Prisca sanctuary: Vermaseren and van Essen (1965) 454 no. 11.

160 Above, n. 80.

161 Heyob (1975) 81–110. Below, pp. 308–9 for the statuses; painting: **12.4e**; hymns: **12.4a**; Veligianni-Terzi (1986).

162 Brooten (1982); Schürer (1973–87) III.1.107; Trebilco (1991) 104–26. Cf. *CIL* VI 29756 = Noy (1995) no. 577 = **12.6d(ii)**; *CIL* VI 29758 = Noy (1995) no. 616 ('not Jewish').

163 Deacons: Pliny, *Letters* X.96.9 = **11.11b**. 'Order' of widows: Hippolytus, *Apostolic Tradition* 10, 23, 30. Martyrs: *Martyrdom of St. Perpetua and Felicitas* (partly in **6.8b**,

Some women no doubt found an opportunity within these cults for all kinds of religious expression not available within the civic cults of Rome. For some women, it may even have been precisely that opportunity which first attracted them to an alternative cult. On the other hand, there is no evidence to suggest that women were particularly powerful within these cults in general or that they dominated the membership in the way suggested by the conventional stereotype of the literature of the period. In the cult of Isis the principal offices were held by men, and the names of cult members recorded in inscriptions do not suggest that women predominated numerically.[164] In Christianity likewise, women were not incorporated into the male hierarchy of priestly office-holding that emerged in the second century A.D. And the 'orthodox' male authorities were uneasy about specifically female groups within the church; many, in fact, came to regard the prominence of women as a marker of 'heretical' or 'heterodox' sects, and roundly condemned it, whether in the theology or in the social organization of Christian communities.[165]

The literary stereotype, in other words, almost certainly exaggerates the number and importance of women in the cults, by representing them effectively as 'women's cults'. Why is this? In part the explanation may lie in the exclusively élite vision of most of the literary sources. Even if women did not dominate the new religions, it seems certain that upper class women were involved in these cults before their male counterparts: wives of senators, that is, were participating in the worship of Isis at a period when no senator was involved in the cult; and wives of senators are attested as Christians from the late second century A.D., before any Christian senator. In fact in the early third century A.D., Callistus the bishop of Rome allowed high status Christian women to cohabit with (rather than marry) Christian men of lower status, even slaves and ex-slaves – for, according to Roman law, they would have lost all senatorial privileges by formal marriage to a man of such lower rank.[166] The literary stereotype, in other words, may reflect a (temporary) difference between the involvement of élite men and women, that did not necessarily apply at other levels of society.

Much more fundamentally, however, the claims of female fascination with foreign religion are embedded in the vast literary and cultural traditions of Graeco-Roman misogyny. Women were regularly associated with the 'Other' in all its forms – the alien world of distant lands, the antitypes

---

7.9b). Heresies: Justin, *First Apology* 26 = **12.7a(i)**, 'Thought of Norea' = **12.7e(i)**; Irenaeus, *Against Heresies* I.6.2–4 = **12.7e(ii)**, I.11.1; Prophets (in Montanism): Eusebius, *Ecclesiastical History* V.16 (cf. below, n. 184); Bishops: Epiphanius, *Against Heresies* 49.2.5 (*Griech. christ. Schrift.* XXXI.243). Fourth century, below, pp. 375–6.

164 Heyob (1975) 81–110, though she tries to argue that the negative stereotype conceals a 'women's religion'; Mora (1990) II.1–29.

165 Gryson (1972); Pagels (1979); Lane Fox (1986) 308–11, 336–74, 404–11; McNamara (1985); Brown (1988) 145–53; Witherington (1990); Kraemer (1992).

166 Hippolytus, *Refutation* IX.12.24–5 = **12.7c(iii)**, with Gülzow (1967); Eck (1971).

of civilization, the wild, transgressive madness of those who broke the rules of civic life. And, at the same time, foreign and 'different' peoples and places were conceptualized or denigrated in specifically female terms. So, for example, one of the commonest themes in the Roman construction of the 'Orient' is the effeminacy of the Oriental man, with his soft skin, perfumes and long hair. In traditional Roman ideology, 'Oriental' cults would inevitably raise questions of gender: the idea that they were 'women's religions' is one important part of this.[167]

Throughout this section we have seen how ancient (and modern) claims about the membership of the various new cults are deeply implicated in the symbolic claims made by (or about) those cults – with their themes of foreignness, poverty and gender. So are any generalizations possible at all about the social composition of these cults and the social range of their members?[168] It is easy enough to imagine how a rootless immigrant, lost in a great city, might have found attraction in the community of worshippers of Isis. But there is no reason to suppose that such people made up the majority of the cult's adherents or explain its success. Likewise it is easy enough to see what 'problems' might in theory be solved by the teaching of the new cults (whether issues of mortality and immortality, or feelings of exclusion from the political order that was sustained by civic cults). But to ascribe the success of these religions to the 'failings' of the civic cults, or the problems to which traditional religion had provided no answer, is only speculation. There is no reason to suppose that significant sections of the population of Rome had long been searching for some kind of spiritual satisfaction which was eventually offered by the new cults; a counter-suggestion holds that the new cults were themselves instrumental in creating the very needs which they satisfied.

We may get further with general questions of membership and appeal by going back to the one cult whose adherents are relatively well known to us. We have already seen that the cult of Mithras recruited heavily from soldiers in the ranks, as well as slaves and ex-slaves. The fixed progression through the Mithraic grades provided such initiates with a structured hierarchy that paralleled the rigid military ranks of their day-to-day life, as well as offering different goals and different rates of progress through this hierarchy – outstripping or transcending their daily experience. The example of Mithraism might, in other words, prompt us to see that the transformation offered by these cults was not a simple rejection of (or escape from) the everyday world, but was rooted and legitimated in the social and political lives of its adherents – that it was tied to the structures of civic life, as much as it rejected them. One important factor here was almost certainly social

---

167 Effeminacy: Juvenal 6.511–21 = **8.7b**; cf. C. Edwards (1993) 63–97. Women: Juvenal 6.314–41 = **13.4**. See above, pp. 165–6.

168 Social composition of Christianity: Malherbe (1977); Judge (1980–1); Meeks (1983) 51–73; Lane Fox (1986) 317–35; Kyrtatas (1987).

mobility. Although sharply socially stratified, the Roman empire worked on the assumption that self-advancement was both desirable and possible: slaves could gain freedom; sons of ex-slaves could enter local councils; members of local élites could enter equestrian service or even the Roman senate.[169] If the adherents of the new cults can be defined as those particularly open to the varied possibilities of transformation, part of that openness may stem from their own position (as freedmen, for example) within the structure of advancement in the social and political world around them. Their everyday experience, that is, found an echo in the promise of the cults to transform lives.[170]

All kinds of other factors were, of course, at work too – different, no doubt, in the different cults; and all of them, as briefly expressed, are inevitably crude oversimplifications of the complex motives any individual, or group, would have in joining a new religion. Our point is to emphasize the relationship between the appeal of these cults to certain groups and the Roman social political order, a relationship much closer than a first glance at their sometimes very 'foreign' symbolism might suggest.

5. Homogeneity and exclusivity

The new cults, which we have examined so far through the context of Rome, also flourished in other parts of the empire; we now return finally to consider how far their structures and practice were similar in different parts of the empire; how far the *same cult title* denoted what was effectively the *same cult*, empire-wide.

The distribution pattern of the different cults differs widely. The cult of Isis in the Hellenistic period is found in Greece, but its expansion under the empire was largely western (Africa, Spain and Gaul); Jupiter Dolichenus appears mainly in Rome and along the Rhine-Danube frontier zone. Mithras was common in Italy, and again in the Rhine-Danube area, but appears hardly at all in Greece, Asia Minor, Syria, Egypt, North Africa or Spain. Jewish communities in the early empire existed in most parts of the eastern Mediterranean: Judaea, Egypt, Syria, Asia Minor, mainland Greece and various islands; in the Latin-speaking west in this period they are attested mainly in Italy. After the Jewish War of A.D. 66–73 they are also found in North Africa, Spain and Gaul. There were, in addition, important

---

169 In other words, we are not dealing here, as has been suggested in other societies, with the problem of 'status dissonance' (disparity between status achieved by an individual and the way others saw him or her) underlying the growth of new cults; in a world where there was a structural expectation of advancement 'status dissonance' is hardly a meaningful category.

170 This is a different point from the stress by I. M. Lewis (1989) on the incidence of spirit possession among the sexually or socially disadvantaged. For criticism of this 'relative deprivation thesis', B. R. Wilson (1982) 115–18.

Jewish communities outside the empire to the east, in the Parthian (later Sassanian) kingdom. The spread of Christianity, by contrast, seems to have followed no such definable geographical pattern, at least not by region; from the early second century A.D., there were professed Christians in many different parts of the empire, numerous in some areas, almost entirely absent in others.[171] The main feature of their distribution is their concentration in the cities of the Graeco-Roman world, rather than the countryside; up until at least the early fourth century A.D. (when the number of Christian communities was far greater, even if forming a small minority of the total population of the empire) professed Christians were still overwhelmingly concentrated in the towns – although some Christian 'heresies' were thought to be particularly located in rural areas.[172] In fact, the term 'pagan' (Latin *paganus*), which can be used from the fourth century onwards by Christians to designate non-Christians, carried with it (rightly or wrongly) pejorative associations with country-dwellers as opposed to townsfolk.[173]

It is only possible to plot the distribution of these cults across the empire because there *is* a degree of uniformity in their material remains. Dedications to Jupiter Dolichenus from Syria, Rome and Austria have a very similar iconography. The inscribed hymns to Isis from the Greek world, which range in date from the second century B.C. to the second or third centuries A.D., are similar both to one another and to the version in Apuleius' novel. And when Lucius went from Corinth to Rome, at the instruction of Isis, it was recognisably the same cult into which he was initiated. The surviving evidence for the cult of Mithras is also broadly similar across the empire.[174] Shrines excavated in Britain or Germany have the same basic features as those in Rome or Dura Europus on the Euphrates frontier. At the sanctuary at Dura Europus, in fact, simply because of its location, we might have expected clear elements of some 'eastern' traditions of the cult; but at least in the second phase of the shrine (when it was patronized by soldiers), the iconography, if not the style, of the frescoes closely follows a standard pattern found in the west.

The explanation of such similarities lies in various factors. The existence

171 Isis: Malaise (1984). Jupiter Dolichenus: Hörig and Schwertheim (1987). Mithras: Clauss (1990) 33–7. Jews: Schürer (1973–87) III.1.3–86; Barnes (1985) 282–5, 330. Christians: Pliny, *Letters* X.96 = **11.11b**; Lane Fox (1986) 265–93. The only statistic concerns the Roman church in A.D. 251 which supported 154 ministers and more than 1500 widows and poor: Eusebius, *Ecclesiastical History* VI.43.11; above, n. 66.

172 S. Mitchell (1993) II documents the importance of 'heretical' Christian groups in some rural areas of Asia Minor.

173 The earliest associations of the word are perhaps with '*civilians*', rather than the 'military'; but this was not relevant to fourth-century usage: O'Donnell (1977).

174 Cf. Burkert (1987) 30–53. Jupiter Dolichenus: e.g. Hörig and Schwertheim (1987) nos. 5, 386, 512. Isis: *Inschriften von Kyme* 41 = **12.4a**; Apuleius, *Metamorphoses* XI.5–6, 23–5 = **12.4b**. Mithras: Vermaseren (1963) ch. 7; Beck (1984) 2016–17 on Dura.

of specialized priests, who could carry the traditions of the cult from place to place, was a feature of the cult of Isis and Christianity. But this could not have been so in other religions. There seems, for example, to have been no organized priesthood of Mithras, nor in Judaism outside Judaea. The existence of sacred books in some cults (Isis, Jews, Christians), prescribing rituals or orthodox doctrine, and transportable from place to place, might also have been a factor in promoting uniformity. Surviving fragments of a papyrus book, for example, seem to preserve the formulae of a 'catechism' of the cult of Mithras initiates, in which an officiant questions an initiate, who must give the required answers:

He will say: 'Who is the father?' Say: 'The one who [begets?] everything ...' [he will say: 'How (?)] ... did you become a Lion?' Say: 'By the ... of the father.'

But neither personnel nor books are sufficient on their own to explain the apparent uniformity in these cults across such wide areas of the empire. The crucial point must be that these cults defined themselves as international; that their adherents perceived and wanted these cults not to be limited to one town, but to transcend any single place. As was said in the cult of Mithras, 'Hail to the Fathers from East and West.'[175] This was surely enhanced by the movement of people around the empire. The interaction of traders, officials and soldiers, as well as of priests, helped to promote a degree of homogeneity in the various cults; while, at the same time, the cults responded to similar social conditions in different parts of the empire. It is a striking fact that (with the exception of Judaism, Christianity and Manichaeism) they are not found outside the boundaries of the Roman empire – a further indication that, for all their foreignness, they were essentially 'Roman'.[176]

But we should not exaggerate the extent of this uniformity. We have already stressed that, even with their strikingly similar material remains, it is highly unlikely that these cults 'meant' the same to their practitioners in different parts of the empire. Given the vast differences in local religious and cultural traditions, Isis in Gaul *must* have been a significantly different phenomenon from Isis in Egypt. We can sometimes detect differences even within the broad similarities we have noted. None of the Isiac hymns is identical with any of the others, although they all share a series of family resemblances. And in the cult of Mithras the side scenes regularly shown around the main figure of Mithras and the bull, depicting parts of the Mithraic myth, do not appear in any fixed sequence: there seem to be two major geographical areas, along the Rhine and the Danube, where some of

---

175 Catechism: Brashear (1992), though whether it is Mithraic is questioned by Turcan (1992), (1993) 152–6. 'Hail': Vermaseren and van Essen (1965) 179–84 (= **12.5h(xv)**).

176 Manichaeism, a 'successor' to Christianity, moved into the empire from across its eastern frontier in the mid third century A.D., and was propagated by active missionary activity. Cf. **11.12**.

the scenes at least commonly appear in a local 'standard' order; but Italy was different and even within the two areas there was much diversity. It is clear that no orthodox 'pattern-book' can have been used by Mithraic groups across the empire in commissioning their major cult icon.[177]

This pluralism can be more fully documented within Judaism. As we noticed earlier, before A.D. 70 Jews in the empire sent contributions to the temple in Jerusalem, and instructions and information no doubt came back in return. But even within Judaea itself there was a great variety of Jewish religious practices and philosophies, and there was no attempt to create 'orthodoxy' among communities outside Judaea (in the 'diaspaea'). After the suppression of the Jewish revolt and the destruction of the temple, and even more after the failure of further revolts in the early second century A.D., Jerusalem was no longer a practical centre for Judaism. Within Palestine (and then Babylon) wise men (rabbis) emerged as a new and important feature of Judaism, but there is little evidence for them in other parts of the empire – still less that they imposed authoritative rules and norms on the widely spread communities.[178] Common descent, a collective historical memory, shared rituals, and the synagogues sufficed to define the Jewish communities in the early empire; though definition of Jewish identity is an issue that must have become more pressing, both in theory and in practice, in the second century with the imposition by the Romans of a special tax on all Jews.[179]

Christianity laid far greater stress than any of the other cults on its internal organization and central control. Within Rome by the third century A.D. there was a strong central authority in the bishop of Rome; from A.D. 235 the bishops' status was marked by their separate burial in a special crypt in the cemetery of Callistus. The emperor Decius is alleged (by a Christian, of course) to have said that he was less worried by the news of a pretender to the throne than of the appointment of a new bishop of Rome. Under the bishop, Rome was divided into seven pastoral districts, a division which roughly took over and eventually superseded the civil division of the city into fourteen regions established under Augustus. By the early

---

177 Isis: **12.4a**. Mithras: **12.5b**; R. L. Gordon (1980b); Beck (1984) 2075–8. On Mithraic use of planetary gods and planetary orders Beck (1988) argued for homogeneity, but see Price (1990). On 'local jargons' within Mithraism, R. L. Gordon (1994) .

178 Neusner, Green and Frerichs (1987). See now Sanders (1992), who argues for a core of common Jewish practices and theology in the first century A.D. Contributions: Philo, *Embassy to Gaius* 156 = **12.6c(ii)**; below, p. 341. Information: Acts of the Apostles 28.21 = **12.7b(i)**. Christian sources allege coherent Jewish 'missions' against Christianity, but these are probably fictitious (see Goodman (1983) 111–18 against Harnack (1908) I.57–9, 327–30). Rabbis: Cohen (1981–2). Late Jewish sources claim a *yeshibah* (academy) in second-century Rome (Reynolds and Tannenbaum (1987) 33, 83) but it is quite uncertain whether there were any academies outside Palestine and Babylon.

179 Goodman (1989); Cohen (1993). Goodman (1994b) on the possibility of continuing pluralism after A.D. 70.

fourth century the city included about twenty places in all for Christian worship, though none of them need have been purpose-built churches.[180] It is hard to trace the history of the office of bishop in Rome in the first two centuries A.D., partly because later Christian writers, from the mid third century on, attempted to draw a direct line of succession from the apostle Peter as 'first bishop of Rome' (the so-called 'doctrine of apostolic succession'). But, in general, as far as we can tell episcopal authority developed only in the course of the second century A.D.[181]

Outside Rome, Christian communities throughout the empire had their own bishops. Later, as the doctrine of the primacy of the Roman church developed, these bishops (at least in the west) were clearly under the formal authority of the bishop of Rome. In the earliest Christian centuries, that authority was only informal – resulting partly from the size and importance of the city, and partly from the association of its church with the apostles and famous martyrs (such as Peter and Paul). Thus in the second and third centuries A.D. Rome sought to advise other churches, and was appealed to as an arbiter in matters of church discipline.[182] But other churches (Corinth, Philippi, Ephesus) could claim that they too had been founded by apostles, and churches in other large cities of the empire also operated as major focuses in the hierarchy of Christian organization. The Roman church was of particular importance, but it did not yet have the status of 'Christian capital'. The Christian community was still a complex network of different focuses of authority.

The development of internal structures of organization within the Christian church was, in fact, closely connected to the variety of beliefs and practices within Christianity; for these structures of authority were established partly to deal with the problems of such variety – while, at the same time, of course, exposing and even emphasizing (as we shall see) the sometimes irreconcilable differences of view within the church.[183] The first regional meetings of bishops of which we hear were held from c. 180 A.D. onwards in Asia and elsewhere to deal with the 'heresy' of Montanus (a Christian movement originating in Phrygia).[184] By the end of the second

180 Burial: above, n. 77. Decius: above, pp. 243–4. Division of city: by Fabianus (A.D. 236–50) according to the Liberian catalogue, *Liber Pontificalis* (ed. Duchesne) I.4–5, 148, 123 n. 6. Churches: Saxer (1989) 920; above, p. 184. Cf. Pietri (1989).

181 Hobbs and Wuellner (1980); Lane Fox (1986) 493–517; Lampe (1989) 334–45; Brent (1995) 398–457. It is crucial not to use the anachronistic term 'pope' for the bishop of Rome, which implies acceptance of the primacy of Rome. *Papa* emerges in the fourth century as a term particularly associated with the bishop of Rome, with the implication of fatherly and traditional authority: Pietri (1976) II.1609–11. For the fourth century, below, p. 377.

182 E.g. Cyprian, *Letters* 59, 67.5, 68.

183 Cf. R. Williams (1989). S. G. Hall (1991) is an introduction to the theological debates.

184 The movement, based on charismatic men and women, claiming the authority of the Holy Spirit, prophesies the end of the world, and was marked by strongly ascetic

century A.D. the long-standing differences over whether the Easter fast should end on the fourteenth day of the lunar month, like the Jewish Passover, or on the nearest Sunday, came to a head. Each party claimed authority for their practice stretching back to the apostles and the very foundation of the church. Various regional councils (Palestine, Pontus, Osrhoene, Asia, Corinth, Rome and Gaul), covering the church from east to west, debated the issue. They separately agreed on a common position, with the exception of the Asian bishops, who upheld the fourteenth-day dating. The bishop of Rome sought to impose his own (the majority) view on Asia, but his action was rejected for its autocracy. The various councils had only the authority derived from mutual consent. Subsequently, other meetings of bishops from particular areas were held to thrash out organizational problems; the first one recorded in North Africa was on the issue of re-baptism for those who moved from a 'heretical' to an 'orthodox' church.[185] Inevitably to some extent, under their parade of unity (unparalleled in any other cult of the day), Councils must have effectively advertised the 'heresy' they set out to control; they must also have served to imperil the authority of particular bishops, and groups of bishops, while consolidating their ascendancy in general, as they successfully claimed through the Councils the right to make decisions on 'orthodox' Christian doctrine and practice.

Internal strength and coherence was of course promoted (just as we saw in the pagan context in chapter 5) by the maintenance of boundaries, and by the construction of internal enemies. From the mid second century A.D., the ideal of a coherent central tradition of Christian practice and belief was delineated in the denunciation of variant traditions as 'heresies'. Irenaeus, in Gaul, wrote the first extant treatise against 'heretics', followed by Hippolytus in Rome.[186] Protesting against doctrines they saw as dangerous or untraditional, they effectively created the idea of Christian 'orthodoxy' – even though, as we shall see in chapter 8, the institutions for enforcing orthodoxy were created only in the fourth century, and the goal of a single agreed set of doctrines across the whole of the Christian world was never (and has never been) achieved.

practices. It continued into the sixth century. See Eusebius, *Ecclesiastical History* V.16.7–8 = **7.6b**; Fischer (1974) on councils; Frend (1984); S. Mitchell (1993) II.39–40, 104–5 (and above, n. 162).

185 Eusebius, *Ecclesiastical History* V.23–5, with Huber (1969) 1–88; C. C. Richardson (1973). On the relationship to the Jewish Passover, see below, p. 310. North Africa: Cyprian, *Letters* 70.1.2, 71.4.1, 73.3.1. The council of Nicaea (below, pp. 370–1) was the largest assembly of bishops to that date, and was, at least later, described as 'worldwide'.

186 Justin, *First Apology* 26 = **12.7a(i)**; extracts of Irenaeus in **12.7e(ii–iii)** and of Hippolytus in **12.7c(iii)** and **12.7e(iv)**. Cf. Eusebius, *Ecclesiastical History* II.25.5–7 = **12.7f(iii)**. The term 'heresy' was influenced by the usage of the medical schools: Staden (1982).

Our final question concerns the degree of exclusivity of these new cults; or how far it was possible, or likely, for people be adherents of more than one such cult. We have already characterized these cults as shifting 'clusters' of people and ideas; and we have questioned the simple notion of cult 'membership', suggesting instead all kinds of different degrees of adherence. These factors, combined with the expectations of traditional Graeco-Roman polytheism (that the various gods had particular, but overlapping, functions to serve at particular times and in particular circumstances) would imply that multiple adherence was possible – in much the same way as we have seen that traditional deities could be honoured within the sanctuaries of the new cults. On the other hand, some of the complex (and seemingly mutually exclusive) theologies we have detected within these different cults must raise the question of how far any individual could live with the flagrant incompatibilities between them. Would it be possible at any level to accept the tenets of both the cult of Isis and of Mithras?[187]

There is some evidence that this was indeed possible. In addition to the imagery in the Aventine sanctuary of Jupiter Dolichenus (which included both Mithras and Isis and Sarapis), a fine Mithraic relief from Italy illustrates the possibility that an individual could support more than one cult. At the bottom of the relief, an inscription runs: 'Apronianus the civic treasurer made it at his own expense'. It so happens that on another inscription from the same town the same man proclaims that he had paid for the erection of statues of Sarapis and Isis.[188] This point is reinforced by the terminology of the cults themselves. It is not only *our* caution which queries the notion of 'membership' of these cults; it seems also that the initiates of most of the cults did not generally use any particular term of self-description, to define them as potentially exclusive adherents of the cult concerned. Modern scholars may talk of 'Mithraists', but there is no corresponding word in the ancient sources; while the titles of the grades of initiation were precisely that – not terms regularly used outside a specifically cultic context. The most we can detect are some much vaguer terms of self-description (*syndexios* – 'he who has performed the ritual handshake', or *sacratus* – 'devotee'). Only 'Isiacs', 'Jews' and 'Christians' have equivalent ancient words, but even these are not quite as straightforward as they seem at first sight. 'Isiacus', though it is apparently the self-designation of a devotee of Isis, is only very rarely attested. The range of meanings of 'Judaeus' reflects the fact that Judaism was both an ethnic and an elective religion: it can refer simply to inhabitants of Judaea or people from there, as well as to Jews in a religious sense, including converts to Judaism. The word 'Christianus' is

187 Polytheism: Versnel (1981a). Scholars who specialize in one or another of the various cults tend to imply that exclusivity was normal.
188 **12.5b**; *ILS* 4381 = Vidman (1969) no. 477. See further Malaise (1972b) 461–8. Such multiple allegiances make very problematic the application of the term 'sect', which was devised for exclusive (Christian) groups: B. R. Wilson (1982) 101–2.

probably most like modern usage. Certainly by the early second century A.D., Pliny can use it quite unselfconsciously when writing to Trajan. But the history of even this word is complex: it is rare in Christian texts until the mid second century, when it was still possible to talk to 'us so-called Christians', and other terms remained commonly in use as self-designations of Christians.[189]

In some cults there is a difference between those whose religious, and maybe social, identity had come to depend on the worship of their particular deity (and who were rarely involved in more than one of the new cults) and those nearer the margins (who were much less likely to be so exclusive). In the cult of Magna Mater, for example, we can detect a difference between the *dendrophori*, 'tree-bearers' (who formed a sub-group within the cult, with particular ritual duties), and the castrated cult servants the *galli*: the *dendrophori* are found playing other roles; not so the *galli*. This exclusivity is predictable, insofar as their castration marked them out in perpetuity as belonging to this one deity; for the *galli*, that is, this religious role *was* their principal role, their claim to status and their self-definition – as is suggested by the fact that some chose to have themselves represented on their tombstones in the costume of, and with the symbols of, their religious office.[190] It is probably significant in this context that the only two Italian tombstones to record allegiance to Mithras commemorate members of the highest Mithraic grade: as if it was only at the very top of the sequence of initiation that Mithraic grade defined social identity.[191]

In the cult of Isis, however, religious identity, as defined by a particular cultic role, was more commonly paraded; and there were some priests and worshippers whose physical appearance (shaven heads) signified to the world that they belonged to Isis.[192] At the end of Apuleius' novel Lucius' newly shaven head, though in part a good joke, also emphasizes that Lucius had no time for any other deity but Isis. Funerary inscriptions also suggest that some people were deeply attached to the cult of Isis. Some funerary monuments represent those they commemorate (mainly women) as servants of Isis, others define the deceased through numerous Isiac positions: a temple warden of Isis Pelagia who had held office for ten years; a

189 Mithraic terms: R. L. Gordon (1994) 109–10. 'Isiacus': Vidman (1969) nos. 487–8, 536 (= **12.4c**), 538–9, 560. 'Judaeus': Schürer (1973–87) III.1.87–91; Kraemer (1989). 'Christianus': first in Acts of the Apostles 11.26; Pliny, *Letters* X.96 = **11.11b**; Athenagoras, *Embassy* 1; *RAC* II.1131–8.

190 *Dendrophori* might, like other associations, share a burial ground (e.g. *CIL* V 81, Pula; X 8107–8, Volceii; above, p. 270), but they did not parade the peculiar imagery of the *galli* (e.g. **8.7c**).

191 *ILS* 4270 = *CIMRM* 511 (Rome); *CIMRM* 708 (Milan). We do not know how far, in practice, these were the distinctive features of only a small group of religious 'overachievers', or more widespread within the cult; for the idea of religious 'overachievement', Lane Fox (1986) 336–40.

192 Shaven heads: **5.6d** (relief sculpture of four Isiac officials).

man who had paid for a major festival of Isis; women described as Bubastiaca or Memphiana; or a wife commemorated by her husband as 'chaste worshipper of the Pharian goddess <i.e. Isis>, diligent and beautiful in appearance'.[193] Maybe the display of Isiac attachments on public funerary monuments stemmed from the connection between Isis and the afterlife. On the other hand, they do not read like an attempt to maximize the chances of the deceased in the (Isiac) after-life; rather, they pick out Isiac attachments as crucial attributes of the living. Little of this need imply that allegiance to the cult was regularly exclusive, even among those who were commemorated in an Isiac role; and we have already seen clear evidence for overlaps between the cult of Isis and other cults. Nevertheless, it may suggest that, in contrast to the cult of Magna Mater, the cult of Isis much more regularly offered a religious status that could be paraded also as a marker of social and public status.

The exclusivity of Judaism and Christianity is difficult to assess because of the dominance in each case of later orthodoxies, which sought to exclude any possibility of overlap with traditional or other alternative cults. Among the Jews, 'godfearers' were probably not expected to reject all their own religious heritage; and some Jews certainly would have been more separatist than others – though, at most, this meant *keeping apart;* they did not (so far as we know) produce treatises on the nature and inferiority of the cults they shunned.[194] By contrast, some strands in early Christianity did seek to explain how Christianity was superior both to Judaism and to the traditional cults. The relationship between Judaism and Christianity, a crucial issue from the earliest days of the Christian Church, was articulated in various ways. Marcion, teaching in Rome in the mid second century A.D., distinguished between two gods, a good but very distant god, and a creator god who is inferior to him; the latter god, who is concerned with justice but subject to passions and perhaps partly evil, Marcion identified with the god of the Jews. He also went so far as to reject the whole Old Testament, on the grounds that it could not be reconciled with the New Testament.[195] He was a controversial figure, condemned by Justin and other 'orthodox' writers as a 'heretic', but the founder of a long-lived church. Justin, despite his criticisms of Marcion, agreed with him on the profound differences between Judaism and Christianity. In his *Dialogue with Trypho,* he argued that Christianity replaced the Mosaic law, which had only temporary validity; that Christ was God; and that those nations who followed Christ were the new Israel.

At around the same time in the mid second century, Christians also began to write 'Apologies', defences of Christianity normally addressed to

193 Eingartner (1991); Vidman (1969) nos. 373, 396, 422–4, 428, 433, 451 (= **9.6b**). Above, p. 298 on women.
194 'Godfearers': above, p. 275.
195 Blackman (1948).

the reigning emperor, attacking the traditional cults. They were written in the form of documents seeking to persuade the Roman authorities and other non-Christians of the merits of Christianity; but in practice the Apologies seem not to have been much read by non-Christians, their importance lying in their internal consumption within the church. One of the most famous of these treatises in the second century, again by Justin, criticized the official Roman treatment of the Christians, expounded Christian doctrine and explained the misleading nature of the traditional gods; although Greek mythology had many superficial similarities to Christianity, suggesting that the history of Christ was a mere myth on a par with the Greek poets' myths about the various sons of Zeus, it was the product of demons who wished to lead people astray. Nor was this merely a matter of evil stories: the practices of the Mithraic cult, for example, were a demonic imitation of the Christian eucharist.[196] The Apologies and other Christian texts attempted to define a clear and unambiguous boundary round the new movement; and it is clearly a marker of Christianity's claims to exclusivity that it, alone of all the new religions, so far as we know, explicitly defined the other cults as rivals.[197]

The hard-line rejection of both Judaism and 'paganism' was, however, only one strand in second- and third-century Christianity. If one way of understanding the origin of Christianity is as a break-away Jewish cult, then connections between Judaism and Christianity are likely to have been close. Marcion's rejection of the Old Testament was not the norm; Christians adopted a variety of different positions towards Judaism. Some practised circumcision and followed an obviously Jewish way of life. Others who rejected Judaism as a system nonetheless were much indebted to Jewish thought; for example, the homily *On Easter* by Melito of Sardis (in Asia Minor) draws on Jewish Passover traditions and recitations. And the second-century debates about the date of Easter hinged on the question whether (as people like Melito held) Easter should keep in step with the Jewish Passover.[198]

There were also debates about how much Christians should borrow from pagan learning: for example, should philosophical logic be applied to the interpretation of the Bible? Some Christians held that they could take part in traditional cults, for example by eating sacrificial meat, without themselves being corrupted. Others held that traditional cults contained

---

196 Millar (1977) 561–6 stresses the form of the Apologies. Justin, *First Apology* 54–8, 66, partly in **12.7a(i)**; cf. his *Dialogue with Trypho* 70, with Clauss (1990) 151–2, 175–9. Cf. Alföldy (1989) 66–70. The rejection of the Mithraic cult was just one element, and not a particularly important one, in the Christian critique of contemporary Greek and Roman cults.

197 Walsh (1970) 186–7 argues that Apuleius' *Metamorphoses* was written in part to counter the spread of Christianity, but the polemic is at most implicit.

198 'Jewish Christianity': e.g. Irenaeus, *Against Heresies* I.26.2 = **12.7e(iii)**; Segal (1992). Melito: S. G. Hall (1979); Easter, above, n. 185.

part of the divine message. The Naassenes (one of the Christian 'heresies' condemned by Hippolytus) were said to believe that the performance of the mysteries of Attis were under the guidance of providence; without themselves being castrated, they attended the mysteries of Magna Mater 'considering that they can actually observe their own mystery in these rites'.[199] In Hippolytus' horrified report of their actions, we should see not just 'heresy' on the part of the Naassenes; but also the drive of Hippolytus and others like him to define the limits of acceptability for Christian thought and behaviour. They were ultimately successful; which is to say their vision of Christianity was accepted by subsequent generations as the authoritative and 'orthodox' tradition. We may well reflect how different Christianity might have been if a different tradition had become dominant. For Hippolytus represented just one side of a set of debates in the first centuries A.D., concerning not only the relationship between different versions of Christianity, but also that between Christianity and other religions (whether Judaism or the cult of Magna Mater). And it was all no doubt taking place against a background of Christian behaviour, in which many more 'Christians' probably took a quiet interest in other cults, or even participated without much trouble in 'pagan' sacrifices, than vowed themselves exclusively to the Christian faith – even unto a painful death.[200]

In the next two chapters we shall develop some of these arguments further, and farther afield. Imperial Rome was by no means a typical city – and it is hard to know in any detail how far the kinds of religious choices we have characterized in the imperial capital were matched in different areas of the empire. For the western part of the empire, at least, we rely to a very great extent on the material remains of cult. And although these allow us to say for certain that there is not a single elective cult found in Rome that is not found somewhere else in the empire, they only rarely come together to offer any relatively complete picture of the religious options in any particular place.[201] In the east, we gain a picture of the ancestral Olympian deities remaining the dominant religious focus. Even in the great city of Ephesus the only non-Greek gods attested on inscriptions are Isis and Sarapis, and we hear of few elective religious associations; though here (and this point may be connected to the last one) Christian evangelizing was all the more intrusive. On the other hand, the framework of ancestral cults in both east

---

199 Logic: Eusebius, *Ecclesiastical History* V.28.13–14 = **12.7e(v)**. Sacrifices: e.g. I. Corinthians 8.10; Revelation 2.14–15, 20; Irenaeus, *Against Heresies* I.6.2–4 = **12.7e(ii)**. Naassenes: Hippolytus, *Refutation of all Heresies* V.6–9 = **12.7e(iv)** in part.

200 The complexities of interacting religious positions in Asia Minor: S. Mitchell (1993) especially II.43–51. Fourth- and fifth-century attempts to retain parts of the traditional religious heritage: below, pp. 381–8.

201 The religion of Carthage: Rives (1995a).

and west was itself, as we can clearly demonstrate, affected by Rome; and it is to this impact of Rome we turn next in chapter 7.

In the final chapter we shall return to Christianity. As we saw in chapter 5, persecution of the Christians, whether haphazard or systematic, reinforced a sense of religious identity for the Roman élite; while overt official backing for the ancestral cults defined, for the first time, all the accepted religious practices of the empire as a single category, in opposition to Christianity – so that it is only from this point, and directly under the influence of Christianity, that it is possible to speak of 'paganism' as a *system* rather than as an amalgam of different cults.[202] But another effect of the growing popularity of Christianity was that by the fourth century A.D. the official cults of Rome, once a traditional set of practices embedded unproblematically in a stable social order, had become one option among many. It is to this new world of choice that we return in chapter 8, to consider in particular the religious allegiances of the Roman élite in the fourth century.

202 Only now is it proper to speak of 'paganism'. It is a paradox that Christianity invents paganism, not just as a term, but also as a system.

7 *Roman religion and Roman Empire*

What was the impact of Roman religion on the provincial communities of the Roman empire? We have already discussed the spread of so-called 'oriental religions' outside the city of Rome itself. But what of the 'official' cults? How far did the inhabitants of the empire acquire *Roman* religious identities? Was the impact of Rome strikingly different in different parts of the empire? Was it different at different periods? Or among different classes and groups of people? As we shall see, the historical development of imperial religion produced some remarkably idiosyncratic effects (the emperor Augustus, for example, depicted in traditional Egyptian style as a pharaoh offering cult to Egyptian gods), as well as some curiously ironic enigmas (as when the Roman governor of Egypt circulated the emperor Claudius' message to the Alexandrians that they should *not* worship him as a god – with a covering edict calling him precisely that, 'our god Caesar').[1] In what follows, we shall explore such representations as part of the operation of imperial power across the Roman world.

The point of this chapter is to show, first, that Roman imperialism *did* make a difference to the religions of its imperial territory; and, second, to explore how we might trace the impact of Roman religion outside Rome, principally in the period after the reign of Augustus. Of course military conquest and the imposition of foreign control (whether in the form of taxation, puppet government or military occupation) inevitably impacts on cultural life – both in the imperial centre and in the provincial territories. No one can be culturally unaffected by imperialism. But its impact comes in a wide range of forms, and is experienced very differently by the parties involved – whether conquering or conquered, peasant or aristocrat, the native resistance or the local collaborators. Imperialism is, besides, constantly *re-interpreted* in culture and religion, as we can see very simply in the different images of the emperor himself that are found throughout the Roman provinces – not just the relatively standardized portraits on the coins that flood the Roman world, but the (to us) almost unrecognizable images from Nile sanctuaries with the emperor in the distinctive guise of

---

1 See, for example, the temple from Dendur, now on display in the Metropolitan Museum, New York: Aldred (1978) figs. 14–18, 28–33, 38–9. Claudius: E.M. Smallwood, *Documents Illustrating the Principates of Gaius, Claudius and Nero* (Cambridge 1967) no.370 (trans. Sherk (1988) 83–6).

Egyptian pharaoh or Ptolemaic king. Religion and culture are regularly put to work on imperialism's behalf, incorporating the conquering power into local traditions. But at the same time religion and culture may always work against imperialist power, in reasserting the distinctiveness of native traditions against the forces (whether military or cultural) of occupation. It is a plausible suggestion that 'native' rebellions in the Roman empire tended to fight under the banner of local deities.[2]

Within these different perspectives, we shall delineate some of the most characteristic features of Rome's religious impact on the empire. Rome did not generally seek to eradicate 'native religious traditions' nor systematically to impose her own religious traditions on her conquered territories. (Roman religion's identity as a 'religion of place' – strongly focussed on the city of Rome – would anyway make unlikely any wholesale direct export.) On the other hand there was borrowing and interchange at various levels between Roman cults and religious practices through the empire; Roman gods, for example, or at least (and this may not be the same thing at all) gods with Roman names, were widespread across the imperial territories, throughout our period. But such borrowing was not the same everywhere, from Scotland to the Sahara. We shall disentangle some of the factors which affected the impact of Roman religion on the world outside Rome, and how that impact was experienced. These factors include formal political rights and privileges (communities of Roman citizens outside Rome being much closer to the religion of Rome itself than non-citizens), as well as wealth and class (local élites in the provinces showing greater interest in ostensibly *Roman* deities than their poorer compatriots). But we shall also consider how different religious and cultural traditions in the conquered territories affected patterns of 'Romanization': the Roman authorities treated the Jews, for example, differently from the Druids; while the western part of the empire, with only a limited history of urban culture on the 'classical' model, imported Roman institutions, (whether willingly or not) more directly than did the eastern part; there, by contrast, Greek civic life and cults often worked towards the *accommodation* of Rome; there, the Roman conquerors found religious traditions that they recognized as already like their own, or even as the ancestors of their own.[3]

All these factors (and others, as we shall see) intersect – and sometimes conflict – to produce the complex pattern of Rome's religious influence on its empire. In section 1, however, we concentrate on the legal status of the different provincial communities and their constitutional relationship with

2 Egypt: Dunand (1983). Rebellions: below, pp. 347–8.
3 Issues of similarity and difference between the Greek east and Rome have been central to debates on Roman culture since ancient times – see on Dionysius above, pp. 171–4. Throughout this chapter we use the distinction between east and west, while also arguing that some features are common to different parts of the empire. For a stronger version of that position see Woolf (1994).

Rome. In one sense influence literally radiated from Rome: it was strongest in Italy itself and in the camps of the Roman army, wherever it was stationed; elsewhere it was felt in proportion to the official *Roman* status of the town or group concerned, and their formal links to Rome itself. If some Roman pressures were exercised everywhere, the particular legal status of the community made a fundamental difference to its religious life. Let us explain first how these statuses differed.

Throughout the first two centuries A.D. (until, that is, the emperor Caracalla completed the restructuring of such distinctions by granting citizenship to most of the free population of the empire) there were three principal types of provincial community under the empire: *coloniae*, *municipia*, and towns without any specifically *Roman* status at all. Roman *coloniae* were, with the army, the main context in which the Roman religious system was replicated abroad.[4] *Coloniae* were communities of Roman citizens settled outside Italy. In the middle Republic they were mostly landless citizens from Rome itself, and in the first centuries B.C. and A.D. mostly ex-legionaries who received land in return for their military service; these foundations ceased altogether after the early second century A.D. They were designed to be clones of Rome in all respects: Latin was the official language, even when they were established in the Greek world; some *coloniae* made a point of boasting 'seven hills', just like Rome. So too, in their religious institutions, these 'mini-Romes' abroad explicitly mirrored the institutions of the capital.

In the Latin west (especially in North Africa, Spain and Southern France) there was also a second category of towns with Roman status, known as *municipia*.[5] These towns had been granted the so-called 'Latin right' by the Romans, which meant that individual members of the community gained some of the rights of Roman citizens and their ex-magistrates automatically became full citizens. It seems that when they received this status the new *municipia* also received a new constitution directly from Rome. After Vespasian granted the Latin right to towns in Spain, these municipal constitutions were standardized (under Vespasian's son, Domitian); fragments of seven copies of the standard municipal regulation survive from Spain which clearly show the direct influence of Roman practice on institutions outside Rome.

Communities *without* Roman status fell into two main types: towns in the East, whose principal language was Greek, and whose own ancient religious traditions were deeply embedded in the fabric of urban life; and towns without municipal status in the West, often of much more recent foundation, in areas that were themselves more recently conquered, or

---

4 Levick (1967); Gargola (1995) 71–101; Fear (1996) 63–104. Above, p.157 for the late republican context.
5 Fear (1996) 131–69. That *municipia* were not as closely modelled on Rome as *coloniae* is stated in Aulus Gelius, *Attic Nights* XVI.13.4–9.

without a long history of loyalty to Rome. Both these types of community (though much more commonly and directly those in the west) borrowed elements from the Roman system, though less directly than *coloniae* or *municipia*; and their religious institutions might be subject to Roman regulation. We shall discuss the religious impact of Rome on communities without Roman status in section 2.

Of course, as we have already implied, juridical status – even if a useful starting point – was not everything. The adoption and adaptation of Roman religious custom by local communities depended on much more than constitutional position (and on more, for that matter, than any of the other factors that we have so far mentioned): individual interests within the province, local perceptions of cultural and religious identity, calculations of advantage, no doubt, in relation either to the Roman government or the 'native' élite, or both. Besides, the religious practice or beliefs of individuals might always (as at Rome itself) go against the grain of the regulations laid down for the community as a whole. Just as there must have been some individuals in *municipia* or *coloniae* who lived in a resolutely *non-Roman* religious world, so too in towns without any formal Roman status, there must have been some whose religious experience was in many respects Roman.

The religious history of other empires may also help us at the outset to understand the pattern of religious influence in the Roman empire. The religious impact of the centre in the periphery of empires varies greatly, often depending on how *integrated* the empire is (a theme we touched on in chapter 5). In some cases the central power makes stringent religious demands on its dependent territories. This is particularly clear, for example, in the highly integrated Inca empire (where the nobility directly administered their provincial territories and there were strong reciprocal obligations between rulers and subjects). Significantly, the Inca transported the images of the major gods of the vanquished to their capital and, in return, the subjects were compelled to accept new, Inca, idols and to maintain places of worship in the same manner as in the capital. A hostile contemporary account claims that the eleventh Inca king killed all priests of the subject peoples and destroyed even their less important shrines – because the priests had refused to give him information. At all events the Incas attempted to create a tightly centralized system, of administration *and* religion.[6] Likewise, in the late nineteenth and twentieth centuries, the massive overseas expansion of Japan was accompanied by the export of state Shintoism: shrines were built, for example, in Formosa, Korea and

6 Cobo (1653/1979) 187–8, 211–12, 241–2, a seventeenth-century Spanish historian. Hostile account: Guamán Pomo de Ayala (1567–1615?/1978) 70. For subtle studies of the reception of Inca cults see S.J. Stern (1982) 20–2 and MacCormack (1991). Contrast the less integrated Aztec empire. The Aztecs removed conquered deities to the centre, without replicating the centre in the provinces: Sahagún (1950) II.168.

Manchuria, not just for the Japanese residents overseas, but as part of a new-found 'world civilizing mission'.[7] This is a model not far different from the British empire, which also attempted to impose its own religion (Christianity) on its colonies and to eradicate 'unacceptable' or 'uncivilized' native religious practices, though unsystematically, with varying energy and many varieties of self-deception and chauvinism.[8]

The Roman empire, on the other hand, operated according to a quite different pattern. In general, it was relatively diffuse and unintegrated – neither systematically imposing its own cults on the conquered, nor systematically removing the cults of their subjects to the capital.[9] But, as we have already implied, one aspect of integration *was* particularly important within the vast geographical and political extent of the Roman empire: that is, Roman citizenship. The bearers of Roman citizenship were, it seems, expected to recognize *Roman* gods; an expectation which overlaps neatly with the juridical status of the different communities we have outlined (from *coloniae* as full citizen communities to towns without Roman status, which might have included no Roman citizens at all). Despite increasing religious choices in the imperial period, the identity of religion and state was maintained: those who counted as 'Roman' in civic terms counted as 'Roman' in religious terms too.

In exploring these issues, we shall consider the process by which local and Roman gods apparently merged with each other and were often referred to, and presumably worshipped, under a composite title. In Roman Britain, for example, as in many other provinces in the West, we find a wide variety of these hybrids, 'Mars Alator', 'Sul Minerva' and so on.[10] In most cases, however, we have only the record of a mixed divine *name*; we can only guess what that name *meant*, which deity (Roman or native) was uppermost in the minds of the worshippers, or whether the two had merged into a new composite whole (a process often now referred to as 'syncretism'); we do not know, in other words, how far the process was an aspect of Roman take-over (and ultimately obliteration) of native deities, how far a mutually respectful union of two divine powers, or how far it was a minimal, resistant and token incorporation of Roman imperial paraphernalia on the part of the provincials. Signs of 'syncretism', then, always need to be *interpreted*. For example, to understand why most deities in the eastern part of the empire did not merge with Roman counterparts, but retained their individual personalities and characteristics, whereas in the west pre-Roman gods acquired Roman names, or non-Roman and Roman

---

7 Holtom (1943) 153–73. One might be tempted to see this as an aspect of the growth of modernity in Japan, of peculiarly modern nationalism, but it (like the Inca case) may be accounted for in terms of the growing general integration of the Japanese state.

8 For the British in India, Bayly (1989), Metcalf (1994). Inden (1990) is a critique of western ('imperialist') constructions of Indian society.

9 For the occasional Roman use of *evocatio*, see above, pp. 34–5; 82–3; 132–4.

10 See for different forms *RIB* 307 = **2.9b(i)**, *RIB* 218 = **2.9b(ii)**; below, pp. 344–5.

divine names were linked, we need to investigate much more deeply the nature of Roman religion outside Rome; we need also to attend to the agenda of all those groups involved in developing a new Roman imperial world view – throughout the empire and over the centuries.[11]

Another theme, central to this chapter, is the 'imperial cult' offered to the Roman emperor or his (deified) predecessors, with temples, festivals, prayers and priesthoods in every province of the empire. The historian Cassius Dio in the third century A.D. saw cult of the emperor as one unifying factor in the religions of the vast imperial territory, one aspect of worship that all Roman subjects shared. After noting the establishment of temples to Augustus in Asia and Bithynia, he goes on to say: 'This practice, beginning under him, has been continued under other emperors, not only among the peoples of Greece, but also among all the others insofar as they are subject to the Romans.'[12] We have chosen to consider various aspects of imperial cult together in section 3 partly because of Dio's claim of its universality across the Roman empire, and his suggestion that this form of shared religious practice was one aspect of 'belonging' to that empire. On the other hand, we do not want to suggest (and Dio comes nowhere near claiming) that there was a single entity, the same throughout the empire, that can be identified as '*the* imperial cult'. There was no such thing as '*the* imperial cult'; rather there was a series of different cults sharing a common focus in the worship of the emperor, his family or predecessors, but (as we shall see) operating quite differently according to a variety of different local circumstances – the Roman status of the communities in which they were found, the pre-existing religious traditions of the area, and the degree of central Roman involvement in establishing the cult. Besides, there was no sharp boundary between imperial cult and other religious forms: the incorporation of the emperor into the traditional cults of provincial communities, his association with other deities, was often just as important as worship which focussed specifically and solely on him. Nor was imperial cult necessarily the most powerful marker of Romanization in religion: in specifically Roman communities abroad (*coloniae* and *municipia*), imitations of the transformed system of Augustan Rome were often a far more important aspect of religious Romanization than any direct worship of the emperor.

11 The term 'syncretism' is problematic, not least because it has often been used pejoratively to refer to a meaningless mish-mash of religions (see Berner (1982) and Martin (1983) 134–7 for a history of the term). It has, however, been revived in a neutral sense: Pirenne Delforge (1994); Stewart and Shaw (1994). *Interpretatio romana*, a phrase taken from Tacitus, *Germany* 43.3, which is also commonly used, at least places the emphasis on interpretation (Girard (1980)), but it stresses the role of Romans rather than provincials, and assumes that one-for-one identifications were possible between Roman and local gods. For the processes, see documents and discussion in **2.9** and R. L. Gordon (1990c).

12 Cassius Dio LI.20.7.

The sources for this chapter are different in their emphasis from those we have used before.[13] In attempting to reconstruct provincial viewpoints on the processes of Romanization in the provinces, we have ample evidence from one section of the provincial population only – the educated writers from the Greek world in the first two centuries A.D., some of whom (like Plutarch and Lucian) discuss various aspects of Greek and Roman religion and their interaction.[14] Otherwise the bulk of the evidence for Roman influence on religion in the empire comes from inscriptions or from visual images: sculptured reliefs depicting gods or emperors, for example, may provide evidence for the native or Roman characteristics of a particular deity, or for how an emperor is imagined within the divine system; inscriptions reveal the names of the gods, the religious offices and sometimes the particular rites of towns in Italy and the empire. But at the same time these objects may challenge interpretation. How can you tell, for example, if a statue of Jupiter found in a provincial town is the result of Roman imposition or of enthusiastic provincial imitation of Rome? How can you know whether a temple to Roman deities in a distant province was the focus of loyal worship by the provincial community or the focus of their resentment at Rome's dominance? Besides, it is all too easy to patronize provincial aspirations and ideology. Is a rough, 'unclassical', Celtic image of a Roman deity to be written off as a demonstrably naive failure by the local craftsman to reproduce metropolitan style? Or is it motivated by a desire to assert local, 'tribal' *difference* from the dominant, imperial, classical culture?

This chapter emphasizes the *changes* wrought under Roman rule; so we pay little attention to the relatively unchanging civic cults of the Greek east that continued throughout the period. Yet especially in the west, but also in parts of the near east, the evidence for pre-Roman religious life is very scanty – with few, if any, surviving pre-Roman inscriptions, and few if any images carved in stone, let alone any trace of literary accounts.[15] It is often impossible, then, to specify precisely the individual changes brought about by Rome and Roman influence. We can, however, deploy the evidence we have to assess the overall impact of Rome on the religious life of the empire, and the factors which intensified or diminished that impact – both east and west, from the classical world of the Greek city states to the tribal societies of Britain and Gaul.

---

13 Toutain (1907–20) remains a useful synthesis on the west, but it is unfinished and anyway omits iconographic evidence. The range of epigraphic evidence is presented by MacMullen (1981) and Lane Fox (1986).

14 For an introduction, Swain (1996).

15 Problems of the changing nature of the evidence are compounded by the divisions between different scholarly traditions. For much of the Latin west scholars study *either* the pre-Roman *or* the Roman periods, but not both, thus failing to address issues of continuity and change. See, however, Woolf (1998), ch. 8 on Gaul.

1. Roman religion outside Rome

Throughout the empire the Roman authorities tended to promote a variety of Roman religious practices. Whatever differences there were in the impact of Rome, it was a general rule that governors and other Roman officials favoured Graeco-Roman (rather than 'native') gods in whichever province they were stationed, and the governor's staff regularly included *haruspices* for the proper interpretation of sacrifices performed on the Roman model. Even more important was the expectation that governors right across the empire would ensure that the provincials, presumably in the context of the provincial assemblies (which consisted of representatives of the individual towns), performed the annual *vota* (vows followed by sacrifice) for the emperor and the empire.[16] Evidence for this is widespread: the practice was recorded by the Christian writer Tertullian in North Africa; *coloniae* in southern France and Dacia offered *vota*; a town in Portugal made a dedication to the emperor as a result of the annual vow.[17] Even rabbis in Palestine noted the prevalence of the practice; and Greek cities too sacrificed annually 'on behalf of the emperor' – even though such 'vows', in the technical sense of promising a sacrifice if something did (or did not) happen, were a peculiarly Roman practice in the context of public civic sacrifices.[18] These *vota* were in fact an institution common to all types of provincial community – which is particularly striking given that, as we shall see, communities of different statuses and culture had very different relations to Roman religion.

On the other hand, Roman provinces were not Rome; and the religious rules governing practice in Rome itself did not apply directly elsewhere in the empire. Instead Roman authority was mediated through the governor, according to similar – but not always exactly the same – principles as operated in the city. So, for example, according to Roman lawyers, land in the provinces could not, strictly speaking, be religious or sacred as it was not consecrated by the authority of Rome; it could only be treated *as* religious or *as* sacred.[19] But inevitably such legal rules were not always a clear guide to religious practice. The problem of the two categories of land faced Pliny

16 Tacitus, *Agricola* 21. *Haruspices*: *ILAfr* 592 (Africa Proconsularis); cf. *ILS* 4952a (Lugdunum); *ILS* 8833 = *Inschriften von Ephesus* V 1540. Cf. Eck (1992). Imperial ex-slaves were another source of local pressures: e.g. Tacitus, *Histories* I.76. *Vota*: Pliny, *Letters* X.35–6, 101–2.

17 Tertullian, *On the Crown* 12.3; *Apology* 35.4; cf. Gaius in *Digest* L.16.233.1; *ILS* 112 = **10.1b** (Narbo); Mărghitan and Petolescu (1976) (Sarmizegethusa); *AE* (1950) 217 (Ammaia in Portugal). Cf. Meslin (1970) 30–1.

18 Mishnah, *On Alien Worship* 1.3 = **12.6g**; Plutarch, *Cicero* 2.1. Cf. Lucian's assertion of the Roman character of the festival: *The Mistaken Critic* 8. On *vota* see above, p.196; examples of *vota* by Arval Brothers trans. in Lewis and Reinhold (1990) II. 516–19; private vows were common throughout the empire (for inscribed examples see **9.5a–b**).

19 Gaius, *Institutes* II.7 = **10.4c**. Cf. generally E. De Ruggiero, *Dizionario epigrafico di antichità romane* (Rome 1886–) I.190–200.

when he was governor of Pontus-Bithynia. In relation to religious land (used for burials) he asked the emperor, as *pontifex maximus*, whether he could permit people to rebury the bodies of their relatives which had been disturbed by river erosion. Trajan replied that provincials could not be expected to consult the *pontifices*, and that local custom should be followed.[20] Despite Pliny's uncertainty, in the provinces emperor and governor filled the role occupied in Italy by the *pontifices*. On another occasion, Pliny wrote to the emperor about sacred land. He enquired whether it was religiously proper for the town of Nicomedia to move a temple, though, to his surprise, there was no 'law' which laid down the location of the temple or other conditions applying to it – in Roman terms, that is, no 'law of dedication', laying down the location and other conditions of the temple. Trajan pointed out that only Roman and not foreign territory could receive such a law.[21] The actual Roman rules did not apply to ordinary provincial land, but governors were told firmly in the instructions (*mandata*) issued to them by emperors to preserve sacred places.[22] The role of the governor included supervision of religious matters along essentially *Roman* guidelines.

For the rest of this section, however, we shall be concentrating on the different legal and constitutional statuses that affected how the influence of Rome was felt in different communities. We shall explore Rome's control over the religious practices of the empire and the adoption of Roman religious practices outside the city in a sequence moving out from Rome: Italy, the army, and provincial communities with Roman status, *coloniae* and *municipia*. All these, with the partial exception of *municipia*, consisted of Roman citizens, and all held some consistent patterns of religious practices in common. At the same time we shall show the hybrid complexities that cut across this relatively simple pattern: the very different forms of accommodation with Rome that were attempted even by communities of the same constitutional type; the different significances that could attach to the 'same' religious institutions, rituals and symbols.

Italy formed the core of the empire. All the free-born population of the peninsula up to the Alps had been Roman citizens since the time of Julius Caesar. Italy was not a 'province' (it was not, for example, subject to Roman taxation); but remained, in principle, a collection of self-governing communities. Some towns preserved their religious institutions from pre-Roman days, including practices utterly at variance with *Roman* traditions – burying their dead within the city limits, for example, which was strictly

---

20 Pliny, *Letters* X.68–9 = **10.4d(iii–iv)**; cf. *Codex Justinianus* III.44.1. For the governor and the transport of corpses see *Digest* XI.7.38 (Ulpian), with Gabba and Tibiletti (1960) = *AE* (1992) 813; also imperial rulings in *Digest* XLVII.12.3.4 (Ulpian).

21 Pliny, *Letters* X.49–50 = **10.4d(i–ii)**.

22 Frontinus (?), in Agennius Urbicus, *On Disputes over Land* (ed. C. Thulin, *Corpus agrimensorum Romanorum*), p.48.4–12.

prohibited at Rome.[23] However, at least when it suited them, Roman officials did claim authority over the religious institutions of Italy. This is
neatly illustrated by an incident under Tiberius, when the equestrian order
in Rome vowed a gift to 'the temple of Equestrian Fortune' for the health
of Livia, only to discover that there was no such shrine in Rome itself. But
such a temple *was* discovered at Antium, a town fifty kilometres south of
Rome, where (according to Tacitus) the senate decided that the gift could
be placed, 'since all rituals, temples and images of the gods in Italian towns
fall under Roman law and jurisdiction'. Neither the senate nor any other
group of Roman officials did actually exercise day to day control of Italian
shrines; but in this case at least it was convenient (and presumably seemed
plausible) for them to stake a theoretical claim to Roman power over the
religious institutions of the rest of the peninsula. Likewise when the
Roman authorities moved to expel undesirables from the city, they normally specified expulsion from both Rome and Italy. The Roman college of
pontifices also sometimes gave permissions to Italians to repair tombs or
move corpses from one tomb to another, and, soon after the death of Julius
Caesar, a Roman law seems to have instructed Italian communities to set
up statues of *divus* Julius. Of course, in practice many Italians must have
repaired tombs without the permission of the Roman priests, and we do
not know how many obeyed the order to erect statues of Caesar; but in
both these cases the parade of Roman authority over the peninsula as a
whole is significant.[24]

The uniquely close relationship between Rome and the rest of Italy is
visible most clearly in a series of documents we have already discussed from
different points of view in earlier chapters: the surviving painted and
inscribed calendars of festivals. In all, forty-seven such calendars survive
(often in small fragments), dating mainly to the reigns of Augustus and
Tiberius, and all but one coming from Italy (the exception being a *colonia*
in Sicily).[25] Of these forty-six imperial Italian calendars, twenty-six are
from Rome itself (many, it seems, having been for the use of private associations in the city); the other twenty come mostly from the towns in the
vicinity of Rome – generally on public display in the civic centres of the
towns concerned.[26] The level of detail given in the Italian calendars varies

23 Festus p.146L s.v. 'municipalia sacra'; Ulpian in *Digest* XLVII.12.3.5 on whether such
    municipal laws should now be overridden by general imperial rulings; cf. above, p. 222
    for attitudes towards local peculiarities.
24 Antium: Tacitus, *Annals* III.71.1; Map 5. Expulsions: above pp. 230–2. *Pontifices*:
    Millar (1977) 359–61. Caesar: *ILS* 73, 73a, *AE* (1982) 149, with Alföldy (1991) 305;
    cf. below pp. 329–30 for instructions to *coloniae* outside Italy and pp. 337–8 on the
    quindecimviri.
25 Above, pp. 5–6 on the early calendar; **3.3**; Whatmough (1931); Degrassi (1963); Salz-
    man (1990) 7–8; Rüpke (1995). The only extant earlier calendar, from Antium, dates to
    the early/mid first century B.C. An extract from the Praeneste calendar is given in **3.3b**.
26 Though one was for the ex-slaves and slaves of an imperial villa who formed an associ-
    ation of worshippers of Augustus: Degrassi (1963) 201–12 (Antium).

greatly, but all differ from and apparently replace earlier, pre-imperial, Italian calendars and all are mutually compatible, recognizably versions of the same overall system of religious time-keeping. Strikingly they give practically no festivals peculiar to the local city, but only differing selections from the official festivals of the city of Rome. This raises acutely the question of the relationship between the calendar and religious practice. Would it really have been the case, for example, that such rituals as the Lupercalia, so closely tied to the topography of Rome, would have been celebrated in all the Italian towns that chose to mark it on their calendars? And if it was not celebrated, then what function did those calendars have? Why display in the local forum a series of festivals that your own town did not actually carry out? However we choose to answer such questions, it is clear that some towns in Italy – and this seems not to have been the case in the provinces – chose to parade the official Roman religious calendar as (or as if it were) the framework for their own lives.[27]

Some of the religious links between Rome and the Italian towns derived directly from historical links in the distant past. The ancient communities nearest Rome, for example, had been Rome's 'Latin' allies in the early republican period and shared a variety of common cultural forms stretching back almost into prehistory and to Rome's status as a 'Latin' city. Thus Alba Longa, Lavinium, Tibur and other Latin towns had one or more of the following priests: *flamen Dialis*, Vestal Virgins, *rex sacrorum*, and *Salii*.[28] The *Salii* and the *rex sacrorum* (and, once, the *flamen Dialis*) are also found in a few towns in northern Italy, but otherwise these offices appear almost nowhere else in the Roman empire, except in Rome itself. Interpretation of this common culture could vary, of course. In those early days the religious influence did not necessarily flow from Rome outwards; and some Italian communities might choose to give themselves (not Rome) priority in the relationship – suggesting that if they shared some of Rome's most distinctive practices, that was because Rome had adopted them from the Latins, not the other way round. A shared religious history, in other words, could be the focus of rivalry and conflicting interpretations.

But historical links could also be invented. In the early empire, ancestral ties between the Latin towns and Rome were emphasized by a new flowering of such (allegedly) ancient cults. For example, at Lavinium 30 km south of Rome, where there was no settlement in the late Republic, Italians of equestrian rank from the reign of Claudius on held a priesthood which supposedly continued the cult of the Lavinian *Penates* (the deities that Aeneas had brought from Troy), participating at ceremonies of the Latin League on the Alban Hill, and, on one occasion at least, renewing the ancient

27 For a denial that municipal display of calendars was connected with their religious role, Rüpke (1995) 165–86.
28 Map 5; see **1.5**; Wissowa (1912) 157 n.4, 519–21, 555 n.2; Ladage (1971) 8–10. Most of the surviving evidence is imperial in date.

treaty with Rome, first made in the fourth century B.C.[29] In the second century A.D., after the renewal of civic life at Lavinium, local men from the town began to hold the office, which is attested until the middle of the third century. This is a case of ancestral similarities between the religious practices of Rome and Italy being re-emphasized in the early empire through what was almost certainly an *invented* tradition. For some observers and participants, no doubt, it was all a picturesque, quaintly antiquarian show; but such instances of constructive archaism also served as another way of representing the religious links between Rome and its Italian neighbours.

Outside Italy, the body of men which most clearly stood for Rome was the army. In the professional standing army, established for the first time under the emperor Augustus, Roman citizenship remained a precondition for service in the legions (though it might be granted at recruitment); they were gradually recruited from a wider and wider area, so that, by the early second century A.D., they had only a tiny proportion of men from Italy itself – but the rules of citizenship governing recruitment continued to emphasize that the men were troops in the service of Rome. The other main body of troops, the auxiliaries, were not Roman citizens in the early empire, though they were commanded by officers who were citizens and they themselves might receive citizenship on discharge; later it became not uncommon for those who were already Roman citizens to enlist in the auxiliary forces. The official religious life of both sets of troops was predominantly Roman; though that could mean different things and be interpreted in different ways.

The specifically Roman character of official religious life in the army was enshrined in an official Roman calendar which specified the year's religious festivals for both legionaries and auxiliaries; this was different in form from the civic calendars of Italy we have just discussed, but (crucially, as we shall see) shared some of their major celebrations. The archives of an auxiliary cohort, the 'Twentieth Palmyrene', stationed at Dura Europus on the eastern Euphrates frontier, included a papyrus copy of this calendar which still survives.[30] The calendar was written in Latin, the official language of the army, and in neat capital letters throughout. This particular copy obviously received considerable use before it was discarded; the frequent rolling and unrolling of the papyrus had distorted the original shape of the roll and two patching jobs had been necessary. It was certainly not just an official ordinance kept in the files and ignored.

29 *ILS* 5004 (trans. Braund (1985) no.460); Wissowa (1915); Purcell (1983) 167–79; Saulnier (1984). On the creation of the treaty, in 338 B.C., see Dubordieu (1989) 339–61. For Aeneas sacrificing before a shrine of the Penates (in a sculptured relief from the Ara Pacis), see **4.3c**.

30 Fink, Hoey and Snyder (1940) = **3.5** (A.D. 223–7). Nock (1952) 223 denied there was an official desire to see the soldiers worshipping the gods listed in the calendar rather than any other gods, but see Fishwick (1987–) II.1 593–608.

The festivals to be celebrated by the cohort demonstrate how the restructured religious system of Augustan Rome was, in a modified form, repeated in the army. First, some of the major festivals of Rome (the Vestalia, for example, or the Neptunalia) were marked on the appropriate day by a sacrifice in the army camp too; so too were the circus games established in Rome by Augustus in 2 B.C. at the dedication of the temple of Mars Ultor. The 'Birthday of Rome' also appears, presumably added to the calendar under Hadrian, to replace an earlier celebration of the Parilia (as we saw in chapter 4). A second group of celebrations honours the reigning emperor, his family and predecessors. The deified emperors and empresses whose birthdays were celebrated by the army seem to correspond exactly to those whose birthdays were celebrated at this time by the Arval Brothers at Rome, marked in their inscribed record; that is, the cohort's calendar was in step with at least one version of official practice in Rome. And on 3 January vows were taken for the well-being of the emperor and the eternity of the Roman empire, with sacrifices to the Capitoline triad – again in accordance with practice at Rome itself.[31]

The forms of ritual prescribed for the army unit were also the same as those performed in Rome – including (as in state cult) both animal sacrifices and offerings of wine and incense (*supplicatio*). The rules for animal sacrifices were also for the most part identical to those followed in the capital: male deities were offered male victims, and female ones, female victims; Mars received a bull, as was standard; the *genius* of the emperor received a bull and the *divi* received oxen. The overlap with the Arval record is again striking: the military calendar even used the same abbreviations for 'ox' ('b.m.') and 'cow' ('b.f.') as the Arval Brothers, abbreviations which are not otherwise attested outside Rome. On the other hand, there were a few differences too. At Dura deified empresses (*divae*) received only *supplicationes*, not cows in sacrifice as in Rome.

Of course, both officers and men also worshipped other gods, apart from those honoured and listed in the calendar. We have already noted, for example, the popularity of Mithras in the Roman army. There was, in fact, a temple of Mithras at Dura which was used by soldiers – although no mention is made of the god in our document; and we shall return below to other examples of the varied religious life of a military unit. Presumably this calendar was not intended to regulate the private religious worship of individual soldiers; rather it formed the basis of the official cycle of ceremonies carried out by (or on behalf of) the cohort as a whole, as a Roman institution. Although the Dura calendar is the only surviving example, it is a fair guess that all army units possessed, and in principle followed, a ritual calendar on this model – which may, in fact, with alterations and adaptations, go back to a calendar first issued to the legions under Augustus himself. Rome, in other words,

---

31 These military *vota* happened in parallel with those performed by civilians throughout the empire; see above, p. 320.

made a version of its own religious system the basis of the religion of the Roman army.

This guess is supported by a variety of evidence suggesting a common basis to the official religious activity of army units. There is certainly a good deal of material to show that the gods and festivals recorded in the Dura calendar did recur in other military contexts throughout the army.[32] For example, from the Roman fort at Maryport, just south of Hadrian's Wall, a series of 21 altars and plaques survives officially dedicated to Jupiter Optimus Maximus in the course of the second century A.D. by three different regiments, perhaps on 3 January when vows were made 'for the wellbeing of the emperor and the eternity of the empire'. Or again, at another fort near Hadrian's Wall (the third century A.D. legionary supply base at Corbridge) we can see the traces of the rituals that the legion's official calendar prescribed, even though we do not possess any written version of the document itself. Inscriptions and carvings from Corbridge attest many of the cults known in the Dura calendar: Jupiter, Victoria, Concordia; and the 'rose festival of the standards', which appears twice in the Dura calendar, is depicted there on a decorative relief which probably formed part of the shrine for the standards. The specifically Roman focus of the legion's official religious activity is further attested by a shrine in the base which clearly evoked the foundation of Rome: a relief carving on the pediment showed the wolf suckling Romulus and Remus, This scene was repeated in another camp halfway across the empire: an early third-century inscription from a fort on the Danube refers to the dedication of a *signum originis*, that is a statue of the wolf with Romulus and Remus.[33]

In general the arrangement and personnel of army camps throughout the empire conformed to the system implied by the Dura calendar.[34] In the centre of the camp, at the rear of the headquarters building, was the shrine which housed the legionary standards and imperial and divine images. This shrine is actually called a Capitolium on one inscription.[35] In front of the headquarters building was a platform where the commander took omens from the flight of birds. The army had on its staff specialist religious personnel: the *victimarii*, who killed the animals, and the *haruspices*, who took the omens from the animals' entrails. Scenes of military sacrifice, on exactly

32 Ankersdorfer (1973); Helgeland (1978); Birley (1978); Rüpke (1990) 184–98, 250–8.
33 Maryport: *RIB* 813–35; cf. the dedications to Jupiter Optimus Maximus on altars dedicated by *beneficiarii*, adjutants (Schallmayer (1990)). Corbridge: Richmond (1943); E.J. Phillips (1977) 12–13, 34, 55; the shrine with the carving of the wolf may have been dedicated to Dea Roma; a sculptured panel from the shrine showed a rustic scene of a faun, perhaps alluding to the first inhabitants of the later site of Rome. On the rose festival see Hoey (1937) and *ILS* 4918 = **3.7**. Danube: *AE* (1982) 849 = J. Kolendo et al. (eds), *Inscriptions latines de Novae* (Poznán 1992) no.28, with Kolendo (1980) and Sarnowski (1989) (A.D. 208).
34 Petrikovits (1975) 75–8; Johnson (1983) 111–17; Rüpke (1990) 165–83.
35 *AE* (1989) 581 (A.D. 208) from Aalen.

Fig. 7.1 A scene from Trajan's column showing the ritual purification of the Roman army, before an assault on the Dacians. A bull, sheep and pig – to form the sacrifice known as *suovetaurilia* – are led in procession round a Roman camp and in through a gate; they are followed by the *victimarii* (shown semi-clad) whose function was to perform the killing of the victims. Within the camp the emperor Trajan, head duly veiled, pours a libation over an altar in front of the standard-bearers. (Height, *c.* 0.80m.)

the standard Roman pattern and attended by the appropriate specialists, are depicted on reliefs from Trajan's column in Rome (in scenes from Trajan's campaigns in Dacia, modern Romania) and from the Antonine Wall in Scotland.[36] (Fig. 7.1) This re-enactment of the most central and characteristic ritual of *Roman* official religion was one of the most striking ways in which the army paraded that religion across the known world; in the case of Trajan's column, that diffusion was then monumentalized in Rome itself, displaying in the very centre of the city the Roman army ritually enacting their 'Romanness' on the frontier.

The official prescription of Roman gods did not, however, prevent the worship of other gods. After all, by the second century A.D., most Roman soldiers came from places other than Rome and Italy and may well have wished to maintain their original identity within a Roman framework; their religious interests must have been as cosmopolitan as those of any group of 'Romans'. For example, an auxiliary cohort from Emesa in Syria, which was raised in the 160s and served for a long period (from the later second to the mid third century A.D.) in Pannonia on the Danube frontier, maintained a dual allegiance to Roman and to Syrian gods, to Jupiter Optimus Maximus and to Elagabalus.[37] This was not just a matter of

36 Domaszewski (1967) index A1 under '*haruspices*' and '*victimarii*'; *victimarii* now attested in the legions, J.C. Balty, *JRS* 78 (1988) 99; Antonine Wall: Henig (1984) 86–7.
37 Fitz (1972) 177–95. Cf. dedication at Carnuntum (in Austria) by an *eques* in a Canathene regiment to two Arab gods peculiar to the area of the Hauran in which

individual devotion. Both gods were worshipped officially by the cohort as a whole as well as by individual officers and men. In contrast, the civilian community outside the camp honoured neither Jupiter Optimus Maximus nor Elagabalus, but a variety of local and other gods.[38] By the second century most soldiers served close to their homeland (the distance of the Emesene cohort from their native territory was unusual in this period), and soldiers and even high-ranking officers sometimes made offerings to local deities.[39] This must have made it easier, for those soldiers who wished, to maintain all kinds of 'native' traditions of worship. But even so the dominant religious system of the army as an institution remained modelled on that of Rome.

After the army, it was Roman *coloniae* that mirrored the religious institutions of Rome itself most closely. This is clearly illustrated by the regulations for the *colonia* founded by Caesar in 44 B.C. at Urso in southern Spain that we noted in chapter 3. The surviving copy of the regulations is a re-inscription of the original rules, dating from the late first century A.D. — effectively reaffirming the peculiarly *Roman* nature of Urso more than a century after its foundation (perhaps to maintain her superiority over other Spanish towns which had received the 'Latin right').[40] This Roman character is evident in almost all the regulations for the life of the *colonia*, but is particularly striking in the detailed, and well-preserved, clauses of the document that refer to priesthoods. As we saw, the two main priestly groups were *pontifices* and *augures*; and 'as at Rome' (the regulations specifically refer to the model of Rome) the priests were to be free from military service and public obligation; they also had the right to wear special clothes at games and sacrifices and to sit at games in the same privileged seats as the town-councillors. Their functions too were similar to those of their Roman prototypes: the *augures*, for example, were to have jurisdiction over the auspices and all matters concerning them.[41]

Canatha lies: *ILS* 4349, revised in J. Češka and R. Hošek, *Inscriptiones Pannoniae Superioris in Slovacia Transdanubiana Asservatae* (Brno 1967) no.12. See generally Haynes (1993).

38 A fresco from Dura, which used to be interpreted as a sacrifice by the commander of the Twentieth Palmyrene cohort to three gods from Palmyra, may in fact show a sacrifice before three statues of emperors: Pekáry (1986).

39 E.g. the 'Aufaniae Matres' in Lower Germany: Birley (1978) 1525–7. Cf. Wissowa (1916–19) 21–3; Drexel (1922) 8; Eck (1989b) 44–5; above, p. 230.

40 *ILS* 6087 = Crawford (1996) I.393–454, part in **10.2a**; translation of more in Lewis and Reinhold (1990) I.453–61 and of all in Crawford (1996) I.421–32. Cf. above, p. 157; D'Ors (1953) 167–280; Mackie (1983) 222–3. It is possible that the original rules were revised for this publication, but for arguments against see Gabba (1988). Cf. Scheid (1991), (1995) on Trier, and Rives (1995a) on Carthage.

41 *ILS* 6087 = Crawford (1996) I.400–2 sects 62, 66–8 = **10.2a**. Cf. Ladage (1971) 11–14, 18–19, 32–5, 39–41, 51–4, 79–80, 88, 103; Galsterer (1971) 59–61; Canto (1981) on *AE* (1978) 402 (Italica). Unfortunately, the relevant part of the charters of the Spanish *municipia*, which probably stood at the beginning of the standard charter, is not preserved in any of the surviving copies.

Much the same priestly organisation and duties are found in all other *coloniae*. As late as A.D. 322, some 200 years after it had become a *colonia*, an embassy from Zama Regia in north Africa to the governor consisted of ten men, of whom the first named were the four *pontifices* and two *augures*; similarly, at Timgad (also in North Africa), over 250 years after the foundation of the *colonia*, the council included the four members of the colleges of *pontifices* and *augures* as well as other priests of the cult of the emperor.[42] An inscribed altar from the *colonia* of Salona (on the eastern Adriatic coast) gives a glimpse of a local *pontifex* at work: the inscription records that at the dedication of the altar a *pontifex* dictated the words to the local magistrate – just the procedure that was adopted at Rome.[43] Of course, local priestly functions could never be exactly identical to those in the capital: the authority of both *pontifices* and *augures*, for example, was restricted by that of the governor (who himself had the right to authorize the moving of corpses – in Rome a pontifical responsibility). But overall the symbolic structures of *coloniae* emphasize their status as 'mini-Romes' from the very moment of their foundation, conducted with rites that echoed the mythic foundation rituals of Rome itself: the auspices were taken and – like Romulus in the well-known myth – the founder ploughed a furrow round the site, lifting the plough where the gates were to be;[44] within this boundary, which replicated the *pomerium* of Rome, no burials could be made; the land within the *pomerium* was public land which could not be expropriated even by the local council.[45]

Much of this similarity is due to direct Roman initiative. The original religious regulations for the *coloniae* and the form of their foundation rituals were devised by the Roman authorities; and *coloniae* in the late Republic and early empire may also have received specific instructions, directly from Rome, on the establishment of new Roman practices. Priests of the deified Julius Caesar (*flamines divi Julii*), who was officially deified at Rome, are found outside Rome only in Roman *coloniae*, in both the eastern and western parts of the empire. A relief honouring one such flamen in the *colonia* of Alexandria Troas in north west Turkey even shows the distinctive hat

42 Zama: *CIL* VI 1686; Timgad: Chastagnol (1978) 26–31 (the document dates to the mid to late 360s A.D.). See generally Dupuis (1992).

43 *ILS* 4907 = **10.1c**. For Rome see Varro, *Latin Language* VI.61; Tacitus, *Histories* IV.53.

44 Above, p. 175 for Romulus and the Parilia; relief showing ploughing in **10.2b**; Plutarch, *Romulus* 11.1–4 = **4.8a**; Levick (1967) 35–7 and *Sammlung von Aulock Index* (1981) 224 s.v. 'Koloniegründer'.

45 Boundary stones: *ILS* 6308 (Capua). Burials: *ILS* 6087 (Urso) = Crawford (1996) I.403–4 sect 73; Frontinus, *On Disputes* (ed. C. Thulin) p.7.2–5 (the section is misplaced in the text but ancient). After the taking of the auspices, the professional land-surveyors could proceed, laying out the land divisions of the *colonia* and orienting them in accordance with the direction of the mid-day sun: Hyginus Gromaticus, *Disposition of Boundaries* (ed. Thulin) p. 135.1–14; also Frontinus pp. 10–11. Cf. Le Gall (1975) 301–8.

(*apex*) worn by *flamines* in Rome.[46] The fact that this cult is found only in *coloniae* may suggest that they were responding to official instructions from Rome, issued perhaps in 42 B.C. when Caesar's deification was finally ratified. Certainly in A.D. 19, when the senate passed a lengthy decree on the funeral honours for the emperor Tiberius' son Germanicus, provincial *coloniae* were explicitly instructed to set up a copy, and their magistrates were barred from transacting public business on the anniversary of the death of Germanicus.[47] At this period, *coloniae* were expected to move in step with Rome.

But even without direct instructions, throughout their history *coloniae* might themselves choose to follow, and parade, Roman models. This was clearly the case in the inscription from Salona, whose introductory formulae involving *pontifex* and magistrate we have just mentioned. What follows this introduction are the regulations governing the rituals at the altar (the 'law of dedication', which Pliny had wrongly expected to find in a non-Roman town):[48] some of these are spelled out; for the rest it is stated that they 'shall be the same as the law pronounced for the altar of Diana on the Aventine'. This ancient set of rules in the Aventine sanctuary in Rome originally governed the relations between Rome and her Latin allies.[49] Here the *colonia* of Salona, some 170 years after its foundation, chose to adapt this model to articulate its own ritual rules and at the same time to emphasize its privileged relationship to Rome. Two other similar documents from Roman *coloniae*, one from Narbo in southern France, the other from Ariminum (Rimini) in Italy, refer to the Aventine model in framing their own cult regulations.[50]

How exactly the population of more distant *coloniae* gained access to the Roman ritual knowledge implied by these and other rules is unclear. It is certainly possible that in some cases they had very little access to that knowledge; and that Roman models were more of a display than a rule book to be followed to the letter. On the other hand, the governor's staff and army units stationed in the provinces included Roman religious experts (*haruspices* and *victimarii*), who might have been able to offer

46 Weinstock (1971) 405, 408–10, pl. 31.2, though he does not note the connection with *coloniae*; M. Walbank (1996) on Corinth. Above, pp. 140–9 for deification of Caesar.

47 *AE* (1984) 508 frr. II a and b (Tabula Siarensis), translated in Sherk (1988) no. 36. Note also the birthday of Germanicus (24 May) in the calendar from Dura: Fink, Hoey and Snyder (1940) 45 (and 136–8) = **3.5**.

48 Pliny, above, p. 321.

49 Inscriptions of these rules in archaic lettering survived in the sanctuary to at least the Augustan period: Dionysius of Halicarnassus IV.26.5; Festus p.164L s.v. 'nesi'. For the creation of the temple see Livy I.45 = **1.5d**.

50 Salona: *ILS* 4907 = **10.1c** (A.D. 137); Narbo: *ILS* 112 = **10.1b** (A.D. 11); Ariminum: *CIL* XI 361 (first century A.D.); the procedure was so standard that the terms were given in highly abbreviated forms. Though these documents have been much studied, it seems important to us to stress the 'colonial' status of the towns concerned.

advice on points of detail; so too might the governor himself.[51] More puzzling, in fact, is the question of what *general* idea of 'Roman religion' (if, by that, we mean the religious institutions and practices of the capital) the population of such places would have had – who, though Roman citizens, might have been resident hundreds of kilometres from Rome for generations. One possible channel is Varro's *Religious Antiquities*. This treatise, of the mid first century B.C., remained even under the empire the only general work on the Roman religious system. That provincials did turn to it for inspiration is suggested by the effective (polemical) use made of it by the Christian Tertullian, writing in north Africa.[52] But even this book will have been hard going, and difficult to apply to particular local issues. The problem is a useful reminder, however, that any such statement as 'the *coloniae* imitated the religion of Rome' is always liable to be a shorthand for 'the *coloniae* imitated their own image (or conflicting images) of the religious institutions of the capital'.

This is not to say that the population of a *colonia* was always in danger of 'misunderstanding' the religion of Rome; but rather that imitation of the religion of the capital must in practice always have been a creative process, involving adaptation and change. Two altars from the *colonia* of Carthage illustrate different ways in which images of (and derived from) Rome might be represented and constructively reinterpreted in a *colonia*. One, a grand public altar, of Augustan date, stood on the outskirts of the Augustan *colonia*. (Fig. 7.2) Two of its large sculpted panels survive. One represents Mars Ultor standing between Venus Genetrix and a figure probably to be identified with *divus* Julius. The other shows a seated female figure, with children in her arms, her lap full of fruit, animals at her feet. This figure is closely based on the scene of 'Earth' on Augustus' Ara Pacis in Rome, though the personified breezes which flank the figure on the original monument have been replaced with a sea god (a Triton) and a female divinity carrying a torch.[53] On the other face, the figures of Mars, Venus and (probably) *divus* Julius are almost certainly derived from statues (not necessarily cult-statues) from the temple in the Forum of Augustus; Mars and Venus are even represented on statue bases, marking them out as statues, not simply deities. It is likely that the altar was produced locally, in Carthage, though we do not know how knowledge of the Roman monuments was disseminated. That is, the *colonia* here, in its own religious monuments, was explicitly combining themes

---

51 A man is shown reading from a book (once) on a military sacrificial relief: Henig (1984) 86–7.

52 Tertullian, *To the Gentiles* II. Augustine later made a similar use of Varro in his *City of God* (e.g. VI.5 = **13.9**). Cf. Price (forthcoming).

53 Find spot: Gsell (1920–8) VIII.117. Wuilleumier (1928) 40 showed that the two reliefs are of exactly the same dimensions. Cf. Zanker (n.d.) 18–20; Fittschen (1976) 187–9; Torelli (1982) 39–42; Kleiner (1992) 100–2. On the Augustan *colonia* see generally Gros (1990); Rives (1995a). On Mars Ultor see above, pp. 199–201 and **4.2**; on Ara Pacis above, Fig. 4.6, and **4.3**.

Fig. 7.2 Two
reliefs from altar in
Carthage.
(a) Left to right:
Venus, Mars;
probably *divus*
Julius, as strongly
implied by the star
on his forehead,
rather than an
Augustan 'prince'.
Mars must be Mars
Ultor, the cult-
image from his own
temple in the
Forum of Augustus
(see **4.2a**). If, as is
now suggested (*see*
Steinby (1993–)
II.291–2 for
discussion), the
temple had only a
single cult-image,
then Venus and
divus Julius must
have been located
elsewhere in Mars'
temple – as statues,
but not cult-images.
(Height, 0.98m;
width, 1.13m.)
(b) 'Earth', flanked
by deities. For the
Roman prototype,
see fig.4.6.
(Preserved height
0.80m., width
1.13m.)

from two of the major Augustan buildings at Rome itself; with direct 'quo-tations' (as in the statues), adaptations (as in the new flanking figures for Earth, perhaps deities with a particular local relevance) and, of course, a wholly new juxtaposition of scenes. The *colonia* was expressing its own ver-sion of Roman identity, through a creative imitation of Rome itself.[54]

The second, and much smaller, altar was found close to an inscription recording the building of a temple to the Augustan family – by a wealthy individual (probably an ex-slave) at his own expense, on private land near the centre of the *colonia*; the donor (so the inscription also records) became perpetual priest of the new cult. Almost certainly the altar belongs to this temple, and dates to the last decade of Augustus' reign.[55] (Fig. 7.3) The scenes on the four sides of the altar again reflect central Roman themes. On the front is Roma, seated on her armour, with a miniature shield and winged victory on her outstretched right hand. The figure may be a version of the Roma (now very fragmentary) which balanced 'Earth' on one side of the Ara Pacis; but, if so, the altar with its globe and cornucopia in front of her must be adaptations of the original design; while the figure of Victory on her hand carries a shield modelled on the 'Shield of Virtue' awarded to Augustus by the senate.[56] The scenes on either side of the altar show Aeneas leading Ascanius and carrying his father Anchises out of Troy (a scene immortalized in Virgil's *Aeneid*, and represented in the Forum of Augustus);[57] and sacrificers, who perform their ritual in the distinctively Roman manner with togas over their heads (perhaps recalling similar scenes on the Lares altars of Rome). Finally, on the rear of the altar, to match the figure of Roma, is Apollo (whose temple Augustus had built on the Palatine), seated in front of a tripod. This altar is also a creative juxta-position of Augustan themes and images, Roma, Aeneas and Apollo, per-haps again influenced by specific monuments in the capital. In this case, the imagery particularly serves the interest of the donor, ineligible (as an ex-slave) for membership of the local council, but nonetheless here proudly asserting his position within the community and within the Roman impe-rial world. If indeed we read (as may be intended) the main officiant in the sacrificial scene as the donor himself, we see him displaying his own (Roman) piety within a version of imaginary Rome.

Imitation of Roman religion in the *coloniae* was, then, less rigid than the regulations we started with might have suggested. And although *coloniae* in general borrowed, sometimes closely, from Rome, there was no immutable

---

54   Though art historians have generally treated the two reliefs separately and simply as evi-dence for Augustan Rome, the real interest of the reliefs lies in the light they cast on Carthage.

55   *ILAfr* 353 = Z.B. Ben Abdullah, *Catalogue des inscriptions latines païennes du Musée du Bardo* (1986) 253 no.7, with Rostovtzeff (n.d.); Poinssot (1929); Rives (1995a) 53–7.

56   A similar allusion is found on one of the Lares altars from Rome: above, p. 186.

57   Above, Fig. 1.1 for an early statuette; Forum of Augustus, **4.2**.

blueprint. Different *coloniae* were Roman in very different ways and made different kinds of accommodation with the central imperial power. This is illustrated very clearly in their choice and layout of temples, and (particularly) in the varied distribution of Capitolia throughout the different *coloniae*.[58] A Capitolium, in the sense of a temple of Jupiter, Juno and Minerva on the model of the Capitoline temple at Rome, provided a very clear link with the capital. Some *coloniae* certainly built Capitolia immediately at the time of their foundation: there are second-century B.C. *coloniae* in Spain with their own Capitolia, and the regulations from Urso specify major games in honour of the Capitoline triad (though we do not know if the town actually had a Capitolium).[59] Other *coloniae* built Capitolia only later, if at all. The *colonia* of veteran soldiers at Timgad, for example, established in A.D. 100, did not include a Capitolium in the forum, where there was only a small temple which may have related to the emperor; and, when building of a Capitolium began circa A.D. 160, it was sited outside the original area of the *colonia*.[60] The options were even wider when a *colonia* was not founded completely afresh, but when an existing town received some Roman colonists – and so took on the status of a *colonia*. For example, at Heliopolis (modern Baalbek in Lebanon), which lay in the territory of the *colonia* of Berytus, a great new civic temple was begun in the Augustan period when ex-soldiers were settled there. The basic design is Roman (with some local adaptations) and the expense of construction, plus the use of imported red Egyptian granite for the portico, strongly suggests financing from Rome, even from the emperor himself. But the name of the main deity, Jupiter Optimus Maximus *Heliopolitanus*, shows clearly how even the Capitoline god could absorb and display the influence of local culture and conditions.[61]

Towns with the status of *municipia* (where local citizens had the so-called 'Latin right' and some even full Roman citizenship) shared some of the Roman religious features of *coloniae*; their principal priesthoods, for example, were named after, and modelled on, Roman institutions – *pontifices*, *augures* and *haruspices*. And from the second century A.D. onwards *municipia* in north Africa also began to build their own Capitolia;

---

58 **10.2c**; Bianchi (1950); I.M. Barton (1982); Todd (1985). Cologne: Ristow (1967); Follmann-Schulz (1986) 735–8. Corinth: M. Walbank (1989), with architectural observations of C.K. Williams (1989). Jerusalem: Schürer (1973–87) I.542, 550–1, 554. For increased emphasis on the Capitoline triad at Ostia, an ancient *colonia*, under Augustus and Hadrian see Meiggs (1973) 352, 380–1.

59 Spain: Keay (1988) 117, 145, 148. Urso: *ILS* 6087 = Crawford (1996) I.403, sects 70–1.

60 Timgad: I.M. Barton (1982) 308–10; cf. Xanten: Follmann-Schulz (1986) 766–9.

61 Seyrig (1954); Liebeschuetz (1977) 485–9; Millar (1990) 10–23 and (1993) 281–5, who notes that the nature of any prior local cults is very obscure, and in particular that the triad postulated by Hajjar (1985) is very hypothetical. We are grateful for the advice of Dr H. Dodge on the construction of the temple. Cf. above, p. 283 and below pp. 384–6 for a sanctuary of the god in Rome.

Fig. 7.3 Altar from Carthage. (a) Roma. (b) Aeneas carrying Anchises and leading Ascanius. (c) Sacrifice at an altar. (d) Apollo. (Total height, 1.18m.; width, 1.16m.; depth 1.03m.)

Thubursicu Numidarum in Algeria, for example, which became a *municipium* after A.D. 100 (perhaps *c.* A.D. 106), dedicated a Capitolium in A.D. 113. A cult that in the first century A.D. had been confined to *coloniae* (and Rome itself) was taken over by *municipia* as part of their display of Roman status. But interestingly, that sequence may also be reversed; and on more than one occasion we can see the building of a Capitolium as part of a claim for Roman status (rather than a boast of Roman status already acquired). At Numluli, which lay in the territory of Carthage, some local citizens who had achieved high status in Carthage dedicated a Capitolium for the local Roman citizens and for the village itself. The building of the temple clearly displayed allegiance to Rome, but it was almost certainly a part of an attempt to gain the status of *municipium* for Numluli which it certainly later held. Similarly at neighbouring Thugga, which also consisted of a group of Roman citizens and a village in the territory of Carthage, a

335

Capitolium was built at just the time that the group of Roman citizens was granted imperial permission to receive legacies; the building of the Capitolium, with its Roman-style cult of the Capitoline triad, was presumably intended to promote their recognition as an independent community.[62] Roman religious institutions in the provinces were not merely reflections, then, of different levels of Romanization; they were also useful counters in the competition for prestige, honour and status that was one of the defining features of provincial culture across the Roman world.

Roman citizens did not, of course, live only in *coloniae* and *municipia*; even in the early empire, when Roman citizenship was a privilege virtually restricted to members of the élite, groups of citizens were found (as at Numluli and Thugga) outside communities with any formal Roman status. In many respects these citizens would have lived and worked indistinguishably from their non-citizen neighbours; but for some purposes they might have formed distinct groups within their non-Roman communities. The religious activity of these groups was, no doubt, one of the ways in which they re-affirmed and displayed their 'Roman' status; and at the same time it must have been one of the channels that spread specifically Roman religion more widely through the provinces. At Thinissut, a non-Roman town in north Africa, the Roman citizens who traded there made a dedication to 'Augustus god'.[63] They probably had in mind the living emperor, who (as we have seen) was not usually the recipient of direct dedications in Rome itself; but, in this alien context, worship of the emperor may have served to mark the boundary between Roman citizens and the non-citizen subjects of Rome. The position of the dedication may itself be significant: for the inscription comes from a site overlooking a Punic sanctuary of Baal and Tanit. This juxtaposition is in one way a striking illustration of the varied religious culture of this small north African town – but at the same time it must have served to emphasize the difference between the Roman cult of the emperor and the Punic traditions of Baal and Tanit.

Individual Roman citizens too could adopt similar strategies. At Vaga, another non-Roman town in north Africa where there had long been Italian traders and Roman citizens, one Marcus Titurnius Africanus restored a shrine of Tellus (Earth), dating the record – in conventional Roman form – by the consuls of 2 B.C.; and in the Greek city of Nicaea (in Bithynia) an Italian trader dedicated statues of the Capitoline triad to the

---

62 Bianchi (1950); I.M. Barton (1982); Rives (1995a) 114–32. Thubursicu: Syme (1951). Numluli: *CIL* VIII 26121; Ferchiou (1984) on decoration. Thugga: *CIL* VIII 15513 (A.D. 166–9), temple; 26582b (A.D. 168), legacies; below, p. 351.

63 *ILS* 9495 = *ILAfr* 306 = Z.B. Ben Abdullah, *Catalogue des inscriptions latines païennes du Musée du Bardo* (1986) 73 no.190. Fishwick (1987–) II.1 452–3 argued that this is a dedication to an Augustan god, of the type discussed below, p. 352. See also a dedication to the Capitoline triad by Roman citizens resident at Troesmis, a non-Roman town near a legionary camp near the mouth of the Danube: *CIL* III 6167 (A.D. 138–61).

local god, albeit with a Greek inscription.[64] We also read of celebrations of the festival of Saturnalia by Roman students studying in Athens – or by one retired soldier living in the Egyptian Fayum, who wrote to his son to order ten cocks from the local market for the festival.[65] Individuals no doubt reminded themselves (as much as the community at large) of their Roman status by making specifically Roman religious gestures.

This general pattern of Roman religious influence in the empire – with its concentration on those groups and places with some formal Roman status – is cut across by a whole variety of different factors. We conclude this section by exploring two of those complexities: first the spread of different forms of what could count as 'Roman' cult among provincial communities; secondly the different impact of Roman deities on the élite and non-élite.

Throughout the Roman world there were wildly different images of 'Roman' religion; as we saw in our discussion of *coloniae*, different communities in the provinces must have constructed their own versions of what they thought was Roman. Of course in earlier chapters of this book we have raised just this question in relation to Rome itself: what was to count as official Roman religion? The negotiability of that category even at the very centre of the Roman world, the changing definitions of 'Romanness', is obviously relevant to the 'export' of Roman religion to provincial communities – as is clearly illustrated in the cult of Magna Mater.

This cult, as we have seen, was 'officially' introduced to Rome in the late third century B.C. From there, it became a common feature of the towns of Italy and the provincial *coloniae* and *municipia* in North Africa, Spain, the Danube region and especially Gaul;[66] at first the cult members seem to have been limited to ex-slaves and others of low formal status, but from the mid second century A.D. local dignitaries too are found within it. In other words, a cult of eastern origin spread through the Roman world not from its eastern 'home', but from Rome and so as a 'Roman' cult. By the mid second century A.D., in fact, the cult in Italy and at least the western provinces was under the general authority of the Roman priests, the *quindecimviri*, who had originally been responsible for the introduction of the cult to Rome. The priests of Magna Mater in Italy and Gaul are sometimes even given the title 'quindecimviral priests'; and an inscription from the territory of the *colonia* at Cumae in southern Italy preserves the text of a letter from the college of *quindecimviri* in Rome, authorizing the local priest of Magna Mater, whom the town had recently

64 Vaga: *CIL* VIII 14392, with Smadja (1980) 153. Nicaea: Robert (1978) 275–6.
65 Aulus Gellius, *Attic Nights* XVIII.2; *Fayûm Towns and their Papyri*, ed. B.P. Grenfell (London 1900) 119.28–9 (c. A.D. 100).
66 Above, pp. 96–8; Wissowa (1912) 320–7; Vermaseren (1977) 60–9, 126–44; Schillinger (1979); Turcan (1989) 61–8.

elected, to wear the special armlet and crown (the priestly badge of office) within the territory of the *colonia*.[67]

There is also a striking reference to a direct link with the city of Rome in an inscription from the *colonia* of Lugdunum (modern Lyons), recording the performance of a *taurobolium* (the cult's characteristic sacrifice of a bull). This text refers to the 'powers' ('vires' – probably the genitals of the sacrificed animal) being 'transferred' from the Vatican sanctuary ('Vaticanum'). It is not exactly clear what that means. It seems unlikely (though not impossible) that the bull's genitals should have been taken from the Vatican in Rome to Lugdunum. More likely, perhaps, there was a 'Vatican sanctuary' in Lugdunum itself – but, if so, its name (and no doubt other aspects of its cult) derived directly from the Roman model.[68] In either case, the direct or indirect dependence of the Lugdunum cult on Rome was unusual. Unlike, for example, the cults of Isis or Mithras, which had no 'headquarters' there, the cult of Magna Mater claimed authority from the centre, which had officially adopted the original cult.

Significantly the inscription also states that this *taurobolium* was performed (as many were at Rome) on behalf of the emperor, as well as the local community – another link with the capital.

The cult of Magna Mater exposes the shifting ambiguities of Roman status, and the expanding definition of what might count as Roman in the provinces: under the general authority of the *quindecimviri,* she counted both as a 'foreign' god (the *quindecimviri* had, as we have seen, specific responsibilities for cults of Greek origin in the city of Rome) and as a 'Roman' god (overseen even in provincial contexts by *Roman* priests). One of the most striking features of Roman imperialism is that (especially in the west) the spread of Roman religious culture through the empire was marked by the diffusion of cults that in the context of Rome itself claimed a 'foreign' origin. It was not only the Capitoline triad, but Magna Mater and Mithras, who could stand for 'Roman' religion in the provinces.

Wealth and power are also factors that we have not so far considered in plotting the patterns of Roman religious influence in provincial communities. By and large, in every kind of community the local élite tended to display less interest in local indigenous cults than in the universal deities associated with the Roman empire.[69] For example, in the *colonia* of Timgad, magistrates and priests in the course of the second and third centuries A.D. made a series of dedications in return for their offices to principally Roman

---

67 *ILS* 4175 = **10.4b** (A.D. 289); cf. *ILS* 4131 = **6.7b** (A.D. 160). The *quindecimviri* also authorized the *dendrophori* ('tree-bearers') of Cumae who served the same cult: *ILS* 4174 (A.D. 251). Wissowa (1912) 320–1; Schillinger (1979) 358–60.

68 *ILS* 4131 = **6.7b**; there was certainly a 'Vatican hill' at Mainz-Kastel: *ILS* 3805. If this text does refer to the sanctuary in Rome (Map 2 no.6; below, p. 384), then the original *taurobolium* must have been performed there.

69 Février (1976); Le Glay (1984) 156–7; Rives (1995a) 100–72 stresses their interest also in native cults. See below, p. 357 on imperial priests.

deities: Jupiter, Victoria, Mars, Fortuna and so on; one text neatly indicates that the declared purpose of its dedicator was 'the celebration of public *religio* and the embellishment of his noble city'.[70] In southern France, which had been under Roman control since the late second century B.C., we can detect a significant distinction between (in one aspect at least) the religious practice of the local urban élite and those outside that group. 'Mars', the most prominent god of the area, appears in inscribed dedications sometimes with a range of local epithets and sometimes without: the dedications with local epithets are usually associated with dedicators who did not come from old established or distinguished families; Roman functionaries and members of the local élites are much more commonly associated with those without local epithets. In addition, 90% of the dedications to Mars with local epithets are found outside the towns.[71] Even in this area, which seems at first sight to be strongly Roman in tone overall (note, for example, the name 'Mars'), those of higher local status chose to display their relationship with gods who were more obviously part of the Roman system.

Religious display must have been central in the competition for status, both inside and outside the local community. We can only guess how different it might have *felt* to make a dedication to Mars rather than Mars Alator; we can only guess what costs (as well as benefits) there might have been in publicly displaying allegiance to explicitly Roman gods. But it is clear enough that local élites expressed their own status, as against their social and political inferiors, by parading close ties with the gods of Rome.

2. Controls and integration

The religious impact of Rome on communities without formal Roman status was quite different; it was much less a matter of imitation, much more a question of various forms of control and integration. Roman authorities moved to suppress (or 'emend') religious forms that seemed to be a focus of opposition to Roman rule – whenever and wherever they found them. But in other respects there appears to be a clear distinction between their approach to the pre-Roman religions in the west and those in the east. In the Greek east the civic cults seem to have continued, outwardly unaffected by Rome; but in the west local gods were transformed and integrated into the Roman pantheon. This distinction, however, raises the question of how we can identify different degrees of 'Romanization'; what counts as the transformation of religion under the impact of a conquering power; how far we can assess fundamental changes in religious ideology from its outward forms.

---

70 *AE* (1987) 1078; cf. Pavis d'Escurac (1980–1); above, p. 217. Note also the Roman cults of the *colonia* of Savaria, though they receded in importance in the second and third centuries A.D.: Balla (1967).
71 Lavagne (1979); also Carré (1981).

Priesthood was an area of particular concern. In four different areas, we can see how the Romans restricted the power of native priests in the provinces; in all these cases, the priesthoods were organized quite differently from the traditional model of Graeco-Roman city-states (where priests were civic officials, with strict limitations on their authority, drawn in rotation from the local élites) and, to the Romans at least, represented an alternative system of power capable of rivalling their own; often these priesthoods were based on rich and powerful temple institutions.[72]

Egypt was annexed to the Roman empire in 30 B.C.; here temples, with their powerful priesthoods and widespread landholding, had traditionally been a major focus of religious and political authority. After annexation the Romans were faced with the problem of negotiating their relationship with these powerful religious institutions.[73] In detail, the pattern of Roman action in Egypt is very varied: some temple lands were confiscated in 24–22 B.C. (the temples either leased these lands back to be cultivated for revenue or accepted a direct state subsidy); but extensive lands were also granted (or confirmed) to a temple of Isis in the south of Egypt, and some 'sacred land' continued to be administered directly by religious officials. Overall, however, even where existing religious institutions were not abolished by the Romans, there is a clear trend towards increasing Roman supervision, if not direct control. All people attached to sanctuaries had to be registered from 4 B.C. onwards; from the mid first century A.D. onwards temple property and dues owed to the state by the temples also had to be recorded. The temples fell within the responsibility both of the office of the so-called 'Idios Logos' (the 'Special Account', which handled financial and administrative matters) and of the Roman governor, aided by a separate Roman official, known as the High Priest of Alexandria and All Egypt. This High Priest vetted requests to circumcise candidates for the Egyptian priesthood,[74] and adjudicated on the qualifications of those already in the priesthood. The Romans probably did not devise all these regulations entirely themselves; they represent in part at least a development of the practices of earlier rulers of the country, the dynasty of Ptolemaic kings (for after all temple power was likely to be a challenge to any secular authority, not just the Romans). However they illustrate a strong assertion of Roman control of Egyptian religious institutions – not just in general, but right down to the level of individual priests, their qualifications and marks of office.

The religious organization of two other parts of the eastern

72 See R.L. Gordon (1990c) 240–5.

73 The conventional view holds that Rome took a series of measures of increasing scope to bring both temple lands and temple personnel under the control of Roman administration: Swarney (1970) 57–9, 83–96; Whitehorne (1980–1); Stead (1981); cf. Thompson (1988) 271–6 on Memphis. For a revisionist view see the forthcoming book by P. Glare.

74 From Antoninus Pius onwards circumcision was illegal except for Jews and for Egyptian priests.

Mediterranean also posed problems for Rome and similar methods of control were introduced. When Judaea passed from the rule of a client king to direct Roman administration in A.D. 6, the Roman governor (as earlier King Herod) appointed or dismissed the High Priest of the temple; as a further attempt to restrict its potential power base, the office was made technically an annual one – even though in practice (as a compromise, perhaps, between Roman authority and Jewish tradition) the holder was regularly re-appointed. The Romans oversaw the finances of the temple and restricted the competence of the Jewish council, the Sanhedrin. But otherwise the day to day temple organization was unaffected by Rome (though new sacrifices on behalf of the empire were now offered there); and Jews in other provinces and in Italy were permitted to continue sending a regular tax and gifts to the temple – until, that is, it was violently destroyed by the Romans following the Jewish revolt of A.D. 66–70. At that point a special, humiliating Roman tax replaced these contributions to the temple: Jews now had to pay not towards the temple at Jerusalem, but in perpetuity for the rebuilding of the temple of Jupiter Capitolinus in Rome (burned down the previous year).[75]

In Asia Minor too there were temples whose priests wielded considerable secular power. Again Roman responses varied; but all tended towards neutralizing any threat that the priestly organization might represent. When a Roman *colonia* was established at Pisidian Antioch, for example, the sanctuary of the god Men lost its territories and its sacred slaves, but elsewhere the Romans encouraged a gradual evolution towards priesthood much more on the Graeco-Roman norm. In Cappadocia and Galatia there had been four major temple estates, inhabited by 'sacred serfs' (*hierodouloi*) and ruled by priests. Under Rome, the cults continued to be prestigious, but the communities were transformed into Greek-style city-states and the priesthoods tended to become multiple and to be held (annually) by the local hellenized aristocracy.[76]

In the west any indigenous priesthoods that predated the conquest by the Romans came under pressure. The Romans attempted actively to suppress the Druids for their 'magical' practices and promotion of *superstitio*, though repression may, in fact, have increased their self-consciousness and cohesion.[77] In other cases the message to local élites was clear, even without drastic action by the Roman authorities: local styles of priesthoods were transformed into a Roman pattern. Occasionally, the ancient names were preserved, but the ubiquitous Roman titles of *flamen* and *sacerdos* in towns

---

75 Schürer (1973–87) I.376–9, II.218–23; Goodman (1989). Sacrifices: Philo, *Embassy to Gaius* 157 = **12.6c(ii)**; below p. 361. Gifts to Jerusalem seen as 'barbarous *superstitio*': Cicero, *On Behalf of Flaccus* 67; cf. Tacitus, *Histories* V.5.

76 Debord (1982) 56–61; S. Mitchell (1993) I.81–2. Antioch: Strabo XII.8.14 (p.577C); Levick (1967) 85–7.

77 Above, pp. 221; 234.

in the Latin west sometimes at least were the result of a reinterpretation of indigenous priestly offices. Civic priesthood on the Graeco-Roman pattern was the norm and as a result, with the exception of the Druids, no indigenous priestly group in the west appears to have posed a threat to the Roman order.

Roman forms of control operated in broadly similar ways, with broadly similar aims everywhere; but in other respects the effects of Roman rule on religious life in the east appear very different from those in the west. In mainland Greece and Asia Minor, where Greek language and culture were dominant and respected by Rome, the religious life of the towns did not, to all appearances, change radically under Roman rule. In Athens, for example, the central cult remained that of Athena Polias on the Acropolis, and the Eleusinian Mysteries continued to have immense prestige.[78] Since time immemorial the celebration of the mysteries had involved a grand annual procession between the city of Athens and the sanctuary at Eleusis. In A.D. 220 the people of Athens in fact voted to enhance the grandeur of the procession by increasing the participation of the youth (*ephebes*) of the city: 'Since we continue now as in previous periods to perform the mysteries, and since ancestral custom along with the Eumolpidae <sc. the Athenian clan with charge over the mysteries> ordains that care be given that the sacred objects be carried grandly here from Eleusis and back from the city to Eleusis...'[79] 'Ancestral custom' could be the sanction not for fossilization but for the evolution of cults within a traditional framework. Earlier, probably in the Augustan period, there was a major reorganization of sanctuaries throughout Attica (the region around Athens): new leases of sacred properties were drawn up, to place the finances of the cults again on a proper footing. This 'restoration' of ancestral cults even involved moving several earlier temples from outlying sites in Attica in to the agora in the centre of the city – presumably allowing worship to continue in a new 'heritage' setting.[80] The ancestral cults formed the core of religious life in Athens (and other Greek cities): Isis and Sarapis were important as they had been in the Hellenistic period, but the other elective cults attested in Rome made little impact on Athens.

On the other hand, there was inevitably a good deal of adaptation as a consequence of Roman conquest; at the very least, traditional cults would have taken on new meanings in the context of a Roman province. We shall see in the next section how ancestral Greek religion provided the framework

---

78 Nilsson (1961–7) II.327–58; Lane Fox (1986) 27–101; Price (1998) ch.8. Above, p. 223 for Roman initiates.

79 *IG* II² 1078 = F. Sokolowski, *Lois sacrées des cités grecques* (1969) no.8.

80 Sacred properties: *IG* II² 1035, dated by Culley (1975) to 10/9 – 3/2 B.C. Temples: Camp (1986) 184–7; Alcock (1993) 192–5. The claim that these moved temples also housed the imperial cult is not founded on secure epigraphic evidence. (Gaius Caesar, Augustus' son, is called 'new Ares' not in the agora, but in the Theatre of Dionysus.)

for various forms of worship of the Roman emperor. It is also clear that the Roman calendar had an increasing influence in the east – though it was not here a question of simple provincial imitation of the central model. When the province of Asia decided to honour Augustus by creating a new calendar, the assembly chose to start the year not, as in the orthodox Roman calendar, on 1 January, but on another date of Roman significance, 23 September, which was the emperor's birthday. (According to the inscription recording this change of calendar, the precise date of 23 September came as a suggestion of the Roman governor – a glimpse of the complex background that must lie behind many decisions of this kind.)[81] The Roman authorities also sometimes sought to control the finances of civic sanctuaries. In the very early Augustan period a Roman official in the province of Asia issued an extensive regulation to Ephesus on religious finances, a regulation known from its subsequent revision in A.D. 44: for example, priests (who would no longer have to buy their offices) would not receive subventions from the city, and public slaves were not to dedicate to the goddess their own slaves who would then be reared at the expense of the goddess. Whether this reform was driven by Roman desire to ensure the financial stability of local cults, or by their desire to eradicate religious practices that did not conform to their own model of piety, it is a clear case of Roman intervention in a civic cult of the Greek world.[82]

In most cases, however, we are not dealing with a straightforward opposition between the continuity of local civic cults and Roman interference. All Roman activity in relation to the cults of the Greek world (from generous subvention to drastic eradication) must have been open to various interpretations. If, for example, a Roman official had paid for the restoration of a Greek temple, would that have counted as Roman respect for traditional civic cults? Or would it have been instead (or at the same time) a mark of Roman take-over, of Rome's domination of those cults? At the very least, a restoration by Rome must have carried a different significance from a restoration by the local city itself. Even if not outwardly 'Romanized', traditional religion was now operating within a context of Roman power and empire. And it was often the local inhabitants themselves who were instrumental in parading the Roman associations of traditional cult. We do not know who placed the statue of the emperor Hadrian that (as Pausanias records) once stood within the Parthenon – but at the very least it must have been authorized by the local Athenian officials. It was, however, certainly they who decided to honour the emperor Nero, emblazoning his

---

81 Calendar: Samuel (1972) 171–88; cf. Price (1984) 106. The governor's suggestion itself followed a request by the province for ideas.

82 E.M. Smallwood, *Documents Illustrating the Principates of Gaius, Claudius and Nero* (Cambridge 1967) no.380 = *Inschriften von Ephesos* Ia 17–19 (trans. Braund (1985) 213–15). Cf. Debord (1982) 211–12; Price (1984) 69, 103. For Roman control of asylum see above, p. 224.

name across the architrave of the Parthenon.[83] In both these cases we can easily understand how the Roman presence could have seemed to some like an outrageous intrusion of the imperial power into one of the most holy cult places of Greece; or, equally, like the incorporation of Rome within the venerable traditions of Greek religion. 'Continuity' or 'change' can be matters of interpretation.

In the west, however, where Latin was the dominant language and where there was no unified and prestigious cultural system when the Romans arrived, the religious position of Rome's subjects was very different from in the Greek east. There was, unsurprisingly, a range of religious continuities as well as resistances to the cults practised in Rome: a calendar in general use in Gaul in the late second century A.D. perpetuated local traditions, and (to judge from names of adherents that are recorded) the 'Oriental' cults were of little importance among the indigenous populations.[84] However, a crucial aspect of religious change (quite different from anything we saw in the east) was that indigenous gods became widely reinterpreted, by the locals and others, in a Roman form. As we noted at the beginning of this chapter, this process of transformation is difficult to plot – not least, we may now add, because the native deities generally become visible to us only under Roman rule, with increased use of writing on durable surfaces and more iconographic representations in stone. However, the excavation of a sanctuary in the Italian Dolomites, an area conquered by Rome only in the first century B.C., offers a glimpse into the changes in one sanctuary from pre-Roman times onwards.[85] Among the finds, which run from the third or second century B.C. through to A.D. 340, are bronze dippers used for drinking the sacred waters from a sulphurous spring. They were inscribed with the name of the god (Trumusiatis or Tribusiatis), initially in the local language (Venetic), then with the same name transcribed into Latin characters and, only in the most recent ones, with the Graeco-Roman name Apollo. It would be a crude oversimplification to suggest that under the sign of Apollo the cult lost all trace of its native roots; after all there is no suggestion of any major change in the rituals through this period. But at the same time it would be little short of a romantic fallacy to argue that nothing had really changed, and exactly the same native god lurked behind his new classical name. The change (or not) of language and names is not merely a cosmetic issue. At the very least, to call a god not Trumusiatis, but Apollo, was to relate the local healing god to the broader classical pantheon.

The reinterpretation of local gods (by both Romans and members of the local communities) was widespread in the western provinces, from the

---

83   Hadrian: Pausanias I.24.7; Arafat (1996) 163. Nero: Price (1984) 149; Arafat (1996) 153–4.

84   Duval and Pinault (1986); Olmsted (1992). 'Oriental' cults: Toutain (1907–20) II; Le Glay (1984) 156; Alföldy (1989) 74–5.

85   Pascal (1964) 140–4; Pauli (1984) 152–5.

north-west of the Iberian peninsula to the Danube.[86] As part of his effort to describe and explain to a Roman readership the culture and society of Gaul, Julius Caesar identified and interpreted in Roman terms a number of gods (for example, Mercury and Vulcan) as characteristic of the area at the time of the Roman conquest; while evidence from the imperial period shows how these gods did indeed become assimilated to Graeco-Roman deities, verbally or iconographically – so becoming part of the mixed religious world of Roman Gaul in the combinations that Caesar himself identified, predicted or invented.[87] At the same time, the design of local temples and sanctuaries was also changed; some elements of Roman architecture were incorporated into the facades, though the overall groundplan remained basically unchanged and distinctively unRoman.[88] It is striking that in central and southern Gaul dedications to these reinterpreted local gods were not, by and large, made by local élites, who, as we noted in the case of Mars, tended to parade their connections with specifically Roman gods; nor for that matter were such dedications regularly made by Roman officials, soldiers and others from outside Gaul. The overwhelming majority of the worshippers seem to have been relatively humble people – confirming that (however exactly they are to be interpreted) these hybrid deities appealed to those who related themselves less fully to the Roman order.[89]

The complexities of the local divine hierarchies, and the changes prompted by Roman influence, can be illustrated by two examples, from Spain and Germany. In the north west of the Iberian peninsula the pattern of religious activity was very different from that on the east and south coasts, which had been a Roman province since the second century B.C. and where religious forms on a strongly Graeco-Roman model were well-established.[90] In the north and west (conquered only under the emperor Augustus) the religious picture was much more varied. So, for example, instead of the cults of the Lares Augusti, the category of Lares was taken over and joined with a variety of local protective deities; likewise, though Jupiter Optimus Maximus does appear both in official and in indigenous contexts, Jupiter alone or with various other titles was more widely worshipped. In

---

86 Alföldy (1989) 79–82 on preponderance of local deities.

87 Caesar, *Gallic War* VI.17 (= **2.9a**), 21; cf. inscriptions in **2.9b**, Tacitus, *Germania* 9.

88 Horne (1986).

89 Toutain (1907–20) I.297–314, 388–92, III.193–467; Clavel-Lévêque (1972); Lavagne (1979); Letta (1984). Wightman (1985) 177–87 and (1986) shows that the pattern is less clear in Belgica, because there were far fewer unambiguously Roman deities. Cf. Derks (1991); Van Andringa (1994) on Aventicum. For cults of pre-Roman Gaul see Brunaux (1988); Roymans (1990); Goudineau et al. (1994) include studies of both pre-Roman and Roman Gaul.

90 Below, p. 355 n. 120; Lambrino (1965); Pastor Muñoz (1981); Nicols (1987). Cf. Fear (1996) 227–69 on differences within Baetica. For religions in Spain: Mangas (1986); Keay (1988) 145–71; Vázquez y Hoys (1982), testimonia.

both these cases an earlier local god (or group of gods) may have been rein-terpreted in Roman guise. The way Jupiter could be reinterpreted (and then re-placed) within a local divine hierarchy is well illustrated in an inscription of the Danigi, a people in what is now Portugal, which lists the sacrificial ani-mals due to a range of deities: Nabia Corona; Nabia; Jupiter; -urgus; and Ida(?).[91] Jupiter, we should note, was in second place to the local Nabia (wor-shipped in two forms); and he received as sacrifice not his usual Roman ox but a lamb and a suckling calf – emphasizing his different role within the local context. There is a Roman tinge in the style of the altar and in the use of a Roman date (given by the consuls of that year), perhaps because the two local landowners who presided over the sacrifices were Roman citizens; but the complex divine hierarchy of the rural Danigi, with its specifically local and regional gods, was only partly integrated into the Roman divine system.

The second example concerns 'Jupiter columns' – columns up to fifteen metres high dedicated to Jupiter Optimus Maximus, which were a com-mon type of religious monument in parts of eastern France and Germany from the mid second to mid third centuries A.D. These columns also illus-trate borrowing from Rome, reinterpreted within a local religious hierar-chy. They take two different regional forms. The first type, with Jupiter on horseback trampling a giant, is characteristic of the Rhine land between Mainz and Strasbourg.[92] (Fig 7.4) The second type, prevalent in lower Germany and Gallia Belgica, features a Jupiter enthroned. The prototype for both was the column erected at Mainz by the local population in hon-our of Nero in A.D. 60, which was itself probably directly based on a Jupiter column in Rome; hence its largely classical iconography. The subsequent Jupiter columns, all a century and more later, included round the base of the column a more eclectic range of deities, often shown in two tiers: the members of the Capitoline triad were usually depicted, but not usually as a triad; and otherwise the combinations of deities were novel, including a range of much less 'classical' gods. Though they may have been inspired by the early Mainz column to Nero, the columns were not simply Roman. Their interpretation has been much debated: are the gods local (German or Celtic), or Roman? And in this case it is much less clear that they are to be connected with a particular social group, as we have argued for the dedica-tion of the Danigi: the columns seem to have been erected in towns, sanc-tuaries and, especially, on estates by all sorts of people from private individuals to local groups to soldiers and officials. They do, however, demonstrate very clearly the flexibility and shifts of 'Roman' religion as it was incorporated into provincial ideology: in these columns Roman and

---

91   *AE* (1973) 319 (A.D. 147) with Le Roux (1994b). For a nice example from western Gaul see *ILS* 7053 and *AE* (1969–70) 405 with Chastagnol (1980) and Scheid (1991) 51. In Africa too one needs to distinguish between Jupiter Optimus Maximus, an offi-cial deity, and Jupiter without the epithet: Kallala (1992).

92   Bauchhenss and Noelke (1981); in English, Schutz (1985) 66–7.

Fig. 7.4 Jupiter column from Butzbach (Wetteraukreis, Germany), c. A.D. 230; height c.4m. The bottom four panels depict Juno, Minerva, Hercules and Mercury. The next tier up features the seven gods that gave their names to the days of the week: Saturn, Sol, Luna, Mars, Mercury, Jupiter and Venus. On the top of the column is a rider on horseback standing on a defeated giant.

native religious forms were combined, and re-combined, into a new celestial hierarchy that guaranteed the cosmic order.

Religion, however, was not always an effective buttress of Roman rule, or a flexible integrator of the traditions of conquered and conquering. Roman cults and deities could stand all too clearly for the oppressive demands of Roman imperialism. When a rebellion broke out in Germany one local priest of the imperial cult at the Ara Ubiorum tore off his fillets, the symbol of his office, and went over to join the rebels. In the British revolt, the temple to Claudius, seen as 'a citadel of eternal domination' at which the provincial priests wasted their money 'in the guise of *religio*', was totally destroyed. When the Jewish revolt broke out in A.D. 66 the first move of the rebels was to end the sacrifices in the temple on behalf of Rome.[93]

Conversely local cultic traditions could become the rallying ground for opposition to Roman rule.[94] The stories of Alexandrian Greeks protesting against the perceived tyranny of Rome include appeals to the Alexandrian Sarapis. Prophecies, originating in the Hellenistic period but still circulating under the Roman empire, foretold the liberation of Egypt and her gods from the foreign oppressor.[95] In actual revolts, local religious figures are often claimed to have stimulated or even led the rebels. In an Egyptian rebellion of A.D. 172–173 the leader was a priest.[96] An incursion into the empire from Thrace was led by a priest of Dionysus, who gained a following by his performance of rites; he was probably acting to recover the sanctuary of Dionysus which had earlier been made over by the Romans to another tribe.[97] In Gaul, at a time of political chaos in Rome, the Druids allegedly prophesied that the (accidental) burning of the Capitoline temple in Rome signified the end of Roman rule over the Gauls. At around the same time, a revolt on the Rhine frontier started with a feast in a sacred grove and a religious vow and was strongly supported by a local

---

93   Tacitus, *Annals* I.39.1, 57.2; XIV.31.4, 32.3. Jews: Josephus, *Jewish War* II. 409–21; Roth (1960); above, p. 341.

94   Momigliano (1987); Goodman (1991). Pekáry (1987) lists cases of unrest and revolts. See also S.J. Stern (1982) 51–71 for religious millenarian opposition to Spanish rule in Peru.

95   Musurillo (1954) 4–5, 45 (= **12.6f**). Koenen (1970); also (1984).

96   Cassius Dio LXXII.4.

97   Cassius Dio LI.25.5 (29 B.C.), LIV.34.5–7 (11 B.C.).

prophetess.[98] The Jewish revolts against Rome, which were much more significant in military terms than any we have just mentioned, were also aided by the fact that the Jewish faith could be interpreted to offer a coherent religious basis for revolt. At least some of the rebels in Judaea in A.D. 66–70 and 132–135 were inspired by the principle that their god alone should be master of Israel and, in the revolt of A.D. 116–117 which flared up in Egypt, North Africa and Mesopotamia, the rebels in Cyrene seem to have damaged or destroyed temples of the pagan gods.[99] The subsequent massacre of the Jews in Egypt was probably due in part to traditional enmity to the Jews as religious enemies of Egypt's gods and the 'victory' was still celebrated in Egypt eighty years later by civic festivals.[100]

Local religion operating as a focus of opposition to Rome is a further reminder of the sheer complexity of religious life in the provinces. Individual gods, whether local or Roman, did not stand for just one thing; cults were not combined according to a single standard blueprint which equated one deity unproblematically with another. Religious forms were constantly re-interpreted and deployed in different combinations for quite different purposes. The god that was joined in worship with Jupiter one day might be leading the rebels the next.

3. Imperial rituals

Various forms of what we call 'the imperial cult' are found right across the empire. The army sacrificed to the Capitoline triad on behalf of the living emperor and also to his officially deified predecessors; provincials performed *vota* to the gods and sacrificed the *taurobolium* to Magna Mater on behalf of the emperor; and (in the province of Asia) celebrated Augustus' birthday as the start of their year. In other words, as we have already seen (both in chapter 4 in relation to Rome itself and again at the start of this chapter), cults of the emperor were not an independent element of religious life: sometimes the emperor was placed under the protection of the Olympian pantheon or linked with the traditional gods (as we shall see in the combination Mars Augustus), sometimes cult was offered directly to him. These forms of cult were rarely a separate export to the provinces from Rome, but developed in different ways in the context of the various forms of Romanized religion that operated there. In this section, we have decided to group together some rather different practices which in a variety of ways across the empire related the emperor to the gods. However, we stress that these are very diverse, because they were located in very different contexts. That is, there is no such thing as '*the* imperial cult'.

98 Tacitus, *Histories* IV.54, 61, 65, V.22, 24. Cf. above, p. 341 on Druids.
99 Schürer (1973–87) I.531, 544–5, II.598–606; cf. Barnes (1989b) on dating.
100 Frankfurter (1992).

The passage of Cassius Dio cited at the start of this chapter shows the significance of the different contexts of imperial cult. Though Dio sees cults of the emperor as a unifying factor across the empire, he draws a crucial distinction between different forms of imperial cult: cults offered to the living emperor by subjects of Rome and the practices of the centre. 'For in the capital itself (he writes) and in Italy generally no emperor, however worthy of renown he has been, has dared to do this <i.e. have lifetime cults of himself>; still, even there various divine honours are bestowed after their death upon such emperors as have ruled uprightly, and in fact shrines are built to them.'[101] That is, official public cults in the capital were restricted to deceased emperors (and members of their families); for the living emperor vows were offered on his behalf to the Olympian gods.[102] Dio further distinguishes between the cults offered by subjects of Rome (Greeks and others) and those to be performed by Roman citizens resident in the provinces. Whereas the subjects of Rome had cults of the living emperor, Roman citizens had cults of the Roman type.

We can draw further distinctions. Cults of the emperor are found in the provinces at two different levels. Most provinces had a provincial assembly, consisting of representatives of the towns of that province; the assembly at its annual meeting conducted business of provincial interest (whether, for example, the governor should be prosecuted in Rome for corruption) and celebrated an imperial festival. When Dio talks of Augustus giving permission in 29 B.C. to the Greeks of the two provinces of Asia and Pontus-Bithynia to establish cults to himself, he is referring to the creation of cults organized by the two provincial assemblies. In addition, outside the organization of the province as a whole, individual communities established their own cults of the emperor: Ephesus, for example, had not only the sanctuary for the Roman citizens of the province of Asia, but also its own Greek-style cults of Augustus.

It is conventional to draw another distinction in analysis of 'the imperial cult' – between the eastern and the western parts of the empire: in the east the cult was a voluntary matter, absorbed within pre-existing structures, while in the west it was imposed by Rome. We shall notice various differences between east and west in the course of this section, but we have decided to treat the whole empire together, in order to draw out significant patterns right across the Roman world. In so far as Rome had religious expectations of Roman citizens resident in the provinces, it did not matter whether they were in east or west; and civic cults in the west may have arisen from local dynamics similar to those in Greek cities. Rather than stress the east/west distinction, we shall emphasize again the importance of the *status* of the community offering cult.

101 Cassius Dio LI.20.8.
102 Public cults of Italy did not always follow the Roman model, but rather that of towns in the provinces – suggesting perhaps that Italian towns were perceived (and perceived themselves) as subordinate to the power of Rome, rather than partners in it.

Cult offered to, or on behalf of the emperor, his family or dead ancestors ('imperial cult') is just one part of a wider set of associations between emperor and religion in the empire. A distinctive symbol of the Augustan restructuring of religion was the image of the emperor officiating at sacrifice. As we saw in chapter four, the links between emperor and sacrifice were so emphasized that from the reign of Augustus onwards almost no one other than the emperor (and his immediate family) was depicted at sacrifice in public images. This particular imperial scene is represented in a series of sculptures from Rome and Italy; but one of the most striking examples is found in the *colonia* of Lepcis Magna in North Africa, on an early third-century commemorative arch which was lavishly decorated with four sculptured friezes. One of these friezes shows the offering of sacrifice by the imperial family, probably to the Capitoline triad (Fig. 7.5). Although the centre of the frieze is very damaged, it almost certainly showed Septimius Severus with his two sons; the figure of his wife, Julia Domna, survives on the right of the central group, her hand stretched out to offer incense; behind, a few fragments remain from what appear to be the Capitoline deities – pictured in receipt of the sacrifice. Flanking the central group on the left stands a group of soldiers; and on the right, figures representing Rome and the senate, and a sequence of men clad in togas and other soldiers – in front of whom, from either end, the sacrificial animals are introduced. Other friezes on the arch offer slightly different versions of the place of the imperial family in relation to the gods (one shows the emperor holding an *augur*'s staff (*lituus*), linking hands with his son in front of a group of deities, both 'Roman' and local); but they combine to stress the significance of imperial harmony and the piety of the emperor in ensuring the favour of the gods for the empire.[103]

Scenes of imperial sacrifice were not limited to specifically Roman settlements in the provinces. Often stamped as a design on Roman coins, they were found in pockets and purses all over the Roman world. In Asia Minor one or two temples dedicated to the emperor had cult statues which depicted the emperor in the act of performing a sacrifice. The image even seems to have been stamped on sacrificial cakes distributed to the people at festivals through the empire. A number of curious discoveries made in Britain and Hungary have been identified as the moulds for these cakes – showing the emperor offering sacrifice, among other imperial scenes. The emperor in his religious role was literally imprinted on the ritual food consumed at provincial religious celebrations. The distinctively Roman model of sacrifice became a familiar image almost everywhere.[104]

The emperor was regularly represented as under the particular protection

103 Strocka (1972), with full reconstruction of the frieze; Kleiner (1992) 340–3; also illustrated **6.1d**. For a similar image from Rome see **6.1b**.
104 Asia Minor: Price (1984) 185. Moulds: Boon (1958); E.B. Thomas (1980) 184. Cf. in general R.L. Gordon (1990b) 202–19.

Fig. 7.5 Part of a frieze on a commemorative arch in Lepcis Magna, c. A.D. 206–209. On the far left (originally the centre of the frieze, but now very damaged) are traces of a male figure (?one of the imperial sons, possibly Geta); next the empress Julia Domna; a flute-player; then other figures who may include a personification of Rome (holding a globe) and of the senate. In front the sacrificial attendants are in the act of killing the animal. See also **6.1d**. (Height 1.72m.)

of the gods of the local community. In the Greek east sacrifices were made on behalf of the emperor to the Greek gods of the Olympian pantheon. In the west most often it was specifically Roman gods that were emphasized in this role. At Timgad, for example, some of the deities allude to the emperor ('Victoria Victrix', the 'Conquering Victory' who was responsible for imperial successes); other gods are described explicitly as his protectors ('Mars Augustus, protector of our lords').[105] The magistrates of a community of Roman citizens (perhaps army veterans) in Tunisia who made a dedication to 'the gods of the emperors' probably had in mind the gods that supported the emperor. Thus the Capitolium at Thugga was dedicated to the Capitoline triad 'for the well-being' of Marcus Aurelius and Lucius Verus and its pediment featured a relief of an eagle bearing a man aloft, that is an image of the ascension of the emperor to the heavens, a new god. Jupiter, Juno and Minerva protected the emperor in this life and guaranteed his apotheosis after 'death'.[106] Even in an area such as the north-west of the Iberian peninsula where strictly Roman cults were rare, dedications on behalf of the emperor were made not to local, but to Roman gods.[107] But occasionally local gods too were enlisted in his support. In north Africa, for example, dedications 'for the well-being of the emperor' were also made to Romanized forms of local deities: Saturn, Frugifer and Pluto. The divine associations of the emperor extended beyond the Roman pantheon into local religious traditions.

In fact a wide range of deities was invoked as protectors of the emperor

105   Above, n. 70. 'Lords' refers to the emperors.
106   Tunisia: *AE* (1977) 855. Thugga: I.M. Barton (1982) 317; above, p. 336. Cf. Smadja (1985) on the emperor and the pantheon.
107   Tranoy (1981) 332–3. Cf. Le Glay (1984) 168–9.

or as his equals.[108] Numerous dedications were made in all the western provinces in the form 'Saturnus Augustus', 'Silvanus Augustus', or 'Mars Augustus' and so on. The interpretation of the dedications is difficult: are god and emperor equated, or is 'Augustus' an epithet merely indicating loyalty to the imperial regime? The most likely explanation is that there is a reciprocal relationship between the two terms. On the one hand, the place of the local deity within the Roman order was assured and, on the other, the local deity was a protector of the emperor. The western subjects of Rome, especially those of lowly status, sought to restructure their existing religious systems in order to relate them more or less closely with the gods and emperor of Rome.

More direct cults of the emperor are also found, but their forms vary greatly, partly in relation to the statuses of the individuals and communities concerned. The establishment of cults of Roma and Augustus in 29 B.C. by the provinces of Asia and Pontus-Bithynia was a model for other eastern provinces: for example, the provincial assembly of Syria subsequently inaugurated an annual priesthood of Augustus and games which were on the international Greek athletic circuit.[109] These provincial cults of Roman power were generally an innovation of the imperial period, even when there had been a provincial assembly under the Republic.[110] They were not normally imposed by Rome, but arose from and enhanced the rivalry between individual cities and the standing of those who served as high priests of the provincial cults. In the west the form of the provincial cults varied. Recently conquered and very 'unRoman' areas established cults like those in the Greek east, to the living emperor; and in fact it was part of the Roman élite's image of such subjects that they did worship the emperor directly. A high-ranking Roman recorded with approbation how he had seen in Germany a barbarian chief cross the Elbe in a dugout canoe to touch the divine person of Tiberius (then Augustus' heir); the chief in addressing Tiberius referred to the local worship of the divinity of the emperor.[111] The cult of the emperor alluded to here is quite different from the provincial cults of those western areas with long standing Roman traditions which we shall examine shortly.[112] It was one of a series established in the early empire by Roman commanders in barbarian areas which had just

108 Nock (1925) 91–3; Le Glay (1984) 166–9; Price (1984) 91–100 for the east; Fishwick (1987–) II.1, 446–54.

109 Syria: *AE* (1976) 678; *Inschriften von Magnesia* 149. On provincial cults see Deininger (1965) 7–98, 158–61; Price (1984) 56, 66–7, 72–3, 75–7, 83, 88, 104–5, 128–31, 226. On Galatia see S. Mitchell (1993) I.100–17.

110 For cults of Dea Roma and of Roman governors, above, pp. 158–60.

111 Velleius Paterculus II.107.2 = **10.6a**; cf. address to Nero as god by Tiridates, king of Persia: Cassius Dio LXII.5.2.

112 Fishwick (1987–) I.97–146. Spain: Tranoy (1981) 327–9. Gauls and Germans from across the Rhine were instructed by Rome to offer cult to the memories of Drusus and Germanicus at Mainz: Tabula Siarensis frag.a.29–32, Crawford (1996) I.37; Suetonius, *Claudius* 1.3; cf. Lebek (1989) 67–72.

(they hoped) been conquered. The first of these is found in the north-west of the Iberian peninsula soon after its subjugation by Augustus; a governor serving in 22–19 B.C. dedicated three altars to Augustus (the Arae Sestianae, named after the governor), which probably served as centres for three peoples in this region. In 12 B.C. the three Gallic provinces conquered by Caesar were united in a single provincial assembly at Lugdunum, at an altar of Roma and Augustus, dedicated by Drusus, Augustus' stepson. In Germany an altar (the Ara Ubiorum) was built in the last decade B.C. or the first A.D. on the banks of the Rhine near Cologne, as a focus for the new province of Germany. At a time when Roman power reached beyond the Rhine to the Elbe a governor dedicated an altar there in 2 B.C.; the barbarian chief who greeted Tiberius is probably referring to the cult of Augustus at this altar. Cults to the living emperor continued to be established subsequently in areas conquered or reorganized by later emperors.[113]

Roman citizens, on the other hand, were expected to offer different forms of cult from those offered by people who were *subjects* of Rome. In various provinces Roman citizens formed official organizations with a religious function, separate from the organizations of the provincials. In Asia and Pontus-Bithynia, when Augustus gave permission for the Greek provincials to worship Roma and Augustus, he instructed the Roman citizens of each province to set up temples in different cities to Roma and *divus* Julius. At Ephesus both temple and ritual may have been closely modelled on the cult at Rome, and the association of Roman citizens probably existed at least into the second century A.D.[114] In two Greek-speaking cities in north Africa inscriptions record vows on behalf of the emperor in Latin – in phraseology that is very close to the formulae used in Rome by the Arval Brothers. These records may have been put up by the Roman citizens resident in those towns, the use of Latin, combined with the display of religious allegiance to the emperor, offering a way of marking their difference from other members of the local community.[115]

In the west too Roman citizens formed their own associations. At Lugdunum in fact we find two separate organizations: first the provincial council of the Three Gauls in which both non-Romans and Roman citizens could and did participate; second, as an inscription of A.D. 220 records, an association explicitly of Roman *citizens* from each of the provinces of the Three Gauls, with its own officers and funds, also meeting at Lugdunum.[116]

---

113 Fishwick (1987–) I.298, 301–7; Fitz and Fedak (1993) 265–7. There was an altar, or perhaps even a temple, to Claudius in his lifetime: Simpson (1993) *contra* Fishwick (1987–) I.195–218, (1991). Cf. a temple for the emperor built A.D. 166–9 by a tribe in Arabia on the encouragement of the governor: Bowersock (1975).

114 Cassius Dio LI.20.6; Crawford (1996) I.493–5 (with different interpretation); *Inschriften von Ephesos* II 409, V 1517, VII.1 3019. Price (1984) 76–7, 169, 254.

115 Cyrene and Ptolemais: Reynolds (1962), (1965), (1990) 71–2.

116 *AE* (1955) 210 = P. Wuilleumier, *Inscriptions latines des Trois Gaules* (1963) no.221, a text curiously ignored in recent years.

We have no clear record of any religious activity on the part of this second association, but it is tempting to guess that it was modelled on that laid down for the provinces of Asia and Pontus-Bithynia. Much more puzzling is its composition. Although the inscription refers to Roman citizens specifically, from A.D. 212 almost all free inhabitants of the empire had been granted citizenship – and so it is hard to see the logic or purpose by this date of a special association restricted to *citizens*. We may perhaps guess that this was an organization which united not all citizens, but only those who were of Italian rather than Gallic origin. That is, the idea that a defined group of Roman citizens had a particular relation to the emperor seems to have survived the change that ought to have made that idea redundant.

Similarly, provinces in the west with a significant proportion of Roman citizens followed in general the model of Rome itself.[117] The key episode occurred in A.D. 15, the year after the official deification of Augustus in Rome, when permission was given to the province of Hispania Tarraconensis for a temple to *divus* Augustus in the *colonia* of Tarraco. Its priests were drawn not just from Tarraco but the whole province, and Tacitus, reporting the decision of A.D. 15, notes that it set a precedent for other provinces.[118] There was also a range of divine honours offered to living emperors, beyond the displays of divine protection that we have already noted. In the provincial cult of Gallia Narbonensis and Africa Proconsularis, the living emperor may have been included in the cult alongside the dead and deified; and at the time of Vespasian the cult at Tarraco may have been extended to include the reigning emperor. These developments were a notable divergence from standard practice in Rome itself, and perhaps reflect the influence of other civic communities in the west. But, by and large, the range of religious honours offered to the emperor in these western provincial assemblies seems to have followed the patterns set in the centre.

If we move on now to the cults of individual cities rather than of provinces, we find again significant differences in the forms of cults, depending in part on the status of the cities concerned. As we have already seen, civic priests of *divus* Julius are found outside Rome only in *coloniae* – in both eastern and western parts of the empire. It would seem to follow from this that *coloniae*, at least in the early empire, were expected (and perhaps even instructed) to follow the lead of Rome. The cult of the *numen* ('divine power' or 'nod') of Augustus is instructive here, even though it was a form of cult that did not prove popular. The cult is attested in two towns: a town in Etruria dedicated an altar to the *numen* of Augustus, at which sacrifices were

---

117 Fishwick (1978); (1987–) I.150–68, 219–94. Much of this account necessarily remains hypothetical: Le Roux (1994a).

118 Tacitus, *Annals* I.78. The temple complex was completed only in the later first century A.D., when the provincial priests are first attested, though work on it probably began much earlier: Fishwick (1996) 176–82.

to be made on the birthdays of Augustus and Tiberius; and the *colonia* of Narbo dedicated a similar altar in the forum, at which a series of imperial festivals was celebrated. As the cult of the *numen* focussed closely on the living emperor, it might seem to be overstepping the mark officially set, but there was a precedent from the city of Rome itself. An altar to the *numen* of Augustus had been dedicated there in about A.D. 6, and the two towns were probably responding to this lead.[119] The cult of the Lares Augusti was a much more widespread response to a Roman innovation. Following the major reorganization of the ward cults in Rome in 7 B.C. cults of the Lares Augusti are found throughout the Roman west. At Pompeii a new organization of 'ward officials' took office in the same year as the Roman reorganization and the cult later spread to all of Italy. For example, at Ostia, the port of Rome, the cult was established in A.D. 51 with the building of a shrine to the Lares Augusti in the forum; a purification (*lustratio*) of the area, probably round the forum, was performed, a ritual also carried out by the wards in Rome. Outside Italy, the cults occur in almost every Latin province.[120]

At the other extreme, communities lacking Roman status generally determined the forms of their cults without reference to Rome. Those communities which we know best, those in the Greek east, regularly established cults of the living (rather than the posthumously apotheosized) emperor. At Athens a small round temple to Roma and Augustus was built on the Acropolis in the Augustan period; it lay close to, and directly on the long axis of, the Parthenon and its architecture was modelled on that of the neighbouring classical temple known as the Erechtheum. In other respects the degree of explicit deification far outstripped the mere *association* of emperor and god. Athenians sometimes treated living members of the imperial house as themselves divine. They decreed (in the late 190s A.D.) a series of honours for Julia Domna (wife of the emperor Septimius Severus) which identified her with Athena Polias: there was to be a gold cult statue of Julia Domna in the Parthenon, and various sacrificial rites were to be performed by traditional civic and religious officials, both on 'Roman' dates (the birthday of Julia Domna; the first day of the Roman year) and at the principal festival of Athena Polias.[121]

119 *ILS* 154 (A.D. 18) (trans. Braund (1985) 62); *ILS* 112 = **10.1b** (A.D. 11). Cf. above, p. 207. For a dedication of A.D. 11–12 to the *numen* of Augustus see *AE* (1948) 8 = *Inscriptions of Roman Tripolitania* (1952) 324a (Lepcis), with Fishwick (1992c). These provincial dedications are sometimes seen (wrongly) as overstepping the mark established in Rome.

120 Above, pp. 184–6; Vitucci (1946–85) 403–5; Pascal (1964) 71–3; Ladage (1971) 94–5; Silvestrini (1992); Hänlein-Schäfer (1996). Pompeii: *ILS* 6381. Ostia: Map 5; H. Bloch (1962); Degrassi (1965); Bakker (1994) 118–33. Numerous cults in the Romanized towns of southern and eastern Spain: Alarcão et al. (1969). Also among Italian business men at Alexandria: *CIL* III Supp. 12047 = F. Kayser, *Recueil des inscriptions grecques et latines (non funéraires) d'Alexandrie impériale* (Cairo, 1994) no. 5.

121 Price (1984) 147 n.40; above, pp. 343-4 for Nero and Hadrian. For Rome and Augustus at the provincial level, see above, p. 352. Julia Domna: Oliver (1940) = **10.5c**.

The history of these cults in the western empire shows the initiative coming both from the provincials themselves and, on other occasions, from the central Roman authorities, actively promoting festivals, priesthoods and temples for deified emperors.[122] As we have seen, the cult of *divus* Augustus in Tarraco was the result of a request by the Spaniards.[123] On the other hand, the fact that at roughly the same time, under the emperor Vespasian, three long-established provinces (Gallia Narbonensis, Africa Proconsularis and Spanish Baetica) established (or at least reformulated) cults on Roman lines suggests strong pressure from the centre – perhaps to be connected with Vespasian's desire to promote a focus of loyalty to his new dynasty; the provinces of Mauretania in north Africa may also have established a provincial cult at this point. It is fairly certain too that similarities in the institutions of imperial cult between *coloniae* or *municipia* and Rome were not always a matter of voluntary imitation of the centre. A centrally controlled and changed calendar of festivals 'for the veneration of the imperial house' seems to have been issued to *municipia* (and presumably *coloniae*); and these local communities included the centrally directed imperial festivals alongside their locally determined festivals.[124]

Questions of initiative are not, however, always so easily settled. Often there is simply no evidence to determine the issue: we do not know, for example, who it was who instigated the building of the great imperial temples at Nîmes and Vienne that still stand (the so-called Maison Carrée of Nîmes, dedicated to Gaius and Lucius Caesar; the temple at Vienne to *divus* Augustus and *diva* Livia). In many cases, however, inscriptions on civic temples ascribe the responsibility for them either to prominent locals or to the community as a whole.[125] But even here there may have been a much more complicated history than the simple opposition between local or central initiative suggests. In the case of Tarraco's request to build an imperial temple, for example, all kinds of factors may have lain behind their approach – even a prompt from the local governor.[126] The fact that

---

122 There is here a contrast with the provincial cults in the Greek east, which resulted, as we have seen, from local initiatives, though the contrast is not an east/west one but one of status: Augustus instructed (rather than merely permitted) Roman citizens in Asia and Pontus-Bithynia to establish cults of Roma and *divus* Julius.

123 Above, p. 354. Another Spanish province, Lusitania, follows a similar pattern: a temple of *divus* Augustus in the *colonia* of Merida, and a provincial *flamen* (of Livia) in the Claudian period.

124 *AE* (1986) 333, paras. 31, 90, 92 (Lex Irnitana) (trans. *JRS* 76 (1986) 182–99). Cf. above, p. 251; Herz (1975), (1978); Fishwick (1987–) II.1, 482–501; Rüpke (1995) 540–6.

125 Nîmes: Amy and Gros (1979); Gros (1984). Vienne: Pelletier (1982) 446–52; Hänlein-Schäfer (1985) 244–6; André et al. (1991). Inscriptions: Hänlein-Schäfer (1985) 90–3. For the position of imperial temples in the transformation of urban space, Gros (1987), (1991).

126 Tacitus, *Annals* I.78. Price (1984) 65–75 on the relations between central and local initiatives.

Tacitus records it as a spontaneous gesture from the province does not mean that that is the only story that could be told; and he himself implies that rivalry between different communities for the emperor's attention may have played a part, when he says that Tarraco's gesture 'set an example' to other provinces.

All these different forms of honour and cult required priests and other personnel.[127] Priests of the provincial cult were generally drawn from the local élite, but the forms of priesthood varied between the more and the less Romanized provinces. Some of the regulations for the office of high priest of the province of Gallia Narbonensis are preserved, inscribed on a bronze tablet. These show clearly how in this highly Romanized province the priest's privileges and obligations were partly modelled on Rome: his title was *flamen*; his wife was known as *flaminica* (like the *flaminica* of Jupiter), and she seems to have shared at least some of the *flamen*'s religious duties; the surviving clause which prevents her taking an oath against her will or touching a dead body matches almost exactly equivalent regulations for the *flamen Dialis* and his wife at Rome. On the other hand, there are significant differences: at Rome all the major *flamines* held office for life; here the office is explicitly short-term, and a good part of the surviving regulations are concerned with the honours and privileges of ex-*flamines*.[128] The parade of Roman models contrasts with the forms of cult in less Romanized provinces, where there were no Roman-style *flamines* or temples to the officially deified emperor, but priests whose name (*sacerdotes*) distinguished them from the ancient priesthoods of Rome and altars for worship of the living emperor.

But many other social groups were involved in different aspects of imperial cult. The organization of the cult of the Lares Augusti in the provinces, for example, was similar to that at Rome. The colleges responsible for the cult consisted of three or four members, who were generally drawn from ex-slaves (though the freeborn are also found). Gradually, however, slaves too entered the colleges, perhaps because ex-slaves preferred to join the more prestigious group of *Augustales* – who were also in some way connected with the emperor and his honour.

Augustales, who were common in *coloniae* and *municipia* in Italy and the Latin west, have usually been defined in relation to their performance of cult, as if they were priests of the emperor.[129] They have been taken to be small groups, often six in number (*seviri*), rather like the associations

127 Civic priests in the west, of Roma and Augustus, and to lesser extent of other emperors: Geiger (1913); Etienne (1958) 197–250; Fayer (1976) 213–54. For local games see e.g. *AE* (1992) 374 (territory of Amiternum, A.D. 2).
128 *ILS* 6964 = **10.4e**. The *flamines* of the Three Gauls capitalized on their position by erecting statues of themselves and their families in the sanctuary at Lugdunum: F. Richard (1992). The priests of the cult at Tarraco were also called *flamen*, and also wore the special Roman hat (*apex*).
129 Duthoy (1978); Ostrow (1985); Fishwick (1987–) II.1 609–16.

responsible for the cult of the Lares Augusti. A picture of their role, on this interpretation, comes in an inscription from Narbo – where, after a period of tension between the people and the council, the people decided to appoint six men, three Roman knights from the people and three ex-slaves to perform a series of sacrifices in honour of Augustus and his *numen*.[130] The problem is that this particular inscription makes no explicit mention of 'Augustales'.[131] But suppose (as it normally is supposed) that these officials from Narbo did have that title – they still represent only one type of the groups that throughout the Roman empire were known as 'Augustales'. There is other, and much stronger, evidence to suggest that many *Augustales* were not members of small associations at all (whether they had specifically priestly duties or not), but possessors of a particular local status.[132] The (fragmentary) list of *Augustales* from Herculaneum near Naples has more than 450 names, divided into different units (*curiae*), at least one of which was for the freeborn.[133] *Augustales* ranked immediately below the local council at public festivals. Their officials had the symbols of a magistrate (special toga, lictors, the bundle of rods (*fasces*) and so on), and in return for their office were obliged to repair buildings, erect statues and put on games.[134] They also had, in at least some cases, their own special buildings, with imperial statues.[135] There is no real case for seeing *Augustales* of this kind as priests, but *Augustales*, like other public figures, certainly carried out religious functions in their public role: one of their officials is praised in an inscription for 'imitating bygone piety' in his concern for a local cult; others were responsible for the cult of the Lares Augusti.[136] That is, *Augustales* performed the conventional range of local religious actions, and there is no reason to think of them as particularly connected by definition with 'the imperial cult'. Their name 'Augustales' may in fact not derive from their presumed cult function, but mark the creation of the status by Augustus.

In at least the 'civilised' parts of both east and west the principal social change which accompanied these religious changes was the role of local

---

130   *ILS* 112 = **10.1b**, with Kneissl (1980). The 'knights from the people' were probably inhabitants of the *colonia* who were not colonists but did have the equestrian property qualification. The council could grant honorary membership of the order of *Augustales*: *AE* (1987) 239 (Terracina).

131   This is in fact a classic case of the modern tendency to lump together some rather diverse epigraphic evidence under the heading of *Augustales*.

132   Abramenko (1993a). For a similar problem with '*haruspices*' see above, p. 20.

133   *AE* (1978) 119; cf. (1989) 181.

134   Symbols: Petronius, *Satyricon* 30, 71.9; on tombstones, Schäfer (1989) 55–6, 218–21.

135   R.J.A. Wilson (1990) 111–13, 297; De Franciscis (1991); Patras: *Archaeological Reports 1987–88* (1988) 28–9. However, the building at Sarmizegethusa has now been re-identified as a basilica: Etienne et al. (1990). Statues: Trebula Suffenas (*AE* (1972) 154 = *Supplementa Italica* n.s. 4 (1988) 178 no. 43) and Aquincum (*CIL* III 3847).

136   Jupiter: *AE* (1990) 138 (Terracina). Lares Augusti: Etienne (1958) 275–9; Fishwick (1987–) II.1, 614–16; *AE* (1992) 302; Petronius, *Satyricon* 65 = **8.6b**.

élites in the service of Rome. In regions such as Spain, southern France, Greece, Asia Minor, Syria and north Africa, those who were ambitious could hope to see their sons entering the Roman administration as equestrians and their grandsons even entering the Roman senate. For many of the local offices of the imperial cult, the holders received prestige in their local communities, as they did for holding other offices or priesthoods. In the west, ex-slaves with Roman citizenship who formed a significant upwardly mobile group could aspire to some public status which articulated their position in the framework of the Roman empire. But the higher up the social ladder you went, especially to the priesthoods at the provincial level, the higher the stakes became. From the point of view of the priests, these major priesthoods could be a stepping stone to further social and political advancement – even into the world of the city of Rome itself.[137] From the point of view of Rome, on the other hand, we might see the imperial cult as one of the major ways that the local élites were suborned to the service of Rome.

This raises sharply what has always seemed an intriguing puzzle about cults offered to the emperor and his family: were they just a political tool (in the service of Rome, or of local élites)? or did they have some 'real' religious significance? We have already seen throughout this book from discussion of very earliest Roman religion that the opposition implied between religion and politics is an inappropriate model for thinking about Roman religion. It is hard now to appreciate that Jesus' claim in the Gospels that one should give unto Caesar that which is Caesar's and give unto God that which is God's was, in the context of the first century A.D., utterly startling.[138] The idea, in other words, that there was (or should be) a clear delimitation of the political and religious spheres of authority cut across most of the Roman assumptions about the relationship between religious and political life that we have seen so far. The success of this reading of Jesus' message and the dominance of Christianity in the western political tradition has meant that we come to imperial cults with an inappropriate distinction in mind. Ordinary inhabitants of the Roman empire *expected* that political power had a religious dimension. The opposite was also true: religious cults might quite properly have a political dimension. If we seek to distinguish between cults that were (really) political and those that had a (genuine) spiritual dimension we are doing little more than engaging illicitly in Christian polemic against an alien religious system.

Another piece of illicit Christianizing often colours our understanding of the relation between imperial rituals and rituals for the traditional gods. If Christianity eventually triumphed over paganism, what kind of paganism was it? The old model which viewed traditional cults in the Roman

---

137   So, for example, we must imagine that the office of provincial priest would bring its
      holder into contact with (and within the patronage of) the local Roman governor.
138   Matthew 22.15–22; Mark 12.13–17; Luke 20.20–6.

empire before Constantine as mere decayed survivals has now been largely abandoned. But some would still argue that the traditional cults had been effectively supplanted by worship of the emperor, so that Christianity's victory was in fact over the idolatrous worship of a human being. This too is a misunderstanding. In the east throughout the period we have been considering the primary identities of Greek cities continued to be focussed on their ancestral gods. For the citizens of Ephesus in the first centuries A.D. the key to understanding their city lay in the cult of Artemis. The city boasted that it was the birthplace of Artemis, that it possessed an image of the god that had fallen from heaven, and that cults of Artemis had been diffused from Ephesus all over the world. In the words of an Ephesian decree,

> ... the goddess Artemis, patron of our city, is honoured not only in her native city, which she has made more famous than all other cities through her own divinity, but also by Greeks and barbarians, so that everywhere sanctuaries and precincts are consecrated for her, temples are dedicated and altars are set up for her because of her manifest epiphanies ...[139]

Cults of the emperor, which were modelled on the traditional forms of civic cults of the gods, did not displace traditional cults; they fitted in alongside them. For example, in one Macedonian town, a local citizen volunteered to be priest of Zeus, Roma and Augustus and displayed extraordinary munificence in the monthly sacrifices to Zeus and Augustus and in the feasts and games for the citizens.[140] His activities illustrate clearly how (as we have seen on several occasions) the worship of Augustus could be integrated within local religious and social structures.

The same is true not only of Rome itself, as we have seen in chapter 4, but also of communities closely modelled on Rome. The army placed the Capitoline triad at the centre of its religious life, had cults of other ancient Roman gods, and of the official *divi* and *divae*. There was no opposition between the two types of cult: the army, like many others in the empire, started its year with *vota* to the Capitoline triad on behalf of the emperor and the eternity of the empire. The ancient cults of Rome were the context (if a modified one) within which the emperor fitted.

Whereas Greek cities retained a largely stable (if evolving) religious system, and the army and (some) *coloniae* were artificial creations, the picture is in some ways different for many communities in the Latin west. At first sight it might seem that here the imperial cult was an isolable phenomenon, and hence potentially a more easily identifiable competitor for Christianity, but what we have seen throughout this chapter is that in the west ancient cults across a wide spectrum were transformed, and recentred, at least in part, on Rome. The development of the imperial cult may not be

---

139 *Inschriften von Ephesos* 24. Price (1998) ch.2.
140 *Supplementum Epigraphicum Graecum* XXXV. 744 (A.D. 1). Cf. **10.5**, and generally Price (1984); some criticisms in Friesen (1993) 142–68.

so fully integrated in existing traditions as it was in the east – located in a novel, rather than a stable and familiar symbolic context. But even here it was part of something bigger, and must be seen in a context of wider and more profound religious and political changes. Analyses of the imperial cult in the Latin west which examine only the imperial cult itself suffer from a serious case of scholarly tunnel vision and simply fail to grapple with the problem of the relationship of the new forms of imperial rituals to the local religious context.

Does it then matter whether rituals treated the emperor like one of the ordinary gods or 'merely' placed him under their protection? To modern observers it seems crucial, because in modern world religions there is a uniqueness claimed for divinity, and in Christianity specifically one of the central 'mysteries' is precisely the relationship between humanity and divinity, as summed up in the relationship between god and Jesus. The issue had some importance also for Jews and Christians in the Roman empire. Both were (generally) happy to place the emperor under the protection of their god, by sacrifices or prayers.[141] Normally, they were not expected to do more than that. Even when Christians faced trials before Roman officials, the principal issue was their relationship to the traditional gods, not to the (divine) emperor: the question was – would they perform sacrifice to the *gods*? But behind this lay a further concern: if they would not support the traditional pantheon (which upheld the emperor), how could they support the emperor (given that praying to the Christian god did not count)? It is true that sometimes in this context Christians were expected to sacrifice to the gods *on behalf of* the emperor, and sometimes directly *to* the gods and *to* the emperor.[142] But the pressures exerted on Jews and Christians to conform were not motivated by theological concerns about the nature of divinity.

What was at stake for emperors, governors and members of civic élites was the whole web of social, political and hierarchical assumptions that bound imperial society together. Sacrifices and other religious rituals were concerned with defining and establishing relationships of power.[143] Not to place oneself within the set of relationships between emperor, gods, élite and people was effectively to place oneself outside the mainstream of the whole world and the shared Roman understanding of humanity's place within that world. Maintenance of the social order was seen by the Romans to be dependent on maintenance of this agreed set of symbolic structures, which assigned a role to people at all levels. Emperors in Rome needed to play the role of first citizen (not god), an 'ordinary' (if unequalled) senator, but they also needed to be assured of their superiority over other groups and areas. Roman citizens in the provinces needed to construct identities for themselves which articulated their superiority over mere *subjects* of

141 Philo, *Embassy to Gaius* 355–7 = **10.6b**; above, pp. 284; 341.
142 Price (1984) 220–2; above, pp. 239–41.
143 Above, pp. 36–7; Price (1984) 207–33.

Rome, and so followed the precedent of Rome. As for those mere subjects, the centre might expect that they would and should abase themselves before Rome by worshipping the emperor as a god. One emperor indeed asked a delegation of Jews from Alexandria in Egypt in a pointed and hostile manner why they did not sacrifice to him as to a god.[144] There could be no clearer way of articulating the hierarchy of social, political and religious relations that formed the Roman empire. The subjects themselves responded to such pressures or demands in different ways: by accommodating the power of Rome within their traditional symbolic structures, or by changing everything in favour of Rome. From the point of view of status it might make all the difference whether the emperor was treated as a god or only placed under the protection of the gods.

The patterns of the early empire were maintained to some extent into the second century A.D.: new conquests of the first and second centuries were treated much as those of the Augustan period. Internally, there were developments in the statuses of towns: new *coloniae* were rarely created after the Augustan period, but from the second century A.D. existing towns were granted colonial status. Roman citizenship spread slowly in the course of the first two centuries A.D., but in A.D. 212 was granted dramatically by the emperor Caracalla to almost all the free population of the empire.[145] Most newly enfranchised provincials continued to worship their old gods in the old ways; we have, however, one nice example of what seems to be a religious response to Caracalla's grant of Roman citizenship.

Within three years of this grant a civic temple to Zeus Kapitolios is found at Ptolemais Euergetis in the Egyptian Fayum.[146] The earlier scattering of cults of Zeus Kapitolios and of games called Kapitolia in Greece and Asia Minor had been in Roman *coloniae* and in other cities with especial ties to Rome. At Ptolemais the new cult is very striking. The name 'Zeus Kapitolios' refers to the god worshipped on the Capitol at Rome (while, significantly perhaps, refraining from calling him *Optimus Maximus* – 'Best and Greatest'). This is almost the only cult in Egypt that refers to a specifically Roman god and the calendar of rituals associated with it consists partly of specifically Roman festivals. There were sacrifices on 1 January; 21

---

144 Philo, *Embassy to Gaius* 353–7 = **10.6b**. Admittedly the emperor was the bizarre Gaius Caligula, but he merely made explicit a generally latent issue.

145 Above, p. 241.

146 L. Mitteis and U. Wilcken, *Grunzüge und Chrestomathie der Papyruskunde* (Leipzig 1912) I 96 (trans. *An Economic Survey of Ancient Rome*, ed. T. Frank (Baltimore and London 1936) II.662–8); *Sammelbuch* 9489 = *Papyri della Università degli Studi di Milano* IV (1967) 233 (Tebtunis) *might* refer to this temple. Glare (1994) notes earlier interest in 'the imperial cult' at Ptolemais. Cf. Rübsam (1974) 47–52; M. Walbank (1989) 381–3 for Greek cults. The only Egyptian parallel is the Capitolium at Oxyrhynchus, in existence by the late second century A.D.: *Oxyrhynchus Papyri* 2128 etc.

April, the birthday of Rome; on eight occasions for the reigning emperor, twice for his deceased father and twice for his mother. But there were some very different rituals too. In addition to the Roman cults, there were also festivals of four Egyptian gods: the crocodile god Souchos, who was the principal deity of the town, Harpokrates, the Nile and Sarapis. To us, the combination may seem baffling. But it seems that the town was picking up the religious rhetoric of Caracalla's edict granting Roman citizenship to the empire and creating for itself something to count as a new 'Roman' cult. But the way it proclaimed that Roman status was not just by the replication of Roman festivals, but by the integration of local Egyptian cults and standard Roman festivals within the cult of Zeus Kapitolios – already itself a strangely non-Roman 'Roman' title.[147] In just such ways in communities throughout the empire, distinctively Roman and distinctively local traditions were integrated as a response to (and as an articulation of) the power of Rome. *Roman* religion came in many 'foreign' forms.[148]

147 On Roman religion in the third century A.D., Alföldy (1989).
148 For one aspect of this issue, see Price (1984) 234–48.

8 Roman religion and Christian emperors: fourth and fifth centuries

Roman religion changed fundamentally in the fourth century A.D. The city of Rome itself ceased to be the primary residence of the emperor or the main centre of government from the late third century A.D. The military threats posed by 'barbarians' on the northern frontiers of the Rhine and Danube impelled emperors to spend more of their time in the north: Trier in Germany, Sirmium in Serbia and Milan in northern Italy all developed as imperial centres. No emperor lived in Rome after the early fourth century A.D.; indeed after the reign of Constantine (306–337) there were only two imperial visits to the city in the course of the fourth century. A major factor in Rome's changing role was the division of the empire in A.D. 286 into two halves – east and west. Each half was the primary responsibility of one 'Augustus' aided (from A.D. 293) by a junior 'Caesar'. The east also had its own imperial centres (Nicomedia in north-west Asia Minor and Syrian Antioch; then Constantinople founded by Constantine in A.D. 330). This division of responsibility – which was partly a tactical, military response to external threats to the security of the empire, but also became the basis for a whole new politics of imperial rule – persisted to the end of our period, in the early fifth century, and beyond; even though from time to time one 'Augustus' (like Constantine) proved able to control the whole empire and resembled once more an emperor of the old type. In the eyes of some Rome was still the grand old imperial capital and life went on much as usual; for others, no doubt, it looked more like a 'heritage city', a tourist ghost-town. But even if the image of Rome, as cultural capital, would remain indelibly imprinted on the empire, it was increasingly displaced from the centre of the political and military stage, occupying a marginal position even in the western half of the empire. The history of Roman religion in the fourth century can be seen in part as a response to this displacement of Rome.

The upholders of traditional Roman religion at this period were also faced with a new threat. Christians ceased to be systematically harried by the imperial authorities and became instead the recipients of imperial favour. This did not mean, however, a reversal of some simple dichotomy between pagans and Christians, the latter now victorious over their persecutors. Christians themselves (as we have already seen in earlier chapters) were far from uniform and much imperial attention was devoted to distinguishing 'true' from 'false' Christians. Nor did Christians make a simple, blanket rejection of all 'paganism'; there were serious debates as to what was to count as 'Christian', how far the traditional customs and festivals of Rome were to be regarded as specifically 'pagan', or how far they should be seen as the ancient cultural inheritance of the city and its empire. To what extent, in other words, could Rome reject its 'religion of place' without jeopardizing its own cultural identity?

The major change in the fourth century is not so much the defeat of paganism as its change of status. In the face of an imperially backed Christianity, support for the traditional cults of Rome was no longer taken for granted as part of the definition of 'being Roman'; they became a matter of choice, an elective religion. This situation arose from the actions that Constantine took in favour of Christianity (which we discuss in section 1), as well as from the measures that he and subsequent emperors introduced against practices defined (or re-defined) as unacceptable: heresy, illicit divination and (finally) the official cults of Rome themselves (see below section 2). We trace in Section 3 the growth of the Christian community at Rome (partly, no doubt, a consequence of imperial support), the series of major churches founded at this period as well as the development for the first time of a specifically Christian iconography in visual representation. Finally (in section 4) we explore the continuance of traditional cults at Rome alongside, or in opposition to, Christianity. By the 380s A.D., certainly, some members of the senatorial class were ostentatiously (and piously) maintaining what they defined and championed as the 'traditional' cults of Rome in the face of Christianity. The vitality of this group did not survive the sack of Rome by the Goths in A.D. 410, but our period ends with the death of the western emperor Honorius (A.D. 393–423) and the installation by the eastern emperor of a new emperor in the west in A.D. 425 – a vivid symbol of Rome's now subordinate position in an empire that still clung to its heritage of (lost) cultural omnipotence.[1]

1. Constantine and the church

By the late third century Christians were well established in Rome, and elsewhere in the empire – even though they probably formed only a small minority of the population, and their growth may have been held back by periods of persecution.[2] The persecution initiated by Diocletian in A.D. 303 was still a recent memory[3] when in A.D. 312 Constantine marched on

---

1 Matthews (1975) is the basic account of the years A.D. 364–425. Note Cochrane (1940), and the surveys in Demandt (1989) 413–69, Averil Cameron (1993a) 66–84, 151–69 and (1993b) 57–80, 128–51.

2 Persecution could, of course, have had the opposite effect. Successful (or, at least, public) resistance to persecution may have helped to strengthen the church, and to advertise its virtues to outsiders.

Rome and defeated his rival Maxentius outside the city at the Battle of Milvian Bridge. This battle (which might otherwise have been remembered as just one chapter in the repeated and inglorious story of Roman civil war) is said to have marked a crucial turning point in the history of Christianity – and so in the history of the western world. A Christian, writing at most four years later, claimed that as the result of a dream Constantine had inscribed 'the heavenly sign of God' on his soldiers' shields just before the decisive conflict.[4] That is, on the eve of the Battle of Milvian Bridge, Constantine was believed to have abandoned the traditional deities of Rome in favour of the Christian god.

The conversion of Constantine was among the most unexpected events in Roman history, and remains highly controversial. Even supposing that what happened at and before the battle was central to Constantine's support of Christianity (which is, of course, far from certain), almost every aspect of that support has been debated ever since. Was he sincere in his adherence to Christianity? How far did he conflate Christianity with elements of traditional cults? From what date is Constantine's firm support of Christianity to be dated – from A.D. 312 or later? (He was not formally baptized until his deathbed, but this was not uncommon in early Christianity).[5] The questions are unanswerable. Nonetheless Constantine's own version of what he said and did at that time tells us exactly how to see the matter. We are told that many years later he declared on oath to a Christian bishop, Eusebius, that before the battle he had seen by day a vision in the skies of the cross inscribed with the words 'By this, conquer', and that the following night Christ had appeared to him in a dream bearing the same sign. Constantine himself (according to Eusebius) recalled the victory as a Christian victory, and is said to have put up in Rome a statue of himself holding the cross.[6] Others may have declined to accept this Christian interpretation;[7] but, for his part, Constantine certainly soon proceeded to act in favour of the Christian church.

Within a month or two of the battle Constantine joined with the eastern emperor Licinius in calling for the toleration of Christian meetings and the rebuilding of churches.[8] In the first months of A.D. 313, in what were

---

3   The persecution had ceased in the west under Constantine's father in 305, but continued in the east until 311, with a brief resumption in 312.

4   Lactantius, *On the Deaths of the Persecutors* 44.5.

5   The debate: Baynes (1972) and Lane Fox (1986) 609–62, who both argue that Constantine was a firm Christian from 312. Coin evidence: Fig. 8.1.

6   Eusebius, *Life of Constantine* I.28–9. Statue: Eusebius, *Ecclesiastical History* IX.9.10; *Life of Constantine* I.40.2. However, as Eusebius did not visit Rome his claim that the statue held a cross is not necessarily reliable. The right hand of the colossal statue of Constantine in the Basilica of Maxentius rested on a sceptre or lance, but we cannot know if it was topped by a cross: Helbig (1963–72) II no.1441.

7   *ILS* 694 = *ILCV* 2 (the dedication by the senate on the arch of Constantine ascribes his victory to 'the inspiration of the divine' – not explicitly stating the nature of the *divinitas* involved).

a   b

Fig. 8.1 Two medallions illustrate Constantine's public position. (a) Constantine with Sol (Sun) as a guardian god behind him. Other traditional gods were dropped from the coinage under Constantine; Sol, (which, arguably, had a Christian interpretation), continued until the 320s A.D. (b) Constantine on a silver medallion struck for presentation in A.D. 315. On his helmet is the chi-rho monogram, often used as an abbreviation of 'Christ'. Such Christian emblems remained fairly unobtrusive on coinage until the fifth century A.D.

to be the first of a series of moves by which imperial favour and imperial resources were put behind Christianity, he restored church property in Africa (and doubtless other provinces), made huge donations to the church from the imperial treasury and granted exemption to the clergy from compulsory civic public duties.[9]

These actions were without precedent. Though previous emperors had ended persecution of Christians by restoring property, no previous emperor had given the church money, let alone money on this scale. (The annual rents on the land he gave to the church came to over 400 pounds of gold per year – a substantial sum, though only 10% of the income of the wealthiest senator.) The exemption from the burdens of civic office represents a yet more striking innovation. Such exemption was a privilege that had previously been granted only to groups such as athletes, doctors and teachers that were seen as particularly meritorious within traditional Roman culture. The only priests to have held the privilege were those of Egypt (following a particular local tradition); otherwise ordinary civic priesthoods were compatible with membership of local councils, and entailed only limited immunities. Constantine's extension of exemptions to (orthodox) Christian clergy marked a new recognition that the Christian church was of benefit to the state; or rather perhaps annexed the church *as a benefit* to the state. When the emperor Galerius had ended persecution of the Christians in A.D. 311, he had expressed the hope that the Christians would pray to their god 'for our welfare, and that of the state and their own'. Constantine accepted this logic in stating the reason for the grant: so that the clergy

shall not be drawn away by any deviation or sacrilege from the worship that is due to the divinity, but shall devote themselves without interference to their own law. For it seems that, rendering the greatest possible service to the deity, they most benefit the state.

---

8 Lactantius, *On the Deaths of the Persecutors* 48.2–12 (= **11.13a**). Eusebius, *Ecclesiastical History* 9.12; 9a.11–12.
9 Eusebius, *Ecclesiastical History* X.5.15–17; 6.1–3 (= **11.13b**); 7.2; *CTh* XVI.2.1–2, modified in 3 and 6. Cf. Millar (1977) 577–84.

No longer was the safety and success of Rome entrusted to the traditional state religions alone.[10]

In addition to grants of money to the Christian authorities, Constantine was also personally responsible for the foundation of new church buildings. In Rome he paid for five or six churches, which fundamentally changed the profile of the Christian community.[11] Probably only a year or two after the Battle of Milvian Bridge work began on a great 'basilica' with an adjacent baptistery. Known as the Basilica Constantiniana (now St. John Lateran), this became the principal church of the city. Other buildings were erected in memory of the martyrs of Rome. And a decade later (probably in the mid 320s) the basilica of St. Peter's was started. The significance attached to the earlier monument to St. Peter determined the location and level of the church.[12] The surrounding, largely pagan, cemetery was levelled off to provide a foundation at the appropriate height, and the trophy was enshrined in the apse, projecting about three metres above the floor of the basilica. The Christian community in Rome had now for the first time a monumental setting.

The designs of these Constantinian basilicas varied, but all were derived from a type of secular public building that had long been a feature of Rome and other Roman towns – the traditional basilicas that lined, for example, the Roman forum, with a large central space (or nave) and aisles running down each side. Following this pattern the Basilica Constantiniana was a huge hall, some 100 metres in length, with two side aisles giving a total width of about 54 metres. St. Peter's was on the same scale, but its design differed somewhat. Here the central nave was again flanked by two aisles, but between the nave and the apse was a crossing, wider than the aisles, which focussed the building on the trophy of St. Peter in the apse. The overall dimensions are impressive: the nave was 90 metres long, the total length 119 metres and the width 64 metres. In front of the church was a large open area, equal in size to the body of the church, surrounded by arcades. The dimensions are comparable with the grand imperial buildings of the past: the Forum of Augustus was 125 by 118 metres, and the (secular) Basilica in Trajan's Forum, the largest basilica ever built in Rome, 170 metres (or 120 metres within the apses). The differences between the design of St. Peter's and that of the Basilica Constantiniana relate closely to

---

10 Traditional priests, above, pp. 192–6; Wissowa (1912) 500; A.H.M. Jones (1940) 354 n.33. Galerius: Eusebius, *Ecclesiastical History* VIII.17.10. Constantine: Eusebius, *Ecclesiastical History* X.7.2. Constantine also exempted municipal and provincial *flamines* in Africa in A.D. 335 and 337 (*CTh* XII.1.21, XII.5.2). See above, p. 329 for other priests in the fourth century A.D.

11 Krautheimer (1979) 39–70; (1980) 3–31; Arbeiter (1988). Above, p. 268 for third-century church building outside Rome.

12 Plan, reconstruction and location of St Peter's: **4.15c**; Map 4 no. 61 (with **4.15d**, a fifteenth-century view of 'Old' St Peter's). Basilica Constantiniana: Map 4 no 24. Cf. above, p. 268 for earlier monument.

their different functions. The latter with its contemporary baptistery was the principal church of the city, designed for regular use on festal days, while St. Peter's was a martyr's shrine, used for burials and commemorative feasts. But the crucial point is that both these buildings, in taking the overall design of the secular basilica, strikingly reject the form of traditional religious, temple architecture of the Roman world – whose function had been principally to house the deity. Logically enough (for, unlike pagans, Christians *congregated* in the house of their god), the new, monumental Christian architecture was derived from the vast halls that the traditional pagan culture of Rome associated with law-courts and market-places and other places of public assembly. Despite their size, Constantinian church buildings in Rome remained, literally, peripheral to the city. There is no church building under Constantine in the ancient heart of Rome, with its prestigious temples and shrines. Only the Basilica Constantiniana and a chapel inside an imperial palace were – just – inside the walls of Rome (but outside the *pomerium*), and they both lay on property owned by the emperor. The other Constantinian basilicas were, like St. Peter's, martyrs' shrines and covered cemeteries; they all lay outside Rome in the areas of Christian burial and at least some were again on imperial estates.[13] Constantine sought not to rewrite the religious space of Rome, but to provide Christians with their own, supplementary space alongside.

2. Imperial religious policy

Constantine started a pattern of imperial intervention in favour of Christianity that finally helped Christianity to triumph over paganism. But the process was much more complicated than that apparently simple outcome might suggest. Emperors did not regard all Christians with favour, nor did they at first seek to eliminate all elements of the traditional cults.

From the outset, Constantine's support for Christians was selective. Already in A.D. 313 his interventions in Africa were directed not simply to 'Christians', but to 'the Catholic Church of the Christians'. As he had been informed, there was a division in the African church. One group recognized Caecilian as bishop of Carthage, while the other denied his authority (on the grounds that he had been consecrated by a bishop who had himself handed the Scriptures over to the Roman authorities in the Diocletianic persecutions) and elected a rival bishop. Constantine had decided that Caecilian's church was to be the recipient of his benefactions, but the other party petitioned the emperor to put the matter to ecclesiastical arbitration. After two such arbitrations had gone against them, the opposition, now

---

13 Krautheimer (1960); Guyon (1987). Forum of Augustus: Map 1 no. 9. Trajan's Forum: Map 1 no. 8.

headed by Donatus, appealed to Constantine himself. The emperor had investigations made in Africa, in A.D. 315 gave judgement in favour of Caecilian, and perhaps in A.D. 317 ordered the confiscation to the state of Donatist churches. Constantine was not an indifferent and passive authority. As he wrote in A.D. 314 to one of his officials involved in the Donatist case, 'I consider it absolutely contrary to the divine law (*fas*) that we should overlook such quarrels and contentions, whereby the Highest Divinity may perhaps be roused not only against the human race but also against myself, to whose care he has by his celestial will committed the government of all earthly things.'[14] Although it is hard ever to see such disputes from anything but the winning, 'orthodox' side, it is clear that imperial authority would not tolerate such dissension within the church; in fact, the authority of the emperor over the Christian communities was defined and displayed precisely in his insistence in adjudicating between rival groups, in eradicating dissension. By the same token, the emperor could not stay clear of manipulation by the politicized churches, but was drawn constantly into the arena of socio-religious politics. This was the new currency.

A decade later, after Constantine had defeated the eastern emperor and united the empire in his own hands (A.D. 324), he discovered that the eastern churches were divided even more deeply than the African church was. Whereas the Donatists had disputed the validity of the ordination of a bishop, the new issue was ostensibly doctrinal. A man called Arius argued on philosophical grounds that as God was eternal, unknowable and indivisible, his Son could not properly be called God; though created before all ages, the Son was created after the Father and out of nothing.[15] Doctrinal disputes within the church were not new, but previously it was the church authorities themselves that had sought to define and exclude 'heretics'.[16] But with Arianism Constantine himself took action. In A.D. 325 he moved a forthcoming council of bishops from Ancyra (modern Ankara) to Nicaea (modern Iznik in north-west Turkey), an attractive city more accessible for western bishops, and more convenient for Constantine himself. He personally attended at least the major sessions – and for the first time an emperor, with all the backing of his wealth, influence and temporal power, personally sought to establish Christian orthodoxy. Under his direction the council reached general agreement on the form of words to be used in the statement of Christian beliefs known as the 'creed' (this particular form of words, which still underlies the phraseology used in some modern Christian churches, is given the title the 'Nicene Creed', after the city of

---

14 *CSEL* XXVI.206. Part of the documentation which showed that a Donatist bishop had handed over the Scriptures is given in **4.15b**. Donatism: Frend (1952); Brown (1972) 237–338; Millar (1977) 584–90.

15 Millar (1977) 590–607; R. Williams (1987). Some documents are translated in Stevenson (1987) 321–55, 366.

16 For an earlier example of doctrinal disputes, above, pp. 305–7. **12.7c(iii)**, **e(ii–iii)** are extracts from treatises condemning 'heretics'.

Nicaea). Meanwhile, Constantine exiled those who dissented – Arius, two of his supporters and their followers. Not only had Constantine sought doctrinal unity; he now, again for the first time, imposed the penalties of the criminal law on 'heretics'. The fusion of religious rule and imperial authority could not be more dramatically displayed.

Despite imperial interest and actions in favour of 'orthodoxy', Donatists and Arians continued to be influential, and there were numerous other 'heretical sects' in the fourth century. From Constantine onwards emperors spasmodically penalized such sects, their religious meetings were banned or any place where they met was confiscated.[17] In addition, other measures were sometimes taken that had the effect, or indeed the aim, of marking out these alternative Christian communities as heretical – at the same time as punishing their heresy: rights to bequeath or receive property by inheritance might be restricted; they might be refused exemptions from the burdens of civic office, or banned from the imperial service. But inevitably the definition of 'orthodoxy' varied. Two of Constantine's successors in the east supported Arianism and so acted against the supporters of the Nicene creed. But the principle remained that the sanctions of imperial authority were available to decree and determine orthodoxy; orthodoxy followed imperial power; political resistance could be heresy.

Constantine and later emperors also took action against a range of non-Christian cult practices. In the later fourth century emperors legislated against Judaism: Christian converts to Judaism lost their property, while Jews were banned from an increasing range of public offices, both local and imperial. Though traditional cults as a whole came to be classed as *superstitio*, for much of the fourth century the term remained ambiguous and was a useful tool in the hands of different groups. As Christians had argued since at least the third century A.D., Christianity was the *religio*. But, if so, what was *superstitio*? Until the early fifth century Judaism was termed either a *religio* or a *superstitio*, depending on whether the legislator was favourable or hostile.[18] The ambiguities are neatly encapsulated in a regulation of A.D. 323. Constantine was concerned by reports that the Christian clergy of Rome had been compelled by people 'of different *religiones*' to perform sacrifices; he laid down that they must not be forced to attend rites 'of another's *superstitio*'.[19] And in A.D. 337 Constantine warned a town in Italy that a temple there to his family 'should not be polluted by the deceits of any contagious *superstitio*'.[20] Within a Christian frame of reference this would imply that there were to be no pagan sacrifices at the temple, but

---

17 *CTh* XVI.5.1 (A.D. 326); Eusebius, *Life of Constantine* III.64–5. Cf. A.H.M. Jones (1964) 950–6, 964–70; Noethlichs (1971). S.G. Hall (1991) introduces the theological debates.

18 Linder (1987) 56–67. In fifth-century legislation Jews, pagans and heretics were often bracketed together.

19 *CTh* XVI.2.5; cf. Salzman (1987).

20 *ILS* 705.46–8 (trans. Lewis and Reinhold (1990) II.579–80) (Hispellum).

Constantine was writing to non-Christians, who might interpret him as ruling out (for example) only illicit divinatory types of sacrifice. Constantine may in fact have deliberately played upon the ambiguities of the term, which might usefully evade any very precise definition.

There is certainly no clear evidence for a simple campaign by Constantine and his successors against 'paganism'. Imperial ordinances were directed only at particular aspects of the traditional cults, and might always be seen as part of a long-standing tradition of imperial action against *superstitio*. Thus Constantine threatened severe punishment on those who used 'the magic arts' against someone's life or to arouse sexual desire; however, he exempted magic for medicinal or agricultural purposes. These categories are familiar from the earlier empire.[21] Similarly, Constantine forbade diviners to practise in private houses; 'those who wish to engage in their *superstitio* should practice their own ritual in public'. Again, Roman law had long banned some types of consultations of diviners. From A.D. 357 all divination (with the exception of that performed by state *haruspices*) was assimilated to indubitably noxious magic and banned.[22] The new conflation of divination and magic helped to generate a spate of trials and an atmosphere of fear and suspicion. Accusations of magical practices were levelled in the highest circles; those who had achieved untoward prominence were wide open to accusations of having employed occult arts.[23] Pagans were doubly vulnerable. Christians, who 'knew' that they worshipped demons, could easily and incontrovertibly suggest that they manipulated them to gain vain knowledge and for illicit purposes.

Other elements of paganism, however, which were *superstitio* only in the Christian sense remained untouched by Constantine and for the next few decades. Constantine certainly by A.D. 315 (and perhaps from A.D. 312) declined himself to take part in official sacrifices on the Capitol at Rome (or elsewhere),[24] but he remained *pontifex maximus,* appointing another member of the pontifical college to perform his duties, as emperors had always done when absent from Rome. Though the Saecular Games were not performed, as calculations suggested they should have been, in A.D. 314, the official cults of Rome (and other cities) seem to have continued without restrictions. Thus the Roman priesthoods continued to perform their traditional functions. If lightning struck the palace or other public buildings in Rome, Constantine permitted the *haruspices* to investigate the meaning of the portent; the *pontifices* retained supervision of tombs; and when the (Christian) emperor Constantius II (A.D. 324–361) visited Rome in A.D.

---

21 *CTh* IX.16.3 (= **11.2c**), A.D.317–19. Cf. Curran (1996). Above, pp. 233–6.
22 Constantine: *CTh* IX.16.1, A.D. 320. A.D. 357: *CTh* IX.16.4–6 = *Codex Justinianus* IX.18.5–7, with Martroye (1930).
23 Brown (1970); Grodzynski (1974b).
24 Fraschetti (1986).

356, as *pontifex maximus* he appointed new priests from the senatorial order.[25]

Traditional temples in the city also received imperial protection. Despite Constantius' proclaimed desire to root out all *superstitio*, he decreed that temples at Rome should not be violated – on the grounds, so it is reported, that traditional popular amusements originated there. And he was remembered (by the pagan Symmachus) as taking an intelligent interest in the temples during his visit to Rome: 'He read the names of the gods inscribed on the pediments, enquired about the origin of the temples, expressed admiration for their founders and preserved these rites for the empire, even though he followed different rites himself.'[26] Though a Christian official might in the 370s close a sanctuary of Mithras, pagan officials are found restoring temples at Rome during the fourth century, and until the sixth century emperors ordered that Roman temples be preserved. Only then was a temple in Rome (the so-called Temple of Romulus) converted to Christian usage, and for this imperial permission was needed. Elsewhere, by contrast, from the mid fourth century on emperors ordered that temples should be closed (perhaps from fear of their use for illicit divination), thus giving implicit sanction to zealous Christian bishops who sought actively to destroy them.[27] In Rome itself, temples seem to have been detached from the taint of *superstitio*, partly (as the story of Constantius' curiosity indicates) because of their prominence in the city's history and heritage.

Not all emperors were Christian. The fourth-century sequence of Christian emperors was interrupted, albeit briefly, by Julian (sole emperor A.D. 361–3), who attempted to revive traditional cults throughout the empire; he planned a network of high priests who would take responsibility for promoting cults in their areas. This policy was presumably welcomed in various parts of the empire, and amongst those still loyal to traditional cults. In Rome the sanctuary of the Syrian gods on the Janiculum, which had previously been destroyed, was revived in the fourth century, perhaps during the reign of Julian. But, in general, Julian showed little interest in traditional cults at Rome,[28] and died before his ideas could

---

25 Saecular games: above, pp. 201–6; the pagan Zosimus II.1–7 takes this non-performance as a cause of the current 'crisis'. *Haruspices*: *CTh* XVI.10.1 (A.D. 320); non-harmful haruspicy still licit in A.D. 371: *CTh* IX.16.9. *Pontifices*: *CTh* IX.17.2 (A.D. 349). Constantius II: Symmachus, *Report* 3.7 (trans. Croke and Harries (1982) 37).

26 Temples: *CTh* XVI.10.3 (A.D. 342); Symmachus, *Report* 3.7; cf. Ammianus Marcellinus XVI.10.13–17; below, pp. 381–2. There seems even to have been a Capitolium in Constantine's new foundation of Constantinople (Mango (1985) 30), and a festival of the Lupercalia (Y.–M. Duval (1977) 222–43; Munzi (1994)).

27 Mithras: below, p. 387. *CTh* XVI.10.4 (A.D. 356). Ward-Perkins (1984) 88–91, 208–9. Cf. generally Vaes (1984–86) 326–37; Trombley (1993) I.108–47. Conversions to churches were late (and rare) in Greece; we do not know how early they occurred in Italy outside Rome.

28 Weiss (1978). Cf. above, p. 243 n. 108 on Julian; below, pp. 384–6 on Syrian sanctuary (Map 2 no. 16).

have much effect anywhere. The following, Christian, emperors continued the earlier trend of action against *superstitio*.

Until the 370s these Christian emperors were prepared to accept an arm's length relationship with the official cults of Rome, but in (apparently) A.D. 379 the emperor Gratian resigned the position of *pontifex maximus* and in A.D. 382 decided to remove the financial support of the cults of Rome. Such immunities from public service that the Vestals and the Roman priesthoods enjoyed were abolished; the revenues of their lands were confiscated and used (as an extra affront) to pay the wages of porters and baggage-carriers; the altar of the goddess Victory (Victoria) in the senate house, on which senators, since the time of Augustus, had sacrificed before each meeting, was removed (the altar had already been removed once by Constantius II, but on that occasion had soon been replaced). The senate protested to the emperor Gratian, when he refused the office of *pontifex maximus,* but no emperor was again to be (even nominally) head of Roman religion.[29]

The practice of sacrifice also fell under an imperial ban. Since Constantine, sacrifice had been in disfavour in imperial circles – but he and his successors took action directly only against magic and private divination. So, for example, nocturnal sacrifices, long characteristic of magic, were prohibited; but Vettius Agorius Praetextatus, a well known traditionalist and governor of Achaia at this time, immediately persuaded the emperor not to enforce this ban in Greece – thus permitting the Eleusinian mysteries to continue; and in Rome and other major cities of the empire official sacrifices were for a time left untouched.[30] However, in A.D. 391 the emperor Theodosius prohibited all sacrifices, closed all temples, and threatened Roman magistrates with special penalties if they broke the ban. The following year the prohibitions were repeated and made more specific. Sacrifice for the purpose of illicit divination was to be severely punished, even if it had not involved an enquiry about the welfare of the emperor. The forbidden curiosity that we saw alleged against Apuleius in chapter 5 became part of the rationale for a general prohibition on pagan sacrifice.[31]

---

29 The debate over the altar of Victory: below, p. 386. Matthews (1975) 203–4. Gratian: Zosimus IV.36 = **8.10b**; on the date of Gratian's resignation, against Alan Cameron (1968) see Noethlichs (1971) 198–202 and Paschoud (1975) 63–79 (arguing for 376). *Pontifex* had been used to translate the Greek term *archiereus* ('high priest') applied to Christ, and from the mid fourth century it was used, in classicizing style, for bishops, though the technical term remained *episcopus; pontifex maximus* was generally eschewed, probably because of its pagan associations, and became standard only in the fifteenth century (Pietri (1976) II.1607–8; Kajanto (1981)).

30 Nocturnal sacrifices: *CTh* XVI.10.5 (A.D. 353); IX.16.7 (A.D. 364). Praetextatus: Zosimus IV.3.2 (A.D. 364); an inscription in his honour, **8.9**; above, p. 223 on Eleusis. *CTh* XVI.10.2 (A.D. 341), a ban on sacrifices, continued a law of Constantine's, but 'the law' is presumably a reference to his action against divination, to which Eusebius, *Life of Constantine* II.45.1 may also refer. See, however, Barnes (1989a) 322–33. For Alexandria see Libanius, *Oration* XXX.35–6.

31 *CTh* XVI.10.10 (A.D. 391); XVI.10.12 = **11.14** (A.D. 392); for Apuleius, see above, pp. 235–6.

The effect of Theodosius' prohibitions in Rome was, however, limited. The ban of 391 was promulgated throughout the empire, but by 392 Theodosius was no longer in control of the west, and the western emperor Eugenius attempted to conciliate the pagan aristocracy by restoring the endowments that had been removed by Gratian – not to the priests directly, but to leading pagan senators, who would put them to their proper use. As we shall see, some traditional cults of Rome continued into the fifth century, but repeated imperial enactments continued to clamp down on the practices of paganism.[32] We cannot tell how far the repetition of these bans on traditional religion was a consequence of widespread disobedience; how far the series of different laws addressed subtly different aspects of traditional cult; or how far the point of the legislation was the public declaration of the emperor's support for Christianity. But the overall message is clear enough: true (that is, now, Christian) religion was to be promoted and those addicted to *superstitio* punished.

3. The growth of the Christian church

The general pressure of imperial authority in favour of catholic , i.e. orthodox, Christianity affected the range of choices open to people in Rome. In the second and third centuries A.D. there had been first the state cults and then a great variety of religious groups (followers of Isis, Mithras, Jahveh or Christ). From Constantine onwards the choice was simplified – or reversed. Partly because of imperial patronage, Christianity increasingly became the base-line, while it was the traditional cults that now became the *option*, the matter of *choice*. Even members of the senatorial order, whose religious, political and social identity had long been bound up with traditional cults, now found that the upholding of those cults was something they could choose or reject. At one level these choices were exclusive: it would have been hard, for example, to make a public claim to be a Christian and at the same time to perform animal sacrifices to the Capitoline triad. But, even so, it was not a total polarity. Some Christians, as we shall see, also attempted to incorporate elements of their traditional Roman heritage.[33]

The growth in the number of Christians in Rome (and elsewhere in the empire) continued in the fourth century. Some of these were more visible than others: particularly women of the senatorial order, prominent in the later fourth century for their parade of virginity, self-starvation and other

32 Matthews (1975) 236, 240–3; Trombley (1993) I.1–97 on fifth-century legislation. For the religious significance of the Theodosian code, Hunt (1993); Salzman (1993).

33 Alföldi (1948) argued for a total polarity, but see Novak (1979). Brown (1961), (1982), (1995), Salzman (1990) 193–246 and Markus (1990) offer a more subtle picture. See also Salzman (1992).

ascetic practices. But overall the number of individual Christians is impossible to estimate; we know for certain only that the number of priests in Rome had risen by the end of the fourth century to around 70, and that by the early fifth century Rome had 25 principal centres of worship (and maybe 15 others). Along with this specifically Roman growth, the movement within the church from the Greek language to Latin continued; in the course of the fourth century the liturgy was turned into Latin.[34] The Christian church was now divided, like the empire itself, into east and west.

Church building continued on the lines established by Constantine.[35] The churches were built in all the residential districts of Rome, so that finally (in the fifth century A.D.) there were almost no houses more than 500–600 metres from a church that was regularly open for worship. In the fourth century there were still no churches in the monumental centre of the city, though one was built at the foot of the Palatine near the Circus Maximus. This may be connected to patronage and land-ownership. After Constantine only one more church in our period was an imperial foundation, but to build in the monumental centre (which was mainly 'public land') imperial permission was needed. The rate of the building in the fourth century is not dramatic, but ecclesiastical and private patronage was responsible for five new churches, in addition to other religious buildings. Thanks in part to Constantine, the church itself (as an institution, rather than a building) was now wealthy, and was also successful in tapping the resources of the Roman élite into its monumental building schemes. This was not a simple shift of private patronage from pagan temples to Christian churches, but a striking contrast with the pagan traditions established under Augustus: for since the beginning of the empire, public building in Rome – both religious and secular – had been the monopoly of the emperor himself, from which the rest of the élite were effectively excluded. After three centuries of imperial monopoly, in other words, Christianity found a role once more for the non-imperial, élite patron of monumental religious building in the capital.

The development of St. Peter's is symptomatic of ecclesiastical building in this period, showing the involvement and patronage of the Roman élite, the church hierarchy and the emperor himself: Damasus, the bishop of Rome, drained the marshy area round Constantine's church and added a baptistery (A.D. 366–84); between A.D. 390 and 410 a rich Roman lady

34 Women: Brown (1961); Clark (1986); Salzman (1989), who denies their importance in the spread of Christianity; Elm (1994); cf. above, pp. 298–300. This issue demands more attention than it can receive here. The number of Christians was contested in the debate on the altar of Victory (Matthews (1975) 206–7; below, p. 386). Priests: Harnack (1924) II.833–5. Churches: Pietri (1976) fig.1; Optatus II.4 (*CSEL* XXVI.39) speaks of around 40 Roman churches. Liturgy: above, p. 295; Bardy (1948) 161–4; Klauser (1979) 18–24.

35 Ward-Perkins (1984) 51–84, 236–41; Reekmans (1968), (1989); Saxer (1989), on liturgy and space. On 'heretical' meeting places, see Maier (1995).

built a mausoleum for her husband off the apse of the church; while around A.D. 400 the emperor Honorius built a mausoleum for himself and his family, opening off the south crossing of the church. In addition, the approach to the church was monumentalized (using forms of architecture that had once adorned the secular centres of cities). A monumental portico was built (perhaps in the late fourth century), running due east from the church and linking up with one of the bridges over the Tiber. These lavish schemes helped to make St. Peter's a major focus not just for Rome, but also for Christians from elsewhere. The Christian pilgrims of the early fourth century seem to have ignored Rome in favour of the Holy Land, but by the end of the fourth century they were certainly drawn to Rome.[36]

The martyrs Peter and Paul were of central importance to the Roman church. Bowls, medallions and statuettes commemorated them jointly; they shared a feast day; and under Damasus were seen as citizens of Rome. United in harmony (unlike Romulus and Remus – whose original foundation of Rome was marked by the murder of Remus by Romulus), *they* were now the true founding heroes of the city.[37] Depiction of this harmony formed part of the claim of the Roman church to high status. Peter was believed to have come to Rome with Paul, and from him the bishops of Rome followed in (allegedly) unbroken sequence. But there was as yet no overall claim by the church in Rome to primacy over all the Christian communities in the world. The Roman church had, as in the third century, considerable authority in Italy, Gaul, and Spain (for a time) – but even in Italy this was probably dependent on the vigour of particular bishops; with Africa, on the other hand, the Christian church at Rome had only loose connections, and in the East it had no special standing at all.[38]

The adherence of people in Rome to the Christian church raised problems of identity and status. The celebration of the ancient festivals of Rome seems to have remained popular throughout the fourth century A.D. And the games associated with them (the ostensible reason, as we have seen, for Constantius' preservation of Roman temples) continued to draw great crowds. Maybe all these crowds were entirely pagan; but there is little reason to think so – after all, the Christian writer Ausonius could write an affectionate poem on the Roman festivals.[39] The Christian audience presumably thought of their own attendance at such occasions in a variety of different ways – some little troubled by the contradictions that must have been glaring to others, some (we may guess) seeing no connection between these popular amusements and their own personal religion, some (as at every period)

36 The development of St Peter's is shown at **4.15c**; Reekmans (1970); Ward-Perkins (1984) 63–4. Pilgrims: Bardy (1949); Barnes (1981) 310 n.61.

37 Pietri (1961), (1976) 1537–1626; *Age of Spirituality* (1979) 566–73; Huskinson (1982).

38 Pietri (1976) I.184–7, 866–72, II.1332–47, 1407–9; Baus (1980) 240–1, 245–69; above, p. 305 on the third century.

39 VII.23 (Loeb) = XIV.16 (Green).

being much stricter and more exclusive Christians than others. For many senators, though, the matter must have been particularly pressing. Christian senators, in general, were as determined as their pagan colleagues to maintain the prestige of Rome and the senate in a changed world. And yet the traditional identity of Rome (for the élite at least) was derived from its traditional cults.

By the mid third century some senators had become Christians, but seem to have kept their Christianity a private matter.[40] Later senators were not so circumspect. Junius Bassus, prefect of the city of Rome, died a Christian in A.D. 359. His sarcophagus, which was placed in the crypt of St. Peter's next to the martyr's memorial, uses a classical style, but an iconography derived principally from the Old and New Testaments (Fig. 8.2). This is more revolutionary than it might seem at first sight. In the period before Constantine there was (to our knowledge) no specifically Christian iconography – at least there is no trace of the repertoire of Christian images (the Good Shepherd, Christ Ascending, Christ on the Cross) that were later to become standard. This sarcophagus symbolizes the emergence of Christianity and Christian images onto the public stage. But, even here, at either end of the sarcophagus were representations of winged putti engaged in harvesting grain and grapes, scenes common on non-Christian sarcophagi of the period.[41] A similar pattern is seen in the mausoleum of Constantine's daughter Constantina (a building known now as the church of Santa Costanza), which was built between A.D. 337 and 361. In the cupola were mosaics (now destroyed, but known from earlier drawings) depicting biblical scenes above a marine landscape with putti; while the (surviving) ceiling of the ambulatory around the central cupola, shows grape-harvesting and (among other motifs) medallions with putti and female figures.[42] The newly created Christian imagery did not mark a complete break with traditional, pagan iconography. Though it generated some distinctively Christian images, it also incorporated, and no doubt at the same time re-interpreted, themes from the pagan past.[43]

Upper class Christians also negotiated a delicate relationship to specifically pagan festivals. In A.D. 354 a lavish volume, the work of one of the leading scribes of the day, was presented to a rich Christian in Rome.[44] The

40   They were, however, subject to hostile imperial actions: above, p. 241.
41   Deichmann (1967) no.680; Malbon (1990). Cf. **4.15c** n.3 for its location.
42   H. Stern (1958); Grabar (1967) 165–7, 187–92; Frutaz (1976) 106–118. It was built by the cemetery of Agnes (Map 4 no.13).
43   For studies of such transformations see Murray (1981); Elsner (1995). For examples of 'traditional' iconography which is not 'pagan' or 'anti-Christian' see the mid fourth-century Esquiline Treasure, owned by a Christian: Shelton (1981); the dating remains controversial: Alan Cameron (1985); Shelton (1985). The same 'neutral' interpretation is possible of the representations of Hercules and Tellus in the fourth century Via Latina catacomb (Map 4 no.30), though the excavator argues that these images show that 'pagan' family members were included in this family catacomb housing mainly Christians: Ferrua (1991).
44   H. Stern (1953); Salzman (1990). **3.3d** gives the entry for April and **5.3b** the illustration of the Saturnalia; **3.6** gives the calendar of Christian festivals from this book.

Fig. 8.2 The sarcophagus of Junius Bassus. Upper level of the front: Abraham and Isaac; Peter's arrest; Christ enthroned; Christ's arrest; Pilate's judgement. Lower level: Job's distress; Adam and Eve; Christ's triumphal entry; Daniel; Paul's arrest. On the lid: a mask of Sol; a relief (lost); a verse inscription about Bassus' public funeral; a funerary banquet – common on earlier non-Christian monuments; a mask of Luna. *(continued overleaf)*

book consists primarily of a calendar which lists all the festivals celebrated in Rome, both those in honour of the emperor and those for the traditional gods. The entry for each month is also accompanied by an illustration, which in some cases seems explicitly pagan. For January there is a man offering incense, probably a ward magistrate sacrificing to the Lares Augusti; April has a man dancing, probably at the festival of Magna Mater; a priest of Isis is featured in November; and December depicts the celebration of the Saturnalia. These representations of pagan religious festivals were presumably welcomed by the recipient of the book, but the title page has a strongly Christian dedication, and five of the 12 supplementary texts are also Christian: a list of the dates in which Easter had fallen between A.D. 312 and 358, and a continuation for the future 50 years; the dates of burial of bishops of Rome; a calendar of the martyrs of Rome; the list of bishops of Rome; and a Christian chronicle down to A.D. 334 (though this may not have been part of the original book). Even the lists of Roman consuls in the book record four Christian events (the birth and death of Christ; the arrival in Rome and martyrdom there of Peter and Paul). The juxtaposition of the two traditions is striking – and it raises again the question of the varieties of Christian adherence, and what is to count as 'Christian faith'. One explanation of the text is that there was a category of people (the recipient of this book being one) whose Christianity was purely nominal, and whose

379

(Fig 8.2 continued)
The two ends show
putti harvesting
grapes (this page)
and grain (next
page, top) and with
flowers and birds
(next page,
bottom). (Height of
sarcophagus,
1.41m.; width,
2.43m.; depth,
1.44m.)

hearts were still in the old world. But this seems unlikely at this period: for most of the fourth century, and certainly under Constantius II when the book was created, there was little political advantage in being a Christian; despite curbs on pagan practices, emperors appointed both pagans and orthodox Christians to positions of high responsibility. 'Nominal Christianity' would hardly have been an advantage; indeed, the pressures of the local context on the Roman élite strongly favoured the traditional practices. We are more likely dealing with a group of people who became Christians without seeing the need (or, maybe, being willing) to give up elements of traditional *Roman* practice; without being prepared to jettison what made Rome *Roman*. Maybe, after all, both festivals of Isis and of Peter and Paul could enhance the dignity of Rome.[45]

45 Alföldi (1937) and Alföldi and Alföldi (1976–90) Vol. I argued that medallions ('Contorniates') with images of Isis and other 'pagan' deities were issued by a 'pagan' party in Rome. However, against that argument runs the fact that these medallions were issued as part of the official coinage of Rome, and so are unlikely to be specifically anti-Christian. The Calendar of 354 (with its inclusion of the Isis cult) also makes it unlikely that such images carried a strongly anti-Christian message or could be used

4. The traditional gods

Rome in the fourth century A.D. remained for some people a city characterized by the worship of the ancient gods. Others could find there great
diversity. Scattered through the city were Christian meeting places, which
were gradually receiving distinctive, monumental form, and on the periphery of the city were the prominent Christian foundations of Constantine.
The Jewish community continued to flourish; Jewish catacombs were in
use through the fourth into the fifth century A.D. and the synagogues may
have become more lavish.[46] However, the upholders of the old order might
choose to ignore these monuments. As we have seen, the pagan historian
Ammianus Marcellinus, when describing the visit of the emperor
Constantius II to Rome in A.D. 357, depicted the (Christian) emperor

    against any particular 'party'. See Mazzarino (1951); Salzman (1990) 212–8; Alan
    Cameron in Alföldi and Alföldi (1976–90) II.63–74. Alföldi and Alföldi (1976–90)
    I.193–240 list the 'pagan' types. Cf. traditional gods on fourth-century African lamps
    (Barbera (1985)).

46 Catacombs: Map 4 nos. 62–8; Vismara (1986) 381. Plan of the fourth-century syna-
    gogue at Ostia: **4.14a**. Note *Age of Spirituality* (1979) nos. 347–8. Cf. Ruggini (1959)
    on northern Italy and Millar (1992).

admiring the temples and other ancient ornaments of the city.[47] This account tendentiously suppresses any mention of Christianity or Judaism in Rome. In a similarly tendentious way, two fourth-century catalogues which list many of the buildings of the city area by area note traditional temples, from the Capitolium to the Pantheon; they give a total of 80 'gold gods' and 84 'ivory gods' (the gold and ivory were the material of the cult statues). But they too systematically exclude mention of any Jewish or Christian buildings. What observers *saw* of the religious buildings of Rome very largely depended on what they *chose* or *refused* to see.[48]

The traditional monuments of the city were duly restored in the course of the fourth century A.D. by the Prefect of the City, who had taken over the functions of the Curator of the Sacred Buildings of the early empire. In the mid century one Prefect repaired a temple of Apollo, and another had pulled down private houses that abutted temples and restored the images of the Consenting Gods (Di Consentes) in the Forum, while a little later the emperor ordered another official to restore a temple to Isis at Portus (near Ostia, the port of Rome). The cult of Vesta also retained four days for her rituals in the official calendar and was specifically mentioned in a contemporary description of Rome, though the major series of third-century statues of Vestals, sometimes sponsored by grateful clients of the priestesses, has only two extant successors in the fourth century. Even after the reforms of Gratian, when the responsibility of the Prefect of the City was redirected toward the Christian buildings, instead of the traditional temples, the monuments of pagan religion were not entirely neglected by the imperial authorities. Under the emperor Eugenius (A.D. 392–4) some temples were again restored and as late as the 470s a Prefect of the City is known to have restored an image of Minerva.[49]

The traditional religious practices of Rome were not mere fossilized survivals. They did not incorporate elements of Christianity or Judaism (in this sense they were quite different from Christianity, with its frequent assimilation of pagan symbolism); but there were continuing changes and restructuring through the fourth century. Our best evidence comes, again, from the Calendar of 354.[50] Here we can see that games in honour of the emperor continued to be remodelled and adjusted to the new rulers. There were games to mark the birthdays of Septimius Severus and Marcus

---

47 XVI.10.13–17; cf. above, p. 373.

48 Valentini & Zucchetti (1940–53) I.63–192; above, p. 186. So too the *Description of the Whole World* 55 (= **13.7**), dating to A.D. 359, describes only the traditional cults of Rome.

49 Above, pp. 252–3. Chastagnol (1960) 144–78, with *AE* (1986) 109. Apollo: *ILS* 3222 (A.D.357/9). Houses: Ammianus XXVII.9.10. Consenting Gods: *ILS* 4003 (A.D. 367/8). Portus (Map 5): Chastagnol (1969) (A.D. 375–6?). Vesta: Salzman (1990) 157–61; description: *Description of Whole World* 55 = **13.7**. Minerva: *ILS* 3132 (A.D. 475(?)–482). Cf. Lepelley (1994) on the preservation of 'pagan' art.

50 Above, n.44. Text in Degrassi (1963) 237–62; April in **3.3d**. See above, pp. 322–3 for calendars of the earlier empire.

Fig. 8.3
A sarcophagus from Rome, c. A.D. 350. On the left, four elephants pulling a wagon (on which was presumably a divine or imperial image), preceded by two men in togas. On the right, an image of Magna Mater, with her two lions, is carried on a *ferculum*; behind her an image of Victory. Between them a trumpet is played. The scenes depict the carrying of divine images to the circus, and commemorate the celebration of circus games by the deceased. (Height, 0.40m.; length, 2.05m.)

Aurelius (as there had been in the army calendar found at Dura Europus). But only 29 such occasions in the course of the year were in honour of previous dynasties; the remaining 69 were for birthdays and victories of the house of Constantine. The cycle of festivals in honour of the gods was also reworked – as is clear if we look at the evidence of just one month, April. Ancient festivals were still marked, and we may presume celebrated, over many days: April includes festivals to Venus, Magna Mater, Ceres and Flora, as well as the Birthday of the City, as the Parilia was by now known. But about half of the festivals of the Republic do not feature in this calendar, including in April the Fordicidia, Vinalia and Robigalia. However, other festivals have been added: the celebration of the birthdays of the god Quirinus, and of Castor and Pollux, and a festival in honour of Sarapis. The date at which these festivals entered the official calendar is unknown. Quirinus and Castor and Pollux had had temples in Rome since the republican period, but had no celebrations on these dates in the early empire; Sarapis had a (modest) sanctuary built by Caracalla, under whom the festival may have originated, but there was already a popular festival in the first century A.D.[51] This fourth-century calendar thus honoured a range of deities of diverse origins.

The process of incorporation of once foreign cults into the 'official' religion is most visible in the priesthoods held by members of the senatorial class. Until the end of the fourth century senators continued to be members of the four main priestly colleges, but they were in addition priests of Hecate, Mithras and Isis. For senators to associate themselves with these

---

51 Isis too had a festival, on 5 March. Alföldi (1937) and (1965–6) argued that it was concerned with *vota* (vows) for the emperor, but this is impossible as the *vota* took place on 3 January; the argument also assumes, wrongly, that the 'Contorniates', which included Isiac images, were anti-Christian propaganda: above, n.45; Malaise (1972b) 220–1. For a local calendar in Campania, *ILS* 4918 = Degrassi (1963) 283 = **3.7**.

cults in Rome is an innovation of the fourth century, and this change has been interpreted in many modern accounts of the period as the emergence of a new religious 'party' in Rome: the senatorial supporters of Oriental cults, as against the upholders of ancestral Roman cults.[52] There is, in fact, very little evidence to suggest such a split.[53] Those who did not hold priesthoods of Oriental gods were not necessarily hostile to those who did, and conversely many of the priests of Isis, Hecate and Mithras were also members of at least one of the four ancient priestly colleges. The change is better seen as a trend toward assimilating into 'traditional' paganism cults in Rome which had not previously received senatorial patronage. Though Hecate and Mithras were not incorporated into the official calendar, some senators at least wished to place them within the bounds of *religio*. Faced with the new threat posed by imperial patronage of Christianity, senators redefined (and expanded) their ancestral heritage.

The process of change is also visible in cults long established in Rome which sometimes received new and heady interpretations. In the fourth century the cult of Magna Mater placed a new emphasis on the practice of the *taurobolium*.[54] Inscriptions from the Vatican sanctuary record that some worshippers repeated the ritual after the lapse of twenty years; one claimed that he had been thereby 'reborn to eternity' – which seems to mark a radically new significance. Magna Mater by this date was not simply an 'Oriental' deity; she had after all received official cult in Rome for over five hundred years and was intimately connected with the destiny of Rome. The reinterpretation of the *taurobolium* in what was by now an ancient cult of Rome shows clearly how even such ancestral religions could still generate new meanings: in this case, a new intensity of personal relationship with the divine. The cult at the Syrian sanctuary on the Janiculum also seems to have changed during this period – losing much of its specifically Syrian focus.[55] The sanctuary, which had been destroyed in the mid third century, was rebuilt in the fourth century. (Fig 8.4) Beneath the main cult statue of Jupiter Heliopolitanus a human skull was buried, which probably indicates

---

52 See H. Bloch (1945) and (1963). H. Bloch (1945) after p. 244 tabulated the senatorial priesthoods. The priesthoods of Vettius Agorius Praetextatus, listed on an inscription: *CIL* VI 1778 = **8.9**. Other relevant texts trans. in Lewis and Reinhold (1990) II.584–6. A senator in the cult of Mithras: *ILS* 4267b = **12.5c(iv)**. Hecate: Wissowa (1912) 378–9.

53 Matthews (1973).

54 Map 2 no.6; **6.7a**. Vermaseren (1977) 45–51; Sfameni Gasparro (1985) 107–18; Vermaseren (1977–89) III nos. 225–45. There are puzzling gaps in the evidence here. First, inscribed records of the performance of *taurobolia* in Rome are associated entirely with the Vatican sanctuary, not the Palatine; this may or may not be significant. Second, there is no pre-fourth-century inscription from the Vatican; though the inscription we discussed above, p. 338, implies an association between the Vatican sanctuary and the *taurobolium* at a much earlier date.

55 Map 2 no.16. The earlier phase: above, p. 283, with references; cf. Meneghini (1984); Turcan (1989) 184–9.

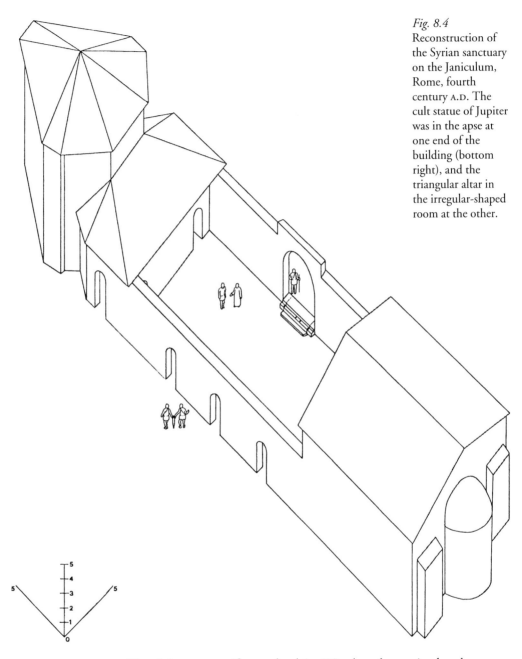

Fig. 8.4
Reconstruction of
the Syrian sanctuary
on the Janiculum,
Rome, fourth
century A.D. The
cult statue of Jupiter
was in the apse at
one end of the
building (bottom
right), and the
triangular altar in
the irregular-shaped
room at the other.

an (illegal) human sacrifice to the deity.[56] In the other main chamber was a large triangular altar surrounded by a number of sculptures: Dionysus in gilded marble, an Egyptian pharaoh of black basalt and a relief of the Seasons(?). Beneath the altar a male bronze idol entwined with a snake lay in a casket with numerous eggs broken over it, presumably to symbolize the

56 This was exactly what Christians had suspected: Eusebius, *Life of Constantine* III.57.2 (p. 110.20 Winkelmann); Rufinus, *Ecclesiastical History* II.24.

385

rebirth of the initiate. In the second-century phase, so far as we know, the main deity was a strongly Romanized form of a Syrian god; in the fourth century, the cult incorporated elements of diverse origin: Syria, Greece, Egypt. And there is some evidence that the cult now offered a form of 'rebirth' to the initiate.[57] The exact reasons for these changes in the cult of Magna Mater and of Jupiter Heliopolitanus are unclear; but a partial explanation at least must lie in the development of Christianity. Though old cults did not adopt elements of Christianity, they did adapt old procedures to offer a new eschatology and to enhance the involvement of the initiate.

Christianity did, however, pose a critical threat to the restructured traditional cults of Rome. When state funding of public rites in Rome was abolished and the altar of Victory removed from the senate house in A.D. 382, Symmachus as Prefect of the city of Rome wrote a lengthy memorandum to the emperor arguing for the restoration of the status quo. The traditional religious customs had served the state well for centuries; the altar of Victory was where senators swore oaths of loyalty to the emperor; the ancestral rites had driven the Gauls from the Capitol (an argument used also by Livy); the imperial confiscation of funding had caused a general famine in the empire. Symmachus' arguments were directed not so much against Christianity, as in favour of toleration of the traditional cults: every people had their own customs and rituals, which were different paths to the truth. His memorandum was countered by two letters from Ambrose, bishop of Milan, to the emperor, which argued forcefully that it was the Christian duty of the emperor to fight for the church.[58] After A.D. 382 with the partial exception of the (brief) reign of Eugenius (A.D. 392–394), the traditional cults did not receive the toleration Symmachus urged; and even Eugenius, himself a Christian, made only limited concessions to 'paganism'. There was now only one true *religio*.

The argument between traditionalists and Christians extended to other contexts. One (Christian) poem, which probably dates either to the period of Symmachus' memorandum or to the period of favour for traditional cults under Eugenius, attacked an unnamed Prefect of the city of Rome and consul for his participation in a wide range of pagan rituals, from Etruscan divination to the *taurobolium*.[59] According to the poem, he supplicated Isis and mourned Osiris, he celebrated the festival of Magna Mater and Attis, with full trappings, including lions to draw the image of Magna Mater through the city,

---

57 The epitaph of Gaionas (*CIL* VI 32316 = W. Peek, *Griechische Vers-Inschriften* I 402 = *IGUR* 1157) does not show that this idea was present already in the second century; it implies only that Gaionas had paid his debt to death by dying (Goodhue (1975) 111–16).

58 All three texts are translated in Croke & Harries (1982) 30–50. Cf. Matthews (1975) 205–11.

59 *Poem against the Pagans*, translated by Croke & Harries (1982) 80–3. The addressee is uncertain. Matthews (1970) argued for Nicomachus Flavianus, Ruggini (1979) for Praetextatus.

he held the festival of Flora, and his heir built a temple to Venus. For some, eclecticism was the way of truth; for others, like the author of this poem, it illustrated the vacuity of paganism.[60] After the fall of Eugenius, Theodosius' ban on sacrifices was more effectively applied, and the secular implications of the old calendar revised. The ancient distinction between 'festival days' dedicated to the gods and 'working days' on which (among other things) law-courts could sit was abolished. Now law cases could be heard on all days, except Easter, Sundays and the conventional breaks for the summer time and autumn harvesting and for imperial and other anniversaries. It was subsequently underlined that 'the ceremonial days of pagan *superstitio*' were not to be counted among the holidays. Traditional public festivals were not thereby banned, but they were officially marginalized in favour of Christian festivals. The last pagan senatorial priests are attested in the 390s: the Arval cult seems to have ended in the 340s, and the sanctuary was dismantled from the late fourth century onwards; the series of dedicatory inscriptions from the sanctuary of Magna Mater on the Vatican runs from A.D. 295 to 390; and the last dated Mithraic inscription from Rome is from A.D. 391 (slightly later than from elsewhere in the empire).[61] Some Christians went on the offensive, destroying pagan sanctuaries, including sanctuaries of Mithras.[62]

But traditional religious rites were very tenacious, and their demise cannot be assumed from the ending of dedicatory inscriptions. Emperors through the fifth into the sixth century elaborated Theodosius' ban on sacrifices – presumably in the face of the continuing practice of traditional sacrifice; while a pagan writer travelling up from Rome through Italy in the early fifth century observed with pleasure a rural festival of Osiris.[63] In Rome the death of Symmachus in A.D. 402 was commemorated by two pairs of small ivory panels with strongly traditional imagery (a woman offering incense on an altar; another woman holding inverted torches, a sign of mourning, in front of a flaming altar), and a few years later the old ways were revived at a time of crisis: during the siege of Rome by the Goths (A.D. 408–9), when Christianity was not obviously helping, the Prefect of the city, after meeting diviners from Etruria, attempted to save the city by publicly celebrating the ancestral rituals with the senate on the Capitol.[64] Around

60 Slightly later, Prudentius also denounced the *taurobolium*: *Crowns of Martyrdom* X.1007–1050 = **6.7a**.

61 Calendar reforms: *CTh* II.8.18–22 (A.D. 386–395); old rules, *lex Irnitana* chs. K and 92 (for trans. *JRS* 76 (1986) 187, 198); Macrobius I.16.2–6 (= **3.1**); cf. **3.7**. *Augur. ILS* 4151 (A.D. 390); Vestal: Zosimus V.38.3–4 (allegedly A.D. 394, perhaps 389). Arvals: Scheid and Broise (1980) 242–8; Scheid (1990b) 739–40. Magna Mater, above, n.54. Mithras: Clauss (1990) 37–41.

62 Mithras: Sauer (1996). Destruction in Rome by Gracchus, A.D. 366–7: Jerome, *Letter* 107.2; Prudentius, *Against Symmachus* I.561–5.

63 Harl (1990). Rutilius Namatianus, *On his Return* I.371–6 = **12.4g**. Cf. Lizzi (1990) and Ruggini (1991) on northern Italy.

64 Ivories: Alan Cameron (1986). Zosimus V.41.1–3; Sozomen IX.6.3. Procopius, *Gothic War* VI.21.16 asserts that Etruscans were still diviners in his day, the mid sixth century

A.D. 430 a Roman writer, Macrobius, sought to recreate the religious learning and debate of the age of Symmachus, a generation before, in a long academic dialogue (including Symmachus himself as one of the 'imaginary' speakers) that centres on the interpretation of Virgil's *Aeneid*, but also covers a vast range of classical culture and learning, from the jokes of the emperor Augustus to the different varieties of fish.[65] But most striking of all (given the date of its composition) is the complete exclusion of Christianity – an exclusion which acted to align classical culture and traditional religion.

This was not the dead hand of antiquarianism. We saw in our Preface how, even at the end of the fifth century A.D., the Lupercalia was still being celebrated in the city – by pagans and Christians; and how the bishop of Rome found it necessary both to argue against the efficacy of the cult (as some Christian writers had done for three hundred years) and to ban Christian participation.[66] We wondered then, at the very start of our exploration of Roman religions, how we should interpret his action; how we should understand the significance of this (or any) pagan ritual over its history of more than a thousand years; or what the Lupercalia could possibly have meant in the Rome of Gelasius.

One thing is clear enough. The action of Christian bishops did not mean the ending of the old festivals, either at Rome or elsewhere in the empire.[67] It was not simply a question of 'paganism' successfully resisting Christianity. There is, after all, no reason to assume that those who continued to watch the scantily clad young men race round the city thought of themselves as 'non-Christian'. The boundary between paganism and Christianity was much more fluid than that simple dichotomy would suggest and much more fluid than some Christian bishops would have liked to allow. Fixing the boundary raised all the issues of interpretation that came with living in a self-consciously *historic* culture: could, in short, the heritage of Roman tradition, its places and rituals, be accommodated within a Christian context? Could Romulus and Numa and the other heroes of early Rome, could the rituals and institutions that were inextricably attached to their names, ever simply be excluded from the cultural inheritance of those who counted themselves *Romans* – whether Christian or not?[68]

A.D. Cf. Thulin (1906–09) III.142. The continuing importance of traditional rites is part of the background to Augustine's polemic in *The City of God*: Barnes (1982).

65 Macrobius, *Saturnalia*, with dating of Alan Cameron (1966), supported by Panciera (1982) 658–60.

66 Bishop of Rome: Gelasius, *Letter* (*Sources chrétiennes* 65, 1959) (16 = **5.2e**), with Y.-M. Duval (1977) 243–60; the letter, normally ascribed to Gelasius, may in fact be by his predecessor Felix III. Cf. Salzman (1990) 235–46.

67 E.g. (in the West) Meslin (1969) and (in the East) Harl (1990), Bowersock (1990) and Trombley (1993). For an example of transformations at Rome, Aronen (1989).

68 The 21 April (the Parilia) is still celebrated in the official calendar of the modern city as the Birthday of Rome.

Bibliography

The following bibliography lists all (and only) the books and articles cited in our footnotes. Those already familiar with the field may find it useful because of its sheer size; others may like some preliminary guidance, especially to works in English. We note here a selection of major reference works and other basic studies.

A general history of Roman religion is found in Liebeschuetz (1979); and discussion of the archaic and republican periods in Dumézil (1970) – though, for a critique of Dumézil's approach, see chapter 1 above. Festivals of the republican calendar are covered by Scullard (1981); for late Roman festivals, see Salzman (1990). Feeney (1998) discusses religious aspects of Latin literature.

Details of the main religious monuments of the city of Rome are given in E. Nash (1968), with excellent photographs; in L. Richardson (1992) and in the major multi-volume (and multi-lingual) topographical dictionary of Rome, Steinby (1993–). Ryberg (1955) illustrates and discusses depictions of Roman rituals in sculpture.

On priesthood in Rome and in the empire, see Beard and North (1990), especially the chapters by Beard, North and Gordon.

For cults outside Rome, see MacMullen (1981), an impressionistic survey, but helpful in showing the range and importance of epigraphic material; Henig (1984), on Britain; Lane Fox (1986), particularly strong on Greek civic cults of the imperial period; Rives (1995), on Roman cults at Carthage.

On 'imperial cult' see Hopkins (1978) 197–242; Price (1984), particularly on the eastern part of the empire; Fishwick (1987–), on the west; Taylor (1931) is still useful; as is the more recent collection of essays, Small (1996).

On 'Oriental cults' in general, the fundamental study of Cumont (1911) still lies in the background of most later studies (even if its explanatory framework and many of its particular conclusions have been challenged); see more recently, Burkert (1987); Turcan (1996). On Magna Mater, Vermaseren (1977) offers a popular introductory account; on Mithras, see Cumont (1903), Vermaseren (1963) and the important re-interpretations in Beck (1984) and R.L. Gordon (1996).

The pluralism of Judaism can be seen in Schürer (1973–87), the essential work of reference; Trebilco (1991), on Asia Minor; Lieu et al., (1992); Rutgers (1995), on Rome.

The growth of Christianity is illustrated by Snyder (1985), an archaeological companion; Lane Fox (1986). On the persecutions, see de Ste Croix (1963) and Barnes (1968); on Christianity in the fourth and fifth centuries, Markus (1990) and Brown (1995).

For those who know even a little German, the great handbook of Roman religion, Wissowa (1912), is still a mine of information.

Abramenko, A. (1993) *Die munizipale Mittelschicht im kaiserzeitlichen Italien. Zu einem neuen Verständnis von Sevirat und Augustalität* (Europäische Hochschulschriften Ser.3, 547). Frankfurt.

Abry, J.H. ed. (1993) *Les tablettes astrologiques de Grand (Vosges) et l'astrologie en Gaule romaine.* Paris.

Abt, A. (1908) *Die Apologie des Apuleius von Madaura und die antike Zauberei* (Religionsgeschichtliche Versuche und Vorarbeiten 4.2). Giessen.

Accame, S. (1942) 'La legislazione romana intorno ai collegi nel 1 secolo a.C.', *Bull.Mus.Imp.Romano* 13: 13–48.

Age of Spirituality (1979) *Late Antique and Early Christian Art, Third to Seventh Century,* edd. K. Weitzmann and M.E. Frazer. New York.

Alarcão, J., R. Etienne and G. Fabre (1969) 'Le culte des Lares à Conimbriga (Portugal)', *CR Acad. Insc.* 1969: 213–36.

Alcock, S.E. (1993) *Graecia Capta. The Landscapes of Roman Greece.* Cambridge.

Aldred, C. (1978) *The Temple of Dendur* (*Met.Mus. of Art Bull.* 36.1). New York.

Alexander, L. ed. (1991) *Images of Empire* (*Journal for the Study of the Old Testament,* Supp.122). Sheffield.

Alföldi, A. (1935) 'Insignien und Tracht der römischen Kaiser', *Röm.Mitt.* 50: 3–158, repr. in his *Die monarchische Repräsentation im römischen Kaiserreiche.* Darmstadt, 1970.

(1937) *A Festival of Isis in Rome under the Christian Emperors of the IVth Century* (Dissertationes Pannonicae 2nd ser., 7). Budapest.

(1948) *The Conversion of Constantine and Pagan Rome.* Oxford.

(1965) *Early Rome and the Latins.* Ann Arbor.

(1965–6) 'Die alexandrinischen Götter und die Vota Publica am Jahresbeginn', *Jahrb.Ant.Christ.* 8–9: 53–87.

(1973) *Die zwei Lorbeerbäume des Augustus.* Bonn.

Alföldi, A. and E. Alföldi (1976–90) *Die Kontorniat-Medallions,* 2 vols. Berlin.

Alföldy, G. (1989) 'Die Krise des Imperium Romanum und die Religion Roms', in Eck (1989a) 53–102.

(1991) 'Augustus und die Inschriften: Tradition und Innovation', *Gymnasium* 98: 289–324.

Alla ricerca di Iside (1992) *Analisi, studi e restauri dell'Iseo pompeiano nel Museo di Napoli.* Rome.

Allen, W. (1944) 'Cicero's house and *Libertas*', *Trans.Amer.Philol.Ass.* 75: 1–9.

Amici, C.M. (1991) *Il foro di Cesare.* Rome.

Ampolo, C. (1971) 'Analogie e rapporti fra Atene e Roma arcaica. Osservazioni sulla Regia, sul *rex sacrorum* e sul culto di Vesta', *PdP* 26: 443–60.

Amy, R. and P. Gros (1979) *La Maison Carrée de Nîmes* (*Gallia* Supp.38). Paris.

Anderson, B. (1983) *Imagined Communities: Reflections on the Origin and Spread of Nationalism.* London.

Anderson, J.C. (1984) *The Historical Topography of the Imperial Fora* (Coll. Latomus 182). Brussels.

André, P., A. Debat, R. Lauxerois and A. LeBot-Helly (1991) 'Données nouvelles sur la Vienne augustéenne', in *Les villes augustéennes de Gaule,* edd. C. Goudineau and A. Rebourg, 61–77. Autun.

Andreussi, M. (1988) 'Roma: Il pomerio', *Scienze dell'Antichità* 2: 219–34.

Ankarloo, B. and G. Henningsen edd. (1990) *Early Modern Witchcraft. Centres and Peripheries.* Oxford.

Ankersdorfer, H. (1973) *Studien zur Religion des römischen Heeres von Augustus bis Diokletian.* Ph.D. Diss. Konstanz.

Appel, G. (1909) *De Romanorum precationibus* (Religionsgeschichtliche Versuche und Vorarbeiten 7.2). Giessen.

Arafat, K. (1996) *Pausanias' Greece.* Cambridge.

Arbeiter. A. (1988) *Alt-St. Peter in Geschichte und Wissenschaft.* Berlin.

Arce, J. (1988) *Funus imperatorum. Los funerales de los emperadores romanos.* Madrid.

Aronen, J. (1989) 'La sopravvivenza dei culti pagani e la topografia cristiana dell'area di Giuturna e delle sue adiacenze', in *Lacus Iuturnae* I (Lavori e Studi di Archeologia pubblicati dalla Soprintendenza Archeologica di Roma 12), ed. E.M. Steinby, 148–74. Rome.

Astin, A. E. (1958) *The Lex Annalis before Sulla* (Coll. Latomus 32). Brussels.

(1964) 'Leges Aelia et Fufia', *Latomus* 23: 421–45.

(1967) *Scipio Aemilianus.* Oxford.

(1978) *Cato the Censor.* Oxford.

Ausbüttel, F.M. (1982) *Untersuchungen zu den Vereinen im Westen des römischen Reiches* (Frankfurter althistorische Studien 11). Kallmünz.

Axtell, H.L. (1907) *The Deification of Abstract Ideas in Roman Literature and Inscriptions.* Chicago, repr. New Rochelle NY, 1987.

Bakker, J.T. (1994) *Living and Working with the Gods.* Amsterdam.

Baldus, H.R. (1991) 'Zur Aufnahme des Sol Elagabalus-Kultes in Rom, 219 n. Chr.', *Chiron* 21: 175–8.

Balla, L. (1967) 'Zur Geschichte des religiösen Lebens von Savaria', *Acta Classica Univ. Scient. Debrecen* 3: 67–76.

Balsdon, J.P.V.D. (1951) 'Sulla Felix', *JRS* 41: 1–10.

(1957) 'Three Ciceronian problems. 1. Clodius' "repeal" of the *lex Aelia Fufia*', *JRS* 47: 15–16.

(1966) 'Fabula Clodiana', *Historia* 15: 65–73.

(1969) *Life and Leisure in Ancient Rome.* London.

Balty, J.C. (1988) 'Apamea in Syria in the second and third centuries A.D.', *JRS* 78: 91–104.

Barbera, M. (1985) 'Lucerne africane nel museo nazionale romano: riflessioni su iconografia e ideologia', *Opus* 4: 153–63.

Bardy, G. (1948) *La question des langues dans l'église ancienne.* Paris.

(1949) 'Pélérinages à Rome vers la fin du IVᵉ siècle', *Analecta Bollandiana* 67: 224–35.

Barnes, T.D. (1968) 'Legislation against the Christians', *JRS* 58: 32–50, repr. in his *Early Christianity and the Roman Empire.* London, 1984.

(1981) *Constantine and Eusebius.* Cambridge MA.

(1982) 'Aspects of the background of the *City of God*', *Revue de l'Université d'Ottawa* 52: 64–80, repr. in his *From Eusebius to Augustine.* London, 1994.

(1985) *Tertullian*, rev. edn. Oxford.

(1989a) 'Christians and pagans in the reign of Constantius', in *L'église et l'empire au IVᵉ siècle* (Fondation Hardt, Entretiens 34), ed. A. Dihle, 301–37. Geneva, repr. in his *From Eusebius to Augustine.* London, 1994.

(1989b) 'Trajan and the Jews', *Journ. Jewish Stud.* 40: 145–62.

Barré, V. et al. (1981) *Panauti. Une ville au Nepal.* Paris.

Barton, I.M. (1982) 'Capitoline temples in Italy and the Provinces (especially Africa)', *ANRW* II.12.1: 259–342.

Barton, J. (1986) *Oracles of God. Perceptions of Ancient Prophecy in Israel after the Exile*. London.

Barton, T. (1994) *Ancient Astrology*. London and New York.

Baslez, M.-F. et al. (1993) *L'invention de l'autobiographie d'Hésiode à Saint Augustine*. Paris.

Bastiaensen, A.A.R. ed. (1990) *Atti e passioni dei martiri*, 2nd edn. Milan.

Bauchhenss, G. and P. Noelke (1981) *Die Iupitersäulen in den germanischen Provinzen* (*Bonner Jarhrb.* Supp.41). Bonn.

Baus, K. et al. (1980) *The Imperial Church from Constantine to the Early Middle Ages* (History of the Church 2). London.

Bayet, J. (1926) *Les origines de l'Hercule romain* (BEFAR 132). Paris.

    (1935) 'Le rite du fécial et le cornouiller magique', *MEFR* 52: 29–76, repr. in Bayet (1971) 9–43.

    (1950) 'Les "Feriae Sementivae" et les indigitations dans le culte de Cérès et de Tellus', *Rev.Hist.Rel.* 137: 172–206, repr. in Bayet (1971) 177–205.

    (1955) 'Les sacerdoces romains et la pré-divinisation impériale', *Bull. Acad. royale Belgique*, cl. des lettres 41: 453–527, repr. in Bayet (1971) 275–336.

    (1957) *Histoire politique et psychologique de la religion romaine*. Paris.

    (1960) 'Les malédictions du tribun C. Ateius Capito', in *Hommages à G. Dumézil* (Coll. Latomus 45) 31–45. Brussels. Repr. in Bayet (1971) 353–65.

    (1969) *Histoire politique et psychologique de la religion romaine*, 2nd edn. Paris.

    (1971) *Croyances et rites dans la Rome antique*. Paris.

Bayly, C.A. (1989) *Indian Society and the Making of the British Empire* (New Cambridge History of India 3.4). Cambridge.

Baynes, N.H. (1972) *Constantine and the Christian Church*, 2nd edn. by H. Chadwick. London. First published in *Proc.Brit.Acad.* 15 (1931) 341–442.

Beagon, M. (1992) *Roman Nature. The Thought of Pliny the Elder*. Oxford.

Beard, M. (1980) 'The sexual status of Vestal Virgins', *JRS* 70: 12–27.

    (1985) 'Writing and ritual: a study of diversity and expansion in the Arval Acta', *Pap.Brit.Sch.Rome* 53: 114–162.

    (1986) 'Cicero and divination: the formation of a Latin discourse', *JRS* 76: 33–46.

    (1987) 'A complex of times: no more sheep on Romulus' birthday', *Proc.Camb.Philol.Soc.* 213, n.s. 33: 1–15.

    (1989) 'Acca Larentia gains a son: myths and priesthood at Rome', in *Images of Authority* (Camb. Phil. Soc., Supp.16), edd. M.M. Mackenzie and C. Roueché, 41–61. Cambridge.

    (1990) 'Priesthood in the Roman Republic', in Beard and North (1990) 17–48.

    (1993) 'Looking (harder) for Roman myth: Dumézil, declamation and the problems of definition', in Graf (1993) 44–64.

    (1994) 'The Roman and the foreign: the cult of the "Great Mother" in imperial Rome', in *Shamanism, History and the State*, edd. N. Thomas and C. Humphrey, 164–9.

    (1995) 'Re-reading (Vestal) virginity', in *Women in Antiquity*, edd. R. Hawley and B. Levick, 166–77. London and New York.

Beard, M. and M.H. Crawford (1985) *Rome in the Late Republic*. London.

Beard, M. and J.A. North edd. (1990) *Pagan Priests*. London.

Beaujeu, J. (1955) *La religion romaine à l'apogée de l'empire*, I. Paris.

(1964) 'La religion de la classe sénatoriale à l'époque des Antonins', in *Hommages à Jean Bayet* (Coll. Latomus 70), 54–75. Brussels.

(1978) 'Le paganisme romain sous le Haut Empire', *ANRW* II.16.1: 3–26.

Beck, R. (1976) 'Interpreting the Ponza zodiac', *J. Mithraic Stud.* 1: 1–19.

(1977–8) 'Interpreting the Ponza zodiac II', *J. Mithraic Stud.* 2: 87–147.

(1984) 'Mithraism since Franz Cumont', *ANRW* II.17.4: 2002–2115.

(1988) *Planetary Gods and Planetary Orders in the Mysteries of Mithras* (EPRO 109). Leiden.

(1991) 'Thus spake not Zarathustra: Zoroastrian pseudepigrapha of the Greco-Roman world', in Boyce and Grenet (1991) 491–565.

(1992) 'The Mithras cult as association', *Studies in Religion/Sciences Religieuses* 21: 3–13.

(1994) 'In the place of the Lion: Mithras in the tauroctony', in Hinnells (1994) 29–50.

Belier, W.W. (1991) *Decayed Gods: Origin and Development of Georges Dumézil's 'Idéologie tripartie'*. Leiden.

Bémont, C. (1960) 'Les enterrés vivants du Forum Boarium. Essai d'interprétation', *MEFR* 72: 133–46.

Benko, S. (1984) *Pagan Rome and the Early Christians*. Bloomington.

Bergesen, A.J. (1977) 'Political witch hunts: the sacred and the subversive in cross-cultural perspective', *Amer.Sociol.Rev.* 42: 220–33.

Berner, U. (1982) *Untersuchungen zur Verwendung des Synkretismusbegriffes* (Göttinger Orientforschungen). Wiesbaden.

Besnier, M. (1902) *L'île Tibérine dans l'antiquité* (BEFAR 87). Paris.

Bianchi, U. (1950) 'Disegno storico del culto capitolino nell'Italia romano e nelle provincie dell'Impero', *Atti Accademia Nazionale dei Lincei, Memorie,* Sc. morali, 8th ser., II (Rome) 349–415.

ed. (1979) *Mysteria Mithrae* (EPRO 80). Leiden.

(1980) 'Iside dea misterica. Quando?', in *Perennitas. Studi in onore di Angelo Brelich*, 9–36. Rome.

Bianchi, U. and M.J. Vermaseren edd. (1982) *La soteriologia dei culti orientali nell'impero romano* (EPRO 92). Leiden.

Bickerman, E.J. (1961) 'Filius Maiae (Horace, Odes I.2.43)', *PdP* 16: 5–19, repr. in his *Religions and Politics in the Hellenistic and Roman Periods*, 453–69. Como, 1985.

(1980) *Chronology of the Ancient World*, 2nd edn. London.

Birley, E. (1978) 'The religion of the Roman army: 1895–1977', *ANRW* II.16.2: 1506–41.

Blackman, E.C. (1948) *Marcion and his Influence*. London.

Bleicken, J. (1957a) 'Oberpontifex und Pontifikalkollegium. Eine Studie zur römischen Sakralverfassung', *Hermes* 85: 345–66.

(1957b) 'Kollisionen zwischen Sacrum und Publicum', *Hermes* 85: 446–80.

Bloch, H. (1945) 'A new document of the last pagan revival in the west, 393–394 A.D.', *Harv.Theol.Rev.* 38: 199–244.

(1962) 'A monument of the *Lares Augusti* in the forum of Ostia', *Harv.Theol.Rev.* 55: 211–23.

(1963) 'The pagan revival in the west at the end of the fourth century', in Momigliano (1963) 193–218.

Bloch, R. (1960) 'L'origine du culte des Dioscures à Rome', *Rev.Phil.* 34: 182–93.

(1963) *Les prodiges dans l'antiquité classique.* Paris.

Boatwright, M.T. (1986) 'The pomerial extension of Augustus', *Historia* 35: 13–27.

(1987) *Hadrian and the City of Rome.* Princeton.

Bömer, F. (1964) 'Kybele in Rom', *Röm.Mitt.* 71: 130–51.

Boëthius, A. (1978) *Etruscan and Early Roman Architecture*, revised by R. Ling and T. Rasmussen. Harmondsworth.

Bonnefond, M. (1987) 'Transferts de fonctions et mutation idéologique: le Capitole et le Forum d'Auguste', *L'urbs* (1987) 251–78.

Boon, G.C. (1958) 'A Roman pastrycook's mould from Silchester', *Antiquaries Journal* 38: 237–40.

Borgeaud, P. (1993) 'Quelques remarques sur la mythologie divine à Rome, à propos de Denys d'Halicarnasse (ant.Rom. 2,18–20)', in Graf (1993) 175–87.

(1996) *La mère des dieux: de Cybèle à la vierge Marie.* Paris.

Bowersock, G.W. (1975) 'The Greek-Nabataean bilingual inscription at Ruwwafa, Saudi Arabia', in *Le monde grec. Hommages à C. Préaux*, 513–22. Brussels.

(1990) *Hellenism in Late Antiquity.* Cambridge.

Boyancé, P. (1950) 'Properce aux fêtes de quartier', *Rev.Et.Anc.* 52: 64–70, repr. in Boyancé (1972) 291–7.

(1954) 'Cybèle aux Mégalésies', *Latomus* 13: 337–42, repr. in Boyancé (1972) 195–200.

(1972) *Etudes sur la religion romaine* (Coll. de l'Ecole franç. de Rome 11). Rome.

Boyce, A.A. (1937) 'The expiatory rites of 207 B.C.', *Trans.Amer.Philol.Ass.* 68: 157–71.

Boyce, M. and F. Grenet (1991) *A History of Zoroastrianism*, vol.3 (Handbuch der Orientalistik I.8.1.2.2). Leiden.

Boyer, P. and S. Nissenbaum (1974) *Salem Possessed. The Social Origins of Witchcraft.* Cambridge MA.

Brandenburg, H. (1984) 'Überlegungen zur Ursprung und Entstehung der Katakomben Roms', in *Vivarium. Festschrift für Theodor Klauser* (*Jahrb.Ant.Christ.* Supp.11), 11–49. Münster in Westfalen.

Brashear, W.M. (1992) *A Mithraic Catechism from Egypt* (*Tyche* Supp.). Vienna.

Braund, D.C. (1985) *Augustus to Nero: A Sourcebook on Roman History 31 B.C. – A.D. 68.* London and Sydney.

Brelich, A. (1949) 'Storia delle religioni: religione romana (1939–48)', *Doxa* 2: 136–66.

(1960) 'Quirinus. Una divinità romana alla luce della comparazione storica', *Studi e materiali di storia delle religioni* 31: 63–119.

(1965) 'Offerte e interdizioni alimentari nel culto della Magna Mater a Roma', *Studi e materiali di storia delle religioni* 36: 27–42.

Bremmer, J. and N. Horsfall (1987) *Roman Myth and Mythography* (*Bull. Inst. Class. Stud.*, Supp.52). London.

Brent, A. (1995) *Hippolytus and the Roman Church in the Third Century* (*Vigiliae Christianae* Supp.31). Leiden.

Briquel, D. (1981) 'Des propositions nouvelles sur le rituel d'ensevelissement de grecs et de gaulois au Forum Boarium', *Rev.Et.Lat.* 59: 30–7.

Briscoe, J. (1973) *A Commentary on Livy Books XXXI–XXXIII*. Oxford.
  (1981) *A Commentary on Livy Books XXXIV–XXXVII*. Oxford.
Brooten, B.J. (1982) *Women Leaders in the Ancient Synagogue* (Brown Judaic
  Stud. 36). Chico, CA.
Brouwer, H.H.J. (1989) *Bona Dea: The Sources and a Description of the Cult*
  (EPRO 110). Leiden.
Brown, P. (1961) 'Aspects of the christianization of the Roman aristocracy', *JRS*
  51: 1–11, repr. in Brown (1972) 161–82.
  (1970) 'Sorcery, demons and the rise of christianity: from late antiquity into
  the middle ages', in *Witchcraft Confessions and Accusations* (Assoc. of Social
  Anthropologists Mono. 9) 17–45; repr. in Brown (1972) 119–46.
  (1972) *Religion and Society in the Age of Saint Augustine*. London.
  (1982) 'Dalla "plebs romana" alla "plebs Dei"', in Brown et al., *Governanti e
  intellettuali: popolo di Roma e popolo di dio, I–VI secolo* (Passatopresento 2),
  123–45. Turin.
  (1988) *The Body and Society. Men, Women and Sexual Renunciation in Early
  Christianity*. New York.
  (1995) *Authority and the Sacred: Aspects of the Christianization of the Roman
  World*. Cambridge.
Brox, N. (1966) 'Zum Vorwurf des Atheismus gegen die alte Kirche', *Trierer
  Theologische Zeitschrift* 75: 274–82.
Bruhl, A. (1953) *Liber pater. Origine et expansion du culte dionysiaque à Rome et
  dans le monde romain* (BEFAR 175). Paris.
Brunaux, J.L. (1988) *The Celtic Gauls: Gods, Rites and Sanctuaries*. London.
Brunt, P.A. (1971) *Social Conflicts in the Roman Republic*. London.
  (1989) 'Philosophy and religion in the later Republic', in *Philosophia Togata:
  Essays on Philosophy and Roman Society*, edd. M. Griffin and J. Barnes,
  174–98. Oxford.
Buraselis, K. (1989) *Theia Dorea: Meletes pano stin politiki tis dinasteias ton
  Seviron kai tin Constitutio Antoniniana* (Academy of Athens, Research
  Centre for Antiquity Mono.1). Athens.
Burkert, W. (1987) *Ancient Mystery Cults*. Cambridge MA and London.
Burnett, A. (1983) [review of A. Rainer, *Das Bild des Augustus auf den frühen
  Reichsprägungen*], *Gnomon* 55: 563–5.
Calzini Gysens, J. and F. Duthoy (1992) 'Nuovi elementi per una cronologia del
  santuario siriaco del Gianicolo', *Ostraka* 1: 133–5.
Cameron, Alan (1966) 'The date and identity of Macrobius', *JRS* 56: 25–38.
  (1968) 'Gratian's repudiation of the pontifical robe', *JRS* 58: 96–102.
  (1985) 'The date and owners of the Esquiline treasure', *Amer.J.Arch.* 89:
  135–45.
  (1986) 'Pagan ivories', in *Colloque genévois sur Symmache*, ed. F. Paschoud,
  41–64. Paris.
Cameron, Averil (1993a) *The Later Roman Empire AD 284–430*. London.
  (1993b) *The Mediterranean World in Late Antiquity AD 395–600*. London
  and New York.
Camp, J.M. (1986) *The Athenian Agora*. London.
Campenhausen, H. von (1972) *The Formation of the Christian Bible*. London.
Cannadine, D. and S. Price edd. (1987) *Rituals of Royalty: Power and Ceremonial
  in Traditional Societies*. Cambridge.
Canto, A.M. (1981) 'Notas sobre los pontificados coloniales y el origen del

culto imperial en la Betica', in *La religión romana en Hispania*, 141–53. Madrid.

Capdeville, G. (1995) *Volcanus: recherches comparatistes sur les origines du culte de Vulcan* (BEFAR 288). Rome.

Carcopino, J. (1926) *La basilique pythagoricienne de la Porte Majeure*. Paris.

Cardauns, B. (1960) *Varros Logistoricus über die Götterverehrung*. Diss. Köln, Würzburg.

(1976) *M. Terentii Varronis Antiquitates Rerum Divinarum* (Akademie der Wissenschaften und der Literatur in Mainz, Abh. der Geistes – und sozialwiss. Kl. Einzelveröffentlichung), 2 vols. Wiesbaden.

(1978) 'Varro und die römische Religion', *ANRW* II.16.1: 80–103.

Carettoni, G. (1978–80) 'La domus virginum Vestalium e la domus publica del periodo repubblicano', *Rendiconti della Pontificia Accademia Romana di Archeologia* 51–2: 325–55.

et al. (1960) *La Pianta Marmorea di Roma Antica*, 2 vols. Rome.

Carlsen, J. (1994) '*CIL* X 8217 and the question of temple land in Roman Italy', in *Landuse in the Roman Empire* (*Analecta Romana* Supp.22), edd. J. Carlsen, P. Ørsted, and J.E. Skydsgaard, 9–15. Rome.

Carré, R. (1981) 'Cultes et idéologie religieuse en Gaule méridionale', *Memorias de Historia Antigua* 5: 131–42.

Cassatella, A. and S. Panella (1990) 'Restituzione dell'impianto adrianeo del tempio di Venere e Roma', *Arch.Laz.* 10.2: 52–4.

Castagnoli, F. (1979) 'Il culto della Mater Matuta e della Fortuna nel Foro Boario', *Stud. Rom.* 27: 145–52.

(1981) 'Influenze Alessandrine nell'urbanistica della Roma augustea', *Rivista di filologia* 109: 414–23.

(1983) 'L'introduzione del culto dei Dioscuri nel Lazio', *Stud. Rom.* 31: 3–12, repr. in his *Topografia Antica: un metodo di studio, I Roma*, 341–52. Rome, 1993.

Catalano, P. (1960) *Contributi allo studio del diritto augurale* I (Università di Torino. Memorie dell'Istituto Giuridico ser. 2, Mem. 107). Turin.

(1978) 'Aspetti spaziali del sistema giuridico-religioso romano. *Mundus, templum, urbs, ager*, Latium, Italia', *ANRW* II.16.1: 440–53.

Caute, D. (1978) *The Great Fear: the Anti-communist Purge under Truman and Eisenhower*. London.

Chadwick, H. (1957) 'St. Peter and St. Paul in Rome: the problem of the Memoria Apostolorum ad Catacumbas', *J.Theol.Stud.* n.s. 8: 31–52, reprinted in his *History and Thought of the Early Church*. London, 1982.

(1966) *Early Christian Thought and the Classical Tradition*. Oxford.

Chalmers, W.R. (1965) 'Plautus and his audience', in *Roman Drama*, edd. T.A. Dorey and D.R. Dudley, 21–50. New York.

Champeaux, J. (1982–7) *Fortuna. Recherches sur le culte de la Fortune à Rome et dans le monde romain des origines à la mort de César*, 2 vols. (Coll. Ecole franç. de Rome 64). Rome.

Chastagnol, A. (1960) *La préfecture urbaine à Rome sous le bas-empire*. Paris.

(1969) 'La restauration du temple d'Isis au *Portus Romae* sous le règne de Gratien', in *Hommages à Marcel Renard*, 3 vols. (Coll. Latomus 102), II.135–44. Brussels.

(1978) *L'album municipal de Timgad*. Bonn.

(1980) 'L'organisation du culte impérial dans la cité à la lumière des inscriptions de Rennes', in A.M. Rouanet-Liesenfelt, *La civilisation des Riedones*, 187–99. Brest.

Chausson, F. (1995) '*Vel Iovi vel Soli*: Quatre études autour de la Vigna Barberini (191–354)', *MEFRA* 107: 661–765.

Chiarucci, P. (1983) *Lanuvium*. Rome.

Cichorius, C. (1922) 'Staatliche Menschenopfer', *Römische Studien*, 7–20. Leipzig.

Cirilli, R. (1913) *Les prêtres danseurs de Rome. Etude sur la corporation sacerdotale des Saliens*. Paris.

Clark, E.A. (1986) *Ascetic Piety and Women's Faith* (Studies in Women and Religion 20). Lewiston, NY and Queenston, Ont.

Clarke, G.W. (1984–) *The Letters of Cyprian of Carthage* (Ancient Christian Writers 43–). New York.

Clarke, J.R. (1991) *The Houses of Roman Italy, 100 BC – AD 250: Ritual, Space, and Decoration*. Berkeley.

Clauss, M. (1990) *Mithras. Kult und Mysterien*. Munich.

(1992) *Cultores Mithrae. Die Anhängerschaft des Mithras-Kultes*. Stuttgart.

Clavel-Lévêque, M. (1972) 'Le syncrétisme gallo-romain: structures et finalités', in *Praelectiones patavinae*, ed. F. Sartori, 91–134. Rome.

Clay, D. (1983) *Lucretius and Epicurus*. Ithaca NY.

Clinton, K. (1989) 'The Eleusinian mysteries: Roman initiates and benefactors, second century BC to AD 267', *ANRW* II.18.2: 1499–1539.

Coarelli, F. (1971–2) 'Il complesso pompeiano del Campo Marzio e la sua decorazione scultorea', *Rendiconti della Pontificia Accademia Romana di Archeologia* 44: 99–122.

(1977a) 'Public building in Rome between the Second Punic War and the death of Sulla', *Pap.Brit.Sch.Rome* 45: 1–23.

(1977b) 'Il comizio dalle origini alla fine della repubblica: cronologia e topografia', *PdP* 32: 166–238.

(1979) 'Topografia mitraica di Roma (con una carta)', in Bianchi (1979) 69–79.

(1982) 'I monumenti dei culti orientali in Roma. Questioni topografiche e cronologiche', in Bianchi and Vermaseren (1982) 33–67.

(1983a) *Roma*, 3rd edn. Rome.

(1983b) 'Il Pantheon, l'apoteosi di Augusto e l'apoteosi di Romolo', *Città e architettura nella Roma imperiale*, 41–6 (*Analecta Romana*, Supp.10). Odense.

(1983–5) *Il Foro Romano*, 2 vols (1. Periodo arcaico , 2. Periodo repubblicano e augusteo). Rome.

(1986a) 'La tombe d'Antinous à Rome' (with J.-C. Grenier), *MEFRA* 98: 217–53.

(1986b) 'L'urbs e il suburbio', in Giardina (1986) 1–58.

(1987) 'La situazione edilizia di Roma sotto Severo Alessandro', in *L'urbs* (1987) 429–56.

(1988) *Il Foro Boario*. Rome.

Coarelli, F. et al. (1981) *L'area sacra di Largo Argentina* (Studi e materiali dei musei e monumenti comunali di Roma). Rome.

Cobo, B. (1653/1979) *History of the Inca Empire*. Austin TX and London.

Cochrane, C.N. (1940) *Christianity and Classical Culture*. Oxford.

Cohen, S.J.D. (1981–2) 'Epigraphical rabbis', *Jewish Quart.Rev.* 72: 1–17.

(1993) ' "Those who say they are Jews and are not": How do you know a Jew in antiquity when you see one?', in *Diasporas in Antiquity*, edd. Cohen and E.S. Frerichs, 1–45. Atlanta, GA.

Cohn, N. (1975) *Europe's Inner Demons*. New York.

Colini, A.M. (1935) 'La scoperta del santuario delle divinità Dolichene sull'Aventino', *BCACR* 63: 145–59.

(1961–2) 'Compitum Acili', *BCACR* 78: 147–57.

Combet-Farnoux, B. (1980) *Mercure romain: le culte public de Mercure et la fonction mercantile à Rome de la république archaïque à l'époque augustéenne* (BEFAR 238). Rome.

Comella, A. (1981) 'Tipologia e diffusione dei complessi votivi in Italia in epoca medio- e tardo-repubblicana', *MEFRA* 93: 717–803.

Cornell, T.J. (1981) 'Some observations on the "crimen incesti"', in *Le délit religieux* (1981) 27–37.

(1995) *The Beginnings of Rome*. London.

Countryman, L.W. (1980) *The Rich Christian in the Church of the Early Empire: Contradictions and Accommodations*. New York and Toronto.

Cramer, F. H. (1951) 'Expulsion of astrologers from ancient Rome', *Class.& Med.* 12: 9–50.

(1954) *Astrology in Roman Law and Politics* (Mem.Amer.Philos.Soc. 37). Philadelphia.

Crawford, M.H. (1973) 'Foedus and sponsio', *Pap.Brit.Sch.Rome* 41: 1–7.

(1974) *Roman Republican Coinage*, 2 vols. Cambridge.

(1976) 'Hamlet without the prince', *JRS* 66: 214–17.

ed. (1996) *Roman Statutes*, 2 vols (*Bull.Inst.Class.Stud.* Supp. 64). London.

Croke, B. (1984–5) 'The era of Porphyry's anti-Christian polemic', *J.Rel.Hist.* 13: 1–14, repr. in his *Christian Chronicles and Byzantine History, 5th–6th Centuries*. London, 1993.

Croke, B. and J. Harries (1982) *Religious Conflict in Fourth-century Rome*. Sydney.

Crook, J.A. (1996) 'Political history, 30 B.C. to A.D. 14', *CAH*, 2nd edn, 10: 70–112. Cambridge.

Culley, G.R. (1975) 'The restoration of sanctuaries in Attica', *Hesperia* 44: 207–23.

Cumont, F. (1896–9) *Textes et monuments figurés relatifs aux mystères de Mithra*, 2 vols. Brussels.

(1903) *The Mysteries of Mithra*. London.

(1911) *The Oriental Religions in Roman Paganism*. Chicago.

Curran, J. (1996) 'Constantine and the ancient cults of Rome: the legal evidence', *Greece & Rome* 43: 68–80.

Darsy, F.M.D. (1968) *Recherches archéologiques à Sainte-Sabine sur l'Aventin* (Monumenti dell'Antichità Cristiana 2nd ser. 9). Vatican.

Debord, P. (1982) *Aspects sociaux et économiques de la vie religieuse dans l'Anatolie gréco-romaine* (EPRO 88). Leiden.

De Cazanove, O. (1987) '*Exesto*. L'incapacité sacrificielle des femmes à Rome', *Phoenix* 41: 159–73.

De Fine Licht, K. (1968) *The Rotunda in Rome. A Study of Hadrian's Pantheon* (Jutland Arch.Soc.Pub. 8). Copenhagen.

De Franciscis, A. (1991) *Il sacello degli Augustali a Miseno*. Naples.

Degrassi, A. (1939) 'Frammenti di elogi e di una dedica a Romolo del Foro d'Augusto', *BCACR* 67: 5–12, repr. in Degrassi (1962–71) I.211–19.

(1951–2) 'Le dediche di popoli e re asiatici al popolo Romano e a giove Capitolino', *BCACR* 74: 19–47, repr. in Degrassi (1962–71) I: 415–44.

(1962–71) *Scritti vari di antichità*, 4 vols. Rome.

(1963) *Inscriptiones Italiae, vol. XIII – Fasti et elogia, fasc. II – Fasti anni Numani et Iuliani*. Rome.

(1965) 'Epigraphica II', *Memorie dell'Accademia Nazionale dei Lincei*, Classe di Sc. mor., stor. e filol., 8th ser., 11: 233–47, repr. in Degrassi (1962–71) III.35–87.

(1969) 'Epigraphica IV', *Memorie dell'Accademia Nazionale dei Lincei*, Classe di Sc. mor., stor. e filol., 8th ser., 14: 111–41, repr. in Degrassi (1962–71) IV.1–38.

Deichmann, F.W. (1967) *Repertorium der christlich-antiken Sarkophage I. Rom und Ostia*. Wiesbaden.

Deininger, J. (1965) *Die Provinziallandtage der römischen Kaiserzeit von Augustus bis zum Ende des dritten Jahrhunderts n. Chr.* (Vestigia 6). Munich.

Demandt, A. (1989) *Die Spätantike: römische Geschichte von Diocletian bis Justinian 284–565 n.Chr.* (Handbuch der Altertumswissenschaft III.6). Munich.

Dench, E. (1995) *From Barbarians to New Men: Greek, Roman and Modern Perceptions of the Peoples of the Central Apennines*. Oxford.

Derks, T. (1991) 'The perception of the Roman pantheon by a native elite: the example of votive inscriptions from Lower Germany', in *Images of the Past*, edd. N. Roymans and F. Theuws, 235–65. Amsterdam. (More briefly in *MEFRA* 104 (1992) 7–23.)

Derow, P.S. (1979) 'Polybius, Rome and the east', *JRS* 69: 1–15.

Derow, P. S. and Forrest, W. G. (1982) 'An inscription from Chios', *Ann.Brit.Sch.Athens* 77: 79–92.

De Ste. Croix, G.E.M. (1954) 'Aspects of the "great" persecution', *Harv.Theol.Rev.* 47: 75–113.

(1963) 'Why were the early Christians persecuted?', *Past & Present* 26: 6–38, repr. in *Aspects of Ancient Society*, ed. M.I. Finley, 210–49. London and Boston MA.

De Sanctis, G. (1907–64) *Storia dei Romani*, 4 vols. Turin.

Detienne, M. and J.-P. Vernant edd. (1989) *The Cuisine of Sacrifice among the Greeks*. Chicago and London.

De Vos, M. (1993) 'Il tempio di Iside in via Labicana a Roma', in *I grandi santuari della Grecia e l'Occidente*, ed. A. Mastrocinque, 81–91. Trento.

Diels, H. (1890) *Sibyllinische Blätter*. Berlin.

Dihle, A. (1958) 'M. Verrius Flaccus (Verrius 2)', *RE* 2. Reihe, 8: 1636–45.

Di Stefano Manzella, I. (1994) 'Accensi velati consulibus apparentes ad sacra', *ZPE* 101: 261–79.

Dobesch, G. (1966) *Caesars Apotheose zu Lebzeiten und sein Ringen um den Königstitel: Untersuchungen über Caesars Alleinherrschaft*. Baden bei Wien.

Domaszewski, A. von (1967) *Die Rangordnung des römischen Heeres*, 2nd edn by B. Dobson (*Bonner Jahrb.* Supp. 14). Köln.

Dondin-Payre, M. (1987) 'Topographie et propagande gentilice: le *compitum Acilium* et l'origine des *Acilii Glabriones*', in *L'urbs* (1987) 87–109.

Dorcey, P.F. (1992) *The Cult of Silvanus: a Study in Roman Folk Religion.* New York.

Dörner, F. K. and Gruber, G. (1953) 'Die Exedra der Ciceronen', *Ath.Mitt.* 68: 63–76.

D'Ors, A. (1953) *Epigrafía jurídica de la España romana.* Madrid.

Douglas, M. (1966) *Purity and Danger: An Analysis of Concepts of Pollution and Taboo.* London.

Drexel, F. (1922) 'Die Götterverehrung im römischen Germanien', *Bericht der römisch-germanischen Kommission* 14: 1–68.

Dubourdieu, A. (1989) *Les origines et le développement du culte des Pénates à Rome* (Coll. Ecole franç. de Rome 118). Rome.

Dumézil, G. (1941–5) *Jupiter Mars Quirinus*, 3 vols. Paris.
    (1957) 'Augur', *Rev.Et.Lat.* 35: 126–51, repr. in Dumézil (1969) 79–102.
    (1968-73) *Mythe et épopée*, 3 vols. Paris.
    (1969) *Idées romaines.* Paris.
    (1970) *Archaic Roman Religion*, 2 vols. Chicago.
    (1974) *La religion romaine archaïque*, 2nd edn. Paris.
    (1975) *Fêtes romaines d'été et d'automne, suivi de dix questions romaines.* Paris.

Dunand, F. (1980) 'Cultes égyptiens hors d'Égypte. Essai d'analyse des conditions de leur diffusion', in *Religions, pouvoir, rapports sociaux* (Ann. litt. Univ. Besançon 237), 71–148. Paris.
    (1983) 'Culte royal et culte impérial en Égypte. Continuité et ruptures', in *Das römisch-byzantinische Ägypten* (Aegyptiaca Treverensia 2). Mainz.

Dupuis, X. (1992) 'Les pontifes et les augures dans les cités africaines au bas-empire', in *Histoire et archéologie de l'Afrique du Nord, Ve Colloque int.*, 139–51. Paris.

Durand, J.-L. and J. Scheid (1994) '"Rites" et "religion". Remarques sur certains préjugés des historiens de la religion des Grecs et des Romains', *Arch.Sc.Soc.Rel.* 39: 23–44.

Dury-Moyaers, G. (1981) *Énée et Lavinium. A propos des découvertes archéologiques récentes* (Coll. Latomus 174). Brussels.

Duthoy, R. (1978) 'Les *Augustales', *ANRW* II.16.2: 1254–1309.

Duval, P.-M. and G. Pinault (1986) *Recueil des inscriptions gauloises III. Les calendriers* (*Gallia* Supp. 45). Paris.

Duval, Y.-M. (1977) 'Des Lupercales de Constantinople aux Lupercales de Rome', *Rev.Et.Lat.* 55: 222–70.

Duviols, P. (1971) *La lutte contre les religions autochtones dans le Pérou colonial: 'l'extirpation de l'idolâtrie' entre 1532 et 1660.* Lima and Paris.

Eck, W. (1971) 'Das Eindringen des Christentums in den Senatorenstand bis zu Konstantin d. Gr.', *Chiron* 1: 381–406.
    (1979) 'Christen im höheren Reichsdienst im 2. und 3. Jahrhundert?', *Chiron* 9: 449–64.
    (1984) 'Senatorial self-representation: developments in the Augustan period', in *Caesar Augustus: Seven Aspects*, edd. F. Millar and E. Segal, 129–67. Oxford.
    (1987) 'Römische Grabinschriften. Aussageabsicht und Aussagefähigkeit im funerären Kontext', in *Römische Gräberstrassen. Selbstdarstellung – Status – Standard* (Bayerische Akad. der Wiss., phil.-hist. Kl., Abh new ser.96), edd. H. von Hesberg and P. Zanker, 61–83. Munich.
    ed. (1989a) *Religion und Gesellschaft in der römischen Kaiserzeit. Kolloquium zu*

Ehren von Friedrich Vittinghoff (Kölner historische Abhandlungen 35). Vienna.

(1989b) 'Religion und Religiosität in der soziopolitischen Führungsschicht der hohen Kaiserzeit', in Eck (1989a) 15–51.

(1992) 'Die religiösen und kultischen Aufgaben der römischen Statthalter in der hohen Kaiserzeit', in *Religio deorum*, ed. M. Mayer, 151–60. Barcelona.

Edelstein, E.J. and L. Edelstein (1945) *Asclepius: a Collection and Interpretation of the Testimonies*. Baltimore.

Edwards, C. (1993) *The Politics of Immorality in Ancient Rome*. Cambridge.

Edwards, M.J. (1990) 'Atticizing Moses? Numenius, the Fathers and the Jews', *Vigiliae Christianae* 44: 64–75.

(1992) 'Some early Christian immoralities', *Anc.Soc.* 23: 71–82.

Ehlers, W. (1948) 'Triumphus', *RE* 2.Reihe, 7: 493–511.

Ehrenberg, V. (1964) 'Caesar's final aims', *Harv.Stud.Class.Philol.* 68: 149–61.

Eingartner, J. (1991) *Isis und ihre Dienerinnen in der Kunst der römischen Kaiserzeit* (*Mnemosyne* Supp.115). Leiden.

Eisenhut, W. (1955) 'Ver sacrum', *RE* 2.Reihe, 8: 911–23.

Elm, S. (1994) *'Virgins of God'. The Making of Asceticism in Late Antiquity*. Oxford.

Elsner, J. (1995) *Art and the Roman Viewer: The Transformation of Art from the Pagan World to Christianity*. Cambridge.

Erikson, K.T. (1966) *Wayward Puritans: a Study in the Sociology of Deviance*. New York.

Erkell, H. (1952) *Augustus, Felicitas, Fortuna. Lateinische Wortstudien*. Göteborg.

(1969) 'Ludi saeculares und ludi Latini saeculares', *Eranos* 67: 166–74.

Etienne, R. (1958) *Le culte impérial dans la péninsule ibérique d'Auguste à Dioclétien* (BEFAR 191). Paris.

Etienne, R., I. Piso and A. Diaconescu (1990) 'Les deux forums de la colonia Ulpia Traiana Augusta Dacica Sarmizegetusa', *Rev.Et.Anc.* 92: 273–96.

Fantham, E. (1992) 'The role of Evander in Ovid's *Fasti*', *Arethusa* 25: 155–71.

Faraone, C.A. and D. Obbink edd. (1991) *Magika Hiera. Ancient Greek Magic and Religion*. New York and Oxford.

Fasolo, F. and G. Gullini (1953) *Il santuario della Fortuna Primigenia a Palestrina*. Rome.

Fayer, C. (1976) *Il culto della dea Roma* (Coll. di Saggi e Ricerche 9). Pescara.

Fear, A.T. (1996) *Rome and Baetica. Urbanization in Southern Spain c. 50 B.C. – A.D. 150*. Oxford.

Feeney, D.C. (1991) *The Gods in Epic: Poets and Critics of the Classical Tradition*. Oxford.

(1992) *'Si licet et fas est*: Ovid's *Fasti* and the problem of free speech under the principate', in *Roman Poetry and Propaganda in the Age of Augustus*, ed. A. Powell, 1–25. London.

(1998) *Literature and Religion at Rome: Cultures, Contexts and Beliefs*. Cambridge.

Fenelli, M. (1975) 'Contributo per lo studio del votivo anatomico: i votivi anatomici di Lavinio', *Arch. Class.* 27: 206–52.

Ferchiou, N. (1984) 'Un décor architectonique du IIe siècle en Afrique Proconsulaire (Tunisie): les vestiges du Capitole de Numlulis', *Pap.Brit.Sch.Rome* 52: 115–23.

Ferrary, J.-L. (1988) *Philhellénisme et impérialisme* (BEFAR 271). Rome.

Ferrua, A. (1991) *The Unknown Catacomb*. New Lanark.

Festugière, A.J. (1954) 'Ce que Tite-Live nous apprend sur les mystères de Dionysos', *MEFR* 66: 79–99, repr. in his *Etudes de religion grecque et hellenistique* (Paris 1972) 89–109.

Février, P.-A. (1976) 'Religion et domination dans l'Afrique romaine', *Dial. d'Hist.Anc.* 2: 305–36.

   (1978) 'Le culte des morts dans les communautés chrétiennes durant le IIIe siècle', in *Atti del IX Congresso Internazionale di Archeologia Cristiana*, 2 vols, I.211–74. Vatican.

Fink, R.O., Hoey, A.S. and Snyder, W.F. (1940) 'The *Feriale Duranum*', *Yale Class.Stud.* 7: 1–222.

Finney, P.C. (1994) *The Invisible God. The Earliest Christians on Art*. New York and Oxford.

Fischer, J.A. (1974) 'Die antimontanistischen Synoden des 2./3. Jahrhunderts', *Annuarium Historiae Conciliorum* 6: 241–73.

Fishwick, D. (1967) '*Hastiferi*', *JRS* 57: 142–60.

   (1969) '*Genius* and *Numen*', *Harv.Theol.Rev.* 62: 356–67, revised in Fishwick (1987–), II.1, 375–87.

   (1978) 'The development of provincial ruler worship in the western Roman empire', *ANRW* II.16.2: 1201–53.

   (1987–) *The Imperial Cult in the Latin West* (EPRO 108). Leiden.

   (1991) 'Seneca and the temple of Divus Claudius', *Britannia* 22: 137–41.

   (1992a) 'On the temple of Divus Augustus', *Phoenix* 46: 232–55.

   (1992b) 'The statue of Julius Caesar in the Pantheon', *Latomus* 51: 329–36.

   (1992c) 'Le *numen* impérial en Afrique romaine', in *Histoire et archéologie de l'Afrique du Nord, Ve Colloque int.*, 83–94. Paris.

   (1996) 'Four temples at Tarraco', in Small (1996) 165–84.

Fittschen, K. (1976) 'Zur Panzerstatue in Cherchel', *Jahrb.deut.Arch.Inst.* 91: 175–210.

Fitz, J. (1972) *Les Syriens à Intercisa* (Coll. Latomus 122). Brussels.

Fitz, J. and J. Fedak (1993) 'From Roman Gorsium to late-antique Herculia', *J.Rom.Arch.* 6: 261–73.

Flambard, J.-M. (1977) 'Clodius, les collèges, la plèbe et les esclaves. Recherches sur la politique populaire au milieu du 1er siècle', *MEFRA* 89: 115–56.

Follmann-Schulz, A.-B. (1986) 'Die römischen Tempelanlagen in der Provinz Germania inferior', *ANRW* II.18.1: 672–793.

Fordyce, C.J. ed. (1961) *Catullus: A Commentary*. Oxford.

Fox, M. (1996) *Roman Historical Myths: The Regal Period in Augustan Literature*. Oxford.

Fraccaro, P. (1911) *I processi degli Scipioni*. Pisa.

Frankfurter, D. (1992) 'Lest Egypt's city be deserted: religion and ideology in the Egyptian response to the Jewish revolt (116–117 C.E.)', *Journ.Jewish Stud.* 43: 203–20.

Fraschetti, A. (1981) 'Le sepolture rituali del Foro Boario', in *Le délit religieux* (1981) 51–115.

   (1984) 'La sepoltura delle Vestali e la città', in *Du châtiment dans la cité. Supplices corporels et peine de mort dans le monde antique* (Coll. Ecole franç. de Rome 79), 97–129. Rome.

   (1986) 'Costantino e l'abbandono del Campidoglio', in Giardina (1986) 59–98, 412–38.

(1990) *Roma e il principe*. Rome and Bari.

Fraser, P.M. (1960) *Samothrace II.1. The Inscriptions on Stone*. London and New York.

Frend, W.H.C. (1952) *The Donatist Church*. Oxford.

    (1965) *Martyrdom and Persecution in the Early Church*. Oxford.

    (1984) 'Montanism: research and problems', *Riv. di storia e lett.rel.* 30: 521–37, repr. in his *Archaeology and History in the Study of Early Christianity*. London, 1988.

Frier, B.W. (1979) *Libri annales pontificum maximorum. The Origins of the Annalistic Tradition* (Papers and Monographs of the American Academy in Rome 27). Rome.

Friesen, S.J. (1993) *Twice Neokoros. Ephesus, Asia, and the Cult of the Flavian Imperial Family*. Leiden.

Frutaz, A.P. (1976) *Il complesso monumentale di Sant'Agnese*, 3rd edn. Rome.

Fugier, H. (1963) *Recherches sur l'expression du sacré dans la langue latine*. Paris.

Funaioli, H. (1907) *Grammaticae Romanae Fragmenta*. Leipzig. Repr. Stuttgart, 1969.

Gabba, E. (1988) 'Reflessioni sulla Lex Coloniae Genetivae Iuliae', in *Estudios sobre la Tabula Siarensis*, edd. J. González and J. Arce, 157–68. Madrid.

    (1989) 'Rome and Italy in the second century B.C.', *CAH*, 2nd edn. 8: 197–243.

    (1991) *Dionysius and 'The History of Archaic Rome'*. Berkeley.

Gabba, E. and G. Tibiletti (1960) 'Una signora di Treveri sepolta a Pavia', *Athenaeum* n.s.38: 253–62.

Gagé, J. (1930) 'Romulus-Augustus', *MEFR* 47: 138–81.

    (1931) 'Les sacerdoces d'Auguste et ses réformes religieuses', *MEFR* 48: 75–108.

    (1933a) 'Recherches sur les jeux séculaires II. Ce que nous apprennent les nouveaux fragments épigraphiques', *Rev.Et.Lat.* 11: 172–202, repr. in his *Recherches sur les Jeux Séculaires*, 45–75. Paris, 1934.

    (1933b) 'Recherches sur les jeux séculaires III. Jeux séculaires et jubilés de la fondation de Rome', *Rev.Et.Lat.* 11: 400–35, repr. in his *Recherches*, 77–111.

    (1936a) 'Actiaca', *MEFR* 53: 37–100.

    (1936b) 'Le "Templum Urbis" et les origines de l'idée de "Renovatio"', *Mélanges F. Cumont*, I.151–87. Brussels.

    (1955) *Apollon romain. Essai sur le culte d'Apollon et le développement du 'ritus Graecus' à Rome des origines à Auguste* (BEFAR 182). Paris.

    (1966) 'Quirinus fut-il le dieu des Fabii?', *Mélanges A. Piganiol* III: 1591–1605.

Gager, J.G. ed. (1992) *Curse Tablets and Binding Spells from the Ancient World*. New York and Oxford.

Galinsky, G. K. (1969) *Aeneas, Sicily, and Rome*. Princeton NJ.

Gallagher, E.V. (1982) *Divine Man or Magician? Celsus and Origen on Jesus* (SBL Diss. Ser. 64). Chico CA.

Gallini, C. (1962) 'Politica religiosa di Clodio', *Studi e materiali di storia delle religioni* 33: 257–72.

    (1970) *Protesta e integrazione nella Roma antica* (Bibliotheca di cultura moderna 698). Bari.

Galsterer, H. (1971) *Untersuchungen zum römischen Städtewesen auf der iberischen Halbinsel* (Madrider Forschungen 8). Berlin.

(1976) *Herrschaft und Verwaltung im republikanischen Italien*. Munich.

Gargola, D.J. (1995) *Lands, Laws, and Gods. Magistrates and Ceremony in the Regulation of Public Lands in Republican Rome*. Chapel Hill NC and London.

Garnsey, P. (1984) 'Religious toleration in classical antiquity', in *Persecution and Toleration* (Studies in Church History 21), ed. W.J. Sheils, 1–27. Oxford.

Garosi, R. (1976) 'Indagine sulla formazione del concetto di magia nella cultura romana', in *Magia. Studi di storia delle religione in memoria di Raffaella Garosi*, ed. P. Xella, 13–93. Rome.

Gatti lo Guzzo, L. (1978) *Il deposito votivo dall'Esquilino detto di Minerva Medica* (Studi e materiali di etruscologia e antichità italiche 17). Rome.

Geiger, F. (1913) *De sacerdotibus Augustorum municipalibus*. Diss. Halle.

Gelzer, M. (1935) 'Die Glaubwürdigkeit der bei Livius überlieferten Senatsbeschlüsse über römische Truppenaufgebote', *Hermes* 70: 269–300, repr. in Gelzer (1962–4) III.209–55.

(1936) 'Die Unterdrückung der Bacchanalien bei Livius', *Hermes* 71: 275–87, repr. in Gelzer (1962–4) III. 256–69.

(1962–4) *Kleine Schriften*, 3 vols. Wiesbaden.

Gesche, H. (1968) *Die Vergottung Caesars* (Frankfurter althistorische Studien 1). Kallmünz.

Giardina, A. ed. (1986) *Società romana e impero tardoantico* II. Rome.

Girard, J.-L. (1980) 'Interpretatio romana. Questions historiques et problèmes de méthode', *Rev.Hist. et Phil.Rel.* 60: 21–7.

Glare, P.M. (1994) 'The temple of Jupiter Capitolinus at Arsinoe and the imperial cult', in *Proc. 20th Int.Congr.Papyr. Copenhagen 1992*, ed. A. Bülow-Jacobsen, 550–4. Copenhagen.

Goldhill, S. (1987) 'The Great Dionysia and civic ideology', *J.Hell.Stud.* 107: 58–76, revised in *Nothing to do with Dionysos?*, edd. J.J. Winkler and F.I. Zeitlin, 97–129. Princeton NJ.

Goodhue, N. (1975) *The Lucus Furrinae and the Syrian Sanctuary on the Janiculum*. Amsterdam.

Goodman, M. (1983) *State and Society in Roman Galilee, A.D. 132–212*. Totowa NJ.

(1989) 'Nerva, the *fiscus Judaicus* and Jewish identity', *JRS* 79: 40–44.

(1991) 'Opponents of Rome: Jews and others', in Alexander (1991) 222–38.

(1994a) *Mission and Conversion*. Oxford.

(1994b) 'Sadducees and Essenes after 70 CE', in *Crossing the Boundaries*, edd. S.E. Porter, P. Joyce and D.E. Orton, 347–56. Leiden.

Gordon, A. E. (1938) *The Cults of Lanuvium* (Univ.California Publ.Class.Arch. 2.2). Berkeley.

(1952) *Quintus Veranius, Consul A.D. 49* (Univ.California Publ.Class.Arch. 2.5). Berkeley.

Gordon, R.L. (1972) 'Mithraism and Roman society', *Religion* 2: 92–121, repr. in Gordon (1996).

(1975) 'Franz Cumont and the doctrines of Mithraism', in *Mithraic Studies*, ed. J.R. Hinnells, I.215–48. Manchester.

(1977–8) 'The date and significance of CIMRM 593 (British Museum, Townley Collection)', *J. Mithraic Stud.* 2: 148–74, repr. in Gordon (1996).

(1980a) 'Reality, evocation and boundary in the mysteries of Mithras', *J. Mithraic Stud.* 3: 19–99, repr. in Gordon (1996).

(1980b) 'Panelled complications', *J. Mithraic Stud.* 3: 200–27, repr. in Gordon (1996).

ed. (1981) *Myth, Religion and Society.* Cambridge.

(1987a) 'Lucan's Erictho', in *Homo Viator. Classical Essays for John Bramble*, edd. M. Whitby et al., 231–41. Bristol and Oak Park, IL.

(1987b) 'Aelian's peony: the location of magic in Graeco-Roman tradition', in *Comparative Criticism*, ed. E.S. Shaffer, 9: 59–95.

(1989) 'Authority, salvation and mystery in the mysteries of Mithras', in *Image and Mystery in the Roman World*, edd. J. Huskinson et al., 45–80. Gloucester, repr. in Gordon (1996).

(1990a) 'From Republic to Principate: priesthood, religion and ideology', in Beard and North (1990) 177–98.

(1990b) 'The veil of power: emperors, sacrificers and benefactors', in Beard and North (1990) 199–231.

(1990c) 'Religion in the Roman empire: the civic compromise and its limits', in Beard and North (1990) 233–55.

(1994) 'Mystery, metaphor and doctrine in the mysteries of Mithras', in Hinnells (1994) 103–24.

(1996) *Image and Value in the Graeco-Roman World.* Aldershot, Hampshire and Brookfield VT.

Goudineau, C., I. Fauduet and G. Coulon edd. (1994) *Les sanctuaires de tradition indigène en Gaule romaine.* Paris.

Grabar, A. (1967) *The Beginnings of Christian Art, 200–395.* London.

Graf, F. ed. (1993) *Mythos in mythenloser Gesellschaft. Das Paradigma Roms* (Colloquium Rauricum 3). Stuttgart and Leipzig.

(1994) *La magie dans l'antiquité gréco-romaine.* Paris.

Graillot, H. (1912) *Le culte de Cybèle, mère des dieux, à Rome et dans l'empire.* Paris.

Grandazzi, A. (1993) 'La *Roma quadrata*: mythe ou réalité', *MEFRA* 105: 493–545.

Grande Roma (1990) *La Grande Roma dei Tarquini* (Exhibition Cat. Palazzo delle Esposizioni, 12 June–30 Sept 1990). Rome.

Grant, M. (1971) *Cities of Vesuvius.* London.

(1973) *Roman Myths.* Harmondsworth.

Gratwick, A.S. (1982) 'The early Republic', in *Cambridge History of Classical Literature. II Latin Literature*, edd. E.J. Kenney and W.V. Clausen, 60–171. Cambridge.

Greenleaf, R.E. (1969) *The Mexican Inquisition of the Sixteenth Century.* Albuquerque.

Griffin, M.T. (1984) *Nero, the End of a Dynasty.* London.

Grodzynski, D. (1974a) 'Superstitio', *Rev.Et.Anc.* 76: 36–60.

(1974b) 'Par la bouche de l'empereur', in *Divination et rationalité*, ed. J.-P. Vernant, 267–94. Paris.

Gros, P. (1976) *Aurea templa. Recherches sur l'architecture religieuse de Rome à l'époque d'Auguste* (BEFAR 231). Rome.

(1984) 'L'*Augusteum* de Nîmes', *Rev. arch. de Narbonnaise* 17: 123–34.

(1987) 'Un programme augustéen: le centre monumental de la colonie d'Arles', *Jahrb.deut.Arch.Inst.* 102: 339–63.

(1990) 'Le premier urbanisme de la Colonia Julia Carthago', in *L'Afrique dans l'occident romain*, 547–73. Rome.

(1991) 'Les cultes des Caesares et leur signification dans l'espace urbain des villes julio-claudiennes', in *L'espace sacrificiel dans les civilisations méditerranéennes de l'antiquité* (Publ. de la Bibliothèque Salomon-Reinach 5), 179–86. Paris.

Gruen, E.S. (1990) *Studies in Greek Culture and Roman Policy* (Cincinnati Classical Studies 7). Leiden.

(1993) *Culture and National Identity in Republican Rome*. London.

Gryson, R. (1972) *Le ministère des femmes dans l'église ancienne*. Gembloux.

Gsell, S. (1920–8) *Histoire ancienne de l'Afrique du Nord*, 8 vols. Paris. (Repr. Osnabrück, 1979.)

Guamán Poma de Ayala (1567–1615?/1978) *Letter to a King*. London.

Guarducci, M. (1971) 'Enea e Vesta', *Röm.Mitt.* 78: 73–118, repr. 198–256 in her *Scritti scelti sulla religione greca e romana e sul cristianesimo* (EPRO 98). Leiden.

Guittard, C. (1976) 'Recherches sur la nature de Saturne, des origines à la réforme de 217 av. J.-C.', in Bloch (1976) 43–71.

Guizzi, F. (1968) *Aspetti giuridici del sacerdozio romano. Il sacerdozio di Vesta.* Naples.

Gülzow, H. (1967) 'Kallist von Rom. Ein Beitrag zur Soziologie der römischen Gemeinde', *Zeit.Neutest.Wiss.* 58: 102–21.

Guterman, S.L. (1951) *Religious Toleration and Persecution in Ancient Rome*. London.

Gutschow, N. (1982) *Stadtraum und Ritual der newarischen Städte im Kathmandu-Tal.* Stuttgart.

Guyon, J. (1987) *Le cimetière aux Deux Lauriers* (BEFAR 264). Rome.

Habinek, T.N. (1992) 'Grecian wonders and Roman woe', in *The Interpretation of Roman Poetry*, ed. K. Galinsky, 227–42. Frankfurt am Main.

Hajjar, Y. (1977) *La triade d'Héliopolis-Baalbek. Son culte et sa diffusion à travers les textes littéraires et les documents iconographiques et épigraphiques* (EPRO 59), 2 vols. Leiden.

(1985) *La triade d'Héliopolis-Baalbek*. Montreal.

Halkin, L. (1953) *La supplication d'action de grâces chez les Romains* (Bibl. de la Faculté de Phil. et Lettres de l'Univ. de Liège 128). Paris.

Hall, A. S. (1973) 'New light on the capture of Isaura Vetus by P. Servilius Vatia', *Akten des VI Int. Kongresses für Griechische und Lateinische Epigraphik* (*Vestigia* 17), 568–71. Munich.

Hall, S.G. ed. (1979) *Melito of Sardis, On Pascha*. Oxford.

(1991) *Doctrine and Practice in the Early Church*. London.

Hamnett, I. ed. (1990) *Religious Pluralism and Unbelief.* London and New York.

Hänlein-Schäfer, H. (1985) *Veneratio Augusti. Eine Studie zu den Tempeln des ersten römischen Kaisers*. Rome.

(1996) 'Die Ikonographie des *Genius Augusti* im Kompital- und Hauskult der frühen Kaiserzeit', in Small (1996) 73–98.

Hansen, V. (1990) *Changing Gods in Medieval China, 1127–1276*. Princeton.

Hanson J. A. (1959) *Roman Theater-Temples*. Princeton.

Harl, K.W. (1990) 'Sacrifice and pagan belief in fifth- and sixth-century Byzantium', *Past & Present* 128: 7–27.

Harmon D.P. (1978) 'The public festivals of Rome', *ANRW* II.16.2: 1440–68.

Harnack, A. von (1905) 'Der Vorwurf des Atheismus in den drei ersten Jahrhunderten', *Texte und Untersuchungen* 28.4: 3–16.
   (1908) *The Mission and Expansion of Christianity in the First Three Centuries.* London.
   (1924) *Die Mission und Ausbreitung des Christentums in den ersten drei Jahrhunderten,* 2 vols, 4th edn. Leipzig.
Harries, B. (1989) 'Causation and the authority of the poet in Ovid's *Fasti*', *Class.Quart.* 38: 164–85.
Harris, W.V. (1979) *War and Imperialism in Republican Rome 327–70 B.C.* Oxford.
Hassel, F.J. (1966) *Der Trajansbogen in Benevent. Ein Bauwerk des römischen Senates.* Mainz.
Häuber, R.C. (1990) 'Zur Topographie der Horti Maecenatis und der Horti Lamiani auf den Esquilin in Rom', *Kölner Jahrbuch für Vor- und Frühgeschichte* 23: 11–107.
Hayman, P. (1991) 'Monotheism – a misused word in Jewish studies?', *J.Jewish Studies* 42: 1–15.
Haynes, I.P. (1993) 'The romanization of religion in the *auxilia* of the Roman imperial army from Augustus to Septimius Severus', *Britannia* 24: 141–57.
Helbig, W. (1963–72) *Führer durch die öffentlichen Sammlungen klassischer Altertümer in Rom,* 4th edn. Rome.
Helgeland, J. (1978) 'Roman army religion', *ANRW* II.16.2: 1470–1505.
   (1979) 'Christians and the Roman army from Marcus Aurelius to Constantine', *ANRW* II.23.1: 724–834.
Henderson, J. (1996) 'Footnote: representation in the *Villa of the Mysteries*', in *Art and Text in Roman Culture,* ed. J. Elsner, 235–76. Cambridge.
Henig, M. (1984) *Religion in Roman Britain.* London and New York.
Herz, P. (1978) 'Kaiserfeste der Prinzipatszeit', *ANRW* II.16.2: 1135–1200.
Heurgon, J. (1957) *Trois études sur le 'ver sacrum'* (Coll. Latomus 26). Brussels.
   (1959) 'The date of Vegoia's prophecy', *JRS* 49: 41–5.
Heyob, S.K. (1975) *The Cult of Isis among Women in the Graeco-Roman World* (EPRO 51). Leiden.
Hijmans, B.L. (1994) 'Apuleius orator: "Pro se de magia" and "Florida"', *ANRW* II.34.2: 1708–84.
Hinds, S. (1992) '*Arma* in Ovid's *Fasti*', *Arethusa* 25: 81–153.
Hinnells, J.R. (1985) *Persian Mythology,* 2nd edn. Feltham, Middlesex.
   ed. (1994) *Studies in Mithraism.* Rome.
Hobbs, E.C. and W. Wuellner edd. (1980) *The Role of the Christian Bishop in Ancient Society* (Center for Hermeneutical Studies). Berkeley.
Hoey, A.S. (1937) 'Rosaliae signorum', *Harv.Theol.Rev.* 30: 15–35.
Hoffmann, W. (1933) *Wandel und Herkunft der Sibyllinischen Bücher in Rom.* Diss. Leipzig.
Holland, L.A. (1937) 'The shrine of the *Lares Compitales*', *Trans.Amer.Philol.Ass.* 68: 428–41.
Holloway, R.R. (1994) *The Archaeology of Early Rome and Latium.* London.
Hölkeskamp, K.-J. (1988) 'Das Plebiscitum Ogulnium de sacerdotibus', *Rhein.Mus.* 131: 51–67.
Holtom, D.C. (1943) *Modern Japan and Shinto Nationalism.* Chicago.
Hommel, P. (1954) *Studien zu den römischen Figurengiebeln der Kaiserzeit.* Berlin.

Hopkins, K. (1978) *Conquerors and Slaves*. Cambridge.
   (1983) *Death and Renewal*. Cambridge.
   (1991) 'From blessing to violence', in *City States in Classical Antiquity and Medieval Italy*, edd. A. Molho et al., 479–98. Stuttgart.
Hörig, M. (1984) 'Iupiter Dolichenus', *ANRW* II.17.4: 2136–2179.
Hörig, M. and E. Schwertheim (1987) *Corpus cultus Iovis Dolicheni* (EPRO 106). Leiden.
Horne, P.D. (1986) 'Roman or Celtic temples? A case study', in *Pagan Gods and Shrines of the Roman Empire* (O.U. Committee for Archaeology, Mono.8), edd. M. Henig and A. King, 15–24. Oxford.
Horsley, G.H.R. (1981–) *New Documents Illustrating Early Christianity*, 5 vols. North Ryde N.S.W.
Huber, W. (1969) *Passa und Ostern. Untersuchungen zur Osterfeier der alten Kirche*. Berlin.
Hull, J.M. (1974) *Hellenistic Magic and the Synoptic Tradition*. London.
Hume, D. (1757) *The Natural History of Religion* (ed. A.W. Colver, Oxford 1976), originally first of the *Four Dissertations* (London 1757).
Humphrey J.H. (1986) *Roman Circuses*. London and Berkeley.
Hunt, D. (1993) 'Christianising the Roman empire: the evidence of the Code', in *The Theodosian Code*, edd. J. Harries and I. Wood, 143–58. London.
Huskinson, J.M. (1982) *Concordia Apostolorum. Christian Propaganda at Rome in the Fourth and Fifth Centuries* (Brit.Arch.Rep. Int. Series 148). Oxford.
Hutchinson, G.O. (1993) *Latin Literature from Seneca to Juvenal*. Oxford.
Iacopi, I. (1968–9) 'Area Sacra dell'Argentina: considerazioni sulla terza fase del Tempio A', *BCACR* 81: 115–25.
Inden, R. (1990) *Imagining India*. Cambridge MA and Oxford.
Jal, P. (1962) 'Les dieux et les guerres civiles dans la Rome de la fin de la République', *Rev.Et.Lat.* 40: 170–200.
Janssen, L.F. (1979) '"Superstitio" and the persecution of the Christians', *Vigiliae Christianae* 33: 131–59.
Jocelyn, H. D. (1990) 'Forme letterarie e vita sociale', in *Storia di Roma*, ed. A. Schiavone, II.1: 595–629. Turin.
Johnson, A. (1983) *Roman Forts of the First and Second Centuries A.D. in Britain and the German Provinces*. New York.
Jones, A.H.M. (1940) *The Greek City from Alexander to Justinian*. Oxford.
   (1964) *The Later Roman Empire, AD 284–602*. Oxford.
Jones, C.P. (1976) 'The Plancii of Perge and Diana Planciana', *Harv.Stud.Class.Philol.* 80: 231–7.
   (1986) *Culture and Society in Lucian*. Cambridge MA and London.
Judge, E.A. (1980–1) 'The social identity of the first Christians: a question of method in religious history', *J.Rel.Hist.* 11: 201–17.
Kähler, H. (1937) 'Zum Sonnentempel Aurelians', *Röm.Mitt.* 52: 94–105.
Kaiser Augustus (1988) *Kaiser Augustus und die verlorene Republik* (Exhibition catalogue, Berlin). Mainz am Rhein.
Kajanto, I. (1957) *God and Fate in Livy*. Turku.
   (1981) 'Pontifex maximus as title of the Pope', *Arctos* 15: 37–52.
Kallala, N. (1992) 'L'autre aspect du culte de Jupiter en Afrique', in *Histoire et archéologie de l'Afrique du Nord, Ve Colloque int.*, 193–200. Paris.
Kätzler, J.B. (1952–3) 'Religio. Versuch einer Worterklärung', *Jahresbericht des Bischöflichen Gymnasiums Paulinum in Schwaz* 20: 2–18.

Keay, S.J. (1988) *Roman Spain*. London.

Kellum, B. (1985) 'Sculptural programs and propaganda in Augustan Rome: the temple of Apollo on the Palatine', in *The Age of Augustus* (Archaeologia Transatlantica 5), ed. R. Winkes, 169–76. Providence RI and Louvain-La-Neuve.

Kelly, J.N.D. (1978) *Early Christian Doctrines*, 5th edn. San Francisco.

Kienast, D. (1982) *Augustus. Prinzeps und Monarch*. Darmstadt.

Klauser, T. (1979) *A Short History of the Western Liturgy*, 2nd edn. Oxford.

Kleiner, D.E.E. (1992) *Roman Sculpture*. New Haven and London.

Kloppenborg, J.S. and S.G. Wilson edd. (1996) *Voluntary Associations in the Graeco-Roman World*. London and New York.

Klotz, A. (1940–1) *Livius und seine Vorgänger* (Neue Wege zur Antike, 2. Reihe 9–11). Leipzig (repr. Amsterdam 1964).

Kneissl, P. (1980) 'Entstehung und Bedeutung der Augustalität. Zur Inschrift der Ara Narbonensis (*CIL* XII 4333)', *Chiron* 10: 291–326.

Koch, C. (1937) *Der römische Juppiter* (Frankfurter Studien zur Religion und Kultur der Antike 14). Frankfurt.

(1954) 'Der altrömische Staatskult im Spiegel augusteischer und spätrepublikanischer Apologetik', *Convivium. Festschrift Konrat Ziegler*, 85–120. Stuttgart, repr. in Koch (1960) 176–204.

(1958) 'Vesta', *RE* 2. Reihe, 8: 1717–76.

(1960) *Religio. Studien zu Kult und Glauben der Römer*. Nürnberg.

(1963) 'Quirinus', *RE* 24: 1306–21.

Koenen, L. (1970) 'The prophecies of a potter: a prophecy of world renewal becomes an apocalypse', 249–54 in *Proc. XII Int. Cong. of Papyrology* (American Studies in Papyrology 7), ed. D.H. Samuel. Toronto.

(1984) 'A supplementary note on the date of the oracle of the potter', *ZPE* 54: 9–13.

Koep, L. (1962) ' "Religio" und "Ritus" als Problem des frühen Christentums', *Jahrb.Ant.Christ.* 5: 43–59.

Koeppel, G.M. (1983) 'Die historischen Reliefs der römischen Kaiserzeit I', *Bonner Jahrb.* 183: 61–144.

(1984) 'Die historischen Reliefs der römischen Kaiserzeit II', *Bonner Jahrb.* 184:1–65.

Kolb, A. (1993) *Die kaiserliche Bauverwaltung in der Stadt Rom. Geschichte und Aufbau der* cura operum publicorum *unter dem Prinzipat*. Stuttgart.

Kolendo, J. (1980) 'Le rôle du *primus pilus* dans la vie religieuse de la légion, en rapport avec quelques inscriptions des *principia* de Novae', *Archeologia* (Polish Academy) 31: 49–60.

Konstan, D. (1983) *Roman Comedy*. Ithaca.

Köves-Zulauf, T. (1972) *Reden und Schweigen*. Munich.

(1978) 'Plinius der Ä. und die römische Religion', *ANRW* II.16.1: 187–288.

Kraemer, R.S. (1989) 'On the meaning of the term "Jew" in Greco-Roman inscriptions', *Harv.Theol.Rev.* 82: 35–53.

(1992) *Her Share of the Blessings: Women's Religions among Pagans, Jews and Christians in the Greco-Roman World*. New York and Oxford.

Kraft, K. (1952–3) 'Der goldene Kranz Caesars und der Kampf um die Entlarvung des Tyrannen', *Jahrb.Num.Geld.* 3/4: 7–98.

Krautheimer, R. (1960) 'Mensa-coemeterium-martyrium', *Cahiers archéologiques*

11: 15–40, repr. in his *Studies in Early Christian, Medieval and Renaissance Art* (London, 1971).

(1979) *Early Christian and Byzantine Architecture*, 3rd. edn. Harmondsworth.

(1980) *Rome. Profile of a City, 312–1308*. Princeton.

Kuhn, P.A. (1990) *Soulstealers: the Chinese Sorcery Scare of 1768*. Cambridge MA.

Künzl, E. (1988) *Der römische Triumph: Siegesfeiern im antiken Roma*. Munich.

Kyrtatas, D.J. (1987) *The Social Structure of the Early Christian Communities*. London and New York.

Labriolle, P. de (1934) *La réaction païenne. Étude sur la polémique antichrétienne du Ier au VIe siècle*. Paris.

Labrousse, M. (1937) 'Le *pomerium* de la Rome impériale', *MEFR* 54: 165–99.

Ladage, D. (1971) *Städtische Priester- und Kultämter im lateinischen Westen des Imperium Romanum zur Kaiserzeit*. Diss. Köln.

Lambrechts, P. (1951) 'Cybèle, divinité étrangère ou nationale?', *Société royale belge d'anthropologie et de préhistoire* 62: 44–60.

(1952) 'Les fêtes "phrygiennes" de Cybèle et d'Attis', *Bulletin de l'Institut historique belge de Rome* 27: 141–70.

(1962) *Attis: van herdersknaap tot god*. Brussels.

Lambrino, S. (1965) 'Les cultes indigènes en Espagne sous Trajan et Hadrien', in *Les empereurs romains d'Espagne*, 223–42. Paris.

Lampe, P. (1989) *Die stadtrömischen Christen in den ersten beiden Jahrhunderten*, 2nd edn (Wissenschaftliche Untersuchungen zum Neuen Testament, 2nd series, 18). Tübingen.

Lane Fox, R. (1986) *Pagans and Christians*. Harmondsworth and New York.

La Piana, G. (1927) 'Foreign groups in Rome during the first centuries of the empire', *Harv.Theol.Rev.* 20: 183–403.

Larner, C.J. (1981) *Enemies of God: the Witch-hunt in Scotland*. London and Baltimore.

La Rocca, E. (1984) *La riva a mezzaluna. Culti, agoni, monumenti funerari presso il Tevere nel Campo Marzio occidentale*. Rome.

Latte, K. (1926) 'Über eine Eigentümlichkeit der italischen Gottesvorstellung', *Archiv Rel.Wiss.* 24: 244–58, repr. in Latte (1968) 76–90.

(1960a) *Römische Religionsgeschichte* (Handbuch der Altertumswissenschaft v.4). Munich.

(1960b) 'Der Historiker L. Calpurnius Frugi', *Sitz.Deut.Ak.Wiss., Berlin*, Kl. für Sprache..., no.7: 3–16, repr. in Latte (1968) 837–47.

(1968) *Kleine Schriften*. Munich.

Laurin, J.-R. (1954) 'Le lieu du culte chrétien d'après les documents littéraires primitifs', *Analecta Gregoriana* 70: 39–57.

Lausberg, M. (1970) *Untersuchungen zu Senecas Fragmenten*. Berlin.

Lavagne, H. (1979) 'Les dieux de la Gaule Narbonnaise: "romanité" et romanisation', *Journal des Savants* 1979: 155–97.

Lebek, W.D. (1989) 'Die Mainzer Ehrungen für Germanicus, den älteren Drusus und Domitian', *ZPE* 78: 45–82.

Le Bonniec, H. (1958) *Le culte de Cérès à Rome des origines à la fin de la république* (Etudes et commentaires 27). Paris.

Le délit religieux dans la cité antique (1981) (Coll.Ecole franç.Rome 48). Rome.

Lefèvre, E. (1989) *Das Bild-Programm des Apollo-Tempels auf dem Palatin* (Xenia 24). Konstanz.

Le Gall, J. (1953) *Le Tibre, fleuve de Rome dans l'antiquité*. Paris.
  (1975) 'Les Romains et l'orientation solaire', *MEFRA* 87: 287–320.
  (1976) 'Evocatio', *Mélanges J. Heurgon* I: 519–24 . Rome.
Le Glay, M. (1966) *Saturne africain* (BEFAR 205). Paris.
  (1984) 'Les religions populaires dans l'occident romain', *Praktika tou H'
  diethnous sinedriou ellinikis kai latinikis epigraphikis*, 2 vols, I.150–70.
  Athens.
Lehmann, K. (1962) 'Ignorance and search in the Villa of the Mysteries', *JRS*
  52: 62–8.
Lembke, K. (1994) *Das Iseum Campense in Rom* (Archäologie und Geschichte
  3). Heidelberg.
Lenaghan, J. O. (1969) *A Commentary on Cicero's Oration, De Haruspicum
  Responso*. The Hague.
Leon, H.J. (1960) *The Jews of Ancient Rome*. Philadelphia.
Leone, M. (1976) 'Il problema del flaminato di Cesare', in *Studi di storia antica
  offerti dagli allievi a E. Manni*, 193–212. Rome.
Lepelley, C. (1994) 'Le musée des statues divines', *Cahiers archéologiques* 42:
  5–15.
Le Roux, P. (1994a) 'L'évolution du culte impérial dans les provinces
  occidentales d'Auguste à Domitien', *Pallas* 40: 397–411.
  (1994b) 'Cultes indigènes et religion romaine en Hispanie sous l'Empire',
  in *L'Afrique, la Gaule, la religion à l'époque romaine: Mélanges à la
  mémoire de M. Le Glay*, ed. Y. Le Bohec (Coll. Latomus 226) 560–7.
  Brussels.
Letta, C. (1984) 'Amministrazione romana e culti locali in età altoimperiale – il
  caso della Gallia', *Riv.Stor.Ital.* 96: 1001–24.
Levene, D.S. (1993) *Religion in Livy* (*Mnemosyne* Supp. 127). Leiden.
Levick, B. (1967) *Roman Colonies in Southern Asia Minor*. Oxford.
Lewis, I.M. (1989) *Ecstatic Religion*, 2nd edn. London and New York.
Lewis, M.W.H. (1955) *The Official Priests of Rome under the Julio-Claudians*
  (Papers and Monographs Amer. Acad. Rome 16). Rome.
Lewis, N. and M. Reinhold (1990) *Roman Civilization*, 3rd edn, 2 vols. New
  York.
Liebeschuetz, J.H.W.G. (1967) 'The religious position of Livy's History', *JRS*
  57: 45–55.
  (1977) 'Epigraphic evidence on the Christianization of Syria', *Limes. Akten des
  XI internationalen Limeskongresses*, 485–508. Budapest.
  (1979) *Continuity and Change in Roman Religion*. Oxford.
Liegle, J. (1942) 'L. Aemilius Paullus als Augur maximus im Jahre 160 und das
  Augurium des Heils', *Hermes* 77: 249–312.
Lieu, J. et al. edd. (1992) *The Jews among Pagans and Christians in the Roman
  Empire*. London and New York.
Linder, A. (1987) *The Jews in Roman Imperial Legislation*. Detroit and
  Jerusalem.
Linderski, J. (1965) 'Constitutional aspects of the consular elections in 59 B.C.',
  Historia 14: 423–42.
  (1982) 'Cicero and Roman divination', *PdP* 37: 12–38.
  (1986) 'The augural law', *ANRW* II.16.3: 2146–312.
Ling, R. (1991) *Roman Painting*. Cambridge.
Lintott, A. W. (1968) *Violence in Republican Rome*. Oxford.

(1978) 'The Capitoline dedications to Jupiter and the Roman people', *ZPE* 30: 137–44.

Liou-Gille, B. (1980) *Cultes 'héroïques' romains. Les fondateurs*. Paris.

(1993) 'Le pomerium', *Mus.Helv.* 50: 94–106.

Lissi-Caronna, E. (1986) *Il mitreo dei* Castra Peregrinorum (*S. Stefano Rotondo*) (EPRO 104). Leiden.

Little, A.M.G. (1972) *A Roman Bridal Drama at the Villa of the Mysteries*. Kennebunk.

Lizzi, R. (1990) 'Ambrose's contemporaries and the Christianization of northern Italy', *JRS* 80: 156–73.

Luce, T.J. (1977) *Livy: the Composition of his History*. Princeton NJ.

Luciani, R. ed. (1984) *Roma sotteranea*. Rome.

Lugli, G. (1952–69) *Fontes ad topographiam veteris urbis Romae pertinentes...*, 8 vols. Rome.

Luhrmann, T.M. (1989) *Persuasions of the Witch's Craft. Ritual Magic and Witchcraft in Present-day England*. Oxford and Cambridge MA.

L'urbs (1987) *L'urbs. Espace urbain et histoire (Ier siècle av. J.-C. – IIIe siècle ap. J.-C.)*. (Coll.Ecole franç. de Rome 98). Rome.

MacBain, B. (1982) *Prodigy and Expiation: a Study in Religion and Politics in Republican Rome* (Coll. Latomus 177). Brussels.

MacCormack, S. (1991) *Religion in the Andes*. Princeton NJ.

MacDonald, W.L. (1976) *The Pantheon. Design, Meaning and Progeny*. London.

Macfarlane, A. (1970) *Witchcraft in Tudor and Stuart England*. London.

McKay, A.G. (1977) *Houses, Villas and Palaces in the Roman World*. London.

Mackie, N. (1983) *Local Administration in Roman Spain* A.D. *14–212* (Brit.Arch.Rep. Int. Ser. 172). Oxford.

MacMullen, R. (1966) *Enemies of the Roman Order: Treason, Unrest and Alienation in the Empire*. Cambridge MA.

(1981) *Paganism in the Roman Empire*. New Haven and London.

(1993) 'The unromanized in Rome', in *Diasporas in Antiquity*, edd. S.J.D. Cohen and E.S. Frerichs, 47–64. Atlanta GA.

McNamara, J.A. (1985) *A New Song: Celibate Women in the First Three Christian Centuries*. New York.

Magdelain, A. (1964) 'Auspicia ad patres redeunt', in *Hommages à J. Bayet* (Coll. Latomus 70), 427–73. Brussels. Repr. in Magdelain (1990) 341–83.

(1968) *Recherches sur l' 'Imperium', la loi curiate et les auspices d'investiture*. Paris.

(1977) 'L'inauguration de l'*urbs* et l'*imperium*', *MEFRA* 89: 11–29, repr. in Magdelain (1990) 209–28.

(1990) *Jus, Imperium, Auctoritas* (Coll.Ecole franç. de Rome 133). Paris and Rome.

Magie, D. (1950) *Roman Rule in Asia Minor*. Princeton NJ.

Maier, H.O. (1995) 'The topography of heresy and dissent in late-fourth-century Rome', *Historia* 44: 232–49.

Maiuri, A. (1931) *La villa dei Misteri*. Rome.

Malaise, M. (1972a) *Inventaire préliminaire des documents égyptiens découverts en Italie* (EPRO 21). Leiden.

(1972b) *Les conditions de pénétration et de diffusion des cultes égyptiens en Italie* (EPRO 22). Leiden.

(1981) 'Contenu et effets de l'initiation isiaque', *Ant.Class.* 50: 483–98.

(1984) 'La diffusion des cultes égyptiens dans les provinces européennes de l'empire romain', *ANRW* II.17.3: 1615–91.

Malbon, E.S. (1990) *The Iconography of the Sarcophagus of Junius Bassus.* Princeton.

Malcovati, H. (1955) *Oratorum Romanorum Fragmenta Liberae Rei Publicae,* 2nd edn. Turin.

Malherbe, A.J. (1977) *Social Aspects of Early Christianity.* Baton Rouge and London.

Mangas, J. (1986) 'Die römische Religion in Hispanien während der Prinzipatszeit', *ANRW* II.18.1: 276–344.

Mango, C. (1985) *Le développement urbain de Constantinople (IVe – VIIe siècles).* Paris.

Manzano, P. di (1984) 'Note sulla monetazione dei Ludi secolari dell'88 d.C.', *BCACR* 89: 297–304.

Mărghitan, L. and C.C. Petolescu (1976) '*Vota pro salute imperatoris* in an inscription at Ulpia Traiana Sarmizegetusa', *JRS* 66: 84–6.

Markus, R.A. (1990) *The End of Ancient Christianity.* Cambridge.

Martin, L.H. (1983) 'Why Cecropian Minerva? Hellenistic religious syncretism as system', *Numen* 30: 131–45.

Martínez Díez, G. and F. Rodriguez (1984) *La colección canónica Hispaña* (Monumenta Hispaniae Sacra, Serie Canónica) IV. Madrid.

Martroye, F. (1930) 'La répression de la magie et le culte des gentils au IVe siècle', *Revue historique de droit français et étranger*, 4th ser., 9: 669–701.

Massonneau, E. (1934) *La magie dans l'antiquité romaine.* Bourdeaux.

Matthews, J.F. (1970) 'The historical setting of the "Carmen contra paganos" (Cod.Par.Lat. 8084)', *Historia* 20: 464–79, repr. in Matthews (1985).

(1973) 'Symmachus and the oriental cults', *JRS* 63: 175–95, repr. in Matthews (1985).

(1975) *Western Aristocracies and Imperial Court,* A.D. *364–425.* Oxford.

(1985) *Political Life and Culture in Late Roman Society.* London.

Mattingly, H. (1960) *Roman Coins from the Earliest Times to the Fall of the Western Empire,* 2nd edn. London.

Maule, Q. F. and Smith, H. R. W. (1959) *Votive Religion at Caere: Prolegomena.* Berkeley-Los Angeles.

Mazzarino, S. (1951) 'La propaganda senatoriale nel tardo imperio', *Doxa* 4: 121–48.

Mazzoli, G. (1984) 'Il problema religioso in Seneca', *Riv.Stor.Ital.* 96: 953–1000.

Méautis, G. (1940) 'Les aspects religieux de l' "affaire" des Bacchanales', *REA* 42 (*Mélanges Georges Radet*): 476–85.

Meeks, W.A. (1983) *The First Urban Christians. The Social World of the Apostle Paul.* New Haven and London.

Meier, C. (1995) *Caesar.* London.

Meiggs, R. (1973) *Roman Ostia,* 2nd edn. Oxford.

Mélanges J. Heurgon (1976) *L'Italie préromaine et la Rome républicaine. Mélanges offerts à J. Heurgon* (Coll.Ecole franç. de Rome 27). Rome.

Mele, M. ed. (1982) *L'area del 'santuario siriaco del Gianicolo'. Problemi archeologici e storico-religiosi.* Rome.

Mellor, R. (1975) *Thea Rome. The Worship of the Goddess Roma in the Greek World* (Hypomnemata 42). Göttingen.

Meneghini, R. (1984) 'Il santuario siriaco del Gianicolo', *Romana Gens* n.s.1.2 (May–Aug.): 6–10.

Merkelbach, R. (1961) 'Aeneas in Cumae', *Mus.Helv.* 18: 83–99.

   (1984) *Mithras.* Königstein.

Meslin, M. (1969) 'Persistances païennes en Galice, vers la fin du VIᵉ siècle', in *Hommages à Marcel Renard* (Coll. Latomus 101–103), 3 vols, II.512–24. Brussels.

   (1970) *La fête des kalendes de janvier dans l'empire romain. Etude d'un rituel de Nouvel An* (Coll. Latomus 115). Brussels.

   (1978) *L'homme romain, des origines au Iᵉʳ siècle de notre ère. Essai d'anthropologie.* Paris.

Metcalf, T.R. (1994) *Ideologies of the Raj* (New Cambridge History of India 3.4). Cambridge.

Metzger, B.M. (1987) *The Canon of the New Testament.* Oxford.

Michels, A.K. (1967) *The Calendar of the Roman Republic.* Princeton.

   (1976) 'The versatility of religio', in *The Mediterranean World. Papers Presented in Honour of Gilbert Bagnani*, 36–77. Peterborough, Ontario.

Mielsch, H. (1975) *Römische Stuckreliefs* (*Röm.Mitt.* Supp.21). Heidelberg.

Miles, G.B. (1995) *Livy: Reconstructing Early Rome.* Ithaca and London.

Millar, F. (1977) *The Emperor in the Roman World (31 B.C. – A.D. 337).* London.

   (1990) 'The Roman *coloniae* of the Near East: a study of cultural relations', in *Roman Eastern Policy and Other Studies in Roman History* (Commentationes Humanarum Litterarum 91), edd. H. Solin and M. Kajava, 7–58. Helsinki.

   (1992) 'The Jews of the Graeco-Roman diaspora between paganism and Christianity', in Lieu et al. (1992) 97–123.

   (1993) *The Roman Near East 31 B.C. – A.D. 337.* Cambridge MA and London.

Miller, D. ed. (1993) *Unwrapping Christmas.* Oxford.

Miller, J.F. (1991) *Ovid's Elegiac Festivals* (Studien zur klass. Phil. 55). Frankfurt.

Mitchell, S. (1988) 'Maximinus and the Christians in A.D. 312: a new Latin inscription', *JRS* 78: 105–24.

   (1993) *Anatolia*, 2 vols. Oxford.

Mitchell, T. N. (1986) 'The *Leges Clodiae* and *obnuntiatio*', *Class.Quart.* 36: 172–6.

   (1991) *Cicero: The Senior Statesman.* New Haven and London.

Moatti, C. ed. (forthcoming) *La mémoire perdue*, Vol. II. Paris.

Mol, H. (1976) *Identity and the Sacred.* Oxford. (New York, 1977).

   (1985) *Faith and Fragility: Religion and Identity in Canada.* Burlington, Ontario.

Momigliano, A.D. (1938) 'Thybris pater', (unpublished), repr. in his *Terzo Contributo* 609–39.

   (1941) [rev. of A.N. Sherwin-White, *The Roman Citizenship*], *JRS* 31: 158–65, repr. in his *Secondo Contributo*, 389–400.

   (1955–95) *Contributi alla storia degli studi classici (e del mondo antico).* Rome. *Secondo Contributo* (1960), *Terzo* (1960), *Quarto* (1969), *Ottavo* (1987).

   (1967) 'L'ascesa della plebe nella storia arcaica di Roma', *Riv. Stor. Ital.* 79: 297–312, repr. in his *Quarto Contributo*, 437–54.

(1971) 'Il *rex sacrorum* e l'origine della repubblica', in *Studi in onore di E. Volterra* I.357–64. Milan. Repr. in his *Quarto Contributo*, 395–402.

(1983) 'Premesse per una discussione su Georges Dumézil', *Opus* 2: 329–42, revised as 'Georges Dumézil and the trifunctional approach to Roman civilization', in his *On Pagans, Jews, and Christians*, 289–314. Middletown, CT, 1987.

(1984) 'The theological efforts of the Roman upper classes in the first century B.C.', *Class.Philol.* 79: 199–211, repr. in his *Ottavo Contributo*, 261–77.

(1987) 'Some preliminary remarks on the "religious opposition" to the Roman empire', in *Opposition et résistances à l'empire d'Auguste à Trajan* (Fondation Hardt, Entretiens 33), 103–29. Geneva. Repr. in his *On Pagans, Jews, and Christians*, 120–41. Middletown, CT, 1987.

(1990) *The Classical Foundations of Modern Historiography*. Berkeley.

Mommsen, T. (1890) 'Der Religionsfrevel nach römischem Recht', *Historische Zeitschrift* 64: 389–429, repr. in his *Gesammelte Schriften* 3 (1907) 389–422.

(1899) *Römisches Strafrecht*. Leipzig.

Montanari, E. (1988) *Identità culturale e conflitti religiosi nella Roma repubblicana*. Rome.

Monter, W. (1990) *Frontiers of Heresy. The Spanish Inquisition from the Basque Lands to Sicily*. Cambridge.

Moore, R.I. (1987) *The Formation of a Persecuting Society: Power and Deviance in Western Europe, 950–1250*. Oxford.

Mora, F. (1990) *Prosopographia Isiaca*, 2 vols (EPRO 113). Leiden.

Morel, J.-P. (1989) 'The transformation of Italy, 300–133 B.C.', *CAH*, 2nd edn 8: 477–516.

Moretti, L. (1980) 'Chio e la lupa Capitolina', *Rivista di Filologia* 108: 33–54.

(1982–4) 'Frammenti vecchi e nuovi del Commentario dei Ludi secolari del 17 A.C.', *Rendiconti della Pontificia Accademia Romana di Archeologia* 55–6: 361–79.

Morgan, M. G. (1990) 'Politics, religion and the games in Rome, 200–150 B.C.', *Philologus* 134: 14–36.

Mudie Cooke, P.B. (1913) 'The paintings of the Villa Item at Pompeii', *JRS* 3: 157–74.

Müller, H.W. (1969) *Der Isiskult im antiken Benevent* (Münchner ägyptologische Studien 16). Berlin.

Münzer, F. and Jörs, P. (1901) 'Ti. Coruncanius (Coruncanius 3)', *RE* 4: 1663–5.

Münzer, F. (1920) *Adelsparteien und Adelsfamilien*. Stuttgart.

Munzi, M. (1994) 'Sulla topografia dei *Lupercalia*: il contributo di Costantinopoli', *Studi Classici e Orientali* 44: 347–64.

Murray, C. (1981) *Rebirth and Afterlife: A Study of the Transmutation of Some Pagan Imagery in Early Christian Funerary Art* (BAR Int.Ser. 100). Oxford.

Mussies, G. (1982) 'Cascelia's prayer', in Bianchi and Vermaseren (1982) 156–67.

Musurillo, H. (1954) *The Acts of the Pagan Martyrs*. Oxford.

(1972) *The Acts of the Christian Martyrs*. Oxford.

Mysteries of Diana: the Antiquities from Nemi in Nottingham Museums (1983). Castle Museum, Nottingham.

Nash, D. (1976) 'Reconstructing Poseidonius' Celtic ethnography: some considerations', *Britannia* 7: 111–26.

Nash, E. (1968) *Pictorial Dictionary of Ancient Rome*, 2nd edn. London.

Needham, R. (1975) 'Polythetic classification: convergence and consequences', *Man* n.s.10: 349–69.

Neusner, J. (1979–80) 'Map without territory: Mishnah's system of sacrifice', *History of Religion* 19: 103–27.

Neusner, J., W.S. Green and E.S. Frerichs edd. (1987) *Judaisms and their Messiahs at the Turn of the Christian Era*. Cambridge.

Newlands, C. E. (1995) *Playing with Time: Ovid and the Fasti*. Ithaca and London.

Nicols, J. (1987) 'Indigenous culture and the process of Romanization in Iberian Galicia', *Amer.J.Philol.* 108: 129–51.

Niebling, G. (1956) 'Laribus Augustis Magistri Primi. Der Beginn des Compitalkultes der Lares und des Genius Augusti', *Historia* 5: 303–31.

Nilsson, M.P. (1920) 'Saeculares ludi', *RE* 2 Reihe, I: 1696–1720.

  (1957) *The Dionysiac Mysteries of the Hellenistic and Roman Age*. Lund.

  (1961–7) *Geschichte der griechischen Religion*, 2 vols., 2nd–3rd edns. Munich.

Nisbet, R.G.M. and Hubbard, M (1970) *A Commentary on Horace, Odes, Book 1*. Oxford.

Nock, A.D. (1925) 'Studies in the Graeco-Roman beliefs of the empire', *JHS* 45: 84–101, repr. in Nock (1972) I.33–48.

  (1930) '*A diis electa*: a chapter in the religious history of the third century', *Harv.Theol.Rev.* 23: 251–74, repr. in Nock (1972) I.252–70.

  (1934) 'Religious developments from the close of the Republic to the reign of Nero', *CAH* 10: 465–511. Cambridge.

  (1938) *St. Paul*. London.

  (1952) 'The Roman army and the Roman religious year', *Harv.Theol.Rev.* 45: 186–252, repr. in Nock (1972) II.736–90.

  (1972) *Essays on Religion and the Ancient World*, 2 vols. Oxford.

Noethlichs, K.-L. (1971) *Die gesetzgeberischen Massnahmen der christlichen Kaiser des vierten Jahrhunderts gegen Häretiker, Heiden und Juden*. Diss. Köln.

North, J. A. (1975) 'Praesens Divus' [review of Weinstock (1971)], *JRS* 65: 171–7.

  (1976) 'Conservatism and change in Roman religion', *Pap.Brit.Sch.Rome* 44: 1–12.

  (1979) 'Religious toleration in Republican Rome', *Proc.Camb.Philol.Soc.* 25: 85–103.

  (1980) 'Novelty and choice in Roman religion', review article, *JRS* 70: 186–91.

  (1986) 'Religion and politics, from republic to principate', *JRS* 76: 251–8.

  (1990) 'Family strategy and priesthood in the late Republic', in *Parenté et Stratégies Familiales dans l'Antiquité*, edd. J. Andreau and H. Bruhns, 527–43. Rome.

  (1992) 'Deconstructing stone theatres', *Apodosis. Essays Presented to Dr W.W. Cruickshank*, 75–83. London.

  (1993) 'Roman reactions to empire', *Scripta Classica Israelica* 12: 127–38.

  (1995) 'Religion and rusticity', in *Urban Society in Roman Italy*, edd. T.J. Cornell and K. Lomas, 135–50. London.

Novak, D.M. (1979) 'Constantine and the senate: an early phase of the
   Christianization of the Roman aristocracy', *Anc.Soc.* 10: 271–310.
Noy, D. (1995) *Jewish Inscriptions of Western Europe. 2. The City of Rome.*
   Cambridge.
O'Donnell, J.J. (1977) '*Paganus*: evolution and use', *Classical Folia* 31: 163–9.
Ogilvie, R.M. (1965) *A Commentary on Livy Books 1–5.* Oxford.
Oliver, J.H. (1940) 'Julia Domna as Athena Polias', in *Athenian Studies ... W.S.
   Ferguson* (*Harv.Stud.Class.Philol.* Supp.1), 521–30. Cambridge MA.
Olmsted, G.S. (1992) *The Gaulish Calendar.* Bonn.
Ostrow, S.E. (1985) '*Augustales* along the bay of Naples: a case for their early
   growth', *Historia* 34: 64–101.
Pagels, E. (1979) *The Gnostic Gospels.* New York.
   (1988) *Adam, Eve, and the Serpent.* New York.
Pailler, J.-M. (1976) '"Raptos a diis homines dici ...." (Tite-Live, xxxix, 13): les
   Bacchanales et la possession par les nymphes', *Mélanges J. Heurgon* (1976)
   II.731–42. Rome.
   (1983) 'Les pots cassés des Bacchanales', *MEFRA* 95: 7–54.
   (1988) *Bacchanalia: la répression de 186 av. J.-C. à Rome et en Italie* (BEFAR
   270). Rome.
Palmer, R.E.A. (1965) 'The censors of 312 B.C. and the state religion', *Historia*
   14: 294–324.
   (1974) *Roman Religion and Roman Empire. Five Essays* (The Harvey
   Foundation Series 154). Philadelphia.
   (1990) *Studies of the Northern Campus Martius in Ancient Rome*
   (Trans.Amer.Philos.Soc. 80.2). Philadelphia.
Panciera, S. (1970) 'Tra epigrafia e topografia – I', *Arch.Class.* 22: 131–63.
   (1970–1) 'Nuovi documenti epigrafici per la topografia di Roma antica',
   Rendiconti della Pontificia Accademia di Archeologia 43: 109–34.
   (1980) 'Nuovi luoghi di culto a Roma dalle testimonianze epigrafiche',
   Arch.Laz. 3: 202–13.
   (1982) 'Iscrizioni senatorie di Roma a dintorni', in *Epigrafia e ordine senatorio*
   (Tituli 4), I.591–678. Rome.
   (1987) 'Ancora tra epigrafia e topografia', in *L'urbs* (1987) 61–86.
Parke, H.W. (1988) *Sibyls and Sibylline Prophecy in Classical Antiquity.*
   London.
Pascal, C.B. (1964) *The Cults of Cisalpine Gaul* (Coll. Latomus 75). Brussels.
Paschoud, F. (1975) *Cinq études sur Zosime.* Paris.
Pastor Muñoz, M. (1981) 'Reflexiones sobre la religión de los Astures en epoca
   romana', in *La religión romana en Hispania*, 263–76. Madrid.
Pauli, L. (1984) *The Alps. Archaeology and Early History.* London.
Pavis d'Escurac, H. (1974) 'Pour une étude sociale de l'Apologie d'Apulée',
   Antiquités africaines 8: 89–101.
   (1980–1) 'La publica religio a Timgad', *Centre ricerche e documentazione
   sull'antichita classica. Atti* 11: 321–37.
Pekáry, T. (1986) 'Das Opfer vor dem Kaiserbild', *Bonner Jahrb.* 186: 91–103.
   (1987) '*Seditio*. Unruhen und Revolten im römischen Reich von Augustus bis
   Commodus', *Anc.Soc.* 18: 133–50.
Pelletier, A. (1982) *Vienne antique.* Roanne.
Pensabene, P. et al. (1980) *Terracotte votive dal Tevere* (Studi Miscellanei 25).
   Rome.

Pergola, P. (1986) 'Le catacombe romane: miti e realtà (a proposito del cimetero di Domitilla)', in Giardina (1986) 333–50.

Pesce, G. (1953) *Il tempio d'Iside in Sabratha*. Rome.

Peter, H. (1906–14) *Historicorum Romanorum Reliquiae*, 2nd edn. Leipzig.

Petrikovits, H. von (1975) *Die Innenbauten römischer Legionslager während der Prinzipatszeit*. Opladen.

Phillips, C.R. (1986) 'The sociology of religious knowledge in the Roman Empire to A.D. 284', *ANRW* II.16.3: 2677–2773.

    (1992) 'Roman religion and literary studies of Ovid's *Fasti*', *Arethusa* 25: 55–80.

Phillips, E.J. (1977) *Corpus Signorum Imperii Romani (Great Britain)*. I.1. Oxford.

Piccaluga, G. (1965) *Elementi spettacolari nei rituali festivi romani*. Rome.

    (1974) *Terminus. I segni di confine nella religione romana*. Rome.

Piccottini, G. (1994) *Mithrastempel in Virunum* (Aus Forschung und Kunst 28). Klagenfurt.

Pieper, J. (1977) *Die anglo-indische Station oder die Kolonisierung des Götterberges. Hindustadtkultur und Kolonialstadtwesen im 19. Jahrhundert als Konfrontation östlicher und westlicher Geisteswesen* (Antiquitates Orientales 1). Bonn.

Pietilä-Castrén, L. (1987) *Magnificentia Publica: the Victory Monuments of the Roman Generals in the Era of the Punic Wars* (Commentationes Humanarum Litterarum 84). Helsinki.

Pietri, C. (1961) 'Concordia Apostolorum et Renovatio Urbis. Culte des martyrs et propagande pontificale', *MEFR* 63: 275–322.

    (1976) *Roma christiana. Recherches sur l'église de Rome, son organisation, sa politique, son idéologie de Miltiade à Sixte III (311–440)* (BEFAR 224), 2 vols. Rome.

    (1978) 'Recherches sur les *domus ecclesiae*', *Rev.Etudes Augustiniennes* 24: 3–21.

    (1989) 'Régions ecclésiastiques et parroises romaines', in *Actes du XIe Congrès international d'archéologie chrétienne*, 3 vols. (Coll.Ecole franç. de Rome 123), II.1035–62. Rome.

Piganiol, A. (1923) *Recherches sur les jeux romains* (Publication de la Faculté des Lettres de l'Université de Strasbourg 13). Strasbourg.

Piggott, S. (1968) *The Druids*. London.

Pighi, G.B. (1965) *De ludis saecularibus*, 2nd edn. Amsterdam.

Pirenne-Delforge, V. (1994) 'Du "bon usage" de la notion de syncrétisme', *Kernos* 7: 11–27.

Platner S.B. and T. Ashby (1929) *A Topographical Dictionary of Ancient Rome*. London.

Poe, J.P. (1984) 'The Secular Games, the Aventine, and the Pomerium in the Campus Martius', *Classical Antiquity* 3: 57–81.

Poinssot, L. (1929) *L'autel de la Gens Augusta à Carthage* (Notes et documents 10). Tunis and Paris.

Pomeroy, S. (1976) *Goddesses, Whores, Wives, and Slaves*. London (New York 1975).

Poole, F.J.P. (1986) 'Metaphors and maps: towards comparison in the anthropology of religion', *J.Amer.Acad.Rel.* 54: 411–57.

Potter, D.S. (1994) *Prophets and Emperors: Human and Divine Authority from Augustus to Theodosius*. Cambridge MA and London.

Poupon, G. (1981) 'L'accusation de magie dans les actes apocryphes', in *Les acts apocryphes des apôtres. Christianisme et monde païen*, edd. F. Bovon et al., 71–93. Geneva.

Price, S.R.F. (1984) *Rituals and Power: the Roman Imperial Cult in Asia Minor*. Cambridge.

(1987) 'From noble funerals to divine cult: the consecration of Roman emperors', in Cannadine and Price (1987) 56–105.

(1990) [Review of Beck (1988)]. *Phoenix* 44: 194–6.

(1998) *Religions of the Ancient Greeks*. Cambridge.

(forthcoming) 'Latin Christian apologetics' in *Ancient Apologetics*, edd. M. Edwards, M. Goodman, S. Price and C. Rowland. Oxford.

Purcell, N. (1983) 'The *Apparitores*: a study in social mobility', *Pap.Brit.Sch.Rome* 51: 125–73.

(1986) 'Livia and the womanhood of Rome', *Proc.Camb.Philol.Soc.* 212, n.s.32: 78–105.

(1996) 'Rome and its development under Augustus and his successors', *CAH* 2nd edn. 10: 782–811. Cambridge.

Quet, M.H. (1993) 'Parler de soi pour louer son dieu: le cas d'Aelius Aristide', in Baslez (1993) 211–51.

Radke, G. (1963) 'Quindecimviri', *RE* 24: 1114–48.

(1979) *Die Götter Altitaliens* (Fontes et Commentationes 3), 2nd edn. Münster.

(1981) 'Die *dei Penates* und Vesta in Rom', *ANRW* II.17.1: 343–73.

(1987) *Zur Entwicklung der Gottesvorstellung und der Gottesverehrung in Rom* (Impulse der Forschung 50). Darmstadt.

Rawson, E. (1971) 'Prodigy lists and the use of the *Annales Maximi*', *CQ* 21: 158–69, repr. in Rawson (1991) 1–15.

(1973) 'Scipio, Laelius, Furius and the ancestral religion', *JRS* 63: 161–74, repr. in Rawson (1991) 80–101.

(1974) 'Religion and politics in the late second century B.C. at Rome', *Phoenix* 28: 193–212, repr. in Rawson (1991) 149–68.

(1975) *Cicero: a Portrait*. London.

(1976) 'The first Latin annalists', *Latomus* 35: 689–717, repr. in Rawson (1991) 245–71.

(1985) *Intellectual Life in the Late Roman Republic*. London.

(1987) '*Discrimina ordinum*: the *lex Julia Theatralis*', *Pap.Brit.Sch.Rome* 55: 83–114, repr. in Rawson (1991) 508–45.

(1991) *Roman Culture and Society. Collected Papers*. Oxford.

Reekmans, L. (1968) 'L'implantation monumentale chrétienne dans la zone suburbaine de Rome du IVe au IXe siècle', *Riv.Arch.Crist.* 44: 173–207.

(1970) 'Le développement topographique du Vatican à la fin de l'antiquité et au début du moyen âge (300–850)', in *Mélanges d'archéologie et d'histoire de l'art offerts au Professeur Jacques Lavalleye*, 197–235. Louvain.

(1989) 'L'implantation monumentale chrétienne dans le paysage urbain de Rome du 300 à 850', in *Actes du XIe Congrès international d'archéologie chrétienne*, 3 vols. (Coll.Ecole franç. de Rome 123), II.861–915. Rome.

Remus, H. (1983) *Pagan-Christian Conflict over Miracle in the Second Century* (Patristic Monograph Series 10). Cambridge MA.

Reynolds, J.M. (1962) 'Vota pro salute principis', *Pap.Brit.Sch.Rome* 30: 33–6.

(1965) 'Notes on Cyrenaican inscriptions', *Pap.Brit.Sch.Rome* 33: 52–4.

(1990) 'Some inscriptions of Roman Ptolemais', in *Giornata Lincea sulla Archeologia Cirenaica*, 65–74. Rome.

Reynolds, J.M. and R. Tannenbaum (1987) *Jews and Godfearers at Aphrodisias* (Camb. Philological Soc., Supp.12). Cambridge.

Rich, J. W. (1976) *Declaring War in the Roman Republic in the Period of Transmarine Expansion* (Coll. Latomus 149). Brussels.

(1990) *Cassius Dio. The Augustan Settlement.* Warminster.

Richard, F. (1992) 'Une nouvelle inscription lyonnaise d'un *sacerdos* Sénon des Trois Gaules: Sextus Iulius Thermianus', *CR Acad. Insc.* 1992: 489–509.

Richard, J.-C. (1965) 'La victoire de Marius', *MEFR* 77: 69–86.

(1966) 'Les funérailles de Trajan et le triomphe sur les Parthes', *Rev.Et.Lat.* 44: 351–62.

(1968) 'Sur quelques grands pontifes plébéiens', *Latomus* 27: 786–801.

(1978) *Les origines de la plèbe romain. Essai sur la formation du dualisme patricio-plébéien* (BEFAR 232). Paris.

(1982) '"M. Laetorius primi pili centurio"; à propos de la dédicace du temple de Mercure', in *Scritti in memoria di A. Brelich*, edd. V. Lanternari et al., 501–9. Bari.

Richardson, C.C. (1973) 'A new solution to the Quartodeciman riddle', *J.Theol.Stud.* 24: 74–84.

Richardson, L. jnr (1987) 'A note on the architecture of the Theatrum Pompei in Rome', *Amer.J.Arch.* 91: 123–6.

(1992) *A New Topographical Dictionary of Ancient Rome.* Baltimore and London.

Richmond, I.A. (1943) 'Roman legionaries at Corbridge, their supply-base, temples and religious cults', *Archaeologia Aeliana* 4th ser., 21: 127–224.

Ristow, G. (1967) 'Götter und Kulte in der Rheinlanden', in *Römer am Rhein*, 57–69. Cologne.

Rives, J.B. (1994) 'Tertullian on child sacrifice', *Mus.helv.* 51: 54–63.

(1995a) *Religion and Authority in Roman Carthage from Augustus to Constantine.* Oxford.

(1995b) 'Human sacrifice among pagans and Christians', *JRS* 85: 65–85.

Robert, L. (1969) 'Théophane de Mytilène à Constantinople', *CR Acad. Insc.* 42–64, repr. in his *Opera Minora Selecta* (Amsterdam 1969–90) V.561–83.

(1978) 'Malédictions funéraires grecques', *CR Acad.Insc.* 241–89, repr. in his *Opera Minora Selecta* (Amsterdam 1969–90) V.697–745.

Rohde, G. (1936) *Die Kultsatzungen der römischen Pontifices* (Religionsgeschichtliche Versuche und Vorarbeiten 25). Berlin.

Romanelli, P. (1963) 'Lo scavo al tempio della Magna Mater sul Palatino e nelle sue adiacenze', *Mon. Ant.* 46: 202–330.

Rose, H. J. (1926) *Primitive Culture in Italy.* London.

(1950) 'Myth and ritual in classical civilisation', *Mnemosyne* 4th ser. 3: 281–7.

(1960) 'Roman religion 1910–1960', *JRS* 50: 161–72.

Rosenstein, N.S. (1990) *Imperatores Victi: Military Defeat and Aristocratic Competition in the Middle and Late Republic.* Berkeley.

Rostovtzeff, M.I. n.d. [c.1922]. 'Augustus', *University of Wisconsin Studies in Language and Literature* 15.

Roth, C. (1960) 'The debate on the loyal sacrifices, A.D. 66', *Harv.Theol.Rev.* 53: 93–7.

Roymans, N. (1990) *Tribal Societies in Northern Gaul. An Anthropological Perspective*. Amsterdam.

Rubino, C.A. (1974) 'Myth and mediation in the Attis poem of Catullus', *Ramus* 3: 152–75.

Rübsam, W.J.R. (1974) *Götter und Kulte in Faijum während der griechisch-römisch-byzantinischen Zeit*. Bonn.

Ruggini, L.C. (1959) 'Ebrei e Orientali nell'Italia settentrionale fra il IV e il VI secolo d. Cr.', *Studia et documenta historiae et iuris* 25: 186–308.

    (1979) 'Il paganesimo romano tra religione e politica (384–394 d.C.): per una reinterpretazione del "Carmen contra paganos"', *Atti Accademia nazionale dei Lincei, Memorie, Sc. morali*, 8th ser, 23: 3–141.

    (1991) 'La cristianizzazione nelle città dell'Italia settentrionale (IV–VI secolo)', in *Die Stadt in Oberitalien und in den nordwestlichen Provinzen des römischen Reiches* (Kölner Forschungen 4), edd. W. Eck and H.Galsterer, 235–49. Mainz.

Rüpke, J. (1990) *Domi militiae. Die religiöse Konstruktion des Krieges in Rom*. Stuttgart.

    (1995) *Kalender und Öffentlichkeit. Die Geschichte der Repräsentation und religiösen Qualifikation von Zeit in Rom* (RGVV 40). Berlin and New York.

Rutgers, L.V. (1990) 'Überlegungen zu den jüdischen Katakomben Roms', *Jahrb.Ant.Christ.* 33: 140–57.

    (1992) 'Archaeological evidence for the interaction of Jews and non-Jews in late antiquity', *Amer.J.Arch.* 96: 101–18.

    (1995) *The Jews in Late Antique Rome*. Leiden.

Ryberg, I.S. (1955) *Rites of the State Religion in Roman Art* (Mem. Amer. Acad. Rome 23). New Haven.

Rykwert, J. (1976) *The Idea of a Town. The Anthropology of Urban Form in Rome, Italy and the Ancient World*. Princeton.

Sabbatucci, D. (1954) 'L'edilità romana: magistratura e sacerdozio', *Atti Accademia Nazionale dei Lincei, Memorie, Sc. morali*, 8th ser. (Rome) 8.6: 255–334.

Sachot, M. (1991) '"Religio/superstitio". Historique d'une subversion et d'un retournement', *Rev.Hist.Rel.* 208: 351–94.

Sahagún, B. de. (1950–82) *General History of the Things of New Spain*. Sante Fe.

Said, E.W. (1978) *Orientalism*. New York.

Salomonson, J.W. (1956) *Chair, Sceptre and Wreath. Historical Aspects of Their Representation on Some Roman Sepulchral Monuments*. Diss. Groningen.

Salzman, M.R. (1987) ' "Superstitio" in the Codex Theodosianus and the persecution of pagans', *Vigiliae Christianae* 41: 172–88.

    (1989) 'Aristocratic women: conductors of Christianity in the fourth century', *Helios* 16: 207–20.

    (1990) *On Roman Time. The Codex-Calendar of 354 and the Rhythms of Urban Life in Late Antiquity*. Berkeley.

    (1992) 'How the west was won: the Christianization of the Roman aristocracy in the west in the years after Constantine', in *Studies in Latin Literature and Roman History* (Coll.Latomus 217), ed. C. Deroux, 6: 451–79. Brussels.

    (1993) 'The evidence for the conversion of the Roman empire to Christianity in Book 16 of the *Theodosian Code*', *Historia* 42: 362–78.

Samter, E. (1909) 'Fetiales', *RE* 6: 2259–65.

Samuel, A.E. (1972) *Greek and Roman Chronology*. Munich.

Sanders, E.P. (1992) *Judaism, Practice and Belief 63 B.C.E.–66 C.E.* London and Philadelphia.

Santero, J.M. (1983) 'The "Cultores Augusti" and the first worship of the Roman emperor', *Athenaeum* 61: 111–25.

Sarikakis, T.C. (1965) 'Aktia ta en Nikopolei', *Archaiologiki Ephimeris* 1965: 145–62.

Sarnowski, T. (1989) 'Zur Statuenausstattung römischer Stabsgebäude. Neue Funde aus den Principia des Legionslagers Novae', *Bonner Jahrb.* 189: 97–120.

Sauer, E. (1996) *The End of Paganism in the North-Western Provinces of the Roman Empire: The Example of the Mithras Cult* (BAR Int.Ser. 634). Oxford.

Saulnier, C. (1980) 'Le rôle des prêtres fétiaux et l'application du "ius fetiale" à Rome', *Rev. hist. de droit franç. et étr.* 58: 171–99.

 (1984) 'Laurens Lavinas. Quelques remarques à propos d'un sacerdoce équestre à Rome', *Latomus* 43: 517–33.

Saunders, T.J. (1991) *Plato's Penal Code*. Oxford.

Sauron, G. (1984) 'Nature et signification de la mégalographie dionysiaque de Pompéii', *CR Acad.Insc.* (1984) 151–74.

 (1987) 'Le complexe pompéien du Champ de Mars: nouveauté urbanistique à finalité idéologique', in *L'urbs* (1987) 457–73.

 (1994) *Quis deum? L'expression plastique des idéologies politiques et religieuses à Rome* (BEFAR 285). Paris and Rome.

Savage, S.M. (1940) 'The cults of ancient Trastevere', *Mem.Amer.Acad.Rome* 17: 26–56.

Saxer, V. (1989) 'L'utilisation par la liturgie de l'espace urbain et suburbain: l'exemple de Rome dans l'antiquité et le haut moyen âge', in *Actes du XIe Congrès international d'archéologie chrétienne*, 3 vols. (Coll.Ecole franç. de Rome 123), II.917–1033. Rome.

Schäfer, T. (1989) *Imperii Insignia. Sella Curulis und Fasces. Zur Repräsentation römischer Magistrate* (*Röm.Mitt.* Supp.29). Mainz.

Schallmayer, E. et al. (1990) *Der römische Weihebezirk von Osterburken I. Corpus der griechischen und lateinischen Beneficiarier-Inschriften des römischen Reiches* (Forschungen und Berichte zur Vor- und Frühgeschichte in Baden-Württemberg 40). Stuttgart.

Scheid, J. (1975) *Les frères Arvales. Recrutement et origine sociale sous les empereurs julio-claudiens*. Paris.

 (1978) 'Les prêtres officiels sous les empereurs julio-claudiens', *ANRW* II.16.1: 610–54.

 (1981) 'Le délit religieux dans la Rome tardo-républicaine', in *Le délit religieux* (1981) 117–71.

 (1983) 'G. Dumézil et la méthode experimentale', *Opus* 2: 343–54.

 (1984) 'Le prêtre et le magistrat', in *Des ordres à Rome*, ed. C. Nicolet, 243–80. Paris.

 (1985a) *Religion et piété à Rome*. Paris.

 (1985b) 'Religion et superstition à l'époque de Tacite: quelques reflexions', in *Religión, superstición y magia en el mundo romano* (Departamento de historia antigua, Universidad de Cádiz), 19–34. Cádiz.

 (1986) 'La thiase du Metropolitan Museum', in *L'association dionysiaque dans les sociétés anciennes* (Coll.Ecole franç. de Rome 89), 275–90. Rome.

 (1987) 'Polytheism impossible; or, the empty gods: reasons behind a void in the history of Roman religion', in *The Inconceivable Polytheism* (History and Anthropology 3), ed. F. Schmidt, 303–25. Paris.

(1990a) *Le collège des frères Arvales. Etude prosopographique du recrutement (69–304)*. Rome.

(1990b) *Romulus et ses frères. Le collège des frères Arvales, modèle du culte public romain dans la Rome des empereurs* (BEFAR 275). Rome.

(1991) 'Sanctuaires et territoire dans la Colonia Augusta Treverorum', in *Les sanctuaires celtiques et leurs rapports avec le monde méditerranéen* (Actes du colloque de St-Riquier, 8–11 Nov.1990), ed. J.-L. Brunaux, 42–57. Paris.

(1992a) 'Myth, cult and reality in Ovid's *Fasti*', *Proc.Camb.Philol.Soc.* n.s.38: 118–31.

(1992b) 'The religious roles of Roman women', in *A History of Women: from Ancient Goddesses to Christian Saints*, ed. P. Schmitt Pantel, 377–408. Cambridge MA.

(1993) 'The priest', in *The Romans*, ed. A. Giardina, 55–84. Chicago.

(1995) 'Les temples de l'Altbachtal à Trèves: un "sanctuaire national"?', *Cahiers du Centre G. Glotz* 4: 227–43.

(1996) 'Graeco ritu. A typically Roman way of honouring the gods', *Harv.Stud.Class.Philol.* 98.

Scheid, J. and H. Broise (1980) 'Deux nouveaux fragments des Actes des frères arvales de l'année 38 ap. J.-C', MEFRA 92: 215–48.

Schilling, R. (1954) *La religion romaine de Vénus* (BEFAR 178). Paris.

(1960) 'Les "castores" romains à la lumière des traditions indo-européennes', *Hommages à G. Dumézil* (Coll. Latomus 45) 177–92. Brussels, repr. in Schilling (1979) 338–53.

(1962) 'À propos des "exta": l'extispicine étrusque et la "litatio" romaine', *Hommages à A. Grenier* (Coll. Latomus 58) III.1371–8, repr. in Schilling (1979) 183–90.

(1969) 'Ovide interprète de la religion romaine', *Rev.Et.Lat.* 46: 222–35, repr. in Schilling (1979) 11–22.

(1972) 'Les études relatives à la religion romain (1950–1970)', *ANRW* I.2: 317–47.

(1979) *Rites, cultes, dieux de Rome* (Études et Commentaires 92). Paris.

Schillinger, K. (1979) *Untersuchungen zur Entwicklung des Magna Mater-Kultes im Westen des römischen Kaiserreiches*. Diss. Konstanz.

Schneider, E.E. (1987) 'Il santuario di Bel e delle divinità di Palmira. Comunità e tradizioni religiose dei Palmireni a Roma', *Dialoghi di Archeologia*, 3rd ser., 5: 69–85.

Schofield, M. (1986) 'Cicero for and against divination', *JRS* 76: 47–65.

Scholz, U.W. (1970) *Studien zum altitalischen und altrömischen Marskult und Marsmythos* (Bibliothek der klass. Altertumswissenschaften n.s.2, 35). Heidelberg.

(1981) 'Zur Erforschung der römischen Opfer (Beispiel: die Lupercalia)', in *Le sacrifice dans l'antiquité* (Fondation Hardt, Entretiens 27), 289–340. Geneva.

Schürer, E. (1973–87) *The History of the Jewish People in the Age of Jesus Christ*, rev. edn. by G. Vermes, F. Millar and M. Goodman, 3 vols. Edinburgh.

Schulz, F. (1946) *History of Roman Legal Science*. Oxford.

Schutz, H. (1985) *The Romans in Central Europe*. New Haven.

Schwarte, K.-H. (1989) 'Die Christengesetze Valerians', in Eck (1989a) 103–63.

Schwenn, F. (1915) *Die Menschenopfer bei den Griechen und Römern* (Religionsgeschichtliche Versuche und Vorarbeiten 15.3). Giessen.

Scott, K. (1925) 'The identification of Augustus with Romulus-Quirinus', *Trans.Amer.Philol.Ass.* 56: 82–105.

Scott, R.T. (1993) 'Excavations in the Area Sacra of Vesta, 1987–89', in Scott and Scott (1993) 161–81.

Scott, R.T. and A.R. Scott edd. (1993) *Eius Virtutis Studiosi. Classical and Postclassical Studies in Memory of Frank Edward Brown (1908–1988)*. Hanover and London.

Scullard, H.H. (1973) *Roman Politics 220–150 B.C.*, 2nd edn. Oxford.

—— (1981) *Festivals and Ceremonies of the Roman Republic*. London.

Seaford, R.A.S. (1981) 'The mysteries of Dionysos at Pompeii', in *Pegasus: Classical Essays from the University of Exeter*, ed. H.W. Stubbs, 52–68. Exeter.

Segal, A.F. (1981) 'Hellenistic magic: some questions of definition', in *Studies in Gnosticism and Hellenistic Religions Presented to Gilles Quispel* (EPRO 91), edd. R. van den Brink and M.J. Vermaseren, 349–75. Leiden.

—— (1992) 'Jewish Christianity', in *Eusebius, Christianity and Judaism*, edd. H.W. Attridge and G. Hata, 326–51. Leiden.

Seyrig, H. (1954) 'Questions héliopolitaines', *Syria* 31: 80–98, repr. in his *Antiquités syriennes* 5 (1958) 99–177.

Sfameni Gasparro, G. (1985) *Soteriology and Mystic Aspects in the Cult of Cybele and Attis* (EPRO 103). Leiden.

Shackleton Bailey, D. R. (1965–70) *Cicero's Letters to Atticus*, 7 vols. Cambridge.

Shelton, K.J. (1981) *The Esquiline Treasure*. London.

—— (1985) 'The Esquiline treasure: the nature of the evidence', *Amer.J.Arch.* 89: 147–55.

Sherk, R.K. (1984) *Rome and the Greek East to the Death of Augustus*. Cambridge.

—— (1988) *The Roman Empire: Augustus to Hadrian*. Cambridge.

Sherwin-White, A.N. (1973) *The Roman Citizenship*, 2nd edn. Oxford.

Silvestrini, M. (1992) 'Una nuova idenzione per i Lari Augusti dal territorio do Vibinum', *MEFRA* 104: 145–57.

Simón, F.M. (1996) *Flamen Dialis: el sacerdote de Júpiter en la religión romana*. Madrid.

Simon, M. (1979) 'Mithra et les empereurs', in Bianchi (1979) 411–28, repr in his *Le Christianisme antique et son contexte religieux*, 2 vols, II.803–17. Tübingen.

Simpson, C.J. (1993) 'Once again Claudius and the temple at Colchester', *Britannia* 24: 1–6.

Skinner, M.B. (1993) 'Ego mulier: the construction of male sexuality in Catullus', *Helios* 20: 107–31.

Skorupski, J. (1976) *Symbol and Theory. A Philosophical Study of Theories of Religion in Social Anthropology*. Cambridge.

Skutsch, O. (1985) *The Annals of Q. Ennius*. Oxford.

Smadja, E. (1980) 'Remarques sur les débuts du culte impérial en Afrique sous le règne d'Auguste', in *Religions, pouvoir, rapports sociaux* (Ann. litt. Univ. Besançon 237), 151–69. Paris.

—— (1985) 'L'empereur et les dieux en Afrique romaine', *Dial. d'hist.anc.* 11: 541–55.

Small, A. ed. (1996) *Subject and Ruler: The Cult of the Ruling Power in Classical Antiquity* (*J.Rom.Arch.* Supp.17). Ann Arbor MI.

Smith, J.Z. (1978) *Map is not Territory. Studies in the History of Religions.* Leiden. (Repr. Chicago 1993.)

(1987) *To Take Place. Toward Theory in Ritual.* Chicago and London.

(1990) *Drudgery Divine. On the Comparison of Early Christianities and the Religions of Late Antiquity.* London and Chicago.

Smith, M. (1978) *Jesus the Magician.* New York.

Snyder, G.F. (1985) *Ante Pacem. Archaeological Evidence of Church Life before Constantine.* Macon.

Sokolowski, F. ed. (1955) *Lois sacrées de l'Asie Mineure.* Paris.

Solin, H. (1971) *Beiträge zur Kenntnis der griechischen Personennamen in Rom* I. Helsinki.

(1983) 'Juden und Syrer im westlichen Teil der römischen Welt', *ANRW* II.29.2: 587–789.

(1996) 'Namen in alten Rom', in *Namenforschung. Eine internationales Handbuch zur Onomastik* II.1041–8. Berlin.

Spaeth, B.S. (1996) *The Roman Goddess Ceres.* Austin TX.

Staden, H.von (1982) 'Hairesis and heresy: the case of the *haireseis iatrikai*', in *Jewish and Christian Self-definition*, edd. B.F. Meyer and E.P. Sanders, III.76–100, 199–206. Philadelphia and London.

Stambaugh, J.E. (1978) 'The functions of Roman temples', *ANRW* II.16.1: 554–608.

Stead, M. (1981) 'The High Priest of Alexandria and All Egypt', *Proc. of the XVI International Congress of Papyrology* (Amer.Stud.Papyr. 23), 411–18. Chico CA.

Steinby, E. M. (1993–) *Lexikon Topographicum Urbis Romae.* Rome.

(1993) 'Sulla funzione della rampa situata fra l'area di Giuturna e l'*atrium Vestae*', in Scott and Scott (1993) 149–59.

Stern, H. (1953) *Le calendrier de 354.* Paris.

(1958) 'Les mosaïques de l'église de Sainte-Constance à Rome', *Dumb.Oaks Pap.* 12: 157–218.

Stern, S.J. (1982) *Indian Peoples and the Challenge of Spanish Conquest: Huamanga to 1640.* Madison WI.

Stevenson, J. (1978) *The Catacombs. Rediscovered Monuments of Early Christianity.* London.

(1987) *A New Eusebius. Documents Illustrating the History of the Church to* A.D. *337*, revised edn. by W.H.C. Frend. London.

Stewart, C. and R. Shaw edd. (1994) *Syncretism/Anti-Syncretism. The Politics of Religious Synthesis.* London and New York.

Stibbe, C.M. et al. (1980) *Lapis Satricanus* (Nederlands Instituut te Rome, Scripta Minora 5). The Hague.

Strocka, V.M. (1972) 'Beobachtungen an den Attikareliefs des severischen Quadrifrons von Lepcis Magna', *Antiquités africaines* 6: 147–72.

Stübler, G. (1941) *Die Religiosiät des Livius.* Stuttgart. (Repr. Amsterdam 1964.)

Sumner, G. V. (1963) 'Lex Aelia, Lex Fufia,' *Amer.J.Philol.* 84: 337–58.

Swain, S. (1996) *Hellenism and Empire. Language, Classicism and Power in the Greek World* A.D. *50–250.* Oxford.

Swarney, P.R. (1970) *The Ptolemaic and Roman Idios Logos* (Amer.Stud.Papyr. 8). Toronto.

Syme, R. (1939) [Review of Koch (1937)], *JRS* 29: 108–10.

    (1951) 'Tacfarinas, the Musulamii and Thubursicu', *Studies in Roman Economic and Social History in Honor of Allan Chester Johnson*, 113–30. Princeton. Repr. in his *Roman Papers* (Oxford 1979–91) I.218–30.

    (1978a) *History in Ovid*. Oxford.

    (1978b) 'The *pomerium* in the Historia Augusta', *Bonner Historia-Augusta - Colloquium 1975–76* (Antiquitas 4th. ser., 13), 217–31. Bonn. Repr. in his *Historia Augusta Papers*, 131–45. Oxford, 1983.

    (1980) *Some Arval Brethren*. Oxford.

Szemler, G. J. (1972) *The Priests of the Roman Republic: a Study of Interactions between Priesthoods and Magistracies* (Coll. Latomus 127). Brussels.

Talbert, R.J.A. (1984) *The Senate of Imperial Rome*. Princeton.

Tamassia, A.M. (1961–2) 'Inscrizioni del Compitum Acili', *BCACR* 78: 158–63.

Tatum, W.J. (1990) 'Cicero and the *Bona Dea* scandal', *Class.Philol.* 85: 202–8.

Taylor, L.R. (1931) *The Divinity of the Roman Emperor* (Amer. Philol. Assoc., Philol. Mono. 1). Middletown. (Repr. New York, 1975.)

    (1934) 'New light on the history of the Secular Games', *Amer.J.Philol.* 55: 101–20.

    (1935) 'The *sellisternium* and the theatrical *pompa*', *Class.Philol.* 30: 122–30.

    (1941) 'Caesar's early career', *Class.Philol.* 36: 113–32.

    (1942) 'The election of the *pontifex maximus* in the late Republic', *Class.Philol.* 37: 421–4.

    (1949) *Party Politics in the Age of Caesar*. Berkeley.

    (1951) 'On the chronology of Caesar's first consulship', *Amer.J.Philol.* 72: 254–68.

    (1962) 'Forerunners of the Gracchi', *JRS* 52: 19–27.

    (1966) *Roman Voting Assemblies from the Hannibalic War to the Dictatorship of Caesar*. Ann Arbor MI.

Testini, P. (1966) *Le catacombe e gli antichi cimiteri cristiani in Roma*. Bologna.

Thomas, E.B. (1980) 'Religion', in *The Archaeology of Roman Pannonia*, edd. A. Lengyel and G.T.B. Radan, 177–206. Lexington, KY.

Thomas, E. and C. Witschel (1992) 'Constructing reconstruction: claim and reality of Roman rebuilding inscriptions from the Latin West', *Pap.Brit.Sch.Rome* 60: 135–77.

Thomas. G. (1984) 'Magna Mater and Attis', *ANRW* II.17.3: 1500–35.

Thomas, K. (1971) *Religion and the Decline of Magic*. London and New York.

Thompson, D.J. (1988) *Memphis under the Ptolemies*. Princeton.

Thulin, C. O. (1906–09) *Die etruskische Disciplin*, 3 vols. Göteborg.

    (1910) 'Haruspices', *RE* 7: 2431–68.

Tierney, J.J. (1947) 'The senatus consultum de Bacchanalibus', *Proc.R. Irish Ac.* 51: 89–117.

Timpanaro, S. ed. (1988) *Della divinazione: introduzione, traduzione e note*. Milan.

Todd, M. (1985) 'Forum and Capitolium in the early empire', in *Roman Urban Topography in Britain and the Western Empire* (CBA Research Report 59), edd. F. Grew and B. Hobley, 56–66. London.

Torelli, M. (1975) *Elogia Tarquiniensia*. Florence.

    (1982) *Typology and Structure of Roman Historical Reliefs*. Ann Arbor.

(1992) 'Topografia e iconologia. Arco di Portogallo, *Ara Pacis, Ara Providentiae, Templum Solis*', *Ostraka* 1: 105–31.

Toutain, J. (1907–20) *Les cultes païens dans l'empire romain*, 3 vols. Paris.

Toynbee, A.J. (1965) *Hannibal's Legacy*. London.

Toynbee, J.M.C. (1929) 'The *Villa Item* and a bride's ordeal', *JRS* 19: 67–87.

(1955–6) 'Still more about Mithras', *Hibbert Journal* 54: 107–14.

(1971) *Death and Burial in the Roman World*. London.

(1986) *The Roman Art Treasures from the Temple of Mithras [London]*. London.

Toynbee, J. and J. Ward-Perkins (1956) *The Shrine of St. Peter and the Vatican Excavations*. London.

Tranoy, A. (1981) *La Galice romaine. Recherches sur le nord-ouest de la péninsule ibérique dans l'antiquité*. Paris.

Trebilco, P.R. (1991) *Jewish Communities in Asia Minor*. Cambridge.

Trombley, F.R. (1993) *Hellenic Religion and Christianization c.370–529*, 2 vols. (Religions in the Graeco-Roman World 115.1–2). Leiden.

Tuchelt, K. (1979) *Frühe Denkmäler Roms in Kleinasien I: Roma und Promagistrate* (*Ist.Mitt.* Supp.23). Tübingen.

Turcan, R. (1969) 'Le démone ailée de la Villa Item', in *Hommages à Marcel Renard*, 3 vols. (Coll. Latomus 102), III.586–609. Brussels.

(1972) 'Religion et politique dans l'affaire des Bacchanales' [review of Gallini (1970)], *Rev.Hist.Rel.* 181: 3–28.

(1975) *Mithras Platonicus. Recherches sur l'hellénisation philosophique de Mithras* (EPRO 47). Leiden.

(1976) 'Encore la prophétie de Végoia', *Mélanges J. Heurgon* (1976) II: 1009–19.

(1981) 'Le sacrifice mithriaque: innovations de sens et de modalités', in *Le sacrifice dans l'antiquité* (Fondation Hardt, Entretiens 27), 341–80. Geneva.

(1982) 'Salut mithriaque et sotériologie néoplatonicienne', in Bianchi and Vermaseren (1982) 173–91.

(1989) *Les cultes orientaux dans le monde romain*. Paris.

(1991) 'Les autels du culte mithriaque', in *L'espace sacrificiel dans les civilisations méditerranéennes de l'antiquité* (Publ. de la Bibliothèque Salomon-Reinach 5), 217–25. Paris.

(1992) 'Un "catéchisme" mithriaque?', *CR Acad. Insc.* 1992: 549–64.

(1993) *Mithra et le mithriacisme*, 2nd edn. Paris.

(1996) *The Cults of the Roman Empire*. Oxford. Trans. of Turcan (1989).

Turchi, N. et al. (1954, 1956, 1958, 1961, 1963, 1967, 1971, 1975, 1977, 1978, 1983, 1985, 1988, 1989, 1990, 1991, 1992, 1993) 'Studi sulla religione romana', *Studi Romani* 2: 570–7; 4: 590–4; 6: 591–4; 9: 301–7; 11: 581–9; 15: 70–8; 19:315–22; 23: 195–205; 25: 401–12; 26: 78–86; 31: 307–13; 33: 109–17; 36: 97–107; 37: 123–30; 38: 125–34; 39: 111–18; 40: 109–13; 41: 106–13.

Ulf, C. (1982) *Das römische Lupercalienfest*. Darmstadt.

Vaes, J. (1984–6) 'Christliche Wiederverwendung antiker Bauten: ein Forschungsbericht', *Anc.Soc.* 15–17: 305–443.

Valentini, R. and G. Zucchetti (1940–53) *Codice topografico della città di Roma*, 4 vols. Rome.

Valenzani, R.S. (1991–92) 'ΝΕΩΣ ΥΠΕΡΜΕΓΕΘΗΣ. Osservazioni sul tempio di piazza Quirinale', *BCACR* 94: 7–16.

Valeton, J. (1895) 'De templis Romanis', *Mnemosyne* 23: 15–79.

Valette, P. (1908) *L'Apologie d'Apulée*. Paris.

Van Andringa, W. (1994) 'Cultes publics et statut juridique de la cité des Helvètes', in *Roman Religion in Gallia Belgica and the Germaniae* (Bull. des Antiquités Luxembourgeoises 22), 169–93. Luxembourg.

Van Doren, M. (1953) 'L'évolution des mystères phrygiens à Rome', *Ant.Class.* 22: 79–88.

Vanggaard, J.H. (1988) *The Flamen: a Study in the History and Sociology of Roman Religion*. Copenhagen.

Van Son, D.W.L. (1960) *Bacchanalia: Livius' behandeling van de Bacchanalia*. Amsterdam.

Vasaly, A. (1993) *Representations: Images of the World in Ciceronian Oratory*. Berkeley.

Vázquez y Hoys, A.M. (1982) *La religión romana en Hispania. Fuentas epigraficas, arqueologicas y numismaticas*, 2 vols. Diss. Madrid.

Veligianni-Terzi, C. (1986) 'Bemerkungen zu den griechischen Isisaretalogien', *Rhein.Mus.* 129: 63–76.

Vermaseren, M.J. (1963) *Mithras, the Secret God*. London.

   (1977) *Cybele and Attis. The Myth and the Cult*. London.

   (1977–89) *Corpus cultus Cybelae Attidisque* (EPRO 50), 7 vols. Leiden.

Vermaseren M.J. and C.C. van Essen (1965) *The Excavations in the Mithraeum of the Church of Santa Prisca in Rome*. Leiden.

Vernant, J.-P. (1983) *Myth and Thought among the Greeks*. London.

Versnel, H.S. (1970) *Triumphus. An Enquiry into the Origin, Development and Meaning of the Roman Triumph*. Leiden.

   (1976) 'Two types of Roman *devotio*', *Mnemosyne* 29: 365–410.

   (1980) 'Historical implications', in Stibbe et al. (1980) 95–150.

   (1981a) 'Religious mentality in ancient prayer', in *Faith, Hope and Worship*, ed. Versnel, 1–64. Leiden.

   (1981b) 'Self-sacrifice, compensation and the anonymous gods', in *Le sacrifice dans l'antiquité* (Fondation Hardt, Entretiens 27), 135–94. Geneva.

   (1982) 'Die neue Inschrift von Satricum in historischer Sicht', *Gymnasium* 89: 193–235.

   (1990) *Inconsistencies in Greek and Roman Religion. 1. Ter Unus. Isis, Dionysos, Hermes. Three Studies in Henotheism* (Studies in Greek and Roman Religion 6.1). Leiden.

   (1991) 'Some reflections on the relationship magic-religion', *Numen* 38: 177–97.

   (1993) *Inconsistencies in Greek and Roman Religion. 2. Tradition and Reversal in Myth and Ritual* (Studies in Greek and Roman Religion 6.2). Leiden.

Veyne, P. (1976) *Le pain et le cirque. Sociologie historique d'un pluralisme politique*. Paris.

Vidman, L. (1969) *Sylloge inscriptionum religionis Isiacae et Sarapiacae* (Religionsgeschichtliche Versuche und Vorarbeiten 28). Berlin.

Vielliard, R. (1941) *Recherches sur les origines de la Rome chrétienne*. Mâcon. (Repr. Rome, 1959.)

Vigna Barberini (1990) 'Les activités archéologiques en 1989. Rome: le Palatin (Vigna Barberini)', *MEFRA* 102: 443–72.

Vismara, C. (1986) 'I cimiteri ebraici di Roma', in Giardina (1986) 351–92.

Vitucci, G. (1946–85) 'Lares', in *Dizionario epigrafico di antichità romana*, ed. E. de Ruggiero, 4: 394–406.

Vogt, J. (1953) 'Zum Herrscherkult bei Julius Caesar', in *Studies Presented to D. M. Robinson*, edd. G. E. Mylonas and D. Raymond, II: 1138–46. St. Louis.

Vovelle, M. (1973) *Piété baroque et déchristianisation en Provence au XVIIIᵉ siècle*. Paris.

Wagenvoort, H. (1956a) *Studies in Roman Literature, Culture and Religion*. Leiden.

(1956b) 'The crime of fratricide (Horace *Epode* 7,18)', in Wagenvoort (1956a) 169–83.

Walbank, F.W. (1957–79) *A Historical Commentary on Polybius*, 3 vols. Oxford.

(1967) 'The Scipionic legend', *Proc.Camb.Philol.Soc.* 13: 54–69.

(1972) *Polybius*. Berkeley.

Walbank, M.E.H. (1989) 'Pausanias, Octavia and Temple E at Corinth', *Ann.Brit.Sch.Athens* 84: 361–94.

(1996) 'Evidence for the imperial cult in Julio-Claudian Corinth', in Small (1996) 201–13.

Wallace-Hadrill, A. (1983) *Suetonius: The Scholar and his Caesars*. London.

(1987) 'Time for Augustus: Ovid, Augustus and the *Fasti*', in *Homo Viator. Classical Essays for John Bramble*, edd. M. Whitby, P. Hardie and M. Whitby, 221–30. Bristol and Oak Park IL.

Walsh, P.G. (1970) *The Roman Novel*. Cambridge.

Waltzing, J.-P. (1895–1900) *Étude historique sur les corporations professionnelles chez les romains ...*, 4 vols. Louvain.

Warde Fowler, W. (1899) *The Roman Festivals*. London.

(1911) *The Religious Experience of the Roman People*. London.

Ward-Perkins, B. (1984) *From Classical Antiquity to the Middle Ages. Urban Public Building in Northern and Central Italy, AD 300–850*. Oxford.

Wardman, A. (1982) *Religion and Statecraft among the Romans*. London.

Watson, A. (1992) *The State, Law and Religion: Pagan Rome*. Athens GA.

Weber, M. (1951) *The Religion of China*. Glencoe.

Weiland, A. (1992) 'Bemerkungen zur Datierung der ehemaligen Luperkal-Kapelle im Vicus Patricius zu Rom', in *Memoriam Sanctorum Venerantes. Miscellanea in onore di Monsignor Victor Saxer*, 773–93. Vatican.

Weinrib, E.J. (1970) 'Obnuntiatio: two problems', *Zeitschrift der Savigny-Stiftung für Rechtsgeschichte (Romanistische Abteilung)* 87: 395–425.

Weinstein, S. (1987) *Buddhism under the T'ang*. Cambridge.

Weinstock, S. (1932) 'Tarentum', *RE* 2. Reihe, 4: 2213–6.

(1934) 'Templum', *RE* 2. Reihe, 5: 480–5.

(1937a) 'Nonalia sacra', *RE* 17: 861–2.

(1937b) 'Penates', *RE* 19: 417–57.

(1937c) 'Clodius and the Lex Aelia Fufia', *JRS* 27: 215–22.

(1958) 'Victoria', *RE* 2. Reihe, 8: 2501–42.

(1960) 'Two archaic inscriptions from Latium', *JRS* 50: 112–18.

(1971) *Divus Julius*. Oxford.

Weismann, W. (1972) *Kirche und Schauspiele. Die Schauspiele im Urteil der lateinischen Kirchenväter unter besonderer Berücksichtigung von Augustin* (Cassiacum 27). Würzburg.

Weiss, J.-P. (1978) 'Julien, Rome et les Romains', in *L'empereur Julien. De l'histoire à la légende (331–1715)*, edd. R. Braun and J. Richer, 125–40. Paris.

Wells, C.M. (1992) *The Roman Empire*, 2nd edn. London.

Whatmough, J. (1931) 'The calendar in ancient Italy outside Rome', *Harv.Stud.Class.Philol.* 42: 157–79.

White, L.M. (1990) *Building God's House in the Roman World. Architectural Adaptation among Pagans, Jews and Christians*. Baltimore and London.

Whitehorne, J.E.G. (1980–1) 'New light on temple and state in Roman Egypt', *J.Rel.Hist.* 11: 218–26.

Wiedemann, T. (1986) 'The *fetiales*: a reconsideration', *Class.Quart.* 36: 478–490.

Wightman, E.M. (1985) *Gallia Belgica*. London.

  (1986) 'Pagan cults in the province of Belgica', *ANRW* II.18.1: 542–89.

Wild, R.A. (1984) 'The known Isis-Sarapis sanctuaries of the Roman period', *ANRW* II.17.4: 1739–1851.

Wilhelm, J. (1915) *Das römische Sakralwesen unter Augustus als Pontifex Maximus*. Diss. Strassburg.

Williams, C.K. (1989) 'A re-evaluation of Temple E and the west end of the forum of Corinth', in *The Greek Renaissance in the Roman Empire* (*Bull.Inst.Class.Stud.*, Supp.55), edd. S. Walker and Averil Cameron, 156–62. London.

Williams, R. (1987) *Arius: Heresy and Tradition*. London.

  (1989) 'Does it make sense to speak of pre-Nicene orthodoxy?', in *The Making of Orthodoxy. Essays in Honour of Henry Chadwick*, ed. Williams, 1–23. Cambridge.

Wilson, B.R. (1982) *Religion in Sociological Perspective*. Oxford.

  (1990) *The Social Dimensions of Sectarianism*. Oxford.

Wilson, R.J.A. (1990) *Sicily under the Roman Empire*. Warminster.

Winkler, J.J. (1985) *Auctor & Actor. A Narratological Reading of Apuleius' Golden Ass*. Berkeley.

Winter, J.G. (1910) 'The myth of Hercules at Rome', in *Roman History and Mythology*, ed. H.A. Sanders, 171–273. London.

Wiseman, T.P. (1974) *Cinna the Poet and Other Roman Essays*. Leicester and New York.

  (1984) 'Cybele, Virgil and Augustus', in *Poetry and Politics in the Age of Augustus*, edd. T. Woodman and D.West, 117–28. Cambridge.

  (1985) *Catullus and his World: A Reappraisal*. Cambridge.

  (1987) '*Conspicui postes tectaque digna deo*: the public image of aristocratic and imperial houses in the late Republic and early Empire', in *L'urbs* (1987) 393–413, repr. in his *Historiography and Imagination* (Exeter, 1994) 98–115.

  (1989) 'Roman legend and oral tradition', *JRS* 79: 129–37.

  (1991) *Death of an Emperor. Flavius Josephus*. Exeter.

  (1995) *Remus. A Roman Myth*. Cambridge.

Wissowa, G. (1907) 'Evocatio', *RE* 6: 1152–3.

  (1912) *Religion und Kultus der Römer* (Handbuch der Altertumswissenschaft), 2nd edn. Munich (repr. 1971).

  (1915) 'Die römischen Staatspriestertümer altlateinischer Gemeindekulte', *Hermes* 50: 1–33.

(1916–19) 'Interpretatio romana. Römische Götter im Barbarenlande', *ARW* 19: 1–49.

Witherington, B. (1990) *Women and the Genesis of Christianity*. Cambridge.

Woolf, G. (1994) 'Becoming Roman, staying Greek: culture, identity and the civilizing process in the Roman east', *Proc.Camb.Philol.Soc.* 40: 116–43.

(1998) *Becoming Roman: the Origins of Provincial Civilization in Gaul.* Cambridge.

Wrede, H. (1983) '*Statuae Lupercorum habitu*', *Röm.Mitt.* 90: 185–200.

Wuilleumier, P. (1928) *Musée d'Alger. Supplément* (Musées et collections archéologiques de l'Algérie et de la Tunisie). Paris.

Zaidman, L.B. and P. Schmitt Pantel (1992) *Religion in the Ancient Greek City.* Cambridge.

Zanker, P. (1969) 'Der Larenaltar im Belvedere des Vatikans', *Röm.Mitt.* 76: 205–18.

(1970) 'Das Trajansforum in Rom', *Arch.Anz.* 1970: 499–544.

(1970–1) 'Über die Werkstätten augusteischer Larenaltäre und damit zusammenhängende Probleme der Interpretation', *BCACR* 82: 147–55.

(1983) 'Der Apollontempel auf dem Palatin', in *Città e architettura nella Roma imperiale* (Analecta Romana Supp.10), 21–40. Odense.

(1988) *The Power of Images in the Age of Augustus*. Ann Arbor MI.

n.d. [c.1968] *Forum Augustum. Das Bildprogramm*. Tübingen.

Ziolkowski, A. (1992) *The Temples of Mid-Republican Rome and their Historical and Topographical Context.* Rome.

Zuntz, G. (1963) 'On the Dionysiac fresco in the Villa dei Misteri at Pompeii', *Proc.Brit.Acad.* 49: 177–201.

Details of illustrations

Index

abstractions, deified 62

Acts of the Apostles 227, 237

Aebutius 92–3

aediles (plebeian) 64–5; and *ludi* 101

Aemilianus (Publius Cornelius Scipio Africanus Aemilianus, *consul* 147, 134 B.C.) 109, 111

Aemilius *see* Lepidus, Paullus

Aeneas 1–2 fig 1.1, 5, 53–4, 84, 89, 173, 257; in Carthage 333 fig. 7.3; and Magna Mater 198; in temple of Mars Ultor 200; and Parilia 175–6; and Vesta 189–90; in *vici* 185–7 fig. 4.3

Aesculapius: introduction of 69–70; name of 70; temple of (Map 1 no. 27) 69

after-life: Christian 290–1; Isis and 290; Jewish 290; Mithras and 290; in new cults 289–91; traditional attitude to 289

Agorius *see* Praetextatus

agriculture 11, 45, 194

Agrippa (Marcus Vipsanius Agrippa, *consul* 37, 28, 27 B.C.): and the Saecular Games 202; and the Pantheon 257–8 fig. 6.1

Agripinilla, cult-group of 271; includes women 298

Alba Longa 89, 187 fig. 4.3, 189, 323

Alexander the Great *see* Scipio; Victoria, temple of

Alexandria: 254, 255; and Claudius 313

Alexandria Troas (*colonia* in Asia Minor): *flamen* in 329–30

altar(s): to Augustus in Cologne 352; to Augustus (three) in north-west Spain 352; at Carthage (two) 331–3 fig. 7.2, 7.3; of Lares 185–7 fig. 4.3; of Augustus' *numen* 207; *see also* Terentum

Ambarvalia (May) 50

Ambrose (bishop of Milan, c. 340–397): polemic against Symmachus 386

ancilia 43, 173

animism 13–14, 30–1

Antinous (companion of emperor Hadrian, died A.D. 130) 272; *see also* Diana

Antioch (*colonia*, in Pisidia, Asia Minor): cult of Men in, diminished 341

antiquarianism 110–13, 151–3; in practice 323–4

Antoninus Pius (emperor A.D. 138–61) *see divus* Antoninus

Antony *see* Mark Antony

Aphrodisias: Jewish community of 275, 293

Apollo 33 fig. 1.5 (c), 63; Augustan iconography of 199; Augustan temple of (Map 1 no. 14) 198–9; in Carthage 333 fig. 7.3; republican temple of (Map 1 no. 33) 198; and Saecular Games 203; games of *see ludi*

apotheosis see deification

Apronianus: Mithraic relief of 307; Isiac dedication of 307

Apuleius (writer and orator, born c. A.D.125) 238; *religio* and 217; magic in 233, 235–6; claims initiations 235; *The Metamorphoses* 287–8

Ara Maxima (Greatest Altar, Map 1 no. 21) 2, 68,173–4

Ara Pacis (Altar of Peace, Map 1 no. 30) 203–4 fig. 4.6; in Carthage 331–3 figs. 7.2, 7.3

Aricia (Map 5): statue of Ceres from fig.1.8

Arius (Christian heretic, c. A.D. 260–336): 370–1

army: auxiliaries in 324–5, 327–8; calendar of 251, 324–5; camps, religious structure of 326–7; Christians and 295; festivals in 325; local deities in 328; Mithraism and 293, 295, 325; religion of 324–8; vows in 325

Arval Brothers 194–6; Augustus joins 186, 194; pre-Augustan, our ignorance of 194; compared to Dura Europus calendar 251, 325; end of

Germanicus (Germanicus Caesar, 15 B.C. – A.D. 19): his funeral honours 330; and magic 234

god-fearers 293, 309

gods, goddesses *see* deities

gods, Augustan 351–2

governor(s), provincial 235, 237, 238, 239, 241–2, 320; Pliny as 237–9; Claudius not obeyed by 313; accompanied by *haruspices* 320, 330; religious role of 321

Granius Flaccus (antiquarian, first century B.C.) 152

Gratian (emperor, A.D. 367–83), resigns as *pontifex maximus* 374

Greeks, influence of 62–3, 64–6, 69, 70–1, 75, 79–80, 141, 161–3, 165; architectural 90; on divine honours 145–7; and mystery-cults 247; on Roman mythology 172; in philosophy 151

Greece (mainland): cults not radically changed 341; adaptations to Roman rule 342–4; *see also* Athens

'Greek rite' 2, 27, 70–1, 173–4

Greeks and Gauls, burial of 80–2

groups: ethnically based 271–2; elective 272–3; initiatory 287–8; moral rules of 288–9; specifically religious 42, 95–6, 98, 161, 231–3, 273–8; of Bellona 273; of Diana and Antinous 272–3, 287; of Magna Mater 273; *see also* Christianity; *collegia*; heresy; cults, new; Isis; Judaism

Hadrian (emperor, A.D. 117–38): against foreign cults 228; and the Pantheon (Map 1 no. 310) 257; statue in the Parthenon 343; temple to Venus and Rome (Map 1 no. 6) 257, 263

haruspex (haruspices) 19–20 fig. 1.4, 101–2, 113, 137–8; accompany governors 320, 330; in the army 326; not a college 20, 100; debate over 137–8, 261; senate decree about 101–2, 113; in fifth century A.D. 387; foreignness and 20; importance of 102; prodigies and 38, 137; tolerated by Constantine 372

health-cults: in Dolomites 344; *see also* Aesculapius; incubation; votives

hearth, cult of 51–3, 191 *see also* Vestal Virgins

Hecate: senators as priests of 383–4

Hannibalic War 79–87

Heliopolis (Baalbek), and Jupiter Heliopolitanus 283; Capitolium of 334; *see also* Jupiter Heliopolitanus

Hephaestus 12

Herculaneum, list of *Augustales* from 358

Hercules 2, 68, 90,173–4; Olivarius 91 fig. 2.3; and Pompey 122; and Septimius Severus 255

hermaphrodites *see* prodigies

heresy 248, 284–5, 302, 305–7; Arianism 370–1; Donatism 369–70; Montanism 305

hierarchy: Christian 243–4, 299; of Jupiter Dolichenus 275; in Mithraism 295

High Priest: (in Egypt) controls priesthood 340; (in Judaea) appointed by governor 341

Hippolytus (Bishop, c. A.D. 170–c. 236) on heresy 311

Hispala 92–3

Hispellum (modern Spello): warned of *superstitio* 371

Honorius (emperor, A.D. 393–423), extends St. Peter's Basilica 377

Honos (Honour) 105; *see also* Virtus

honours, divine 146–7, 148; to Pompey 147; *see also* deification, *divi*

Horace (Quintus Horatius Flaccus, poet, 65–8 B.C.), on religious decline 118, 181–2; on fratricide 183–4; Saecular Hymn of 203

Hostilius *see* Mancinus

hyenas, women as 298

identity, religious 41–2, 212–14, 288–9; Roman 313, (adapted) 333; Isiac 308

image: of Elagabalus 256; interpretation of 319

imperial cult (so-called)169, 318, 348; Cassius Dio on 318, 349; importance of, exaggerated 360; *see also* emperors: worship of

imperialism: and religion 156–7, 313 and ch. 7 *passim*; re-interpretation of 313

incest, charges of 225–6; discounted 226

incubation 13, 69–70

individuals 42–3, 48–51, 79; *see also* cults, new

initiation 50, 247, 287–8; Bacchic 162–3; of Jupiter Dolichenus 275; repeated, of Lucius in *The Metamorphoses*, 287–8; Mithraic 288

initiative, in cult of emperor, 356; ascribed to locals 356

innovation, religious 61–72, 79–84, 244, 252, 256, ch. 8 *passim*; mediation of 70, 80, 84

integration *see* Romanization

intercalation 46–7

Isaura Vetus 133

Isis, cult of: after-life in 308; Apuleius on 287–8; devotion required by 289, 308–9; geographical distribution of 301; Egyptian emphasis of 279,